INTELLECTUAL PROPERTY

INTELLECTUAL PROPERTY

Second Edition

DAVID I BAINBRIDGE

BSc, LLB, PhD, CEng, MICE, MBCS

Lecturer in Law, Aston University

PITMAN PUBLISHING
128 Long Acre, London WC2E 9AN

A Division of Longman Group Limited

First published in 1992
Second edition published in 1994

© David Bainbridge 1992, 1994

A CIP catalogue record for this book can be obtained from the British Library.

ISBN 0 273 60422 8

3 5 7 9 10 8 6 4 2

Typeset by PanTek Arts, Maidstone, Kent
Printed and bound in Great Britain by Page Bros, Norwich

The Publishers' policy is to use paper manufactured from sustainable forests

Contents

Preface

The purpose of this book is to provide students with a reasonably substantial view of intellectual property law, dealing with principles, academic issues and, where appropriate, practical considerations. Whilst the book is primarily intended for undergraduate law students, it should also be useful to commercial law students whose course includes some intellectual property law and to students taking non-law degrees where the practical implications of the exploitation and marketing of intellectual property are relevant. It is also hoped that the book will find favour amongst practitioners who wish to find out more about this exciting and dynamic area of law.

United Kingdom intellectual property law is described in this book but in addition the impact of EC law is discussed. The nature and effect of international conventions are also considered, bearing in mind that the exploitation of intellectual property is rarely confined to national boundaries. It should be noted that intellectual property law is, for the most part, uniform throughout the United Kingdom and that a significant amount of harmonization throughout the Community (and beyond) has taken place and will continue in the future. International conventions have also played an important role in laying down mimimum standards and providing mechanisms for reciprocal protection between individual nations.

The sequence of this book reflects my preferred order in teaching the various intellectual property rights. Copyright is dealt with first because in my experience most students have some notion of copyright law and are aware of its existence through copyright notices on films, music recordings, and in books and notices to be found near photocopying machines and so on. The importance and far-reaching scope of copyright law is beyond doubt. There is an argument for putting patent law first because it is the strongest and oldest form of intellectual property. However, because it involves complex formalities, I have considered it better to be left until later. Another argument can be made for considering the law of confidence first as it is often the precursor of other intellectual rights, although it is of more recent origin than patent law and copyright law. Ultimately, the choice of sequence lies with the reader, lecturer or teacher, as each section is relatively self-contained and it is not essential to follow the precise order of the book.

The book is divided into six parts. The first part deals with preliminary matters and should be read before proceeding to the other parts as it contains basic principles of intellectual property law and cross-cutting themes. The rest of the book is subdivided into the major areas of copyright, confidence, patents, designs and business goodwill and reputation (trade marks and passing off). There is a glossary, the first part of which contains explanations of some of the terms and phrases commonly used in intellectual property law, bearing in mind that some of the terminology used will be new or unfamiliar to many students. The second part of the glossary is concerned with computer terms and phrases; this will be useful for Chapter 8 on new technology and copyright, parts of Chapter 14 on patent law including a discussion on the patentability of computer programs, and that part of Chapter 19 on the design right which deals with the protection of semiconductor products.

I have been helped by many people during the research for and preparation of this book. In particular, I would like to express my thanks to Pat Bond of Pitman Publishing for his efficiency and suggestions with the text of the manuscript. Professor Bryan Niblett made many useful, incisive and helpful recommendations for which I thank him. Thanks are also due to the reviewers of the manuscript. Susan Singleton very kindly agreed to write the section on careers in intellectual property which appears in Chapter 1. I should also like to thank Lorraine Keenan for helping to read the drafts and for assisting with the preparation of the tables and index. Several organizations and their staff proved very helpful including the Patent Office and European Commission, and I extend my thanks to those which gave their permission to reproduce materials. Finally, I want to mention my wife Sylvia for her support, encouragement and patience.

I have attempted to state the law as at 1 January 1992.

David I. Bainbridge

Preface to second edition

It is two years since the first edition of this book was published. Intellectual property law is a fast-changing subject and there have been a number of important developments recently resulting from case law, legislation and the work of the European institutions. It was, therefore, thought timely to bring the book up to date and to deal with these issues. The opportunity has also been taken to expand the treatment given to patents, design law and trade marks.

Copyright law has seen the implementation of the controversial Directive on the legal protection of computer programs and this has been fully described. Other Directives dealing with rental, lending and other rights and satellite broadcasting have been adopted and await implementation in the near future. There are also some proposals for Directives on the protection of databases and the term of copyright. The implications of these are discussed as appropriate. The scope of copyright protection for computer programs has received detailed judicial consideration in *John Richardson Computers Ltd* v *Flanders* [1993] FSR 497 and this is fully examined in Chapter 8.

Patent law has seen a number of important cases (including a decision of the European Court of Justice throwing doubt on the validity of section 48 of the Patents Act 1977), the introduction of supplementary protection certificates for medicinal products and further work on a proposal for a Directive on legal protection of biotechnological inventions. The sensitive field of genetic engineering and patent law is becoming increasingly important. In design law we have seen the first major case on the design right and a case of far-reaching importance on the 'must-match' exception to registered designs. Here too, European influences are starting to loom on the horizon.

Perhaps the single most important development has been the introduction of a long-awaited Parliamentary Bill for a new Trade Mark Act. This will make the greatest changes to trade mark law that have been felt for over 50 years and the new law will be a significant improvement over the Trade Marks Act 1938 which has, for some time, been seen by many to be obscure and substantially outdated. The Bill and its implications are dealt with comprehensively in Chapter 20. However, the 1938 Act still receives a full treatment as it will continue to remain important in a number of respects. The law of passing off appears to have been extended as a result of the fascinating case of *Taittinger SA* v *Allbev Ltd* [1993] FSR 641 on the subject of Elderflower Champagne.

Writing the second edition has proved to be both enjoyable and demanding. I have been helped and encouraged by a number of persons and I learnt a great deal by talking to practising solicitors, barristers and others whose work brings them into contact with intellectual property rights, in addition to the staff and students at Aston University. My wife, Sylvia, deserves a special mention. I extend my sincere thanks to them all. I have attempted to state the law as at 1 February 1994.

David I Bainbridge
1 March 1994

Table of cases

Table of legislation

Glossary

Terms and phrases common in intellectual property law

Anton Piller order: an order of the High Court permitting the aggrieved party to enter the premises of an alleged wrongdoer and remove materials that are important evidentially. Named after the case of *Anton Piller KG v Manufacturing Processes Ltd.* [1976] 1 Ch 55. The order must be executed by a solicitor. Its purpose is the preservation of evidence, that is to prevent the destruction or concealment of evidence by an alleged wrongdoer. The order is common in intellectual property cases, for example to allow a copyright owner to take possession of alleged pirate copies of his work. The successful applicant for an Anton Piller order usually has to give a cross-undertaking in damages to compensate the other person should the applicant lose the case at trial.

Assignment: the transfer of the title in a chose in action. For example, ownership of copyright is transferred by means of an assignment in writing which is signed by or on behalf of the previous owner of the copyright, that is the assignor. In intellectual property law, an assignment must be distinguished from an exclusive licence, which is similar in many practical respects, but which does not involve the transfer of the title in the right.

Character merchandising: this occurs when the owner of the rights in some popular character or personality grants licences to others allowing them to apply drawings, photographs or other representations of the character to goods and articles which those others make or sell. Typically, the character will be a famous fictitious character popularized by television or film. Examples are Mickey Mouse, the Pink Panther, Denis the Menace, Indiana Jones, Teenage Mutant Hero Turtles, etc.

Collecting society: a society that collects revenue in respect of the exploitation of an intellectual property right and distributes that revenue amongst the right owners. In some cases, the owners of the right will assign part of their rights to the collecting society. An important example is the *Performing Right Society* which takes an assignment of the performing rights in music, grants blanket licences and distributes the revenue thus earned between the authors of the music. For example, the owner of premises such as a shop to which the public have access will pay a fee to the *Performing Right Society* which will allow him to play popular music in the shop. The same applies to hotels, restaurants and the like playing background music. This arrangement is much more convenient to the shop owner or hotelier and removes the problem of trying to negotiate separate licences with individual copyright owners.

Comptroller of Patents, Designs and Trade Marks: the head of the Patent Office with responsibility for the administration and grant of patents, registered designs and trade marks. Under trade mark legislation and design legislation the Comptroller is referred to as the *Registrar*. The Comptroller has other duties. Examples are: the conduct of hearings and proceedings, the production of statistics and an annual report, increasing public awareness of the work of the Patent Office in addition to working with, advising and participating with the European Patent Office, the World Intellectual Property Organization and the Council of Europe. In 1992, the Patent Office employed over 1,000 persons and had a turnover of nearly £52 million.

Exhaustion: a doctrine emanating from EC law. Basically, the owner of an intellectual property right which relates to articles which have been put into circulation by him or with his consent anywhere within the EC cannot exercise that right to prevent the subsequent import, export or sale of those particular articles. The right is said to be exhausted. This will only apply where trade between Member States is affected.

Infringement: intellectual property law gives rights to the owner of that property permitting him to do certain acts in respect of the thing in which the right subsists. Any person who does one of these acts without the permission or authority of the right-owner is said to infringe the right unless the act concerned is permitted by law or a defence applies. Thus, it is usual to speak of an infringement of copyright or to say that a patent has been infringed. Strictly speaking, it is incorrect to say that a person is in breach of copyright (although even High Court judges have been guilty of this *faux pas*). However, it is accurate to talk of a breach of confidence.

Licence: a licence is a permission given by the owner of a right (the licensor) to another person (the licensee) allowing that other person to do certain specified things in respect of the subject matter of the right. For example, the owner of the copyright subsisting in a musical work may grant a licence to a publishing company allowing it to print and sell copies of the work in the form of sheet music. Another example is where the proprietor (owner) of a patent grants a licence to another person permitting the working of the patent by that other person. Intellectual property licences are usually contractual in nature and the licensor will usually receive royalties by way of consideration for the permission.

Licences may be exclusive or non-exclusive. An *exclusive licence* is one where the licensee has the exclusive right to do certain things to the exclusion of all others including the licensor. Several *non-exclusive licences* may be granted to different persons in respect of the same work and the same activities. For example, the owner of the copyright in a dramatic work may grant several non-exclusive licences to theatre companies permitting each of them to perform the dramatic work live on stage.

Compulsory licences may be granted under the provisions of an Act of Parliament. For example, the Patents Act 1977 gives the Comptroller of Patents, Designs and Trade Marks the power to grant a compulsory licence to an applicant if the patent in question is not, *inter alia*, being worked commercially in the United Kingdom. In some cases, licences are available as of right. This may be the ultimate result of a report from the Monopolies and Mergers Commission (for example, if a patent or design is not being sufficiently worked and this is contrary to the public interest), or because of a statutory provision, for example as regards designs subject to the design right during the last five years of the right, or because the owner has volunteered that such licences be available

(in the case of a patent, the proprietor may do this and from then on he will only pay half the usual renewal fees).

If there is a defect in an assignment or a misunderstanding as to the ownership of a right, a court might be prepared to imply a licence. For example, if a person commissions the making of a work of copyright and there is no express agreement for the assignment of that copyright, the court might be able to imply a licence so that the commissioner can use the work for certain purposes consistent with the purpose of the commission. Alternatively, the concept of beneficial ownership may be used to similar effect.

Mareva injunction: an injunction freezing the assets of a defendant thus preventing him removing them abroad. This is useful where the defendant is not resident within the jurisdiction of the English courts. So named after the case *Mareva Compania Naviera SA v International Bulk Carriers SA* [1980] 1 All ER 213.

Moral rights: the rights that the author of a work of copyright has independent to the economic rights of the copyright owner. The moral rights are: to be identified as the author of the work (or the director of a film) and to be able to object to a derogatory treatment of the work. These rights leave the author with some control over his work even if he does not own the copyright. Any person also has a right, under copyright law, not to have a work falsely attributed to him.

Public domain: refers to all material which is available to the public at large (or a portion of it) and which may be freely used and exploited by anyone without infringing anyone's intellectual property rights. Material may be in the public domain because: (a) it is commonplace, (b) it has been put there deliberately by the 'owner', and (c) the intellectual property rights concerning the material have expired or lapsed. It is possible that material has fallen into the public domain through a breach of confidence, in which case only those persons who have come across the material in good faith without notice of the breach of confidence will be free to make use of it. Such cases will be rare.

Reverse engineering: the process where information about the design or construction of an article is determined by an examination of the article itself, frequently after dismantling or measuring the dimensions of the article. Another manufacturer can copy articles by this process without having to inspect drawings and other design documents made for the article. For example, one company copied another's exhaust pipes by removing an exhaust system from a car and measuring it.

Royalty: a payment mechanism, normally calculated on a percentage of the income derived from sales of works or articles subject to an intellectual property right. This is a common method of paying for a licence to exploit a work subject to an intellectual property right. For example, the author of a literary work may grant a licence to a publisher permitting him to print and sell copies to bookshops. The publisher may then pay the author 10 per cent of the price he receives from the booksellers. Sometimes, royalty figures will have to be fixed by the Comptroller of Patents, Designs and Trade Marks or by the Copyright Tribunal (for example, where a compulsory licence is obtained and the parties cannot agree a royalty). A percentage based on sales is not the only method of payment and a single lump sum or series of sums can be agreed between the parties.

Computer terms and phrases

Assembly language: see low-level programming language

Computer memory: the storage facilities of a computer. Computers can store vast amounts of data. Some of the computer's storage is internal, such as that provided for by integrated circuits and an internal magnetic disk. Other forms of storage are external, for example, 'floppy' diskettes, magnetic tape, CD ROM disks. Older forms of external storage include punched cards and paper tape. Internal computer memory can be classified as being ROM (read only memory) or RAM (random access memory). ROM contains programs such as the start up program and parts of the computer's operating system. ROM cannot be altered; it is permanent. RAM is transient memory, the contents are alterable. It is used to store application programs and associated data during the operation of a computer program which has been loaded from a disk or tape. When the computer is switched off, the contents of RAM are erased.

Computer program: a series of instructions which control or condition the operation of a computer.

Decompilation and disassembly: disassembly is an operation whereby the object code of a computer program is converted into assembly language (a low-level programming language). This is relatively easy to do using an appropriate computer program. Much more difficult is decompilation. This is where the object code is converted into its original form in a high-level language. For this to be feasible, the type and version of the high-level language in which the program was originally written must be known. Quite often the word decompilation is used to describe disassembly (in essence, the process is the same, retrieving the original source code program from its object code version). Reverse analysis of computer programs is usually undertaken using a disassembler program.

High-level programming language: a language that resembles natural language more closely than machine code (object code) or assembly language. High-level language is relatively remote from the machine language which can be directly 'understood' by the computer's central processing unit (processor). It is usually easier to write programs using a high-level language. However, for the program to operate, it must be converted permanently (compiled) or temporarily (interpreted) into machine code. Each statement in a high-level language corresponds to several statements in machine code. From reading a listing of a computer program written in a high-level language, it is possible to obtain a good insight into the ideas used and the program's algorithm. Examples of high-level languages are COBOL, BASIC, PASCAL and FORTRAN.

Low-level programming language: (or assembly language) a language which is very close to the machine code directly executable by the computer. Each statement is directly equivalent to a machine code operation. Assembly language is usually written using mnemonics and memory addresses.

Programming language: a set of words, letters and numbers which, according to the particular syntax of the language, describe a computer program, directly or indirectly, to a computer.

Object code: the machine code resulting from compiling a program written in a high-level language. Alternatively, it is produced by 'assembling' a program written in a low-level language. Object code is directly executable by a computer. Object code is not directly intelligible and must be converted by disassembly before it can be understood by humans. Most computer programs are marketed in object code form. It is faster and far less easy to modify than a source code program.

Reverse analysis: this is the computer equivalent of reverse engineering. It is the process where a computer program is analysed by converting object code into assembly language or high-level language to determine features about the program. Reverse analysis can be used to discover interface details, that is information which will enable the writer of another program to make his program (or the files generated by his program) compatible with the other program. Reverse analysis can also be used to determine a program's algorithm and structure and to facilitate the writing of a program which will perform the same task. Hence, the scope and permissibility of reverse analysis are of utmost importance to the computer industry.

Source code: a program in a high-level language which must be converted into object code before it can be executed. See also, **object code.**

Table of abbreviations

AC	Appeal Cases
All ER	All England Reports
Ch	Chancery
CLSR	Computer Law and Security Report
CMLR	Common Market Law Reports
CPC	Community Patent Convention
Cr App R	Criminal Appeal Reports
CTM	Community Trade Mark
ECR	European Court Reports
EIPR	European Intellectual Property Review
EPO	European Patent Office
EPOR	European Patent Office Report
FSR	Fleet Street Reports
IIC	International Review of Industrial Property and Copyright Law
KB	King's Bench
Mac CC	MacGillivray's Copyright Cases
MLR	Modern Law Review
QB	Queen's Bench
OJ	Official Journal of the European Community
RPC	Reports of Patent, Design and Trade Mark Cases
SI	Statutory Instrument
USC	United States Code
WIPO	World Intellectual Property Organization
WLR	Weekly Law Reports
WPC	Webster's Patent Cases

Part One

PRELIMINARY

1

Introduction

The content of this chapter goes further than a simple introduction of the subject of intellectual property in which the various forms of intellectual property are briefly described. The chapter also addresses some of the basic principles underlying this area of law, examines the nature of intellectual property law and discusses some issues that transcend boundaries between individual forms of intellectual property rights. Some practical considerations are also dealt with briefly at this stage such as the essential rationale for intellectual property and its importance in a commercial sense. Finally, the nature of the study of intellectual property is discussed followed by a brief description of the prospects open to an intellectual property lawyer. The purpose of this chapter is to give the reader a feel for intellectual property law and to introduce some of the important issues, laying the foundations for the more detailed study which follows.

WHAT IS INTELLECTUAL PROPERTY LAW?

Intellectual property law is that area of law which concerns legal rights associated with creative effort or commercial reputation and goodwill. The subject matter of intellectual property is very wide and includes literary and artistic works, films, computer programs, inventions, designs and marks used by traders for their goods or services. The law deters others from copying or taking unfair advantage of the work or reputation of another and provides remedies should this happen. There are several different forms of rights or areas of law giving rise to rights that together make up intellectual property. These are:

- Copyright
- Rights in Performances
- The Law of Confidence
- Patents
- Registered Designs
- Design Right
- Trade Marks
- Passing Off
- Trade Libel.

This list is not exhaustive and there are other rights, for example the rights associated with plant and seed varieties protection, but these will not be dealt with in detail in this book.

Taxonomy of intellectual property rights

Obviously, there are many similarities and differences between the various rights that make up intellectual property law. For example, there is common ground between patents and registered designs, as there is between copyright and rights in performances. Some rights give rise to monopolies whilst others merely prevent the unfair use by others of an existing work or article. The various rights are not necessarily mutually exclusive and two or more of the rights can co-exist in relation to a certain 'thing'. Sometimes, the rights will progressively give protection, one right taking over from another over a period of time during the development of an invention, design or work of copyright.

A practical distinction that can be used to subdivide the various rights is whether there is a requirement for registration, that is whether the right is dependent upon the completion of formalities, or whether it automatically springs into life at a specified time. Another distinguishing feature is the nature of the right, whether it applies to something which is primarily creative or has to do with goodwill in a wide commercial sense. Creative things can be further subdivided into those that are creative in an artistic or aesthetic sense, such as an oil painting, music or literature, or those that are inventive in an industrial context such as a new type of machine or engine or a new way of making a particular product. Before looking briefly at each type of right, consider Table 1.1 which shows how, somewhat imperfectly, intellectual property rights conform to the above taxonomy. The word 'artistic' is used in an everyday and wide sense and should not be confused with the artistic category of copyright works where the word has a special significance.

Table 1.1 Taxonomy of intellectual property

	Basic nature of the right		
	Creative		Commercial reputation & goodwill
Whether formalities required	*Artistic*	*Industrial*	
Formalities required	Registered designs	Patents Plant varieties	Trade marks
Formalities not required	Copyright Rights in performances	Design right	Passing off Trade libel
		The law of confidence	

Formalities

Some intellectual property rights, in respect of particular ideas, works or things, are secured by the successful completion of a formal application and registration procedure. The necessary formalities are not simply satisfied by depositing details with an appropriate authority because such rights are not granted lightly. They do, after all, put the owner of the right in a privileged position whereby he can restrain others from doing certain things whilst exploiting the right for himself. The rights impinge upon the freedom of action of others. The owner has a form of property which he can use as he likes, subject to some constraints, and he can take legal action either to deter would-be trespassers or to obtain damages against those who have trespassed just as the owner of real property can do.[1]

For those rights that require registration, the applicant will succeed in obtaining such registration only if certain rigorous standards are achieved. The rationale for this is that rights subject to formalities are generally monopolistic in nature. Another distinction is between those rights that are provided for and governed by statute and those that derive from the common law (although the latter are given statutory recognition). There is no correlation between the need for formalities and whether the area of intellectual property law is rooted in statute as a comparison of Table 1.1 above and Table 1.2 shows.

Table 1.2 Statute and common law rights

Statute	Common law
Copyright	Breach of confidence
Patent	Passing off
Trade marks	Trade libel
Registered designs	
Design right	
Rights in performances	
Plant varieties	

Industrial property

Traditionally, a number of intellectual property rights were known collectively as *industrial property*. Such rights include patents, trade marks and designs. This term was used in the Paris Convention for the Protection of Industrial Property, 1883. Included in this term by implication are the law of confidence and passing off. When other rights such as copyright are added to industrial property the phrase used to describe the entirety of rights is *intellectual property* and this has become the phrase normally used to describe these individual, and sometimes disparate, rights collectively. Significant moves have been made in terms of the international harmonization of intellectual property law, but it should be remembered that the early development of copyright, patents and trade mark law in England set the pattern that was largely adopted throughout the common law countries of the world. Even before the beginning of the twentieth century, international collaboration and cooperation was well under way, reflecting the world-wide importance of intellectual property.

Before discussing further the nature of intellectual property, it will be useful to describe briefly each right individually using non-technical language.

1 This also extends to other persons having rights under intellectual property law such as an exclusive licensee of a copyright or patent as it does to lessees and licensees of real property.

Copyright

Copyright is a property right which subsists (exists) in various 'works', for example literary works, artistic works, musical works, sound recordings, films and broadcasts. The author of a work is the person who creates it[2] and he (or his employer) is normally the first owner of the copyright which will last until 50 years after the author's death or 50 years after it was created depending on the type of work. Copyright gives the owner the right to do certain things in relation to the work which include making a copy, broadcasting or giving a public performance. Anyone else who does any of these things, known as the acts restricted by copyright, without the permission of the owner, infringes copyright and may be sued by the owner for that infringement. Ownership of a copyright is alienable and it can be transferred to another or a licence may be granted by the owner to another, permitting him to do one or more specified acts with the work in question.

Copyright does not protect ideas, only the expression of an idea (that is, its tangible form), and it is free to others to create similar, or even identical works as long as they do so independently and by their own efforts. In other words, copyright does not create a monopoly in a particular work. In addition, certain things may be done in relation to a work of copyright without the permission of the copyright owner such as making a copy of a work, for example for the purposes of research, private study, criticism or review. Such acts are known as the 'permitted acts' and limit the scope of copyright protection. Copyright gives rise to two forms of rights: the proprietary or economic rights in the work, for example the right to control copying, and, secondly, moral rights which leave the author, who may no longer be the owner of the copyright, with some control over how the work is exploited in the future. The author has a right to be identified as such and has a right to object to derogatory treatment of the work. The moral rights are independent of the economic rights and hence the importance of the distinction between the author of a work and the owner of the copyright subsisting in it. There are some forms of infringement which can be grouped together as being of a commercial nature, such as importing or dealing with infringing copies, that carry criminal penalties.

International protection of copyright works is effected mainly through two international conventions, the Berne Copyright Convention and the Universal Copyright Convention, both of which lay down minimum standards of protection to be attained and for reciprocity of protection between those countries that are signatories to the conventions. The conventions have been responsible for the measure of harmony that now exists on the world stage, albeit far from complete. The effect is that a foreign national can sue in the United Kingdom for copyright infringement occurring there as if he was a British subject.[3] The United Kingdom is a member of both conventions.

Rights in performances

Live performances give rise to two different rights, the performer's right and a recording right. The former is not dissimilar to the author's moral right in copyright, whilst the latter is akin to the copyright owner's economic right. A live performance will frequently involve copyright materials, for example where a recently written piece of music is performed. Sound recordings, films and

2 For some types of works, the author is the person by whom the arrangements necessary for the creation of the work are undertaken.

3 *Hanfstaengl v Empire Palace* [1894] 2 Ch 1. All three judges in the Court of Appeal commented on this then novel state of affairs.

broadcasts of the performance will all be protected by copyright law. However, these rights in performances are required to give the performer himself some rights that he will not otherwise have, unless he is performing a song which he has written himself, to prevent someone (colloquially known as a 'bootlegger') making a recording of the performance without permission for the purpose of making and selling copies. Rights in performances are also important if the work being performed is out of copyright such as a piece of classical music. Another factor is that, if the music is still protected by copyright, the copyright owner might be unwilling to take action. Rights in performances are not restricted to music and are available in respect of a dramatic performance, the reading or recital of a literary work and, a recent addition, the performance of a variety act such as by a juggler.

Rights in performances last for 50 years and the performer's consent is required by any person wishing to make a recording of the performance or transmit it. The person entitled to the recording right is the person who has an exclusive recording contract with the performer. The recording right is infringed by making copies without consent or by dealing with infringing copies. The performing right may not be assigned (although it may pass on the death of the performer), indicating its similarity with moral rights, although the recording right is assignable. Like copyright, there are similar exceptions to infringement and criminal offences associated with certain types of infringement.

The law of breach of confidence

The law of breach of confidence developed as a way of protecting confidential information by preventing its use by persons to whom the information has been divulged in confidence or the further disclosure of the information by such persons. A wide variety of types of information are protected, ranging from industrial or trade secrets to details of a personal nature to secrets about the Government or defence of the realm. In the context of intellectual property it is with trade and industrial secrets that we are primarily concerned. The rationale of the law of confidence is that it stops a person making wrongful use of information beyond the purposes for which it was disclosed to him. The law of confidence protects ideas and is a useful ally to other intellectual property rights, often being the only form of protection when the subject matter is still in its embryonic state.

Patent law

A patent right, because it gives its owner a monopoly, is the form of intellectual property *par excellence*. A patent may be granted in respect of a new invention capable of industrial application and gives a monopoly right that can last for up to 20 years. This very strong form of protection is reserved for inventions that satisfy rigorous standards (for example, novelty and inventiveness) and an application for a patent has to be drawn up precisely and accurately stating the scope of the invention and the claims made in respect of it for which protection is sought. A patent may be for a product such as a new type of longer lasting light-bulb or a new type of ignition system for a petrol engine or it may be for a new industrial process, for example a new way of making synthetic rubber tyres or a novel technique for making plate glass.

Patents can be assigned and licences may be granted in respect of them. The owner of a patent is the person who is registered as the proprietor. A large number of inventions are made by employees and usually, in such cases, the employer will be the proprietor although the inventor will still be named as such. If the invention turns out to be of outstanding benefit to the employer, the employee may apply for a compensation award. By their nature, patents usually protect ideas but there are several controls on the monopoly status they confer upon proprietors. For example, compulsory licences may be available after the first three years from the grant of a patent or it may be indicated on the register of patents that a licence is available as of right. A compulsory licence would be appropriate if the patent was not being worked or if the proprietor was limiting supply of a patented product in order to maintain unrealistically high prices.

It is probably in respect of patents that the greatest strides have been made towards international harmonization, particularly within Europe. The European Patent Convention permits the application for a bundle of patents covering a specified number of Member States including the United Kingdom. The administration of the convention, patent applications, patent grant and resolution of patent disputes are within the remit of the European Patent Office, situated in Munich, which has its own Boards of Appeal.[4] The growing significance of this route to international patent protection cannot be underestimated and, before long, it should be possible to obtain a Community-wide patent. Protection in other countries may be obtained through the Patent Cooperation Treaty, a system which facilitates the application procedure where several countries are concerned although it does not enjoy the level of concordance between members that the European Patent Convention can boast.

4 Applications can also be made through the Patent Office in London. This would be the normal procedure for a United Kingdom applicant.

Design law – registered designs and the design right

A new object or article may be designed which is not sufficiently novel or inventive to satisfy the exacting requirements for the grant of a patent. Designs that are applied to articles may be protected by design law. There are two systems of design law in place in the United Kingdom (some European countries use a watered down version of patent law for designs known as petty patents or utility patents). Of the two United Kingdom systems, one requires registration, has some features in common with patent law in a very broad sense, and applies to designs that have and are intended to have eye-appeal. Examples are household ornaments, toys, display packaging and some electrical appliances. These designs can be described as being aesthetic. The other system of design protection is called the design right and is provided for along copyright lines. This right applies to designs that can be said to be functional in nature such as a new design for an engine cover, fan cowling or plastic printer ribbon container. It can, however, also apply to many registrable designs and there is a large overlap between the two forms of design rights. Both forms of design right relate to the design aspects of the shape or configuration of an article and, for registered designs only, also to pattern and ornament.

The registered design lasts for up to 25 years, initially granted for five years and then subject to renewal every five years, whereas the design right can last for 15 years but this will be reduced if the design is applied commercially during its first five years. Confusingly, the creator of a registered design is known as its author whereas the creator of a design in which the design right subsists is known as the designer. The owner (proprietor for a registered design) will normally be the creator unless the design was created by an employee or under a commission. Both rights are transmissible. There is potential overlap between the two rights themselves and between the two rights and copyright. This is a complex issue which is dealt with in detail in Part 5 of this book.

Trade marks

Trade marks may not have the glamour of inventions or creative works but they are, nevertheless, of substantial importance in an industrial and commercial sense. Trade marks are closely associated with business image, goodwill and reputation. Goods or services are often requested by reference to a trade mark and the public rely on many marks as indicating quality, value for money or origin of goods or services.

Trade marks are registered in respect of certain classes of goods or services. Service marks have been registrable since 1986 as a result of the Trade Marks Amendment Act 1984. However, the separate description of 'service mark' will soon disappear and all marks will be known as trade marks. Registrations for trade marks may be renewed indefinitely. Registration for trade marks began in 1876 and some of the first marks registered (including the very first mark, the Bass Red Triangle label mark) are still in use today. In addition to marks applied to or used in connection with goods or services, there are also certification marks indicating the origin or quality of the goods, for example the 'wool mark'. All registered marks must be used and they can be revoked if they are not used for five or more years. A basic principle is that a trade mark should identify a connection in the course of trade between a trader and his goods (or a provider of services and those services).

Significant changes to trade mark law are underway and, at the time of writing, a new Trade Marks Bill is before Parliament. This will replace the Trade Marks Act 1938 which is widely recognized as an obscure and difficult piece of legislation, and a thorough overhaul of trade mark law is long overdue. In addition to bringing trade mark law up to date, the new Act will allow the United Kingdom to comply with the European Community Directive on the approximation of the laws of Member States relating to trade marks.[5] The implications of the new forthcoming Act are fully discussed in Chapter 20.

5 OJ [1989] L 40/1. The United Kingdom should have complied with the Directive before 1 January 1993.

Passing off

The tort of passing off is, in effect, a common law version of trade mark law. Indeed, trade mark law developed from passing off which in turn developed from the tort of deceit. Being common law, passing off can be more flexible than trade mark law and can apply to marks that would not be sufficiently distinctive for registration as a trade mark. As with trade mark law, passing off is concerned with the protection of business goodwill and reputation and this has the secondary effect of protecting the buying public from trade deception. One area of interest is character merchandising, usually a massive commercial activity whereby famous and often fictional characters are used to promote the sale of goods, for example by applying pictures of the characters to the goods. Mickey Mouse watches and Ninja Turtle T-shirts are examples. The law is belatedly showing signs of recognizing rights in this field of commerce, extending the boundaries of intellectual property.

NATURE OF INTELLECTUAL PROPERTY

Intellectual property as property

Intellectual property rights give rise to a form of property that can be dealt with just as with any other property and which can be assigned, mortgaged and licensed. Table 1.3 below shows a classification scheme for property and how intellectual property fits in with this scheme.

Table 1.3 Classification of property and examples

Real property		Personal property	
Tangible (immovable)	*Intangible*	*Tangible (movable)*	*Intangible*
Land	Easement *Profit à prendre*	Car Desk Book Box of chocolates	Cheque Shares Intellectual property, e.g. copyright

Intellectual property is property in a legal sense: it is something that can be owned and dealt with. Statutory forms of intellectual property are declared to be property rights but even common law forms have been recognized as producing a form of property right.[6] Most forms of intellectual property are 'choses in action', rights that are enforced only by legal action as opposed to possessory rights. Channell J. described a chose in action in the following terms in *Torkington* v *Magee*:

> 'Chose in action' is a known legal expression used to describe all personal rights which can only be enforced by action, and not by taking physical possession.[7]

This has implications as regards the transfer of rights (assignment) and the requirement for consideration. In many cases, the assignment of intellectual property rights is expressly governed by statute and, where this is so, assignment requires no consideration.[8] Otherwise, assignment of a chose in action (meaning 'thing in action') is governed by section 136 of the Law of Property Act 1925 which requires the assignment to be written and signed by the assignor, to be absolute and followed by express notice.[9] However, there is one major exception to the classification of intellectual property rights as choses in action. Patents are declared to be personal property without being a thing in action by section 30(1) of the Patents Act 1977. This strange anomaly seems to be without purpose or consequence as the provisions for ownership and assignment are contained in detail in the Act itself.

6 For example, in the passing off case of *Leather Cloth Co. Ltd.* v *American Leather Cloth Co. Ltd.* (1863) 4 De GJ & S 137, the Court of Chancery recognized that the plaintiff had acquired a property in a trade mark which was valid in equity. However, the right afforded to a performer is not, strictly speaking, a property right nor is the right to take action to prevent a breach of confidence.

7 [1902] 2 KB 427 at 430.

8 *Re Westerton, Public Trustee* v *Gray* [1919] 2 Ch 104.

9 This has been recognized as extending to equitable choses in action. It is possible to have an equitable assignment of an equitable chose in action.

Jurisprudential character

Intellectual property gives rise to rights and duties. It establishes property rights, which give the owner the right to do certain things in relation to the subject matter. For example, if the right is a copyright and the subject matter is a piece of music, the owner of the copyright has the exclusive right to make copies of the sheet music, to make an arrangement of the music and to control the performance of the music. However, the owner also has the negative right to prevent others from doing such things in relation to the music. The right can arise automatically, on the creation of the thing to which the right pertains, an example being copyright which springs to life automatically upon the recording of a work.[10] In other cases, the right depends on the completion of an application and registration procedure, patents and trade marks being examples of such rights. In one area of intellectual property, the right comes into existence only after goodwill has been established. This is the tort of passing off where one trader is attempting to take unfair advantage of another trader's goodwill. For the law to give remedies here, the aggrieved trader must have built up goodwill associated with his business and this could take several years or just a few days depending on the circumstances.

We have seen that intellectual property law is concerned with rights. Conversely, it must create duties, for according to the legal theorist Hohfeld, every right has an associated duty – there cannot be one without the other. It is instructive to take the Hohfeldian analysis of legal rules further, particularly in terms of his legal correlatives and oppositions as shown in Figure 1.1.

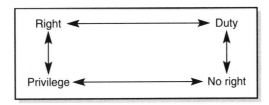

Figure 1.1 Hohfeld's correlations and oppositions

10 Recording, in this sense, means putting ideas into some tangible form, for example by writing down on paper, recording on magnetic tape or entering into a computer memory.

11 Hohfeld, W.N. *Fundamental Legal Conceptions as Applied in Judicial Reasoning*, reprinted in part in Lloyd, Lord (of Hampstead), *Introduction to Jurisprudence* (London: Stevens, 4th edn, 1979) at pp. 260–266.

12 Knowledge of the existence of the right may be relevant in terms of the applicability and measure of some of the remedies for infringement. For example, in an action for infringement of copyright, damages are not available against an 'innocent' infringer, section 97(1) of the Copyright, Designs and Patents Act 1988.

13 Justifiable on the grounds of protecting private interests and promoting investment whilst providing benefits for society at large in terms of increased wealth, knowledge and employment.

Rights and duties have a distinct relationship and are called legal correlatives by Hohfeld.[11] In terms of intellectual property, the right is a right to do certain things such as making copies of a work of copyright, making articles to a design covered by a design right or making products in accordance with a patented invention. The correlative duty is a duty owed by all others not to infringe the right. This duty exists even if the person infringing the right does not know of it.[12] Looking at Hohfeld's scheme again, it can be seen that there are associated privileges and 'no-rights'. The right resulting from the operation of intellectual property law gives the owner of that right a corresponding privilege, that is the privilege to exploit the work. The correlative no-right is to the effect that persons other than the owner do not have this privilege.

In this overall scheme of things, certain provisos must be added. In the area of intellectual property, the law strives to reach a balance between conflicting interests, to reach a justifiable compromise.[13] Therefore, the duty not to infringe is often curtailed by way of exceptions to infringement. For example, the right given by registration of a design does not extend to features dictated solely by function.[14] Copyright law permits many things to be done that would otherwise infringe, for example the so-called 'fair dealing' provisions. Infringement in areas of intellectual property provided for by statute is carefully and precisely defined and any act that falls outside can be freely done by anyone, regardless of the right-owner's wishes. An example in copyright law is lending a book to a friend; copyright law does not control such an act however much the author or the publisher may argue that a sale has been lost as a result.[15]

The honest use by a trader of his own name will not infringe a trade mark comprising the same name. Hohfeld's 'no-right' is also compromised as it is possible, under certain circumstances, to obtain compulsory licences to exploit intellectual property even if the owner of the right is vehemently opposed to this. For example, it may be possible to obtain a compulsory licence to exploit an intellectual property right irrespective of the owner's wishes. The final limitation on intellectual property rights concerns their duration. Most of the rights are limited in time. As a rule of thumb, it can be said that the duration of the right is inversely proportional to its power. For example, a patent gives a monopoly right which is limited to 20 years maximum but a copyright, which is not a monopoly right, will last for at least 50 years.[16] Some rights may, however, endure for longer.[17] Trade mark rights are of indefinite duration and last as long as the proprietor of the mark is prepared to continue both renewing his registration and using the mark. The law of passing off will give protection to the goodwill of a trader as long as this still exists. The law of breach of confidence will be available to protect the information concerned for as long as it can be kept confidential.

Purchasers' rights and intellectual property

The theoretical nature of intellectual property has many practical ramifications. Of particular interest in the understanding of intellectual property law is the question of what rights a purchaser of an article that embodies an intellectual property right obtains. An examination of this question is best carried out by means of an example and that following is set in the context of copyright law, although some of the principles are relevant to other rights. Consider the situation where a person, Georgina, goes to a bookshop to purchase a copy of a best-selling novel. The text of the novel itself will be protected by copyright as a literary work.[18] Georgina picks up a copy of the novel, takes it across to the cash point and buys it. Georgina has become the owner of the book and she now has legal title to it – or does she? She certainly has legal title to the paper, the cover and the printer's ink which are the physical embodiment of the story. But what are her rights in relation to the literary work expressed in the book – does she own it and can she do with it as she pleases? The answer emphatically is NO, the copyright in the literary work still belongs to the publisher of the novel or the author as the case may be. Georgina can do certain things such as reading the book or she may burn it because neither of these acts are controlled by copyright. However, Georgina may not make a copy of the book or translate it into a foreign language because these acts are controlled by copyright.

What if Georgina wishes to lend the novel to her friend John? Lending (as opposed to hiring or renting) is not a restricted act so at first sight this would

14 Section 1(1)(b) of the Registered Designs Act 1949.

15 Attempts to control lending contractually by way of a notice inside a book are of dubious status at law. For one thing, the person buying the book has a contract with the bookseller, not the author nor the publisher and, secondly, it is questionable whether the notice would qualify as a contractual term in any case. This is particularly interesting with respect to 'shrink-wrap' licences common to computer software, see Bainbridge, D.I. *Introduction to Computer Law* (London: Pitman, 2nd edn., 1993) at pp.136–137.

16 In many cases, the period will be significantly longer. However, typographical arrangements of published editions and industrially exploited artistic work are limited to 25 years' protection.

17 Until 1 August 1989, copyright contemplated perpetual rights in respect of works the copyright in which was vested in the Universities of Oxford and Cambridge and some other colleges.

18 Unless the copyright has expired. Copyright endures for 50 years after the end of the calendar year during which the author dies. The typographical arrangement will also be protected by copyright but this is not considered further in the example.

19 Or the author depending upon which of those two own the copyright.

seem to be perfectly lawful. However, if Georgina looks inside the flyleaf of her book she will find a notice stating that certain things cannot be done without the permission of the publisher and lending might be one of them. This brings into question Georgina's status *vis-à-vis* the publisher.[19] The sale of the book was a sale of goods contract between Georgina and the proprietors of the bookshop – there is no privity of contract between Georgina and the publisher. Even if there was, it is extremely doubtful whether the notice was a term of that contract. The only way a contractual link can be forged between Georgina and the publisher would be on the basis of a copyright licence but this would be unrealistic as Georgina does not need a licence to be able to read the book, she would only need a licence if she intended to perform one of the acts controlled by copyright. Therefore, it would seem that, apart from those parts of the notice that refer to the acts restricted by the copyright, Georgina can ignore it and lend the book to her friend.[20]

Another issue is what remedy Georgina has should the novel turn out to be very poorly written, lacking a good plot. In essence, nothing at all unless there has been some misrepresentation by the bookseller concerning the quality of the novel which is sufficient to make the contract between Georgina and the bookseller voidable.[21] Of course, if the tangible matter is defective, for example the printer's ink is poor and has smudged destroying the legibility of the book, or if the binding is poor and the book falls apart, Georgina may obtain redress from the bookseller under section 14(2) of the Sale of Goods Act 1979. However, the absence of a contractual link between Georgina and the publisher robs her of any remedy if the story itself turns out to be very badly written and it does not appear that the implied terms of merchantable quality, fitness for purpose and sale by description contained in sections 13 and 14 of the Sale of Goods Act 1979 apply to a work of copyright.[22] Finally, suppose that the book is not a novel but a cookery book and one of the recipes contains a mistake that can lead to food poisoning if that recipe is used. If Georgina suffers as a result, can she sue for negligence and, if so, whom? The bookseller might be liable in negligence on the basis of *Donoghue* v *Stevenson*[23] or on the basis of the contract between them[24] or the publisher might be liable under the product liability provisions of the Consumer Protection Act 1987. However, the definition of 'product' and 'goods' in the Act would appear not to include intellectual property.[25]

These issues are complex and, in the main, largely unresolved. The problems are compounded tenfold where the transaction includes a licence from the right-owner in addition to a normal sale or service contract, for example where the contract relates to computer software. The 'sale' of computer software must include a licence because using the software will normally require the performance of an act restricted by copyright, unlike the case of reading a book. The licence may be express but will otherwise be implied. This may result in a hybrid contract involving a sale of goods contract for the physical items such as floppy disks together with a licence to use the computer programs included in the package.[26] The legal ramifications should the software prove to be defective and the applicability of the terms implied by statute and controls over exclusion clauses have yet to be fully considered by the courts in the United Kingdom although it does appear from an Australian case *Toby*

---

20 A restriction on lending 'by way of trade or otherwise' is common. Trade lending might be a restricted act if it amounts to renting or if it qualifies as a secondary infringement of copyright. It is arguable whether this extends to the loan of a book to a friend (the application of the *ejusdem generis* rule could restrict 'otherwise' to lending for gain). In any case, the free loan to a friend does not infringe copyright and even if it did control would be totally impracticable. Just why some publishers attempt to control such an act which does not infringe copyright is beyond comprehension and is an undesirable practice in that it unjustly attempts to limit the rights of purchasers and third parties.

21 A publisher who sold a book written by Alastair MacNeill, based on an outline for a story made by the famous novelist the late Alistair Maclean was found guilty of offences under the Trade Descriptions Act 1968 because the relative prominence of Alistair Maclean's name compared to the actual author's name was such that the buying public thought that there were acquiring a book *written by Alistair Maclean*. The publisher was fined £6,250: *The Times*, 28 September 1991.

22 By section 61(1) 'goods' includes all personal chattels other than things in action and money. Copyright is a thing in action, and therefore, outside the provisions of the Act. However, it should be noted that a patent is personal property without being a thing in action and the Sale of Goods Act might apply to an assignment of a patent although it is difficult to forecast whether this is of any relevance.

23 [1932] AC 562. But is it realistic to expect a bookseller to check the safety of instructions in books which he sells? Even if he wants to check, the bookseller will be ill-equipped to validate the integrity of the contents of many books.

24 For example, compare with the latent defect in a catapult giving rise to damages for breach of contract in *Godley* v *Perry* [1960] 1 WLR 9.

25 See section 45(1) of the Consumer Protection Act 1987.

26 For a discussion of the nature

Construction Products Pty. Ltd. v *Computa Bar (Sales) Pty. Ltd.*[27] that the proportionate cost of the hardware (subject to a sale of goods type of contract) and the software (subject to a licence) may provide a clue as to the direction the courts will be prepared to take. The fact of the matter is that intellectual property law is a well developed, refined and advanced branch of law of which other areas of law fail to take proper notice and make due allowance. In dealings involving intellectual property, full account must be made of the failure to address intellectual property by the general laws of contract and of tort and suitable express provisions must be incorporated in any agreement, remedying such defects.

CROSS-CUTTING THEMES

Two particular features or aspects permeate through all or most forms of intellectual property rights. The first is concerned with the control of an abuse of the rights, for example by the proprietor of a patent who is manipulating the market to his own advantage. Obviously, a line will have to be drawn because part of the rationale for intellectual property is that it provides a mechanism for exploiting ideas and the tangible expression of those ideas, but sometimes there is a danger that the exploitation will reach unacceptable levels. The second aspect concerns the international pressures and opportunities presented by intellectual property law and of particular importance in this respect is the European Community.

Abuse of intellectual property

The owner of an important and prominent item protected by intellectual property law might be tempted to use his position to control a market to the disadvantage of competitors and consumers alike. He can prevent or deter potential competitors from developing similar products to his own and he can charge high prices for the product. To some extent, this is to be expected in a capitalistic society; there must be sufficient rewards for the risks of investment in new products and entrepreneurial creation of employment and wealth. Nevertheless, human nature being what it is, some will try to take an 'unfair' advantage of their status as intellectual property right holders. Some rights, such as patents, give a monopoly and this can lead to obvious abuse. However, there are provisions in domestic United Kingdom patent law and in European Community law to control abuse. Section 48 of the Patents Act 1977 allows any person to apply for a compulsory licence to work the patent after three years of the patent being granted, on the basis of specified grounds, for example when the demand for the product is not being met on reasonable terms. Article 85 of the Treaty of Rome[28] controls restrictive trade practices and Article 86 prohibits the abuse of a dominant position within the European Community where either affects or is likely to affect trade between Member States. There seems to be an irreconcilable conflict between the basic monopoly concept of a patent and Article 86. However, European Community law recognizes the existence and utility of patents and does not prevent dominant trading situations developing, it only controls abuse of such dominant positions where this affects trade between Member States.

26 *Continued*
of a contract for the acquisition of computer software, see Bainbridge, D.I., *Introduction to Computer Law* (London: Pitman, 2nd edn., 1993) Chapter 13; Reed C. (ed.), *Computer Law* (London: Blackstone, 2nd edn., 1993) Chapters 2 & 3 and Tapper, C., *Computer Law* (London: Longman, 4th edn., 1990) Part 2.

27 [1983] 2 NSWLR 48 in which it was held that sale of goods law applied to a contract for hardware and software, the bulk of the consideration payable, around 85 per cent, was for the hardware. The judge in this case and some subsequent commentators have failed to grasp the nature of a software copyright licence.

28 Establishing the European Economic Community.

29 In the United States of America, it appears that many companies faced with lawsuits for copyright infringement related to computer software settle out of court because they do not have the money to fight a protracted lawsuit. See, for example, *Computing*, 23 May 1991 at p.4.

30 Section 70 of the Patents Act 1977.

31 Section 60 of the Trade Marks Act 1938. There is an equivalent provision for registered designs, section 35 of the Registered Designs Act 1949.

32 Section 253 of the Copyright, Designs and Patents Act 1988. The Trade Mark Bill 1993 contains a remedy for groundless threats of infringement proceedings in relation to trade marks.

33 See Chapter 21. For a description of the tort of malicious falsehood, see Cornish, W.R., *Intellectual Property: Patents, Copyright, Trade Marks and Allied Rights* (London: Sweet & Maxwell, 2nd edn., 1989) at pp.427–431.

Another way in which the owner of an intellectual property right can abuse his position is to threaten potential competitors with legal action. In some cases the threats may be groundless, but the victim might be prepared to cease the relevant activities or pay a royalty rather than risk the court action and its attendant costs. Litigation can be very expensive[29] and this may deter the person threatened from challenging the validity of the right concerned or otherwise defending the alleged infringement. Patent law contains remedies for groundless threats of infringement proceedings[30] and it is an offence to falsely represent that a trade mark is registered.[31] Although there is no such control over groundless threats of infringement proceedings with respect to an alleged copyright infringement, there is for design rights.[32] Bearing in mind the commercial importance of copyright and the possibility of legal tactics by dominant companies to control the market this seems a serious omission. However, the tort of malicious falsehood (trade libel) might be available in limited cases to provide a remedy.[33]

European and international considerations

Intellectual property law has long been set upon an international stage and, therefore, it is not surprising that the United Kingdom's membership of the European Community has a great influence on copyright, patents, trade marks and the like. Three particular issues mark the impact of the European Community on intellectual property law:

(a) the drive towards greater harmonization of the laws of individual Member States;

(b) the move to Community-wide intellectual property rights;

(c) the impact of the Treaty of Rome on the use and abuse of intellectual property rights.

Each of these aspects is discussed in the context of individual intellectual property rights in the relevant parts of the book. However, a brief overview of basic principles is given below.

Harmonization

34 All the Member States of the European Community now belong to the European Patent Convention.

35 The date that the Patents Act 1977 came into force.

Trade between Member States is facilitated if the intellectual property rights implemented in each State are alike. The process of harmonization of national laws in the field of intellectual property has been proceeding for some time and has not been restricted to the European Community. Harmonization of patent law was effected through the European Patent Convention which has a different membership to that of the European Community.[34] United Kingdom patent law was changed on 1 June 1978 as a result of this Convention.[35] European Community Directives have been instrumental in changing domestic laws protecting computer programs and semiconductor products and trade mark law is in the process of being modified in line with a Directive. European Community Regulations have also had an impact on domestic intellectual property laws and a number of Directives await implementation. There are also some proposals under consideration at the time of writing for Directives that will further affect intellectual property laws.

Community-wide rights

It would be ideal if identical intellectual property rights were recognized and given effect throughout the European Community. Work has been done towards this goal in respect of patent law and trade mark law. A Community Patent Convention was produced in 1975.[36] The Community patent differs from a patent under the European Patent Convention in that the Community patent system will be a unitary system, granting patents that will take effect throughout the Community, whereas a grant obtained under the European Patent Convention gives a bundle of national patents. The Community patent will be administered by the European Patent Office. The Patents Act 1977 contains the necessary mechanism for recognition of the Community patent.[37]

There have also been plans for a Community-wide trade mark system, a 'Euromark' (or CTM). The latest draft Directive dates from 1984 but there are more serious problems to be overcome here compared to patent law. For one thing, similar trade marks may be registered and used in different countries by different proprietors and reconciling these conflicts will prove difficult. There is the added difficulty of the impact of the law of passing off in the United Kingdom and other similar laws, such as the law of unfair competition in Germany. However, it may be that only new and non-conflicting marks can be accepted as Euromarks. There is as yet no date fixed for implementation of the Euromark system and it may be better postponed until after the process of harmonization of national laws has had time to settle.

Conflicts with the Treaty of Rome

The control of abuses of intellectual property rights by provisions in the Treaty of Rome has been noted previously. Those provisions are: Articles 30 to 36 which promote the free movement of goods, Article 85 which prohibits restrictive trade practices and Article 86 which is designed to prevent the abuse of a dominant market position. It must be stressed that these controls are relevant only if trade between Member States is affected or is likely to be affected. By their very nature, the rights given by intellectual property law can easily offend against the Treaty of Rome. For example, the proprietor of a patent will wish to exploit that patent to its best advantage and to do this he may be selective about markets and persons to whom licences are granted and this may operate against the free movement of goods. However, Community law recognizes the advantage of intellectual property law and is sufficiently realistic to appreciate the value of licensing arrangements and the like. Article 222 of the Treaty of Rome states that nothing in the Treaty shall prejudice the rules in Member States governing the system of property ownership and, as already mentioned, intellectual property is a form of property. Nevertheless, the worst abuses are struck down without hesitation by the Commission or the European Court of Justice and this has been sometimes controversial, as evidenced by opportunistic parallel importing and the doctrine of exhaustion of rights.[38]

International aspects

On a wider international stage, it is worth mentioning briefly the importance of uniform laws and reciprocal protection. The vast majority of the world's developed nations play a role and are members of one or more of the various

36 Convention for the European Patent for the Common Market (Community Patent Convention), (76/76/EEC), OJ [1976] L17/1.

37 Sections 86 and 87.

38 See Chapter 9 for an explanation of these terms.

international conventions relating to intellectual property rights. Several of these conventions are administered by the World Intellectual Property Organization (WIPO) which is part of the United Nations. One of the most important and earliest conventions is the Paris Convention for the Protection of Industrial Property, 1883, to which there are currently 114 signatories, including the United Kingdom. This convention, which is updated and amended occasionally (last revision 1979), applies to inventions, trade marks, industrial designs, indications of origin and unfair competition. It establishes basic principles for laws in individual countries and reciprocal protection and, also, priority rights in respect of patents, trade marks and industrial designs. The World Intellectual Property Organization also administers, *inter alia,* the Berne Copyright Convention and the Madrid Agreement which concerns the international registration of trade marks. The United Kingdom will soon become a member of this latter agreement which has 37 signatories at the time of writing. Another important convention on copyright law is the Universal Copyright Convention. Most countries belong to one of the copyright conventions and 61 countries are members of the Patent Cooperation Treaty which provides a streamlined method of obtaining a patent internationally.[39]

39 The membership of this Treaty has increased rapidly over the last few years.

PRACTICAL CONSIDERATIONS

Rationale and justification for intellectual property law

Various justifications have been put forward for the existence of intellectual property law and these have usually been set in the context of patents. A more detailed discussion of the justification for intellectual property rights is therefore contained in Chapter 13 concerning patent law. The basic reason for intellectual property is that a man should own what he produces, that is, what he brings into being. If what he produces can be taken from him, he is no better than a slave. Intellectual property is, therefore, the most basic form of property because a man uses nothing to produce it other than his mind.[40] It is claimed that investment should be stimulated by the presence and enforcement of strong laws that provide a framework ensuring that the publication of new works and the manufacture of new products will be profitable, assuming, of course, that they are sufficiently meritorious, useful and commercially attractive to attain a viable level of sales. If investment is stimulated this should lead to increased prosperity and employment, although these days, sadly, this new employment may be outside the United Kingdom. Another justification is that the existence of strong laws in this area encourages the publication and dissemination of information and widens the store of available knowledge. For example, details of patents are published and are available for public inspection. In due course, when the patent expires, anyone is free to make the product or use the process, as the case may be. This is ample vindication for offering a monopoly protection in the case of patents.

40 I am indebted to Professor Niblett for suggesting this simple but powerful reason.

Another reason is that a person who creates a work or has a good idea which he develops has a right, based partly on morality and partly on the concept of reward, to control the use and exploitation of it and he should be able to prevent others from taking unfair advantage of his efforts. Why should others be able to save themselves all the time and effort required to create or invent the thing concerned? Surely, on this basis, the law should provide remedies against those who appropriate the ideas of others and a person who has devoted time and effort to create something has a right to claim the thing as his own and also has a right to obtain some reward for all his work. The tendency in the United Kingdom has been to encourage innovation through economic incentives but, in other countries, stress has been placed on moral aspects although there have been moves in the United Kingdom to afford rights to the creator independent from the ownership of the right.

Other considerations come into the study of the place of intellectual property law in modern society. Counterfeiting is a serious problem which should be attacked, not so much to protect the interests of legitimate traders but to protect society from being deceived into buying substandard goods. In some cases, safety is at issue, for example, where the counterfeit is a poorly made toy covered in a paint containing high levels of lead.

Combination of intellectual property rights

The lifespan of an invention or a work of copyright can comprise several different and distinct stages and, during these stages, different intellectual property rights may afford protection to the invention or work. For example, an idea for an invention will be protected by the law of confidence until such time as a patent application is published. Once a patent has been granted in respect of the invention, patent law takes over. Other rights might be appropriate such as the law of trade marks or passing off if a mark or name is applied to the product. Intellectual property rights work together to provide legal protection throughout the life of the product until such time as all the rights have expired for one reason or another. Tables 1.4 and 1.5 on pages 19 and 20 give examples of how the various intellectual property rights work together to give continuity of protection.

Note that, in the first example, copyright protection might be all but exhausted because, by section 47 of the Copyright, Designs and Patents Act 1988, documents submitted in a patent application are open to public inspection and may be copied (with the authority of the Comptroller of Patents, Designs and Trade Marks). Copyright still provides limited protection to these documents, for example if copied without such permission.

In the tables, solid lines represent the duration of the right and a broken line signifies that the right still exists but in a weaker form.

The nature of the study of intellectual property

Intellectual property law is a demanding subject but this is compensated by it being one of the most enjoyable and diverse of all substantive law areas. Many aspects of procedural law are also highly relevant. As much as any subject in the study of law, intellectual property law cuts across boundaries and makes the oft-imposed compartmentalization of legal subjects seem awkward and inappropriate. A study of intellectual property law embraces property law (real and personal), contract law, tort, criminal law, commercial law, competition law, European Community law and evidence. An understanding of the subject is enhanced by a knowledge of the basic principles of equity, some legal philosophy and at least a superficial grasp of other disciplines such as economics,

Table 1.4 The life of an invention

Stage in the life of an invention	Form of intellectual property right				
	Confidence	*Copyright*	*Patent*	*Trade marks*	*Passing off*
The bare idea, in the inventor's mind only	***				
Discussion with friends and colleagues	Maintain air of confidence				
Idea expressed in tangible form, e.g. in writing, on drawings, in a computer memory		***			
Preliminary negotiations with potential manufacturers	Maintain air of confidence				
Patent application (assumed successful)	Only in respect of things not disclosed in the patent application		*** From priority date		
Further negotiations with potential manufacturers					
Put invention into production and sell articles made to it				*** If applied for	
Establish a reputation associated with the product					***
		Protected for author's life plus 50 years	Up to a maximum of 20 years	For as long as renewed	For as long as reputation associated with article

*** Signifies the commencement of the right.

Table 1.5 The life of a play

The life of a play	*Form of intellectual property right*			
		Copyright		
	Confidence	*Dramatic work*	*Typographical arrangement*	*Rights in performance*
The bare idea for the play in the playwright's mind only	***			
Preliminary negotiations with potential publishers	Maintain air of confidence			
Play is recorded by writing, typing or using word processor, for example		***		
Further negotiations with potential publishers	Maintain air of confidence			
Publish play	Ideas now in public domain		***	
Performance of play made in public				***
		Dramatic works protected for author's life plus 50 years	For 25 years from end of year of first publication	For 50 years from end of year of performance

*** Signifies the commencement of the right.

Note: rights in performance are for the benefit of the performers and any person with whom they have a recording contract.

sociology and industrial history. A liking for, or sympathy with, science and technology is also helpful. A number of practitioners in the field of intellectual property including members of the Chancery bar, solicitors, patent agents and trade mark agents have science degrees in addition to law degrees and this dual educational background can be very much an advantage in the practice of intellectual property law. A command of one or more foreign languages may also be useful. As the demand for specialists in this area of law is high and the number of graduates emerging from educational establishments who have received formal teaching in the subject is still relatively low, intellectual property is a good area in which to pursue a career.

Careers in intellectual property[41]

41 I am grateful to Susan Singleton for writing this section. Susan is the author of *Introduction to Competition Law* (London: Pitman, 1992).

Intellectual property is a fascinating and constantly developing area of law. Careers in this field can be varied and stimulating. Some solicitors' firms specializing in intellectual property look favourably on science graduates with degrees in chemistry, physics or other such subjects which will facilitate the solicitor in understanding the client's technology. However, a science degree is by no means a strict requirement. Law degrees are, of course, perfectly acceptable.

Those who have studied intellectual property as part of their law degree will find themselves at an advantage, having a basic understanding of copyright, patents, trade marks, etc. Those wishing to practise in this area may join one of the specialist intellectual property niche firms, principally concentrated in London, or, on qualification, take a position in one of the intellectual property departments which most of the larger firms now have. Legal directories provide information concerning which firms are regarded as pre-eminent in this field.

Intellectual property work is not the sole preserve of solicitors. The specialist intellectual property bar thrives in the increasingly litigious business world of today. Those with a bent for advocacy, who wish to be barristers, would be advised to seek pupillage in intellectual property chambers. Other openings include lecturing in this popular subject or working in industry. Many large companies hold huge patent and trade mark portfolios, which require lawyers and others to preserve and monitor. The tracking-down of counterfeiters is another area which requires private investigators or trading standards officers versed in this area of law.

Finally, an intellectual property training at undergraduate level is clearly an advantage for those who wish to qualify as patent or trade mark agents. Their work will comprise filing and keeping up to date registrations of patents and trade marks throughout the world.

Work in the intellectual property field varies across a wide spectrum of subject areas, even within the career routes described above. In a solicitor's practice the work could be divided into litigation and non-litigation. On the litigation side the pursuit of patent, trade mark or copyright infringers through the courts would be the principal work. For example, a firm is instructed by its client to bring proceedings against a rival which is manufacturing widgets in apparent infringement of the client's patent. Proceedings will be issued, a writ served, and the case may proceed to trial. There will be much discussion concerning the evidence. Both sides will bring in their own experts, who will act as witnesses in the trial.

Another client discovers that a new company is copying its product, say a T-shirt. It believes that unless prompt action is taken the evidence of the infringement of its rights in the garment will be destroyed. The solicitors advise that an Anton Piller order should be obtained from the court, permitting the solicitors to seize the allegedly infringing articles. Such orders require speed by the solicitors, subsequent attendance at the premises of the defendant, and the seizure of the articles concerned. This can be a much more proactive role for a solicitor than can be the case in other fields of law. In intellectual property litigation, speed is of the essence.

Joe Bloggs has left a client's firm under a cloud. He has taken with him secret information, know-how and customer lists. The solicitors are asked to advise whether he can be prevented from using that information and if so what practical steps can be taken to achieve that end.

On the non-contentious side, intellectual property work is principally concerned with agreements. Patents, trade marks, copyright and allied rights are licensed and sold regularly in the course of ordinary commercial life. They are valuable assets for any company. Solicitors will be asked to draft agreements effecting intellectual property transactions and to represent the client in negotiations concerning the terms of such agreements. Advice in this field will cover not only basic intellectual property law, but also contract law, issues such as the exclusion of liability, choice of law and jurisdiction, competition law of the European Community and United Kingdom (particularly where restrictions are sought to be imposed on the parties) and tax law, which may often govern the nature of an intellectual property transaction.

What make the intellectual property field interesting are the niceties and sophisticated variants of its many forms. As perhaps its name implies, it is intellectually challenging and requires individual expertise of those called on to advise in connection with it. It is very much a specialist area, but one without the narrow confines of some other such areas, as it covers the full range of industries and their respective problems, from the licensing of copyright in computer software to patents on greasy valves. It is low-tech and high-tech. It demands attention to detail combined with the ability to see the whole of any problem, and requires urgent action in a proactive, practical and commercial way.

Intellectual property law, then, combines the challenge of the difficult legal issue with the excitement and force of major litigation.

Framework for description of rights

In this book, each of the various rights is described, examined and discussed within the following framework:

- Overview and history
- Nature of the right and its subsistence
- Ownership of the right
- Infringement of the right
- Exceptions and defences
- Remedies
- International aspects.

This framework is followed wherever possible, although it has been modified for some of the rights. Because of the nature of these rights, it is usual to speak of infringement rather than breach. Breach is suggestive of a pre-existing contractual or tortious duty owed by and to specific persons although it does apply to the law of confidence. Therefore, a person *infringes* a copyright, a patent or a trade mark, he is *not* in breach of copyright, etc. However, many judges talk in terms of breach of copyright. With passing off, it is usual to say that a person has committed the tort of passing off or is guilty of passing off.

Part Two

COPYRIGHT

(including rights in performances)

2

Background and basic principles

WHAT IS COPYRIGHT?

Copyright is a property right that subsists in certain specified types of works as provided for by the Copyright, Designs and Patents Act 1988. Examples of the works in which copyright subsists are original literary works, films and sound recordings. The owner of the copyright subsisting in a work has the exclusive right to do certain acts in relation to the work such as making a copy, broadcasting or selling copies to the public. These are examples of the acts restricted by copyright. The owner of the copyright can control the exploitation of the work, for example by making or selling copies to the public or by granting permission to another to do this in return for a payment. A common example is where the owner of the copyright in a work of literature permits a publishing company to print and sell copies of the work in book form in return for royalty payments, usually an agreed percentage of the price the publisher obtains for the books.

If a person performs one of the acts restricted by copyright without the permission or licence of the copyright owner, the latter can sue for infringement of his copyright and obtain remedies, for example damages and an injunction. However, there are limits and certain closely drawn exceptions are available, such as fair dealing with the work. An example would be where a person makes a single copy of a few pages of a book for the purpose of private study. Other acts may be carried out in relation to the work if they are not restricted by the copyright, for example, borrowing a Rolling Stones recording to listen to in private.

A broad classification can be made between the various types of copyright work. Some such as literary, dramatic, musical and artistic works are required to be original. As will be seen later, this is easily satisfied and the work in question need not be unique in any particular way. Other works such as films, sound recordings, broadcasts, cable programmes and typographical arrangements can be described as derivative or entrepreneurial works and there is no requirement for originality; for example, repeat broadcasts each attract their own copyright.[1] Copyright extends beyond mere literal copying and covers acts such as making a translation of a literary work, performing a work in public and other acts relating to technological developments such as broadcasting the work or storing it in a computer.

Fundamentally and conceptually, copyright law should not give rise to monopolies and it is permissible for any person to produce a work which is similar to a pre-existing work as long as the later work is not taken from the first. It is theoretically possible, if unlikely, for two persons independently to produce identical works, and each will be considered to be the author of his work for copyright purposes. For example, two photographers may each take a

1 Under previous copyright legislation, original works were described as Part I works and derivative works were described as Part II works. See the Copyright Act 1956.

photograph of Nelson's Column within minutes of each other from the same spot using similar cameras, lenses and films after selecting the same exposure times and aperture settings. The two photographs might be indistinguishable from each other but copyright will, nevertheless, subsist in both photographs, separately. The logical reason for this situation is that both of the photographers have used skill and judgment independently in taking their photographs and both should be able to prevent other persons from printing copies of their respective photographs.

Another feature of copyright law which limits its potency is that it does not protect ideas, it merely protects the expression of an idea. Barbara Cartland does not have a monopoly in romantic novels. Anyone else is free to write a romantic novel since the concept of a romantic novel is an idea and not protected by copyright. However, writing a romantic novel by taking parts of a Barbara Cartland novel infringes copyright, because the actual novel is the expression of the idea. Just how far back one can go from the expression as formulated in a novel to the ideas underlying the novel is not easy to answer. If a person gleans the detailed plot of a novel and then writes a novel based on that detailed plot, there is an argument that there has been an infringement of copyright even though the text of the original novel has not been referred to further or copied during the process of writing the second novel.[2] A detailed plot, including settings, incidents and the sequence of events can be described as a non-literal form of expression. However, the boundary between idea and expression is notoriously difficult to draw.[3] Suffice it to say at this stage that judges have been reluctant to sympathize with a defendant who has taken a short cut to producing his work by making an unfair use of the plaintiff's work, especially when the two works are likely to compete.

Copyright is also restricted in its lifespan; it is of limited duration although it must be said that copyright law is rather generous in this respect. For example, copyright in a literary work endures until the end of the period of fifty years from the end of the calendar year in which the author dies. Approximately, therefore, copyright lasts for the life of the author plus fifty years.[4] This temporal generosity can be justified on the basis that copyright law does not lock away the ideas underlying a work. Ownership of the copyright in a work will often remain with the author of the work, the author being the person who created it or made the arrangements necessary for its creation, depending on the nature of the work. However, if a literary, dramatic, musical or artistic work is created by an employee working during the course of employment, his employer will own the copyright. Additionally, copyright, like most other forms of property right, can be dealt with; it may be assigned, it may pass under a will or intestacy or operation of law and licences may be granted in respect of it.

Full acknowledgement of moral rights is a relatively recent concept in United Kingdom copyright law though well established in other European countries, reflecting differences in the historical development and conceptual foundations of copyright between the United Kingdom and continental Europe. These moral rights, such as the right to be recognized as the author of a work and the right to object to a derogatory treatment of the work, remain with the author irrespective of subsequent ownership and dealings with the ownership of the copyright. They recognize the creator's contribution, a way of giving legal effect to the fact that the act of producing a work is an act of creation and that the cre-

2 *Corelli* v *Gray* [1913] TLR 570.

3 For example in *Nichols* v *Universal Pictures Corporation* (1930) 45 F.2d 119 the eminent U.S. judge Learned Hand said of the boundary between idea and expression 'Nobody has ever been able to fix that boundary, and nobody ever can' (at 121).

4 This is likely to be modified soon to life plus 70 years.

ator has a link or bond with the work which should be preserved regardless of hard economic considerations. The tort of defamation has, of course, long been available and could provide remedies if an author's work were to be distorted or if a work was falsely attributed to someone, depending on the circumstances, for example if a dreadful musical composition was falsely attributed to a famous and brilliant composer. But the difficulties of suing in defamation and the attendant expense and uncertainty are good reasons for the author–work nexus to be specifically recognized and enforceable in copyright law.[5] However, just how straightforward the enforcement of moral rights is remains to be seen.

Copyright law adopts a very practical posture and takes under its umbrella many types of works which lack literary or artistic merit and may or may not have commercial importance. Thus everyday and commonplace items such as lists of customers, football coupons, drawings for engineering equipment, tables of figures, a personal letter and even a shopping list can fall within the scope of copyright law.[6] One important reason for this is that such works are of economic value and will usually be the result of investment and a significant amount of work. Without protection there are many who would freely copy such things without having to take the trouble to create them for themselves and would be able, as a consequence, to sell the copied items cheaper than the person who developed or produced the original. If this were to happen, the incentive for investment would be severely limited. Nor is copyright generally concerned with the quality or merit of a work, the rationale being that it would be unacceptable for judges to become arbiters of artistic or literary taste or fashion. Copyright implicitly accepts that tastes differ between people and over a period of time. If the converse were true, many avant-garde works would be without protection from unauthorized copying and exploitation.

The pace of technological development over the twentieth century has been unprecedented, but here too, copyright law has striven to keep pace and the current legislation, the Copyright, Designs and Patents Act 1988, has attempted to provide a framework which will be resilient to future changes. A recent example of copyright being adapted to prevent the unfair use of works created by or associated with modern technology is the way that many countries have extended copyright to expressly include computer programs in the fold of copyright works.[7]

BRIEF HISTORY

Dating back almost to the beginnings of civilization there have been those eager to profit from the work of others. In ancient times, the idea that the author of a work of literature had economic rights to control dissemination and copying was not particularly well established and yet those who falsely claimed a work were considered contemptible. Most authors were primarily teachers, hence the emphasis on moral rights. The word 'plagiarist', meaning one who copies the work of another and passes it off as his own, is derived from the latin 'plagiarius' meaning kidnapper. The problems of unauthorized copying of works produced by others stretch back into antiquity.

Copyright law has a relatively long history and its roots can be traced back to the advent of printing technology which permitted the printing of multiple

5 Legal aid is not available for defamation but it may be for false attribution.

6 The protection of design and engineering drawings by copyright law is considerably curtailed by the law of designs as a result of the Copyright, Designs and Patents Act 1988, section 51.

7 For example, in the United Kingdom, the Copyright (Computer Software) Amendment Act 1985 (now repealed); in France, 1985 Law art. 46 (Law No. 85-660 of 3 July 1985); in the Federal Republic of Germany, BGbl 1985 I 1137 amending the Copyright Law of 1965 and, in the United States, Pub. L. No. 96-517, 12 Dec 1980, 94 Stat 3028, amending the Copyright Act of 1976.

copies quickly and at relatively little expense. Before the late fifteenth century, works of literature were mainly religious and were written by scholarly monks who would work painstakingly for considerable periods of time preparing their gloriously illuminated books. Obviously, because of the massive human labour and skill required to produce such works, plagiarism of books was not usually a viable consideration. Additionally, there was not a market for books due to the general illiteracy of the population at large. The religious books which were produced were made mainly for use within the monastery or within churches.

Two inventions in the late fifteenth century changed everything. It could be claimed that printing has had a greater impact on civilization than any other single invention. Gutenberg invented moveable type, first used in 1455, and Caxton developed the printing press and published Chaucer's *Canterbury Tales* in 1478, the first 'best seller'. Until the early sixteenth century, the art of printing was practised freely and England was quickly established as an important centre for printing in Europe. But Henry VIII, desiring to restrict and control the printing of religious and political books, eventually banned the importation of books into England. In an Act of 1529 Henry VIII set up a system of privileges and printing came to be controlled by the Stationers' Company, originally a craft guild. With the backing of the infamous Court of Star Chamber, the Government and the Stationers' Company maintained an elite group of printers and regulated publishing. Only registered members of the Stationers' Company could print books, the titles of which had to be entered on the Company's Register before publication. Members of the Company had the right to print their books in perpetuity and this right became known as 'copyright', the right to make copies. The Stationers' Company had powers to enable it to control printing and it could impose fines, award damages and confiscate infringing copies.

This system of privileges, registration and control survived, going through phases of varying effectiveness and licensing systems, until its ultimate collapse in 1695 and, following a brief period when piracy of books flourished, the Statute of Anne was passed in 1709,[8] the first true Copyright Act in the world. The effect of widescale piracy of books was described in the Act, in words bordering on the emotional, as being 'to their [Authors and Proprietors of Books and Writings] very great Detriment and too often to the Ruin of them and their Families'. The importance of the law as a means of encouraging the dissemination of information was also recognized in the Preamble which described the Act as being for:

> '. . . the Encouragement of Learning by vesting the Copies of Printed Books in the Authors or Purchasers of such Copies . . .'

The Statute of Anne gave 14 years' sole right of printing to authors of new books (books already published by 1710 were given 21 years' protection). At the end of that period, the right returned to the author and, if still alive, he was granted an additional 14 years. Infringers were to pay a fine of 1 penny for every sheet of the infringing book, one moiety of which went to the author, the other to the Crown. By modern standards, this was a considerable fine. In addition, infringing books and parts of books were forfeit to the proprietor who 'shall forthwith damask and make waste paper of them'. A system of registration was still in place and an action could be brought only if the title had been entered in the register book at the Stationers' Company, before publication. The

8 8 Anne c.19.

'copy', by the Act was the 'sole liberty of printing and reprinting' a book and this liberty could be infringed by any person who printed, reprinted or imported the book without consent. The Act was also the first clear acknowledgement of the legal right of authorship. The 1709 Act did not extend to certain universities and libraries, but some doubt about the scope and effectiveness of this was remedied by the Copyright Act of 1775[9] which gave a perpetual copyright to copies belonging to the Universities of Oxford and Cambridge and the Colleges of Eton, Westminster and Winchester. This survived until the Copyright, Designs and Patents Act 1988 which substituted a period of 50 years from the end of 1989, after which such rights expire.[10]

Later, there was some argument as to whether the author had, apart from statute, a perpetual common law right to print or publish his work (a right that could be assigned to a publisher in perpetuity). In *Donaldson v Beckett*,[11] it was held that the author did have common law rights that were potentially perpetual (that is, the right of first printing and publishing) but once the work was published, this common law right was extinguished and the author's rights were to be determined solely from the Statute of Anne 1709.[12]

The duration of copyright was gradually increased and its scope widened to include other works such as engravings, prints, lithographs, sculptures, dramatic and musical works. These changes did not go unchallenged; for example, the historian Macaulay described copyright as 'a tax on readers for the purpose of giving bounty to writers'.[13] In the meantime, it was becoming recognized that copyright was important in an international context and the Berne Copyright Convention was formulated in 1886 with the purposes of promoting greater uniformity in copyright law and giving copyright owners full protection in all Member States. Reciprocal protection was based on the place of publication and not by reference to the nationality of the author. The Berne Convention was remarkable in that it successfully reconciled the fundamentally different nature of English copyright law with the French tradition of *droit d'auteur*.[14] In the Berlin revision of 1908 (the Berlin Act), *inter alia*, the term of copyright protection was increased to the life of the author plus 50 years and copyright was extended to cover choreographic works, works of architecture and sound recordings. The revision also introduced the compulsory licence and removed formalities (works still had to be registered in the United Kingdom). Major changes to United Kingdom copyright law were introduced by the Copyright Act of 1911, heavily influenced by the Berlin revision. The 1911 Act formed the basis of copyright law throughout the British Empire and accounts for similarities in copyright law between the United Kingdom and countries such as Australia, New Zealand and South Africa.

Since the Berne Convention and subsequent revisions (and the later Universal Copyright Convention, first promulgated in 1952), the impetus for change in copyright law has been largely the result of the Conventions rather than internal national considerations. The 1911 Act was replaced in the United Kingdom by the Copyright Act 1956 which added three new forms of works: cinematograph films, broadcasts and the typographical arrangement of published editions. The Performing Right Tribunal was created.[15] The 1956 Act classified works as being either original works (Part I works – literary, dramatic, musical and artistic works) or Part II works sometimes known as derivative works or entrepreneurial works (namely, sound recordings, cinematograph films, broadcasts and the typo-

9 15 Geo. III c.53.

10 Schedule 1, para. 13. The Whitford Committee found that the universities and colleges concerned were not overly anxious to retain perpetual copyright. *Copyright and Design Law*, Cmnd. 6732, (London: HMSO, 1977).

11 (1774) 2 Bro PC 129.

12 In the earlier case of *Millar v Taylor* (1769) 4 Burr 2303, it was held that the author did have a common law right which was not extinguished by publication. Both *Millar v Taylor* and *Donaldson v Beckett* were about the same book – Thomson's poem, 'The Seasons'.

13 Hansard, HC Deb vol. 56 (5 February 1841).

14 Authors' rights.

15 Now replaced by the Copyright Tribunal.

graphical arrangement of published editions). These works could be described as derivative as they were usually based on a Part I work. For example, a sound recording may be made of the live performance of a musical work. The link was not essential and a Part II work could be subject to copyright protection without an equivalent Part I work, for example a sound recording of a bird singing could qualify for copyright protection.

Finally, in response to major technological developments, the current Act, the Copyright, Designs and Patents Act 1988 was passed. This Act takes due account of 'moral rights', inalienable rights which belong to the author irrespective of the ownership of copyright.[16] These are equivalent to the *droit moral* of the Rome Act of 1928 of the Berne Convention; that is a right to claim authorship of a work and the right to object to any distortion, mutilation or other modification of a work which could be prejudicial to the honour and reputation of the author.[17] This also has the effect of pulling English copyright law closer to that subsisting in most other European countries.

COPYRIGHT AND ITS RELATIONSHIP TO OTHER INTELLECTUAL PROPERTY RIGHTS

Similar to other intellectual property rights, copyright does not stand in splendid isolation. The unfair taking or use of the results of the application of human intellect may infringe more than any one single right. An act giving rise to infringement of copyright may be associated with or accompany a breach of confidence. For example, if an employee copies a confidential report belonging to his employer without permission and then passes on the copy to a competitor of the employer, there will be an infringement of copyright by the act of making a copy without permission and a serious breach of confidence by the employee giving the copy to the competitor and also by the latter if he realizes or ought to realize that the report is confidential. Additionally, the employee will be in breach of his contract of employment. The action taken by his employer may depend on the remedies available and, in the example quoted, it is likely that the employer would dismiss the employee (for being in breach of the contract of employment) and an injunction would be sought (for breach of confidence) against the competitor restraining him from using the information and from divulging it further. It is unlikely that there would be much to be gained by suing the employee for infringement of copyright, although this could be a case where 'additional damages' might be appropriate (see Chapter 6).

Generally, things that fall within the ambit of copyright law are excluded from the grant of a patent,[18] but preliminary materials such as plans, sketches, specifications and the like will be protected, in principle, by copyright. That is, copyright will subsist in each of these items irrespective of any patent granted for the invention with which the items are concerned.

However, there are two limitations to this, the first being where the details of the invention represented in drawings fall within the scope of design law[19] and, secondly, copies may be made of patent applications (including the specification) by permission of the Comptroller of Patents, Designs and Trade Marks without infringing copyright.[20] Ideas for a new invention, whilst outside the scope of copyright until such time as these are given some tangible form of

16 With the exception of the *droit de suite*, the author's right to payment on subsequent sale of his work of art or manuscript, Berne Convention, article 14[ter].

17 Article 6[bis] of the Berne Convention.

18 Section 1(2) of the Patents Act 1977. But see Chapter 14 for instances when a computer program (which is a literary work under copyright law) can indirectly achieve patent protection.

19 Indirect infringement of a drawing of a design by making the article represented does not infringe the copyright in the drawing, section 51(1) of the Copyright, Designs and Patents Act 1988.

20 Section 47 of the Copyright, Designs and Patents Act 1988.

expression, will be the subject matter of the law of confidence. There is also a close relationship between copyright and the law of designs and many articles that are subject to design law will have been prepared from drawings and written specifications. However, any potential overlap between design law and copyright is expressly removed by the Copyright, Designs and Patents Act 1988.[21]

Sometimes, different rights may be relevant at different times during the life of a work. For example, if a musician has an idea for a piece of music, that idea will be protected by the law of confidence unless it is already in the public domain. When the music is written down, it will be protected by copyright both before and after publication. After publication, of course, confidentiality will be lost. Live performances of the music will be protected by Part II of the Copyright, Designs and Patents Act 1988 which deals with rights in performances (replacing the Performers' Protection Act 1963) and any recordings made will be protected as sound recordings. If a copy is made of a record, cassette tape or compact disc of the music, the copyright both in the sound recording and the original music will be infringed. If the music is a song, the lyrics will be independently protected as a literary work. Thus, it can be seen that a single item may be subject to several copyrights. This is essential as different interests may be involved. For example, in the case of a song, the music may have been written by one person, the lyrics by another. The recording company will also require direct protection of the sound recording so that they may take action against anyone making duplicates of the recordings. The performer and, if recorded live, the recording company, also require protection against persons making unauthorized 'bootleg' recordings of the live performance.

COPYRIGHT AS A MEANS OF EXPLOITING A WORK

Copyright provides a very useful and effective way of exploiting a work economically. It provides a mechanism for allocation of risks and income derived from the sale of the work. For example, if a poet compiles an anthology of poems, this will be protected as a literary work even if unpublished. Copyright provides remedies in respect of published and unpublished works. If an unpublished work is copied and sold by someone without the permission of the copyright owner, remedies such as damages, additional damages, accounts of profits and injunctions are available depending on the circumstances. They are, however, available only to the owner of the copyright or an exclusive licensee. An equitable owner of the copyright cannot obtain damages or a perpetual injunction without joining the owner of the legal title to the copyright, although an equitable owner may be able to obtain a interlocutory injunction on his own. If the poet in the example wants his anthology of poems published, he might decide to approach prospective publishers, and if one agrees to publish, the poet might grant an exclusive licence to the publisher allowing him to print and sell copies of the poems in book form. Alternatively, the poet might agree to assign the copyright to the publisher. In either case, the publisher usually takes the risk, he pays the cost of printing, binding, marketing and distributing. In return the poet will be paid a royalty of, say, 10 per cent of the income obtained by the publisher on sales of the anthology.

21 With respect to the unregistered design right, see section 236 of the Copyright, Designs and Patents Act. By section 1(5) of the Registered Designs Act 1949, as amended, the Secretary of State may make rules excluding from registration articles of primarily literary or artistic (in the copyright meaning) character.

An added attraction, in the case of an exclusive licence – a licence granting the exclusive rights of, for example publishing the work in the United Kingdom – is that the publisher has the right to sue for infringement and if he is successful, the poet will be entitled to a share of the damages awarded equivalent to his lost royalties attributable to the infringement.[22] Depending on the terms of the exclusive licence, the poet may be free to make agreements in respect of other modes of expression of the poems, such as a sound recording of the poems being recited by a famous actor. Of course, if the poet assigns the work to the publisher, the publisher will be entitled to sue for infringement as owner of the copyright and the assignment agreement will usually provide for a division of the damages awarded between the author and the publisher. A major attraction of the exclusive licence, or for that matter an assignment, to a publisher is that copyright actions tend to be fairly expensive and daunting for an individual to pursue but a reputable publishing company will not hesitate in enforcing its rights under copyright law and, indirectly, the rights of the author.

A copyright can be considered to comprise a bundle of rights, associated with the acts restricted by the copyright. These are the acts that only the copyright owner is allowed to do or authorize. They include copying, issuing copies to the public, performing, playing or showing the work in public and broadcasting the work. These can be exploited separately and a copyright owner must be careful not to assign or grant more than he need to. For example, the owner of the copyright in a dramatic work might grant an exclusive right to publish the work in book form to a literary publisher. The owner may then later grant other rights to others, such as the right to perform the work on stage or even the right to make it into a film. In this way, the income the owner derives from the work can be maximized.

22 By section 102 of the Copyright, Designs and Patents Act 1988 the owner or exclusive licensee may not proceed, unless the other is joined in the action, without the leave of the Court.

3

Subsistence of copyright

INTRODUCTION

Fundamentally, copyright law exists to prevent others taking unfair advantage of a person's creative efforts. The courts have displayed very little sympathy for plagiarists and frequently have demonstrated that copyright law ought to be interpreted in such a way as to protect the interests of the copyright owner. This approach is best summed up in the words of Peterson J in *University of London Press Ltd.* v *University Tutorial Press Ltd.*, where he said:

> . . . there remains the rough practical test that what is worth copying is prima facie worth protecting.[1]

The Copyright, Designs and Patents Act 1988 is the legislative source of copyright law. This voluminous Act comprising 306 sections and eight Schedules[2] also deals with designs, rights in performances and has miscellaneous provisions concerning patent law and trade mark law. The copyright provisions of the Act came into force on 1 August 1989. Although some significant changes were made to copyright law by the Act, it was not intended to change fundamental copyright principles and much of the case law developed prior to the coming into force of the Act may still be used as an aid to the construction of the Act and for determining whether the previous law has been departed from.[3] Also, copyright provisions under the Act which correspond to provisions under the previous law are not to be taken to depart from previous law merely because of a change of expression.[4]

Some of the primary effects of the 1988 Act in terms of copyright law are that it:

(a) takes account of new technology and it attempts to use definitions that will prove to be sufficiently flexible to take future technological developments in its stride;

(b) provides more effectively for 'moral rights' for authors, in accordance with the Berne Convention;

(c) removes some of the anomalies under the old law (for example, under the Copyright Act 1956, the owner of the copyright in a photograph was the person who owned the film, not the photographer).

Copyright can subsist only in specified descriptions of works. Section 1(1) lists the works in which copyright can subsist, subject to the qualification requirements (discussed later), as being:

(a) original literary, dramatic, musical or artistic works,

(b) sound recordings, films, broadcasts or cable programmes, and

(c) the typographical arrangement of published editions.

Each of these categories is now examined in detail.

1 [1916] 2 Ch 601 at 610.

2 In its original form. The Act has been amended and some new sections inserted.

3 Section 172(3). Statutory references are to the Copyright, Designs and Patents Act 1988 unless otherwise stated.

4 Section 172(2).

ORIGINAL LITERARY, DRAMATIC, MUSICAL OR ARTISTIC WORKS

Originality

All of these descriptions of works, unlike the other categories of works of copyright, must be *original* for copyright to subsist in them. Before looking at each of the types of works, the meaning of 'original' must be investigated. One can be excused for believing that this means that the work must be new or innovative in some sense but, in copyright law, the word 'original' does not have its ordinary dictionary meaning and the courts have interpreted originality very loosely. The work does not have to be unique or even particularly meritorious. Rather, originality is more concerned with the manner in which the work was created and is usually taken to require that the work in question originated from the author, its creator, and that it was not copied from another work. In *Ladbroke (Football) Ltd.* v *William Hill (Football) Ltd.*, Lord Pearce said that the word original requires:

> . . . only that the work should not be copied but should originate from the author.[5]

5 [1964] 1 WLR 273 at 291.

A drawing of an existing object may not be original because the design of the object was not created by the act of drawing. Harman J came to this conclusion in *The Duriron Company Inc.* v *Hugh Jennings & Co. Ltd.*[6] in the context of an inaccurate drawing of an existing design for an anode, described as being of the most jejune and simple character. It would be unthinkable if this view of originality were applied to drawings made by artists. The act of drawing a representation of a flower or wild bird requires skill and judgment even if a faithfully accurate reproduction is the purpose. Although the thing drawn already exists it is in respect of the drawing that the test of originality must be applied. In this respect the judgment of Harman J is very questionable. It would have been better if he had based his decision on a lack of skill or judgment or that the drawing was not a 'work'.

6 [1984] FSR 1

In another way, the utility of this rule that the work in question must not have been copied from another work is limited because if the work is a copy the very act of copying would most likely infringe the copyright, if any, in the prior work. As a consequence, the maker of the second work would find it difficult if not impossible to exploit his work. One situation of more practical import where originality would be denied on the basis of copying is where the copyright in the earlier work has expired or it is not a work of copyright at all but, for example, a functional article. Otherwise any person, whether a stranger or the owner of the copyright which had subsisted in a work, would be able to extend the duration of copyright simply by making another work which was largely a copy of the prior work, for example by making a copy which incorporates some minor alterations. In *Interlego AG v Tyco Industries Inc.*[7] small modifications made to existing drawings of 'Lego' bricks were held not to give rise to new works independently protected by copyright even though the modifications were technically significant. To hold otherwise would result in the possibility that copyright in what was essentially the same work could be extended indefinitely. Sometimes, originality is equated with the degree of skill, labour and judgment that went into the creation of the work.[8] However, any skill, labour or judgment used merely in the process of copying an existing work cannot be sufficient to make a work original. It is submitted that the require-

7 [1989] 1 AC 217. (Judicial Committee of the Privy Council).

8 See, for example, the judgment of Whitford J. (at first instance) in *LB (Plastics) Ltd.* v *Swish Products Ltd.* [1979] RPC 551 where, talking in terms of artistic copyright, he suggested that the question of originality depended upon the amount of labour, skill and judgment expended on the creation of the work.

ment for 'skill, labour and judgment' is a test to be used to determine whether the thing concerned is a 'work' rather than a test of originality and is more concerned with questions of adequacy and the *de minimis* principle, discussed below.

Peterson J gave the issue of originality detailed consideration in *University of London Press Ltd.* v *University Tutorial Press Ltd.* where he said:

> The word 'original' does not in this connection mean that the work must be an expression of original or inventive thought. Copyright Acts are not concerned with the originality of ideas, but with the expression of thought, and, in the case of a 'literary work', with the expression of thought in print or writing. The originality which is required relates to the expression of thought.[9]

He went on to say that the work must not be copied from another work but that it should originate from the author. The implication of this is that the constituent parts of the work themselves need not be new in any sense and that the work as a whole can be made up from commonplace and pre-existing materials. In a case concerning a street directory, *Macmillan & Co. Ltd.* v *K & J Cooper*,[10] it was held that although many compilations have nothing original in their parts, yet the sum total of the compilation may be original for the purposes of copyright. The basic argument for holding that copyright can subsist in such things is that a reasonable amount of work involving judgment and selection has been used in making the compilation.

Meaning of 'work'

As mentioned above, the search for a reasonable amount of effort expended in the creation of a work is one way in which some judges have tested for originality. For copyright to subsist in a literary, dramatic, musical or artistic work, it must qualify as a 'work' and one way of determining this is to consider the amount of skill or labour which has gone into its creation. Judges have displayed some inconsistency in the formulae they have used, for example, 'work or skill or expense' per Lord Pearce in *Ladbroke (Football) Ltd.* v *William Hill (Football) Ltd.*,[11] 'knowledge, labour, judgment or literary skill or taste' per Lord Atkinson in *Macmillan & Co. Ltd.* v *Cooper & Co. Ltd.*,[12] and 'skill and labour' per Lord Templeman in *British Leyland Motor Corp. Ltd.* v *Armstrong Patents Co. Ltd.*[13] But, nevertheless, it is clear that some measure of skill or effort must have been expended in the production of the work before it can attract copyright protection. In *Baily* v *Taylor*,[14] a case concerning the copying of tables of values of leases and annuities, a request for an injunction to restrain publication of a work containing the copied tables was refused partly on the grounds that any competent person could have recalculated the tables in a few hours. However, this case would probably be decided differently today, a work in which copyright subsists may be created in a relatively short time, for example an artist's freehand sketch.[15]

The question arises as to whether the application of sheer effort alone is sufficient to bestow copyright upon the resulting work. The United States Supreme Court held not in *Feist Publications Inc.* v *Rural Telephone Service Co. Inc.*[16] in denying copyright protection to purely factual compilations, laying to rest the 'sweat of the brow' doctrine.[17] In that case it was held that the 'White Pages' in a telephone directory were not protected by copyright because that section of

[1916] 2 Ch 601 at 608–9.

10 (1923) 40 TLR 186.

11 [1964] 1 WLR 273 at 291.

12 (1923) 93 LJPC 113 at 121.

13 [1986] 2 WLR 400 at 419.

14 (1829) 1 Russ & M 73.

15 The tables would now be protected as a literary work and the issue now would be whether a substantial part had been copied.

16 (1991) S.Ct. 1282.

17 According to this doctrine copyright was a reward for the hard work that went into compiling facts.

the directory was the result of effort only and did not require the application of skill and judgment. It was basically a question of arranging names in alphabetical order and including addresses and telephone numbers. On the other hand, 'Yellow Pages' in telephone directories could be copyright material because of the skill and judgment expended in selecting the classification system and the fact that other copyright materials such as advertisements were also included.

This approach is not contrary to the position in the United Kingdom and, apart from the wooliness of some judgments on this point, it appears that the same principle applies. For example, in *Cramp* v *Smythson*,[18] a diary containing the usual information contained in diaries, such as a calendar, tables of weights and measures and postal information failed to attract copyright. The reason was that the commonplace nature of the information left no room for taste or judgment in the selection and organization of the material.

However, in *Waterlow Directories Ltd.* v *Reed Information Systems Ltd.*[19] the subsistence of copyright in legal directories containing lists of names and addresses of firms of solicitors and barristers was not put in issue. The defendant simply denied infringement. In *Cobbett* v *Woodward*[20] it was suggested that a Post Office directory which was purchased by the public could be subject to copyright although it was held that there could be no copyright in a trade catalogue, a fact that must be seriously doubted now. Though there must be some doubt about the copyright status of compilations that require no skill or selectivity in their making, as soon as some additional material is included that does require skill or judgment then copyright will subsist in the compilation. That additional material may be a set of headings for a classification scheme[21] or a credit rating appended to each client in a database of customers. This approach complies with German copyright law which requires a work to be a 'personal intellectual creation'[22] and the European Community approach which requires a copyright computer program to be the author's 'own intellectual creation'[23] Where the creation of the work itself does not require skill or judgment, it may still attract copyright if there is sufficient skill or judgment expended in the work carried out in preparing for its creation. Aldous J so held in *Microsense Systems Ltd.* v *Control Systems Technology*[24] in relation to a list of mnemonics designed to control pelican crossings. He said it was at least arguable that the skill and labour in devising the functions and operations of the controller should be taken into account.

One way of looking at the requirement for skill or judgment to have been used in the creation of a work of copyright is to consider it as an example of the basic principle, as alluded to by Peterson J in the *University of London Press* case, that copyright does not protect ideas, merely the expression of ideas.

Idea/expression

The United States has a well-defined legal principle that copyright protects expression but not ideas; indeed the Copyright Act of 1976 specifically states that ideas, procedures, processes, systems, methods of operation, concepts, principles and discoveries are excluded from copyright protection.[25] Blank forms for accounts were denied protection by the Supreme Court in *Baker* v *Selden*[26] and the idea/expression dichotomy has been developed to high levels of sophistication by the United States courts ever since. The distinction is important in two respects:

18 [1944] AC 329.

19 [1992] FSR 409.

20 (1872) 14 Eq 407 LR.

21 It was held that there was copyright in a set of headings in a trade catalogue in *Lamb* v *Evans* [1893] 1 Ch 218.

22 German Copyright Act 1965, section 2(2).

23 Article 1(3) Council Directive on the legal protection of computer programs OJ [1991] L122/42.

24 (unreported) 17 July 1991 (Chancery Division).

25 United States Copyright Act of 1976, 17 USC § 102 (a).

26 101 US 99 (1880).

(a) some things can be expressed only in one way, the expression is dictated by its function or external factors, and

(b) if copyright were limited only to the actual words used (in a literary work), it would be too easily circumvented by re-writing the work using different words.

Therefore, as a direct result of these points, some forms of expression are not protected as being ideas (or equivalent to, or dictated by, ideas) and some forms of expression are not directly perceivable (they are non-literal forms of expression).

United Kingdom law does not explicitly make the distinction between idea and expression either in legislation or case law.[27] However, English judges have decided cases in such a way to produce similar results. In *Page v Wisden*[28] (which was cited in *Baker v Selden*) it was held that a cricket scoring sheet was not protected by copyright. This is not unlike the blank form exclusion in *Baker v Selden*. In *Kenrick v Lawrence*[29] copyright was denied to a drawing showing a hand holding a pen and marking a ballot paper. The intention of the person commissioning the drawing was that it could be used to show persons with poor literacy skills how to vote. It was held that a similar drawing did not infringe because it was inevitable that any person who attempted to produce a drawing to show how to vote would create a similar drawing. In other words it was an unprotectable idea.[30] Non-literal expression has been recognized as being within the scope of copyright protection in *Rees v Melville*[31] and *Corelli v Gray*[32] concerning the plot of a play. The idea/expression distinction and, particularly non-literal copying, has become very relevant in terms of computer programs and is discussed further in Chapter 8.

De minimis principle

It is clear that it would be ridiculous to afford copyright protection to works that are trivial in the extreme or so small as to be entirely insignificant. However, a line has to be drawn separating works that are the proper subject matter of copyright and those that are not. The courts will often, though not always, use the principle *de minimis non curat lex*,[33] that is, that the work is insufficiently significant to be afforded copyright protection. For example, in *Sinanide v La Maison Kosmeo*,[34] it was held that to quote a bit of a sentence of a literary work was too small a matter on which to base a copyright infringement action. *A fortiori* a name cannot be subject to copyright. For example, the name of the fictional television detective 'Kojak' was not protected by copyright.[35] In the *Sinanide* case, the plaintiff had used an advertising slogan 'Beauty is a social necessity, not a luxury' and complained unsuccessfully about the defendant's use of the phrase 'A youthful appearance is a social necessity'. Generally, copyright will not subsist in advertising slogans and titles because they are usually fairly brief and the song title 'The Man who Broke the Bank at Monte Carlo' was held to be insufficiently substantial for copyright purposes.[36] Nevertheless, there may be circumstances where a title is of such an extensive nature and important character that it will be the proper subject matter of copyright.

If the name or title is represented in a particular way it seems possible that copyright might subsist in it. It was held in *News Group Newspapers Ltd. v Mirror Group Newspapers (1986) Ltd.*[37] that the use by one newspaper in its

27 Judges may sometimes recognize the principle, for example Whitford J in *Geo. Ward (Moxley) Ltd. v Sankey* [1988] FSR 66 and Ferris J, applying U.S. authorities, in *John Richardson Computers Ltd. v Flanders* [1993] FSR 497.

28 (1869) 20 LT 435.

29 (1890) 25 QBD 99.

30 However, the judge went on to say that if the drawing had been an exact duplicate, there would have been an infringement of copyright. In other words, exact copies would infringe, inexact copies would not.

31 [1911–1916] Mac CC 168.

32 [1913] TLR 570.

33 The law does not concern itself with trifles. In *Exxon Corporation v Exxon Insurance Consultants International Ltd.* [1981] 3 All ER 241, it was held that the word 'EXXON' could not be an 'original literary work' without recourse to the *de minimis* principle.

34 (1928) 139 LT 365.

35 *Tavener Rutledge Ltd. v Trexapalm Ltd.* [1977] RPC 275.

36 *Francis Day & Hunter Ltd. v Twentieth Century Fox Corporation Ltd.* [1940] AC 112.

37 (unreported) *The Times* 27 July 1988 (Chancery Division).

advertisements of the logo of another newspaper (*The Sun*) gave rise to an arguable case of copyright infringement. Of course, unauthorized use of a name or title could infringe a trade mark or be passing off.

Tangibility

We have seen that copyright does not protect ephemeral things such as an idea for a novel or a play.[38] As such, ideas may have some protection under the law of confidence, depending upon the circumstances. Copyright law is, because of the nature of the drafting of the current Act and previous Acts, directed to the expression of ideas rather than the ideas themselves.[39] The method used by copyright law is to require that the work has some tangible form. In the case of some works, such as sound recordings and films, their very existence implies tangibility. The same applies to artistic works. For example, according to Lawton LJ in *Merchandising Corp. of America v Harpbond*[40] a painting is not an idea: it is an object. However, literary, dramatic and musical works clearly can exist without any material form. For example, a person may compose a poem and recite it from memory without ever having written it down. A musician may devise a tune whilst sitting at a piano keyboard without recording it in some way. Therefore, for literary, dramatic and musical works the Copyright, Designs and Patents Act 1988 declares that copyright does not subsist in such works unless and until they are recorded, in writing or otherwise.[41] 'Writing' is defined by section 178 (the interpretation section)[42] as including any form of notation or code, whether by hand or otherwise and regardless of the method by which, or medium in which, it is recorded. These definitions are deliberately couched in language which should ensure that copyright will not be defeated by technological advances; hence the use of the phrase 'or otherwise'. The requirement for some tangible existence is also important in that it dates the creation of the work; that is, the work is deemed to have been made when it is recorded.

Of course, one would expect that the record is made by the author or with the author's permission but this is not essential and section 3(3) states that it is immaterial whether the work is recorded by or with the permission of the author. Therefore, if a person delivers an impromptu unscripted speech without having made any notes previously, and a member of the audience writes the speech down verbatim, then the speaker will be the author of the written work for copyright purposes. If the member of the audience uses skill and judgment and makes a selective record of the speech, perhaps adding his own comments and interpretation, then it is arguable that he may be considered to be the author of the notes for copyright purposes. In *Walter v Lane*,[43] it was held that copyright subsisted in a newspaper report of a speech by Lord Roseberry prepared from a reporter's shorthand notes and that the newspaper for whom the reporter worked for, *The Times*, owned that copyright.[44]

Literary work

Section 3(1) of the Copyright, Designs and Patents Act 1988 defines a literary work as any work, other than a dramatic or musical work, that is written, spoken or sung, and includes a table or compilation, a computer program, and preparatory design material for a computer program.[45] It should already be clear that a literary work does not have to be a work of literature and this is

38 Provided that they are not so detailed as to be considered a non-literal form of expression.

39 This distinction is evident in the Berne Copyright Convention, see Chapter 9.

40 [1983] FSR 32.

41 Section 3(2).

42 Section 178 contains several important definitions but other definitions are scattered throughout the Act. However, the Act is very helpful in that an index is provided to assist in the location of definitions – section 179. Other indexes are provided for the parts of the Act dealing with rights in performances and the design right.

43 [1900] AC 539.

44 At the time of this case there was no requirement for originality. It may depend on whether the person making the record exercises some skill thus bringing some originality to the report, see *Roberton v Lewis* [1976] RPC 169 and Cross J's comments on *Walter v Lane*. In *Express Newspapers plc v News (UK) Ltd.* [1990] 1 WLR 1320 it was held that *Walter v Lane* was still undeniably good law.

45 Preparatory design material was added by the Copyright (Computer Programs) Regulations 1992, SI 1992 No. 3233.

implied by the inclusion of tables, compilations, computer programs and preparatory design material for computer programs in the category of literary works. The courts have long since been prepared to take a very wide view of what constitutes a literary work; for example, Peterson J said in *University of London Press Ltd.* v *University Tutorial Press Ltd.*:

> It may be difficult to define 'literary work' as used in this Act [Copyright Act 1911], but it seems to be plain that it is not confined to 'literary work' in the sense in which that phrase is applied, for instance, to Meredith's novels and the writings of Robert Louis Stevenson ... In my view the words 'literary work' cover work which is expressed in print or writing, irrespective of the question whether the quality or style is high. The word 'literary' seems to be used in a sense somewhat similar to the use of the word 'literature' in political or electioneering literature and refers to written or printed matter.[46]

This must be expanded nowadays to cover material recorded on computer storage media and compact discs. For example, a report produced using a word processor is a literary work the moment it is stored on a computer disk because it is then recorded 'in writing or otherwise'.

Examples of works afforded literary copyright are books of telegraphic codes,[47] examination papers,[48] football coupons,[49] consignment notes,[50] headings in a trade directory[51] and business letters.[52] Tables and compilations expressly fall within the meaning of literary work, examples of tables being railway timetables, company balance sheets, actuarial tables and mileage charts. Compilations include things such as lists of customers, directories and the 'Top Twenty' best-selling records. Although it has been accepted in the past that a compilation can comprise both literary and artistic materials,[53] a change in terminology in the 1988 Act may mean that there is no copyright protection in a compilation of artistic works only because a literary work must be written, spoken or sung and it can be argued that artistic works are not written.[54] Of course, the artistic works may be protected in their own right.

The Copyright, Designs and Patents Act 1988 affords copyright protection to computer programs and preparatory design material for computer programs as literary works. The Act, very wisely, does not attempt to define what a computer program is.[55] In view of the rate of development of computer technology, any precise legal definition would prove to be inappropriate in the future or, at least, would unduly inhibit flexibility in the law. Where the Act does contain definitions, they tend to be very widely drawn. The classification of computer programs as literary works follows international developments and is in line with European Community developments on the subject. Computer programs, preparatory design material for computer programs and computer databases are considered more fully in Chapter 8.

For a work to be an 'original literary work', it must accord with that phrase taken as a whole. It is not sufficient that a work satisfies each word individually. This is another limitation on the scope of copyright, the effect of which is similar to the *de minimis* principle. In particular, the word 'original' should not be looked at in isolation. In *Exxon Corporation* v *Exxon Insurance Consultants International Ltd.*,[56] the plaintiff was a multinational oil company. It decided to choose a new corporate name and after considerable research and consultation, the word 'Exxon' was decided upon. The plaintiff contended that

46 [1916] 2 Ch 601 at 608.

47 *Ager v Peninsula & Oriental Steam Navigation Company* (1884) 26 Ch D 627 and *DP Anderson & Co. Ltd. v Lieber Code Co.* [1917] 2 KB 469.

48 *University of London Press Ltd. v University Tutorial Press Ltd.* [1916] 2 Ch 601.

49 *Ladbroke (Football) Ltd. v William Hill (Football) Ltd.* [1964] 1 WLR 273.

50 *Van Oppen & Co. Ltd. v Van Oppen* (1903) 20 RPC 617.

51 *Lamb v Evans* [1893] 1 Ch 218.

52 *British Oxygen Co. Ltd. v Liquid Air Ltd.* [1925] 1 Ch 383.

53 For example, *Purefoy Engineering Co. Ltd. v Sykes Boxall & Co. Ltd.* (1955) 72 RPC 89, concerning a trade catalogue containing literary and artistic materials.

54 Monotti, A., 'The Extent of Copyright Protection for Compilations of Artistic Works' [1993] 5 EIPR 156.

55 Neither does the Computer Misuse Act 1990 define computer program. However, there are some legal definitions, for example the Banks Committee described a computer program as: 'a series of instructions which control or condition the operation of a data processing machine' *Committee to Examine the Patent System and Patent Law*, 1970, Cmnd. 4407, para. 471, p.140. The United States has a statutory definition in an amendment to the Copyright Act of 1976 which is: 'a set of statements or instructions to be used directly or indirectly in a computer to bring about a certain result', 17 USC § 101. This begs the question 'what is a computer?'!

56 [1981] 3 All ER 241

the word 'Exxon', being first used by it, was *original*, that it was *literary* because it was expressed in letters and that it was a *work*, being the result of considerable research and effort. Therefore, the plaintiff argued that the word 'Exxon' was an 'original literary work' within section 2(1) of the Copyright Act 1956. However, it was held that the term 'original literary work' was a composite expression denoting a literary work intending to offer information, instruction or pleasure in the form of literary enjoyment.[57] For a word or expression to be within the meaning of 'original literary work', it was not enough that the work could be described as 'original', 'literary' and a 'work'. Although 'Exxon' could be described thus separately, it was not an original literary work because it conveyed no information, provided no instruction and gave no pleasure. There was, therefore, no copyright in the word 'Exxon'.[58] However, the requirement for literary enjoyment must be questioned now because of the addition of computer programs to the categories of literary works.

Dramatic work

A dramatic work includes a work of dance or mime.[59] Under previous law, it was possible, theoretically, for a work to be both a dramatic work and a literary work, for example a script for a play could fall into both of these categories. This was of no consequence as the rights provided for were identical for both types of work. Under the Copyright, Designs and Patents Act 1988, this sterile overlap is removed and a literary work is defined to exclude a dramatic work. Dramatic works in common with literary and musical works must be recorded for copyright to subsist in them. In *Tate v Fullbrook*[60] it was held that a visual skit for a music hall sketch involving the use of a firework was not the subject matter of copyright because it had not been reduced to writing.[61] More recently, in *Green v Broadcasting Corporation of New Zealand*,[62] it was held that the dramatic format of a television show had to be certain for that format to be entitled to copyright protection. The appellant, Hughie Green, devised the television show 'Opportunity Knocks' and claimed copyright in the scripts and dramatic format of the show. The latter comprised catch phrases, the use of a 'clapometer' and sponsors to introduce competitors. Finding for the respondents, Lord Bridge said that the protection which copyright gave was a monopoly and that there had to be certainty in the subject matter of such a monopoly. However, Lord Bridge erred in this respect because copyright certainly does not give a monopoly, it being free to anyone else to produce a similar work as long as they do so independently. A better rationale is that Mr. Green's dramatic format could not be protected either because it lacked certainty for want of material form or that the respondent had only copied the ideas and not the expression of those ideas. It is difficult to reconcile this case with earlier cases such as *Rees v Melville*[63] concerning the plot of a dramatic work in which it appears that the plot of the play, in addition to the written expression, may be afforded some protection. It depends on the level of abstraction from the literal expression. The closer it is, the more likely it can be considered to be protected. The further away it is, the more likely it will be considered to be an unprotected idea.[64]

57 Based on the definition of a literary work given by Davey J in *Hollinrake v Truswell* [1894] 3 Ch 420 at 427–8. This seems to be a narrower definition than that adopted by Peterson J in *University of London Press Ltd. v University Tutorial Press Ltd.* [1916] 2 Ch 601.

58 The word 'Exxon' was previously registered as a trade mark by the plaintiff both within the United Kingdom and elsewhere.

59 Section 3(1).

60 [1908] 1 KB 821.

61 See also, *Tate v Thomas* [1921] 1 Ch 503.

62 [1989] RPC 700 (The Judicial Committee of the Privy Council).

63 [1911–1916] Mac CC 168.

64 Legislative action is needed to clarify the protection of the dramatic format of 'game shows'. An opportunity to include suitable measures in the Broadcasting Act 1990 was not taken advantage of.

Musical work

A musical work is one consisting of music, exclusive of any words or action intended to be sung, spoken or performed with the music. A song will, therefore, have two copyrights, one in the music and one in the words of the song, the latter being a literary work. This is convenient as it is common for different persons to write the music and the lyrics. Once again, the work must be reduced in writing or otherwise. The Copyright, Designs and Patents Act 1988 gives no guidance as to what a musical work is but, in practice, this does not seem to cause any problems; what is beautiful music to one man might be a dreadful cacophony to another. It would seem that a relatively small number of notes and chords are sufficient for copyright protection as a dispute as to the ownership of the copyright in the old Channel 4 logo music, comprising a four note theme in an orchestral setting, demonstrated.[65]

Making an arrangement of an existing piece of music may attract its own copyright in addition to and running alongside the copyright subsisting in the prior work. For example, a musician who expends a reasonable amount of skill in arranging and adapting a piece of music originally written for a rock group so that it is suitable for a traditional orchestra will have a copyright in the orchestral work.[66] Of course, he could be guilty of infringing the copyright in the earlier piece of music if he makes his arrangement without the permission of the copyright owner.[67]

Artistic works

The artistic work category is a diverse one and includes several different types of works. It is a category that causes special problems because it overlaps with design law and the relationship between copyright and design law is not at all clear cut. Section 4(1) of the Copyright, Designs and Patents Act 1988 defines 'artistic work' as meaning:

(a) a graphic work, photograph, sculpture or collage, *irrespective of artistic quality,*
(b) a work of architecture being a building or a model *for* a building, or
(c) a work of artistic craftsmanship.

[emphasis added.]

As copyright is stated to subsist in the first category irrespective of artistic quality, a painting of coloured rectangles by Mondrian or a Jackson Pollock painting made up of coloured squiggles is as deserving of copyright protection as is a portrait or a landscape painted in a traditional manner. This formula ensures that personal taste or preference is no bar to copyright protection and it also safeguards utilitarian and functional works such as drawings for engineering equipment, photographs made for scientific or record purposes, weather charts and plans for civil engineering and building works. However, it appears that for works falling into the last category, that is, works of artistic craftsmanship, some qualitative characteristic is required, as will be discussed later.

Section 4(2) expands on the definitions and states that a graphic work includes:

65 *Lawson* v *Dundas* (unreported), *The Times*, 13 June 1985 (Chancery Division).

66 *Wood* v *Boosey* (1868) LR 3 QB 223.

67 This falls within the meaning of making an adaptation, one of the acts restricted by copyright, section 21(3)(b).

(a) any painting, drawing, diagram, map, chart or plan, and

(b) any engraving, etching, lithograph, woodcut or similar work.

The scope of some artistic works is very difficult to fix with any certainty. For example, the meaning of sculpture could be particularly wide. Section 4(2) provides a non-exhaustive definition stating that sculpture includes a cast or model made for the purpose of sculpture. Whilst a three-dimensional object carved from a block of wood or stone and bronze or porcelain figures are obviously sculptures it is doubtful that any three-dimensional article would qualify. Presumably the collection of bricks laid out in the Tate Gallery is a sculpture but a casing for a gearbox, a moulded plastic chair and a bath are not. What about a moving sculpture such as a 'mobile' or Chinese windcharms? Dictionary definitions of 'sculpture' are suggestive of works of art but this contradicts the phrase 'irrespective of artistic quality'. If we require the work to have been produced by a sculptor, this is difficult to reconcile with the fact that graphic works are not required to be made by an artist as engineering drawings qualify as artistic works.

There is very little case law on sculptures. In *J & S Davis (Holdings) Ltd.* v *Wright Health Group Ltd.*[68] it was held that a cast for making a denture was not a sculpture because it was not made for the purposes of sculpture. A generous view of the meaning of sculpture was taken in the New Zealand case of *Wham-O Manufacturing Co.* v *Lincoln Industries Ltd.*[69] in which it was held that a wooden model, from which moulds were made in order to produce plastic flying discs known as Frisbees, was a sculpture.[70] The moulds were held to be engravings, following the decision of Judge Paul Baker in *James Arnold & Co. Ltd.* v *Miafern Ltd*[71] in which he held that the term 'engraving' encompassed not only the final image made by the engraved plate but the plate itself also.

A photograph means a recording of light or other radiation on any medium on which an image is produced or from which an image may by any means be produced, and which is not part of a film. Copyright may subsist in a photograph of a painting providing skill and judgment has been expended, for example by selecting part of the painting only and/or choosing lighting conditions, aperture settings, etc. In *Groves' Case*[72] it was held that copyright subsisted in a photograph of an engraving taken from a picture – three potential copyrights! The definition of photograph is particularly wide, presumably to keep pace with future technological change. Like literary, dramatic and musical works, artistic works must be 'original'. However, there is no requirement for them to be recorded as their very existence implies some form of tangibility.

A building includes any fixed structure, and a part of a building or fixed structure. Buildings effectively have double protection, as works of architecture and through the plans drawn up for the buildings. Models for buildings, such as a model made for a proposed building to show to prospective investors and clients, are specifically protected but models of buildings are not. However, if a model made of an existing building is copied, the copyright in the building itself and in the drawings made for the construction of the building will be infringed. With the exception of works of artistic craftsmanship, artistic copyright is very generous in what it can protect and in the scope of the protection. Some fairly simple things have been afforded artistic copyright such as a bare design of a hand,[73] a simple label[74] and a working sketch of machinery.[75]

68 [1988] RPC 403.

69 [1985] RPC 127.

70 The provisions of section 2 of the New Zealand Copyright Act, 1962 defining artistic works were equivalent to those under the United Kingdom Copyright Act 1956.

71 [1980] RPC 397.

72 (1869) LR 4 QB 715.

73 *Hildesheimer and Faulkner* v *Dunn & Co.* (1891) 64 LT 452. But see also *Kenrick* v *Lawrence* (1980) 25 QBD 93 involving a simple design of a hand showing voters how to cast their votes.

74 *Charles Walker Ltd.* v *The British Picker Co. Ltd.* [1961] RPC 57.

75 *B O Morris Ltd.* v *F Gilman (BST) Ltd.* (1943) 60 RPC 20.

Typefaces are not specifically mentioned in section 4 among the categories of artistic works. Nevertheless, it is beyond doubt that a typeface is an artistic work. Indeed, there are references in the Act to typefaces as a form of artistic work. For example, sections 54 and 55 (permitted acts in relation to typefaces) are stated in terms of the 'copyright in an artistic work consisting of the design of a typeface'. In the past, typefaces would have been within the ambit of registered designs (common features such as a new type of serif would have been registrable) but now typefaces are usually stored as computer software and not applied to metal type. Thus, copyright protection is more appropriate.

Artistic craftsmanship

Works of artistic craftsmanship give rise to the greatest difficulty amongst artistic works. Normally, one might expect this category to include such things as jewellery to a special design, 'designer' goods such as furniture and clothing and quality hand-made items intended to appear attractive or 'rustic' in some way and as found in craft shops.[76] Certainly, the phrase 'artistic craftsmanship' conjures up items made by hand by skilled workers which are bought because of the quality of workmanship and because of their eye-appeal. Better examples of hand carved cuckoo clocks made in Switzerland should clearly be works of artistic craftsmanship. But where is the line drawn? What about mass-produced cuckoo clocks which are crudely assembled from machine jigged plywood, incorporating a cheap timepiece and a plastic cuckoo? And what about a mock-up for furniture to be mass-produced, roughly made with a light timber frame held together with nails and covered in upholstery but too flimsy to be able to support a person sitting on it? The case of *George Hensher Ltd.* v *Restawhile Upholstery (Lancs.) Ltd.*[77] concerned such a prototype made for a suite of furniture, described as 'boat-shaped'. The House of Lords held that the prototype was not a work of artistic craftsmanship and that for something to fall into this category it must, in addition to being the result of craftsmanship, have some artistic quality. None of their Lordships seemed able to lay down a workable test for the required artistic quality but agreed that the work must be viewed in a detached and objective manner. The question of whether a particular item possessed that quality is one of fact and evidence, in particular, expert evidence, is an important factor in reaching a decision. Lord Reid said that a work of artistic craftsmanship would have the necessary artistic quality if any substantial section of the public genuinely admired and valued the thing for its appearance even though others may have considered it common or vulgar.

Lords Reid and Kilbrandon considered that the intention of the maker of the article was an important though not conclusive issue. Whilst Viscount Dilhorne considered that mass produced articles could not be works of artistic craftsmanship, Lord Simon of Glaisdale said that the word 'artistic' was not incompatible with machine production. However, the claim of copyright infringement concerned the appellant's prototype, not the furniture made from it, and the real obstacle standing in the way of copyright protection for it was that the appellant was unable to convince any of their Lordships that the prototype was, in any sense, artistic. It was likely that the design of the mock-up chair would have been accepted for registration under the Registered Designs Act 1949 because it

76 In some cases, an article which might properly be considered to be a work of artistic craftsmanship might also qualify for protection as a sculpture. For example, a three dimensional wood carving.

77 [1976] AC 64.

was new and designed for eye-appeal, albeit somewhat vulgar, and the failure to apply for this relatively inexpensive form of protection against copying reduces the sympathy one can feel for the appellant. Nevertheless, a substantial amount of thought lay behind the design, aimed to revive falling sales, and the respondent simply copied the appellant's furniture made in accordance with the prototype, saving itself the trouble of designing furniture that would appeal to the public and sell in large numbers. The respondent took unfair advantage and the decision in the House of Lords is difficult to square with Peterson J's oft-quoted dictum that a thing worth copying is worth protecting.[78]

However, the *Hensher* case has done nothing to clarify the meaning of 'artistic craftsmanship' and whilst items such as Chippendale chairs, hand-crafted jewellery and fashion clothing are clearly within the meaning, utilitarian and mass-produced works are left vulnerable in terms of copyright protection even though they will often be subject to large commercial investment and risk. For once, the pragmatic and commercially sound approach of copyright law founders on the rock of taste and one might ask why atrocious or feeble paintings and sculptures are protected by copyright law whilst other things such as furniture, that have proven visual appeal, fail to attract protection and why the *Hensher* principles have not been discarded by the Copyright, Designs and Patents Act 1988. The one saving grace is that many of the articles that will fail to be classed as works of artistic copyright will be protected either as registered designs or under the recently introduced design right. However, the former requires registration and the payment of a fee and both rights require a standard of novelty which is probably higher than is the case for copyright.

The question of artistic craftsmanship was considered again later in the High Court in *Merlet* v *Mothercare plc*.[79] Walton J, applying *Hensher*, held that a prototype cape for a baby, called a 'Raincosy', was not a work of artistic craftsmanship. He said that the test was whether the thing itself was a work of art and, consequently, the garment had to be considered by itself and not as worn or containing a baby. The Raincosy was a work of craftsmanship only and not a work of artistic craftsmanship because the garment itself was not aesthetic, although seeing the ensemble of mother, child and garment may have given an onlooker some sense of aesthetic satisfaction. On the issue of the maker's intention he said that the purpose of the garment was to protect a child from the rigours of the Scottish climate and the plaintiff had not been concerned with the creation of a work of art.

SOUND RECORDINGS, FILMS, BROADCASTS OR CABLE PROGRAMMES

These are the derivative works. They are usually based on original literary, dramatic, musical and artistic works, for example a recording of pop tunes, where the record is protected as a sound recording and each tune will have musical copyright and literary copyright in any lyrics. Sometimes, however, a derivative work is not based on one of the 'original' works. For example, a recording of the Flying Scotsman building up steam will be a sound recording but there is no other underlying work. Sound recordings, films, broadcasts and cable programmes[80] need protection so that the investors and entrepreneurs involved in such works can take direct action in case of infringement. The fact that several

78 *University of London Press Ltd.* v *University Press Ltd.* [1916] 2 Ch 601 at 610.

79 [1986] RPC 115. The case went to the Court of Appeal but only on the issue of whether there had been an infringement of the copyright in the drawings of the garment concerned.

80 Note the spelling 'programme'; this is presumably to distinguish these from computer programs. The spelling 'program' has become accepted in terms of computer technology. However, in spite of the common view to the contrary, the '-am' ending is the better and accords with the traditional English spelling. It is not an 'Americanism', the '-amme' ending was adopted in the nineteenth century when French words and spellings were popular.

different original works may be encapsulated in a single film or sound recording makes it much more convenient for the owner of the rights in the latter to sue directly for any infringement. To take an example, consider a musical film such as *South Pacific;* there may be separate copyrights in the music, the lyrics to the songs and the dramatic parts of the film. If a part of the film is copied without permission, the owner of the copyright in the film can sue, otherwise it would be necessary to identify which rights were affected and who owned those rights and what the relationships were between those persons and the owner of the film. The situation could become very complex and this could work to the detriment of the film industry, the ensuing confusion making it easier for film piracy to flourish. Of course, if the owner of the copyright in a film successfully sues for infringement of copyright, he may distribute part of the award in damages to the various copyright owners in accordance with the contractual arrangements. In the case of an award of account of profits in respect of concurrent rights under an exclusive licence, the court will apportion the profit between the licensor and licensee.[81]

81 Section 102(4).

Compared to the 'original' works of copyright, these derivative works give rise to far fewer problems relating to the question of copyright subsistence. There is no requirement that these works be original because many would fail; for example, in a broadcast of a play, the play may be an original dramatic work in the copyright sense but the broadcast cannot be original in the popular sense.

Sound recordings

By section 5(1) of the Copyright, Designs and Patents Act 1988, a sound recording is:

(a) a recording of sounds, from which the sounds may be reproduced, or
(b) a recording of the whole or any part of a literary, dramatic or musical work, from which sounds reproducing the work or part may be produced,

regardless of the medium on which the recording is made or the method by which the sounds are reproduced or produced.

Note that the language of the Act talks of 'sound' not music so that recordings of non-musical sounds will come within the definition and a recording of a person reciting a passage from a book or a poem falls within the meaning of a sound recording. The definition is very wide in terms of storage media to take account of changes in technology. There is nothing to prevent several persons making recordings of the same thing at the same time and each having their own copyright. For example, if several persons make a sound recording of Concorde passing through the sound barrier each will own the copyright in their own recording and can sue for infringement if someone makes a copy of *their* recording without permission.

Films

Films are also defined by section 5(1) and are a recording on any medium from which a moving image may by any means be produced. Again notice the width of the definition: 'any medium' and 'by any means'. As the definition only refers to the image, a sound track is not included but will have a separate copyright as a sound recording. Merely copying an old film or an old sound recording does not bring about a new copyright, for, by section 5(2), copyright does not subsist in a sound recording or film which is, or to the extent that it is, a copy taken from a previous sound recording or film. If a recording company make a new record of a song, it will use a master recording to produce cassettes, vinyl records and compact discs for sale to the public. These cassettes, records and discs will not themselves have copyright as a result of section 5(2). However, making a copy of one without permission will *indirectly* infringe the copyright in the master recording.

Broadcasts

Copyright subsists in broadcasts and cable programmes. By section 6 of the Copyright, Designs and Patents Act 1988, a broadcast, which consists of visual images, sounds or other information, is a transmission by means of wireless telegraphy of visual images, sounds or other information which is capable of being lawfully received by members of the public, or which is transmitted for presentation to members of the public. Before the 1988 Act, this was limited to the BBC and the IBA. Now, even satellite television such as BSkyB is covered. By section 6(2), if a transmission is encrypted it is still regarded as capable of being lawfully received by members of the public if decoding equipment has been made available to the public by or with the authority of the person making the transmission or the person providing the contents of the transmission. An example of a transmission for presentation to the public is where a boxing match is transmitted to a sporting arena in a different part of the country from where the match is held, to be displayed on a large screen to members of the public who pay an entrance fee. By section 6(6), copyright does not subsist in a broadcast which infringes (or to the extent that it infringes) the copyright in another broadcast or cable programme.

It is important to know where the broadcast is made from as this will determine whether it attracts United Kingdom copyright. This could be an issue where the broadcast is made by satellite and, therefore, section 6(4) states that such a broadcast is made at the place from which the signals carrying the broadcast are transmitted to the satellite. Thus, a satellite broadcast where the signal is transmitted to the satellite from within the United Kingdom will attract United Kingdom copyright even though the satellite is over another country or international waters at the time.

Cable programmes

The content of a broadcast is defined as visual images, sounds or other information. A cable programme service is similar, consisting wholly or mainly of visual images, sounds or other information. The difference between a broadcast and a cable programme service is that a broadcast is a transmission by wireless telegraphy, that is over the airwaves, whereas a cable programme service is a transmission by means of a telecommunications system other than wireless telegraphy, for example by cables laid in the ground. Therefore, the two are mutually exclusive. It is the cable programme which is protected by copyright (not the cable programme service) and this is defined by section 7(1) as meaning any item included in a cable programme service. There are certain exceptions in section 7(2) which can be added to or modified by the Secretary of State. These exceptions include interactive systems, that is where visual images, sounds or other information can be transmitted back to the person providing the service, and certain 'closed' systems which are not connected to any other telecommunications system.

By section 7(6), if the cable programme included in a cable programme service merely involves the reception and immediate re-transmission of a broadcast, it is not protected by copyright, although the broadcast itself will be. Also, copyright is declared not to subsist in a cable programme if it infringes, or to the extent that it infringes, the copyright in another cable programme or broadcast.

Typographical arrangement of published editions

Section 8 defines a published edition, in the context of a typographical arrangement of a published edition, as the whole or any part of one or more literary, dramatic or musical works. The protection of the typographical arrangement of published editions gives some protection to the publisher of a work which is itself out of copyright and also gives some recognition to the skill expended in work such as selection of typestyles, format and typesetting. Artistic works are not included. If a publisher produces a book from a literary work which is still in copyright and a person copies a substantial part of the book, say by photocopying, then both the copyright in the literary work and the copyright in the typographical arrangement will be infringed.[82] If the copyright in the content of the book has expired, for example in the case of a Shakespeare play, copying the book will infringe the typographical arrangement only.

This form of copyright is increasingly important because of the recent advances in photocopying technology. To prevent publishers extending the life of their typographical arrangement of copyright indefinitely, copyright is declared not to subsist in the typographical arrangement of a published edition if, or to the extent that, it reproduces the typographical arrangement of a previous edition.

QUALIFICATION

For copyright to subsist in a work, by section 1(3) of the Copyright, Designs and Patents Act 1988, the qualification requirements must be satisfied. This can be achieved in two ways, either by reference to the author of the work or by reference to the country of first publication or, in the case of a broadcast or cable programme, the country of first transmission.[83] In most cases, qualification will be easily satisfied such as where the work is created by a United Kingdom citizen (or an individual domiciled or resident in the United Kingdom) or is first published in the United Kingdom. Also, international copyright conventions will give protection to works that would not otherwise qualify. Basically, these conventions, of which there are two, afford reciprocal protection to member countries and most developed countries belong to one or other or both. The United Kingdom is a signatory to both the Berne Copyright Convention and the Universal Copyright Convention. As a result, if a work is first published in or transmitted from a convention country or if the author of the work is a citizen of or is domiciled in a convention country the owner will be able to take

82 However, if the person types the book into a computer, there will be an infringement of the literary work but not the typographical arrangement.

83 Section 153. In relation to Crown Copyright, the qualification requirements are waived in the case of a work made by an officer of servant of the Crown in the course of his duties, section 163(1)(a). Similarly in respect of Parliamentary copyright, section 165(1).

action for infringement in the United Kingdom. Similarly, works first published or transmitted in the United Kingdom or having an author who is British or is domiciled in the United Kingdom will be protected in all the other convention countries.

Qualification by reference to the author

As will be seen in the following chapter, authorship and ownership of copyright are two distinct concepts and it is quite common for copyright to be owned by non-living legal persons such as corporations. However, it is self-evident that the author of a literary, dramatic, musical or artistic work will be a living (or lately deceased) person. In the case of computer-generated literary, dramatic, musical and artistic works and sound recordings, films, broadcasts and cable programmes the Copyright, Designs and Patents Act 1988 still defines the author in terms of a 'person', that is the person who makes the arrangements necessary for the creation of the work, makes the work or the broadcast or provides the service, but in relation to these works it would seem that all forms of legal persons, including artificial persons such as corporations can be the author of the work. The author of the typographical arrangement of a published edition is the publisher and this will often be a corporation such as a limited company. For this reason, the qualification requirements cover the situation where the author is a corporate body.

By section 154(1) a work will qualify for copyright protection if the author comes within any of the following categories:

(a) a British citizen, a British Dependent Territories citizen, a British national (Overseas), a British subject or a British protected person within the meaning of the British Nationality Act 1981;
(b) an individual domiciled or resident in the United Kingdom or another country to which the relevant copyright provisions apply;
(c) a body incorporated under the law of a part of the United Kingdom or another country to which the relevant copyright provisions apply.

The countries to which these provisions apply can be extended by Order in Council to the Channel Islands, the Isle of Man or any colony.[84] A work also qualifies if at the 'material time' the author was a citizen of or a subject of or domiciled or resident in another country or if the author was a body incorporated under the law of another country to which the provisions have been extended.[85]

The 'material time' is defined by section 154(4) as being, in the case of an unpublished literary, dramatic, musical or artistic work, the time it was made or, if it was made over a period of time, a substantial part of that period. If published, the material time is the time of first publication. If the author dies before first publication, the material time is the time immediately before the author's death. For sound recordings, films and broadcasts, the material time is the time they were made. For cable programmes it is the time they were included in a cable programme service and for a typographical arrangement of a published edition it is the time when the edition was first published.

A work of joint authorship qualifies for copyright protection if, at the material time, any of the authors satisfies the requirements for qualification by reference to the author, and only those who do satisfy those requirements are to be

[84] Section 157.

[85] Section 159.

taken into account for the purpose of first ownership of copyright and duration of copyright.[86]

Qualification by reference to country of first publication or transmission

There is a distinction between transmitted works, namely broadcasts and cable programmes, and all other forms of works. In the case of the latter, by section 155, they qualify for protection if they are first published in the United Kingdom, any convention country or any country to which the copyright provisions are extended by Order in Council. A publication can still be a first publication even if it is simultaneously published elsewhere and a period not exceeding thirty days is considered simultaneous. As an example, if a musical work is made by an author who fails to meet the qualification requirements (such as an Iranian living in Tehran) and the work is first published in Iran but is then published in the United Kingdom within the following thirty days, the music will attract United Kingdom copyright protection under the provisions contained in section 155. The music will be deemed to have been simultaneously published in Iran and the United Kingdom.

The meaning of publication is central to these provisions and it is defined in section 175 as being the issue of copies to the public, including by means of electronic retrieval systems in the case of literary, dramatic, musical and artistic works. The construction of a building is equivalent to publication of the work of architecture it represents and any artistic works incorporated in the building.[87] In order to clarify the meaning further some specified acts are declared not to amount to publication, for example a performance of a literary, dramatic or musical work, an exhibition of an artistic work, the playing or showing of a sound recording or film in public or the broadcast of or inclusion in a cable programme service of a literary, dramatic, musical or artistic work or a sound recording or film. Also excluded are the issue to the public of copies of a graphic work (for example, a sketch) representing, or photographs of, a work of architecture in the form of a building or a model for a building, a sculpture or a work of artistic craftsmanship.[88]

Thus, selling sheet music or video films to the public will be regarded as publication but selling prints made from an original painting will not be. Whether the sale of the original oil painting to a member of the public is to be regarded as publication is a moot point and it may be stretching the language of section 175 too far, especially as it talks in terms of the plural. This is reinforced by subsection 5 which excludes publication which is 'merely colourable and not intended to satisfy the reasonable requirements of the public'. This means that a non-qualifying author who intends to sell copies of his work to the public in large numbers in a non-convention country cannot obtain the international benefits of the conventions simply by putting a few copies on sale at the same time in a convention country. However, selling or offering for sale small numbers of copies may still be deemed to be publication if the intention is to satisfy public demand as in *Francis Day & Hunter Ltd.* v *Feldman & Co.*[89] in which the sale of six copies of the song 'You Made Me Love You (I Didn't Want To Do It)' was deemed to be good publication because of the publisher's intention from the outset to satisfy public demand in the United Kingdom. Section 175(6) states that no account is to be taken of any unauthorized acts, therefore publication

86 Section 154(3).

87 Section 175(3).

88 Section 175(4).

89 [1914] 2 Ch 728.

by a person without the permission of the copyright owner will not have any consequences as regards the qualification requirements for the work involved.

For transmitted works, broadcasts and cable programmes, the qualification requirements are satisfied if it is sent from the United Kingdom or any country to which the copyright provisions are extended by Order in Council. Qualification is determined by reference to the country of transmission and not the country or countries of reception. There is no provision here for dealing with simultaneous transmissions within a 30-day period.

It can be seen that qualification for copyright protection will rarely be in issue, particularly as a result of the operation of the Berne Convention and the Universal Copyright Convention and the reciprocity they provide for. In case there are any shortcomings in the protection offered for British works in another country, section 160 of the Copyright, Designs and Patents Act 1988 permits, by Order in Council, the restriction of rights conferred to authors connected with that country. It is unlikely that any such Orders will be made.

DURATION OF COPYRIGHT

The Copyright, Designs and Patents Act 1988 has simplified the provisions relating to the duration of copyright. Under the Copyright Act of 1956 there were three rules for the duration of copyright in artistic works, depending on which variety of artistic work they were.[90] There were also different rules for works published or unpublished at the time of the author's death.[91] Now things are much clearer, although the transitional arrangements which apply to works in existence at the time when the 1988 Act came into force are not particularly straightforward.[92]

The rules for determining the duration of copyright depend on the nature of the work in question, but as a basic rule of thumb copyright lasts for at least 50 years, sometimes considerably more, except in the case of typographical arrangements of published editions and certain artistic works that have been commercially exploited where the period is 25 years. There are also special rules for the duration of Crown Copyright, that is in respect of works of which Her Majesty the Queen is the first owner of the copyright, and Parliamentary copyright. Perpetual copyright previously enjoyed by the Universities of Oxford and Cambridge and the Colleges of Eton, Winchester and Westminster in relation to certain works under the Copyright Act 1775 is abolished and such works existing at the time the Copyright, Designs and Patents Act 1988 came into force are given a 50 year copyright, commencing at the end of 1989.[93]

Literary, dramatic, musical and artistic works

As a rule, the identity of the author of a work will be known and commonly the author will have produced his work on his own, not in collaboration with another author. The copyright in a literary, dramatic, musical or artistic work of known authorship, having a single author, expires at the end of the period of 50 years from the end of the calendar year during which the author dies.[94] Therefore, when the work is made, it is impossible to pinpoint the exact time when the copyright will expire; a work created by a relatively young author should have a long copyright, perhaps close to or even exceeding 100 years. If

90 Section 3 of the Copyright Act 1956.

91 Section 2 of the Copyright Act 1956.

92 See Schedule 1 to the Copyright, Designs and Patents Act 1988, para. 12.

93 Schedule 1, para. 13.

94 Section 12(1).

the work is the result of the collaboration of two or more authors and the contribution of each is not distinct from the other or others it is a work of joint authorship and, by section 12(4), the 50-year period runs from the end of the calendar year during which the last surviving author dies. If the identities of all the authors are not known, the period is calculated by reference to the end of the calendar year during which the last surviving known author dies.

It is conceivable, though unlikely, that a work might be created by a person unknown.[95] The work may still qualify for protection on the basis of the country of first publication and section 12(2) of the Act makes provision for the duration of copyright for works of unknown authorship. The 50-year period runs from the end of the calendar year in which the work was first made available to the public. 'Making available to the public' includes, in the case of a literary, dramatic or musical work, a public performance, broadcast or inclusion in a cable programme service. For artistic works, it includes public exhibitions, showing a film including the work in public or inclusion in a broadcast or cable programme service. The definitions are not exhaustive and should also cover acts such as selling or offering to sell to the public copies of the work. In determining whether the work has been made available to the public, no account is taken of any unauthorized act so that the period of 50 years does not start to run if the work has been performed in public without the permission of the copyright owner. Copyright in a work of unknown authorship is potentially perpetual, if the work is not made available to the public which seems to be an anomaly difficult to justify. However, the practical effect of this is diluted because, by section 57(1), the copyright in a literary, dramatic, musical or artistic work is not infringed if it is not possible by reasonable enquiry to ascertain the identity of the author and it is reasonable to assume that the copyright has expired or that the author died 50 years or more before the beginning of the calendar year in which the relevant act was done. If the work involved is truly anonymous, there may be considerable difficulties regarding the ownership and enforcement of the copyright although, in such circumstances, section 104(4) contains a presumption that the publisher of the work as first published was the owner of the copyright at that time. If the identity of the author becomes known after the expiry of the copyright then, under section 12(2), this has no effect. The period of copyright cannot be extended by such an occurrence. However, if the identify of the author becomes known before the expiry of copyright under section 12(2), normal rules apply.

The final form of literary, dramatic, musical or artistic work having special provision is where the work is 'computer-generated', being a work generated by computer in circumstances such that there is no human author.[96] Without the life of a human author to measure the term of copyright, the starting date for the 50-year period is sensibly calculated, by section 12(3), from the end of the calendar year in which the work was made. This is the only form of literary, dramatic, musical or artistic work in which the actual time the work was made is relevant to the duration of copyright.

The duration of subsistence of copyright in certain types of artistic work will be considerably shortened if they are 'commercially' exploited. By section 52, where an artistic work has been exploited by or with the licence of the copyright owner by making articles which are copies of the work by an industrial process and marketing them, the copyright subsisting in the artistic work will

95 Of course, there may be situations when, for reasons of his own, the author does not want to be identified and his identity remains a secret between the author and his publisher. In such circumstances, it would appear that the work would be one of unknown authorship for copyright purposes.

96 Section 178. Computer-generated works are fully explained and discussed in Chapter 8.

effectively expire at the end of the period of 25 years from the end of the calendar year during which the articles were first marketed. The copyright in the artistic work still runs its full course notionally but, after the 25-year period, the work may be copied by making articles of any description or doing anything for making such articles without infringing the copyright. The fine detail has been left to the Secretary of State and by the Copyright (Industrial Processes and Excluded Articles) (No.2) Order 1989[97] an artistic work is deemed to have been exploited for the purposes of section 52 if more than 50 articles have been made or goods manufactured in lengths or pieces not being hand-made have been produced.[98] Certain types of artistic work are excluded from this provision, for example works of sculpture, wall plaques, medals, medallions and printed matter primarily of a literary or artistic character. Typically, works of artistic craftsmanship would be caught by this reduction in term of copyright if exploited. This limitation is further discussed in Chapters 7 and 18.

There is at the present time a proposal for a European Community Council Directive harmonizing the term of protection of copyright and certain related rights.[99] This will, *inter alia*, extend copyright in the original works to life of author plus 70 years and will, if adopted in its present form, apply to works in which copyright still subsists at the end of 1994.

Sound recordings and films

Both sound recordings and films are governed by the same rules and, for either, the duration of copyright may depend on when the work was made or, in some circumstances, when it was released. By section 13(2) of the Act, a sound recording or film is 'released' when it is first published, broadcast or included in a cable programme service or, in the case of a film or film sound-track (a sound recording associated with a film), the film is first shown in public.[100] As regards what constitutes a public showing, this can have a wide meaning and is discussed further in Chapter 6. The copyright in a sound recording or film expires 50 years from the end of the calendar year in which it is released with the proviso that, if it is not released, the copyright will expire at the end of the period of 50 years from the end of the calendar year in which it is made.[101] Therefore, the duration of copyright can be extended by delaying the release of the sound recording or film and can be, potentially, around 100 years if released just before the completion of 50 years from the end of the calendar year in which it is made.

Broadcasts and cable programmes

Again, a period of fifty years is part of the formula for calculating duration. In this case, section 14(1) of the Act states that the copyright expires at the end of the period of 50 years from the end of the calendar year in which the broadcast was made or the programme included in a cable programme service.[102] Copyright is deemed to exist in a repeat broadcast or cable programme but expires at the same time as the original, subject to there being no copyright in a repeat broadcast or cable programme made after the expiry of the copyright in the original. Copyright in repeats may seem unnecessary as the concept of indirect copying has been accepted by the courts for some time[103] and is now given statutory effect by section 16(3) of the Copyright, Designs and Patents Act

97 SI 1989 No.1070.

98 Regulation 2.

99 COM(92) 602 final – SYN 395 OJ [1993] C27/7.

100 For the meaning of 'publication' see section 175, discussed above.

101 Section 13.

102 Section 14(2)

103 For example, see *British Leyland Motor Corporation Ltd.* v *Armstrong Patents Co. Ltd.* [1986] 2 WLR 400 and *Purefoy Engineering Ltd.* v *Sykes Boxall Ltd.* (1955) 72 RPC 89.

1988. At first sight, copyright in repeats might seem useful when no tangible copy is made such as where a person without permission receives a broadcast and simultaneously relays it to others, but broadcasting a work or including it in a cable programme service are amongst the acts restricted by copyright.

Section 14(3) states that a repeat broadcast or cable programme is one which is a repeat either of a broadcast previously made or of a cable programme previously included in a cable programme service. This means that a repeat broadcast can be made from a cable programme and will qualify for copyright protection as a repeat, expiring at the same time as the original cable programme and vice versa.

Typographical arrangements of published editions

The copyright in a typographical arrangement of a published edition expires at the end of the period of 25 years from the end of the calendar year in which the edition was first published.[104] By section 175(1)(a), first publication for typographical arrangements of published editions occurs when copies were first issued to the public.

Crown and parliamentary copyright

Crown copyright subsists in works made by Her Majesty or by an officer or servant of the Crown in the course of his duties. Crown copyright in a literary, dramatic, musical or artistic work lasts until the end of the period of 125 years from the end of the calendar year in which the work was made or, if the work is published commercially before the end of the period of 75 years from the end of the calendar year in which it is made, copyright continues to subsist until the end of the period of 50 years from the end of the calendar year in which it was first published commercially.[105] Therefore, if a work of Crown copyright is published in the first year it was created, it will have copyright protection for only 50 years from the end of that year. In relation to a literary, dramatic, musical or artistic work, commercial publication means, by section 175(2), issuing copies to the public at a time when copies made in advance of the receipt of orders are generally available to the public or when the work is available to the public by means of an electronic retrieval system.

There are no special provisions for Crown copyright as regards the other types of copyright work so the usual rules will apply. In the case of a work of joint authorship where one or more of the authors, but not all, fall within the requirement for Crown copyright, the provisions in section 163 apply only in relation to those authors and the copyright subsisting by virtue of their contribution to the work.[106] Does this mean that the rights of the other joint author(s) are unaffected by Crown copyright? This could be problematical as section 10(1) provides that, by definition, a work of joint authorship is a collaborative one in which the work of each joint author is not distinct. Taken to its logical conclusion, this could mean that the copyright subsisting in such a work of joint authorship would have, theoretically, two durations, which is a nonsense.

Acts of Parliament and Measures of the General Synod of the Church of England are protected by copyright from Royal Assent until the end of the period of 50 years from the end of the calendar year in which the Act or Measure

104 Section 15.

105 Section 163(3).

106 Section 163(4).

Table 3.1 Duration of copyright

Type of work	Event	Duration: from end of year of event
Literary, dramatic, muscial, artistic		
Known author	Author dies	50 years
Unknown author	Work first made available to public	50 years
Computer-generated work	Work made	50 years
Joint authors	Death of last author to die	50 years
Sound recordings and films		
	Sound recording or film made	50 years ↖ release
	Or, if released within above period	50 years from end of calendar year of release
Broadcasts and cable programmes		
	Broadcast made or cable programme included in a cable programme service	50 years
Typographical arrangts of pub. edns		
	First publication	25 years
Crown & Parliamentary Copyright etc.		
Literary, dramatic, muscial, artistic	Work made	125 years ↖ commercial publication
	Or, if published commercially within first 75 years	50 years from end of calendar year of commercial publication
Acts and Measures	Royal Assent	50 years
Parliamentary copyright	Work made	50 years
Bills	Bill made (presumably)	(until Royal Assent/ rejection)

Notes:

1. Duration is measured from end of the calendar year in which the event occurred.
2. Copyright subsists before the commencement of the period shown, from the time at which the work is made.
3. In effect, copyright in certain types of artistic works which have been exploited is reduced to 25 years.

107 Section 164(2).

108 Section 165.

received the Royal Assent.[107] Parliamentary copyright, in a literary, dramatic, musical or artistic work, continues to subsist until the end of the period of 50 years from the end of the calendar year in which the work was made.[108] Works within this category include reports of select committees. The duration of copyright in sound recordings, films, live broadcasts or cable programmes is in accordance with the usual rules. Parliamentary Bills are separately provided for by section 166 and copyright in a Bill expires when the Bill receives the Royal Assent, at which time the copyright in the new Act commences, or, if the Bill does not receive Royal Assent, copyright expires when the Bill is withdrawn or rejected or at the end of the Session.

Peter Pan by Sir James Matthew Barrie

Although the copyright in the play *Peter Pan* expired on 31 December 1987, the Copyright, Designs and Patents Act 1988, by section 301 and Schedule 6, provides for the payment of royalties to the Hospital for Sick Children, Great Ormond Street, London in respect of any public performance, commercial publication, broadcasting or inclusion in a cable programme service of the whole or a substantial part of the play or an adaptation of it. This is similar in practical effect to granting a potentially perpetual copyright to the play for the benefit of the hospital, although strictly speaking it is not a copyright but a *sui generis* right. However, the right is not absolute and will come to an end if the hospital ceases to have a separate identity or no longer cares for sick children. Apart from such occurrences, this new extraordinary right, like *Peter Pan* himself, will not grow old.

Table 3.1 shows the duration of copyright as it applies to the various types of works.

4

Authorship and ownership of copyright

INTRODUCTION

As copyright is a property right, this raises important questions about ownership and the mechanisms for exploiting copyright. Authorship and ownership are, in relation to copyright, two distinct concepts, each of which attract their own peculiar rights; the author having moral rights and the owner of the copyright possessing economic rights. Sometimes, the author of a work will also be the owner of the copyright in the work, but this is not always so and many works have separate authors and owners as far as copyright is concerned. Ownership flows from authorship; the person who makes the work is normally the first owner of the copyright in the work, providing that he has not created the work in the course of employment in which case his employer will be the first owner of the copyright. The owner of the copyright in a work may decide to exploit the work by the use of one or more contractual methods. He may grant a licence to allow a third party to carry out certain acts in relation to the work, such as making copies, in which case, he retains the ownership of the copyright. Alternatively, the owner may assign the copyright to another, that is transfer the ownership of the copyright to a new owner, relinquishing the economic rights under copyright law. One point to bear in mind is that a third party can carry out certain acts in relation to the whole or a part of a work protected by copyright without the permission of the owner of the copyright in the work and without infringing the copyright in the work, for example by performing one of the acts falling within the fair dealing provisions or because the act is not restricted by the copyright. There is little that the owner of the copyright can do about these limitations and exceptions to copyright protection apart from denying access to the work itself, for example by refusing to publish the work.

Consider a single work in which copyright subsists. There may be several relationships and activities connected with the work and the copyright to the work. Figure 4.1 shows the relationships that might exist in relation to a work.

(a) The author is the person who has created the work in question.
(b) The copyright in the work is owned by a person who might be the author or the author's employer or a person who has become the owner of the copyright because the title to the copyright has been transferred to him.
(c) With respect to the work, there are certain acts which are restricted by the copyright. These 'restricted acts' (an example is making a copy of a work) can only be carried out by the owner of the copyright or by someone having the owner's permission, such as a licensee. Otherwise, subject to certain exceptions, the copyright in the work will be infringed.
(d) The copyright owner can grant licences in respect of the work which will allow the licensee to do all or some of the restricted acts, in accordance with the terms of the licence. Sometimes, a licensee will be permitted to grant sublicences to others.

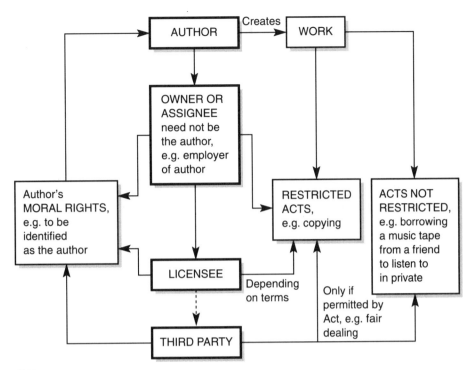

Figure 4.1 Mechanism of copyright

Note:
1. The third party may be a member of the general public or a sublicensee.
2. The licensee may also carry out the permitted acts and any acts not restricted by the copyright, subject to the terms of the agreement.
3. A licence may impose obligations on the licensor preventing him from doing certain acts himself.

(e) The copyright owner and any licensees and sublicensees, subject to the terms of the licence agreement, will be able to carry out all or some of the restricted acts.

(f) A third party, for example a member of the general public, can carry out a restricted act *only* if it is permitted by copyright law (the permitted acts, for example the fair dealing provisions for criticism or review). The requirements for the permitted act in question must be complied with, for example by giving a sufficient acknowledgement.

(g) Any person can carry out acts in relation to the work that are *not* acts restricted by copyright, such as lending to a friend a book or a music cassette or reading a book. There may, however, be contractual restrictions affecting such acts.

(h) All persons including the owner of the copyright, licensees, sublicensees and members of the public generally must respect the author's moral rights. The author may be able to enforce his moral rights irrespective of the identity of the present owner of the copyright (provided that author has asserted his right to be identified as author and has not otherwise waived it).

AUTHORSHIP

The author of a work is the person who creates it.[1] In terms of some types of

1 Section 9(1) of the Copyright, Designs and Patents Act 1988. Unless otherwise stated, statutory references are to the Copyright, Designs and Patents Act 1988.

works this will be self-evident; for example, the author of a work of literature is the person who writes it, the author of a piece of music is its composer, the author of a photograph is the photographer and so on. However, with some types of works, further explanation is required and this is furnished by the Act. By section 9(2), the author of a sound recording or a film is the person by whom the arrangements necessary for its making are undertaken; the author of a broadcast is the person making the broadcast including, in the case of a broadcast relaying another broadcast by reception and immediate retransmission, the person making that other broadcast; the author of a cable programme is the person providing the cable programme service in which it is included. The publisher of the typographical arrangement of a published edition is considered to be its author. Notice that, normally, the director of a film will have no claim of authorship because it is the producer (or the film company employing the producer) who makes the arrangements necessary for the making of the film, not the director. A director of a film can, however, still have moral rights, as will be seen in Chapter 5.[2] If the work is a computer-generated literary, dramatic, musical or artistic work, that is generated by computer in circumstances such that there is no human author, the author is deemed to be the person by whom the arrangements necessary for the creation of the work are undertaken,[3] a similar formula to that for sound recordings and films.

Because copyright protects only the expression of an idea, there may be occasions when the originator of the information that forms the basis of the work in question will not be considered to be the author of the work. For example, in *Springfield* v *Thame*[4] the plaintiff, a journalist, supplied newspapers with information in the form of an article. The editor of the *Daily Mail,* from that information, composed a paragraph which appeared in the newspaper. It was held that the plaintiff was not the author of the paragraph as printed in the newspaper. Similarly, a person making a speech in public will not be the author of a report of the speech made by reporters. In *Walter* v *Lane,*[5] reporters for *The Times* made reports of the speeches of Lord Roseberry which were printed verbatim after they had been corrected and revised. It was held that the reporters were the authors of the reports and, as a result of the terms of the reporters' employment, the copyright in the reports belonged to *The Times*. In the latter case, it can be argued that the reporters had used skill and judgment in making, correcting and revising the reports. However, if a person is simply writing down dictation, the person dictating will be the author for copyright purposes as the person doing the writing is simply the agent by which the work is made.[6] The distinction is a fine but important one as authorship will usually determine ownership of the copyright.

In principle, there is nothing to prevent a corporate body being the author of a work as section 154(1)(c) recognizes that a work may qualify for copyright protection if the author is a body incorporated under the law of the United Kingdom. This may apply in the case of derivative works, for example a sound recording or film, where the work in question is the result of arrangements made by senior officers of a music or film company,[7] in which case the company can be deemed to be the author. If the person who makes the arrangements in practice is lower down in the company hierarchy so that his actions are not automatically deemed to be the actions of the company, the company will probably still *own* the copyright (as opposed to being the author) on the basis of the employer/employee relationship or because of some contractual

2 The principal director of a film will soon be treated as one of its authors as regards certain acts. Council Directive of 19 November 1992 on rental right and lending right and on certain rights related to copyright in the field of intellectual property OJ [1992] L346/61.

3 Section 9(3).

4 (1903) 19 TLR 650. Originality would be in issue now.

5 [1900] AC 539.

6 The principle cannot apply when a person at a seance produces a work under the influence of a person long since dead. In *Cummins* v *Bond* [1927] 1 Ch 167, the medium who had written down the work was the author, not the extra-terrestial psychic being. The judge said he must confine his inquiry to persons alive at the time the work was made.

7 An analogous principle in criminal law is that of corporate liability where a company can be criminally liable on the basis of acts or omissions of its senior officers who are deemed to be the brains of the company. See the judgment of Lord Denning MR in *H L Bolton (Engineering) Co. Ltd. v T J Graham & Sons Ltd.* [1957] 1 QB 159 at 172.

provision. The identification of the author is important for determining the first ownership of copyright and also for measuring the duration of the copyright. In the case of many original works, the copyright expires at the end of the period of 50 years from the end of the calendar year during which the author died.

The Copyright, Designs and Patents Act 1988 recognizes that the identity of the author may not always be known. A work is of 'unknown authorship' if the identity of the author is unknown, meaning that it is not possible for a *person* to ascertain the identity of the author by reasonable enquiry.[8] It is not clear who the person referred to might be. One possibility is that it is the person wishing to copy the work, making the test subjective[9]; on the other hand, it may be the ubiquitous reasonable man, an objective test. The work may be truly anonymous or it may be pseudonymous, that is the author does not wish his identity to be disclosed. The Berne Copyright Convention, by Article 15, makes presumptions in the case of anonymous and pseudonymous works and there is no requirement under United Kingdom copyright law that the identity of the author be disclosed to ultimate purchasers of material incorporating the copyright work, for example purchasers of books written by the author. This has little significance other than with respect to the duration of the copyright in the work concerned but it also may be relevant in terms of infringement[10] and evidentially as regards ownership.

Frequently, a work will be the result of the efforts of more than one person. Several employees may work together to produce a written report, a team of computer programmers and systems analysts together may produce a computer program, two or more persons may collaborate in the writing of a work of literature, a piece of music or the painting of a landscape in oils. Collaboration between two or more persons will result in a work of joint authorship only if their respective contributions to the finished work are not distinct from each other, by section 10(1). That is, the work cannot be broken down so that each author's contribution can be separately identified. Thus, an abstract oil painting created by two painters applying paint to create an effect previously agreed by them would be a work of joint authorship as would be a sound recording made of an impromptu jazz session involving several musicians. A book comprising separate chapters written by different authors is not a work of joint authorship neither is a song where one person has written the music and another has written the words, as in a Gilbert and Sullivan operetta. In the latter cases, each person involved will be the author of their own distinct work and, in the case of a song, the person writing the music will be the author of the musical work whilst the person writing the lyrics will be the author of those lyrics, as a literary work. Two copyrights will exist in the song, each having different authors (and, possibly, different owners) and the duration of the copyright in the music and the lyrics will differ according to the dates when the composer and lyricist die.

In the case of a broadcast, section 10(2) of the Act provides that it will be treated as a work of joint authorship where more than one person is to be taken to be making the broadcast. The person making the broadcast is, by section 6(3), the person transmitting the programme if he has any responsibility to any extent for the content of the broadcast and any person providing the programme who makes, with the person transmitting it, the arrangements necessary for its transmission.

8 See sections 9(4) and 9(5). Section 9(5) further states that once the author's identity is known, it cannot subsequently be regarded as unknown.

9 See Merkin, R., *Copyright, Designs and Patents: The New Law* (London: Longman, 1989) at p.50.

10 Section 57(1) provides for permitted acts on the basis of certain assumptions as to the expiry of copyright or death of the author in relation to anonymous and pseudonymous works. See Chapter 7.

OWNERSHIP

Section 11 of the Act states the basic rule that the author of a work is the first owner of the copyright. This will apply in a good number of cases, for example to persons creating works for their own pleasure or amusement, independent persons not employed under a contract of employment and even to employed persons if the work in question has not been created in the course of their employment. However, there are some exceptions to this basic rule and where a literary, dramatic, musical or artistic work is made by an employee in the course of his employment, his employer is the first owner of the copyright subsisting in the work subject to any agreement to the contrary.[11] In *Noah* v *Shuba*[12] it was held that the copyright in a work created by an employee in the course of his employment could still belong to the employee on the basis of a term implied on the grounds of past practice. If the employee's name appears on the work or copies of the work, there is a presumption that the work was not made in the course of employment.[13]

[11] Section 11(2).

[12] [1991] FSR 14.

[13] Section 104(2).

Other exceptions relate to Crown copyright and Parliamentary copyright. Her Majesty the Queen is the first owner of the copyright in her own works and in works produced by an officer or servant of the Crown in the course of his duties and of the copyright subsisting in Acts of Parliament and Measures of the General Synod of the Church of England.[14] If a work is made by or under the direction or control of either or both Houses of Parliament, the first owner of the copyright is the appropriate House or Houses.[15] This includes Bills, public, private and personal. A final exception to the general rule applies to original literary, dramatic, musical or artistic works made by an officer or employee of certain international organizations or published by the organization and which does not otherwise qualify for copyright by reference to the author or country of first publication. In such cases, by section 168(1), copyright is declared to subsist in the work and the organization concerned is deemed to be the first owner of the copyright in the work. The relevant international organizations are designated by Order in Council and include the United Nations and the Organization for Economic Co-operation and Development. Unlike the position under the Copyright Act 1956, the copyright in certain commissioned works no longer vests in the first instance in the commissioner of the work.[16]

[14] Sections 163 and 164.

[15] Section 165.

[16] This applied to commissioned photographs, portraits (painted or drawn) and engravings provided they were made for money or money's worth, section 4(3) of the Copyright Act 1956.

The ownership of the copyright subsisting in anonymous works can present problems as there is no author available or willing to give evidence as to the ownership. To cope with the evidential difficulties associated with anonymous works, section 104(4) of the Act contains a presumption that the publisher of an anonymous work is the owner of the copyright in the work at the time of first publication unless the contrary is proved, providing that the work qualifies for protection by reason of the country of first publication and the name of the publisher appears on copies of the work as first published. In *Warwick Film Productions Ltd.* v *Eisinger*,[17] the plaintiff failed to rebut the equivalent presumption under the Copyright Act 1956 in relation to an anonymous work 'Oscar Wilde: Three Times Tried', first published in or around 1911.

[17] [1967] 3 All ER 367.

If a work is a work of joint authorship, unless they are employees acting in the course of business, the joint authors will automatically become the joint first owners of the copyright in the work. They will own the copyright as ten-

18 [1892] 3 Ch 402. However, where the co-owners have some relationship such as husband and wife it may be reasonable to infer that they hold the copyright as joint tenants and not tenants in common, see *Mail Newspapers plc v Express Newspapers plc* [1987] FSR 90. On of the death of one joint tenant the other automatically takes the whole copyright.

19 *Cescinsky v George Routledge & Sons Ltd.* [1916] 2 KB 325. This restriction on co-owners should be compared to patent law, where one co-patentee can exploit the patent without the permission of his co-patentees but cannot licence, assign or mortgage his share without the consent of the others. Patents Act 1977, section 36.

ants in common and not as joint tenants; *Lauri* v *Renad*.[18] This means that effectively each owner's rights accruing under the copyright are separate from the others and he can assign his rights to another without requiring the permission of the other owners and, on his death, his rights will pass, as part of his estate, to his personal representatives. However, as far as infringement of the copyright is concerned, any one or combination of the joint owners may take action. By way of contrast, one co-owner of a copyright may not perform or authorize infringing acts to be done in relation to the work without the permission of his co-owners.[19]

As an example, consider the copyright subsisting in a sound recording that has joint owners either because it was created by joint authors or because the copyright has been assigned to more than one person. The sound recording is to be reproduced and sold commercially and each joint owner will be entitled to an agreed share of the profits arising from the sales. One joint owner may be anxious to obtain some immediate capital. To do this, he will be able to 'sell' his future share of the profits to a third party for a lump sum, assigning his copyright interest to that person. He can do this without having to seek or obtain the permission of the other co-owners. However, the co-owner cannot grant a licence to a third party allowing that third party to make and sell copies of the sound recording without the agreement of all the other co-owners. Another example is where a co-owner of a copyright dies leaving all his property to his widow. In such a case, his copyright interests pass to his widow who will, from then on, be entitled to a share of the royalties or profits accruing from the sale or other commercial exploitation of the work.

Employees

The main difficulty with the ownership provisions concerns the employer/employee relationship and the meaning of 'in the course of his employment', or, in the case of Crown copyright, 'in the course of his duties'. There will be many situations where it will be obvious that the work has been made by an employee in the course of his employment, for example a sales manager who, during his normal working hours, writes a report on the last quarter's sales figures for the board of directors of the company he works for. However, difficulties arise if an employee has created the work in his own time, whether or not using his employer's facilities, or if the nature of the work is not that which the employee is normally paid for. To some extent the expectations of the employee and employer as manifested in the contract of employment are important, for example the employee's job description, and whether the nature of the thing produced sits comfortably with that job description, either expressly or by implication. To take an extreme example, say that a woman who is employed as a tea lady writes some music during her own time. She will be the first owner of the copyright in the musical work because she is employed as a tea lady and not as an author of musical works. Even if our tea lady writes the music during the time she should be serving tea as part of her employment, she will still be the first owner of the copyright but may have to answer to her employer for this breach of the contract of employment.

The situation changes if the employee is employed under a contract with a very wide job description, for example as a research and development engineer, and he prepares a work of copyright which is useful to his employer's business. The copyright will probably belong to his employer even if the employee created the work on his own initiative outside normal working hours. A complicating factor may be that the employee's formal job description no longer completely and accurately describes his present duties in which case the actual type of work carried out by the employee will be relevant. A basic test is whether the skill, effort and judgment expended by the employee in creating the work are part of the employee's normal duties (express or implied) or within any special duties assigned to him by the employer. If the answer is 'no', then the employee will be the first owner of the copyright even if he has used his employer's facilities or assistance. In *Stephenson Jordan & Harrison Ltd.* v *MacDonald*,[20] an employed accountant gave some lectures which he later incorporated into a book. It was held that, even though his employer had provided secretarial help, the copyright in the lectures belonged to the accountant because he was employed as an accountant to advise clients and not to deliver public lectures. However, part of the book was based on a report that the accountant had written for a client of his employer and the copyright in this part belonged to his employer. Prudent employers will satisfy themselves that job descriptions accurately reflect the employment and are kept up to date. If there is any doubt about the first ownership of copyright in a work produced by an employee, for example where the employee has been given work beyond his normal duties, agreement should be reached before the employee engages upon the work.

20 [1952] RPC 10.

If the employer wishes, he may allow the employee to be the first owner of the copyright as section 11(2) includes the phrase 'subject to any agreement to the contrary'. Normally, transfer of ownership of copyright must be in writing and signed by or on behalf of the copyright owner[21] but, in this case, it would appear that a verbal or even implied agreement will suffice because this is not a case of assignment, the copyright does not exist until the time it has a first owner.[22] On the other hand, if an employee produces a work, the creation of which lies outside his normal duties (that is, it is not created in the course of his employment), any agreement that the employer will be the owner of the copyright must comply with section 90(3) and must be in writing and signed by or on behalf of the employee. The reason is that the employee automatically will be the first owner and the copyright must, therefore, be assigned to the employer. If there is such an agreement but the formalities are not complied with, the employer may have an implied licence or may be deemed to be the equitable owner of the copyright.

21 Section 90(3).

22 *Noah* v *Shuba* [1991] FSR 14 provides an example of an implied agreement that the employee owned the copyright in a work created during normal working hours.

Freelance workers and consultants may be difficult to classify as employees in the normal sense of the word. By section 178 of the Act, 'employed', 'employee', 'employer' and 'employment' refer to employment under a contract of service or of apprenticeship. The categorization of a person as an employee or self-employed person is so crucial to the question of ownership of copyright that it requires further exploration and employment law may provide some guidance as to how the distinction may be made. A person's status as employee or self-employed is important in employment law as many of the statutory safeguards, such as the right to claim unfair dismissal and the entitlement to redundancy pay, depend upon this question. Although the case law on this subject is far from satisfactory, questions such as who controls the work, whether the person is entitled to sick pay, who provides a pension, the method of payment (for example, weekly or monthly or on the basis of a lump sum for an agreed item of work), whether tax is deducted at source and financial responsibility (for example, for faulty work) may combine to provide an overall test.[23] However, none of these factors can be considered to be conclusive as such. In *Hall* v *Lorimer*[24] Mummery J said that the court could not run through a check list of items pointing one way or the other. He went on to suggest that a whole picture should be painted and viewed from a distance to reach an informed and qualitative decision. Emphasis has been placed on 'mutuality of obligation', described by Kerr LJ in *Nethermere (St. Neots) Ltd.* v *Taverna*[25] in the following terms:

> [The alleged employees] must be subject to an obligation to accept and perform some minimum, or at least reasonable, amount of work for the alleged employer.

Because of the difficulty of predetermining the status of a person carrying out work for another, it is preferable, if there is any doubt whatsoever, to provide contractually for the ownership of copyright subsisting in anything produced by the worker. Certainly, there is a good deal of confusion about the ownership of commissioned works, the commissioner often believing, wrongly, that he will automatically own the copyright subsisting in the work created.[26] In these situations, the person commissioning the work should insist that the contract contains provisions for the assignment of the future copyright (legal and beneficial).[27] Of course, in terms of the relationship between employers and employees and between client and consultant, there is the additional factor of the obligation of confidence owed by one to the other.[28] The law of confidence may help the employer or the client prevent the subsequent use of commissioned material by the employee or consultant regardless of the question of copyright ownership.

Consultants

There may be occasions when the operation of the basic rule regarding first ownership results in an injustice. For example, a consultant may produce a work for a client in circumstances where the client expects that he will own the copyright in the finished work and pays the consultant accordingly. However, if there is no provision for the assignment of the copyright and the consultant cannot be classed as an employee working in the course of his employment, the consultant will be the first owner of the copyright. The consultant may realize the implications of this position and may decide later either to interfere with the client's exploitation of the work or to deal with the work himself without the client's permission. The first possibility, that is where the consultant attempts to interfere with the client's use or marketing of the work should be defeated on the basis of non-derogation from grant[29] or, alternatively, on the basis of an implied licence. Both the first and second possibility can be overcome if the court is willing to use equitable principles to infer beneficial ownership. This was done in the case of *Warner* v *Gestetner Ltd.*[30] in which Warner, who was an expert in the drawing of cats, agreed verbally to produce some drawings to be used by Gestetner to promote a new product at a trade fair. Gestetner subsequently used the drawings for promotional literature and Warner complained that this went beyond the agreement and infringed his copyright. Warner

23 *Market Investigations Ltd.* v *Minister of Social Security* [1969] 2 QB 173 per Cooke J at 185.

24 (unreported) *The Times*, 4 June 1992 (Chancery Division).

25 [1984] IRLR 240.

26 This problem has come to light as regards the ownership of the 'Lightman Report' commissioned by the National Union of Mineworkers. A publisher intended to publish the report with the permission of Mr. Lightman QC, in the face of strong objection by the Union which believed it owned the copyright in the report – see *The Times*, 1 October 1990, p.3. However, unless there was a signed written assignment of the copyright, the person commissioned, Mr. Lightman, is the first legal owner of the copyright in the report although the Union might have some rights as beneficial owner of the copyright in equity.

27 Section 91 provides for prospective ownership of copyright.

28 See Chapter 12 for a discussion of the operation of the law of confidence as regards employees.

29 See *British Leyland Motor Corp. Ltd.* v *Armstrong Patents Co. Ltd.* [1986] 2 WLR 400.

30 [1988] EIPR D-89.

remained the owner of the copyright in the drawings because it had not been assigned to Gestetner. However, Whitford J found that he could imply a term granting beneficial ownership of the copyright to Gestetner. Thus, the copyright had two owners, one at law and one at equity and Gestetner, as beneficial owners, could deal with the work as they wished, Warner's legal interest in the copyright being of little practical significance, although infringement actions are much less effective if brought by a beneficial owner without the legal owner being joined as a party.[31]

The concept of two owners, one legal and one beneficial is used extensively in the law of real property but there have been other examples of its application to intellectual property law. For example, in *Ironside* v *Attorney-General*[32] it was held that an agreement for the design of the reverse face of coins gave rise to an equitable assignment or, alternatively, an implied licence.[33] Of course, to be able to imply beneficial ownership the creator of the work should have been paid a fixed sum rather than a royalty as the latter is inconsistent with a transfer of ownership. Both the above cases involved a lump sum payment. However these decisions can be criticized on the grounds that they completely ignore the effects of section 90 of the Act which clearly requires that an assignment of copyright must be in writing signed by or on behalf of the assignor.

A less contrived approach than implying beneficial ownership which would have had the same effect in practical terms would have been for the court to imply a term to the effect that the commissioner of a work has a licence to continue to use the works. This approach was taken by Lord Denning MR in *Blair* v *Osborne & Tomkins*[34] in which an architect was commissioned to draw building plans for the purpose of obtaining planning permission for some houses. The site for which the plans had been drawn was then sold with the benefit of the planning permission and the plans were transferred to the purchaser who employed his own surveyors who modified the plans for building regulations approval and put their name on the plans. Eventually, houses were built in accordance with the plans and the architect sued for infringement of copyright. It was held that the architect owned the copyright in the plans and there had been an infringement by the surveyors who had submitted the plans to the council in their own name, but only nominal damages were appropriate as no harm was suffered by the architect as a result of this.[35] On the issue of the building of houses by the purchaser of the land in accordance with the architect's plans it was held that the purchaser had an implied licence to use the plans for this purpose. The person who commissioned the architect had such an implied licence which extended to the making of copies of the plans to be used in respect of that site only and not for any other purpose and this implied licence extended to any purchaser of the site. The rationale for thus deciding this case was that the architect had received his fee once and failure to imply a licence would have meant that the architect would have been able to charge a second fee to the purchaser of the site without having to carry out any further work. It must be noted that the scope of the licence was limited to building the houses on that site only and the purchaser would have been prevented from building further houses in accordance with the plans on other sites.

The concept of the implied licence can be criticized because it may destroy the copyright owner's control on the use of the work by others. The initial agreement is for the person paying for the work to have the right to use it for a

31 Generally, on his own, a beneficial owner will only be entitled to interlocutory relief.

32 [1988] RPC 197

33 See also *Performing Right Society Ltd.* v *London Theatre of Varieties Ltd.* [1924] AC 1, discussed later.

34 [1971] 2 WLR 503.

35 Nowadays, the architect would have an action under section 77 for infringement of his right to be identified as the author, providing he had asserted this right.

particular purpose and its use by others is outside this agreement. An implied licence could operate unfairly in some circumstances. For example, a builder (Acme Construction Ltd.) has agreed to design and build a factory for a client (Rapid Developments plc). It was agreed that Acme will prepare all the drawings and specifications for the building work. Two-thirds of the way through the contract, Rapid Developments go into receivership and the receiver decides to engage another company (Quickbuild Ltd.) to complete the factory and he hands over the plans and specifications to Quickbuild. The receiver, in his wisdom, considers that he can obtain the best deal for the creditors of Rapid Developments by completing the factory and that Quickbuild will do this at less expense than Acme even though the latter wish to continue with the construction work. The use of the plans and specifications in this way seems grossly unfair and it may be that, in these special circumstances, the courts will not be prepared to extend an implied licence to the second builder. In terms of tactics, Acme might be well advised to apply immediately for a *quia timet* injunction on the basis that the intended use of the materials will almost certainly involve copyright infringement.

Complexity of rights

For the derivative works of copyright there will usually be several rights associated with the work and the exploitation of works in which numerous rights exist can be fairly complex although collecting societies such as the Performing Right Society do lead to some simplification. As an example of the number of rights that can subsist in a work, consider a song which has been recorded on a sound recording. The following rights can exist:

- musical copyright
- literary copyright
- copyright in the sound recording
- performance rights (these are neighbouring rights to copyright – the performer and recording company have rights)
- composer's moral rights
- lyricist's moral rights

The exploitation of the sound recording must take account of all these rights by way of assignments, licences or waivers. The rights themselves can be subdivided, for example in the above case the following cross-cutting rights are important:

- right to make copies of the sound recordings
- right to play the sound recording in public
- right to permit rental of copies of the sound recording

It should be noted that the EC Council Directive on rental and lending rights will increase complexity rather than reduce it.[36] For example, a film may be subject to many rights. The screenplay will be a dramatic work and may be based on a novel produced as a book. The novel will have literary copyright which will initially be owned by the novelist. The copyright in the film itself will be owned, in the first instance, by the producer (the person making the arrangements necessary for its creation). However, under the Directive, the director of a film shall be considered as one of its authors and will, consequently, have a right to authorize or prohibit rental or lending.[37] Add to this the various rights associated with the sound track, performance rights and moral rights and it becomes clear that lawyers will be kept busy in drawing up all the necessary agreements and consents. Mechanisms for exploiting works of copyright are described in the subsequent sections of this chapter.

DEALING WITH COPYRIGHT

As has been previously mentioned, copyright is a property right and as such the owner of that right can deal with it. He can transfer the right to another or he can grant licences to others, permitting them to do some or all of the acts restricted by copyright in relation to the work. However, it must be remembered that the author of a work has certain moral rights and the owner of the copyright and his assignees or licensees, indeed the public in general, must take notice of and respect these moral rights.[38] Therefore, the ultimate owner of a copyright is not entirely free to do as he wishes with the work that is the subject matter of the copyright. However, in most cases, respecting the author's moral rights will not be a hindrance to the economic exploitation of copyright.

Why should the owner of a copyright wish to transfer his ownership of the copyright or grant licences in respect of it? Bearing in mind that the author of a work of copyright will often be the owner of the copyright, the owner may not be in the best position to exploit the work commercially. For example, the author of a work a literature, such as a romantic story (if he is the first owner of the copyright as will usually be the case), will find it more advantageous in terms of the balance between financial reward and the degree of risk involved, to approach a well-established publisher who will arrange for the printing, marketing and sale of books of the story. Not only that, but the publisher will also be better placed to take legal action against persons infringing the copyright. Similarly, the composer of a piece of music may approach a record company who might arrange for the recording of the music by a well-known orchestra and for the manufacture, distribution and sale of records, cassettes and compact discs on a world-wide scale. Copyright can also be a form of investment. A lump sum can be invested to acquire the copyright in works which will continue to provide income over many years.[39] Alternatively, copyright may be used as security for a loan or other financial transaction. Finally, transfer of ownership of copyright will occur on the death of the owner or a part-owner of the copyright.

There are two ways of dealing with copyright: by assignment and by licensing. Licences may be exclusive or non-exclusive. In the case of an assignment of copyright or an exclusive licence, the transaction, to be effective, must be in writing and signed by or on behalf of the present copyright owner.[40] Although this can be seen as a safeguard for the copyright owner who may be negotiating with powerful publishing organizations from an unequal bargaining position, it can lead to difficulties in the case of commissioned works because it clearly means that the commissioner cannot have any legal rights of ownership under copyright law unless a written signed agreement exists.[41] Because the language of the statute is very clear on this point, the implication by the courts of terms

37 Article 2. See Dworkin, G. 'Authorship of Films and European Commission Proposals for Harmonising the Term of Copyright' [1993] 5 EIPR 151 for a discussion of this provision.

38 The right to be identified a the author must, however, hav been asserted, section 78. Questions of author's consent and waiver may also be relevant, section 87.

39 This may be advantageous in terms of tax liabilities. For the tax implications of intellectual property, see Gallafent, R. J.; Eastaway, N. A. and Dauppe V. A. F., *Intellectual Property: Law an Taxation* (London: Longman, 4th edn., 1992).

40 Sections 90(3) and 92(1).

41 However, by section 85(1), the commissioner of a photograph or film made for private and domestic purposes has certain rights, for example a right not to have the work issued to the public.

42 See the discussion on
Warner v *Gestetner Ltd.*
1988] EIPR D-89, above.

into the contract for the commissioned work which deal with ownership is unlikely though not an impossibility.[42]

Assignment and transmission of copyright

One point that must be made at this stage is that physical possession of an object containing or representing a work of copyright or a copy of such a work does not by itself give any rights under copyright law. For example, mere possession of a book does not give a right to perform any of the restricted acts such as making copies of the book. The same principle applies to a painting and the sale of a painting, no matter how expensive, does not automatically assign the copyright in it. The purchaser obtains a property right in the physical object but, in the absence of an assignment or licence, no interest in the copyright. This may be inconvenient and the courts will construe any documents, such as a receipt, generously to keep the two forms of property together. For example, in *Savory (EW) Ltd.* v *The World of Golf Ltd.*,[43] it was held that a written receipt for card designs 'inclusive of all copyrights' was sufficient to assign the copyright to the purchaser.

3 [1914] 2 Ch 566.

An assignment of copyright can be thought of as a disposal of the copyright by way of sale or hire or by will. The present owner (the assignor) can assign the copyright to another and, by section 90(3), such an assignment must be in writing signed by or on behalf of the assignor. However, the assignment, and other transmission, of the copyright need not be total and absolute, it can be partial. By section 90(2), the assignment or other transmission of copyright can be limited either in terms of the things the copyright owner can do or be limited in terms of the period of subsistence of copyright. As an example, consider a play, a dramatic work, the copyright in which will expire in 40 years' time (William, the author having died some ten years ago). The current owner, William's wife Ann (the assignor), may decide to assign the total copyright in the play to another person, Frances. Alternatively, she might decide to assign only the public performance right to Frances for the remainder of the duration of the copyright whilst retaining the other rights, allowing her to make and issue printed copies of the play either personally or by granting a licence to Richard to do this. Finally, she might decide to assign all the rights to Frances for a period of five years only, after which the copyright will revert to her.

Assignments limited in time need careful thought as to what happens to any copies of the work that have not been sold at the time of the reversion of the copyright. In *Howitt* v *Hall*[44] it was held that the defendant who had been assigned the copyright in a book for four years could continue to sell copies printed during that four-year period after the copyright reverted to the original owner.

4 (1862) 6 LT 348

If the formalities of the Act are not complied with, it may be that a court will be prepared to infer that there has been an assignment of the copyright in equity only: see *Warner* v *Gestetner* above. In these circumstances, there will be a legal owner of the copyright and an equitable owner, the legal owner being the purported assignor and he will still be the legal owner because of some defect in the formalities, for example the written assignment was not signed by him or on his behalf, or the attempted assignment was made orally. Being an owner in equity only does have some disadvantages. In *Performing Right Soci-*

ety Ltd. v *London Theatre of Varieties Ltd.*,[45] it was held that the owner of an equitable interest in the performing rights of a song entitled 'The Devonshire Wedding' could not obtain a perpetual injunction without joining the legal owner of the copyright as a party to the action. This case was applied in *Weddel v J A Pearce & Major*,[46] a bankruptcy case, in which it was held that, although an equitable assignee could sue in his own right, he could not obtain damages or a perpetual injunction without joining as a party the assignor in whom the legal title of a chose in action was vested.[47] Normally, joining another party in an action would mean both appearing as co-plaintiffs, but the requirement is satisfied if the other party is the defendant. For example, in *John Richardson Computers Ltd.* v *Flanders*[48] the equitable owner sued the legal owner.

Of course, the person who executes the assignment may be acting as the agent of the assignor and the general rules of agency apply. It is in the intended assignee's interests to satisfy himself as to the authority of the agent. The case of *Beloff v Pressdram Ltd.*[49] involved the publication of a memorandum written by the plaintiff (an employee of *The Observer* newspaper) by *Private Eye*. The memorandum referred to a conversation between the plaintiff and a prominent member of the government in which the latter said that if the Prime Minister were to run under a bus, he had no doubt that a certain Mr M would take over as Prime Minister. *The Observer* owned the copyright in the memorandum and the editor attempted to assign it to the plaintiff so that the plaintiff could sue the publishers of *Private Eye*. However, as the editor had never before executed an assignment on behalf of *The Observer* and had no express authority to do so, the purported assignment was ineffective. Neither could there be any imputed authority because any representation made by the editor that he had authority had not induced the plaintiff to enter into the assignment or take any relevant steps.[50]

Sometimes, there may be an assignment of copyright in a work which has not yet come into existence. Such prospective ownership of copyright and its assignment is provided for by section 91 of the Act. If an author decides to write a play, he will be the first owner of the copyright in the play when it is written, providing he is not writing the play as an employee in the course of his employment. The author is the prospective owner of the future copyright and he can deal with that future copyright by assigning it to another. By section 91(2), 'future copyright' means copyright which will or may come into existence in respect of a future work or class of works or on the occurrence of a future event. The prospective owner can assign the copyright by an agreement signed by him or on his behalf and the actual assignment will take effect automatically when the copyright in the work in question comes into existence. The assignment can be whole or partial. Before the Copyright Act 1956, it was not possible to assign a future copyright, even if in writing and signed by the prospective owner.[51] This was changed by the 1956 Act and in *Chaplin v Leslie Frewin (Publishers) Ltd.*[52] it was held that a contract for writing an autobiography between the infant son of Charlie Chaplin and a publisher was effective to transfer the copyright in the work when it came into existence.[53]

An assignment may be declared by the court to be unenforceable if it is unconscionable or contrary to public policy being in restraint of trade. In *Schroeder Music Publishing Co. Ltd.* v *Macaulay*[54] a young and unknown song

45 [1924] AC 1.

46 [1987] 3 All ER 624.

47 Copyright is, of course, a chose in action.

48 [1993] FSR 497.

49 [1975] QB 613.

50 *Freeman & Lockyer* v *Buckhurst Park Property* [1964] 1 All ER 630 applied.

51 *Performing Right Society Ltd.* v *London Theatre of Varieties Ltd.* [1924] AC 1. An attempted assignment of a future copyright could only take effect in equity, regardless of the formalities used in practice.

52 [1966] Ch 71.

53 The son was 19 years old a the time, but still classed as an infant for legal purposes. The son tried to avoid the contract fearing passages in the work might be libellous but it was held that the contract was analogous to a beneficial contract of service and was, therefore, not voidable at the infant's option.

54 [1974] 3 All ER 616

writer assigned the world-wide copyright in any musical composition produced by him for five years to a music publishing company. The agreement was very one-sided, the company did not undertake to publish any of the writer's work and could terminate by giving one month's notice. The song writer could not terminate and was paid only £50 (although he would receive royalties on any of his songs actually published). The House of Lords held that the agreement was unenforceable, being in restraint of trade. It required total commitment from the song writer but virtually no obligation was placed upon the company. Lord Diplock said that it was not without significance that successful and established song writers were not offered the standard form agreement given to the respondent in this case.

Licensing of copyright

A licence is, in essence, a permission granted by the owner of a right or interest to another person allowing him to do something in respect of that right or interest. For example, it may be a licence to enter land for some purpose, such as for accommodation or to take a short cut across a field. Licences may be contractual, in which case they can be enforced in a court of law, for example the owner of a field allows a neighbour to graze his sheep there in return of an annual fee of £100. In relation to copyright, a licence is an agreement between the owner of the copyright (the licensor) and another person (the licensee) whereby that person is permitted to do certain acts in connection with the work involved that would otherwise infringe the copyright in the work. In return for this arrangement, the licensee will pay the licensor either by way of a lump sum or by making royalty payments. For example, the owner of the copyright in an artistic painting might agree with a publisher of art works that the publisher can make and sell prints made of the painting and in return, the publisher will pay the copyright owner £5 for each print he sells. Normally making the prints would be an infringement of copyright, being an act restricted by copyright, that is making a copy of the work.[55]

55 For infringement generally, see Chapter 6. Making a copy of a literary, dramatic, musical or artistic work is defined as reproducing the work in any material form, section 17(2).

Like an assignment of copyright, a licence can be limited in terms of either the scope or the duration or both. Scope can be limited either in terms of the acts the licensee is permitted to do or territorially. The licence may be for the whole of the remainder of the period during which copyright will continue to subsist in the work or may be for a shorter period. There will usually be provisions in the licence agreement for its earlier termination, for example if one of the parties is in breach of certain of his obligations under the agreement.

A licence may be exclusive. By section 92(1) of the Act, an exclusive licence is a licence in writing signed by or on behalf of the copyright owner authorizing the licensee, to the exclusion of all other persons *including the owner,* to exercise a right that would otherwise be exercisable exclusively by the copyright owner. The licensee is exclusively granted rights to do certain things in relation to the work and the owner (licensor) will not grant those equivalent rights to anyone else or even exercise them himself. For example, the owner of the copyright in a work of literature may grant an exclusive licence to a book publisher for the purpose of publication of the work. The owner of the copyright will not grant the right of publication to anyone else whilst the exclusive licence is in existence and, indeed, if he attempts to do so, he will be in breach of the exclusive licence. However, although the licence is exclusive, it need not apply to all the acts restricted by copyright and may encompass only one or some of the acts restricted by copyright, such as publishing a book, and the owner will be free to deal with other rights, such as the broadcasting of extracts of the work recited by a famous actor. In the case of a non-exclusive licence, the licensee may make several agreements in respect of the same acts restricted by copyright. For example, the owner of the copyright in a play may allow several theatrical companies to make public performances of the play.

By section 90(4) of the Act, a licence granted by a copyright owner is binding on every successor in title to his interest in the copyright, except a purchaser in good faith for valuable consideration without actual or constructive notice, and persons deriving title from such a person. So, 'equity's darling', the bona fide purchaser for value without notice is given protection that overrides the interests of licensees which is one reason why a commercial organization, such as a publisher, wishing to exploit a work of copyright might prefer to take an assignment of the copyright rather than to operate on the basis of an exclusive licence. However, in practice it would be very difficult for a purchaser of the copyright to show that he did not have constructive notice especially if the work had already been exploited commercially. Note that only a purchaser of the copyright is protected, and a person who receives the copyright as a gift or on the death of the owner must acknowledge any existing licences in respect of the work.

Future copyright can be licensed by the prospective owner by section 91(3), but again protection is given to a purchaser in good faith for valuable consideration without actual or constructive notice as against a licensee. Thus, when a work is eventually created that is subject to a previously executed licence agreement, the owner of the copyright will be bound by the terms of the licence. If the owner later dies and the copyright passes to his wife, she will also be bound. If the wife then assigns the copyright to Andrew, a person who knows about the licence, he will be bound. If Andrew then gives the copyright to Bernard who does not know, nor could be expected to know of the licence, Bernard will be bound by the licence because he has not purchased the copyright, he has taken under a gift. However, if Bernard then assigns the copyright to Cyril who acts in good faith and does not know of the licence and could not be expected to know, Cyril will take free of the licence. Furthermore, if Cyril later disposes of the copyright to Duncan who knows of the licence and is acting in bad faith, Duncan can take free of the licence because he has derived his title from a purchaser in good faith. The licence is effectively destroyed by the intervention of the purchaser in good faith for valuable consideration without notice. It may be, however, that the licensee has a remedy against his licensor under the original agreement as there may be a contractual provision in the agreement requiring successors in title of the owner to be given notice before the copyright is assigned. However, this measure can only be really effective until the chain of notification of the licence between assignors and assignees is broken.

As an example of the exploitation of the various rights associated with the copyright in a particular work, consider the author (and owner) of a dramatic play. He decides to deal with the play in terms of its publication, its performance in public and also, because of the popularity of the play is able to negotiate the making of a film based on the play and the making of sound recordings

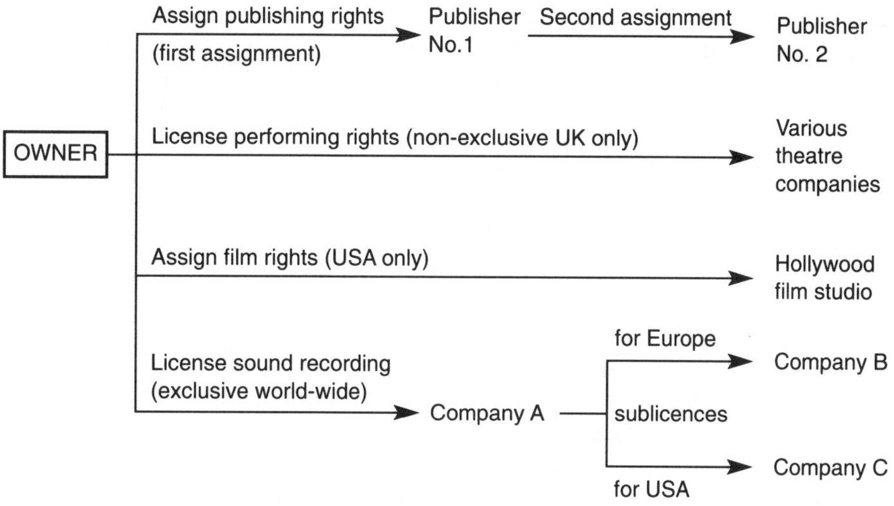

Figure 4.2 Assignment and licensing

of famous actors and actresses reading the play. Figure 4.2 above shows the types of relationships in terms of assignments and licensing that could ensue. In the case of a work such as a computer program, the use of which normally involves a restricted act, the ultimate 'purchaser' of a copy will usually receive a non-exclusive sublicence.

Differences between assignments and licences

An exclusive licence agreement can appear, at first sight, to look like an assignment and it is sometimes difficult to distinguish between the two. Both an assignment and a licence agreement may provide for the payment of royalties which might be thought of as normally being associated with a licence. In *Jonathan Cape Ltd.* v *Consolidated Press Ltd.*,[56] there was an agreement between the author (being the first owner of the copyright) and the plaintiff publishing company granting the latter, its successors and assigns 'the exclusive right to print and publish an original work . . . provisionally entitled *A Mouse is Born* in volume form'. The agreement was partial in terms of the copyright acts (printing and publishing) and in the territorial scope (a specified area including Australia). The defendant substantially reproduced the work but argued that the agreement was a licence and that, as a result, the plaintiff could not bring an action without joining the author. It was held that the question of whether an agreement was an assignment or a licence was a matter of construction and, in this case, the words used inferred that the agreement was a partial assignment of the copyright. Even the use of the words licensor and licensee in an agreement is not conclusive that it is a licence.[57]

The payment of royalties is inconsistent with an assignment and is, therefore, highly suggestive of a licence. Indeed, the owner of a copyright would be foolish to assign that copyright in return for royalty payments. If the copyright is subsequently re-assigned to a third party, the terms providing for royalty payments will be unenforceable against that third party, on the basis of privity of con-

6 [1954] 3 All ER 253.

7 See, for example, *Messager* v *British Broadcasting Co. Ltd.* [1929] AC 151.

tract. It was held in *Barker* v *Stickney*[58] that a person acquiring a copyright is not bound by mere notice of a personal covenant by a predecessor in title.

Other differences between assignments and licences are that only the owner has a right to sue (although an exclusive licensee may sue after joining the owner or by leave of the court) and a right to alter,[59] subject to the author's moral rights. In the absence of express provisions to the contrary, an assignment will generally be assignable but a licence will not be assignable unless expressly provided for. There are also differences as regards the effect of the insolvency of the assignee or licensee.[60]

New forms of exploitation

In time, new ways of exploiting a work of copyright might be discovered and the effect on existing licence agreements may be disputed, for example whether the new form of exploitation falls within the scope of the licence. It will be a question of construction of the licence on the basis of what was properly regarded as being in the contemplation of the parties when the agreement was made. In *Hospital for Sick Children* v *Walt Disney Productions Inc.*[61] the question arose as to whether a licence granted in 1919 by Sir James Barrie in respect of all his literary and dramatic works was limited to silent films or extended to sound films.[62] More recently, in the United States, Peggy Lee was awarded $3.8 million in respect of her contributions to the Walt Disney cartoon film *The Lady and the Tramp* on the basis that her contract with Walt Disney did not extend to selling videos of the film.[63] The contract was drawn up before video technology existed.

COLLECTING SOCIETIES

It may be inconvenient for the owner of copyright to agree licences and collect fees or, alternatively, the copyright owner may want the backing of a powerful body to help to defend his rights in a court of law, if it comes to that. On the other hand it is much more convenient if a user of copyright material can negotiate a single licence with respect to a range of works rather than having to agree separately with all the individual owners. Therefore, a proprietor of a hairdressing salon can obtain a licence from the Performing Right Society and Phonographic Performance Ltd., to be able to play sound recordings of music to the shop's clients. Of course, there is a danger that bodies such as the Performing Right Society (PRS) and Phonographic Performance Ltd. (PPL) can abuse their position. PRS operate by taking an assignment of the copyright in the performance and broadcasting of musical works, administering that copyright, collecting fees and distributing them amongst its members.[64]

Normally, the person wishing to play or broadcast musical works will obtain a blanket licence to do so in respect of all the works managed by PRS. Because of the very large number of works administered by PRS, it clearly has a dominant position and might be tempted to try to control the proportion of music played during a broadcast or the relative proportions of live and recorded work or to charge high fees. To prevent such abuse, the Performing Right Tribunal was set up by the Copyright Act 1956 to regulate the licensing of performing rights and this has now become the Copyright Tribunal, having extended jurisdiction and powers in comparison with the Performing Right Tribunal.

58 [1919] 1 KB 121.

59 *Frisby* v *British Broadcasting Corporation* [1987] Ch 932. A licensee may, expressly or by implication, not be allowed to alter the work.

60 For a fuller description of these aspects see Skone-James E. P., Mummery J., Rayner-James J. E. and Garnett K. M., *Copinger and Skone-James on Copyright* (London: Sweet & Maxwell, 13th edn., 1991) at 470–478.

61 [1966] 1 WLR 1055.

62 The first sound film shown to cinema audiences was *The Jazz Singer* in 1927.

63 *The Times*, 7 October 1992 at 16.

64 Other schemes are appearing, for example the Copyright Licensing Agency, which operates in the field of educational copying. The need for such a scheme can be equated with developments in the technology of photocopying and other means of copying. The issue of a blanket licence is one way that copyright owners can obtain at least some recompense for the vast amount of reproduction of copyright material that takes place nowadays.

LICENSING SCHEMES

The provisions in the Copyright, Designs and Patents Act 1988 concerning licensing schemes are designed to prevent abuse of monopoly powers by copyright owners. The Copyright Tribunal is given control over licensing schemes and over licences granted by licensing bodies. The Tribunal can also grant compulsory licences, discussed later. A *licensing scheme* is, by section 116(1), a scheme setting out the classes of case in which the operator of the scheme, or the person on whose behalf he acts, is willing to grant copyright licences, and the terms on which licences would be granted in those classes of case. That is, it is a scheme concerning the licence fees to be charged in respect of specific types of works, for example a tariff of licence fees to be charged for performing musical works in public. A *licensing body* is a society or other organization that has as its main object, or one of its main objects, the negotiation or granting of copyright licences, including the granting of such licences covering the works of more than one author. The body will be negotiating or granting licences either as owner or prospective owner of the copyright or as the agent of the owner or prospective owner.[65]

65 Section 116(2).

As regards licensing schemes, by section 117, the Copyright Tribunal has jurisdiction in relation to:

(a) schemes operated by a licensing body relating to literary, dramatic, musical and artistic works or films (or film soundtracks when accompanying a film) concerning the copying, performance, broadcasting and inclusion in a cable programme;
(b) all licensing schemes (whether or not operated by a licensing body) in relation to sound recordings (other than film soundtracks when accompanying a film), broadcasts, cable programmes and the typographical arrangements of published editions;
(c) all licensing schemes in relation to the rental of sound recordings, films and computer programs.

Any of the above schemes can be referred to the Copyright Tribunal. In the case of a proposed scheme to be operated by a licensing body referral to the Tribunal can be made by an organization claiming to be representative of users of the copyright material to which the scheme would apply under section 118. If a licensing scheme is already in operation and there is a dispute between the operator of the scheme and a person claiming that he requires a licence under the scheme or an organization representing users, by section 119, that person or organization may refer the matter to the Tribunal. The Tribunal may, in either case, confirm or vary the scheme (existing or proposed) as the Tribunal thinks reasonable in the circumstances. There are also provisions for reference to the Tribunal if a person has been refused a licence by the operator of the scheme or the operator has failed to procure a licence for him, for example if the person is seeking a licence for a work that is in a category of case excluded from the scheme.

Sections 124 to 128 of the Act apply to licences granted by a licensing body otherwise than in pursuance of a licensing scheme, for example the Copyright Licensing Agency's licence with education authorities. The provisions are very similar to those for licensing schemes in respect of the works covered and the scope of the licences.[66] However, reference must be made by a prospective licensee in the case of a proposed licence or, in the case of an existing licence, by the licensee on the ground that it is unreasonable that the licence should cease to be in force. That is, if the licence is due to expire under the terms of the licence. An application by an existing licensee cannot be made until the last three months before the licence is due to expire. The Tribunal may confirm or vary the terms of a proposed licence or may, in the case of an existing licence, extend the licence either for a fixed period or indefinitely.

66 Section 124.

The Copyright Tribunal has to make its determinations on the basis of what is reasonable in the circumstances and, by section 129, this means that the Tribunal shall have regard to the availability of other schemes, or the granting of licences to other persons in similar circumstances and the terms of those schemes or licences. Furthermore, the Tribunal shall exercise its powers so that there is no unreasonable discrimination between licensees (existing or prospective) under the scheme or licence that is subject to the referral, and licensees under other schemes operated by, or other licences granted by, the same person. Further guidelines relating to specific works or forms of use are given in sections 130 to 134. For example, section 130 covers the reprographic copying of published literary, dramatic, musical or artistic works or the typographical arrangement of published editions. With respect to such works, the Tribunal shall have regard to the extent to which published editions of the works are available, the proportion of the work to be copied and the nature of the use to which the copies are to be put. Also, for these types of works, by section 137, the Secretary of State can extend a licensing scheme, under sections 118 to 123, operated by a licensing body or a licence, under sections 125 to 128, to works of a description similar to those covered by the scheme or licence that have been unreasonably excluded from the scheme or licence. This is providing that making them subject to the scheme or licence would not conflict with the normal exploitation of the works or unreasonably prejudice the legitimate interests of the copyright owners. Appeal from section 137 orders lies with the Copyright Tribunal which can confirm, discharge or vary the order.

Section 140 gives the Secretary of State powers of investigation as to the need for a licensing scheme or general licence to authorize educational establishments to make for the purposes of instruction reprographic copies of published literary, dramatic, musical or artistic works or the typographical arrangement of published editions. The Secretary of State may within one year of making a recommendation under section 140 grant a statutory licence free of royalty if provision has not been made in accordance with the recommendation.

Additionally, by section 143, the Secretary of State may certify licensing schemes on application from the person operating or proposing to operate the scheme in question. The Secretary of State shall certify the scheme by way of statutory instrument if he is satisfied that the scheme enables the works to which it relates to be sufficiently identified by persons likely to require licences and clearly sets out the terms of the licences and charges payable, if any. Such schemes cover some of the acts permitted under copyright, such as the educational recording of broadcasts or cable programmes or the making of copies of abstracts of scientific or technical articles, so that, if a certified licensing scheme is in operation, anyone carrying out one of the particular permitted acts included in the certified licensing scheme will infringe copyright, unless covered by the scheme. Some of the permitted acts can thus be nullified by certification.[67]

67 This is acknowledged in Chapter III of the Copyright, Designs and Patents Act 1988, the part dealing with the permitted acts. See, for example, section 35(2), 60(2) and 66(2).

COMPULSORY LICENCES AND LICENCES AS OF RIGHT

Compulsory licences may be granted by order of the Secretary of State in respect to the rental to the public of copies of sound recordings, films or computer programs under section 66, unless there exists a certified licensing scheme under section 143. It is unlikely that the provisions in section 66 will ever be used and they can be thought of as an ultimate safeguard against abuse of copyright. Indeed, these provisions caused a great deal of concern to copyright owners, especially owners of the copyright subsisting in computer programs during the passage through Parliament of the Copyright, Designs and Patents Bill. Should section 66 ever be used, by section 142, the Copyright Tribunal has the power to settle the royalty payable if the parties cannot agree on a royalty.

Licences as of right may become available following a report by the Monopolies and Mergers Commission. By section 144, if the public interest is or has been or may be prejudiced because of conditions in licences restricting the use of the work or the right of the copyright owner to grant further licences or because the copyright owner refuses to grant licences on reasonable terms, a Minister may act on the Commission's report and cancel or modify the conditions or provide that licences shall be available as of right. The terms of the licence will be settled by the Copyright Tribunal in the absence of agreement. A proviso is that the relevant Minister may only exercise his powers under section 144 if he is satisfied that to do so will not contravene the conventions to which the United Kingdom is a party, that is, the Berne Copyright Convention and the Universal Copyright Convention.

THE COPYRIGHT TRIBUNAL

The Copyright Tribunal is the old Performing Right Tribunal with more powers and a much wider scope of operation as has been noted above. Section 145 states that the Performing Right Tribunal which was established under section 23 of the Copyright Act 1956 to regulate the licensing of performing rights, is renamed the Copyright Tribunal. The Copyright Tribunal is made up of a chairman and two deputy chairmen appointed by the Lord Chancellor after consulting the Lord Advocate and between two and eight ordinary members appointed by the Secretary of State. Persons appointed as chairman or deputy chairmen must be barristers, advocates or solicitors of at least seven years', standing or who have held judicial office. Section 146 of the Act contains provisions for the resignation or removal of members of the Tribunal and provision is made for the payment of members in section 147 as well as for the appointment of staff for the Tribunal.

The constitution of the Tribunal for the purpose of proceedings is to comprise a chairman, either the chairman or a deputy chairman, and two or more ordinary members.[68] Voting on decisions is by majority with the chairman having a further casting vote if the votes are, otherwise, equal. The jurisdiction of the Tribunal is set out in section 149 as being to hear and determine proceedings under:

68 Section 148.

(a) reference of a proposed or existing scheme, for example by an organization representing persons claiming they require licences which are covered by the scheme;
(b) application with respect to entitlement to a licence under a licensing scheme, for example where a person has been refused a licence by the operator of a licensing scheme;
(c) the reference or application with respect to licensing by a licensing body, for example as regards the terms of a proposed licence or the expiry of an existing licence in the case of certain types of works and acts;
(d) appeals against the coverage of a licensing scheme or licence as regards the power of the Secretary of State to extend the coverage of schemes and licences relating to the reprographic copying by educational establishments;
(e) applications to settle royalty payments in respect of compulsory licences granted by the Secretary of State in respect of sound recordings, films and computer programs under section 66;
(f) applications to settle the terms of licences available as of right consequential of a report of the Monopolies and Mergers Commission;
(g) applications to give consent under Part II of the Act which concerns rights in performances;
(h) determination of the royalty or other payment to be made to the trustees for the Hospital for Sick Children, Great Ormond Street, London.

The Copyright, Designs and Patents Act 1988 has further provisions as regards the making of procedural rules for the Tribunal[69] and fees to be charged and, by section 151, the Tribunal can make orders as to costs. Finally, by section 152, appeals may be made to the High Court, or the Court of Session in Scotland, on any point of law arising from a decision of the Tribunal. It should be noted that the Tribunal is not a proactive body and can only respond to applications and references made to it.

69 Copyright Tribunal Rules 1989, SI 1989 No. 1129, as amended.

5

Moral rights

INTRODUCTION

1 The Rome Act 1928 added the *droit moral* to the Berne Convention, being the right to claim first authorship of a work and the right to object to any distortion, mutilation or other modification which would be prejudicial to the honour or reputation of the author. See, Stewart, S. M., *International Copyright and Neighbouring Rights* (London: Butterworths, 2nd edn., 1989) at pp.106–107.

In tardy recognition of parts of the Berne Copyright Convention[1] and in acknowledgement of the importance with which moral rights are regarded in much of the rest of Europe, the Copyright, Designs and Patents Act 1988 gives overt recognition and legal effect to such rights given to the creator of a work in which copyright subsists. United Kingdom copyright law has a tradition of emphasizing the economic rights associated with copyright, whilst the French model stresses the author's rights to control and be identified with his work regardless of the ownership of the economic rights. The Copyright, Designs and Patents Act 1988 bundles a collection of rights together under the appellation 'moral rights' even though some might not be thought to fall within this description, an example being the false attribution right and the right to privacy in certain photographs and films. There are four rights within the 'moral right' designation, being:

(a) the right to be identified as the author of a work or director of a film, the 'paternity right' (sections 77–79);
(b) the right of an author of a work or director of a film to object to derogatory treatment of that work or film, the 'integrity right' (sections 80–83);
(c) a general right that every person has not to have a work falsely attributed to him (section 84);
(d) the commissioner's right of privacy in respect of a photograph or film made for private and domestic purposes (section 85).

Notice that the Act refers to the director of a film. Usually, the director will not be the author for copyright purposes as the author of a film is, by section 9(2)(b), the person by whom the arrangements necessary for the making of the film are undertaken and this will typically be the producer of the film. It is his job to make the practical arrangements, the director's function is to provide artistic guidance and direction. Although the director of a film is not normally considered to be the author, he is in an analogous position to the author of, say, a literary or dramatic work; that is, he plays a creative role, hence the provision for moral rights for film directors.

In typically half-hearted fashion, these rights do not apply globally to all types of copyright work and, additionally, there are many exceptions to the application of the rights. The rights can be waived or even fail for lack of positive assertion on the part of the author or director. That the rights can be waived at all is unsatisfactory bearing in mind the economic pressure the creator of a work may be subject to.

To supporters of moral rights, the way in which they have been dealt with by the Act seems to be very much a compromise. Often there will be a conflict between a moral right and an economic right, an example being in the case of employee-authors. Bearing in mind that, as regards a literary, dramatic, musical or artistic work made by an employee in the course of his employment, the employer will be the first owner of the copyright by section 11(2), the Act effectively overrides the author's right to be identified as the author in relation to anything done by or with the authority of the copyright owner.[2]

Moral rights were hailed as a novelty in United Kingdom copyright law.[3] However, this is not really so; other areas of law could give remedies to the author. A licence agreement or assignment of copyright could have contained terms requiring that the author's name be placed prominently on copies of the work and that the work must not be modified. A treatment of an author's work which is derogatory or the false attribution of a work might give rise to an action in defamation. For example, an eminent and distinguished author, Edward, might write a serious and noble play about love conquering adversity and assign the copyright to a television company. If that television company then rewrites the play and changes it into a smutty farce and broadcasts it and Edward's name appears in the credits as being associated with the writing of the play, Edward will have an action in defamation on the basis that his reputation would be significantly harmed by this. The same might apply if an inferior and tasteless musical work has been falsely attributed to a celebrated and highly regarded composer with a high international reputation.

An author's moral rights can be protected indirectly because the act complained of might also involve a normal infringement of copyright. For example, if another person, without permission of the copyright owner makes a parody of the work, the author might feel aggrieved and the copyright owner might decide to sue for infringement because the parody contains a substantial part of the original work. However, only the copyright owner could bring a legal action and an author who did not own the copyright in his work had to stand by helplessly unless the treatment of the work was defamatory. It should be noted that the right to object to a derogatory treatment of the work is likely to be actionable in wider circumstances than would be the case in defamation because it extends to treatment which distorts or mutilates the work without necessarily affecting the author's reputation. In fact a distortion or mutilation of a work is, from the language of section 80(2)(b), prejudicial to the honour or reputation of the author or director, *per se*.

RIGHT TO BE IDENTIFIED AS THE AUTHOR OR DIRECTOR OF A WORK (THE PATERNITY RIGHT)

The right to be identified as the author of a literary, dramatic, musical or artistic work or as the director of a film is a new departure for United Kingdom copyright law. But it is not as wide ranging as it should be and there are a number of exceptions to it. Additionally, the author or director must assert the right for it to be effective. The right does not apply to other types of works, such as sound recordings and broadcasts where it would be inappropriate in any case; nor does the right apply to works in which copyright does not subsist – the work must be a 'copyright' work. Furthermore, the right does not apply to all forms of the works included – for example, the right does not apply to computer programs even though these are literary works.

2 This also applies to the director's right to be identified in the case of a film where the director's employer is the first owner of the copyright, section 79(3)(b) of the Copyright, Designs and Patents Act 1988. (Unless otherwise indicated, statutory references in this chapter are to this Act.)

3 De Freitas, D. 'The Copyright, Designs and Patents Act 1988 (2)', (1989) 133 *Solicitors Journal* 670 at 675. De Freitas recognizes correctly that the right not to have a work falsely attributed to a person is of older vintage, see section 43 of the Copyright Act 1956.

Section 77(1) of the Copyright, Designs and Patents Act 1988 states that the right to be identified as author or director applies to literary, dramatic, musical, artistic works and to films. However, the right is not infringed unless it has been asserted in accordance with section 78 so as to bind the person who carries out an activity which gives rise to the right to be identified. By section 78(2), the right may be asserted generally or in relation to specified acts either:

(a) on assignment, by including a statement in the instrument effecting the assignment – for example, a term in the assignment stating that the author or director asserts his moral right to be identified as such (an assignment must, of course, be in writing and signed by or on behalf of the assignor by section 90);

(b) by written instrument signed by the author or director – for example, by including a suitable term in a licence agreement. However, it may simply be a written notification of the right and not part of some contractual document.

There is no requirement that the right must be asserted before or at the time of any assignment or licence and it would appear that the right may be asserted at any time even subsequent to the transfer of the economic rights in the work. However, there may be a term in an assignment or licence agreement to the effect that the author or director must not at some future date assert this right. If this is so, the author or director will be in breach of contract if he subsequently asserts the right. The Act does not make clear whether the effect of any written notice is retrospective, that is whether an author or director can make this right apply to things done prior to the assertion. This could be extremely awkward for an assignee or licensee but for the fact that the Act does allow a court to take into account any delay in asserting the right when considering remedies.[4] As section 78(2) refers to signature by the author, it would seem that the right to be identified as author cannot be brought to life after the author's death, say by the author's widow.

Under the transitional arrangements contained in paragraphs 22 to 24 of Schedule 1 to the Act, the right to be identified as author applies to literary, dramatic, musical and artistic works made before the commencement of the 1988 Act if the author was still alive at that date.[5] Therefore, the right to be identified as author can be asserted in respect of a pre-existing work, by a written instrument signed by the author. There are certain safeguards – for example, nothing done before the commencement date is actionable as an infringement of moral rights, and assignees and licensees may continue to perform acts covered by an assignment or licence granted before the commencement date.

There are additional means of asserting the right to be identified that apply in relation to public exhibitions of artistic works. By section 78(3), when the author or first owner of copyright parts with possession of the original, or a copy is made under his direction or control, the right may be asserted by identifying the author on the original or copy, or on a frame, mount or other thing to which it is attached. Also, in relation to a public exhibition of an artistic work made in pursuance of a licence agreement, the right may be asserted by including in a licence authorizing the making of copies of the work a statement to that effect.

4 Section 78(5).

5 The commencement date of the copyright provisions of the Copyright, Designs and Patents Act 1988 is 1 August 1989.

It is one thing to assert a right but quite another to enforce it against third parties and, therefore, there must be provisions for determining whether a person is bound by the assertion and whether notice, actual or constructive, is required. In terms of the paternity right, the formula depends on the mode of assertion and section 78(4) states the circumstances when assignees, licensees and the like are bound by an assertion of the right to be identified as the author or director. In the case of an assignment, the assignee and anyone claiming through him are bound by the right regardless of notice. For example, if a person takes an assignment of the copyright in a literary work and the agreement includes a statement to the effect that the author asserts his right to be identified as author and that person, the original assignee, subsequently assigns the copyright to a third person, then the latter will be bound by the right even if he has no knowledge of it and could not reasonably be expected to know of its existence. This will apply also to subsequent licensees and even to a situation where a person obtains ownership of the copyright by way of a gift. Any person without knowledge of the assertion subsequently obtaining rights in the copyright will be bound even if he is acting in good faith provided that he derives his right or interest in the copyright through the original assignee. If observing the right to identification is likely to be inconvenient, a person acquiring a licence or assignment of copyright in a literary, dramatic, musical, artistic work or film should, if at all possible, have sight of the original assignment of the rights he now wants to acquire before concluding the agreement.[6]

Where the assertion is other than by assignment, only persons to whom notice of the assertion is brought are bound by it. The plain language of section 78 seems to be to the effect that the notice must be actual notice and that constructive or imputed notice will not suffice to bind the person with respect to the right. It is clear, therefore, that as far as the author or director is concerned, the right to be identified is far better asserted through an assignment than by any other means. Of course, if the author or director is also the first owner of the copyright, he may make contractual provisions safeguarding this right, for example by including a term that infringement of the right is to be considered a breach of condition and that sublicences may not be granted except with the owner's consent and such sublicences must include a term asserting the right. Least effective of all is the position where the right is asserted by a written and signed non-contractual document.

In relation to public exhibitions of artistic works, terms in licences asserting the right to be identified as author bind everyone, regardless of notice, into whose hands a copy made in pursuance of the licence comes. In the case of identification placed on the original or copy, frame, mount or other thing to which the artistic work is attached, any person into whose hands the original or copy comes is bound even if the identification is no longer present or visible. Therefore, the right is not to be defeated simply because an intermediate possessor of the artistic work deliberately or accidentally removed the identification.

Scope of the right to be identified as the author or director

The right to be identified as the author or director does not apply to every act that can be performed in relation to the work. For example, the right does not apply when a dramatic work is performed privately, say to a group of friends,

6 Of course, in most circumstances, applying the author's name to copies of the work will not be onerous.

or in the case of non-commercial publication. The scope of the right varies according to the nature of the work, as is to be expected and is provided for in section 77. It is interesting to note that the classification of copyright works given in section 1 of the Act is not followed precisely and some regrouping is required to make sense of the scope of the right. In particular, a literary work consisting of words intended to be sung or spoken with music is treated the same as a musical work.[7]

In relation to literary works (other than words intended to be sung or spoken with music) and dramatic works, the author has the right to be identified whenever:

(a) the work is published commercially, performed in public, broadcast or included in a cable programme service; or
(b) copies of a film or sound recording are issued to the public.[8]

The right also applies to these acts in respect of adaptations. That is, the author has the right to be identified as the author of the work from which the adaptation was made. For example, if an author, Florence Smith, writes a story in English and another person later translates the story into German and publishes copies of the German translation commercially, then, providing that Florence has asserted her paternity right, copies of the German version must contain a clear and reasonably prominent notice to the effect that the story has been translated from the original English version written by Florence Smith.

The author of a musical work or literary work consisting of words intended to be spoken or sung with music, for example the lyrics of a song, has the right to be identified as the author of the work whenever:

(a) the work is published commercially; or
(b) copies of a sound recording of the work are issued to the public; or
(c) a film of which the sound-track includes the work is shown in public or copies of such a film are issued to the public.[9]

As with dramatic works and the remainder of literary works, the right also applies to the above events in relation to an adaptation; that is, that the original author has the right to be identified as the author of the work from which the adaptation was made.

The author of an artistic work has, by section 77(4), the right to be identified whenever:

(a) the work is published commercially or exhibited in public or a visual image of it is broadcast or included in a cable programme service; or
(b) a film including a visual image of the work is shown in public or copies of such a film are issued to the public; or
(c) in the case of a work of architecture in the form of a building or model for a building, a sculpture or a work of artistic craftsmanship, copies of a graphic work representing it, or of a photograph of it are issued to the public.

Also, by section 77(5), the author of a work of architecture in the form of a building (that is, the architect) has the right to be identified on the building as constructed or, where more than one building is constructed to the design, on the first to be constructed. However, it is unlikely that names of architects will

7 Section 77(3).

8 Section 77(2).

9 Section 77(3).

be found on the first example of a mass-produced design, such as on a speculative builder's housing estate because, as will be seen below, all moral rights can
be waived. It is likely that a property developer commissioning an architect will
press for a waiver of this moral right unless, of course, the architect is very
famous, and the fixing at or near the entrance of the finished building of a suitable plaque upon which the architect's name is inscribed would be a good selling point. Alternatively, the fame and reputation of the architect may be such
that he is in a strong bargaining position and can insist on exercising his right
to be identified. There is no provision for the right in respect of adaptations of
artistic works, the reason being that it is not an infringement of an artistic work
to make an adaptation of it.[10]

10 See section 21.

Section 77(6) gives the director of a film the right to be identified whenever
the film is shown in public, broadcast or included in a cable programme service
or copies of the film are issued to the public. An example of the latter would be
when video recordings of the film are made available to the public either by
way of sale or rental.

The Act provides that the right to be identified applies in relation to the
whole or any substantial part of the work.[11] For example, if a short extract
from a literary work is printed and published commercially, the right still
applies providing that the extract represents a substantial part of the whole
work. It would be ridiculous if the copying and publication of a short extract
would infringe the economic right but not the moral right and, therefore, it is to
be expected that 'substantial' in the context of moral rights will have the same
meaning developed by the courts for economic rights, remembering that, by section 16(3)(a), acts restricted by copyright apply in relation to the work as a
whole or any substantial part of it. The transitional provisions in Schedule 1
confirm this approach in that paragraph 23(3) links infringement of moral
rights to infringement of the economic rights under copyright, although this is
in the context of things permitted under assignments or licences. It would seem
sensible that infringement of moral rights should be on all fours with the
infringement of economic rights concerning the requirement for substantiality.

11 Section 89(1).

Method of identification

Having the right to be identified as the author or director would be greatly
diluted if there were not also provisions relating to the prominence of the
notice containing the identification. Section 77(7) deals with this important
matter and requires that the identification must be clear and reasonably prominent. The manner of identification depends to some extent on the nature of the
act making the work available. In the case of the commercial publication of the
work or the issue to the public of a film or sound recording, the author or
director (or both if appropriate) should be identified on each copy, or if that is
not appropriate, in some other manner likely to bring his identity to the notice
of a person acquiring a copy.[12] Where the identification relates to a building, it
should be by appropriate means visible to persons entering or approaching the
building, for example by means of a plaque on the wall adjacent to the
entrance. In any other case, the author or director should be identified in such
a manner likely to bring his identity to the attention of a person seeing or hearing the performance, exhibition, showing, broadcast or cable programme in

12 Although the wording of
section 77(7)(a) dealing with
this mode of identification is
not absolutely clear, it seems
almost certain that commercial
publication relates to literary,
dramatic, musical and artistic
works and not to films and
sound recordings.

question. For example, if a play is performed in public, notices, advertisements and the like, and programmes or brochures sold to the audience should contain the author's name in a prominent place. If there are no written or printed materials, the author's name should be clearly stated to the audience prior to the performance.

By section 77(8), the author or director may specify a pseudonym or initials or some other form of identification and, if so, that form shall be used as the means of identification. In all other cases, any reasonable form of identification may be used.

Exceptions to the right to be identified

The exceptions to the right to be identified as the author or director are contained in section 79 of the Act. These exceptions have the effect of significantly weakening the paternity right in respect of certain types of works or as regards authors with a particular status. Coupled with the fact the right must be asserted and that the right, in common with the other moral rights, is capable of being waived by the person entitled to it, this reduces the practical importance of the right to what is, perhaps, a regrettable extent.[13] If an author has been commissioned to create the work, he might be under pressure to waive his moral rights by his paymaster who may be of the view that moral rights are an undesirable hindrance to the commercial exploitation of the work, or just plain inconvenient.

The exceptions to the right to be identified as the author or director of a relevant work are classified by reference to:

(a) **The type of work** (section 79(2)). Computer programs, designs of typefaces and computer-generated works are excluded from the province of the paternity right. This confirms the uncomfortable categorization of computer programs as literary works.[14] A typeface includes an ornamental motif used for printing and would normally fall within the graphic work category of artistic works.

   If justification is required for these first two exceptions, it may be on the basis that a large number of persons could be involved in the design, development and subsequent modification of the program or typeface and it may be inconvenient to allow the right.[15] Another argument could address the fact that they are more of a commercial character and less of an 'artistic' nature than the other works to which the right applies. As computer-generated works have no human author by definition (section 178), it seems reasonable that they must be excluded.[16]

(b) **The employment status of authors and directors** (section 79(3)). If the first owner of the copyright in the work is the author's employer by virtue of section 11(2) or the first owner of the copyright is the director's employer by virtue of section 9(2)(a), then the right does not apply in respect of acts done by or with the authority of the copyright owner.

(c) **The permitted acts.** There are exceptions relating to some specific permitted acts which are:
   (i)   Section 30, fair-dealing to the extent that it relates to the reporting of current events by means of a sound recording, broadcast or cable programme.

13 Waiver of moral rights is provided by section 87.

14 However, the international trend is to protect computer programs as literary works.

15 This could also be true for many works of architecture.

16 A nice conundrum is that a computer-generated work is one created in circumstances such that there is no human author, section 178, yet section 9(3) states that the author for computer-generated works is the person making the arrangements necessary for the creation of the work. This will often be a human-being (it could also be an artificial legal person such as a corporation). If the author, so defined is a human then surely the work cannot, by definition, be computer-generated because it has a human author after all.

(ii)   Section 31, incidental inclusion of a work in an artistic work, sound recording, film, broadcast of cable programme. It would obviously be troublesome and difficult to give credits identifying the author or director, for example if, in a live television news report, some music could be heard playing in the background.

(iii)   Section 32(3), examination questions. However, it is normal practice for the author of a work quoted in an examination paper to be acknowledged.

(iv)   Section 45, parliamentary and judicial proceedings and sections 46(1) & 46(2), Royal Commissions and statutory inquiries. Again, it is unlikely that the author or director would not be acknowledged as a matter of courtesy.

(v)   Section 51, permitted acts in relation to designs documents and models and section 52, relating to copyright in artistic works that have been exploited in a commercial sense.

(vi)   Section 57, in respect of acts permitted on assumptions as to the expiry of copyright or the death of the author in the case of anonymous or pseudonymous works.

(d)   **Works made for the purpose of reporting current events** (section 79(6)). A matter of convenience again. To some extent, the difficulty in identifying the author depends on the nature of the work involved. In the case of newspaper reports, there should be no real difficulty except in so far as the report has been 'taken' from another source, such as a rival newspaper, or if the original report has been edited and rewritten by one or more other persons. The problem is worse in the case of a television newscast that will include a good number of reports written by different individuals or teams of individuals and may have been edited or modified by others. Whilst long credits may be acceptable in the case of feature films, it would be burdensome to have to identify all the various authors (and film directors) and the time taken to roll the credits might be nearly as long as the newscast itself.

(e)   **Publication in various types of publications** (section 79(6)). This exception applies to literary, dramatic, musical and artistic works that are published in newspapers, magazines or other similar periodicals and in an encyclopaedia, dictionary, yearbook or other collective work of reference. However, for the exception to apply, the author must have created the work for the purpose of such publication or it must have been made available with the consent of the author for the purposes of such publication. In many works falling into these categories, authors tend to be identified anyway, if only by way of a list of contributors. However, if there are many authors, identifying each would be onerous, especially if their contributions are interleaved in any way. A question arises as to whether this provision is limited to materials published in paper form as many of the works described are available, additionally or alternatively, in electronic form. If it is so limited, then presumably, the exception will not apply to these things if they are published in electronic form. For example, certain academic journals are available using the LEXIS computer-based legal information retrieval system.[17] If the exception only extends to hard copy publications, the author must be identified in the case of works stored electronically including computer storage, magnetic storage and compact discs, an irrational and absurd result.

17 LEXIS is a registered trade mark of Butterworths Telepublishing Limited. Some publishers of journals seek the agreement of authors to the inclusion of the author's article in such a computer database.

(f) **Crown and parliamentary copyright** (section 79(7)). As might be expected, works in which Crown or parliamentary copyright subsists are excepted from the author's or director's right to be identified. Also excluded are works in which the copyright originally vested in an international organization by virtue of section 168. This exception does not apply if the author or director has previously been identified as such in or on published copies of the work.

RIGHT TO OBJECT TO DEROGATORY TREATMENT OF THE WORK

In addition to having a paternity right (subject to exceptions and conditions), the author of literary, dramatic, musical or artistic work and the director of a film has an 'integrity right', a right to object to derogatory treatment of the author's or director's work. It has always been possible for a copyright owner to limit the extent and nature of alterations that can be made to a work by a licensee. A copyright owner who is also the author can thus provide for the continuing integrity of the work by contractual means. Before the right to object to derogatory treatment existed, in the absence of express or implied terms in a licence agreement, the licensee had the right to make alterations but this was not necessarily an absolute right and, in *Frisby* v *British Broadcasting Corp.,*[18] it was said that the court would, in appropriate circumstances, limit that right to make alterations.[19]

The integrity right is described by section 80(1) as the right belonging to the author or director not to have work subjected to derogatory treatment. For the right to apply, the work must be a 'copyright' work, that is a work in which copyright subsists; furthermore, the right is subject to exceptions and only applies as regards certain acts carried out in relation to the work. As with all other moral rights, the right can be waived with the consent of the person entitled to the right, who might be the author or director or a person taking the right after the death of the author or director. The integrity right also applies to works which existed prior to the commencement date of the Copyright, Designs and Patents Act 1988, subject to certain conditions.[20]

'Derogatory treatment' is described in section 80(2) as being a treatment which amounts to distortion or mutilation of the work or is otherwise prejudicial to the honour or reputation of the author or director. If the treatment does injure the honour or reputation of the author or director, it is possible that it may give rise to a claim in defamation in addition to an action for infringement of the moral right. 'Treatment' is defined as meaning the addition to, deletion from, or alteration to, or adaptation of the work but not including a translation of a literary or dramatic work or an arrangement or transcription of a musical work involving no more than a change of key or register. Notice that the meaning of treatment is not the same as the very technical meaning of adaptation given in section 21 of the Act. In some respects, treatment is wider than adaptation because it includes additions and deletions but narrower in the sense that translations and arrangements are not included. The definition of treatment is directed towards the activities that could offend the author, whereas a straightforward translation of a literary work should not upset any author. The right to object applies in relation to the whole or any part of the work by section 89(2)

[18] [1967] Ch 932.

[19] The BBC wished to remove words from a script which it considered would be offensive to a large proportion of the viewing public even though the plaintiff author considered that the words were important.

[20] See Schedule 1 to the Act, paragraphs 22–25. The provisions are similar to those for the right to identified as author or director.

of the Act. There is no stipulation that the part must be substantial and, theoretically, the right could arise in relation to a small part (in terms of quality or quantity), although the smaller the part, the less likely it is that its treatment would be considered to be derogatory.

An important aspect of the integrity right is the question of what amounts to a derogatory treatment of a work. Certainly, reducing the aesthetic content or damaging the literary style of the work by altering it, in other words reducing the merit or quality of the work, would probably fulfil the requirements. An example is where a parody is made of music intended to be taken seriously or in the case of a performance of a send-up of a worthy drama. An indication of the meaning can be gleaned from the French case of *Rowe* v *Walt Disney Productions*,[21] heard in the *Cour d'Appel* in Paris. In this case it was argued that moral rights under French law had been infringed, including the author's right to integrity. The plaintiff, a citizen of the United States resident in France, had written a story about an aristocratic family of cats resident in one of the better, more elegant areas of Paris, believing that a film would be made using live animals. Eventually, the defendant made a film based on the story not by using live animals but in the form of an animated cartoon, called *Aristocats*. The plaintiff, the author of the story claimed, *inter alia*, damages for the harm done to the integrity of his work.[22] The plaintiff's various claims failed because of a number of factors, not the least being that the original assignment was subject to English law and the then current English copyright legislation, the Copyright Act 1956, did not expressly recognize moral rights.[23]

Scope of the right to object to derogatory treatment

There are, as might be expected some similarities in the scope of this right when compared to the right to be identified. However, the scope of this particular right is expressed in terms of a classification of works which is more faithful to that given in section 1 of the Act. In the case of literary, dramatic and musical works, the right is infringed by a person who:

(a) publishes commercially, performs in public, broadcasts or includes in a cable programme service a derogatory treatment of the work; or

(b) issues to the public copies of a film or sound recording of, or including, a derogatory treatment of the work.[24]

In the case of an artistic work, by section 80(4), the right is infringed by a person who:

(a) publishes commercially or exhibits in public a derogatory treatment of the work, or broadcasts or includes in a cable programme service a visual image of a derogatory treatment of the work;

(b) shows in public a film including a visual image of a derogatory treatment of the work or issues to the public copies of such a film; or

(c) in the case of a work of architecture in the *form of a model for a building*, a sculpture or a work of artistic craftsmanship, issues to the public copies of a graphic work representing, or of a photograph of, a derogatory treatment of the work.

However, unlike the paternity right, this right does not apply to works of architecture in the *form of a building*. Nevertheless, by section 80(5), where the

21 [1987] FSR 36.

22 Initially, the author had asked for further payment in respect of his authorship of the story.

23 A citizen of the United States resident in France enjoys the same moral rights as French authors. However, the law of the country in which the contract is signed becomes the law of the parties and neither the Universal Copyright Convention nor any other provisions of international law, could give the plaintiff moral rights afforded by French law which were denied to him under the law of contract. The assignment had been signed in London.

24 Section 80(3).

author is identified on the building and the building is subjected to a derogatory treatment, the author has the right to have the identification removed. Other remedies will not, therefore, be applicable in this latter situation.

As regards films, the right to object to a derogatory treatment is infringed by a person who:

(a) shows in public, broadcasts or includes in a cable programme service a derogatory treatment of the film;
(b) issues to the public copies of a derogatory treatment of the film; or
(c) along with the film, plays in public, broadcasts or includes in a cable programme service, or issues to the public copies of a derogatory treatment of the film soundtrack.

Section 80(7) provides that the right extends to apply to the treatment of parts of a work resulting from a previous treatment by a person other than the author or director, if those parts are attributed to, or are likely to be regarded as the work of the author or director. Thus, derogatory treatments of versions of the work that have already been altered by a third party are covered by the right. For example, an author, Joe Brown, writes a story in English and assigns the copyright to a publishing company. The story becomes well known. Another person is engaged by the publishing company to translate the story into French. The publishing company grants a licence to a French theatre company permitting the latter to perform the French version in public. The French theatre company decide to perform a send-up of the story in the form of a farce. If this treatment is judged to be derogatory and the work is likely to be attributed to him, Joe Brown's moral right has been infringed. Ironically, the enhanced position given to authors and directors by the paternity right increases the possibility that the author or director will have his integrity right infringed. The more strong the association between the author or director and the work, the greater the likelihood of the integrity right, as regards treatments of previous treatments, being infringed, as indeed is the likelihood that a treatment will harm the honour or reputation of the work. Some authors and directors may find it embarrassing to be so clearly identified as such.

Exceptions and qualifications to the right to object to a derogatory treatment of a work

The right is limited in its scope by exceptions and qualifications provided for by sections 81 and 82 of the Act respectively. The right to object to derogatory treatment of a work is subject to exceptions as follows:

(a) **The right does not apply to computer programs and computer-generated works** (section 81(2)). Although there may be a great deal of creative effort involved in computer programs and, indirectly, in computer-generated works, any right to integrity could be seen as an unwanted potential restriction on the future modification of the work. Nevertheless, professional reputation will be associated with computer programs particularly and it seems anomalous to omit computer programs from the ambit of this right and, indeed, the right to paternity. Computer programs are the result of a great deal of skill, judgment and experience and the author–work bond will be as great as with any other form of literary work and in many cases it will be greater.[25] As regards computer-generated works, it is accepted that the right, at first sight, seems inappropriate. Computer-generated works are defined as being created in circumstances such that there is no human author by section 178, and there should be a human author to feel aggrieved if the work is subsequently subjected to derogatory treatment. However, by section 9(2)(a), a computer-generated work does have an author who may be a living individual and who may feel angry or distressed by the treatment of the work by a subsequent copyright owner or licensee. For example, the work may be subjected to treatment which makes it derisory and this reflects on the author.

(b) **The right does not apply in relation to any work made for the purpose of reporting current events** (section 80(3)). As with the paternity right, this reflects worries expressed by the media during the passage of the Computer, Designs and Patents Bill through Parliament, that providing for moral rights in such circumstances would be very onerous.

(c) By section 80(4), **the right does not apply in relation to the publication of a literary, dramatic, musical or artistic work** in:

(i) a newspaper, magazine or other similar periodical; or

(ii) an encyclopaedia, dictionary, yearbook or other collective work of reference. However, for the exception to apply, the author must have made the work for the purposes of such publication or the work must have been made available with the consent of the author for the purposes of such publication. Furthermore, the right does not apply to any subsequent exploitation elsewhere of such a work without modification of the published version. As the author's work will be one of many in the publication, the purpose of this exception is to facilitate the modification of the works included in the publication and, for example, the later storage in a computer database. If only one author could object on the basis of his right to integrity, it could hamper or delay the subsequent publication of the entire work. In many cases, editors of collective works reserve the right to modify the author's original manuscript to produce the finished version for publication. An example of a case in which a single author could hamper publication is where the editor of the compendium work wishes to reduce the length of a submitted article by leaving out a few paragraphs against the wishes of the author. This exception can be seen as recognizing the editor's role, his skill and judgment and allows the editor the discretion he needs to carry out his work.

(d) **The right is not infringed by an act which by virtue of section 57 would not infringe copyright** (section 80(5)). Section 57 deals with permitted acts based on assumptions as to the expiry of copyright or the death of the author in the case of anonymous or pseudonymous works.

(e) By section 80(7), **the right is not infringed by anything done for the purpose of:**

(i) avoiding the commission of an offence;

(ii) complying with a duty imposed by or under an enactment; or

(iii) in the case of the British Broadcasting Corporation, avoiding the inclusion in a programme broadcast by them of anything which offends against good taste or decency or which is likely to encourage or incite crime or to lead to disorder or to be offensive to public feeling.

25 Some computer programs and suites of programs are the result of many years of work.

If the author or director is identified at the time of the relevant act or has previously been identified in or on published copies of the work, there must be a sufficient disclaimer. One of the main purposes of this exception is to allow the BBC to censor parts of works which are to be broadcast without falling foul of the integrity right. The latter exception only applies to the BBC, therefore, the independent television companies and, for that matter, satellite broadcasters and proprietors of cable programme services must choose whether to run the risk of being sued for infringement of the right if they make cuts, whether to screen the work in full or whether to refuse to use the work at all.[26] A sufficient disclaimer would be to the effect that certain scenes which, for example, would be offensive to many people, have been omitted. Examples of scenes that could fall within this provision are:

(i)   explicit or pornographic sex;
(ii) showing how a terrorist makes bombs;
(iii) violence at a demonstration;
(iv) a live recording of a speech by a member of the IRA

The latter also is covered by the second exception in the list, that is statutory duty.

Section 82 is described in the sub-heading as 'qualification of right in certain cases'. It is really just another list of exceptions to the right and applies to employee works (where the first owner of the copyright is the author's or director's employer), Crown and parliamentary copyright and works in which the copyright originally vested in an international organization under section 168. In respect of these works, the right to object to derogatory treatment does not apply to anything done by or with the authority of the copyright owner unless the author or director:

(a) is identified at the time of the relevant act, or
(b) has previously been identified in or on published copies of the work.

In other cases concerning the works included in the provisions of section 82, that is where the right still does apply (for example, if the author is not and has not been identified), the right is not infringed if there is a sufficient disclaimer.

Infringement by possession of or dealing with an infringing article

Almost as a parallel to the secondary infringements of copyright, the right to object to derogatory treatment can be infringed by possessing or dealing with infringing articles. An infringing article is defined by section 83(2) as a work or a copy of a work that has been subjected to derogatory treatment and that has been or is likely to be the subject of any of the acts within the scope of the right in circumstances infringing that right.[27] By section 83(1), a person also infringes the integrity right if he:

(a) possesses in the course of business,
(b) sells or lets for hire, or offers or exposes for sale or hire,
(c) in the course of business exhibits or distributes,
(d) distributes otherwise than in the course of business so as to affect prejudicially the honour or reputation of the author or director,

an article which is, and which he knows or has reason to believe is, an infringing article.

26 Alternatively, the author or director may be asked to waive his integrity rights.

27 Note that the definition is different to that for 'infringing copies' as given by section 27(2) which relates to secondary infringement of copyright.

These activities are the same or very similar to those relating to some of the secondary infringements of copyright and the associated criminal offences. However, the above activities do not, in terms of the integrity right, give rise to criminal liability, but there is a requirement for knowledge on the part of the person infringing the right. The criminal penalties provided by section 107 are expressed in terms of an 'infringing copy' and it therefore would seem that the criminal penalties do not apply to infringement of the integrity right alone as this is expressed in terms of an 'infringing article'.[28]

28 An infringing article is defined in section 83(2).

FALSE ATTRIBUTION OF A WORK

Any person could be angered or distressed if a work of poor quality or a work containing scandalous or outrageous comment is falsely attributed to them. For example, an artist with a high standing in the art world would be likely to object if another person paints a substandard work in the artist's style and tries to pass it off as being made by the artist. Obviously, the artist's reputation could be harmed by this unless the painting was an obvious 'fraud'. Of course, the law of defamation may be available to give some remedy to the person to whom an inferior work is attributed and substantial damages may be available in appropriate cases.[29] In cases such as the one described, an action in defamation may be the most attractive route to follow for the aggrieved person, especially as such cases tend to attract considerable publicity.

29 Defamation cases are often heard before a jury and the amount awarded to a successful plaintiff can be seen as being something of a lottery as it is the jury who decide the measure of damages.

However, the ingredients necessary for an action in defamation may be missing. The work that has been falsely attributed might be of a high standard. The person who has created it may be hoping to 'cash in' on the reputation and standing of a famous person or may be intending to embarrass some other persons.[30] An example of the latter situation is the work of the exceptionally skilled artist, the late Tom Keating, who produced many paintings in the style of important artists such as Constable, Turner and Palmer. The paintings were not copies of original paintings but Mr Keating adopted the style used by famous artists and his work was of such a high standard that several reputable art dealers and art collectors were fooled.[31] Mr Keating later appeared in a television series showing how he created his 'masterpieces'.

30 In such circumstances, there may be an action in passing off.

31 Criminal proceedings against Mr Keating in respect of his activities were halted because of his ill-health.

It is difficult to know whether the 'false attribution right' is a moral right in the true sense as it does not concern any work created by the person to whom the right accrues. Nevertheless, the Copyright, Designs and Patents Act 1988 places the right firmly amongst the other moral rights and also includes another right which is somewhat out of place in terms of traditional moral rights, that is a right to privacy in relation to certain photographs and films. The false attribution right is not new and was originally provided for in section 43 of the Copyright Act 1956. For example, in *Moore* v *News of the World Ltd.*,[32] the plaintiff, Mrs Edna May Moore (known professionally as Dorothy Squires) alleged that an article which appeared in the *News of the World* falsely attributed authorship to her and was defamatory. The article was entitled 'How My Love For The Saint Went Sour' and was claimed to be by Dorothy Squires talking to a reporter Weston Taylor. The plaintiff claimed that the article inferred that she was an unprincipled woman who had prepared sensational articles about her private life for substantial payment. The case was heard before a jury which awarded £4,300 for the libel and £100 for false attribution.

32 [1972] 1 QB 441. The case was notable in that it was the first to come before the United Kingdom courts on the question of false attribution.

Where there is a court action which involves a claim in defamation together with a claim in respect of false attribution, the general rule is that double damages will not be awarded – there can be no duplication of damages but the jury might properly take the defamation award into account in quantifying damages. In the above case, Lord Denning considered that the jury had decided upon an overall figure of £4,400 and had split this between defamation and false attribution in the proportions £4,300 and £100 respectively.

There must be a work that has been attributed and in *Noah* v *Shuba*[33] it was held that two short sentences by themselves could not be a work for copyright purposes. The defendant had quoted, with acknowledgement in a magazine article, the whole of a passage from a guide on hygiene and sterilization procedures with respect to electrolysis (a method of hair removal) written by the plaintiff. Two sentences in the passage had not been written by the plaintiff and they gave the impression that the plaintiff agreed with the defendant's view that if proper procedures were followed, there would be no risk of viral infections after treatment. It was held that the whole of the quoted passage had been attributed and because it was not taken verbatim from the plaintiff's work, the *whole of the passage* had been falsely attributed even though the differences were small. Even a slight change in wording can significantly alter the meaning of a written work. The plaintiff was awarded £250 for the false attribution and a further £7,250 for defamation.[34]

Persons quoting extracts from the works of others must be careful to use verbatim extracts only and check carefully for typographical errors. For example, if the word 'not' is omitted from a quoted passage and the author's name is acknowledged it would seem that the whole passage has been falsely attributed. The omission of the word would change the meaning of the passage or part of it and would, therefore, amount to a distortion of the work, making an action on the basis of the integrity right an alternative claim.

The false attribution right applies to the same categories of works as do the other moral rights but there are no exceptions. Therefore, unlike the paternity right, it applies to computer programs, typefaces and computer-generated works. A 'person', which presumably can also be an artificial legal person, has the right not to have a literary, dramatic, musical or artistic work falsely attributed to him as author or to have a film falsely attributed to him as director.[35]

Attribution means an express or implied statement as to who is the author or director of the work. The right is infringed in a number of circumstances as follows:

(a) issuing copies of a falsely attributed work to the public (section 84(2)(a));[36]
(b) exhibiting a falsely attributed artistic work or copy thereof in public (section 84(2)(b));
(c) performing in public, broadcasting or including in a cable programme service a literary, dramatic or musical work as being the work of a person knowing or having reason to believe that the attribution is false (section 84(3)(a));
(d) showing in public, broadcasting or including in a cable programme service a film as being directed by a person knowing or having reason to believe that the attribution is false (section 84(3)(b));

33 [1991] FSR 14.

34 There was a further award of £100 for copyright infringement. The judge refused to award additional damages in respect of the copyright infringement.

35 Section 84.

36 The false attribution may be in or on the offending copy of the work.

(e) with respect to the above acts, issuing to the public or publicly displaying material containing a false attribution (section 84(4)); this would include publicity materials such as leaflets distributed informing the public of a performance or posters advertising some event;

(f) possessing or dealing with a copy of falsely attributed work (a work with a false attribution in or on it) in the course of business, knowing or having reason to believe that there is such an attribution and that it is false (section 84(5)). In the case of artistic works, possessing and dealing with the work itself is caught. Dealing is defined in section 84(7) as selling or letting for hire, offering or exposing for sale or hire, exhibiting in public, or distributing;

(g) in the case of an artistic work, dealing with a work, which has been altered after the author parted with possession of it, as being the unaltered work of the author or dealing with a copy of such a work as being a copy of the unaltered work of the author knowing or having reason to believe that the work or the copy is not unaltered (section 84(6)). 'Dealing' has the same meaning as above.

The false attribution provisions also apply to adaptations of literary, dramatic and musical works and to copies of artistic works that are falsely represented as being copies made by the author of the artistic work; section 84(8). By section 89(2), the right of a person not to have a work falsely attributed to him applies in relation to the whole or any part of a work. As regards false attribution before the commencement date of the 1988 Act, section 43 of the Copyright Act 1956 applies.[37]

As before, it is unlikely that many persons will feel the need to turn to the false attribution provisions, as in serious cases the law of defamation is more appropriate and, if the false attribution has affected the commercial sales of some article incorporating a copyright work, an action in passing off might be relevant and provide greater recompense.

RIGHT TO PRIVACY IN PHOTOGRAPHS AND FILMS

English law recognizes no general right to privacy. Prior to the 1988 Act, the right to privacy in relation to photographs or films could only be achieved through the application of the economic rights, for example by obtaining an injunction to prevent publication. In *Mail Newspapers plc v Express Newspapers plc*,[38] an injunction was granted to prevent the publication of wedding photographs of a married couple. The wife had suffered a brain haemorrhage, however, when 24 weeks pregnant and was kept on a life support machine in the hope that the baby could be born alive. The husband had granted exclusive rights to the plaintiff in respect of the photographs together with an undertaking that he would pose for photographs with the baby within 24 hours of its birth. The defendants had intimated that they would also publish copies of the couple's wedding photographs.[39]

The inclusion of the right to privacy in photographs and films was considered necessary because of the power of visual media and the danger that photographs and films made for private purposes would later be published against the wishes of the person who commissioned the photograph, as happened in the

37 Schedule 1 to the 1988 Act, para. 22(2).

38 [1987] FSR 90.

39 The case hinged on whether the husband could grant exclusive rights as it appeared that the husband and wife were joint owners of the copyright in the wedding photographs. However, it was very questionable whether the wife was alive or clinically dead. If the former, her consent would be required for the exclusive licence but she was plainly not in a position to give it.

40 [1960] 1 WLR 1072. See
Chapter 6 for a discussion of
this case.

case of *Williams* v *Settle*.[40] One reason this right is required is that the first owner of the copyright in, for example, a commissioned photograph is the photographer and not the commissioner. The owner of the copyright in a film is the person by whom the arrangements necessary for the making of the film are undertaken. Therefore, commissioners of films and photographs, in common with other works of copyright, will not be able to control the subsequent use of the work through the medium of ownership. Of course, it is open to the commissioner to make contractual arrangements to protect privacy such as taking an assignment of the copyright or becoming an exclusive licensee. However, it will often be the case that the person commissioning the photograph or the film gives no thought to this matter. This new right gives him some safeguards to prevent a publication that would be an unwelcome invasion of his privacy or that of the persons appearing in the photograph or film or, at least, to provide him with some legal redress.

By section 85, the right to privacy applies in the case of a copyright photograph or film which has been commissioned for private and domestic purposes. The scope of the right is not to have:

(a) copies of the work issued to the public (here the difficulty with the scope of this phrase is unlikely to be a problem as it will usually be the first issue to the public that causes the complaint),
(b) the work exhibited or shown in public, or
(c) the work broadcast or included in a cable programme service.

41 The relevant permitted acts
are those under sections 31, 45,
46, 50 and 57.

42 Section 89(1).

The right may be infringed indirectly, such as where a person authorizes the act complained of. There are some minor exceptions to the application of the right connected with a number of the permitted acts.[41] However, the right does not apply to photographs and films made before the commencement of the 1988 Act. The right does apply in relation to a substantial part of the film or photograph as well as the whole of it.[42] This will include a single frame from a film.

JOINT WORKS

43 Section 10 and section
88(5).

The fact that many works are the result of the effort of joint authors (or joint directors), defined as being collaborative works where the respective contributions of the authors or directors are not distinct from the others,[43] requires that the moral rights provisions in the Act have to contain some rules to be applied in such cases. Not only does the Act have to address infringement of the paternity and integrity rights associated with joint works but it also has to consider the possibility that a work might be falsely attributed to joint authors or that a photograph or film may be subject to a joint commission. Section 88 deals with joint works and, briefly, makes the following provisions:

(a) for a joint author (or director) to take advantage of the paternity right he must assert the right himself. An assertion by one joint author will not benefit the other;
(b) the right to object to derogatory treatment applies to each joint author or director individually. The consent of one to the treatment does not prejudice the right of the other;

(c) the false attribution right is infringed by any false statement as to the authorship of a work of joint authorship and by falsely attributing joint authorship to a work of sole authorship. Similar provisions apply to the directorship of films;

(d) the right to privacy in certain films and photographs applies to each commissioner individually. The consent of one to the relevant act does not prejudice the right of the other.

DURATION

The duration of moral rights is provided for in a fairly straightforward way by section 86. In all cases except the false attribution right, they endure as long as copyright subsists in the work in question. As the duration of copyright is, in most cases where moral rights are likely to be in issue, the life of the author plus fifty years this can be seen as fairly generous. However, it could be argued that the rights of paternity and integrity should have no time limit. Why should a person be able to subject a play written by Shakespeare to a derogatory treatment and yet be prevented from doing the same in respect of a work written by an author who is still living or who died not more than fifty years ago? One possible answer is that given the passage of time, it is less likely that anyone would feel aggrieved personally (others might feel angered simply because the work of a great author was being debased). If the rights were perpetual, eventually, it would be difficult to say who had a right of action, that is *locus standi*; it might no longer be clear who could enforce the right. Finally, the law tends to dislike perpetual property rights as evidenced by the development of technical rules to prevent perpetual rights, for example in the law of real property, and especially, as exhibited in the Act itself which removes perpetual copyright from certain universities and colleges granted under the Copyright Act 1775.[44]

As regards the right not to have a work falsely attributed to a person, this continues to subsist for a period of 20 years after the person's death.[45] Of course, in this case, there is no copyright of which the person concerned is the author to measure the duration of the right. It is questionable whether 20 years is sufficient to give the widow or children of the person falsely attributed an action to prevent or claim damages for false attribution. There seems to be no good reason why this right should not endure for a longer period of time, say 50 years, after the person's death.

[44] Para. 13, Schedule 1 to the Copyright, Designs and Patents Act 1988.

[45] This was the period provided for under section 43 of the Copyright Act 1956.

WAIVER

The major chink in the armour in moral rights in the United Kingdom is that they may be waived by the author or director by whom they are owned. It is very likely that copyright owners (unless the owner is the author or director), assignees and licensees will seek to avoid the inconvenience of having to respect the author's or director's moral rights and that pressure may be brought to bear in the hope of obtaining a waiver. Those authors and directors who are in a weak bargaining position may be tempted to acquiesce.

One safeguard for the author or director is that the waiver must be by written instrument signed by the person giving up the right by section 87(2) and the waiver may be conditional or unconditional and may be expressed to be subject to revocation (section 87(3)(b)). The waiver may relate to a specific work or specified description of works or to works generally and may cover existing and future works. For example, an author of plays (dramatic works) may agree in writing to waive his moral rights in:

(a) a play entitled *A Long Summer,* or
(b) all the existing plays in a series written for television, or
(c) all his works up to the 31 December 1996, or
(d) a play, yet to be written, entitled *A Short Winter.*

If the author or director intends to waive all or some of his moral rights in an assignment or licence agreement, he would be wise to insist on a term to the effect that the waiver is to be revoked if the assignor or licensee commits a breach of the agreement.

There is a presumption that a waiver, made in favour of the owner or prospective owner of the copyright in the works affected by the waiver, extends to licensees and successors in title unless a contrary intention is expressed. The author or director will be bound, in respect of the waiver, as regards third parties who subsequently acquire economic rights in the work or works involved unless there is a term in the agreement to the contrary effect. If the formalities required for a waiver are imperfect, for example a written unsigned waiver coupled with an oral agreement, the general law of contract or estoppel is available. An example would be where the author was the first owner of the copyright and he assigned the copyright to another person who was acting in good faith and the author orally assured the other that he would waive his moral right to be identified as author. If the author later attempted to exercise that right, he might be estopped by the courts on the basis of his conduct.[46] Generally, a waiver by a joint author or joint director does not affect the moral rights of the others.[47]

REMEDIES

An infringement of a moral right is actionable as a breach of statutory duty owed to the person entitled to that right.[48] Mandatory injunctions will be relevant such as where a judge orders that the author's name is added to copies of the work remaining in stock and to future copies or that an architect's name is placed in a prominent place at or near to the entrance of a building. Prohibitory injunctions may be granted to prevent subsequent infringement of the integrity right and a *quia timet* injunction may be appropriate to prevent the planned publication of, or broadcast of, a derogatory treatment of the work.

Normally, damages are available for a breach of a statutory duty and, in the case of infringement of moral rights, this would appear to include damages for non-economic loss for the simple fact that moral rights are not economic in nature. Whether aggravated or exemplary damages are available is difficult to say with any certainty. Additional damages were granted in *Williams* v *Settle*,[49] a case involving the publication of a photograph showing a man who had been murdered. Although the effect of the case was to give a remedy for compromising privacy in relation to a photograph, it was done on the basis of an infringe-

46 For examples of the doctrine of promissory estoppel in contract law, see *Central London Property Trust Ltd.* v *High Trees House Ltd.* [1947] KB 130 and, in the context of a non-exclusive licence in respect of a patented process, *Tool Metal Manufacturing Co. Ltd.* v *Tungsten Electric Co. Ltd.* [1955] 2 All ER 657.

47 Section 88(3) and 88(6).

48 Section 103(1).

49 [1960] 1 WLR 1072.

ment of the economic rights of copyright for which the remedy of additional damages was clearly available, and this remains so under section 97(2) of the Act.[50] However, the case of *Moore* v *News of the World Ltd.*,[51] indicates that damages for false attribution may be slight, certainly in comparison with those available for defamation.

The final point on remedies is that a court has a discretion, in a case involving the alleged infringement of the right to object to derogatory treatment, to conditionally grant a prohibitory injunction requiring that a disclaimer is made dissociating the author or director from the treatment of the work, the disclaimer being in such terms and in such manner as may be approved by the court.[52] This could be appropriate where the copyright owner intends to broadcast a much abbreviated version of a play and the author objects, complaining that this is a mutilation of his original work. This power is unlikely to be used if the nature of the version subjected to the treatment complained of is such that, despite the disclaimer, the reputation of the author is at some risk however small. One reason is that the long-term effectiveness of even a strong disclaimer may be doubtful and that in years to come the author may be causally linked to the work as so treated.

50 In principle, exemplary damages are more appropriate for infringement of moral rights than they are in respect of infringements of economic rights.

51 [1972] 1 QB 441.

52 Section 103(2).

6

Infringement and remedies

RIGHTS OF COPYRIGHT OWNERS

The Copyright, Designs and Patents Act 1988 marks out the rights of copyright owners by reference to certain acts which only the owner can do or authorize; he is given exclusive rights in respect of these acts. These are the *acts restricted by copyright*. Other activities, which are mainly of a commercial nature such as dealing with infringing copies of a work, if they are done without the licence of the copyright owner, are described as secondary infringements. Anyone who does one of the acts restricted by the copyright without the permission or licence of the copyright owner infringes copyright, unless any of the exceptions known collectively as the *permitted acts* apply.[1] Strictly speaking, the permitted acts, although so described in the Act, are better described as exceptions to copyright infringement. This is because any activity in relation to a copyright work which is neither a restricted act nor a secondary infringement of copyright can be performed by anyone without the permission of the copyright owner. For example, lending a book to a friend does not infringe copyright, neither does making an artistic work from a literary work.[2] Therefore, unless there is an issue of infringement, the relevance of the permitted acts does not enter into the equation. If there is no infringement, there is no need to rely on the permitted acts to excuse the particular activity concerned. Copyright may be infringed vicariously, where a person without the permission of the copyright owner *authorizes* another to do a restricted act.[3]

As well as giving an aggrieved copyright owner civil remedies for copyright infringement, the Act also provides criminal penalties which generally, though not exactly, mirror the secondary infringements of copyright. Secondary infringements will normally be dealt with by the Crown Prosecution Service on reference from the police or by Trading Standards Officers. A private prosecution may be possible although, in reality, this will be a rare occurrence and the likelihood of a compensation order being made in favour of a copyright owner in criminal proceedings is very small bearing in mind that copyright law makes ample provision for civil remedies.[4]

THE ACTS RESTRICTED BY COPYRIGHT

The copyright owner has, by section 16(1) of the Copyright, Designs and Patents Act 1988, the exclusive right:

(a) to copy the work;
(b) to issue copies of the work to the public;
(c) to perform, show or play the work in public;
(d) to broadcast the work or include it in a cable programme;
(e) to make an adaptation of the work or do any of the above in relation to an adaptation.

See Chapter 7.

Brigid Foley v *Ellot* [1982] RPC 433. It was held that a literary work comprising the words and numerals in a knitting guide was not infringed by the making of garments by the defendant using the knitting guide.

Section 16(2) of the Copyright, Designs and Patents Act 1988. Unless otherwise stated, in this chapter statutory references are to this Act.

The Director of Public Prosecutions has certain powers in respect of private prosecutions including a power to intervene and undertake the conduct of proceedings even if the purpose is to offer no evidence and thereby abort those proceedings. Section 6 of the Prosecution of Offenders Act 1985.

The copyright subsisting in a work is infringed by any person who does or authorizes another to do any of these acts restricted by copyright without the licence (that is, without permission, contractual or otherwise) of the copyright owner.[5] Copyright may be infringed if the act complained of only relates to a part of the work for, by section 16(3), the doing of an act restricted by copyright includes doing it to any *substantial* part of the work. The question of substantiality has been taken by the courts as referring to the quality of what has been taken rather than its quantity in proportion to the whole. In *Ladbroke (Football) Ltd.* v *William Hill (Football) Ltd.*, Lord Pearce said:

> Whether a part is substantial must be decided by its quality rather than its quantity. The reproduction of a part which by itself has no originality will not normally be a substantial part of the copyright and therefore will not be protected.[6]

However, to speak of the reproduction of a part which has no originality *per se* is misleading. Many works have nothing original, if viewed in terms of their constituent parts, yet it is clear that compilations of commonplace material may still be works of copyright; the rationale is that sufficient skill and judgment has been expended in making the compilation.[7]

In *Ladbroke* v *William Hill*, Lord Evershed alluded to the substantial significance of the part taken and suggested that the question of substantial reproduction is incapable of precise definition but is, rather, a matter of fact and degree.[8] On this basis it is clear that copying a small portion of a work can infringe copyright if that part is important in relation to the whole work. For example, in *Hawkes & Sons (London) Ltd.* v *Paramount Film Service Ltd.*,[9] a newsreel contained 28 bars comprising the main melody of the well-known march 'Colonel Bogey'. This portion lasted only 20 seconds whereas the full march lasted for some four minutes. Nevertheless, the newsreel was held to infringe the copyright in the march. It was said that what is substantial is a matter of fact, and value as well as quantity must be considered.

In evaluating substantiality, the court should focus on the parts of the plaintiff's work reproduced by the defendant where the defendant's work contains other materials. In *Spectravest Inc.* v *Aperknit Ltd.*,[10] Millet J said (at 170):

> In considering whether a substantial part of the plaintiff's work has been reproduced by the defendant, attention must primarily be directed to the part which is said to have been reproduced, and not to those parts which have not.

The test seems to be, therefore, to identify the parts taken by the defendant, to then isolate them from the remainder of the defendant's work and then, finally, consider whether those parts represent a substantial part of the plaintiff's work. That comparison will be based on a test that is, according to Millet J, qualitative and not, or not merely, quantitative.

An alternative and, at first sight, very attractive test is to consider whether the act complained of is likely to harm the copyright owner's economic interests. In *Cooper* v *Stephens*,[11] it was said that even copying a small portion of an author's work would be restrained if used in a work which competes with the author's work or with a work that the author may publish in the future. However, such a test, taken literally, would be very difficult to apply and could mean that even copying a small unimportant part could infringe copyright which is plainly not the result intended by the Act. Basically, if the part taken is

5 Section 16(2)

6 [1964] 1 WLR 273 at 293.

7 For example, see *Macmillan & Co. Ltd.* v *K & J Cooper* (1923) 40 TLR 186.

8 The Copyright Act 1956 contained a restricted act of reproducing a work in a material form, equivalent to copying a work under the 1988 Act. Indeed, for literary, dramatic, musical and artistic works, copying is defined in section 17(2) as reproducing the work in any material form

9 [1934] Ch 593.

10 [1988] FSR 161.

11 [1895] 1 Ch 567.

significantly important, regardless of actual size, it is very likely to be detrimental to the copyright owner's interests. Another point is that, in a number of situations, the copyright owner may not wish to exploit the work commercially. For example, the work may have been produced for personal pleasure or interest such as in the case of a private diary.

The Copyright, Designs and Patents Act 1988 explicitly provides for indirect infringement of copyright by section 16(3), regardless of whether any intervening acts themselves infringe copyright. This is particularly valuable in the context of articles made to drawings so that a person making copies of the articles will indirectly infringe the copyright subsisting in the drawings. In *L B (Plastics) Ltd.* v *Swish Products Ltd.*,[12] the plaintiff manufactured a plastic 'knock-down' drawer system of furniture, known as 'Sheer Glide', in accordance with working drawings. The House of Lords upheld the plaintiff's claim that the copyright subsisting in the drawings had been infringed by the defendant who had copied the drawers. There was some evidence that the defendant had directly used the drawings in question but the trial judge, Whitford J, based his judgment on indirect copying of the drawings by the defendant's use of the plaintiff's drawer as a model for making similar drawers and this approach was affirmed in the House of Lords.

Recalling that copyright subsists in drawings as artistic works irrespective of artistic quality, even functional articles sometimes were afforded protection through their working drawings under the Copyright Act 1956. However, the 1988 Act, whilst expressly reinforcing the notion of indirect infringement of copyright, reduces its scope because of an overlap with design law. Section 51(1) of the Copyright, Designs and Patents Act 1988 states that the copyright in a design document (or model recording or embodying a design) is not infringed by making articles to the design unless the design is, itself, an artistic work. A design document is by section 263 any record of a design, whether in the form of a drawing, a written description, a photograph, data stored in a computer or otherwise.[13]

The individual infringing acts will now be considered in more detail. Sections 17 to 21 of the Act expand upon the meaning and scope of the acts restricted by copyright. Infringements of the rights associated with the restricted acts were described in the 1956 Act as 'primary infringements'. They are no longer so called although the Act still classifies some activities as secondary infringements and some writers still refer to these as primary infringements to distinguish them from the secondary infringements. It should be noted at this stage that the scope of the acts restricted by copyright varies according to the nature of the work involved.

Copying

Making a copy of a work is the act which most people think of in terms of copyright infringement. For example, making a photocopy of part of a book or duplicating a music cassette. But 'copying' has a technical meaning which varies depending on the nature of the work in question. Section 17 of the Act comprehensively deals with the concept of copying and, generally, copying is a restricted act for all categories of copyright works.[14] When considering the definitions of copying, it is essential to recognize that many of the words and terms used are themselves widely defined in the Act.

2 [1979] RPC 551.

3 This definition applies to Part III of the Act which concerns the design right subsisting in original designs.

4 Section 17(1).

Section 17(2) defines copying, in relation to a literary, dramatic, musical or artistic work as reproducing the work in any material form and this includes storing the work in any medium by electronic means. Thus, recording a copy of any of the 'original' works of copyright in modern computer storage media falls within the meaning of copying, acknowledging the fact that a work can be stored electronically in an intangible form and copied without the need for paper. 'Electronic' has an extremely wide meaning going well beyond an engineer's understanding of the word. By section 178, electronic means actuated by electric, magnetic, electro-magnetic, electro-chemical or electro-mechanical energy. However, section 17(2) is phrased in terms of storing the work *in* any medium rather than storing the work *in or on* any medium although this is unlikely to cause problems in practice because the phrase 'reproducing the work in any material form' should be wide enough in its own right to include any form of storage, given the spirit of the Act.

In respect of artistic works, copying is extended to include the making of a copy of a two-dimensional work in three dimensions and vice versa.[15] Thus, making a three-dimensional model from a drawing is copying as is making a drawing of a three-dimensional sculpture. As mentioned above, copyright can be infringed indirectly and this means that the process of 'reverse engineering'[16], copying an article by inspecting it, taking measurements and examining details of its construction and using the knowledge thus gained to make the copies, may infringe the copyright in any original drawings of the article concerned. In *British Leyland Motor Corp. Ltd.* v *Armstrong Patents Co. Ltd.*,[17] the plaintiff designed and made motor cars and also made spare parts for their cars. The plaintiff also granted licences to other companies permitting them to copy and sell spare parts for the plaintiff's cars in return for a royalty payment. The defendant refused to obtain a licence and manufactured replacement exhaust pipes for the plaintiff's cars by copying the shape and dimensions of the exhaust pipes made by the plaintiff for the Morris Marina car. The defendant simply bought a Morris Marina and removed the exhaust pipe and examined it to see how it was made, what its contours were, etc. The plaintiff claimed that the defendant's exhaust pipes infringed the copyright in the original drawings of the exhaust pipes. It was held that the defendant had infringed the copyright subsisting in the drawings of the exhaust pipes by the process of reverse engineering but the plaintiff would not be allowed to assert its rights under copyright law. It was said, in the House of Lords, that car owners have an inherent right to repair their cars in the most economical way possible and for that purpose it was essential that there was a free market in spare parts. This required the adoption of the non-derogation from grant principle in *Browne* v *Flower*[18] in which Parker J said (at 225):

> . . . the implications usually explained by the maxim that no one can derogate from his own grant do not stop short with easements.

Lord Templeman thought this principle could apply to a car just as easily as to land. He said:

> The principle applied to a motor car manufactured in accordance with engineering drawings and sold with components which are bound to fail during the life of the car prohibits the copyright owner from exercising his copyright powers in such a way as to prevent the car from functioning unless the owner of the car buys replacement parts from the copyright owner or his licensee.[19]

15 Section 17(3).

16 Sometimes referred to as 'reverse analysis', especially in terms of computer programs. See Chapter 8.

17 [1986] 2 WLR 400.

18 [1911] 1 Ch 219.

19 [1986] 2 WLR 400 at 430.

Therefore, although there had been a technical infringement of copyright, the plaintiffs were not allowed to derogate from or interfere with the car owner's right to a free market in spare parts. This case is important because it shows how the courts are prepared to control actual or potential abuse of a copyright but changes to copyright and design law have removed the possibility of infringing artistic copyright by copying an article made to a drawing if the article is subject to a design right and is not itself an artistic work.[20] However, this does not apply until 1 August 1999 to design documents and models created before 1 August 1989.[21]

Under previous copyright law, there was a defence under section 9(8) of the Copyright Act 1956 to the effect that there was no infringement of artistic copyright by a 'dimensional shift' if the alleged infringing object would not appear to persons, not being experts in relation to such objects, to be a reproduction of the artistic work. In other words, for an infringement, the object copied in a different dimension from an artistic work would have to look like the artistic work in the eyes of the layman. He should have been able to recognize the artistic work in the copy. This test became known as the 'lay recognition test' and was neither easy nor fair to apply as many drawings, particularly engineering drawings, do not appear to be much like the objects they represent in the eyes of a layman.[22] For example, in *Merlet* v *Mothercare plc*[23] the defendant had copied a baby's rain cape designed by the plaintiff. On the question of infringement of the drawings made by the plaintiff for the cape, it was held in the Court of Appeal that the section 9(8) defence succeeded because the layman would not recognize the plaintiff's drawing by comparison with garments made by the defendant. The drawing was in the form of a cutting plan and it was not permissible for the purposes of applying the 'lay recognition test' to unstitch the defendant's garment.[24] However, that test which limited the strength of protection in relation to three-dimensional articles offered primarily through the medium of drawings has now been abandoned by the 1988 Act. The test itself was criticized by senior judges and clearly had failed to achieve its purpose of limiting the scope of copyright. It also provided some indefensible anomalies. For example, simple objects produced from simple drawings would be protected whilst complex equipment produced from engineering drawings, difficult for the layman to comprehend, would fail to attract such protection because the notional non-expert would fail to recognize one from the other. Judges had even shown an inclination to fail to take account of differences in scale when applying the test. For example, in *Guildford Kapwood Ltd.* v *Embsay Fabrics Ltd.*,[25] although the defendant's fabric, greatly magnified, did resemble part of the plaintiff's lapping diagram, Walton J, regarding himself as the notional non-expert, did not think that the fabric appeared to be a reproduction of the lapping diagram.

Now that the notional non-expert test has thankfully vanished, the only question is whether the new form of the artistic work is a reproduction in a material form. Potentially, three-dimensional articles are well protected either by copyright if they are artistic works or through the law of designs in the case of aesthetic or functional articles. It would appear that, although copyright law seems to give strong protection to articles through drawings, this is limited by section 51(1) to the effect that design documents can be indirectly infringed only if they embody designs for articles which are, intrinsically, artistic works

20 See Chapter 19 on the design right. It should be noted that British Leyland were offering licences on reasonable terms. There are exceptions to design rights which relate to spare parts. The inclusion of these exceptions and the removal of artistic copyright protection for certain designs are a direct result of the *British Leyland* case and put the extension of the non-derogation from grant principle to spare parts on a statutory footing.

21 See the transitional provisions, para. 19(1) schedule 1 to the Act.

22 In *Merchant Adventurers* v *M Grew & Co. Ltd* [1971] 2 All ER 657 it was held by Graham J that the test was whether the drawings were such that, after inspecting them, a man of reasonable and average intelligence would be able to understand them to such a degree that he could visualize in his mind what a three-dimensional object made from the drawings would look like.

23 [1986] RPC 115.

24 The plaintiff also failed to show that the finished garment was a work of artistic craftsmanship.

25 [1983] FSR 567.

and that being so, making a copy of the article will directly infringe its own distinct copyright. 'Dimensional shift' copying only applies to artistic works. For example, in *Bradbury, Agnew & Co.* v *Day*,[26] the plaintiff owned the copyright in a cartoon in *Punch* magazine. Some actors who enacted the cartoon on stage by dressing up and posing to look like the cartoon were held to have infringed the copyright in the cartoon. The actors formed a three-dimensional representation of a two-dimensional artistic work, that is, the cartoon. However, in *Brigid Foley Ltd.* v *Ellot*,[27] it was held that converting a two-dimensional literary work, a knitting pattern, into a three-dimensional object, a woolly jumper, was not an infringement of the copyright subsisting in the knitting pattern and was not a reproduction in a material form for the purposes of copyright.

As regards films, television broadcasts and cable programmes, copying includes making a photograph of the whole or any substantial part of any image forming part of the film, broadcast or cable programme.[28] Therefore, taking a single photograph of a substantial part of one frame of a film or a photograph capturing a substantial part of a momentary display on a television monitor, being the result of either a broadcast or cable programme, infringes copyright. In *Spelling-Goldberg Productions Inc.* v *BPC Publishing Ltd.*,[29] the plaintiff made a 'Starsky and Hutch' film and the defendant copied and published a photograph of one frame of the film. It was held that the making of a copy of a single frame of the film was an infringement of the copyright in the film because a single frame is a part of the film within the meaning of section 13(10) of the Copyright Act 1956. The generous definition of 'photograph' contained in the 1988 Act should be considered in relation to this form of copying and the fact that photographs and films are mutually exclusive.[30] It should also be noted that section 17(4) states that copying *includes* making a photograph and that making a film of a film or a film of a television broadcast will probably be deemed to fall within the act of copying. It is possible in such examples that photographs of some kind may be used in an intermediate process, in which case, there will be an infringement in respect of the intermediate copies as, by section 17(6), copying includes the making of copies which are transient or incidental to some other use of the work.

Copying in relation to a typographical arrangement of a published edition simply means making a facsimile copy of the arrangement.[31] Section 178 offers some assistance with the meaning of 'facsimile copy' stating that it includes a copy which is reduced or enlarged in scale. It is reasonable to assume that the word facsimile has its ordinary dictionary meaning, an exact copy or duplicate of something, especially in relation to printed material. This is obviously intended to catch copying by the use of photocopying technology. It will also apply to copies transmitted using 'fax' machines (facsimile transmission machines). Not only can the copyright in the typographical arrangement of published editions be infringed by use of a fax machine, but also copyright in other works, especially the original works. For example, a person faxing a drawing will infringe the copyright in the drawing because he has made a copy of it, unless, of course, he has the permission from the copyright owner to do this. Facsimile transmission is carried out by the sender's machine scanning a document and converting the data contained in the document into digital codes which are then transmitted over the telecommunications system to the receiving machine which converts the digital data back to an image. The person receiving

26 [1916] 32 TLR 349.

27 [1982] RPC 433.

28 Section 17(4).

29 [1981] RPC 283.

30 Section 4(2) states that a photograph cannot be a part of a film.

31 Section 17(5).

a facsimile will obtain a faithful copy of the original although there may be some degradation in print quality. Table 6.1 below summarizes the scope of the restricted act of copying as it applies to different categories of works. It should be recalled that, generally, copying is a restricted act for all types of work.

Table 6.1 The restricted act of copying

Work	Restricted act
Literary, dramatic, musical, artistic: section 17(2)	Reproducing the work in any material form, including storing the work in any medium by electronic means
Artistic (additional): section 17(3)	Includes making a copy in 3-D of a 2-D work and making a copy in 2-D of a 3-D work, for example making a painting of a sculpture or constructing a building from a blueprint.
Film, TV broadcast, cable programme: section 17(4)	Includes making a photograph of the whole of any substantial part
Typographical arrangement of a published edition: section 17(5).	Making a facsimile copy of the arrangement
All works: section 17(6)	Includes the making of copies which are transient or are incidental to some other use of the work

Note: 'Photograph' has the meaning given in section 4(2), 'material form' is not defined but should include invisible means of storage such as on compact discs, magnetic tape, computer disks and integrated circuits.

Copying and alteration

Significant difficulties may arise in infringement actions if the defendant has produced his work based on a previous original work but has made considerable alterations. Two approaches are possible: first, it is a question of whether the second work is sufficiently the result of skill and labour so that it becomes itself an original work of copyright; secondly, the distinction between idea and expression may be relevant to this situation. A person might freely admit that he has used another work during the preparation of his own but may claim that he has not copied the expression of the first work and that his use of it was simply to determine the unprotected ideas contained therein. In other words, he has not made use of the copyrightable elements of the work but only the underlying ideas. *Glyn* v *Weston Feature*[32] provides an example of the former approach, that is whether the second person has used sufficient skill and effort to produce a new and distinct original work of copyright. In that case, a film entitled *Pimple's Three Weeks (without the Option)* which was a send-up of a risqué play *Three Weeks* was held not to infringe copyright in the play because very little of the original remained. It could not be said that the film was a reproduction of a substantial part of the incidents described in the play.

32 [1916] 1 Ch 261.

Judges are generally unsympathetic to a person who has created a work by making use of a prior work of copyright. It seems wrong in principle that someone can take a short cut to producing his own work by relying on the skill and effort of others. If there is evidence that the defendant has used the plaintiff's work in some way, judges appear to be reluctant to find for the defendant, regardless of fine distinctions between idea and expression. For example, in *Elanco Products Ltd.* v *Mandops (Agrochemical Specialists) Ltd.*,[33] the defendant started to sell a herbicide invented by the plaintiff and called 'Trifluralin' after the expiry of the patent. The defendant sold the herbicide together with a leaflet and label which were partly identical to those used by the plaintiff. After the plaintiff complained, the defendant produced a second leaflet using a different format and language. The plaintiff still complained and eventually the defendant started using a third version based on the second one, claiming that the information in the plaintiff's leaflet was in the public domain and that, although copyright protected the expression of language, it did not protect the content of it. As a matter of fact, it was found that most of the information in the defendant's leaflet could be traced to the public domain. Nevertheless, the judge still held that there was an arguable case of infringement of copyright, although the plaintiff was refused an injunction. Plainly, if the defendant had simply taken the trouble to locate and use information in the public domain in the preparation of their leaflet there would have been no infringement. But, the fact that the defendant had used the plaintiff's original leaflet did not help his case and Buckley LJ said that, concerning infringement, the question was whether, by using the plaintiff's literature, the defendant was making use of the skill and judgment of the plaintiff.

Of course, if there is a substantial amount of language copying and the same characters and incidents are used, then the fact that the two works may have other differences will not help the defendant's cause. In *Ravenscroft* v *Herbert*,[34] the defendant wrote a work of fiction but had used the plaintiff's nonfictional work as a source to provide credibility in relation to historical facts. The plaintiff's work concerned a spear reputed to have been the one used on Christ at the crucifixion and also to have been a source of inspiration for Nazi Germany. The spear is part of the Hapsburg treasure in the Hofburg Museum in Vienna. The defendant's claim to have used only historical facts from the plaintiff's work was rejected on the basis of substantial copying particularly in terms of language copying, incidents and in the interpretation of events. Altogether, it was held that the infringing part only represented 4 per cent of the defendant's work, but in assessing damages, that 4 per cent was rated as being worth 15 per cent in terms of its value to the whole of the work.

Copyright owners have occasionally complained about parodies of their works, that is satirical or comic send-ups. A parody usually involves a fair amount of alteration but the link with the first work is quite blatant since the effect of the parody might be largely lost otherwise. Particularly since the passing of the 1988 Act, in addition to the question of whether a substantial part of the first work has been copied, infringement of the author's moral rights also may be an important issue.[35] In *Joy Music Ltd.* v *Sunday Pictorial Newspapers (1920) Ltd.*,[36] a song entitled 'Rock-a-Billy' was parodied in another song which used the words 'Rock-a-Philip, Rock' in the chorus, but otherwise, the words of the two songs were different. It was held that the parody did not

33 [1980] RPC 213, an interlocutory hearing.

34 [1980] RPC 193.

35 Especially the right to object to derogatory treatment and the right not to have a work falsely attributed to the author. Cases on parodies prior to the 1988 Act must be viewed in the light of subsequent strengthening of the author's moral rights.

36 [1920] 2 QB 60.

infringe the copyright in the original song. However, in *Schweppes Ltd.* v *Wellingtons Ltd.*,[37] the defendant produced a label for a bottle which was very much like the plaintiff's famous bottle labels, except instead of using the word 'Schweppes' the defendant used the word 'Schlurppes'. Even though it was accepted that the defendant's label was a parody, it was held that the plaintiff's copyright had been infringed. There is no reason why parodies should be treated any differently to other works which are derived from or based on prior works although they do seem to have been looked on more kindly by the judiciary. Any difference in treatment runs counter to the Act and confirmation that the same principles apply to parodies as to other copies of works was indicated in *Williamson Music Ltd.* v *The Pearson Partnership Ltd.*,[38] a case involving a parody of the Rodgers and Hammerstein song 'There is Nothin' Like a Dame' for the purpose of advertising a bus company on television. It was held that the test for determining whether a parody amounted to an infringement of the parodied work was whether the parody made substantial use of the expression of the original work. In other words, to find an infringement by the restricted act of copying, the second work must contain a reproduction in a material form of a qualitatively substantial part of the first work. To this must be added the fact that the 'author' of the second work must have made use of the first work in creating the second, that is there must be some causal connection between the works.[39]

Copying – causal connection

In an action for copyright infringement by copying, proof of copying and the question as to which party bears the burden of proof are frequently important issues. In *Francis, Day & Hunter Ltd.* v *Bron*,[40] it was alleged that the defendant had reproduced the first eight bars of the song 'In a little Spanish Town' in his song 'Why' ('I'll never let you go, Why, because I love you'). The case is also of interest because it deals with the possibility of subconsciously infringing copyright. Willmer LJ accepted counsel's submission that, in order to constitute reproduction:

(a) there must be a sufficient objective similarity between the two works (an objective issue, that is, would the 'reasonable man' consider the two works sufficiently similar), and
(b) there must also be some causal connection between the two works (a subjective question but not to be presumed as a matter of law merely upon proof of access).

In his judgment, Diplock LJ described the issue of proof of copying in very clear terms, he said:

The degree of objective similarity is, of course, not merely important, indeed essential, in proving the first element in infringement, namely, that the defendant's work can properly be described as a reproduction or adaptation of the copyright work; it is also very cogent material from which to draw the inference that the defendant has in fact copied, whether consciously or unconsciously, the copyright work. But it is not the only material. Even complete identity of the two works [i.e. the works are identical] may not be conclusive evidence of copying, for it may be proved that it was impossible for the author of the alleged infringing work to have had access to the copyright work. And, once you have eliminated the impossible (namely, copying), that which

37 [1984] FSR 210.

38 [1987] FSR 97.

39 For the 'original' works of copyright, the act of copying is defined as reproducing the work in any material form. 'Reproduction' implies some creative relationship between the works, a causal link.

40 [1963] Ch 587.

remains (namely, coincidence) however improbable is the truth; I quote inaccurately, but not unconsciously, from Sherlock Holmes.[41]

As indicated by Diplock LJ, factual similarity coupled with proof of access does not raise an irrefutable presumption of copying, at most it raises a *prima facie* case for the defendant to answer. Thus, in such cases, the burden of proof will shift to the defendant who will then have to satisfy the court, on a balance of probabilities, that he had not copied the first work and that any similarity is the result of coincidence, not copying. This approach was later accepted by the House of Lords in *L B (Plastics) Ltd.* v *Swish Products Ltd.*[42] where it was held, *inter alia*, that a striking similarity combined with proof of access raised a *prima facie* case of infringement that the defendant had to answer.

The possibility of subconscious copying has already been mentioned above. Musical works are particularly susceptible to this form of copying where the author of the second piece of music has heard the first music some time before but has no contemporary conscious recollection of the first piece of music and certainly does not deliberately set out to copy it. This is what happened in the *Francis, Day & Hunter Ltd.* v *Bron* case where it was accepted by the judge at first instance that there had been no conscious copying. Nevertheless, the first eight bars of each song were virtually identical (these are reproduced in the law report). Even so, there must be some causal link between the works – truly independent and coincidental similarity is not copyright infringement. In the Court of Appeal, Willmer LJ said (at 614):

> . . . in order to establish liability [on the grounds of subconscious copying] it must be shown that the composer of the offending work was in fact familiar with the work alleged to have been copied.

At first sight, the notion of subconscious copying might appear bizarre but it appears to be accepted also in the law of breach of confidence.[43] Of course, if the first song has been popular, it will be difficult for a defendant to claim that he has not heard of it and has truly written his work independently in ignorance of it. In terms of music and, to some extent also, computer programs, the author should consider taking deliberate measures to make sure that his work does not appear to be similar to an existing work.

The ultimate safeguard against allegations of subconscious copying is for the author to cut himself off from the rest of society or that part of society knowledgeable about the particular class of works and to create his work in a 'clean-room' environment. But, surely, copyright law does not, and should not, intend that authors should have to take such extreme measures. Nevertheless, proof that the defendant has taken such measures will help his argument that he has not infringed copyright. In *Plix Products Ltd.* v *Frank M Winstone (Merchants)*[44] the fact that the defendant had instructed his designer to work alone without talking to others involved in the design of kiwifruit packs and without referring to existing packs showed that there had been no direct copying. However, it was held that the defendant had copied through the medium of the New Zealand Kiwifruit Authority's specification for kiwifruit packs which was, in turn, derived from the plaintiff's design. This New Zealand case is also notable in that it accepts that copyright can be infringed by copying from a verbal description as is, in principle, also a possibility under United Kingdom law as section 16(3)(b) admits infringement by indirect copying.[45]

41 Ibid. at 627.

42 [1979] RPC 551

43 *Seager* v *Copydex Ltd. (No. 1)* [1967] RPC 349.

44 [1986] FSR 63.

45 As, at the time, only the plaintiff's design had been accepted by the Authority (giving the plaintiff a monopoly in kiwifruit packs) the application of the idea/expression merger doctrine from United States copyright law, discussed in Chapter 8, would probably deny copyright protection to the plaintiff's packs. However, the law of designs and passing off could also apply to this type of situation.

Certainly, the restricted act of copying should be construed as being concerned with an intentional act. The remedies available for copyright infringement give some support to this approach because, by section 97(1), the plaintiff is not entitled to damages if it is shown that the defendant did not know and had no reason to believe that copyright subsisted in the first work at the time of the infringement. The difficulty is that, if the burden of proof shifts to the defendant, he may find it almost impossible to show that he did not base his work on a previous work which has become very well known, even though it was popular several years earlier.

Issuing copies of the work to the public

This restricted act applies to all categories of works. It is defined by section 18 as the:

> issue to the public of copies of a work . . . [by] putting into circulation copies *not previously put into circulation* in the United Kingdom or elsewhere . . .
>
> [emphasis added]

It does not apply to the subsequent distribution, sale, hiring or loan of such copies nor to any subsequent importation into the United Kingdom, although it does include the rental of copies of sound recordings, films and computer programs to the public.[46] In effect these limitations mirror the European Community doctrine of exhaustion of rights.[47] That is, the copyright owner loses the right to control the subsequent sale or importation of copies he has put into circulation. Of course, with respect to the rental of sound recordings, films and computer programs, subsequent dealings may be prohibited by provisions in a licence agreement. Therefore, if Andrew, the owner of the copyright in a sound recording, has marketed copies of the recording in Belgium and Beatrice buys some of those copies, she may later import those copies to the United Kingdom and sell them there without infringing copyright. But, if another person, Cecil, makes pirate copies and sells them in Belgium, he will infringe the public issue right even though Andrew has already sold other copies there. Of course, Cecil (or another person) will have infringed the copyright by making the pirate copies in the first place and there will also be some secondary infringements of copyright.

The inclusion of the rental right is important when it is realized that the film *E.T.* became the most popular rented video in the United Kingdom even before it was officially released for rental in the United Kingdom by the copyright owner. This extension to the right of first issue to the public sensibly takes account of the rapidly increasing rental market.[48]

Public performance, showing or playing a work in public.

Public performances and the public playing or showing of certain types of works infringe copyright unless done with the permission of the copyright owner. These performing rights are, in a great many cases, administered by the Performing Right Society which grants 'blanket' licences to persons wishing to perform, play or show copyright works in public. The performance of a work in public is an act restricted by the copyright in literary, dramatic and musical works. It does not apply to other forms of works. Section 19(2) expands upon

46 Rental includes lending by public libraries and museums whether or not a charge is made, para. 8 Schedule 7 to the Copyright, Designs and Patents Act 1988.

47 See Chapter 9.

48 Additional rental and lending rights are provided for in the European Communities Council Directive on rental right and lending right OJ [1992] L346/61. Compliance is required (but unlikely) by 1 July 1994.

the meaning of performance and states that it includes delivery of lectures, addresses, speeches and sermons and, in line with modern technology, it includes in general any mode of visual or acoustic presentation, including by means of a sound recording, film, broadcast or cable programme. By section 19(3), playing or showing a sound recording, film, broadcast or cable programme in public is an act restricted by the copyright in the work. Therefore, playing music to members of the public, for example background music in a café or restaurant to which the public have access, is a restricted act.

An important element is that the performance, showing or playing must be in 'public', a word which has been responsible for much judicial consideration. A consistent strand in the courts' interpretation has been the question of whether the copyright owner's interests have been harmed by the performance complained of. For example, would the copyright owner expect to be paid a royalty for the performance? Does the performance satisfy part of the public demand for the work and thereby reduce the copyright owner's potential income? In *Duck* v *Bates*,[49] the defendant performed a dramatic piece in a room in a hospital for the entertainment of nurses, attendants and other hospital workers without the consent of the copyright owner. No admission charge was made but approximately 170 persons attended each performance. It was held that the room where the drama was presented was not a place of public entertainment and that, consequently, the defendant was not liable to the copyright owner in damages. Brett MR said that such a private representation of the drama would not harm the copyright owner although a public representation in any place where the public were freely admitted with or without payment would.

However, any distinction which might be drawn in this case between the public at large and an audience limited by vocation or membership does not provide a workable formula as there have been several cases involving an audience limited in such a way in which the performance has been deemed to be a performance in public. For example, in *Ernest Turner Electrical Instruments Ltd.* v *Performing Right Society Ltd.*,[50] the owner of a factory relayed music broadcast by the British Broadcasting Corporation and from gramophone records to his 600 employees. Strangers were not allowed access to the factory. Nevertheless, it was held that the performance was a performance in public for the purposes of section 1(2) of the Copyright Act 1911. Lord Greene MR suggested that it was important to consider the relationship between the audience and the copyright owner rather than the relationship between the audience and the person arranging the performance, that is the employer. Economic considerations were also important in that the 'statutory monopoly' granted by the Copyright Act would be, in Lord Greene's opinion, largely destroyed if performances to such groups of persons were permitted.

Some performances can be said to be in the copyright owner's best interests because they publicize his work and whet the public appetite and, as a result, increase ultimate sales of the work. Such an argument can be raised in terms of radio and television broadcasts of pop music. For example, 'Top of the Pops' and similar programmes can influence sales of particular pieces of music. Nevertheless, broadcasters have to pay for a blanket licence to the Performing Right Society. Since 1976, as a result of a change in policy, even record shops have to pay fees for playing recordings of works written by members of the Performing Right Society over loudspeakers in the shops. In *Performing Right Society Ltd.*

49 (1884) 13 QBD 843.

50 [1943] 1 Ch 167. See also, *Jennings* v *Stephens* [1936] Ch 469 concerning the performance of a play in which the audience was limited to members of a Women's Institute.

51 [1979] All ER 828.

v *Harlequin Record Shops Ltd.*,[51] the owner of some record shops refused to pay the requisite fee arguing that playing the records over loudspeakers in the shops promoted sales and increased the composer's royalties and that this playing of recordings did not constitute a performance in public and, consequently, was not an infringement of copyright. However, injunctive relief was granted to the plaintiff and it was held that the performances were in public. The audience comprised members of the public present in shops to which the public at large was permitted and encouraged to enter. Furthermore, it was shown that a prudent record shop owner would pay the society's fee rather than discontinue playing the recordings.

For a performance not to be deemed to be a public performance, it must be to an audience of a domestic nature. It is clear that playing a video film to a group of friends or relatives will not be 'playing the work in public' and enacting a play in the presence of a few friends will not be a performance of the play in public, but the habitual playing of recordings to employees in a factory will be in public even though the employees are not charged anything for this benefit. There are, however, some instances where it is more difficult to draw a line. For example, a private hospital may transmit video films to its patients from a central machine to television monitors in individual rooms. A hotel may provide a similar service for its guests. It is probable, in these circumstances, that the performance or playing will be in public if the service is provided for all the guests or patients and, taken together, they can be said to form part of the public at large, even though only a proportion of them take advantage of the service. If a charge is made, then the question is beyond doubt.

Section 19(4) limits the personalities who can be liable for infringement by performance, showing or playing a work in public. The performers taking part in a public performance are not themselves to be regarded as being responsible for the infringement. In the case of the performance, playing or showing of the work in question by means of apparatus for receiving visual images or sounds conveyed by electronic means, the person by whom the visual images or sounds are sent is not to be regarded as responsible for the infringement. Therefore, a disc jockey at an unlicensed disco will not be liable to be sued for infringement of the public performance right. The language of the subsection appears to be difficult and inconsistent with subsection 2(b) which is expressed in terms of 'any mode of visual or acoustic presentation' whereas subsection 4 deals only with presentation by electronic means and uses the word 'sound' rather than 'acoustic'. Taking a strictly literal interpretation of section 19(4) could produce absurd results. For example, what is the position where the performers have also arranged the infringing public performance? Section 19(4) appears to excuse their infringement, as it clearly states that the performers shall not be regarded as responsible for the infringement. It is unlikely that the courts will take this interpretation as it plainly runs counter to the spirit of the Act. However, the draftsmen of the Copyright, Designs and Patents Act 1988 have already been subject to judicial criticism. In *BBC Enterprises Ltd.* v *Hi-Tech Xtravision Ltd.*,[52] Scott J said that, in his view:

52 *The Times*, 28 November 1989, Chancery Division. However, Scott J's judgment was reversed on appeal to the Court of Appeal, see [1990] 1 Ch 609.

. . . section 298 [of the Copyright, Designs and Patents Act 1988], on any footing, represented inept legislation. The language of the section justified the suspicion that the legislature was under a misapprehension as to the law.

It is inevitable that, given the size and complexity of the Act, there will be interpretational difficulties and it would have been better if, to the end of section 19(4), the words 'to the extent that the infringement relates to their activity as performer' were added to put the matter beyond doubt.

Broadcasting or inclusion in a cable programme service

By the surprisingly brief section 20, the broadcasting of a work or its inclusion in a cable programme service is an act restricted by the copyright in all categories of work except typographical arrangements of published editions. 'Broadcast' is defined in section 6 of the Act and the meaning of 'cable programme service' is to be found in section 7; these meanings are discussed in Chapter 3. They are of vital importance because, if the activity concerned falls outside the definitions, such as a cable programme service run for the purposes of business or an interactive service,[53] then there is no infringement of copyright and, therefore, no need to obtain licences.[54] In many respects, the restricted acts of broadcasting and inclusion in a cable programme service are a wider form of the restricted acts relating to public performance, playing or showing, especially as the meaning of broadcast is expressed in terms of reception by or presentation to members of the public. Similarly, a cable programme service may be one directed at members of the public, although this is only one possibility.

Making an adaptation

In terms of the Copyright, Designs and Patents Act 1988, the word 'adaptation' has some very special meanings depending on the nature of the work concerned and should not be taken in its usual sense. Making an adaptation does not simply mean the same as modifying a work. The restricted act of making an adaptation applies only to literary, dramatic and musical works. Of the original works, artistic works are not covered by the act of making an adaptation. Therefore, if a person represents an existing drawing by producing a list of coordinates he is not making an adaptation of the drawing and does not infringe the copyright in the drawing unless the list of coordinates can be considered to be a copy of the drawing.[55] However, if that person then makes articles in accordance with the coordinates, he will be deemed to have copied the drawing indirectly and infringed its copyright.[56]

An adaptation is made when it is recorded in writing or otherwise, by section 21(1). 'Writing' is defined by section 178 as including any form of notation or code, whether by hand or otherwise, regardless of the method by which, or medium in or on which it is recorded. This definition is very wide and should present no problems in the context of making an adaptation. 'Adaptation' is defined in section 21(3) and means:

(a) in relation to a literary or dramatic work,
    (i)   a translation of the work;
    (ii)   a version of a dramatic work in which it is converted into a non-dramatic work or, as the case may be, of a non-dramatic work in which it is converted into a dramatic work;
    (iii) a version of the work in which the story or action is conveyed wholly or mainly by means of pictures in a form suitable for reproduction in a book, or in a newspaper, magazine or similar periodical;

53 See the definitions in section 6 and 7 and, especially, the exceptions to the definition of 'cable programme service' in section 7(2).

54 However, there may be other restricted acts involved in the activity such as the making of copies, including transient and incidental copies. This also includes, importantly, storing the work in any medium by electronic means, section 17(2). There may also be a secondary infringement – see later.

55 This may be unlikely. However, if the existing work is a sculpture and a person produces a set of coordinates describing its form, that will infringe because a 'dimensional shift' has occurred which brings section 17(3) into play. Note that, by section 21(5) no inference is to be drawn from section 21 as to what does or does not amount to copying.

56 See section 17(3).

(ab) in relation to a computer program, means an arrangement or altered version of the program or a translation of it;[57]

(b) in relation to a musical work, an arrangement or transcription of the work.

57 Inserted by the Copyright (Computer Programs) Regulations 1992, SI 1992 No. 3233.

A translation would typically include a work of literature or a play that has been translated from French to English. But, as literary works include computer programs, the word takes on a special meaning in relation to computer programs and by section 21(4):

> . . . a 'translation' includes a version of the program in which it is converted into or out of a computer language or code or into a different computer language or code, [otherwise than incidentally in the course of running the program].[58]

58 The words in square brackets were repealed by the Copyright (Computer Programs) Regulations 1992, SI 1992 No. 3233.

The significance of adaptations in terms of computer programs is considered further in Chapter 8.

The dramatic/non-dramatic conversion covers situations such as where a biographical book or a true story is dramatized or, alternatively, where the script for a play is reworked as a novel. For example, in *Corelli* v *Gray*,[59] the defendant was found to have written a dramatic sketch by taking material from the plaintiff's novel. The third form of adaptation in relation to literary and dramatic works is where the story or action has been changed to a form which mainly comprises pictures. An example is where a story has been converted into a strip cartoon. To do the converse is not to make an adaptation, however. To change a cartoon or other graphical means of portraying a story into a written work does not fall within the meaning of making an adaptation, it may, however, fall within the meaning of copying. The rationale for this apparent inconsistency is that, presumably, to convert a story told mainly by pictures to a written work requires a great deal of skill, effort and judgment and all that is really taken is the plot or the idea underlying the pictorial work.[60] The wordsmith has many gaps to fill in. On the other hand, to draw pictures depicting a written work leaves less to the imagination of the artist in terms of the telling of the story although, of course, he will have free rein to express that story in his preferred way. The Act presumably considers artistic licence to be more constrained than literary licence.

59 [1913] TLR 570.

60 However, see the discussion on the requirement for tangibility in Chapter 3.

As far as musical works are concerned, arrangements and transcriptions of existing works are adaptations and will, if copyright subsists in the existing work, infringe that copyright. An example of an arrangement is where a piece of music written for one instrument is rewritten so that it is suitable for another or an operatic aria is re-written as an orchestral piece. If there is a sufficient amount of skill and judgment involved in the arrangement, it too might attract its own copyright,[61] although the permission of the owner of the copyright in the first piece of music would be required before the arranged piece could be exploited.[62]

By section 21(2), the doing of any of the other restricted acts, described in sections 17 to 20, in relation to an adaptation, is also an act restricted by the copyright in a literary, dramatic or musical work. This extends to section 21(1) so that making an adaptation of an adaptation also infringes copyright if done without the permission or licence of the copyright owner. For example, if Albert writes a novel in English and Barry, without Albert's permission, trans-

61 For example, see *Wood* v *Boosey* (1868) LR 3 QB 223.

62 Apart from infringing the copyright owner's rights, the moral rights of the author must be considered. By section 80 of the Act, the author of, *inter alia*, a musical work has a right not to have his work subjected to derogatory treatment. 'Treatment' in relation to a musical work does not include an arrangement or transcription involving no more than a change of key or register.

lates the novel into French, Barry is making an adaptation and infringes Albert's copyright. If Celia then makes copies of Barry's translation, Celia also infringes the copyright in the original novel (regardless of whether or not she has Barry's permission to do so). Finally, if Duncan translates Barry's French version of the novel into German, Duncan infringes copyright by making an adaptation of an adaptation. In addition to the economic rights, Albert's moral rights might be infringed by the above actions, for example if he is not identified as the author. Albert will have the right to object to derogatory treatment of his work only if the translations have some additions or deletions and the treatment amounts to a distortion or mutilation of the work or is otherwise prejudicial to Albert's honour or reputation.

SECONDARY INFRINGEMENTS OF COPYRIGHT

In addition to infringement of copyright through the acts restricted by the copyright in the work, there are certain other infringements known as secondary infringements, most of which are associated with criminal offences. These secondary infringements can be distinguished from the acts restricted by copyright by their predominantly commercial nature. Of course, if a secondary infringement has been committed there will almost certainly have been a corresponding infringement of one or more of the acts restricted by copyright.[63] The reason for the distinction between the acts restricted by the copyright contained in sections 16 to 21 and the secondary infringements (sections 22 to 26) is because different mental elements on the part of the infringer are involved. Because secondary infringers are usually proceeded against in the criminal courts, some form of *mens rea* is required in that the person responsible for the secondary infringement must have knowledge or reason to believe that he is infringing. It would seem from the wording that the person involved must have either actual knowledge or, at least, a subjective reasonable belief that the relevant activity involves a secondary infringement. However, under the Copyright Act 1956, only actual knowledge was sufficient for the corresponding secondary infringements but, nevertheless, the courts tended to take a liberal view of this and in *Columbia Picture Industries* v *Robinson*[64] it was held that, *inter alia*, the knowledge required extended to the situation where a defendant deliberately refrained from enquiry and shut his eyes to the obvious. The phrase 'has reason to believe' in sections 22 to 26 of the 1988 Act is new and, in *L A Gear Inc* v *Hi-Tec Sports plc,*[65] it was said that it could not be construed in accordance with the 1956 Act. The test must be objective in that it required a consideration of whether the reasonable man, with knowledge of the facts that the defendant had, would have formed the belief that the item was an infringing copy. In the trial at first instance, Morritt J suggested that, once apprised of the facts, the defendant should be allowed sufficient time to evaluate those facts so as to be in a position to draw the conclusion that he is dealing with infringing copies.[66] This is not inconsistent with an objective approach – the reasonable man also may need time for the facts to 'sink in'. Situations where a defendant does not have 'reason to believe' include where he believes that the copyright has expired, that copyright does not subsist in the work or that the copies have been made with the copyright owner's permission.

63 But, the 'primary infringement' may have been carried out by another person, hence the need for the secondary infringements. This is especially useful when the primary infringer is outside the jurisdiction of the United Kingdom courts.

64 [1987] 1 Ch 38. See also, *Infabrics Ltd.* v *Jaytex Shirt Co. Ltd.* [1987] FSR 457.

65 [1992] FSR 121.

66 Ibid. at 129.

The need to show a mental element on the part of a secondary infringer must be contrasted with the acts restricted by copyright under sections 16 to 21, in which the question of the infringer's mental element does not arise. If he commits one of the acts, he infringes copyright regardless of whether he knows that copyright subsists in the existing work and regardless of whether or not it is reasonable for the infringer to suspect that copyright subsists in the work. The strictness of this state of affairs is tempered by the fact that the availability of the remedy of damages is dependent upon the infringer's mental state.[67]

67 On the basis of the same formula, section 97(1).

Secondary infringement of copyright involves any of the following activities:

(a) importing an infringing copy into the United Kingdom, other than for private or domestic use (section 22);

(b) possessing or 'dealing' with an infringing copy; this includes possession in the course of business, selling, letting for hire, offering or exposing for sale or hire,[68] exhibiting or distributing in the course of business or distributing (otherwise than in the course of business) to such an extent as to affect prejudicially the owner of the copyright (section 23);

68 Exposing an article for sale is an invitation to treat and modern statutes use this or a similar formula to overcome the problem that this does not constitute a contractual offer as identified in cases such as *Fisher* v *Bell* [1961] 1 QB 394 and *Partridge* v *Crittenden* [1968] 2 All ER 421.

(c) making, importing into the United Kingdom, possessing in the course of business or selling, letting for hire, offering or exposing for sale or hire an article specifically designed or adapted for making infringing copies of a work (section 24(1));

(d) transmission of the work by means of a telecommunications system (excluding by broadcast or inclusion in a cable programme service) without the licence of the copyright owner, knowing or having reason to believe that infringing copies of the work will be made in the United Kingdom or elsewhere (section 24(2));

(e) permitting the use of premises, being a place of public entertainment, for an infringing performance; a 'place of public entertainment' includes places that are only occasionally made available for hire for the purposes of public entertainment, for example, a room in a public house which is hired out from time to time for functions such as weddings (section 25);

(f) where copyright is infringed by a public performance of the work, or by playing or showing the work in public, supplying the apparatus or a substantial part of it for the playing of sound recordings, the showing of films or the receiving of visual images or of sounds conveyed by electronic means (section 26);

(g) an occupier of premises who gives permission for the apparatus to be brought onto those premises may also be liable for the infringement (section 26(3));

(h) supplying a copy of a sound recording or film used to infringe copyright (section 26(4)).[69]

69 Strangely, this provision does not extend to computer programs. Computer programs, sound recordings and films are collectively dealt with in other parts of the Act, for example section 18(2), infringement by rental, and the presumptions contained in section 105.

In all cases, apart from those involving public performances, to be liable, the person concerned must have actual knowledge or have had reason to believe, for example, that the copy is an infringing copy or that the copy supplied by him is to be used in such a way so as to infringe copyright. However, there is a subtle difference in the mental element required for the infringement under section 25 in that the person giving permission for the premises to be used for the performance will be liable unless, at the time he gave permission, he believed on reasonable grounds that the performance would not infringe copyright. A similar expression is used in section 26(2) in terms of providing apparatus the normal use of which involves a public performance. Therefore for these two instances, the test is a blend of the subjective and the objective. It is plain from the wording that the defendant will carry the burden of proof. He will have to show that he did not believe that copyright would be infringed and furthermore that this belief was based on reasonable grounds. This might be an onerous burden but the activities involved give rise to civil liability only, which accounts for the difference in mental element compared to the other secondary infringements.[70]

Some of the secondary infringements involve 'infringing copies' of the work and the meaning of this phrase is given in section 27 as being:

(a) an article, the making of which, constituted an infringement of copyright; or
(b) an article which has been or is proposed to be imported into the United Kingdom and its making in the United Kingdom would have infringed copyright or have been a breach of an exclusive licence agreement; or
(c) copies which are infringing copies by virtue of several provisions relating to the 'acts permitted in relation to copyright works'.[71]

However, a copy of a computer program previously sold by or with the consent of the copyright owner in any other Member State is not an infringing copy for the purposes of (b) above.[72] By section 27(5), the provisions relating to imported copies are abrogated in favour of any enforceable Community right within the meaning of section 2(1) of the European Communities Act 1972 This provision is not really necessary and only restates the effects of the United Kingdom's obligations as a member of the European Communities. Community obligations are separate from and prevail over inconsistent national law.[73] Therefore, if the importation into the United Kingdom of an otherwise infringing copy is permitted by European Community law (for example, under the exhaustion of rights principle), that copy will not be deemed to be an infringing copy and the persons involved in its importation and subsequent dealings with it will not be guilty of secondary infringement. However, if a person then makes copies from the imported copy once it is within the United Kingdom, that person will have infringed copyright, unless this also is permitted by prevailing Community Law.[74]

There is a presumption, by section 27(4), that an article is an infringing copy in any proceedings where the question arises. If it is shown that the article is a copy of the work and copyright subsists or has subsisted at any time in the work, it is presumed that the article was made at a time when copyright subsisted in the work unless the contrary is proved. A person copying or dealing with a copy of any type of work should not only satisfy himself that copyright in the work had expired at the time the copy was made, or that copyright did not otherwise subsist in the work at that time, but should be able to adduce proof to that effect to the satisfaction of the court. Bearing in mind that, in this matter, regardless of whether the proceedings are civil or criminal that proof on a balance of probabilities will suffice.[75]

REMEDIES FOR INFRINGEMENT OF COPYRIGHT

The remedies for copyright infringement and supplemental provisions are set out in sections 96 to 115 of the Act. The remedies available include civil reme-

70 By section 107(3), the criminal offences relating to public performances are available only against persons who 'caused' the work to be so performed, played or shown. Furthermore, the mental element is stated to be that the person knew or had reason to believe that copyright would be infringed. It is arguable whether a person providing premises or apparatus 'causes' the work to be performed.

71 The acts permitted in relation to copyright works are described and discussed in Chapter 7.

72 Section 27(3A) inserted by the Copyright (Computer Programs) Regulations 1992, SI 1992 No. 3233.

73 See, for example, *Costa v ENEL* [1964] ECR 585 and Lasok, D. & Bridge, J. W. *Law and Institutions of the European Communities* (London: Butterworths, 5th edn., 1991).

74 It is unlikely that the European Communities would enact legislation inconsistent with the main provisions of the Copyright, Designs and Patents Act 1988.

75 In criminal proceedings, the prosecution must prove the accused's guilt beyond reasonable doubt and the onus is usually also on the prosecution to negative any defence put up by the accused. However, in some circumstances, the accused bears the burden of proving that the defence applies on a balance of probabilities. These circumstances include express or implied statutory provision.

dies and criminal penalties. The main differences in the remedies now available compared to those under the Copyright Act 1956 are the apparent abolition of conversion damages and some easing of the knowledge required for the criminal offences, but there are also some minor changes and both the scope and availability of some of the remedies need to be given careful consideration. Before looking at the remedies, it is appropriate to consider first the problem of obtaining evidence, particularly in civil matters. (Search and seizure provisions are available for the criminal offences and are discussed later.)

Obtaining evidence for civil proceedings

In terms of all the forms of intellectual property, the question of obtaining evidence is of vital importance. If the person infringing the right discovers that he is to be sued for that infringement, he may be tempted to destroy materials and articles, such as pirate copies of video tapes, that would incriminate him. There is a limited power given by the Act to a copyright owner to seize infringing articles, but this will only apply in a small number of cases. Normally, if a copyright owner believes that his rights are being infringed and there is a real danger that the person involved will dispose of the evidence before the trial, the copyright owner should apply to the High Court for an Anton Piller order which will enable him, accompanied by his solicitor, to enter the premises where the offending materials and articles are kept and remove them so they can be produced at the trial.

The Anton Piller order takes its name from a case involving the alleged disclosure of confidential information concerning frequency converters for computers. In *Anton Piller KG v Manufacturing Processes Ltd.*,[76] it was held that, in exceptional circumstances, where the plaintiff has a strong *prima facie* case, where the actual or potential damage to the plaintiff is very serious and where it was clear that the defendant possessed vital evidence which he might destroy or dispose of so as to defeat the ends of justice, the court had the jurisdiction to order the defendant to 'permit' the plaintiff's representatives to enter the defendant's premises and inspect and remove such materials. The object of the Anton Piller order is the preservation of evidence. When an order is granted, the plaintiff has to give a cross-undertaking in damages in case the plaintiff is wrong, and the defendant suffers damage as a result of the execution of the order. However, before the court will grant an Anton Piller order, the plaintiff must be able to convince the court that he has a strong case and that the order is indeed essential to the ends of justice.[77] In *Systematica Ltd. v London Computer Centre Ltd.*,[78] Whitford J said that 'too free a use is being made of the Anton Piller provision'. In this case, the defendant was carrying on his business quite openly and there was only a mere suspicion that he was infringing the plaintiff's copyright. There was nothing to stop the plaintiff simply walking into the defendant's shop and buying the articles in question over the counter. Sometimes, there is a suspicion that the motives for applying for the order are not to obtain evidence but to remove so much material that the alleged infringer is, effectively, put out of business.

It is very important that the plaintiff does not exceed the provisions of an Anton Piller order. In *Columbia Picture Industries v Robinson*,[79] the plaintiffs (there were 35 of them) alleged that the defendant was a video pirate and

76 [1976] 1 Ch 55

77 In *Jeffrey Rogers Knitwear Productions Ltd. v Vinola (Knitwear) Manufacturing Co.* [1985] FSR 184, Whitford J, in discharging an Anton Piller order, said that it was improper to rely on stale evidence used in other proceedings in making application to the court for an order. The applicant must prepare his application to a very high standard, especially if it is made *ex parte*, as will usually be the case.

78 [1983] FSR 313.

79 [1987] 1 Ch 38.

claimed that he had copied 104 films, infringing copyright, registered trade marks and, additionally, being guilty of the tort of passing off. The plaintiffs sought and obtained an Anton Piller order and a Mareva injunction, the purpose of the latter being to freeze the defendant's assets, preventing him from removing them from the jurisdiction of the court. But the plaintiffs were excessive in their execution of the Anton Piller order and they took more material than was identified in the order, virtually emptying the defendant's premises; apparently taking even the defendant's divorce papers and private correspondence. It appeared that the plaintiffs' real motive in obtaining the order was to shut down the defendant's business. It was held that the method of execution was an abuse of the order. Whilst accepting that the defendant had been infringing copyright and awarding an injunction and damages to the plaintiffs, Scott J awarded the sum of £10,000 in compensatory and aggravated damages to the defendant under the plaintiffs' cross-undertaking in damages.

Scott J identified five criteria essential to the execution of an Anton Piller order as being:

(a) The order must be drawn so as to extend no further than the minimum extent necessary to achieve its purpose, that is the preservation of documents or articles which might otherwise be destroyed or concealed. After inspection and copying by the plaintiff's solicitors, the materials should be returned to the owner.
(b) A detailed record should be made by the solicitors executing the order of the materials to be taken before removal from the defendant's premises.
(c) Only materials clearly covered by the order should be taken.
(d) If the ownership of seized material is in dispute, it should be handed over to the defendant's solicitors on their undertaking for its safe custody and production.
(e) The affidavits in support ought to err on the side of excessive disclosure. In the case of material falling in the grey area of possible relevance, the judge, not the plaintiff's solicitor, should be the arbiter.

Because Anton Piller orders have been abused in their exercise in the past, they are granted sparingly. Further guidelines were suggested by Nicholls VC in *Universal Thermosensors Ltd.* v *Hibben*[80] which concerned the execution of an order at a private house at 7.15am. The house was occupied at the time by a woman and her children. The Vice-Chancellor made the following points:

80 [1992] 3 All ER 257.

(a) the order should be executed during normal office hours so that the defendant could take immediate legal advice;
(b) if the order was to be executed at a private dwelling and there was a chance that a woman might be alone there, the solicitor executing the order should be accompanied by a woman;
(c) a list of items taken should be made giving the defendant an opportunity to check it;
(d) if the order contained an injunction restraining the defendant from informing others (for example, co-defendants), the period should not be too long;
(e) in the absence of good reason otherwise, orders should be executed at business premises in the presence of a responsible officer or representative of the defendant's company;

(f) provision should be made to prevent the plaintiff going through all the defendant's documents (for example, where the parties were competitors and the plaintiff could thereby gain useful and sensitive information about the defendant's business unrelated to the alleged infringement);

(g) ideally, the order should be executed by a neutral solicitor who was experienced in the execution of Anton Piller orders.

The controversy about Anton Piller orders and their execution remains and the Lord Chancellor's Department has issued an advisory paper suggesting, *inter alia* that the order be placed on a statutory footing.[81]

The Copyright, Designs and Patents Act 1988 does provide the copyright owner with a limited power of seizure. Bearing in mind that pirated copies of copyright works frequently are sold at 'unofficial' markets, car boot sales and the like, section 100 gives the copyright owner a right of seizure of infringing articles at such places. Notice of the proposed seizure must be given to a local police station and the premises at which the infringing articles are located must not be a permanent or regular place of business. Additionally, the copyright owner must leave a prescribed form giving particulars of the person making the seizure and the grounds for the seizure. Force may not be used in effecting the seizure. It is unlikely that this provision will be used frequently because of the limited circumstances when it is available and because of the attendant conditions.

Civil remedies

The Copyright, Designs and Patents Act 1988 provides an ample range of remedies for copyright infringement. Section 96 states that infringement is actionable by the copyright owner but this is not exhaustive as, by section 101, an exclusive licensee has, except as against the copyright owner, the same rights and remedies as the copyright owner which run concurrent with those of the owner.[82] As far as taking action for infringement of copyright, an exclusive licensee is, effectively, put in the position of an assignee. Of course, an exclusive licensee will only be able to take action if the infringement concerns the subject matter of the licence agreement. For example, if an exclusive licence is granted with respect to the public performance rights in a dramatic work, the licensee will be able to sue a person who performs the dramatic work in public but will not be able to sue a person who simply makes copies of the work.

The civil remedies available for infringement of copyright are as follows:

- damages
- injunctions
- accounts (of profits)
- 'or otherwise'.

These are stated by section 96(2) as being available in respect of a copyright infringement as they are available in respect of any other property right (remembering that section 1(1) describes copyright as a property right). Although the previous legislation included conversion damages, it is conceivable that the addition of the phrase 'or otherwise' still permits the use of conversion damages as they are available as a general rule in tort for wrongfully dealing with another person's property.[83] The phrase will include an order for specific performance, such as an order for a written signed assignment of copyright in a situation

81 *Anton Piller Orders: A Consultation Paper* Lord Chancellor's Department, November 1992.

82 Section 102 deals with the exercise of concurrent rights. Normally, the copyright owner or an exclusive licensee may not proceed alone without joining the other except with the leave of the court. Section 102 also deals with the matter of remedies in cases involving exclusive licensees and copyright owners having concurrent rights.

83 Conversion damages were specifically provided for by section 18 of the Copyright Act 1956. Section 18 does not apply after commencement of the 1988 Act unless proceedings began before commencement, para. 31(2) Schedule 1 of the 1988 Act. Conversion damages could result in a windfall for the plaintiff, for example if the subject matter of the plaintiff's rights was incorporated in some larger material or item. See, Phillips, J. & Firth, A. *Introduction to Intellectual Property Law* (London: Butterworths, 2nd edn., 1990) at pp.167–168.

where a purported assignment has turned out to be defective in some way. However, it should be noted that injunctions and accounts of profits are equitable in nature and factors that might be important are whether the plaintiff acted promptly, whether injustice would be done to innocent third parties and whether the plaintiff came to the court with 'clean hands'. Other remedies available are:

- additional damages (section 97(2))
- delivery up (section 99).

There are special provisions in respect of infringements of a copyright for which a licence is available as of right under section 144 of the Act (powers exercisable in consequence of a report of the Monopolies and Mergers Commission).[84] In such a case, no injunction shall be granted, there may be no order for delivery up under section 99 and the amount recoverable by way of damages or an account of profits shall not exceed double the amount which would have been payable under the licence as of right providing the defendant undertakes to take a licence on terms to be agreed or, failing agreement, on terms to be settled by the Copyright Tribunal under section 144.[85]

84 Section 98.

85 Similar provisions apply to designs.

Damages

The copyright owner (or exclusive licensee) will usually ask the court for damages which can be expected to be calculated, as with other torts, on the basis of putting the plaintiff in the position he would have been in had the tort not been committed, that is to compensate him for the actual loss suffered in so far as it is not too remote.[86] This might be the amount of royalties the copyright owner would have secured had the infringer obtained and paid for a licence to perform whatever the infringing act was.[87] Alternatively, depending on the circumstances, it might be based on the profit the copyright owner would have derived from sales lost as a result of the infringement. It will generally depend on whether the infringement relates to an 'original' work (for example, a literary work) or a derivative work such as a film or sound recording; calculation by reference to lost royalties is more appropriate to the former. Although knowledge on the part of the defendant is not required for establishing liability for the 'primary' infringements of copyright, there is such a requirement before the plaintiff can be entitled to damages. Section 97(1) states that, if it is shown that, at the time of the infringement, the defendant did not know, and had no reason to believe, that copyright subsisted in the work to which the action relates, the plaintiff is not entitled to damages against the defendant. This is without prejudice to other remedies that might be available to the plaintiff, such as an injunction or an account of profits. The formula for the defendant's knowledge is the same as for secondary infringements and what has been said in that context above should apply here also. An award of damages will usually go hand in hand with the granting of an injunction ordering the infringer to cease carrying out the infringing activities. There may also be an order for delivery up, discussed later, for example of pirate copies of sound recordings in the infringer's possession. A wise copyright owner will apply a prominent copyright notice to copies of his work so that infringers cannot claim to be ignorant of the subsistence of copyright in the work.

86 Apart from the criminal offences, infringement of copyright is in the nature of a tort, that is it is a civil wrong independent of contract. That is why it is better to speak of infringement of copyright rather than breach of copyright.

87 See, for example, *Redwood Music* v *Chappell* [1982] RPC 109.

Injunctions

An injunction is an order of the court which prohibits an act or continuance of an act. Alternatively, the injunction might order a person to perform some act.[88] For example, an injunction may be granted by the court ordering a person to cease making infringing copies of a work of copyright or to destroy some article in his possession which is used for making infringing copies. Injunctions are equitable and, therefore, discretionary. They will not generally be granted if ordinary damages would be an adequate remedy. However, in terms of intellectual property rights, injunctions are very commonly asked for and frequently granted.

In a situation where a person is marketing unauthorized copies of articles in which copyright subsists, it is vital that the aggrieved party takes action as quickly as possible.[89] Many items in which copyright subsists have a limited commercial lifespan, for example, records, cassettes and compact discs of 'pop tunes', best-selling novels and computer software. Unless the person infringing the copyright can be stopped quickly, the damage will be considerable and it may be some years before a full civil action can be heard, after which time the person responsible for the infringement may have disappeared or dissipated his finances and be a 'man of straw'. Therefore, the availability and use of interlocutory injunctions is extremely important in terms of all intellectual property rights, including copyright. An interlocutory injunction is an interim or temporary injunction which is intended to take effect pending the full trial. The plaintiff must undertake to pay the defendant's losses resulting from the interlocutory injunction should the defendant succeed at the full trial. Interlocutory injunctions are often sufficient to dispose of a case which never comes to a full trial either because the defendant loses heart and realizes he has little chance of eventual success or because the effects on his business are crippling; therefore, such injunctions are not lightly granted.

Certain criteria are used by the courts in determining whether or not to grant an interlocutory injunction. Obviously, such an injunction will only be granted if the plaintiff has a good chance of success at the full trial; he should, at the very least, have a *prima facie* case. In *American Cyanamid Co. v Ethicon Ltd.*,[90] a case concerning an alleged infringement of the patent relating to a surgical suture, the basis for granting an interlocutory injunction was discussed. Lord Diplock said (at 406):

> The object of an interlocutory injunction is to protect the plaintiff against injury by violation of his right for which he could not be adequately compensated in damages recoverable in the action if the uncertainty were resolved in his favour at the trial; but the plaintiff's need for such protection must be weighed against the corresponding need of the defendant to be protected against injury resulting from his having been prevented from exercising his own legal rights for which he would not be adequately compensated under the plaintiff's undertaking in damages if the uncertainty were resolved in the defendant's favour at the trial. The court must weigh one need against another and determine where the 'balance of convenience' lies.

Obviously, the court must be satisfied that there is a serious issue to be tried. But the question of whether or not to grant the injunction is determined by weighing the plaintiff's and the defendant's needs. This test was later modified by Lord Diplock in *NWL Ltd. v Woods*,[91] which concerned a shipping trade

88 Injunctions are classified as 'prohibitory injunctions' and 'mandatory injunctions'; the latter orders the person to whom it is addressed to carry out some act, such as demolishing a dangerous wall.

89 The doctrine of laches is relevant here.

90 [1975] AC 396.

91 [1979] 1 WLR 1294.

dispute. The test was modified in such cases as where the granting or refusal of the interlocutory injunction would effectively put an end to the matter because the harm done to the losing party would be out of proportion – for example, it might put him out of business. In such cases, Lord Diplock said that the likelihood of the plaintiff succeeding in his claim for an injunction at the full trial was a factor that should be brought into the 'balance of convenience' by the judge in considering the risks of injustice from his deciding the application one way rather than another.

An interlocutory injunction will not be granted if the plaintiff does not have a *prima facie* case or if there is some doubt about whether the plaintiff would be granted an injunction and substantial damages at the full trial. It was so held in *Entec Pollution Control Ltd.* v *Abacus Mouldings*[92] in which it was alleged that the defendant had indirectly infringed the plaintiff's copyright in sketches for flask-shaped septic tanks. It was doubtful that the defendant would have been able to pay substantial damages but it was equally doubtful whether the plaintiff would indeed be awarded substantial damages. As the plaintiff did not have a strong case, the issue would have to be tried at a full trial and not pre-empted. In some cases, the public interest may be relevant and in *Secretary of State for the Home Department* v *Central Broadcasting Ltd.*,[93] it was held that the public interest did not require an interlocutory injunction to prevent the showing of a film, alleged to infringe copyright, which included an interview with the serial killer Nilsen. The appellant's argument that the trial judge had taken too narrow a view of the balance of convenience and had failed to sufficiently consider the risk of distress to the relatives of the killer's victims was rejected by the Court of Appeal.

As mentioned above, any injunction including an interlocutory injunction will not be granted by the court if it appears to the court that damages will fairly compensate the plaintiff. Two questions are relevant in this respect:

(a) Will the loss to the plaintiff be adequately compensated for by damages awarded later? and
(b) Is the defendant likely to be able to pay such damages?

A final point is the speed with which the plaintiff seeks the injunction because if the infringement complained of has been tolerated for some time, the assumption is that the effects cannot be that serious.

Accounts (of profits)

An account of profits may be a useful alternative for the plaintiff in that the infringer may have made a profit from his actions which exceeds in value what would be the normal award of damages. The purpose of the remedy is to prevent unjust enrichment of the defendant.[94] The quantum of an account is the profit, that is the gain, made by the defendant attributable to the infringement and not the wholesale or retail value of the offending articles or materials. Consider the following hypothetical example which, for the sake of simplicity, ignores income tax and value added tax. Arthur makes 2,000 pirate copies of a popular sound recording, the copyright in which is owned by Zenith Ltd., and has sold the copies to a retailer, Nadir Music Ltd. Arthur charged Nadir £3.00 for each one and Nadir sells them at £5.50 each. The cost to Arthur of making the pirate copies, packaging and delivery, etc., is £3,750.00.

92 [1992] FSR 332

93 (unreported) *The Times*, 28 January 1993 (Court of Appeal)

94 *Potton Ltd.* v *Yorkclose Ltd.* [1990] FSR 11 per Millett J.

If Arthur is successfully sued by Zenith for the infringement by making copies, and Zenith asks for an account of profits, Zenith should be entitled to the following sum:

		£
Arthur's income:	$2,000 \times 3.00$ =	6,000.00
Arthur's expenditure:	=	3,750.00
Profit made by Arthur	=	2,250.00

Therefore, an account of profits should yield Zenith £2,250. This may be better than claiming damages which will not be available in some cases (although it is almost certain in the example that Arthur would have known that copyright subsisted in the original sound recording). Damages could be based on the fact that Zenith have been deprived of 2,000 sales and if their profit margin is usually 10 per cent and the normal retail price is £7.50, damages would amount to £1,500:

$$2,000 \times £7.50 \times 10\% = £1,500.00$$

Damages based on a notional lost royalty might only amount to:

$$12\tfrac{1}{2}\% \text{ of } 2,000 \times £3.00 = £750.00, \text{ assuming a typical royalty of } 12\tfrac{1}{2}\%.$$

Attractive though an account of profits might appear, there are likely to be great practical difficulties in determining what the profit was in relation to the infringement and it may be well nigh impossible to isolate this profit from the other profits made concurrently by the defendant in other, legitimate, dealings. Nevertheless, because, unlike ordinary damages, accounts are available regardless of the defendant's knowledge as to whether copyright subsisted in the work, an account of profits may be the only way in which the copyright owner can recover some monetary compensation for the infringement if the defendant's knowledge is likely to be in issue. In practice, the remedies of damages and accounts should be considered to be alternatives, assuming damages are available. The Act does not expressly make any statement to this effect so that it is theoretically possible for the plaintiff to ask for both. However, if this should happen and an account is ordered, the plaintiff will only be awarded nominal damages.

Additional damages

Additional damages are a form of punitive damages and such an award may be fitting if the defendant has acted scandalously or deceitfully or if ordinary damages or an account of profits is not appropriate, for example where the defendant has published a work of a personal nature such as a diary which the copyright owner wished to keep private. The court has a discretion to award additional damages and in exercising its discretion must have regard to all the circumstances, and in particular to:

(a) the flagrancy of the infringement, and
(b) any benefit accruing to the defendant by reason of the infringement.[95]

95 Section 97(2).

Although additional damages are specifically provided for by the Act, it appears that the court has a common law power to award exemplary (punitive) damages in copyright actions, although this is quite rare in tort actions.[96] A situation where exemplary damages might be appropriate is where a defendant has deliberately calculated that his gain will outweigh any award against him although this will be very improbable because of the possibility of an account of profits. However, a defendant might have hoped to gain status and acclaim through his infringement rather than to make money, although the strengthened moral rights contained in the Act should apply in this type of situation.

Flagrancy was described in terms of deceitful and treacherous conduct in order to steal a march on the plaintiff in *Nichols Advanced Vehicle Systems Inc. v Reese & Oliver*[97] in which the defendants, including the chief designer and a racing driver who had held positions of responsibility with the plaintiff's company, had made use of the plaintiff's working drawings for a Formula One racing car to build their own cars. The defendants had inflicted humiliation and loss on the plaintiff that was difficult to compensate and difficult to assess. In the later follow-up case it was held by Whitford J that the award of additional damages (£2,000) should take account of the damages awarded for infringement (£1,000) and conversion (£11,000).[98]

The Copyright Act 1956 required that the court also considered whether effective relief was otherwise available but this has disappeared from the 1988 Act. This may lead the courts to make more use of additional damages as a form of exemplary damages to be used where the defendant's behaviour has been particularly despicable or immoral in some way. An example is provided by the case of *Williams* v *Settle*,[99] in which the defendant, a professional photographer, was commissioned by the plaintiff to take photographs at his wedding, the copyright in the photographs vesting in the plaintiff. The father of the plaintiff's wife was later murdered and the defendant sold photographs of the wedding group, showing the murdered man, to the press. On the basis of additional damages as provided by section 17(3) of the Copyright Act 1956, or, alternatively, because of the court's power to award punitive damages, the plaintiff was awarded damages of £1,000 which were far in excess of the measure of ordinary damages that would have been awarded as the defendant received a relatively small sum from the newspaper proprietors for the photographs.

Delivery up

By section 99, upon application by the copyright owner, a court may order that infringing copies, or articles designed or adapted for making copies of the copyright owner's work, are delivered up to him or such other person as the court may direct.[100] Delivery up is available where a person has an infringing copy of the work in his possession, custody or control in the course of a business or has in his possession, custody or control an article specifically designed or adapted for making copies of a particular copyright work. In relation to articles, there is an added requirement that the person knows or has reason to believe that the article has been or is to be used to make infringing copies.

There is a time limit which applies to applications for delivery up as provided by section 113 which corresponds to limitation of actions. By section 113(1) the

96 See *Williams* v *Settle* [1960] 1 WLR 1072, where the trial judge awarded damages of £1,000 when the normal limit was £400. The award was upheld on appeal.

97 [1979] RPC 127. In *Ravenscroft v Herbert* [1980] RPC 193, Brightman J described flagrancy thus: '. . . in my view implies the existence of scandalous conduct, deceit and such like; it includes deliberate and calculated copyright infringements'.

98 [1988] RPC 71. The Court of Appeal later reduced the interest rate from 15% to 10% over 7 years.

99 [1960] 1 WLR 1072.

100 The order is not based upon any notion that the property in the copies has passed to the plaintiffs, see *Chappell & Co. Ltd.* v *Columbia Graphophone Co.* [1914] 2 Ch 745 per Swinfen Eady LJ at 756.

time limit is six years from the time the infringing copy or article was made. However, this may be extended if the copyright owner had been under a disability (for example, a minor or person of unsound mind) as in the Limitation Act 1980.[101] Another cause for extension of the period is if the copyright owner is prevented by fraud or concealment from discovering the facts entitling him to apply for the order.

A further requirement before an order for delivery up can be made is that the court also makes, or it appears to the court that there are grounds for making, an order under section 114 of the Copyright, Designs and Patents Act 1988, being an order for the disposal of the infringing copies or other articles. The order may state that the infringing copies or other articles be forfeited to the copyright owner or destroyed or otherwise dealt with as the court thinks fit but the court shall consider whether other available remedies would be adequate to compensate the copyright owner and protect his interests. If the order under section 114 is not made immediately, the person to whom the infringing copies or other articles are delivered shall retain them pending the making of the order. If a decision is taken not to make an order under section 114, the items are to be delivered to the person who had them in his possession, custody or control immediately before being delivered up.[102] Rarely will it be necessary or even desirable to deliver up offending articles to the copyright owner – he will normally be fairly compensated by the other remedies. However, an order for destruction of the offending articles under section 114 is a likely proposition, for example, in circumstances where the defendant has a stock of pirate video tapes in his possession.

PRESUMPTIONS

The Act provides for certain presumptions which will apply in proceedings for copyright infringement for the purposes of facilitating those proceedings. Because copyright can endure for a considerable period of time, some presumptions as to the identity of the author, director or publisher of the work are also helpful. Presumptions are made in terms of three classes of works:

(a) literary, dramatic, musical and artistic works (section 104);
(b) sound recordings, films and computer programs (section 105);
(c) works subject to Crown copyright (section 106).

Presumptions relating to literary, dramatic, musical and artistic works

Where a name purporting to be that of the author appeared on copies of the work as published or on the work when it was made, the person by that name shall be presumed to be the author of the work and to have been the first owner of the copyright in the work.[103] That is, the work was not made in circumstances relating to employees in the course of employment, Crown or parliamentary copyright or copyright of certain international organizations.[104] Similar presumptions apply in the case of works of joint authorship. Even where the identity of the owner is not in dispute, the identity of the author is important for establishing the duration of the copyright and, possibly, its territorial scope.

101 See section 38 of the Limitation Act 1980. In Scotland, disability means legal disability within the meaning of the Prescription and Limitation (Scotland) Act 1973 and, in Northern Ireland, the same meaning as in the Statute of Limitations (Northern Ireland) 1958.

102 Section 114(5).

103 Section 104(2).

104 This presumption was used in *Noah v Shuba* [1991] FSR 14 and the defendant was unable to adduce evidence to rebut it.

Where there is no name purporting to be that of the author on copies of the work then, by section 104(4), if the work otherwise qualifies for copyright protection by reference to the country of first publication[105] and a name purporting to be that of the publisher appeared on copies of the work as first published, then that named publisher shall be presumed to have been the owner of the copyright at the time of publication. Although this deals with the question of ownership of the copyright, the identity of the author is still important and section 104(5) provides that if the author is dead, or his identity cannot be ascertained by reasonable enquiry, it shall be presumed in the absence of evidence to the contrary that the work is an original work and the plaintiff's allegations as to what was the first publication of the work and as to the country of first publication are correct. Therefore, in all these matters, if the defendant wishes to challenge any of them, it is he who bears the burden of proof, he must adduce evidence to the contrary. Of course, in many actions for infringement, the defendant will not wish to dispute these matters but may base his defence on another point, for example that he has not, in the circumstances, copied a substantial part of the work. Although the Act recognizes the subsistence of copyright in literary, dramatic, musical and artistic works that are computer-generated, there are no presumptions specifically directed to such works.

Presumptions relating to sound recordings, films and computer programs

Because computer programs are literary works, the presumptions relating to literary works above apply in addition to the presumption in section 105.[106] In the case of sound recordings, where copies are issued to the public bearing a label or other mark stating that a named person was the owner of the copyright in the recording at the date of issue of the copies, or that the recording was first published in a specified year or in a specified country, that label or mark shall be admissible as evidence of the facts stated and shall be presumed to be correct until the contrary is proved.[107] Similar provisions apply in respect of films where copies are issued to the public bearing statements as to the author or director of the film, the owner of the copyright in the film, and the year and country of first publication: section 105(2). Where, by section 105(3), computer programs are issued to the public in electronic form bearing a statement that a named person was the copyright owner at the date of issue or that the program was first published in a specified country or that copies were first issued to the public in electronic form in a specified year, that statement is also admissible as evidence of the facts stated and shall be presumed to be correct until the contrary is proved. In terms of all the three above forms of works, namely, sound recordings, films and computer programs, issuing of copies to the public, by section 18(2), includes any rental of copies to the public. All these presumptions apply equally to infringements alleged to have occurred before the date on which the copies were first issued to the public.

A final presumption in section 105 concerns the public showing, broadcast or inclusion in a cable programme service of a film and section 105(5) provides that if the film bears a statement that a named person was the author or director of the film or that a named person was the owner of the copyright in the film immediately after it was made, then that statement is admissible in evidence of the facts stated and presumed correct until the contrary is proved.

105 By virtue of section 155.

106 Interestingly, the section heading to section 105 does not mention computer programs even though they are specifically dealt with in subsection (3).

107 Section 105(1). Under section 12(6) of the Copyright Act 1956, sound recordings had to be date-stamped to qualify for copyright protection. This is no longer essential but it is obviously prudent to attach a copyright notice including the year of publication as this fixes would-be infringers with knowledge of the subsistence of copyright and may be important in terms of the availability of damages.

Again, this applies equally in proceedings relating to infringements alleged to have occurred before the public showing, broadcast or inclusion in a cable programme service.

Presumptions relevant to Crown copyright

The final presumption is contained in section 106 and relates to literary, dramatic and musical works in which Crown copyright subsists. Where there appears on printed copies of a work a statement of the year in which the work was first published commercially, that statement shall be admissible as evidence of that fact and presumed correct until the contrary is proven.

CRIMINAL OFFENCES

The Copyright, Designs and Patents Act 1988, in line with the Copyright Act 1956, makes provision for certain criminal offences associated with copyright infringement. The criminal offences reflect very closely the secondary infringements of copyright but there are some omissions. For example, there is no equivalent criminal penalty for the secondary infringement of permitting the use of premises for an infringing performance of a literary, dramatic or musical work. Conversely, the criminal offence of making copies for sale or hire relates to the act restricted by copyright of copying and not a secondary infringement.

The offences are not of strict liability and an element of *mens rea* is required. Thus, for a person to be guilty of any of the offences he must possess actual knowledge or have reason to believe that copyright would be infringed or that he was, for example dealing with infringing copies. The penalties available have been strengthened in some cases, for example, with respect to literary works where, by the 1956 Act, the maximum penalty available was a fine of forty shillings.[108] There is evidence that magistrates and judges are prepared to take piracy and counterfeiting of copyright works seriously. For example, in *R v Carter*[109] the Court of Appeal confirmed a sentence of imprisonment of nine months suspended for two years for a conviction of making and distributing infringing copies of video films contrary to section 107.

It was observed that such an activity was really an offence of dishonesty. The offences are contained in section 107 of the Act and are set out below.

Making, dealing, etc. (subsection 1)

A person commits an offence who, without the licence of the copyright owner:

(a) makes for sale or hire, or
(b) imports into the United Kingdom otherwise for his private and domestic use, or
(c) possesses in the course of a business with a view to committing any act infringing the copyright, or
(d) in the course of a business, sells or lets for hire or offers or exposes for sale or hire or exhibits in public or distributes, or
(e) distributes otherwise than in the course of business to such an extent as to affect prejudicially the owner of the copyright,

108 Some intermediate stiffening of penalties and extension of their scope was undertaken, for example, by the ridiculously titled 'Copyright Act 1956 (Amendment) Act 1982' and the Copyright (Amendment) Act 1983.

109 [1993] FSR 303.

an article which is, and which he knows or has reason to believe is, an infringing copy of a copyright work.

These activities are all commercial in nature with the exception of (e) which would apply, for example, to the situation where a private individual makes a large number of copies of a copyright work and distributes them freely, perhaps acting out of misguided social, political or moral beliefs. Some of the offences in this category are triable either way, that is they can be tried either in the Crown Court or a Magistrates' Court. These are the offences relating to making, importing or distributing (whether or not in the course of a business). The maximum penalty available if tried in a Crown Court is a term of imprisonment not exceeding two years or a fine or both. There is no upper limit on the fines which can be imposed by the Crown Court. If the offence is tried in a Magistrates' Court, the maximum penalty is six months' imprisonment or a fine not exceeding the statutory maximum (presently £5,000) or both. All the other offences are triable summarily only, that is in a Magistrates' Court, and carry a maximum of six months' imprisonment or a fine not exceeding level 5 on the standard scale (presently £5,000) or both.[110]

For some of the offences, namely (c) and (d) above, there is a specific requirement that they were committed in the course of a business. The meaning of this might be important if the person involved has other legitimate full-time employment and is carrying out his infringing activities in his spare time or as a hobby. However, it would appear that, in terms of the Trade Descriptions Act 1968, for goods to be dealt with in the course of a trade or business there must be a degree of regularity in such dealing as part of the normal practice of a business.[111] It would appear, therefore, that if the person involved was carrying out the offending activities on a regular basis, it would be considered that he was operating in the course of a business even if he was doing it in his spare time. However, if the person did whatever it was, regardless of the scale, as a one-off activity, there would be no regularity and it would appear that the relevant offences would not apply.

Articles specifically designed or adapted to make copies (subsection 2)

A person commits an offence if he makes an article specifically designed or adapted for making copies of a particular copyright work or has such an article in his possession, knowing or having reason to believe that it is to be used to make infringing copies for sale or hire or for use in the course of a business. This would include making a plate for printing artistic works or a master copy of a sound recording from which many duplicates could be made. The offence only applies if the article is intended to be used for making copies of a particular copyright work and not for copying works generally. Therefore, the manufacture or possession of a dual cassette tape deck is not caught as it is not intended to be used to copy a particular work but may be used to copy all sorts of works (some of which may be copied legitimately). The offence is triable summarily only and carries a maximum of six months' imprisonment or a fine not exceeding level 5 on the standard scale or both.

Public performances, etc. (subsection 3)

This applies where copyright is infringed, otherwise than by the reception of a broadcast or cable programme, by a public performance of a literary, dramatic

110 The penalties are laid out in section 107(4) and (5).

111 See, *Davis* v *Sumner* [1984] 3 All ER 831, adapting the test laid down in *Havering London Borough* v *Stevenson* [1970] 3 All ER 609.

or musical work or by the playing or showing in public of a sound recording or film. Any person who caused the work to be so performed, played or shown is guilty of an offence if he knew or had reason to believe that copyright would be infringed. The person who caused the work to be performed, played or shown will normally be the person who made the arrangements necessary and organized the performance. It is unlikely that a person who supplies the equipment necessary or provides the premises will be deemed to be the person 'causing'. Of course, such persons may be charged with being accomplices. An offence under this subsection carries a maximum of six months' imprisonment or a fine not exceeding level 5 on the standard scale or both, being triable summarily only.

Liability of officers of corporate bodies

By virtue of section 110, where an offence under section 107 has been committed by a corporate body, for example a limited company, and it is proved that the offence was committed with the consent or connivance of a director, manager, secretary or other similar officer of the body, then that person is also guilty of the offence and is liable to be prosecuted. This also applies to persons holding themselves out to act in such a capacity. Therefore, in the case of an offence by a corporate body, there may be two prosecutions, one against the body itself and another against a high ranking officer of the body who has been implicated in the offending conduct. This is to prevent persons hiding behind a corporate identity in order to escape prosecution. Normally, in terms of vicarious liability in criminal law, the action of a high ranking officer of the company will be deemed to be the action of the company, thereby fixing the corporate body with liability.[112] Therefore, there should be no difficulty in a finding of corporate guilt if the activity complained of has been done under the instructions or guidance of a director or company secretary but, there would be difficulty in attaching liability to the individual concerned and this provision in the Act overcomes that problem.

Search warrants and delivery up

Search warrants are available under section 109[113] and now extend to all types of copyright work. Search warrants can be obtained by a constable from a justice of the peace if the latter is satisfied by information given on oath by the constable that there are reasonable grounds for believing that any of the triable either way offences under section 107 have been committed or are about to be committed and that evidence of this is on the premises to which the search warrant will apply. The warrant will authorize the constable to enter and search the premises using such reasonable force as is necessary. The warrant remains in force for 28 days and may authorize persons to accompany the constable in his execution of the warrant. It should be noted that warrants are not available for the offences that are triable summarily only which significantly weakens the effectiveness of these particular offences. Of course, evidence required to secure a conviction may be obtainable in other ways, for example by simply purchasing an infringing copy which is openly on sale. In exercising his duties under the warrant, a constable may seize any article he reasonably believes to be evidence that an offence under section 107(1) has been or is about to be committed. Thus, the scope of the powers of seizure do not reflect exactly the availability of

112 See the judgment of Lord Denning MR in *H L Bolton (Engineering) Co. Ltd.* v *T J Graham & Sons Ltd.* [1957] 1 QB 159 at 172.

113 Search warrants were first provided for by section 21A of the Copyright Act 1956, an amendment made by the Copyright (Amendment) Act 1983.

search warrants. If a constable obtains a search warrant for a suspected offence under section 107(1)(a) (making an infringing copy for sale or hire) the constable can seize infringing copies in the possession of the suspect (and made by others) in the course of a business – a summary offence under section 107(1)(c) – even though the constable could not obtain a search warrant in relation to that particular offence. The word 'premises' in the context of search warrants includes land, buildings, moveable structures, vehicles, vessels, aircraft and hovercraft.

It seems strange that the availability of search warrants does not extend to all the criminal offences, although there is always the danger of over-zealousness coupled with the suspicion that justices of the peace issue search warrants to the police too readily. However, this fear could be overcome by adopting the approach taken in the Computer Misuse Act 1990 in that search warrants in respect of the unauthorized access offence, the basic 'computer hacking' offence, must be obtained from a circuit judge.[114]

114 Computer Misuse Act 1990, section 14.

Section 108 of the Copyright, Designs and Patents Act 1988 also provides for delivery up in criminal proceedings similar in nature to the civil delivery up provisions under section 99. An order for delivery up may be made by the court before which the proceedings are brought if it is satisfied at the time the accused was arrested or charged that:

(a) he had in his possession, custody or control in the course of a business an infringing copy of the work, or
(b) he had in his possession, custody or control an article specifically designed or adapted for making copies of a particular copyright work, knowing or having reason to believe that it had been or was to be used to make infringing copies.

The order may be made by the court on its own motion or on the application of the prosecutor and may be made irrespective of whether the accused is convicted of the offence with which he was charged. The provisions contained in section 113 (limitation period) and section 114 (order as to disposal) also apply to delivery up in criminal proceedings. The general provisions as to forfeiture contained in section 43 of the Powers of Criminal Courts Act 1973 are unaffected.[115]

115 Of course, there are some differences in terms of search, seizure and delivery up in Scotland and Northern Ireland, but the overall effect is generally the same.

The Act contains some controls over the importation of infringing copies along the lines of the previous Act. Section 111 extends the class of prohibited goods to infringing copies of literary, dramatic and musical works (printed copies of these three types of works) and sound recordings and films. The Commissioners of Customs and Excise must be given notice in writing by the copyright owner to the effect that he is the copyright owner. As regards literary, dramatic and musical works, the notice must also specify the period, not exceeding five years or beyond the duration of the copyright, for which the printed copies are to be treated as prohibited goods. For sound recordings and films the action is pre-emptive in nature and the notice must also specify the time and place that the infringing copies are expected to arrive and that the copyright owner requests the Commissioners to treat the copies as prohibited goods.[116]

116 Section 112 gives powers to the Commissioners of Customs and Excise to make regulations concerning the service of notices, payment of fees, providing security and indemnifying the Commissioners against liability or expense as regards the detention of the articles or things done to the articles in consequence of the notice.

Other offences

A person infringing copyright (and, for that matter, infringing a trade mark or a patent) may commit criminal offences other than those contained in the part of the Copyright, Designs and Patents Act 1988 dealing with copyright. For example, there may be an offence under section 1 of the Trade Descriptions Act 1968. It is an offence, in the course of business, to apply a false trade description to any goods or to supply or offer to supply goods to which a false trade description has been applied. A trade description is widely defined in section 2 of the Trade Descriptions Act 1968 and includes direct or indirect indications as to the person by whom the goods are manufactured and the place and date of manufacture. Therefore, making or supplying a duplicate copy of a work such as a sound recording or video film in which copyright subsists without permission of the copyright owner will be an offence under the Trade Descriptions Act if it is done in the course of business and if the copy is dressed up to look like the genuine article.

By section 25(1) of the Theft Act 1968 a person is guilty of an offence if, when not at his place of abode, he has with him any article for use in the course of or in connection with any burglary, theft or *cheat*. 'Cheat' means the same as obtaining by deception. This would cover someone travelling to, say, a market in possession of pirated sound recordings, video films or computer games.[117] However, there may be a difficulty with this offence in that, in such circumstances, the purchasers of these items are unlikely to have been deceived as they will realize that the articles are not legitimate copies. The cost will be considerably lower and the printed materials and covers probably will be of an inferior quality.

Another offence that could be charged is forgery under the Forgery and Counterfeiting Act 1981, section 1 of which states that a person is guilty of forgery if he makes a false instrument, with the intention that he or another shall use it to induce somebody to accept it as genuine, and by reason of so accepting it, to do or not to do some act to his own or any other person's prejudice. It is also an offence to use a false instrument in such a way. By section 8 of the Act, a false instrument includes any 'disc, tape, sound track or other device on or in which information is recorded or stored by mechanical, electronic or other means'. This definition would include sound recordings, films, computer programs and other copyright works stored in or on computer storage media, such as a copy of a computer database. Also covered would be a copy of a work such as the *Encyclopaedia Britannica* stored on CD-ROM discs. However, again there may be problems associated with whether a person would be induced to accept the article as genuine.

If legitimate copies of the original copyright work have a registered trade mark attached to them, anyone making infringing copies who also attaches the trade mark, or a mark nearly resembling it, to his infringing copies, without permission of the proprietor of the trade mark, commits an offence under section 58A of the Trade Marks Act 1938.[118] This offence is triable either way and carries a maximum penalty, if tried on indictment in the Crown Court, of imprisonment for a term not exceeding ten years or a fine or both.

It does not appear to be possible to steal a copyright by making copies because the owner of the copyright will still have the original.[119] The copyright owner has not been permanently deprived of the copyright and can still make

17 A computer game is a form of computer program.

18 Inserted by section 300 of the Copyright, Designs and Patents Act 1988.

19 See *Oxford* v *Moss* (1978) 68 Cr App R 183.

and license the making of copies. The fact that the copyright owner has been deprived of some of the potential income from the work is not sufficient for theft. In *R v Lloyd*,[120] a projectionist at a cinema, in league with some other persons, surreptitiously removed films from the cinema for a few hours so that they could be copied. The infringing (pirated) copies of the films were then sold, making a considerable profit for the video pirates. It was held that a charge of theft (actually a conspiracy to steal in this case) was inappropriate. Obviously, there was no intention to permanently deprive the owners of the films, nor was the copyright in the films stolen. Although borrowing sometimes can be regarded as theft if the period and circumstances are equivalent to an outright taking or disposal by section 6(1) of the Theft Act 1968, this would apply only if the 'goodness' or 'virtue' in the borrowed article had been exhausted by the time it was returned. An example is where a person borrows a radio battery intending to return it when its power is expended, or where a person borrows a football pass intending to return it to the rightful owner at the end of the football season. But, in the case of the films, there was still virtue in them when they were returned; they were still capable of being used and shown to paying audiences, so the convictions were quashed. The fact that the owner of the copyright in the films had been deprived of potential 'sales' of the films by the circulation of pirate copies was not relevant to the offence of theft.

Whether copyright can be stolen in any circumstances is a moot point.[121] For the purposes of the offence of theft, defined as the dishonest appropriation of property belonging to another with the intention of depriving the other of it permanently,[122] 'property' is defined as including money and all other property, real or personal, including things in action and other intangible property.[123] Theoretically theft of copyright is a possibility because copyright, certainly in the context of the acts restricted by the copyright in the work, is a chose in action and thus falls within the meaning of property. However, the question really hinges on whether the owner has been permanently deprived of the copyright. One plausible scenario is where a rogue obtains a written assignment of copyright from the previous owner, perhaps as a result of some fraud or trick, and then assigns the copyright to a bona fide third party without notice of the fraud or trick. Even though the legal assignment to the rogue would be void for fraud, the original owner of the copyright may be unable to exploit his work because of the third party who may have obtained equitable ownership of the copyright.[124] Perhaps in these circumstances the rogue could be prosecuted for theft or, alternatively, for obtaining property by deception under section 15 of the Theft Act 1968.

A final attempt to extend the reach of the criminal law into copyright issues concerned the electronics company Amstrad Consumer Electronics plc and its twin-deck cassette recording machines. The record industry argued unsuccessfully that the sale and advertising of these machines was authorizing copyright infringement or was an incitement to infringe copyright. The way the machines were advertised did nothing to reassure the industry, using phrases such as 'You can even make a copy of your favourite cassettes'. It is certainly true that the great majority of purchasers of these machines use them to make unauthorized copies of sound recordings and computer games. In *Amstrad Consumer Electronics plc v The British Phonograph Industry Ltd*.[125] it was held that supplying machines which would be likely to be used to unlawfully copy pre-recorded

120 [1985] 2 All ER 661.

121 It is unlikely because the owner will not usually have been deprived of the right, see Griew, E. *The Theft Acts 1968 and 1978* (London: Sweet & Maxwell, 5th edn., 1986) at p.57.

122 Section 1 of the Theft Act 1968.

123 Section 4(1) of the Theft Act 1968.

124 Alternatively, the original assignment to the rogue may not have been avoided at the time of the second assignment and the third party may obtain the legal title to the copyright. This is analogous to the exceptions to the *nemo dat quod non habet* rule contained in the Sale of Goods Act 1979, especially under section 23, sale by a seller with a voidable title. See also, *Lewis v Avery* [1972] 1 QB 198.

125 [1986] FSR 159.

cassettes subject to copyright protection was insufficient to make the manufacturer or supplier an infringer of copyright. Neither could Amstrad be said to be authorizing infringement of copyright because it had no control over the way its machines were used once sold.[126] In the second case, *CBS Songs Ltd.* v *Amstrad Consumer Electronics plc*[127] it was claimed that Amstrad, by its advertising literature, was inciting others to commit an offence under section 21(3) of the Copyright Act 1956 which made it an offence to make or be in possession of a plate to make infringing copies, similar to section 107(2) of the present Act. However, it was held that, since section 21(3) of the 1956 Act did not confer the right to sue for breach of that section on a copyright owner, the defendant's incitement if it were proved, did not confer upon the plaintiff the right to sue for an injunction or damages.[128]

26 By section 16(2) of the Act, copyright is infringed by a person who, without the licence of the copyright owner does, *or authorizes another to* do, any of the acts restricted by the copyright.

27 [1987] 3 All ER 151.

28 Amstrad had printed a small warning about infringing copyright in their literature.

7

Defences to copyright infringement

INTRODUCTION

The Copyright, Designs and Patents Act 1988 contains some express defences to copyright infringement known as the acts permitted in relation to copyright works or, more simply, the 'permitted acts'. These are acts that can be performed without attracting liability for copyright infringement but this is without prejudice to other legal rights or obligations.[1] Therefore, even though something may be done in relation to a copyright work that does not infringe by reason of being a permitted act, it may still result in a breach of confidence or in the tort of passing off, for example. Defences to copyright infringement are not restricted to the permitted acts and there are other defences that may excuse or justify an act which at first sight infringes copyright. Of course, a person sued for infringement may claim that copyright does not subsist in the work in question, that the courts in the United Kingdom do not have jurisdiction to hear the action, that the act done does not fall within the scope of the restricted acts or that the act complained of was not done to a substantial part of the work. As regards the secondary infringements of copyright some form of knowledge is required on the part of the alleged infringer or there may be some dispute as to whether the copy dealt with is an infringing copy within the meaning assigned by section 27.

Other issues are whether the copyright owner authorized or consented to the alleged infringement or whether the defence of public interest is relevant. If none of the above points applies then the defendant may attempt to justify his actions by claiming that they fall within the meaning of the permitted acts. Finally a 'Euro-defence' might be applicable.[2] The flowchart in Figure 7.1 indicates a rational way of looking at the question of infringement and the defences.

COPYRIGHT OWNER AUTHORIZED OR CONSENTED TO THE ACT

Copyright in a work is infringed by a person who performs or authorizes another person to perform one of the acts restricted by the copyright unless the licence of the copyright owner has been obtained.[3] By section 173, in the case of a work having joint copyright owners the licence of all the joint owners is required. The meaning of 'licence' should be considered in terms of the authority of the copyright owner or his permission to carry out particular restricted acts. It would appear that the licence does not have to be formal or contractual so that the absence of consideration, *per se*, does not affect the status of the authorization. Of course, if the licence is not contractual, there is the problem that it may be revoked at any time subject to equitable rules and principles.

1 Section 28(1) of the Copyright, Designs and Patents Act 1988. Unless otherwise indicated, in this chapter statutory references are to this Act.

2 See chapter 9.

3 Section 16(2).

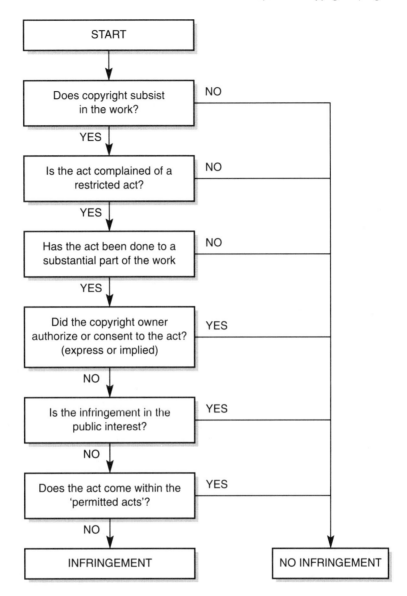

Figure 7.1 Infringement and defences

Under normal circumstances, the licence given by the copyright owner will be formal and contractual in nature, for example a non-exclusive licence in respect of a computer software package for a licence fee of £250. Alternatively, it may be informal and/or non-contractual. If there is no express permission or authority to carry out the restricted act concerned, it may be that the courts will be prepared to imply the copyright owner's licence. This will usually be limited to adding terms to an existing agreement. For example, if a person obtains a licence to use a computer program, the court might imply a term in the licence agreement that the licensee will be the beneficial owner of the copyright in any reports produced by running the program. Of course, it becomes impossible or difficult to imply the copyright owner's authorization or permission in the face of express terms to the contrary in an agreement or if the remaining rights of the owner are prejudiced in some way. An implied licence may overcome difficulties resulting from misunderstandings about the future ownership of copyright, for example where a person commissioning a work of copyright later discovers that he does not own the copyright and the person commissioned to create the work is trying to interfere with the subsequent use of the work.[4] Implying the copyright owner's licence may also be a way of curbing any unconscionable conduct that is proposed by the owner such as taking advantage of an imperfect assignment or a badly drafted licence agreement.

4 See, for example, *Warner v Gestetner Ltd.* [1988] EIPR D-89 and *Blair v Osborne & Tomkins* [1971] 2 WLR 503, discussed in Chapter 4.

PUBLIC INTEREST

'Public interest' is a nebulous concept which can, in some cases, provide a defence for copyright infringement. Cases where the public interest is at issue often concern the publication of information and, frequently, questions of confidence will also be raised. Typically, a person will, without authority of the copyright owner, publish something which embarrasses the copyright owner or some other person. For example, in *Lion Laboratories Ltd.* v *Evans*,[5] the defendant, a newspaper editor, wished to publish information concerning doubts about the reliability of the Lion Intoximeter 3000, a device used to measure levels of intoxication by alcohol. The device had been used to breath test approximately 700 motorists suspected of being unfit to drive through drink. The plaintiff had obtained an injunction preventing the defendant publishing the information on the basis that the information was confidential and also because publication would infringe copyright. The defendant appealed against the injunction.

5 [1984] 2 All ER 417.

The defendant's appeal was allowed. The defence of public interest applied to both the confidence and the copyright issues because it was in the public interest that the information be published and, further, that the operation of the defence was not limited to cases where there had been any wrongdoing on the part of the plaintiff. The court identified matters relevant to the application of the defence of public interest as follows:

(a) There was a difference between what was interesting to the public and what was in the public interest.
(b) It was a fact that the media, for example newspaper proprietors, had a private interest to increase circulation by publishing what appealed to the public.
(c) The public interest might be best served by giving the information to the police or some other responsible body rather than to the press.
(d) The public interest did not only arise when there was an iniquity to be disclosed and the defendant ought not to be restrained solely because what he wanted to publish did not show misconduct on the part of the plaintiff.

If the defence of public interest is raised, the court should weigh up the competing interests. In this particular case, it was unquestionable that it was in the public interest that the information be published. Point (c) above is a little worrying. Surely something either is or is not in the public interest and this test suggests that publication for gain might injure the prospects of the defence succeeding. Surely the motive for publication should be irrelevant – it is the nature of the information that is crucial. In any case, giving the information to a 'responsible body' might lead to a 'cover-up' – if there is some matter which the public should be aware of, the press can serve a very useful function, albeit financially motivated. In *Initial Services Ltd.* v *Putterill*,[6] Salmon LJ recognized that there was very little authority on the status of the person to whom documents or information were given. It was suggested by counsel for the plaintiff that information should have been given to the Registrar appointed under the Restrictive Trade Practices Act 1956[7] and not to the press. However, Salmon LJ said that the law should not lend assistance to anyone proposing to commit or committing a clear breach of statutory duty imposed in the public interest.

Public interest will cover situations involving the disclosure of criminal conduct, both past and contemplated[8] or matters prejudicing the nation's security.[9] In *Attorney-General* v *Guardian Newspapers Ltd.*[10] it was indicated in the House of Lords that the copyright in the Spycatcher novel would not be enforced by the courts because of the conduct of the book's author Peter Wright in divulging national secrets. It could be said that Peter Wright's conduct had harmed the public interest in not keeping secret the activities of 'secret-agents' and the like and the nation's security could have been harmed as a result. As the law of confidence could provide no remedies, the book having been published elsewhere and being widely available, the House of Lords was punishing Mr. Wright the only way it could. The implication was that anyone could publish the book or extracts from it without being liable for copyright infringement.

Freedom of speech can be said to lie within the public interest and as such will not be restrained by way of an interlocutory injunction if the defence of fair dealing is likely to be raised. In *Kennard* v *Lewis*[11] the plaintiff had published a pamphlet entitled *30 Questions and Answers about CND* and the defendant had published a pamphlet called *30 Questions and Honest Answers about CND*, using a layout which was substantially similar. The plaintiff sought an interlocutory injunction to restrain publication of the defendant's pamphlet and the defendant raised a defence of fair dealing (see below). It was held that, as a principle, interlocutory injunctions should not be used to restrain free speech and, *a fortiori*, should not be used to restrain political controversy.[12]

THE PERMITTED ACTS

The acts permitted in relation to copyright works are contained in Chapter III of the Copyright, Designs and Patents Act 1988. The permitted acts are complex and wide ranging in their scope and application, occupying some 52 sections of the Act but, at least, the Act conveniently classifies them by using appropriate sub-headings such as 'Education', 'Libraries and archives', etc. and this classification will be retained in the following description of the permitted acts. At the end of this chapter Table 7.2 shows the basic elements of the permitted acts. The rationale for the permitted acts, allowing what would otherwise be an infringement of copyright, can be seen as a way of limiting the

6 [1968] 1 QB 396.

7 Now repealed. Replaced by the Restrictive Trade Practices Act 1976.

8 Per Lord Denning in *Initial Services Ltd.* v *Putterill* [1968] 1 QB 396. This case involved the disclosure of the operation of a price-fixing ring between laundries.

9 Per Ungoed-Thomas J in *Beloff* v *Pressdram Ltd.* [1973] 1 All ER 241.

10 [1988] 3 All ER 567.

11 [1983] FSR 346.

12 See also *Hubbard* v *Vosper* [1972] 2 QB 84.

strength of the rights associated with copyright. The justification for this restriction is that it provides a fair balance between the rights of the copyright owner and the rights of society at large. Generally, the permitted acts excuse activities which, although technically infringing the copyright in a work, do not unduly interfere with the copyright owner's commercial exploitation of the work. For example, a person writing an academic article is able to include quotations from the writings of other authors. The permitted acts are, therefore, on the whole relatively restricted in their effect on commercial exploitation.

It should be noted that the application of some of the permitted acts depends on the amount of the first work that has been copied or otherwise used whereas, in other cases, the permitted act relates to the whole work. For example, in terms of the permitted act of fair dealing for the purposes of criticism or review it appears that it would not be fair dealing to copy the whole of an existing work of copyright, that fair dealing is limited by some measure which is based on quality or quantity or, perhaps a combination of the two. On the other hand, it is permissible to perform the whole of a dramatic work before an audience of teachers and pupils at an educational establishment.[13]

13 Section 34.

FAIR DEALING

The notion of permitting some use of a copyright work which is considered to be 'fair' is common in many jurisdictions. For example, United States copyright law has its 'fair use' provisions. In the United Kingdom, 'fair dealing' is allowed in relation to a copyright work. It must be noted at once that this has nothing to do with 'dealing' in a trade sense. It can be roughly equated to 'use'. Thus, fair dealing covers research or private study, criticism, review and reporting current events. The fair dealing provisions allow the copying or other use of the work which would otherwise be an infringement and, in many circumstances, the amount of the original work used is very relevant. It may be fair dealing to include 5 per cent of another work for the purpose of criticism or review. It would not normally be fair dealing to incorporate the whole of the other work. Because the proportion of work taken can be relevant to whether the second author can successfully plead the fair dealing provisions, this immediately brings into question the relationship between fair dealing and the taking of a substantial part of a work. If the part taken is not substantial, then there is no infringement of copyright and no need to rely on the permitted acts.

It may be that, in some cases, the existence of the permitted acts is illusory. The problem lies in the determination of the relative thresholds of substantiality and the permitted act in question. In *Independent Television Publications Ltd.* v *Time Out Ltd.*,[14] Whitford J said:

14 [1984] FSR 64.

> Indeed once the conclusion is reached that the whole or a substantial part of the copyright work has been taken, a defence under sections 6(2) or 6(3) [of the Copyright Act 1956, some of the fair dealing provisions] is unlikely to succeed.

If this is true, then there is no such thing as a defence of fair dealing. If the part taken is not substantial there is no infringement and fair dealing is irrelevant, but if the part taken is substantial then, according to Whitford J, the defence will rarely excuse the defendant's use of the work. It is respectfully submitted that this is wrong and that the whole purpose of the fair dealing provisions is to permit, in appropriate circumstances, the taking of a substantial part of a copyright work. It is, however, difficult to say where the boundaries circumscribing substantiality and fair dealing lie.[15]

15 In the New South Wales case of *Copyright Agency Ltd. v Haines* [1982] FSR 331 it was suggested that fair dealing does not permit as much copying as a licensing scheme permitting photocopying by educational establishments.

Consider the case where an author wishes to write a learned article for an academic journal. The author wishes to discuss and critically analyse the work of an eminent professor in the appropriate field. To do this, the author will wish to include extracts from the writings of the eminent professor. But, how much does fair dealing allow him to take? Lord Denning gave a good description of the scope of fair dealing for the purposes of criticism or review in *Hubbard* v *Vosper,* where he said:

> You must first consider the number and extent of the quotations . . . Then you must consider the use made of them. If they are used as a basis of comment, criticism or review, that may be fair dealing. If they are used to convey the same information as the author, for a rival purpose, they may be unfair. Next you must consider the proportions. To take long extracts and attach short comments may be unfair. But short extracts and long comments may be fair. Other considerations may come to mind also. But . . . it must be a matter of impression.[16]

16 [1972] 2 QB 84 at 94.

Apart from the purpose of the inclusion of copyright materials, their overall proportion to the whole must be considered. Although substantiality is determined by a qualitative test, it appears from the above quote that the scope of this particular permitted act is determined at least partly by means of a quantitative test. Hence the difficulty. Consider the following in connection with hypothetical journal articles: the author of the new article is called Aristotle and the author of the earlier article is called Plato. Aristotle uses extracts from Plato's article and quotes and discusses them in his own article. Table 7.1 indicates different proportions of the total volume of the extracts used in relation to both Plato's original article and Aristotle's new article.

Table 7.1 Proportions of extracts and fair dealing

Total of extracts: Plato	Percentage of article written by Aristotle
5%	5%
5%	10%
5%	20%
10%	5%
10%	10%
10%	20%
20%	5%
20%	10%
20%	20%
35%	5%
35%	20%
35%	50%

For example, in the second entry in Table 7.1, Aristotle has copied 5 per cent of Plato's article and this occupies some 10 per cent of Aristotle's work. (In this case, Aristotle's article must be about half the length of Plato's.) It should be apparent from the table that it is not easy to decide which, if any, of these examples represents an infringement of copyright, even assuming a good motive on the part of Aristotle. In some cases, for example, where the total of the extracts represents 5 per cent of both works, it might be considered to be fair dealing yet this might be irrelevant because a substantial part of Plato's work has not been taken. In other cases, such as the last one in the table where the extracts amount to 35 per cent of Plato's work and 50 per cent of Aristotle's work, it can be said with some certainty that a substantial amount of Plato's work has been taken and that this does not fall within the scope of the permitted act of fair dealing. However, there are a range of cases in between where it is difficult to say with any certainty. It depends on other things such as motive and the nature of the two works. In some cases, it may be that the minimum percentage representing a substantial part is the same as the maximum percentage falling within the fair dealing provisions. In other words, there is coincidence in the infringement and permitted act thresholds and, thus, the permitted act is of no consequence.[17]

'Fair dealing' is not defined in the Copyright, Designs and Patents Act 1988 and it is only by reference to case law that the factors that might be considered by a court can be determined. Only sometimes will the factors identified below be said to be conclusive one way or the other – in most cases it will be a matter of combining and weighting the factors. The only thing that can be said with any degree of certainty is that whether a particular act falls within the meaning of fair dealing depends very much upon the circumstances surrounding that act.

(a) **Purpose.** Conceivably, it might be fair dealing to take a copy of an entire work, such as a journal article, for the purposes of research or private study. But, it will not normally be fair dealing to take a large amount of another's work for the purpose of criticism or review.[18]

(b) **Proportion.** Within a particular form of fair dealing, proportion might be important. For example, it may be fair dealing for the purposes of criticism or review to take 5 per cent of a work but not to take 40 per cent.[19]

(c) **Motive.** If the motive for the act was to compete with the other work, this is unlikely to be fair dealing.[20]

(d) **Status of other work,** that is whether confidential or published. It is unlikely to be fair dealing if the work taken has not been published or in the case of a 'leak'.[21]

One thing to note is that an interlocutory injunction will not normally be granted if the defendant is going to raise the defence of fair dealing and has at least an arguable case. This reluctance to grant interlocutory injunctions stems from the desire of the courts to protect freedom of speech, particularly as regards the press or in a political or quasi-political sphere.[22] However, there has to be genuine conflict and a danger that freedom of speech will be prejudiced. For example in *Associated Newspapers Group plc v News Group Newspapers Ltd.*,[23] an injunction was granted because there had been no interference with the press's freedom of speech which would only be interfered with when someone was prevented from saying the truth. The principle that interlocutory

17 Of course, it is unsatisfactory to talk in terms of percentages as substantiality is a qualitative measure. This is one reason why it is so difficult to map out the start of infringement and the end of the permitted acts.

18 See, generally, *Hubbard v Vosper* [1972] 2 QB 84 and Lord Denning's judgment in particular and the quote earlier in this chapter. Also see *Walter v Steinkopff* [1892] 3 Ch 489.

19 *Walter v Steinkopff* [1892] 3 Ch 489.

20 *Weatherby v International Horse Agency & Exchange Ltd.* [1910] 2 Ch 297. Parker J said that the issue of competition is often important and may even be a determining factor in some cases, although he did say that unfair use was wider than this.

21 *British Oxygen Co. Ltd. v Liquid Air Ltd.* [1925] 1 Ch 383 and *Beloff v Pressdram Ltd.* [1973] 1 All ER 241.

22 For example, *Hubbard v Vosper* [1972] 2 QB 84 and *Kennard v Lewis* [1983] FSR 346. It should be noted that *Hubbard v Vosper* pre-dates the *American Cyanamid* guidelines.

23 [1986] RPC 515.

injunctions should not be granted when the defendant raises the fair dealing defence has been questioned recently by Dillon LJ in *British Broadcasting Corporation* v *British Satellite Broadcasting Ltd.*,[24] a case concerning excerpts from broadcasts of World Cup football matches made by the BBC which BSB intended to include in its broadcasts. Nevertheless, the BBC's application for an interlocutory injunction was refused.

Fair dealing for the purposes of research or private study

The defence of fair dealing for research or private study is available in relation to literary, dramatic, musical or artistic works and also applies to the typographical arrangement of published editions of such works.[25] Although this excuses indirect infringement of typographical arrangements, this fair dealing provision is expressly stated by section 29(2) to apply directly to typographical arrangements of published editions. This might apply in the case of a published edition of a literary work, the copyright in which has expired. Although there were calls for fair dealing to be limited to private research, the formula used in the 1956 Act has been retained, that is research and private study. Therefore, fair dealing for the purposes of commercial or industrial research is a distinct possibility, although each case will turn on its particular facts. For example, it would not be considered to be fair dealing to perform an act restricted by the copyright in a work for the purposes of producing a competing work. In *Independent Television Publications Ltd.* v *Time Out Ltd.*,[26] the defendant copied details of forthcoming television programmes from the *TV Times* and the *Radio Times*. The defence of fair dealing (in this case under the head of fair dealing for criticism and review) failed because the purpose was to provide a television programme listing service and had nothing to do with criticism or review.[27]

The financial motive behind making a copy of a work or part of a work for research or private study must surely be considered in determining whether or not it falls within the scope of fair dealing. To this can be added other factors such as the nature of the research or study and the funds available to the researcher or student. Questions such as whether the person concerned is copying simply to save himself the expense of buying a copy of the work or whether it is reasonable to expect a copy to be purchased are important. Take, for example, a postgraduate research student. He will need to refer to hundreds of different journal articles and books. The student will not be able to purchase more than a handful of these, he will have to be selective. The student may decide to purchase those materials which he will need to use over and over again during the research. But many of the articles and books will be used less frequently and only small portions will be referred to. It would not be realistic to expect the student to purchase a book when he only wants to refer to a small part of it. Similarly, in the case of an article in a journal. The student would not be expected to buy the issue of the journal or have to subscribe to the journal just to have access to one particular article.[28]

It is difficult to draw the limits of fair dealing for research or private study; perhaps it can be suggested, partly on the basis of the permitted acts in respect of librarians, that copying the whole of one article from an academic journal would be fair dealing or the copying of part of a book, say no more than one chapter.[29] Any more would not be fair dealing. However, it must be noted that

---

24 (unreported), Court of Appeal, 29 June 1990, Court of Appeal (an appeal against a decision not to grant interim relief). In the subsequent full trial, *British Broadcasting Corporation* v *British Satellite Broadcasting Ltd.* [1991] 3 WLR 174 it was held by Scott J that the defence of fair dealing was available.

25 Section 29(1).

26 [1984] FSR 64.

27 But now, as a result of section 176 of the Broadcasting Act 1990, there is a duty to make information about forthcoming programmes available to other publishers. European Community law also may be appropriate here, especially Article 86 of the Treaty of Rome, see *Magill TV Guide/ITP, BBC and RTE* OJ [1988] L78/43.

28 In some cases, a blanket licence scheme will be in operation allowing more extensive copying such as that administered by the Copyright Licensing Agency.

29 See sections 38 and 39, discussed later.

a great deal of copying in relation to private study is carried out by students and it is difficult to control and monitor the use that students make of photo-copying facilities in libraries. Of course, in many cases, the charges made for photocopying (usually around 10p per sheet) mean that it is not economically viable to copy a whole book – in many cases purchasing the book would be cheaper than copying it. Although photocopying immediately springs to mind, it should be remembered that copyright can be infringed by making a hand-written copy. It is less likely that a substantial part will be taken because of the effort and time required. Making hand-written notes is a selective process and only the materials that are of direct use to the student are likely to be copied out in this way. Also, the materials are read and, usually, analysed by the student during the process. It may be that the notes taken by the student have their own copyright because of the student's expenditure of skill, effort and judgment in adding comments and supplemental notes.

The act involved in fair dealing can be done by another, such as where a librarian makes a copy of an article in a periodical for a student who requires the copy for the purposes of research or private study. However, this is limited by section 29(3) which restricts the making of copies to cases where there are not multiple copies being made or supplied to more than one person at a similar time for purposes that are substantially the same. For example, in *Sillitoe* v *McGraw-Hill Book Co. (UK) Ltd.*,[30] the defendant had published 'study notes' intended to assist students taking GCE 'O' level examinations in literature and had reproduced a substantial part of the plaintiff's works in the study notes. The defendant contended, *inter alia*, that the study notes fell within the fair dealing provisions under section 6(1) of the Copyright Act 1956; that is fair dealing for the purposes of research or private study. This submission failed to find favour as the defendant was not engaged in research or private study but was merely facilitating this for others, that is the students purchasing copies of the study notes.

30 [1983] FSR 545.

Fair dealing for the purposes of criticism, review and reporting current events

Fair dealing for the purpose of criticism or review applies to any form of work or a performance of a work and does not infringe copyright providing a sufficient acknowledgement is given.[31] Section 178 contains a definition of 'sufficient acknowledgement' and requires that it identifies both the work by its title, or other description, and the author. However, if the work is published anonymously, or if the work is unpublished and the author's identity cannot be ascertained by reasonable inquiry there is no requirement for the author's name to be included in the acknowledgement. In *Sillitoe* v *McGraw-Hill Book Co. (UK) Ltd.*[32] it was held that a sufficient acknowledgement must recognize the position or claims of the author.

31 Section 30(1).

32 [1983] FSR 545.

Section 30(1) allows fair dealing with one work in order to criticize or review another work. For example, it is fair dealing to include extracts from a work by T. S. Eliot in a work which is a critical analysis of the work of E. M. Forster.[33] But, otherwise, the work must be subjected to criticism or review. The equivalent defence under the Copyright Act 1956 was held not to apply when

33 Both authors are deceased but literary copyright still subsists in their works.

correspondence between the Duke and Duchess of Windsor was published without any such criticism or review.[34]

Criticism can be scathing and can involve a substantial part of another work and yet still be fair dealing. In *Hubbard* v *Vosper*,[35] the defendant had been a member of the Church of Scientology for some 14 years. After leaving, he wrote a book which was highly critical of the cult of Scientology and used in his book substantial extracts from books, bulletins and letters, some of which were confidential, written by the plaintiff. The defence of fair dealing for the purposes of criticism and review was successfully raised as regards the copyright issues.

Fair dealing for the purpose of reporting current events does not apply in the case of a photograph. It is common practice for newspapers to copy extracts from stories in other newspapers. For example, one newspaper may have an 'exclusive' in its early morning issue and other newspapers carry the story in their later editions giving, of course, a sufficient acknowledgement. This they may do, providing a photograph is not copied without permission. However, these fair dealing provisions are wider than under the previous Act because, apart from the exception of photographs, they are not limited to any particular type of work and can, therefore, apply to broadcasts and cable programmes. Indeed, according to Scott J in *British Broadcasting Corporation* v *British Satellite Broadcasting Ltd.*,[36] this fair dealing provision is not limited to general news bulletins and could apply to a major sporting event such as the World Cup football competition. In this case, there had been an acknowledgement given by BSB as to the source of the film but according to section 30(3) there is no need to give an acknowledgement in the case of reporting current events by means of a sound recording, film, broadcast or cable programme. It seems strange that an exception is made in the case of photographs but not broadcasts.

Incidental inclusion of copyright material

The use of movie and video cameras, still cameras and live broadcasts means that, frequently and inevitably, copyright works will be included in the films, photographs or broadcasts whether by design or accident. To facilitate the making of photographs (and other artistic works), films, broadcasts and cable programmes, the incidental inclusion of a copyright work does not infringe the copyright subsisting in that work: section 31(1). Otherwise, it would be very difficult arranging to make a film or whatever because it would be necessary to avoid the chance inclusion of copyright works. For example, in the case of a television broadcast made in the streets of a city the copyright subsisting in buildings (artistic works) would be infringed[37] as might be the copyright in advertising hoardings. The broadcast may also catch a glimpse of the front page of a newspaper on sale and pick up the strains of a popular tune being played loudly further down the street.

The exception goes further in that the copyright in the work incidentally included is not infringed by other acts such as issuing copies to the public, playing, showing, broadcasting or including in a cable programme anything that was made without infringing copyright under section 31(1). However, as regards musical works and works embodying musical works, incidental inclusion does not extend to deliberate inclusion. This also applies to words spoken

34 *Associated Newspapers Group plc* v *News Group Newspapers Ltd.* [1986] RPC 515.

35 [1972] 2 QB 84.

36 [1991] 3 WLR 174

37 A work of architecture is an artistic work by section 4(1)(a). Section 62 would also excuse – see later. As with other works except typographical arrangements, the copyright in an artistic work can be infringed by broadcasting or inclusion in a cable programme service, section 20.

or sung with music, for example the lyrics of a song. *Hawkes & Sons (London) Ltd.* v *Paramount Film Service Ltd.*,[38] concerning infringement of musical copyright by the inclusion of 28 bars of Colonel Bogey in a newsreel, lives on.

38 [1934] Ch 593.

EDUCATION

Education is treated as a special case by copyright law and there are several exceptions to infringement contained in the Act.[39] Some control is retained – for example, reprographic copying is permitted only in limited circumstances and some of the permitted acts can be done only for or at educational establishments.[40] Section 174 of the Act defines 'educational establishments' as being any school and any other establishment specified by order of the Secretary of State. By the Copyright (Educational Establishments) (No. 2) Order 1989,[41] other establishments include universities established by Royal Charter or Act of Parliament, most institutions for further or higher education and theological colleges. 'School' is defined by reference to the appropriate legislation – for example, in England and Wales, it is as defined in the Education Act 1944.[42] The expressions 'teacher' and 'pupil' include, respectively, any person who gives and any person who receives instruction. Another control is that, in some circumstances where it is permitted to make copies of copyright works, if those copies are subsequently dealt with they are treated as infringing copies. 'Dealt with' means sold or let for hire or offered or exposed for sale or hire.

39 Sections 32–36.

40 Reprographic copying has a wider meaning than simply making photocopies of a work, see section 178.

41 SI 1989 No. 1068.

42 See section 174(3) for the meaning of 'school' in Scotland and in Northern Ireland.

Section 32 deals with things done either for the purpose of instruction or for examination purposes. Unusually for the 'education permitted acts' there is no requirement for the instruction or examination to be done by or on behalf of an educational establishment. It is wider and extends to other institutions such as private colleges for adults and correspondence colleges. Copying in the course of instruction or in preparation for instruction of a literary, dramatic, musical or artistic work is permitted as long as the copying is done by the person giving or receiving the instruction, for example the teacher or the pupil, and the copying is not by a reprographic process. For example, it is permissible for a teacher to ask a pupil to write out by hand a substantial extract from a work of literature. Another example is where a teacher reproduces an artistic work on a blackboard in a classroom for the purpose of instruction. Copying by making a film or a film sound track in the course of, or in preparation for, instruction in the making of films or film sound tracks does not infringe the copyright in a sound recording, film, broadcast or cable programme. Again, the copying must be done by a person giving or receiving instruction. As might be expected examinations are also privileged in that anything may be done for the purposes of the examination by way of setting questions, communicating questions to candidates or answering the questions without infringing copyright. However, there is an exception to this in the case of reprographic copies of musical works for use by an examination candidate in performing the work. Therefore, if the examination requires the candidates to play some music, authorization to make copies must be obtained from the copyright owner or additional copies of the sheet music purchased. The Act prohibits the subsequent dealing with copies made under section 32 by considering such copies to be infringing copies.

Anthologies are dealt with by section 33 which permits the inclusion of a short passage from a published literary or dramatic work in a collection providing that the collection is intended for use in educational establishments and consists mainly of material in which no copyright subsists. Such material would include works in which the copyright has expired.[43] The collection must be described in its title and in any advertisements as being for use in educational establishments. Furthermore, a sufficient acknowledgement is required. But, how short is a short extract? If it is not substantial in copyright terms, then there can be no infringement anyway and the requirements of the exception are meaningless. A further requirement is that no more than two excerpts from the copyright works by the same author can be included in anthologies published by the same publisher over any period of five years. It would seem that this permitted act is extremely parsimonious. Presumably, if there is some criticism of review of the extracts the fair dealing provisions would come into play and larger extracts could be used. Just to place a final and unnecessary imposition, section 33(4) limits the provision to the educational purposes of the educational establishment, though it is hard to think of activities which could be deemed to be non-educational in which anthologies would be useful.

Performances of literary, dramatic and musical works are permitted providing the audience is made up of teachers and pupils at the educational establishment and other persons directly connected with the activities of the establishment.[44] A parent of a pupil is not to be taken as directly connected with the school by reason of being a parent only. Therefore, a play performed by pupils before an audience of parents will fall outside the scope of this permitted act. The performance may be by a teacher or pupil in the course of the school's activities or by any person for the purposes of instruction. For the latter it is required that the performance takes place at the school but as far as teacher and pupil performances are concerned, this limitation does not apply. However, the wording of section 34 seems to suggest that only sole performances fall within the section. The section is termed in the singular as regards the performers. There are similar provisions in respect of the playing or showing of a sound recording, film, broadcast or cable programme for the purposes of instruction before such an audience as described above. Recordings of broadcasts and cable programmes and copies of such recordings can be made by or on behalf of educational establishments for their educational purposes without infringing copyright in the broadcast or cable programme providing there is not an appropriate licensing scheme under section 143 of the Act.[45] However, subsequent dealing is not permitted. Some licensing schemes have been certified, for example in respect of the Open University.[46]

Section 36 permits the reprographic copying of passages of published literary, dramatic or musical works by or on behalf of educational establishments for the purposes of instruction. Nor is the copyright in the typographical arrangement of the published edition infringed. However, the amount that can be copied is extremely small being not more than 1 per cent of any work in any quarter and the authority to copy given by section 36 is subject to the availability of licences and the actual or constructive notice of the person making the copies as regards such licences. A licence may not attempt to reduce the portion that can be copied under section 36. Again, this provision must be considered in the light of what is a substantial part of a work. It is submitted that in most

43 It could also cover material published in a country which is not a member of the copyright conventions and fails otherwise to attract protection in the United Kingdom.

44 Section 34. Such performances are deemed not to be public performances.

45 Section 35.

46 Copyright (Certification of Licensing Scheme for Educational Recording of Broadcasts) (Open University Educational Enterprises Limited) Order 1990, SI 1990 No. 879.

cases, a substantial part of a work will exceed 1 per cent of the total quantity of a work. If this is so, section 36 has no effect whatsoever, it is just so many empty words. Of course, it is very difficult to predict how a court will decide the issue of substantiality, the test being based mainly on quality. However, it would be unlikely that a mere 1 per cent would capture the essence of a work. In *Hawkes & Sons (London) Ltd.* v *Paramount Film Service Ltd.*[47] around 8 per cent was adjudged to be substantial but here the basic melody had been taken. Perhaps a better test would be to look at the effect, if any, on the copyright owner's interests. Has the extent of the copying been such that it would be reasonable to expect that copies of the original work be purchased instead? However, the rapid improvements made in recent times to copying technology perhaps accounts for the attempts to limit unauthorized copying to tiny amounts only.

47 [1934] Ch 593.

LIBRARIES AND ARCHIVES

These provisions apply only to 'prescribed' libraries and archives, that is those prescribed by statutory instrument, which may also provide that, in some cases (also prescribed), a librarian or archivist may only make a copy if the person requesting the copy makes a signed declaration in the prescribed form.[48] In such cases, a librarian or archivist may rely on a signed declaration by a person requesting a copy of part or whole of a work in which copyright subsists unless he is aware that the declaration is false in a material particular. A signed declaration will usually contain a statement to the effect that the copy is required for the purposes of research or private study and that the person requesting the copy has not previously been supplied with a copy from the same work. If a signed declaration is false in a material particular, the copy supplied is considered to be an infringing copy and the person requesting the copy is liable for infringement of copyright as if he made the copy himself. The Act acknowledges that a librarian or archivist may delegate his duties and responsibilities to others.[49] In general, where the copying is permitted of certain types of work, there will be no infringement of accompanying illustrations or in the typographical arrangement. A reproduction of one of the photocopy declarations used by the British Library is shown in Figure 7.2.

48 The Copyright (Librarians and Archivists) (Copying of Copyright Material) Regulations 1989 specifies prescribed libraries and archives and expands on the prescribed conditions and also contains the forms to be used for declarations and written statements required in section 38 to 43 of the Copyright, Designs and Patents Act 1988. For example, the prescribed conditions generally include a requirement for a signed declaration or statement.

49 These preliminary issues are contained in section 37 of the Act.

By section 38, a librarian may make and supply a copy of an article in a periodical to a person requiring the copy for the purposes of research or private study. The person supplied must pay at least the attributable cost which includes a contribution to the general expenses of the library, that is overheads. No person may be supplied with more than one copy of the same article or with more than one article from the same issue of the periodical. Similar provisions in section 39 permit the making and supplying of a copy of a part of a published edition of a literary, dramatic or musical work. The section refers to copying a part of a work without giving any guidance as to the maximum proportion that may be copied. Section 40 of the Act seeks to restrict the making or supplying of multiple copies of the same material by way of regulations made for the purposes of section 38 and 39.

Provisions also exist so that one prescribed library may make and supply copies to other prescribed libraries of:

THE BRITISH LIBRARY DOCUMENT SUPPLY CENTRE

Photocopy Declaration to be retained by the registered BLDSC Customer.

To be obtained by the Librarian of the user library when a declaration or similar undertaking has not otherwise been obtained.

To the Librarian of the [   ] Library

(name of user Library or Library Stamp)

1. I hereby request you to supply me with a copy of item specified on Request Number ....
....
which I require for the purpose of research or private study.

2. I have not previously been supplied with a copy of the same material by you or any other librarian

3. I will not use the copy except for research or private study and will not supply a copy of it to any other person

4. to the best of my knowledge, no other person with whom I work or study has made or intends to make at about the same time as this request, a request for substantially the same material for substantially the same purpose.

5. I understand that if this declaration is false in a material particular the copy supplied to me by you will be an infringing copy and that I shall be liable for infringement of copyright as if I had made the copy myself.

Signature ....   Address ....

Name ....
                    (BLOCK LETTERS)   ....

Date ....

N.B the signature must be the personal signature of the person making the request.

Figure 7.2 Photocopy declaration
(Reproduced by permission of the British Library Document Supply Centre)

(a) articles in periodicals, or
(b) the whole or part of a published edition of a literary, dramatic or musical work.[50]

However, (b) does not apply if, at the time the copy is made, the librarian making it knows or could by reasonable inquiry ascertain the name and address of the person entitled to authorize the making of copies of the work. In the vast majority of cases this will be so – most published editions contain the name of the publisher and the author and, whosoever of these is the copyright owner, the librarian should be able, without undue difficulty, to make contact in order to ask permission.

Subject to certain conditions, the making for another prescribed library or archive of replacement copies of literary, dramatic or musical works which have been lost, destroyed or damaged is permitted by section 42. Making copies in order to preserve the original is also permitted, for example so that the copy may be displayed and the original placed in safe storage. However, such copying is not permitted if it is reasonably practicable to purchase a copy of the item. The copying of certain unpublished works for the purposes of research or private study is also permitted[51] as is the making of copies of articles of cultural or historical importance or interest which are to be exported from the United Kingdom, it being a legal requirement that such a copy is made.[52]

PUBLIC ADMINISTRATION

Copyright is not infringed by certain things done in connection with what might loosely be described as in the course of public administration. This

50 Section 41.

51 Section 43.

52 Section 44.

includes parliamentary and judicial proceedings, Royal Commissions and statutory inquiries, and materials open to public inspection, on a statutory register or contained in a public record. Further, acts done under statutory authority do not infringe copyright, unless the relevant Act of Parliament provides otherwise, and the Crown may copy and issue copies to the public of materials communicated to the Crown in the course of public business.

Thus, the copying of documents for a court trial does not infringe copyright nor does playing a piece of music in court as part of the proceedings, for example if the case concerns a dispute involving an alleged infringement of copyright in a piece of music. Copyright is not infringed by doing anything for the purpose of reporting parliamentary and judicial proceedings or the proceedings of Royal Commissions or statutory inquiries that are held in public. This does not, of course, authorize the copying of published reports of such proceedings. It is permissible to make copies of entries in registers such as the Data Protection Register, the Register of Patents and the Trade Marks Register, to make copies of information contained in electoral registers or to obtain copies of birth, marriage and death certificates, etc. without infringing copyright. The Copyright (Material Open to Public Inspection) (Marking of Copies of Plans and Drawings) Order 1990 contains the text of a statement to be applied to copies of plans and drawings supplied under section 47.[53] Further details of the public administration exceptions to copyright infringement is given in Table 7.2 at the end of this chapter.

53 SI 1990 No. 1427. The statement is contained in regulation 2.

COMPUTER PROGRAMS

The Copyright (Computer Programs) Regulations 1992[54] inserted new sections 50A to 50C providing for some specific exceptions to copyright infringement. Under certain conditions, lawful users of computer programs may make back-up copies of computer programs, decompile programs to achieve interoperability and copy or adapt a computer program. These exceptions are dealt with fully in the following chapter.

54 SI 1992 No. 3233

DESIGNS, TYPEFACES AND WORKS IN ELECTRONIC FORM

The provisions relating to designs are discussed in Part Five which deals with design law; however, these provisions are still contained in Table 7.2 at the end of this chapter for completeness. Basically, the typeface provisions are to limit artistic copyright protection for the design of a typeface[55] which will fall within the graphic work category of artistic works. Using a typeface in the ordinary course of typing, composing text, typesetting or printing, possession of an article for such use or doing anything in relation to the material so produced does not infringe the artistic copyright subsisting in the design of a typeface even if the article is an infringing article.[56] However, section 54(2) goes on to apply certain provisions including secondary infringement of copyright to persons making, importing, dealing or possessing for the purpose of dealing with articles specifically designed or adapted to produce material with a particular typeface.[57] Section 55 of the Act limits the duration of copyright in an artistic work consisting of the design of a typeface to 25 years from the end of the calendar

55 A typeface includes an ornamental motif used in printing, section 178.

56 Section 54.

57 'Dealing with' means selling, letting for hire, offering or exposing for sale or hire, exhibiting in public or distributing.

year during which articles specifically designed or adapted for producing material in that typeface have been marketed by or with the permission of the copyright owner.[58]

Many works are now made available in electronic form, which is defined in section 178 as being in a form usable only by electronic means, 'electronic' having a wide meaning. For example, computer programs, sound recordings, films, information and data are frequently made available in this form. The provision contained in section 56 raises a legal presumption that where a copy of work in electronic form is transferred, the transferee may do anything the original purchaser could do without infringing copyright. Before the provision can apply, the terms under which the copy had been purchased must have allowed, whether expressly, by implication or by operation of law, the purchaser to make copies, to adapt the work or make copies of the adaptation. Furthermore, there must be no express terms interfering with the transfer of the copy or with transferee's rights. Any copies, whether or not adaptations or copies of adaptations, that were made by the purchaser and not transferred are treated as being infringing copies of the work. The provisions also apply to subsequent transfers of the copy of the work. As an example of the workings of section 56, imagine that a person, George, obtains a copy of a word-processing computer program to use on his computer. He may make a back-up copy if the licence agreement permits this or if necessary to his lawful use. Suppose the licence allows George to assign it in the future. After a year of two, George wants to obtain a more powerful word processor program and wants to 'sell' his old one to Robert.[59] George may then:

(a) give Robert the original disk containing the word processing program and the back-up copy (duplicate), or
(b) give Robert the original disk and destroy the back-up copy.

If George retains the back-up copy, this will be treated as an infringing copy. Once Robert receives the original disk, he will be able to make his own back-up copy of the program.

MISCELLANEOUS – LITERARY, DRAMATIC, MUSICAL AND ARTISTIC WORKS

Sections 57 to 65 contain a hotch-potch of provisions relating to various permitted acts in relation to literary, dramatic, musical and artistic works. Section 57 applies to anonymous and so-called 'pseudonymous' literary, dramatic, musical and artistic works and covers the situation where it is not possible by reasonable inquiry to trace the author, it being reasonable to assume that the copyright has expired or that the author died at least 50 years ago. In such a case, copyright is not infringed even if it is later discovered that copyright continues to subsist in the work. Notice that it is the identity of the author and not the owner of the copyright which is at issue. This provision does not apply to works of Crown copyright nor in respect of designated international organizations. If a work is of joint authorship, the provision does not apply if any one of the authors could have been traced by reasonable inquiry or if it is not reasonable to assume that all of the joint authors died at least 50 years ago.

58 'Marketed' means sold, let for hire or offered or exposed for sale or hire anywhere in the world.

59 Strictly speaking, George does not sell the system to Robert: instead, he assigns his licence to Robert. For assignment generally, see Chapter 4.

Other permitted acts include:

(a) the use or copying of a record of spoken words or material from it for the purposes of reporting current events or broadcasting or including in a cable programme service subject to certain conditions: section 58;

(b) the public reading or recitation of a reasonable extract of a published literary or dramatic work, subject to a sufficient acknowledgement: section 59;

(c) copying and issuing to the public abstracts of scientific or technical subjects published in periodicals, subject to the existence of a statutory licensing scheme: section 60;

(d) recording songs for the purpose of inclusion in an archive maintained by a designated body: section 61;[60]

(e) making drawings, paintings, photographs, films, etc. of buildings and, if accessible by the public, sculptures, models for buildings and works of artistic craftsmanship: section 62;

(f) copying an artistic work and issuing copies to the public in order to advertise the forthcoming sale of the work, for example, to distribute photographs of an oil painting to be sold at an auction: section 63;

(g) the making of subsequent artistic works by the author of a previous work (permits an artist to use and develop his style and technique for future works): section 64;[61]

(h) reconstructing buildings: section 65.

MISCELLANEOUS – OTHER WORKS

A miscellany of permitted acts are provided for in sections 66 to 75. Section 66 deals with compulsory rental schemes for sound recordings and computer programs.[62] Further, the duration of copyright in computer programs is slightly compromised by making it permissible to rent copies of a computer program to the public after the elapse of 50 years from the end of the year in which copies of the computer program were first issued to the public. The playing of a sound recording might not infringe copyright if done for charitable, religious, educational or social welfare purposes: section 67. Incidental recording for broadcasting and cable programming is permitted as is recording for supervision and control over programmes and, where appropriate, advertisements, by the BBC, IBA and Cable Authorities.[63]

A large number of video recorders are used domestically to record television programmes for viewing at a later, more convenient time. This is known as 'time-shifting' of broadcasts and cable programmes and is permitted by section 70 if done for private and domestic use. There is no time limit although one of 28 days was proposed at one stage during the passage of the Bill through Parliament but this was finally dropped because it was totally unenforceable.[64]

Strangely, section 71 permits the making, for private and domestic use, of a photograph of an image which is part of a broadcast or cable programme stating that the copyright in the broadcast, cable programme or any included films will not be infringed. Presumably, copyright in other works could still be infringed, such as taking a photograph of a television screen when it is showing a painting or some other artistic work. It is unclear why anyone would want to take photographs from screen images on a television set, although such photographs could be used in advertising and promotions.

60 A list of designated bodies is given in the Copyright (Recordings of Folksongs for Archives) (Designated Bodies) Order 1989, SI 1989 No. 1012. Section 61 of the Act is headed 'Recordings of Folksongs' but the Act nowhere defines a 'folksong' except that from looking at section 61, it appears that a folksong is a song where the words are unpublished and of unknown authorship. In many cases, such songs will be too old for copyright protection under the 1988 Act although they may have qualified under the 1956 Act.

61 It would be unlikely that copyright would be infringed if the artist did not repeat or imitate the main design as required by section 64.

62 At the time of writing, no such schemes exist.

63 Sections 68 and 69.

64 For a discussion of time-shifting and a criticism of section 70, see Merkin, R. *Copyright, Designs and Patents: The New Law* (London: Longman, 1989) at pp.175–176.

The free public showing or playing in public of broadcasts or cable programmes is permitted by section 72, for example to the residents of an old persons home or to members of clubs or societies (unless this is not incidental to the main purpose of the club or society). Reception and immediate retransmission of broadcasts and cable programmes is permissible under certain circumstances by section 73. Designated bodies may, by section 74, modify copies of broadcasts or cable programmes for persons who are hard of hearing or disabled, for example by adding sub-titles, subject to the existence of statutory licensing schemes and, by section 75, recordings of certain broadcasts or cable programmes may be made by bodies such as the British Film Institute and the British Library for archival purposes.[65]

65 The other bodies are the Music Performance Research Centre and the Scottish Film Council: Copyright (Recording for Archives of Designated Class of Broadcasts and Cable Programmes) (Designated Bodies) Order 1989, SI 1989 No. 2510.

ADAPTATIONS

It is possible for the permitted acts to apply to a work which is an adaptation of another work. In these cases, the copyright in the first work (that is, the work from which the adaptation was made) is not infringed. This is the effect of section 76 which prevents infringement of the underlying work from which the adaptation (being a literary, dramatic or musical work) was made, providing the act in relation to the adaptation is permitted.

SUMMARY

Table 7.2 provides a summary of the permitted acts discussed in detail in this chapter.

Table 7.2 The permitted acts: outline

Permitted act	Types of works covered by permitted act	Comments
Fair Dealing, etc.		
Fair dealing – research and private study: s.29	Literary, dramatic, musical or artistic works, typographical arrangements	
Fair dealing – criticism or review: s.30(1)	Any work or performance	Must be accompanied by a sufficient acknowledgement
Fair dealing – reporting current events: s.30(2)	Any work other than a photograph	Must be accompanied by a sufficient acknowledgement except in the case of a sound recording, film, broadcast or cable programme
Incidental inclusion in an artistic work, sound recording, film, broadcast or cable programme: s.31(1)	Any work	But musical work, words spoken or sung with music must not be deliberately included

➤

Table 7.2 cont'd

Permitted act	Types of works covered by permitted act	Comments
Issuing to the public, playing, showing, broadcasting, including in a cable programme service: s.31(2)	Anything, the making of which was not an infringement by virtue of s.31(1) above	

Education

Permitted act	Types of works covered by permitted act	Comments
Copying in the course of instruction or preparation for instruction: s.32(1)	Literary, dramatic, musical or artistic work	Must be done by person giving or receiving instruction and not copied by means of a reprographic process
Copying by making a film or a film soundtrack in the course of, or in preparation for, instruction in the making of films or film sound-tracks: s.32(2)	Sound recording, film, broadcast or cable programme	Must be done by a person giving or receiving instruction
Anything done for the purpose of examination by way of setting questions, communicating questions to candidates or answering the question: s.32(3)	Any work	Making a reprographic copy of a musical work for use by an examination candidate in performing the work is not permitted: s.32(4)
Inclusion of a short passage in a collection intended for use in educational establish-ments and so described in advertisements. The collection must consist mainly of material in which no copyright subsist: s.33	Published literary or dramatic works	Must be accompanied by a sufficient acknowledgement and the work itself must not be intended for use in such establishments and not more than 2 excerpts from copyright works of the same author may be included in collections published by the same publisher over any period of 5 years
Performances before an audience of teachers and pupils at an educational establishment and other persons directly connected with the activities of the establishment: s.34(1)	Literary, dramatic or musical works (such performance is not considered to be a public performance)	Performance must be by a teacher or pupil in the course of the activities of the establishment or the performance may be by any person at the establishment for the purposes of instruction. A person is not 'directly connected' simply because he is a parent of a pupil

Table 7.2 cont'd

Permitted act	Types of works covered by permitted act	Comments
Playing or showing before an audience of teachers and pupils at an educational establishment and other persons directly connected with the activities of the establishment for the purposes of instruction: s.34(2)	Sound recording, film, broadcast or cable programme (such playing or showing is not considered to be a playing or showing in public)	A person is not 'directly connected' simply because he is a parent of a pupil
Making a recording by or on behalf of an educational establish- ment or making a copy of such a recording for educational purposes of that establishment: s.35	Broadcast or cable programme and any included work	Does not apply if or to the extent that there is a certified licensing scheme under s.143
Reprographic copying of passages not exceeding 1% of a work in any quarter by or on behalf of an educational establishment for the purposes of instruction: s.36	Published literary, dramatic or musical works including typographical arrangements of such works	Does not apply if or to the extent that licences are available and the person making the copies knew or ought to have been aware of that fact
Libraries and archives		
Librarians of a prescribed library may, if the prescribed conditions are complied with, make and supply: (a) a copy of an article in a periodical: s.38	Literary work (text) and accompanying artistic works (illustrations) including the typo- graphical arrangement	*Prescribed Conditions:* (a) person supplied must satisfy librarian that he requires the copies for his own research or private study (b) not more than 1 copy of periodical article (or copies from more than 1 article in the same issue) is supplied or, with respect to published literary, dramatic or musical works, not more than 1 copy of the same material or a copy of more than a reasonable proportion of any work is supplied ➤
(b) a copy of part of a published edition: s.39	Literary, dramatic or musical works including the typographical arrangement of such works	

Table 7.2 cont'd

Permitted act	Types of works covered by permitted act	Comments
		(c) the person to whom the copies are supplied must pay at least the cost of making and supplying the copies
Librarian of a prescribed library may make and supply to another prescribed library, a copy of: (a) an article in a periodical, or (b) the whole or part of a published edition: s.41	As above, depending on whether a periodical article or a published work is involved	The prescribed conditions above must be complied with. (b) does not apply if the librarian knows or could by reasonable inquiry ascertain the name and address of the person entitled to authorize the making of the copy
Librarian or archivist of a prescribed library or archive may, if the prescribed conditions are complied with, make a copy from any item in the permanent collection of that library or archive (a) in order to preserve or replace the item (b) to replace a lost, destroyed or missing item in the permanent collection of another prescribed library or archive: s.42	Literary, dramatic or musical works plus accompanying illustrations (artistic works) and including the typographical arrangement	Prescribed conditions include restricting the making of such copies to cases when it is not reasonably practicable to purchase a copy of the item to fulfil the purpose
Librarian or archivist of a prescribed library or archive may, if the prescribed conditions are complied with, make and supply a copy of the whole or part of a work from an unpublished document, providing that the copyright owner has not prohibited copying to the actual or constructive knowledge of the person making the copy: s.43	Literary, dramatic or musical works	Prescribed conditions: (a) person supplied must satisfy the librarian or archivist that he requires the copies for research or private study (b) no person is supplied with more than 1 copy of the same material (c) the person to whom the copies are supplied must pay at least the cost of making and supplying the copies

Table 7.2 cont'd

Permitted act	Types of works covered by permitted act	Comments
Making a copy of an article of cultural or historical importance or interest which cannot be exported from the United Kingdom unless a copy is made and deposited in an appropriate library or archive: s.44	Any work	

Public administration

Permitted act	Types of works covered by permitted act	Comments
Anything done for the purposes of parliamentary or judicial proceedings or for the purposes of reporting such proceedings: s.45	Any work	Does not authorize copying a work which is itself a published report of the proceedings
Anything done for the purposes of the proceedings of a Royal Commission or statutory inquiry or for the purpose of reporting such proceedings held in public or issuing to the public copies of the report of a Royal Commission or statutory inquiry: s.46	Any work	Does not authorize copying a work which is itself a published report of the proceedings
Copying material open to public inspection pursuant to a statutory requirement, or on a statutory register, e.g. entries in the Data Protection Register or the Trade Marks Register: s.47	Any work	Does not include issuing copies to the public except when material contains information about matters of general scientific, technical, commercial or economic interest or to enable the material to be inspected at a more convenient time or place. Includes EPO (European Patent Office) and WIPO (World Intellectual Property Organization) materials ➤

Table 7.2 cont'd

Permitted act	Types of works covered by permitted act	Comments
Copying and issuing copies to the public of works which have been communicated to the Crown by or with the licence of the copyright owner and an item containing the work is in the custody or control of the Crown providing the work has not previously been published otherwise. Communication must have been in the course of public business, which includes any activity carried on by the Crown: s.48	Literary, dramatic, musical or artistic works	Applies only as regards the purpose or related purposes for which the work has been communicated.
Copying and supplying a copy of material contained in public records: s.49	Any work	Must be by or with the authority of any officer appointed under the Public Records Act 1958 (for England & Wales)
Acts specifically authorized by an Act of Parliament unless the Act provides otherwise: s.50	Any work	This does not exclude any defence of statutory authority otherwise available under or by any enactment
Computer Programs		
Making back up copy necessary for lawful use: s.50A	Computer program	Must be by a lawful user. A lawful user is a person having a right to use the program (whether under a licence or otherwise)
Decompiling a computer program by a lawful user: s.50B	Computer program	A number of conditions apply, e.g. it must be necessary to decompile to obtain the information necessary to create an independent program that can be operated with the program decompiled or another program

Table 7.2 cont'd

Permitted act	Types of works covered by permitted act	Comments
Copying or adapting by a lawful user: s.50C	Computer program	For example, for the purposes of error correction. Unlike the two permitted acts above, this can be restricted or prohibited by a term in a licence agreement

Designs

Permitted act	Types of works covered by permitted act	Comments
Making an article to a design or copying an article made to that design. The exception extends to issuing to the public, including in a film, broadcast or cable programme such an article or copy: s.51	Design document or model recording or embodying the design for anything other than an artistic work or typeface. A design document could be a drawing, written description, photograph or data stored in a computer	Relates to articles which are in the province of registered designs (though not all) or the the design right
Copying by making articles, doing anything for purpose of making articles and doing anything in relation to articles, 25 years from end of calendar year in which articles first marketed: s.52	Certain artistic works that have been exploited by making articles by an industrial process and marketing the articles in the UK. Films are not 'articles' for s.52. See Copyright (Industrial Processes and Excluded Articles) (No. 2) Order 1989 for meaning of 'exploitation'	Effectively limits copyright in certain types of artistic works (e.g. works of artistic craftsmanship) that are commercially exploited by making articles which will normally be taken to be copies of the artistic work. Marketing means selling, letting for hire or offering or exposing for sale or hire
In respect of a design registration: (a) things done in pursuance of an assignment or licence granted by the proprietor of a corresponding design (b) things done in good faith in reliance of the registration without notice of proceedings for cancellation or rectification of registration: s.53	Artistic work	'Corresponding design' means a design which if applied to an article would be treated as a copy of an artistic work

➤

Table 7.2 cont'd

Permitted act	Types of works covered by permitted act	Comments
Typefaces		
Using a typeface in typing, composing, typesetting or printing; possessing an article for such use; doing anything in relation to material produced by such use: s.54	Artistic work consisting of the design of a typeface	But making, importing, dealing with, possessing articles specifically designed or adapted for producing material in a particular typeface still infringes – see s.54(2)
Copying by making further such articles, etc. after 25 years from the end of the calendar year in which articles for producing material in a typeface have been first marketed: s.55	Artistic work consisting of the design of a typeface	Limits duration of copyright where the design has been commercially exploited anywhere
Works in electronic form		
Transferee of a work in electronic form may do anything purchaser was allowed to do if the terms of the original purchase allowed the purchaser to copy, adapt or copy adaptations and there are no express terms prohibiting transfer or otherwise interfering with the transferee's rights: s.56	Any work in electronic form	Terms of original purchase may be express, implied or by virtue of any rule of law. Copies and adaptations not transferred are treated as infringing copies
Miscellaneous – literary, dramatic, musical and artistic works		
Acts done in relation to works which are anonymous or pseudonymous where it is not possible to trace the author and it is reasonable to assume that copyright no longer subsists in the work: s.57	Literary, dramatic, musical or artistic works	Note: effects of longer duration of copyright, e.g. Crown copyright, on the assumption as to the time since the author died. Special provisions also for works of joint authorship

Table 7.2 cont'd

Permitted act	Types of works covered by permitted act	Comments
Use of a record of spoken words or material from it, copying the record or material taken from it and use of that copy, subject to conditions: s.58	Literary work (recording, in writing or otherwise, of spoken words for purpose of reporting current events or broadcasting or including in a cable programme service)	Conditions: direct records only, making of which is not prohibited by speaker and did not infringe copyright, use made not of a kind prohibited by speaker or copyright owner, use is by or with authority of lawful possessor of record
Public reading or recitation of a reasonable extract and also the making of a sound recording or broadcasting or including in a cable programme service of such a reading or recitation: s.59	Published literary or dramatic work	Must be accompanied by a sufficient acknowledgement
Copy abstracts of scientific or technical subjects published in periodicals or issue copies to the public: s.60	Literary works (abstracts are almost certain to be literary works)	Does not apply if and to the extent that there is a licensing scheme under s.143
Making a sound recording of a performance of a 'folksong' for inclusion in an archive and subsequent supply of copies for research or private study: s.61	Literary works (words) and musical works (accompanying music)	Certain conditions must be met, words unpublished and of unknown authorship, no other copyright is infringed and not prohibited by any performer
Making a graphic work representing it, making a photograph or film of it, broadcasting or including in a cable programme service a visual image of it. Also issuing copies to the public, broadcasting or including in a cable programme service in relation to the above: s.62	Artistic works being buildings and sculptures, models for buildings and works of artistic craftsmanship if permanently sited in a public place or premises open to the public	
Copying and issuing copies to the public advertising the sale of a work: s.63	Artistic works	For example, in an auction catalogue. However, subsequent dealing excepted ➤

Table 7.2 cont'd

Permitted act	Types of works covered by permitted act	Comments
The making of another work by the author, not being the owner of the copyright in the first work, by copying the first work: s.64	Artistic works	Providing the main design of the earlier work is not repeated or imitated
Reconstructing a building: s.65	Artistic works, that is, the building itself and drawings and plans from which building constructed	As regards the drawings and plans, the building was originally constructed in accordance with them by or with the licence of the copyright owner
Miscellaneous – sound recordings, films and computer programs		
Rental to the public of copies of sound recordings, films and computer programs as provided for by compulsory licence ordered by the Secretary of State: s.66	Sound recordings, films and computer programs	Payment of reasonable royalty (to be determined by the Copyright Tribunal in case of dispute)
Rental of copies of computer programs to the public 50 years after copies first issued to the public in electronic form: s.66(5)	Computer programs	Does not prevent liability for secondary infringement in respect of infringing copies
Playing a sound recording as part of the activities of, or for the benefit of, a club, society or other organization, subject to conditions: s.67	Sound recordings	Main objects of organization must be charitable or for advancement of religion, education or social welfare and proceeds applied solely for the purposes of the organization. (Organization not established or conducted for profit)
Miscellaneous – broadcasts and cable programmes		
Incidental recording for the purposes of broadcasting or inclusion in a cable programme service:		Applies where person is authorized to broadcast or include work in a cable programme by virtue of a licence or assignment of copyright.

Table 7.2 cont'd

Permitted act	Types of works covered by permitted act	Comments
(a) making a sound recording or film of the work or an adaptation (b) taking a photograph or making a film (c) making a copy: s.68	(a) Literary, dramatic or musical work or adaptation of such a work (b) Artistic works (c) Sound recording or film	Such recording is treated as if licensed by the copyright owner. Recording, film, photograph or copy must not be used for any other purpose and shall be destroyed within 28 days of being first used
Making or use of recordings, etc. for the purpose of maintaining supervision and control over programmes by the BBC, IBA or Cable Authority: s.69	Any work	IBA purposes – see Broadcasting Act 1981: s.4(7) Cable Authority – see Cable and Broadcasting Act 1984, Part I, ss.16 & 35
Time shifting broadcasts and cable programmes to view or listen to at a more convenient time: s.70	Broadcasts, cable programmes and included works	Only for private and domestic use
Making a photograph of the whole or any part of an image forming part of television broadcast or cable programme or making a copy of such a photograph: s.71	Broadcasts, cable programmes and included films	Only for private and domestic use
Showing or playing in public to a non-paying audience: s.72	Broadcasts, cable programmes and included sound recordings and films	Section 72 gives guidance as to when an audience has or has not paid admission
Reception of broadcast and immediate retransmission in a cable programme service: s.73	Broadcasts and included works	Only if done under s.13(1) of the Cable and Broadcasting Act 1984 or if broadcast made for reception in area in which cable programme service provided and (broadcast only) not a satellite transmission or encrypted transmission

➤

Table 7.2 cont'd

Permitted act	Types of works covered by permitted act	Comments
Make copies of television broadcasts and cable programmes, issue copies to public if a designated body for purpose of providing people who are deaf, hard of hearing, physically or mentally handicapped in other ways with copies subtitled or modified for their special needs: s.74	Broadcasts, cable programmes and included works	But not if there is a licensing scheme under s.143
Recording and making a copy of such recording for placing in an archive: s.75	Broadcasts, cable programmes and included works	Only with respect to designated classes and only for designated archives
Adaptations		
Any of all of the above acts in respect of an adaptation: s.76	Literary, dramatic or musical works	Does not infringe copyright in the work from which the adaptation was made

8

New technology and copyright[1]

INTRODUCTION

1 For definitions relating to computer technology see the Glossary at the beginning of the book.

Copyright law has a history of change and development that can be partly explained by reference to technological change. Examples of advances in science that have in the past been addressed by copyright law include photography, sound recordings, films and broadcasting. The Copyright, Designs and Patents Act 1988[2] is an attempt to keep abreast of developments in technology coupled with an intention to enact legislation that would take future change in its stride. The phrase 'new technology' conjures up thoughts of computer technology and it is to this exciting and important area that a large part of this chapter is devoted. However, new technology is not restricted to computer systems and other technical advances have been made that need to be examined in the light of copyright law. Two points are worth mentioning at this stage; first, computer technology is not new – universal programmable computing machines have existed for approximately 45 years; secondly, the vast majority of new technical developments involve computer technology even if the developments themselves do not appear at first sight to be connected with such technology. Modern photocopiers, facsimile transmission machines, electronic mail, draughting and design tools, even the humble automatic washing machine, all owe something to computer science.

2 Unless otherwise stated, in this chapter statutory references are to this Act.

'Computer software' is a phrase that, like many phrases in the computer industry, is incapable of precise definition but it is usually taken to include computer programs, databases, preparatory material and associated documentation such as manuals for users of the programs and for persons who have to maintain the programs. Computer programs are considered in detail in this chapter in terms of the extent and scope of copyright protection for them and for the effects that they produce.[3] Particular issues are the 'look and feel' of computer programs in the context of non-literal copying, the decompilation of computer programs, back-up copies and copying and adapting computer programs in manners consistent with their lawful use. After looking at computer programs, the position of databases and other information stored in computer systems and computer-generated works is discussed. Broadcasts and cable programmes are then examined. Following this, the problems stemming from other forms of technology such as photocopying, facsimile transmission and electronic mail are considered. Finally, the growing anxiety over format rights or, more correctly, the lack of them will be discussed.

3 See Chapter 14 for the position of computer programs in patent law.

COPYRIGHT PROTECTION FOR COMPUTER PROGRAMS

Background

It has already been seen that copyright subsists in computer programs as a form of literary work by section 3(1)(b) of the Copyright, Designs and Patents Act

1988.[4] The same prerequisites of originality and qualification must be present as with other forms of literary works for a computer program (or preparatory design material for a computer program) to be the subject matter of copyright. At one time it was not at all clear whether computer programs were protected by copyright. The Copyright Act 1956 made no mention of computers or computer programs. Although at the time that Act was passed computers had been around for a few years, unauthorized copying of computer programs had not become a serious problem. There were only a small number of computers in existence and they were expensive and costly to operate and maintain, and there was no black market in application programs.[5] Many such application programs were specially written and maintained by the staff of computer departments for an organization's own particular needs and would probably have been unsuitable for use by others. However, in spite of the omission of computer programs from the 1956 Act, many writers considered that they were protected as literary works. For example, Laddie et al. suggested that:

> . . . a computer program expressed in writing or other notation on a piece of paper is a 'literary work' within the meaning of [section 2 of the 1956 Act] . . . and if produced as a result of substantial independent skill or useful labour will be 'original' and so qualify for copyright protection.[6]

The issue may have been fairly straightforward and uncontroversial in the case of computer programs that had been printed out, that is listed on paper. After all, if copyright had been extended to books of telegraphic codes as early as 1884, why should copyright be refused for computer programs printed out on paper?[7] However, if this view was accepted, it did not give any assistance in terms of computer programs that were stored in a computer, especially if those programs were in object code form having been compiled from source code programs.[8] A committee, known as the Whitford Committee after its chairman Whitford J, was set up to examine copyright law generally and its report was published in 1977 at a time when the problems of unauthorized copying of computer programs were beginning to be perceived.[9] The report recognized that copyright law was unsatisfactory as regards computer programs and the committee made recommendations to improve the law in this area and to put it beyond doubt that computer programs and works produced with the aid of a computer were protected by copyright. A Green Paper was published in 1981 covering copyright and related matters and included recommendations that copyright law be amended to expressly afford protection for computer programs.[10]

Copyright law remained unchanged after the Whiftford Committee report and during the first few years of the 1980s the problem of computer software piracy[11] became a major concern for the computer industry with the loss attributable to piracy being estimated at some £150 million.[12] There were a handful of interlocutory actions brought alleging infringement of copyright subsisting in computer programs; these actions invariably proceeded on the basis that computer programs were protected by copyright and interlocutory relief was invariably granted. For example, in *Sega Enterprises Ltd.* v *Richards,*[13] the plaintiff owned a computer game called 'FROGGER' which was effected by means of computer programs. The defendant produced a similar program, admitting that his was based on the plaintiff's program. The defendant argued that he had

4 Preparatory design material for a computer program is also a form of literary work, section 3(1)(c).

5 Application programs are designed to perform a specific task such as processing data, producing reports, word processing, etc. They can be distinguished from operating system programs which supply the basic working environment in which the application programs operate.

6 Laddie, H., Prescott, P. and Vittoria, M. *The Modern Law of Copyright* (London, Butterworths, 1st edn. 1980) at p.93.

7 For example, in *Ager* v *Peninsular & Oriental Steam Navigation Co.* (1884) 26 Ch D 627, a book of telegraphic codes was recognized as being suitable subject-matter for literary copyright. See also, *D P Anderson & Co. Ltd.* v *Lieber Code Co.* [1917] 2 KB 469 on the same point.

8 A source code program may be written in a computer programming language, such as COBOL or BASIC, which is fairly easy for computer programmers to understand and write programs in. This source code version will usually be written down on paper or printed out. The source code will then be converted into the language of the computer, that is compiled into object code so that it can run on the computer. The object code will, if printed out in that form, be an apparently meaningless collection of numbers and letters representing binary code.

9 *Copyright – Copyright and Design Law*, Cmnd 6732 (London: HMSO, 1977).

10 *Reform of the Law Relating to Copyright, Designs and Performers' Protection* Cmnd 8302 (London: HMSO, 1981) cl.2.

11 The unauthorized copying and selling of computer programs including, in some cases, documentation. The United States of America was the first country to enact specific legislation directed towards the copyright protection of computer programs, Computer Software Copyright Act 1980, 17 USC §§101, 117.

12 The estimate was produced in 1984 by the Federation Against Software Theft (FAST). A more recent estimate, for the United Kingdom alone, is £300 million, Snell, T. 'Pirates run aground as UK fights IT crime', *Computing*, 21 January 1993 at p.13.

13 [1983] FSR 73. See also, *Gates v Swift* [1982] RPC 339, *Thrustcode Ltd. v W W Computing Ltd.* [1983] FSR 502 and *Apple Computer Inc. v Sirtel (UK) Ltd.* (unreported) 27 July 1983.

14 [1984] FSR 246.

15 A ROM chip is a read only memory integrated circuit which contains, typically, operating system programs. The defendant attacked the copyright in the Apple II programs after it was shown that the names of some of the programmers of the Apple II computer were present in the equivalent programs in the defendant's computer. This raised an almost irrefutable presumption of copying.

16 [1894] 3 Ch. 420. For another recent case in which *Hollinrake v Truswell* was approved, see *Exxon Corporation v Exxon Insurance Consultants International Ltd.* [1981] 3 All ER 241.

17 [1984] FSR 481.

18 HC Deb, 19 April 1985 at c.558.

19 Cmnd 9712 (London: HMSO, 1986).

done much work on the program and that, in any case, copyright did not subsist in computer programs under English law. Goulding J said:

> . . . I am clearly of the opinion that copyright . . . subsists in the assembly code program of the game 'FROGGER'.

He went on to say that the object code derived from the assembly code program (source code) was either a reproduction or an adaptation of the assembly code version and, as a result, also protected by copyright. However, these cases were interlocutory hearings only. Not a single case concerning the issue of the subsistence of copyright in computer programs went to full trial and the computer industry remained nervous.

The industry's fears appeared to be justified when, in 1984, the large and successful Apple Computer Corporation sued in Australia an importer of 'clones' of its computers. Appropriately enough, the clones were called 'WOMBATS'. At first instance, in *Apple Computer Inc. v Computer Edge Pty. Ltd.*[14] it was held that literary copyright did not subsist in the computer programs in question, being the object code programs in the ROM chips in the Apple II computer.[15] A great deal of reliance was placed by the judge on the old English case of *Hollinrake v Truswell*[16] in which Davey LJ said that a literary work is one intended to 'afford either information and instruction, or pleasure, in the form of literary enjoyment'. Although the appeal by the plaintiffs to the Federal Court of Australia was allowed, reversing the decision at first instance, on the basis that the object code programs were adaptations of the source code programs, the dissenting judgment by Shepherd J was the most elegant and well argued.[17] He said that an adaptation of a literary work should be capable of being seen or heard. To put the matter beyond doubt, the Australian Parliament very quickly enacted the Australian Copyright Amendment Act 1984.

The Apple case had serious repercussions for the United Kingdom as Australian copyright law was, at the time, very similar to United Kingdom law. Whilst in the United States of America, the issue was the scope of the protection offered by copyright, in the United Kingdom doubts about whether copyright could subsist in a computer program whatever its form increased. Eventually, after vociferous outbursts by a worried but powerful industry, amending legislation was passed in the United Kingdom but only by way of a Private Member's Bill. The Copyright (Computer Software) Amendment Act 1985 made it quite clear that computer programs were protected by copyright as literary works. When it was passed, this piece of legislation was seen as being a temporary measure and did not directly deal with some of the copyright issues related to computer technology such as the ownership of works produced by or with the aid of a programmed computer.[18] One reason for the brevity and lack of consideration given to the amending legislation was that a wholesale review of copyright and design law was contemplated. That review took place and culminated in the White Paper *Intellectual Property and Innovation*, published in 1986.[19] Many of the recommendations contained in the White Paper found their way into the Copyright, Designs and Patents Act 1988 and it is to this Act and its implications that we will now turn.

COMPUTER PROGRAMS – BASIC POSITION

The Copyright, Designs and Patents Act 1988 does not attempt to define 'computer program'.[20] This is probably sensible and, at least, allows the courts to develop the meaning of the phrase in the light of future technological change. It may, sometimes, be difficult to distinguish between 'hardware' and 'software' such as where a computer program is permanently hard-wired in a microprocessor in the form of 'microcode' or 'microprograms'. The view in the United States is that such programs or codes still fall within the meaning of 'computer program' for the purpose of copyright law. In *NEC Corp.* v *Intel Corp.*[21] it was held that, even though the computer programs were permanently stored in 'read only memory' (ROM), the programs were still copyrightable and the mode of storage did not change the nature of a computer program. In a later hearing between the parties in 1989,[22] an argument that the microcode embedded within a microprocessor was a defining element of a computer and could not, therefore, also be a computer program failed to find sympathy. In the United Kingdom, it is almost certain that microcode will be considered to be a computer program and will be protected by copyright.

The Copyright, Designs and Patents Act 1988 does not elaborate upon the meaning of originality in respect of computer programs. However, the European Community Directive on the legal protection of computer programs[23] describes originality in terms of a program being the author's own intellectual creation.[24] This approximates with the requirement under German copyright law that a work be the author's personal intellectual creation.[25] and appears to be more stringent than the United Kingdom's test based on originating from the author. It has been rigorously applied in Germany in the past and in *Sudwestdeutsche Inkasso KG* v *Bappert und Burker Computer GmbH*[26] it was held that, to be protected by copyright, a computer program must result from individual creative achievement exceeding the average skills displayed in the development of computer programs.[27] However, this case can be seen as an anomaly and, whichever standard is applied, the vast majority of computer programs will attract copyright protection.

The two most important acts restricted by copyright in relation to computer programs are those of copying and making an adaptation. Other acts may be relevant in the context of a computer program such as issuing to the public and the secondary infringements, but it is copying and making adaptations that are of particular interest as regards the scope of protection afforded by copyright. Following the uncertainty as to the copyright protection of computer programs which was finally put to rest by the Copyright (Computer Software) Amendment Act 1985, it is possible that the pendulum has swung too far in the other direction and the extent of the protection now offered by copyright may be too extensive. As a result, innovation and competition within the computer software industry could be unjustifiably inhibited. The problem of finding a balance between conflicting interests has taxed even the European Communities in its search for a balanced Directive on copyright protection for computer programs.[28]

Just as with any other literary work, the copyright in a computer program is infringed if someone makes a copy of the computer program or a substantial part of it.[29] Substantiality is an issue of quality and, therefore, the copyright

---

20 Nor is 'computer' defined.

21 645 F Supp 1485 (D Minn 1985).

22 *NEC Corp.* v *Intel Corp.* (1989) 10 USPQ 2d.

23 OJ [1991] L122/42.

24 Article 1(3).

25 German Copyright Act 1965, section 2(2).

26 (1985) Case 52/83, BGHZ 94, 276.

27 For the background to the Directive, see Wilkinson, A. 'Software Protection, Trade, and Industrial Policies in the European Community' in Lehmann, M. & Tapper, C.F. *A Handbook of European Software Law*, (Oxford: Clarendon Press, 1993) pp.25–38 at pp.28–29.

28 After a great deal of lobbying, the Directive was issued on 15 May 1991: OJ [1991] L122/42.

29 Section 16. In *M S Associates Ltd.* v *Power* [1988] FSR 242, there was an arguable case that a substantial part of the original program had been copied. The second program had 43 line similarities out of a total of 9,000 lines, although there were structural similarities and the same errors were present in both programs.

subsisting in a computer program can be infringed if the 'essence' of the program is copied, even if the part copied is relatively small quantitatively. A difficulty faced by plaintiffs alleging copying of parts of their programs is demonstrating that a substantial part has been taken because of the judge's lack of technical knowledge. In *Total Information Processing Systems Ltd.* v *Daman Ltd.*[30] Paul Baker J considered that the data division of a COBOL program did not represent a substantial part of the program because it did not itself produce executable code nor did it tell anything about the program. The data division in a COBOL program defines the nature and structure of files used by the program and also defines variables used. To many programmers, the data division is considered to be an important and essential part of the program and should certainly be considered to be worthy of protection, at the very least, as a non-literal element of the program. Paul Baker J's judgment is flawed in other respects, for example he said that the considerable steps taken to preserve confidentiality of the file details were suggestive that copyright did not subsist in that element of the program. In many respects, this decision has been overtaken by later events, particularly in terms of non-literal copying, discussed later. In any case, it should be contrasted with *Autodesk Inc.* v *Dyason*[31] which concerned the copying of a hardware device (a 'lock') without which a particular program (AutoCAD) would not run. It was accepted that copying a table of codes contained in the program in the lock infringed copyright. The table was a substantial part of the program in the lock which was a substantial part of the AutoCAD program.

In relation to literary works, 'copying' is defined by section 17 as a reproduction in any material form; this includes storage in any medium by electronic means and making copies which are transient or incidental to some other use of the work. Because of the wide definition of 'electronic' in section 178 there should not be any difficulties concerning existing and future media in or on which a computer program is stored. Copyright has a long duration and, for computer programs, copyright protection subsists until the end of the period of 50 years from the end of the calendar year in which the author dies, or in the case of a computer-generated program, 50 years from the end of the calendar year in which the program was made.[32] This can only be reconciled with the interests of the public at large by limiting the strength of protection. Therefore, generally, other persons can create works similar to existing works providing they do so independently by their own efforts without performing any of the acts restricted by copyright. By implication the actual idea behind a work is not protected by copyright law and a well established principle is that copyright protects the expression of an idea but not the idea itself.[33]

Preparatory design material

The finished code of a computer program is the culmination of a long process involving the creation of a number of preparatory (and intermediate) works. For example, the analysts and programmers working on the development of a new program will usually produce specifications, flowcharts, diagrams, layouts for menus, screen displays and reports and other materials. Prior to the amendments made to the Act by the Copyright (Computer Programs) Regulations 1992 in compliance with the computer program Directive, all these materials

30 [1992] FSR 171.

31 [1992] RPC 575.

32 The European Commission's proposal for a Council Directive on the legal protection of computer programs suggested a term of protection of 50 years from the date of creation, OJ [1989] C91/05, Article 7. However, the Directive as adopted corresponds with the present United Kingdom measures, OJ [1991] L122/42, Article 8.

33 For a discussion of the utility and difficulties associated with this principle, see Pessa, P. 'Evaluating the idea-expression dichotomy: rhetoric or a legal principle', *Computer Law & Practice* (1991) March/April pp. 166–172.

would have been protected in their own right as literary or artistic works as appropriate. In *Japan Capsules Computers (UK) Ltd.* v *Sonic Game Sales*[34] Whitford J accepted that these and other ancillary materials such as music generated by a program could be protected by copyright.[35]

The separate protection of preparatory design material as a literary work by section 3(1)(c) conflicts with the wording of the Directive which states that the term 'computer programs' shall *include* their preparatory design material.[36] In practice, this should not be troublesome though it does mean that the special exceptions for computer programs (sections 50A to 50C) do not apply to preparatory design material. For example, it is not permissible to make a back-up copy of a computer manual unless the other permitted acts generally available for literary works allow this. Why the 1992 Regulations chose to treat preparatory design material separately is inexplicable and unforgivable given that certainty and predictability is so important to the computer industry.[37] Preparatory design material will include works that would previously have been considered to be artistic works such as flowcharts and other diagrams. These are now literary works notwithstanding the resulting implications. For example, there is no requirement for an artistic work to be recorded and infringement and the permitted acts are not precisely the same for literary and artistic works.

DEVELOPMENTS IN THE UNITED STATES

The idea/expression dichotomy is even more ingrained in United States copyright law going back at least to *Baker* v *Selden*[38] where it was held that copyright subsisting in a book describing a method of book-keeping did not extend to protect the method so described and illustrated. If copyright protects expression but not idea, it is obviously important for a court to be able to distinguish between them. If parts of a computer program have been copied, the court must be able to apply a test to determine whether those parts are idea or expression. This issue was considered in the case of *Whelan Associates Inc.* v *Jaslow Dental Laboratory Inc.*,[39] the first so-called 'look and feel' case. It was said that, in relation to a computer program designed to carry out a mundane task (running dental laboratories in that case), anything that was essential to the task was idea whilst anything that was not essential and could have been written in different ways was expression. If these latter parts were copied, then the copyright would be infringed because the expression had been copied. If the programmer had no option but to write a part of the program the way he did because the task to be achieved dictated its form and content then that part was idea and not protected by copyright. Similarly, the purpose of a utilitarian program was idea and the structure of the program, if there were several different possible structures that could have been adopted, was expression. Consequently, not just the actual program code but the structure of a computer program can be protected by copyright if, because of similar structure, the 'look and feel' of the programs are similar.

Whelan has been considered in several later cases. In *Plains Cotton Co-operative* v *Goodpasture Computer Service*,[40] an apparent rejection of the *Whelan* case can be explained by concluding that the structure of the plaintiff's program was idea and not expression because the application itself dictated the structure

34 (unreported) 16 October 1966, Chancery Division

35 For a detailed discussion of this see the 1st edn. of this book, 1992, pp. 172–177.

36 Article 1(1).

37 See Chalton, S. 'Implementation of the Software Directive in the United Kingdom: The Effects of the Copyright (Computer Programs) Regulations 1992', [1993] 9 CLSR 115.

38 101 US 99 (1880).

39 [1987] FSR 1.

40 807 F 2d 1256 (5th Cir 1987).

41 For an argument that *Plains Cotton* is not inconsistent with *Whelan,* see Taylor, W. D. 'Copyright Protection for Computer Software after *Whelan Associates v Jaslow Dental Laboratory*', (1989) 54 *Missouri Law Review* 121.

42 648 F Supp 1127 (ND Cal 1986).

43 The argument by the defendant that there was no other way to structure the screens or design the input formats was quickly overcome by the plaintiff who produced another competing program which performed a similar function (to design greetings cards, signs, banners and posters) but which had screen displays and screen sequences that were very different. Taylor, W.D., op. cit. at 151.

44 659 F Supp 449 (ND Ga 1987).

45 Some commentators argue for strong copyright protection of screen displays subject to a higher standard of originality. See Benson, J. R. 'Copyright Protection for Computer Screen Displays', (1988) 72 *Minnesota Law Review* 1123.

46 740 F Supp 37 (D Mass 1990).

47 A 'macro' is a list of commands that are stored in a separate executable file. The purpose usually is to save time. For example, the user might want to combine several spreadsheets, total them, find the average and change the display format and, rather than having to enter a whole series of commands each time he wants to do this, he can store the instructions in a macro which he can call up and execute in the future at a keystroke. The command language of VP-Planner would have to be the same as that in Lotus 1-2-3 for macros to be compatible.

48 At the beginning of 1991, in the United Kingdom, Lotus 1-2-3 was available at around £200–£300 (depending on the version) whilst VP-Planner was available (for educational use only) at around £8. It must be noted that this version of VP-Planner had a limited overall spreadsheet size compared to Lotus 1-2-3.

of the program. The program's application was to assist in the marketing of cotton and this, by its very nature, could only be expressed in computer programs exhibiting a substantially similar structure; it left no room for alternative structures.[41] Other cases have dealt with screen displays. In *Broderbund Software v Unison World,*[42] the court held that, as there were several means in which the screens could have been structured, sequenced and arranged, the actual way selected by the plaintiff was copyrightable expression.[43] The court also appears to have confirmed that copying the format, structure and sequence of screen displays infringes the copyright in the underlying programs. However, in *Digital Communications Associates v Softklone Distributing Corp.*[44] this view was rejected on the basis that a screen display cannot be a copy of part of the program because the same screen display can be produced by various programs in different ways. Nevertheless, the court did afford protection to the screen display in its own right, and differentiated between idea and expression by regarding the idea of a screen display as being the concept of the screen whereas the means used to communicate the screen's manner of operation, that is, the arrangement of terms, highlighting and capitalization, was the expression of the screen display.[45]

Spreadsheets

A spreadsheet program is, in essence, one which comprises a grid of cells (usually two-dimensional but three-dimensional grids now exist) into which the user can enter text, numbers and/or formulae. A spreadsheet is useful for preparing an easily updated table of calculations from which graphs and barcharts can be derived. Litigation in the United States of America concerning spreadsheet programs demonstrates the strength of copyright protection for computer programs. In *Lotus Development Corp. v Paperback Software International*[46] the defendant had developed a spreadsheet program called VP-Planner. The defendant had realized that, because of the success of the plaintiff's Lotus 1-2-3 spreadsheet program, it was desirable that VP-Planner was compatible with Lotus 1-2-3. To this end, the defendant ensured that the arrangement of commands and menus in VP-Planner conformed to those in Lotus 1-2-3 and this meant that it was possible to transfer spreadsheets from VP-Planner to Lotus 1-2-3 without losing the functionality of any macros in the spreadsheet.[47] Another reason for compatibility and similarity in screen displays and command language was that Lotus 1-2-3 users could transfer to VP-Planner without the need for any further training. When the difference in cost between the two spreadsheets is considered, it is not surprising that Lotus sued the owners of VP-Planner.[48] The defendant claimed that he had not copied the program code of Lotus 1-2-3, so this was a case of 'non-literal copying'. The central issues, therefore, were whether the non-literal elements of the plaintiff's program were protected by copyright, that is the overall organization of the program (structure), the structure of the command system, the screen displays and, especially, the user interface.

In a mammoth judgment in the District Court for Massachusetts, Judge Keeton held that the user interface of Lotus 1-2-3, in particular the two-line moving cursor menu, was protected by copyright and that the defendant had infringed that copyright. The menu command system was said to be copy-

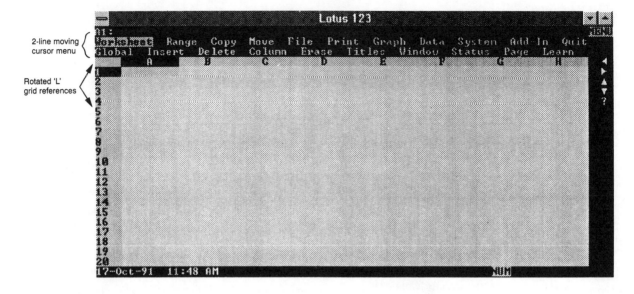

Figure 8.1 Basic screen display for Lotus 1-2-3
(Reproduced with the permission of the Lotus Development Corporation)

rightable because it was effected in different ways in different spreadsheet programs. For example, some use a list of letters (Visicalc uses 'BCDEFGIM-PRSTVW-'), others use a three-line menu or pull down menus. The two-line moving cursor menu used by Lotus 1-2-3 was said to be original and non-obvious and, thus, protected by copyright. Other features such as the rotated 'L' used to contain the grid reference letters and numbers and the use of certain keys to call up commands and perform arithmetical functions, for example the '/', '+', '–' and '*' keys were held not to be protected because they were common to spreadsheets, even though they were not essential (the Excel spreadsheet does not use the rotated 'L').

Judge Keeton went on to lay down some rules for testing for copyrightability. He said that, whilst ideas are not protected and expression is, it does not automatically follow that every expression of an idea is protected by copyright. Four things must be considered:

(a) **Originality** – the expression must be original.
(b) **Functionality** – if the expression does no more than embody elements of an idea which is functional in a utilitarian sense, the expression is not copyrightable.
(c) **Obviousness** – if the expression is obvious it is inseparable from the idea and hence not protected by copyright.
(d) **Merger** – if the particular expression is one of a quite limited number of forms of expression, then it is not copyrightable.

It was accepted that disentangling idea from expression was not an 'either–or' or 'black and white' matter but is a matter of degree and a distinction must be made between the generality and specificity of conceptualizing an idea. A legal test for copyrightability was suggested based on constructing a scale of abstraction from the most generalized conception at one end to the most particularized conception at the other end. The expression being considered was placed on this scale and a decision made based on choice and judgment but earlier judgments by Judge Learned Hand had suggested that this could only be done in an *ad hoc* way.[49] It can be seen from the four points above and the scale of abstraction that the distinction between idea and expression is never going to be clear cut. Even the merger doctrine can be applicable if there exists more than one way of expressing the idea, although the greater the number of possible ways the greater the emphasis on expression rather than idea. However, it is respectfully submitted that the tests laid down in the *Lotus* case will do little to assist a judge in determining whether there has been an infringement of a copyrightable element of a program. Conversely, those tests will do a great deal to confuse and contribute to the uncertainty of litigation in this area.

The *ratio decidendi* in the spreadsheet case is not limited to such programs and applies to all forms of computer programs. It leaves the developer of a new computer program that will perform a similar function to, or compete with, an existing program with some difficult decisions. The compatibility of files created by different programs is of vital importance. Users of computer programs want and expect to be able to transfer information from one program to another. For example, a person may use a spreadsheet program to construct a table of figures and calculations and then want to incorporate that table in a word processed document. Another example is where a person wishes to convert entries in a computer database into a form in which they can be accessed by a word processing program or vice versa. Producers of computer programs usually build in conversion procedures allowing the import and export of data to and from the most popular programs available. The chances of success of a new word processing package, spreadsheet or database will be greatly enhanced if it can match the compatibility and interchangeability of the market leaders and the only way it can do so is if the 'interface details' are the same as the leading products. Interface details include things such as the structure of data files produced by the program, command and macro languages and embedded format and control characters. However, if the person writing the new program copies such details from an existing program, in the United States he is likely to find himself defending a court action, although he may be able to plead fair use. In *Sega Enterprises Ltd.* v *Accolade Inc.*[50] the fair use defence was available to excuse the decompilation, not only of the whole of one program, but of a whole range of computer games cartridges, in order to find the 'key' (the interface – that part of the program that must be present before the program can be used with the games console). The plaintiff was not even allowed to rely on his trade mark, embedded in the interface, to prevent the defendant making games cartridges compatible with the plaintiff's games console. But for the fair use defence, owners of copyright subsisting in computer programs in the United States of America, would have a right that appears to only just stop short of a monopoly.

A new test for non-literal copying

Whelan and subsequent cases can be explained by the need to deal with non-literal copying of computer programs, where the first program has been unfairly

49 For example, *Shipman* v *RKO Radio Pictures* 100 F 2d 533 (2d Cir 1938).

50 (1992) 977 F 2d 1510.

used as a basis for a second program but there is no literal similarity in the actual program code because different programming languages have been used. Non-literal copying is not a problem restricted to computer programs and there have been a number of cases involving plays. In *Nichols* v *Universal Pictures Co.*[51] Judge Learned Hand said (at 121):

> It is of course essential to any protection of literary property . . . that the right cannot be limited literally to the text, else a plagiarist would escape by immaterial variations.

He goes on to discuss the various levels of abstraction from the text to the most general statement of the play (possibly its title only) and the difficulty in determining where, along this spectrum of abstractions, the boundary between copyright and non-copyright material lay. Somewhat discouragingly, he then said 'Nobody has ever been able to fix that boundary and nobody ever can'. In other words, it must depend on the facts of each individual case.

Although the *Whelan* test proved troublesome to apply in practice it has been replaced by a new look and feel test that does nothing to aid predictability. The New York Court of Appeals strongly criticized *Whelan* in *Computer Associates International Inc.* v *Altai Inc.*[52] as taking insufficient account of computer technology. In *Computer Associates*, the defendant had produced a program known as 'Oscar', a job scheduling program for controlling the order in which tasks were carried out by a computer. It had a common interface component allowing the use of different operating systems and this part had been added by a former employee of the plaintiff which had a similar program and interface. The former employee was very familiar with the plaintiff's program and had even taken parts home to work on. As soon as the defendant company realized the problem, it agreed to pay $364,444 in damages and engaged other programmers to re-write the infringing parts of its program. The plaintiff still sued in respect of the defendant's new version but the judge held there was no infringement. The judgment of the court was given by Judge Walker who laid down a new three-stage test for non-literal copying as follows and as shown in Figure 8.2:

(a) **abstraction** – discovering the non-literal elements by a process akin to reverse engineering beginning with the code of the plaintiff's program and ending with its ultimate function. This process retraces and maps out the designer's steps and produces, *inter alia*, structures of differing detail at varying levels of abstraction;

(b) **filtration** – the separation of protectable expression from non-protectable expression material. Some elements will not be protected being ideas, dictated by or incidental to ideas, required by external factors (*scènes a faire* doctrine) or taken from the public domain. These elements are filtered out leaving a core of protectable material – the program's 'golden nugget';

(c) **Comparison** – a determination of whether the defendant has copied a substantial part of the protected expression – whether any aspect has been copied and, if so, whether this represents a substantial part of the plaintiff's program.

The judge recognized that the test will be difficult to apply but expressed the hope that it would become less so with further case law. At first sight, it seems to significantly weaken copyright protection for computer programs. Many

51 45 F.2d 119 (2nd Cir. 1930).

52 (1992) 20 USPQ 2d 1641.

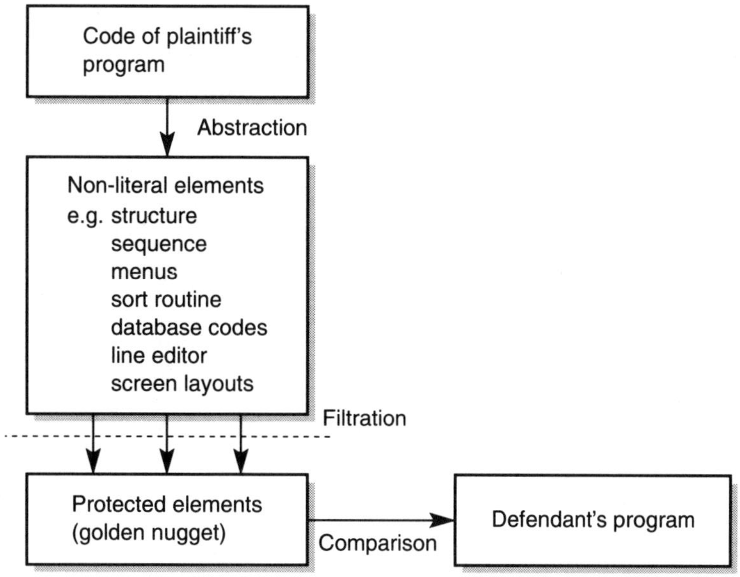

Figure 8.2 Test for non-literal copying

53 (1989) 10 USPQ 2d.

54 This should be compared to the Australian case of *Autodesk Inc. v Dyason* (unreported) Federal Court of Australia, August 7, 1989, in which the reverse analysis of a computer lock (a hardware device, sometimes called a 'dongle', which must be plugged into the computer before a particular computer program can be used) was held to infringe copyright in the computer program contained within the lock. See Goldblatt, M., 'Copyright Protection for Computer Programs in Australia: the Law since Autodesk', [1990] 5 EIPR 170. On appeal, the Autodesk decision was reversed, see Anon. 'Appellate Court gives Green Light to Reverse Engineering', (1991) 2 *Intellectual Property in Business Briefing* 3. However, finally in *Autodesk Inc. v Dyason* [1992] RPC 575 the High Court of Australia reinstated the decision at first instance.

55 [1993] FSR 497.

programs contain parts taken from the public domain (such as commonly used routines to extract data from files, to perform complex arithmetical operations or to sort data into alphabetical order) and other parts will be significantly constrained by ideas or external factors. It would appear that, in some cases, there will be no golden nuggets left after filtration. The plaintiff's gold prospecting will result in bitter disappointment!

Merger of idea/expression

There may be occasions when it is impossible to separate idea from expression because of the constraints which severely limit the ways in which the ideas contained in a computer program can be expressed. In *NEC Corp.* v *Intel Corp.*,[53] such merger of idea and expression was said not to affect the copyright status of a computer program but was an issue of infringement. Even though Intel's microcode programs were declared to be copyrightable material in principle, this case reinforces the look and feel approach in its practical effect because, as Intel's programs were dictated by the instruction set of the microprocessors involved and because there were no alternative ways of expressing the ideas, reverse analysis of the programs did not infringe copyright.[54]

THE UNITED KINGDOM POSITION

Look and feel

John Richardson Computers Ltd. v *Flanders*[55] is the first English case to fully address the look and feel of computer programs and is exceptional in that the test used in the United States for non-literal copying was expressly approved and applied by Ferris J in a comprehensive judgment. Both parties were in the business of developing and marketing computer programs to be used by pharmacists for the purpose of producing labels for prescriptions and for stock control. The judge found the facts of the case difficult to determine (there were a number of disputed points) and the case provides a good example of the need to document the development of copyright works carefully and to make suitable arrangements for ownership.[56]

Mr Richardson, the chairman and managing director of the plaintiff company, who was a pharmacist and self-taught computer programmer, developed a program written in BASIC to produce labels suitable for the Tandy computer. He was not an expert at writing programs and he therefore engaged a self-employed programmer to help complete the program and make it more reliable. In 1983, Mr Flanders joined the plaintiff company as an employee to write an equivalent program in machine code that would have the same look and feel as the original program for the BBC computer. In 1986, Mr Flanders left the employment of the plaintiff company but did further work for it in the capacity of self-employed consultant during which time he re-wrote the program in assembly language, a low-level language, adding some new features. Later, Mr Flanders wrote a new version of the program (in the QuickBASIC language) for the IBM personal computer. The plaintiff was also working on a version for the IBM computer and sued for infringement of its copyright in the BBC version of the program and for breach of confidence.[57]

Ferris J held that there was a limited infringement of the copyright subsisting in the plaintiff's program based on the non-literal elements of the program. A literal comparison was not helpful as the programs had been written in different languages and bore no literal similarity. The judge considered non-literal elements, such as structure and sequence of the plaintiff's program, its input and output routines, menus, formats, facilities and options. He identified 17 objective similarities in the non-literal elements and then went on to consider the reasons for the similarities. The similarities and the reasons for them were classified as follows:

1. Similarities that were the result of copying a substantial part of the plaintiff's program, being the line editor, amendment routines and dose codes. It was in respect of these parts that copyright infringement was found.
2. Similarities that were the result of copying but not in relation to a substantial part of the plaintiff's program. These were the date option, daily figures reset, operation successful message plus double bleep, data entry by quantity first, 4 out of 8 of the pre-printing options and best day's stock control.
3. Similarities that *might* have been the result of copying but, in any case, only related to an insubstantial part of the plaintiff's program. These were the vertical arrangement of prompts and entries and the entry of data within the label routine.
4. Similarities that were not the result of copying, being the date entry, use of the escape key, position of label on screen, drug entry routine, secondary access to the full list of drugs on screen and label entry sequence.

The line editor, amendment routines and dose codes were deemed to have been copied and to represent a substantial part of the plaintiff's program. This approach affects the test of substantiality which has long been accepted as being a question of quality not quantity.[58] As adopted by Ferris J, it implies that rel-

56 The defendant may have been the legal owner of the copyright in parts of the program. The plaintiff was the owner in equity of that copyright and the difficulty beneficial owners can experience in obtaining remedies was overcome here because the legal owner was joined in the action – as defendant.

57 The breach of confidence claim was dropped.

58 *Ladbroke (Football) Ltd.* v *William Hill (Football) Ltd.* [1964] 1 WLR 273.

atively small elements of a program could be used in the comparison process. The manner of Ferris J's application of the test from *Computer Associates* can be criticized because he did not carry out the second stage. He did not filter out those elements that might have been unprotected such as ideas or public domain routines. It should be noted that the programs in this case were by no means exceptional. They performed relatively simple functions. Additionally, both programs made substantial use of what might be termed public domain materials or, at least, techniques and methods commonly used by programmers. For example, there are a limited number of ways that can be used to correct mistakes using a line editor and these are dictated to some extent by the programming language used and other features relating to the type of computer used and its operating system. It is common for standard routines to perform commonly required operations like line editing to be published in textbooks, computer journals and magazines. Even if a line editor could be considered to be protectable expression, there is no doubt that, in terms of the program's function, it could never be said to form a substantial part of the program. Nevertheless, that is what the judge found.

The consideration of a program as a collection of disparate and relatively small and discrete non-literal elements could make it very difficult for ex-employees to write computer programs that perform functions similar to those performed by programs they have written for their previous employers. In this respect, copyright could now become so strong that it operates as a form of restraint of trade. It is also out of step with the law of breach of confidence which is relatively benign as regards mundane information and which generally will permit an employee to make use of what he remembers as long as he does not copy, providing the information concerned is not a trade secret.[59] Computer programs designed to perform mundane functions such as producing labels for pharmacists and handling stock control can hardly be classed as trade secrets.[60]

The idea/expression merger doctrine

The idea/expression merger doctrine takes on a different significance in the context of United Kingdom copyright law. In a case of suspected non-literal copying the person who wrote the alleged copy is simply likely to deny that he copied and both the look and feel test and the merger doctrine become important in an evidential sense. The question to be resolved is whether the defendant copied a substantial part of the original computer program. If the look and feel of the two programs are similar, the fact that there are several different ways in which the program could have been written is persuasive evidence that there has been copying whilst the fact that, because the function dictates the program code or structure, there is only one way the program could have been written significantly weakens the claim that there has been, in fact, copying. Of course, other factors may be relevant such as whether the defendant had access to the plaintiff's program. Nevertheless, as current United Kingdom copyright law declares without caveat that copyright subsists in original computer programs and the fact that one of the acts restricted by the copyright is copying a substantial part of a program, even copying a program or significant part of a program which is dictated by function will infringe copyright. On the other hand, two independently created programs may be similar because function dictates the

59 The position is best summarized by Neill LJ in *Faccenda Chicken Ltd.* v *Fowler* [1986] 1 All ER 617.

60 The phrase 'trade secret' lacks precise definition but has been considered in *Lansing Linde Ltd.* v *Kerr* [1991] 1 All ER 418. See also, Coleman, A. *The Legal Protection of Trade Secrets* (London: Sweet & Maxwell, 1992) at pp.4–28.

program (or simply because of coincidence) and there will be no infringement of copyright. In *Total Information Processing Systems Ltd.* v *Daman Ltd.*[61] it was accepted that where there is only one way of expressing an idea, the idea and expression merged and were not the subject of copyright. But this is to confuse the question of subsistence with evidence of copying. In *Kenrick* v *Lawrence*[62] it was said that a duplicate copy of a simple drawing would infringe.

Indirect copying

It has already been seen that copyright law accepts the notion of indirect copying.[63] Does indirect copying apply to computer programs? Of course there must be copying, which in the *British Leyland* case was done through the medium of a finished exhaust pipe. But consider the position of a person who, having seen a computer program in operation, decides to write a new computer program to perform the same function as the original program. Does that person infringe the copyright subsisting in the original program or preparatory design material even though he has not seen a listing of the program itself or the preparatory materials? In three ways, the Act recognizes that copyright can be infringed indirectly: first by section 16(3)(b) it recognizes that the acts restricted by copyright may be done indirectly: secondly, by section 16(3) the Act contemplates that a work may be infringed even though intervening acts do not infringe copyright; and, thirdly, by section 17(6) the Act states that copying includes the making of copies which are transient or are incidental to some other use of the work. However, the program code in the second program would most likely be significantly different from that in the original, especially if it is written using a different programming language. For this reason, the District Court in *Digital Communications Associates* v *Softklone Distributing Corp.*[64] held that the copyright in the underlying program was not infringed by copying a screen display generated by running the program.

Limits of objective similarity and structure

Perhaps the original program is simply altered in an attempt to disguise its origins or to improve it. Nevertheless, the question of copying still arises as opposed to adaptation which has a precise legal meaning in terms of computer programs. In many cases, the two programs will be similar enough to raise a presumption of copying which can shift the burden of proof as already discussed. But, if the alterations are numerous, it may be more difficult to draw this conclusion. It is a relatively simple matter to change constituent parts of a program, for example the screen displays, the names given to variables used in the program and the line numbering. If this is done, a line for line similarity between the two programs will be obscured. If the changes are merely cosmetic, it will still be possible to use a test of objective similarity based on the structure of the programs, for example whether the flow of the program and the relative positioning of its constituent parts are similar. But even here, a determined programmer can rearrange the parts of the program to defeat this test.

Even more difficult is the situation where the new program is written using a totally different programming technique, using software tools and languages that are fundamentally different from those used to create the original program.

61 [1992] FSR 171.

62 [1890] 25 QBD 99.

63 See Chapter 6, particularly the case of *British Leyland Motor Corp. Ltd.* v *Armstrong Patents Co. Ltd.* [1986] 2 WLR 400.

64 659 F Supp 449 (ND Ga 1987).

In particular, the use of 'fourth generation' languages is relevant to this discussion as they are dissimilar to the older more traditional programming languages, such as BASIC and COBOL, in a way that goes beyond mere syntax. A program written in a traditional programming language is written subroutine by subroutine and line by line. A fourth generation language is effectively a tool which automates the process of developing a computer system to a great extent. It is like a shell into which the developer specifies attributes of the required system such as the structure of database files and the operations to be carried out by the finished system. The file-handling and other operations are then performed by the fourth generation system itself.

In *Computer-Aided Systems (UK) Ltd.* v *Bolwell*,[65] some of the plaintiff's ex-employees devised a computer program using a fourth generation language to carry out a similar function to the programs they had written in COBOL for the plaintiff. The *Whelan* case was cited as authority for the notion that the structure of a computer program was a form of literary expression protected by copyright. However, Hoffmann J did not believe that a seriously triable issue was raised on the questions of copying or the misuse of confidential information. The plaintiff had argued that the output formats and input layouts of the two computer programs would be very similar, especially as the defendants had designed the new system so that it was compatible with the plaintiff's system. The defendants had refused to allow the plaintiff to inspect their program, but it would be highly unlikely that there would be a sufficient similarity in the programs to infer that copying had taken place because of the conceptually different nature of the languages used. Even the structure of the programs would be different.[66] The only plausible similarity might have been in the structure of the databases used by the systems because of the efforts to achieve compatibility in this respect. However, Hoffmann J expressed the opinion that the plaintiff's application for inspection of the defendants' program was little more than a 'fishing expedition' and he refused the application. This decision seems eminently sensible in the context of restraint of trade, after all, computer programmers and analysts should be free to exercise their skill and knowledge for other employers subject to copyright and limited confidentiality issues.[67] However, the potentially wide scope of adaptation may catch even the change from a traditional programming language to a fourth generation language.

MAKING AN ADAPTATION

The second act restricted by copyright that is highly relevant to computer programs is that of making an adaptation. An adaptation of a computer program is defined by section 21(3)(ab) of the Act as an arrangement or altered version of the program or a translation of it. For computer programs, a translation includes (by section 21(4)):

> . . . a version of the program in which it is converted into or out of a computer language or code or into a different computer language or code[, otherwise than incidentally in the course of running the program].[68]

To fully understand the legal issues concerning this definition, it is important that the basic meaning of some computer terms are understood and the definitions given in the Glossary at the beginning of the book should be referred to

65 (unreported) 23 August 1989, Chancery Division.

66 It is not really appropriate to talk of computer systems developed using fourth generation languages (4GLs) as computer programs. 4GLs are more akin to system development tools. The 4GL provides a set of all-purpose computer programs and the system designer develops a set of specifications concerning file structures, calculations and reports which the programs incorporate to produce the finished system.

67 For example, in the South African case of *Northern Office Micro Computers (Pty.) Ltd.* v *Rosenstein* [1982] FSR 124 where it was held, *inter alia*, that an ex-employee would not have to 'wipe the slate of his mind clean'. See also, *Printers & Finishers Ltd.* v *Holloway* [1965] RPC 239.

68 The words in brackets were repealed by the Copyright (Computer Programs) Regulations 1992, SI 1992 No. 3233.

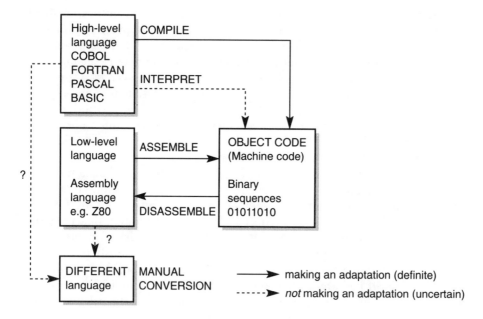

Figure 8.3 Making an adaptation in relation to a computer program

again. The following definitions should also be noted. *Compiling* a computer program means converting a high-level language source code program into object code, being the machine code that can be directly understood by the computer. A permanent version of the program in object code is created which can then be operated without the source code version. This must be contrasted with *interpreting,* a process by which a high-level source code computer program is temporarily converted, line by line, into object code during the operation of the program. This is not as efficient as running a compiled version of the program. *Assembling* computer program means converting a low-level assembly language program into object code. The process of *disassembly* produces assembly language from an object code version of a computer program. Disassembly unlocks the ideas and techniques contained in the object code version of the program.

What then, in the context of making an adaptation, does this mean? Figure 8.3 shows the relevant acts that can be done in relation to a computer program. Suppose that a computer program has been written, either in a high-level programming language such as BASIC or a low-level language such as Z80 assembly language.[69] The legal meaning of making an adaptation would certainly seem to cover the act of compiling or assembling the computer program. If the object code version of a program, produced by compiling or assembling a source code program, is later disassembled, to derive an assembly language version, that too falls within the meaning of making an adaptation.

Now that an adaptation includes an arrangement or altered version of a program, this should cover the situation where a program is manually rewritten in a different computer programming language. The meaning of translation may also extend to a manual translation. There seems to be no reason why translat-

69 Not all computer programming languages are capable of being operated in interpreted form.

ing a computer program cannot be done manually by using a knowledge of grammatical rules and a dictionary of commands and functions. This is highly analogous to translating a work of literature from one natural language into another which is, of course, making an adaptation.

PERMITTED ACTS IN RELATION TO COMPUTER PROGRAMS

In terms of the permitted acts under copyright law, computer technology may be indirectly relevant in many cases. For example, as a computer program is a literary work, all the provisions affecting literary works apply to computer programs, unless the contrary is stated. For example, a teacher can write a listing of part of a computer program on a blackboard for the purposes of instruction. (Obtaining the listing in the first place might, however, infringe.) A design document includes data stored in a computer for the purposes of section 51 which suppresses copyright in design documents where an article is made to a design.

Although the main purpose of the Directive on the legal protection of computer programs[70] in pursuance of which the regulations were passed was the harmonization of copyright protection for computer programs, the aspect that stimulated a most heated debate and controversy was the 'decompilation right'. This is a right given to lawful users of computer programs to reverse engineer other computer programs for the purpose of achieving 'interoperability' with that or another program. In other words, it allows the act of converting a computer program (the target program) into a form easier to understand (expressed in a higher-level language) so that details of its interfaces can be discovered enabling the new program to be compatible with the target program or any other program. Prior to the amendments made by the Copyright (Computer Programs) Regulations 1992,[71] the most important permitted act in terms of achieving the same result was undoubtedly fair dealing for the purposes of research or private study, section 29. It has been seen in Chapter 7 that the scope of this provision is difficult to predict but it was possible that it would extend to the type of situation mentioned above. Indeed, this seems to be the case in the United States where the equivalent act of fair use has been relied on successfully to allow reverse engineering of computer programs to discover details of interfaces.[72]

The Directive provided for other specific exceptions to copyright infringement. These have been included in the Copyright, Designs and Patents Act 1988 by amendment by the 1992 regulations and came into force on 1 January 1993. They are all subject to conditions. Altogether, the special permitted acts for computer programs are:

● decompilation of computer programs
● making back-up copies of computer programs
● making copies or adaptations of computer programs

New sections 50A to 50C are inserted into the Copyright, Designs and Patents Act 1988 under the heading *Computer programs: lawful users*. These exceptions to infringement only apply to acts done by lawful users of computer programs and it is to the meaning of this term that we must now turn.

70 OJ [1991] L122/42.

71 SI 1992 No. 3233.

72 *Sega Enterprises Ltd.* v *Accolade Inc.* (1992) 977 F 2d 1510.

Lawful users

Although the Directive uses the terms 'licensed user', 'person having the right to use' and 'lawful acquirer', depending on the exception concerned the Act as amended uses the term 'lawful user' for all three exceptions. A lawful user is by section 50A(2):

> a person who has a right to use the program, whether under a licence to do any acts restricted by the copyright subsisting in the program or otherwise

This will extend to licensees and, presumably, to persons acting for the licensee such as employees. Unless prohibited by the licence agreement, it should also apply to agents and independent consultants working for the licensee and to many other persons such as students in respect of a site licence granted to an educational establishment or voluntary workers for a charity that has an institutional licence. Others too could fall within the definition of lawful user. It may include a receiver of a company, an external auditor or anyone acting in pursuance of a legal requirement. For example, a policeman executing a search warrant or a solicitor executing an Anton Piller order.

The addition of the words 'or otherwise' could cause the copyright owner to consider carefully how to exploit the program. For example, it could apply to a person who has obtained a copy of a program by rental or loan. A person who has been given a copy of a program for evaluation purposes should also fall within this category. Of course, if a copy has been made in accordance with the exceptions, at the end of the rental or loan period and the right to use the program ceases, subsequent use will infringe copyright. However, the retained copy will not be an infringing copy because section 27 was not amended to cover this possibility.[73] Selling that copy will not, therefore, be a secondary infringement of copyright.[74] This does not apply where the arrangement by which the person concerned obtained the copy within the meaning of section 56 (where a copy of a work in electronic form has been purchased) because any retained copies are treated as infringing copies.[75]

Decompilation of computer programs

The decompilation right[76] allows (subject to certain conditions) a lawful user of a copy of a computer program expressed in a low-level language:

(a) to convert it into a version expressed in a higher-level language, or
(b) incidentally, in the course of so converting the program, to copy it.[77]

Whilst it is up to the legislatures of individual Member States to choose their own form of wording to give effect to a Directive, the differences between the language of the modifications made by the regulations and that of the Directive, which is expressed in terms of reproduction of the code and translation of its form, a much wider rubric, is unfortunate. The Directive does not use the terms 'low-level language' and 'high-level language' nor are they defined in the Act. Although someone wanting to gain access to information about the program's algorithm or its detailed workings would almost certainly want to convert from a low-level language version to a higher-level language version, the Directive is more generous, allowing translation, adaptation, arrangement or alteration. The decompilation right as enacted does not expressly cover the conversion of a

73 Section 27(6) includes as infringing copies any copies made in pursuance of some of the permitted acts but that are subsequently dealt with. The omission of copies made in pursuance of sections 50A to 50C is clearly an oversight.

74 The primary infringement of issuing to the public could apply in some cases, section 18.

75 It is not clear that this could apply in any case because 'purchase' is not the same as obtaining a copy under a licence. This provision may be more appropriate in terms of sound and video recordings.

76 Strictly speaking, this is not a right but is an exception to infringement by virtue of being a permitted act. The act concerned is described as decompilation in the Directive (Article 6) and in the marginal note to section 50B of the Act.

77 Section 50B of the Act, inserted by regulation 8.

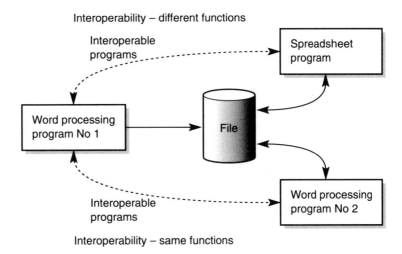

Figure 8.4 Interoperability of computer programs

binary object code program into hexadecimal code, something which is commonly known as performing a 'hex dump', as there is no higher-level language involved at that stage. This would be within the exception as expressed in the Directive.[78]

The conditions that must apply for decompilation to be permitted by section 50B of the Act are stated in subsection (2) and are that:

(a) it is necessary to decompile the program to obtain the information necessary to create an independent program which can be operated with the program decompiled or with another program ('the permitted objective'); and

(b) the information so obtained is not used for any purpose other than the permitted objective.

The purpose of decompilation is to obtain, typically, interface details. For example, Ace Software may wish to develop a new word processing program. Ace will need to know details of various computer operating systems (these systems are a collection of computer programs) so that it can work in the computer's operating environment. Ace must determine how the operating system uses the computer's memory so that its new program can run properly. Also, to stand any chance of being successful, the new program must be compatible with existing programs. Ace's new program must be able to accept (import) word-processed files produced using other word processing programs (and export them in the appropriate format); it would be even better if Ace's new program could accept files from other types of program such as a spreadsheet program or a graphics program. Hence the need for this interface information. Not only does the exception allow decompilation for the purpose of creating a new compatible program (for example, a new word processing program that is compatible with an existing spreadsheet program) it also allows, in principle, the creation of new competing programs (for example, a new word processing program that can import and export files from and to an existing wordprocessing program). Figure 8.4 shows the concept of interoperability.

78 However, this could fall within the normal fair dealing exception in section 29. This is still available for acts not caught by the meaning of decompilation.

The conditions mentioned cannot be met if the lawful user has readily available to him the information necessary to achieve the permitted objective; or if he does not confine the act of decompiling to that objective; if he supplies the information to any person to whom it is not necessary to supply it in order to achieve that objective or if he uses the information to create a program which is substantially similar in its expression to the decompiled program or to do any act restricted by copyright.[79] Most of these conditions are reasonable and, indeed, the latter two are probably redundant. However, it is what constitutes having the information readily available that could be difficult. Of course, the first step that a person who requires interface details of another's program should take is to ask for those details. In some cases the information may be freely given. In other cases, it may even be published in documentation accompanying a licensed copy of the program.

Importantly, the decompilation right cannot be prohibited or restricted by any term or condition in an agreement. Any term in a licence agreement purporting to do this is void, unless the agreement was entered into before 1 January 1993.[80] A considerable number of standard form software licences should be amended as a result of this.

Apart from the decompilation exception, fair dealing for the purposes of research or private study still exists in relation to computer programs.[81] Therefore, it may be permissible for a person to list, copy, inspect and study a program in use for the purposes of understanding the operation of the program and the techniques represented within it for research, including commercial research, and private study. However, the prospective author of an academic journal article cannot disassemble the computer program in order to include an extract of the program expressed in a higher-level language. That does not fall within the permitted objective of decompilation.

Back-up copies of computer programs

Section 50A of the Act permits the making of back-up copies if necessary for the purposes of the lawful use of a copy of a computer program by a lawful user. As with the decompilation right, this right cannot be taken away by any term or condition in an agreement and any such term, in so far as it purports to prohibit or restrict the exercise of this right, is void providing the agreement was made on or after 1 January 1993. Prior to this amendment, there was no equivalent statutory provision although the courts may have been prepared to imply an appropriate term into a software licence where the making of a back-up copy was necessary to the use of the program in question.[82] Of course, many software companies make express provision allowing the user to make one or more back-up copies. It is common for the installation instructions to ask the licensed user to make a copy of the program first and use this as the working copy, placing the original disks in a safe place in case the working disks become damaged or corrupted.

Each lawful user within an organization that has a site licence or a multiple user licence is entitled by section 50A to make his own copy if necessary for his lawful use. In such a situation, it is difficult to predict just how many back-up copies would be deemed to be 'necessary'. If the program is available on a network of computers, presumably the effect of section 50A is to allow the making

79 Section 50B(3).

80 Regulation 12(2).

81 Sections 29(1) and (4) of the Act.

82 However, section 56 of the Act recognizes the possibility that back-up copies may have been made. It makes copies of works purchased in electronic form that are not transferred along with the original, in the case of it being transferred to a third party, infringing copies. However, whether it is right to speak in terms of the purchase of a computer program is uncertain.

of one back-up copy only, to be held by the network manager. Of course, the licence agreement may make specific provision for the making of a greater number of back-up copies.

Copying and adapting

A licence in respect of a computer program will normally state the acts that may be done by the licensee in relation to the program. If it is silent about some particular act which is within the spirit of the agreement, then the courts would imply the appropriate terms permitting that act. Section 50C, in effect, puts this on a statutory footing by allowing a lawful user of a copy of a computer program to copy it or adapt it[83] if that is necessary for his lawful use. Copying or adapting for the purpose of error correction may fall within this exception to infringement and is given as a particular example in section 50C(2) of the Act.

It is common for agreements regulating the lawful use of computer programs to contain a term prohibiting modification by the client and such terms are not controlled by the Act as amended unlike the case with the other two exceptions. However, terms seeking to prevent modification by or on behalf of the licensee might be controlled in other ways. The Court of Appeal, in *Saphena Computing v Allied Collection Agencies*,[84] had an opportunity to consider the position at common law with respect to modification and error correction of licensed computer programs. In that case, the licensee had been given a copy of the source code by the licensor and there was, consequentially, an implied undertaking that the licensee could use it for error correction. Whilst the licensor was still testing and modifying the software, the agreement was determined and it was held that the licensee could continue to use the source code for the purpose of error correction but could not use it for other modifications and improvements to the program. It was said, *obiter,* that there was not an implied duty on a licensor to supply the source code if the agreement only provided for the supply of object code.

If the supplier is no longer able or willing to provide error correction, the principle of non-derogation from grant may be applicable with the result that the client can maintain the program himself or approach third parties with a view to their maintaining it. Even if the supplier is prepared to maintain the program and correct errors (for example, by offering a collateral maintenance contract) the licensee may be able to approach others for this service as the non-derogation principle could still apply. For example, in *British Leyland Motor Corp. Ltd.* v *Armstrong Patents Co. Ltd.*[85] the House of Lords applied the principle to prevent restriction on a free market in spare parts and extended their refusal to enforce copyright to the manufacturers of spare parts and not just to the purchaser. Their Lordships spoke in terms of articles which, by their nature, would require the fitting of replacement parts during their normal lifespan. This principle is most apposite in terms of computer programs. Virtually all computer programs contain errors, a number of which might not be discovered for some considerable time, and the lawful user of the program will require work to be done to it in order to correct those errors. The owner of the copyright subsisting in the program should not be able to use his right to prevent the lawful user asking other persons to repair the program otherwise the copyright owner could charge exorbitant prices for this work and the lawful user would have little option but to pay.

83 'Adaptation' in relation to computer programs, by new section 21(3)(ab), means an arrangement or altered version or translation of it. 'Translation' is further defined by section 21(4) in terms of conversion into or out of a computer language or code.

84 (unreported) 3 May 1989, Court of Appeal.

85 [1986] 2 WLR 400.

Both the Directive and a draft of the 1992 Regulations[86] expressly state that the lawful user can observe, study or test the functioning of the computer program in order to determine the ideas and principles that underlie any element of the program, in the course of loading, displaying, running, transmitting or storing the program as he is entitled to do, for example by virtue of a licence agreement. This reinforces the preamble to the Directive which states that ideas and principles are not protected nor are algorithms, languages and logic that comprise ideas and principles. Express provision is probably unnecessary. First, copyright has long since accepted that copyright does not protect ideas only the expression of an idea and, secondly, those acts mentioned above do not, *per se*, infringe copyright.

COMPUTER PROGRAMMING LANGUAGES

Considerable research effort, investment and skill goes into the development of computer languages and instruction sets. Yet, as it could be argued that these are ideas, there is some doubt about their protection by copyright. However, in the United States, an argument that microcode embedded in a microprocessor representing the computer's instruction set was a defining element of the computer and therefore an idea failed to find sympathy, *NEC Corp.* v *Intel Corp.*[87] In the United Kingdom, the question of copyright protection for an instruction set was considered in *Microsense Systems Ltd.* v *Control Systems Technology Ltd.*[88] The plaintiff made traffic control systems and a controller for pelican crossings, these being programmed using a set of *mnemonics* (a set of three letter symbols, for example SUN for Sunday, MON for Monday)[89] and these were also used to monitor the controllers. The defendant made similar controllers and used a total of 49 of the plaintiff's mnemonics arguing that there was no copyright in them because once the functions had been decided, there was no room for skill and labour in devising the mnemonics. Judge Paul Baker thought that there was an arguable case that the list of mnemonics was protected by copyright because of the work in devising the functions and operations of the controller in the first place. He refused an injunction but ordered the defendant to pay a two per cent royalty into a joint bank account, this being a case where damages would be an adequate remedy for the plaintiff should it be determined at full trial that copyright subsists in the list of mnemonics and the defendant had infringed that copyright. The defendant had argued that it was important, in terms of safety, that there was some degree of standardization in instruction sets for traffic controllers. This is an attractive argument but is the public interest best served by denying a modest royalty to the person who devises a new and original work?

The Directive on the legal protection of computer programs recognizes that programming languages, at least to the extent that they comprise ideas and principles, should not be protected by copyright. Given that this is so one might wonder wherein lies the incentive to create a new language. The answer lies in the fact that, usually, the program, once written, can only be run on a computer if it is converted into object code whether temporarily, using an interpreter program, or permanently, using a compiler program. The licensing of these interpreter and compiler programs, together with appropriate documentation

86 Dated 31 July 1992

87 (1989) 10 USPQ 2d.

88 (unreported) 17 June 1991, Chancery Division.

89 Not all the mnemonics were as obvious. For example, LIT was used to determine the aspect status of the controller. The instruction set was designed so that the engineer could communicate with, monitor or modify the controller or the way it operates.

describing the syntax, semantics and use of the language is the method by which financial reward is usually sought. These interpreter and compiler programs are, of course, protected by copyright.

DATABASES[90]

A computer database is a collection of data stored in a computer or on computer media usually in the form of a computer file. A computer database will contain information which relates to and represents:

- a list of clients and their addresses
- a schedule of rates or prices
- a list of bibliographical references
- an engineering or architectural drawing
- music
- the texts of documents[91]
- mixed text and graphics

Anything can be stored on computer media as long as it can be reduced to a digital form. In the case of text, this is done by using codes to symbolize the letters of the alphabet, for example using ASCII codes.[92] Types of storage media include magnetic disks and tape and compact discs. In earlier times, punched cards and paper tape were commonly used. There is nothing particularly unusual about computer databases compared with collections of information that are written down, typed or printed on paper or index cards. The major difference is that, in the case of a computer database, the information is stored not in its original form, but is translated into a digital representation for the purposes of storage whereas, in the case of traditional paper files, the information is stored in its original form.[93] Some computer databases are available 'on-line', that is they are stored on a central computer and are accessible remotely using a computer with a modem connected to a telecommunications system.[94] Computer programs accessing a computer database convert the digital representation to the original form so that it can be read or printed.

It should be noted that a computer database is generally not a computer-generated work although there is no reason in principle why this should be so. Most computer databases are built up by persons entering information via a keyboard or the information may be entered through the use of an optical character reader. The person compiling the information to be entered will generally be considered to be the author of the database. However, a computer-generated database might be created where a computer program operates on one or more existing databases to produce a new database, for example where two complementary databases are selectively combined into one. Of course, the question of originality as regards the new database must be considered. It will be original if there is sufficient skill and judgment contained within the computer program which is directed towards the task of creating the new database.[95] A 'new' database created in this way might be considered to be a compilation analogous to a directory as in *Macmillan & Co. Ltd. v K & J Cooper*[96] where it was held that a compilation may be original for the purposes of copyright even though the constituent parts are not original because a reasonable amount of work involving judgment and selection has been used in making the compilation.[97]

90 For a good discussion of the problems of database protection see Lea, G. 'Database Law - Solutions beyond Copyright', [1993] 9 CLSR 127.

91 For example, the LEXIS legal information retrieval computer system which contains the full text of transcripts of court cases, statutes, regulations and legal journal articles. LEXIS is a registered trade mark of Butterworths Telepublishing Ltd.

92 ASCII stands for the American Standard Code for Information Interchange.

93 As an example of a digital representation of a letter, the letter 'E' is ASCII code 69 which, in an eight bit computer would be represented as '01000101' using binary notation.

94 These 'on-line' databases may be protected also as cable programmes, see Millard, C. 'Copyright' in Reed, C. (ed) *Computer Law* (London: Blackstone, 2nd. edn., 1993) pp.88–130 at p.99.

95 Only if the skill and judgment of the person writing a computer program is ignored can there be such a thing as a computer-generated work. But a computer-generated work cannot qualify for copyright protection unless it is original. Originality has usually been construed as requiring a minimum of skill, effort or judgment. Unless the skill and judgment of the program writer is taken into account a computer-generated work fails to be protected by copyright. But, if it is taken into account, the work cannot be computer-generated because there is, after all, a human author.

96 (1923) 40 TLR 186.

97 For doubts about the subsistence of copyright in computer databases, see Phillips, J. & Firth, A. *Introduction to Intellectual Property Law* (London: Butterworths, 2nd. edn., 1990) at pp.282–283.

In general terms, it can be said that databases are protected by copyright, usually as literary works. A database containing information relating to bibliographic references including abstracts will be a literary work as will a database containing the full text of literary works such as correspondence, reports, journal articles or other documents. Each document is a literary work in its own right and the collection is also a literary work, being a compilation. If the database comprises data representing three dimensional articles, for example a database of co-ordinates describing sculptures or industrial designs, that database may be considered to be a collection of artistic works so represented, the whole collection being a compilation and, hence, a literary work. The threshold for copyright protection in the United Kingdom has been relatively low compared to some other countries.[98]

The subsistence of copyright in a database *qua* database becomes questionable where its creation has not required the expenditure of skill or judgment. Some databases are the result of effort alone; once the nature of its contents have been determined, there is no room for skill or judgment in the selection of material to be entered into the database. Hence there can be no copyright in the compilation and *G A Cramp & Sons Ltd.* v *Frank Smythson Ltd.*[99] is good authority for this proposition. An example is where a company decides to make a simple database of the names and addresses of all its clients. The 'sweat of the brow' doctrine, affording copyright protection to works which are the result of labour only, has been rejected in the United States Supreme Court in *Feist Publications Inc.* v *Rural Telephone Service Co. Inc.*,[100] in which it was held that the 'white pages' section in a typical telephone directory is not protected by copyright because of a lack of creativity, not owing its origin to an act of authorship. The court did, however, recognize that a compilation of facts could be the subject of copyright because the author has to choose which facts to include and in what order to place them. Thus, the 'yellow pages' section of a telephone directory could be protected because of the presence of original material.[101] This is approximately in line with United Kingdom law. However, an opportunity to examine this question was missed in *Waterlow Directories Ltd.* v *Reed Information Services Ltd.*[102] which concerned an alleged infringement of copyright in a legal directory containing names and addresses of barristers and firms of solicitors by entering extracts into a word processor.

Database structure

If the structure of a computer program is potentially protectable under copyright law, there seems to be no reason why the structure of databases cannot also be protected, providing sufficient skill and judgment has been expended in designing the structure. In most cases, the design of the structure of a database is very important and, once the structure has been decided upon, the entry of data requires relatively little skill. However, in *Total Information Processing Systems Ltd.* v *Daman Ltd.*,[103] it was held that the field and record specifications as expressed in the data division of a COBOL program were not protected because, in this form, the information did not form a substantial part of the computer program as a whole. It is submitted that this approach is wrong and that it would be better to consider the database structure as a form of non-literal expression in its own right and not as part of the computer program. Of

98 For example, German copyright law requires a work to be a personal intellectual creation; German Copyright Act 1965, as amended, section 2(2).

99 [1944] AC 329.

100 (1991) 111 S.Ct. 1282.

101 And the work involved in devising the classification system (a non-literal form of work?).

102 [1992] FSR 409. The issue was whether a substantial part had been taken.

103 [1992] FSR 171.

course, if the structure is dictated by function then it can be said to be an uncopyrightable idea although, often that will not be so; there will be a variety of potential structures possible. Unless the function is very simple and mundane the database structure, that is, the field and record specifications, will require design work involving the exercise of skill and judgment.[104]

Draft Directive

The Commission of the European Communities has prepared a proposal for a Council Directive on the legal protection of databases with a view to harmonizing this area of copyright law throughout the European Community.[105] The proposal has been amended and compliance is required before 1 January 1995.[106] The proposed Directive describes a database as:

> a collection of data, works or other materials arranged, stored and accessed by electronic means, and the materials necessary for the operation of the database such as its thesaurus, index or system for obtaining or presenting information; it shall not apply to any computer program used in the making or operation of the database[107]

The distinction between database so defined and computer program may be very hard to make. For example, is a file containing instructions defining reports to be produced a computer program or a system for presenting information? The proposed Directive gives copyright protection to collections which, by reason of their selection or arrangement, constitute the author's own intellectual creation.[108] However, for databases which fail to come up to that standard a new *sui generis* right to prevent unauthorized extraction is proposed. The normal period of copyright for literary works will apply to databases except for the right to prevent unfair extraction which will last for 15 years. Of course, the materials in a database may have their own copyright and the Directive will not prejudice this copyright. The advantage in having a further copyright in the compilation of such materials is that it gives the database creator a right to sue.

The original text of the proposal attempted to prevent a new copyright (or unauthorized extraction right) springing into life because of insubstantial changes to the database. This was not sufficiently defined and it appeared that an accumulation of insubstantial changes could not give rise to a new right even though the database had been fundamentally changed over a period of time, bearing little resemblance to its original form. Now, by Article 9, a substantial change can give rise to a new copyright where a substantial change means additions, deletions or alterations which involve substantial modification to the selection or arrangement of the contents of a database, resulting in a new edition of that database. This formula will create a legal minefield but, thanks to the generous term of copyright protection, it should not present any problems for the foreseeable future. The unauthorized extraction right is much more simply dealt with. By Article 12, substantial changes (meaning an accumulation of insubstantial additions, deletions or alterations resulting in substantial modification to all or part of the database) will give rise to a new period of protection.

The owner of a database is described by Article 2 as the author or the person to whom the author has lawfully granted the right to prevent unauthorized extraction of material from the database. Presumably this will allow the same provisions to be used as for literary works, for example in relation to employees. The owner of a non-copyright database will be its maker. The owner is

104 In an earlier case, *Computer-Aided Systems (UK) Ltd.* v *Bolwell* (unreported) 23 August 1989, Chancery Division, the mere fact that a new program had file compatibility with an earlier program written by the same people failed to impress the judge.

105 OJ [1992] C156/03.

106 OJ [1993] C194/144 and COM(93) 464 final – SYN 393.

107 Article 1. This definition is slightly different to that originally proposed, for example by the inclusion of the word 'data'.

108 This is similar to the German requirement and that in the Directive on the legal protection of computer programs OJ [1991] L122/42, Article 1(3).

Figure 8.5 A computer-generated work?

given exclusive rights to reproduce the database, change it, distribute it and make it available to the public.[109] There are provisions for some exceptions to infringement in respect of any copyright in the contents of the database in line with the Berne Copyright Convention[110] and in respect of acts consistent with the lawful use of the database.

There is an interesting provision for compulsory licences in terms of the unauthorized extraction right that will apply if the contents of a publicly available database cannot be independently created, collected or obtained from any other source. Article 11 states that the right to extract and re-utilize works or materials from the database shall be licensed on fair and non-discriminatory terms. This also applies as regards certain databases made publicly available by public bodies or having a monopoly status by virtue of an exclusive concession from a public body. The Copyright Tribunal will be empowered to deal with such licences and resolve disputes concerning their availability and terms.

109 Article 5.

110 Article 10 – for quotations and teaching to an extent compatible with fair practice, providing an acknowledgement is given.

COMPUTER-GENERATED WORKS AND ADVICE DERIVED FROM EXPERT SYSTEMS

11 See section 9(3).

The Copyright, Designs and Patents Act 1988 has a curious provision in that it recognizes computer-generated works as a separate species of work with different rules for authorship and duration of copyright. These provisions only apply to literary, dramatic, musical or artistic works.[111] Whilst it is important that works produced using a computer should not be denied the protection of copyright on the basis that the direct human contribution required to make the work is small or negligible, it may be difficult to differentiate between a computer-generated work and other works that have been created with the aid of a computer system.

Section 178 of the Act defines a 'computer-generated work' as being a work that is 'generated by computer in circumstances such that there is no human author'. It is not an easy task to determine the meaning of this definition, nor is it easy to think of examples of such works. All works generated by computer owe their creation to a human being although the human element may be indirect, such as where a computer program contains all the instructions necessary for the creation of the work and the direct human involvement consists of nothing more than switching on the computer and starting up the program. For example, take the artistic work represented in Figure 8.5. It was produced by the author of this book using a computer program containing formulae to generate fractal geometry based on the work of the French mathematician Dr Mandelbrot. The only skill used by the author was to zoom in on an interesting looking part of the main figure. Is this a computer-generated work or has the skill used in selecting an area to be enlarged prevented this result? If the work becomes popular and prints are made of it and sold, to whom should the royalties be paid, the author of this book, Dr Mandelbrot or the person who wrote the program?[112]

112 And what is the position if the author did not zoom in and simply printed the first diagram produced by the programmed computer?

The question of whether a work created using a programmed computer is or is not a computer-generated work is significant because it affects the determination of the authorship and, consequently, the ownership of the copyright subsisting in the work. Of lesser import is the fact that the copyright subsisting in computer-generated works runs from the end of the calendar year in which the work was made and not by reference to the year in which the author dies.[113] For most cases, therefore, the duration of copyright in computer-generated works will be shorter than for other original works.

113 Section 12(3).

Indirect human authorship has been recognized by the courts prior to the 1988 Act, even in the case of a programmed computer intended to select random letters for a competition. In *Express Newspapers plc* v *Liverpool Daily Post & Echo plc*,[114] the defendant claimed that grids of letters produced by computer for a newspaper competition could not be protected by copyright because the grids had no human author.[115] This was rejected by Whitford J who said that the computer was no more than a tool with which the winning sequences of letters were produced using the instructions of a programmer. He said that the defence submission that there was no human author was as unrealistic as saying that a pen was the author of a work of literature.

114 [1985] 1 WLR 1089.

115 A similar example, concerning the making by programmed computer of lists of runners and riders for horse races, is the unreported case of *The Jockey Club* v *Rahim* 22 July 1983, Chancery Division.

There are two possibilities: first that the provisions in the Act concerning computer-generated works are something of a red herring, that there can never be such a thing or, secondly, that the Act overrules the *Express Newspapers* case because it is inconsistent with the Act.[116] If the idea of human authorship can be reconciled with lists of letters drawn randomly by a programmed computer, there seems to be little possibility of a work being considered to be 'computer-generated' within the meaning of the Act because it is difficult to think of a work where the direct human contribution is less. On the other hand, if the concept of a computer-generated work within the meaning assigned to it by the Act is accepted then, as regards works produced with the aid of a computer, it still does not help to draw the line between works that are computer-generated and those that are not. It may be that a suitable test can be derived on the basis of two characteristics relating to the finished work: content and format. Consider the following types of work produced by or with the aid of a computer.

Works produced with the aid of a programmed computer

For example, a document produced using a word processing system. This cannot be a computer-generated work because the author is the person using the computer, or the person who wrote or dictated the text for a word processor operator to enter. The creative link is between the person using the system as a tool and the finished document. The content is entirely that of the person using the system as is the format to a large extent, even though the system may control certain elements such as the printer font, page breaks, etc.

Works produced, to a large extent, by a programmed computer

Examples are rare but might include:

(a) automatically generated weather forecasts produced by a computer receiving signals from satellites,
(b) lists of random numbers – for example, for the Premium Bond draw,
(c) computer code automatically generated from screen layouts designed by the user,
(d) simulations and modelling systems.
(e) fractal diagrams as in Figure 8.5.

In terms of the finished work, all of these systems operate with a minimum of direct human effort or skill. The person operating the system has very little or no control over the format and the content of the output produced by the computer. Section 9(3) of the Copyright, Designs and Patents Act 1988 states that the author of such a work is the person who makes the necessary arrangements for the work to be created. However, to consider such works as being computer-generated is to ignore the skill and expertise of the person or persons who wrote the computer programs used to generate the output.[117] The fact that this skill is indirect could be considered to be akin to a situation where an author of a work of literature dictates to another person who writes it down in shorthand. No-one would suggest that the person recording the work in writing is the author of the work. Similarly with works produced almost exclusively by a programmed computer – the person switching on the computer and setting the program going is merely the agent by which the skill of the computer programmer is brought to fruition, resulting in a recorded work. The author of such a work is either the person by whom the arrangements necessary for the creation

---

[116] It is open to debate whether the provisions as to construction contained in section 172 show that there ha been a sea change as regards works created by a programmed computer. For an argument that there is no such thing as a computer-generated work, see Bainbridge, D.I. 'The Copyright Act: a legal red herring' *Computer Bulletin* Vol.1 Pt.8 October 1989, p.21.

[117] Tapper argues that the computer-generated works provisions are ill-conceived and should be abolished. Tapper C., 'The Software Directive: A UK Perspective' in Lehmann, M. & Tapper, C. *A Handbook of European Software Law*, (Oxford: Clarendon Press, 1993) pp.143–161 at p.150.

118 Section 9(3).

of the work are undertaken,[118] that is the person in control of the programmed computer or the person or persons who wrote the computer program responsible for the creation of the work, whichever view is taken of the legitimacy of computer-generated works.

Intermediate works

Whether or not the potential existence of computer-generated works is accepted, a third type of work will still prove problematic in terms of the identity of the author or authors of the work. Intermediate works can be said to be those in which the human expertise required to produce the work flows from more than one source. The content of the output produced is the result of the skill and judgment of the person operating the programmed computer combined with the skill and judgment of the person or persons responsible for the writing of the computer program. However, the person using the system will probably not have a great influence on the format of the finished work. There are a number of examples of these intermediate works such as a specialized accounting system for a particular business or type of business, a music synthesizer designed to produce music from a basic framework of notes entered by the user and, especially, expert systems. The latter provide an excellent example of intermediate works where the skill and judgment of several people are combined to produce the computer output which may be in the form of a printed report containing advice of some kind together with justification of that advice.

The phrase 'expert system' has been widely used to describe advice-giving computer systems that are somehow different or more special than traditional computer programs. The distinction between expert systems and conventional computer programs is not always clear but there are two ways in which they can be distinguished. One way is to look to the construction of the system. In simple terms, expert systems usually comprise a knowledge-base, an inference engine and an explanation interface. The knowledge-base contains the raw material of the expert system: the rules and facts representing the expertise. The knowledge-base will have been developed using experts in the domain represented who have worked with knowledge engineers to identify, structure and formalize the knowledge. The inference engine is a computer program which attempts to resolve queries put by the user of the system by interacting with the knowledge-base. The inference engine may be either a ready-made program, referred to as a shell, or a program specially written for the particular application. Finally, the interface with the user is simply there to make the system relatively easy to use and to provide a means of inspecting the results and explanations of those results.[119]

119 For a clear structural definition of expert systems, see Winfield, M.J. 'Expert Systems: an Introduction for the Layman', *Computer Bulletin*, December 1982, pp.6–18.

120 Expert systems raise other interesting legal issues in terms of contractual and tortious liability. See Lurie, P.M. & Weiss H.D. 'Computer assisted mistakes: changing standards of professional liability' (1988) II *Software Law Journal* 283 and Bainbridge, D.I. 'Computer-aided Diagnosis and Negligence' (1991) 31 *Medicine, Science and the Law* 127.

The user of the expert system provides expertise because he will have to understand, interpret and respond to questions asked during the operation of the system and he will also have to know what the scope and limitations of the system are. At the present stage of development of expert systems, the user of an expert system must possess a reasonable general knowledge of the domain covered by the system to be able to use it successfully.

What will the law make of the output of expert systems when it comes to deciding the authorship and ownership of that output?[120] To argue that it is computer-generated and has no human author runs counter to common sense, especially because of the significant contribution of the user of the system, not forgetting the considerable skill of those who developed and built the system. To say that the user of the system is its sole author might be convenient but is unrealistic. To attribute authorship to the experts and knowledge engineers who developed the knowledge base is unsatisfactory because they cannot predict how the system will be used and what responses will be made by the user - they have no control over its use. In terms of logical rigour, all those listed above are the joint authors, in differing proportions, of the output resulting from the use of the system. However, it must be said that, if the courts follow this interpretation, it will lead to all manner of complications regarding the commercial use of expert systems and other 'intermediate' systems even though the courts might be willing to imply terms, for example, that the licensee of such systems owns the copyright in any output or to use the concept of beneficial ownership. Of course, it is up to the parties to a licence agreement to include suitable contractual provisions dealing with ownership of output.

SATELLITE BROADCASTING

The broadcasting of television, films and the like by satellite raises fundamental issues of copyright such as where the broadcast is made from. For example, is it made from the earth station or the satellite? This will affect the identity of the national rules of copyright law that will apply. Another problem is where the broadcast is received and then re-transmitted, perhaps by cable, without authorization. A further problem relates to the sale of unauthorized decoders used to receive encrypted broadcasts.

The approach taken by United Kingdom law is straightforward. A satellite broadcast is made from the place from which the signals carrying the broadcast are transmitted to the satellite, that is the earth station.[121] Re-broadcasting or including a broadcast in a cable programme service are restricted acts and will be infringed by anyone doing either without the licence of the copyright owners.[122] It is now an offence to make, import, sell or let for hire any unauthorized decoder by section 297A.[123] Previously, although the fraudulent reception of transmissions (broadcasts and cable) carried criminal penalties by section 297, there were only civil remedies against any person responsible for making, importing, selling or letting for hire unauthorized decoders and this provision had caused considerable problems of interpretation. In *BBC Enterprises Ltd. v Hi-Tech Xtravision Ltd.*[124] the plaintiff provided a satellite television service known as BBC TV Europe. The defendant sold decoders at a price considerably lower than that charged by the distributors authorized by the plaintiff. The offence of fraudulently receiving a programme included in a broadcast or cable programme service in section 297 of the Copyright, Designs and Patents Act 1988, was held to be inapplicable for reasons of jurisdiction. The plaintiff therefore based his claim on section 298 of the Act which controls apparatus, devices or information to assist persons to receive programmes or other transmissions when they are not entitled to do so. In the High Court, it was held that the unauthorized reception of waves in the ether caused by wireless telegraphic transmission did not represent an interference with property rights at common law and that no one had rights of property in those wireless

121 Section 6(4).

122 Section 20. Many rights might subsist in a broadcast. Note the exception to infringement in section 73.

123 Inserted by the Broadcasting Act 1990, section 179.

124 [1990] Ch 609.

transmission waves. Scott J suggested that a right to prohibit reception had to be found outside section 298 before it was possible to say that persons were not entitled to receive programmes and it is not an infringement of copyright to receive a broadcast. Therefore, the foreign viewers of BBC TV Europe could not be described as persons who were 'not entitled to do so' within section 298.[125] Scott J was of the opinion that section 298 was inept legislation and that the legislature was under a misapprehension as to the law.

The Court of Appeal reversed the High Court decision. Whilst the court accepted that the right involved was probably not a proprietary right, it was held that the plaintiff's claim disclosed a good cause of action, rejecting the interpretation of section 298 suggested by Scott J.[126] Staughton LJ said that section 298 contained both the right and the remedy. The person who seeks to charge for encrypted transmissions has the right not to have others making apparatus designed for use by persons not authorized by him to receive the programmes.[127] The defendant's appeal was dismissed by the House of Lords who held that providers of satellite programmes broadcast from the United Kingdom are protected by section 298 and are thus entitled to collect charges for the reception of these programmes and this covered, indirectly, persons receiving the transmissions in other countries that lie within the 'footprint' of the transmissions.[128] As with section 296, it is the copyright owner who has the right and the person responsible is to be treated as infringing copyright. The criminal offence in section 297A carries a maximum penalty of a fine not exceeding level 5, currently £5,000. A 'decoder' is defined as any apparatus designed or adapted to enable (on its own or with other apparatus) an encrypted transmission to be decoded. Apparatus is defined widely as including any device, component or electronic data and will, therefore, include decoders that exist in software form only.[129] The transmission must be one from within the United Kingdom though there is a statutory defence if the person charged did not know and had no reasonable ground for knowing that the decoder was unauthorized. A decoder is unauthorized if it enables an encrypted transmission that is paid for to be viewed without payment. The Council to the European Community has adopted a Directive on the coordination of certain rules concerning copyright and rights related to copyright applicable to satellite broadcasting and cable transmission.[130] The main purpose is harmonization and the protection of such broadcasts throughout the Community. Member States will ensure that copyright and related rights (for example, performers' rights) are observed in relation to programmes from other Member States that are retransmitted by cable into their territory. It will be possible for Member States to exercise the communication rights by way of collecting societies. Compliance is required by 1 January 1995 although there will be some transitional provisions for agreements in force at that date. In the future there may be more problems when transmissions *originate* from satellites, space stations or even the moon.[131]

COPYING TECHNOLOGY

Improvements in copying technology and reductions in the cost of making copies of all manner of copyright works have seriously challenged the efficacy of copyright law as a means of controlling unauthorized copying. For example,

125 *The Times*, 28 November 1989.

126 [1990] Ch 609.

127 There is no similar problem with section 296 as making a copy of a work issued in an electronic form will almost certainly infringe copyright.

128 [1991] 3 WLR 1.

129 Section 297A(3) contains definitions.

130 OJ [1993] L248/15.

131 Sterling J.A.L., *Intellectual Property Rights in Sound Recordings, Film and Video* (London: Sweet & Maxwell, 1992) at pp.374–375.

considerable advances have been made in photocopying in terms of both quality and the cost of making copies in real terms. An additional worry for the owners of copyright in printed materials such as books, magazines and sheet music is the much greater availability of photocopying machines. Most employed persons and students have relatively easy access to a photocopier these days. In 1965, the Society of Authors and the Publishers Association made an announcement, concerning the fair dealing provisions for research or private study, indicating the amount of photocopying which authors and publishers would not normally consider to be unfair. Because of subsequent advances in technology and the dramatic increase in the amount of photocopying, this 'allowance' was withdrawn in 1985.[132] The announcement had, of course, no standing in law and was merely a guideline and, in any case, the fair dealing provisions are not needed unless the amount copied is a substantial part of the work. Another factor rendering the guidelines irrelevant to some extent is the establishment of the Copyright Licensing Agency, which issues blanket licences permitting the copying of substantial parts of works covered by the scheme. This type of arrangement is growing in significance and is likely to continue to do so as a means of obtaining income to be distributed amongst copyright owners and it is likely that such schemes will be developed in the future for other kinds of works.[133] One major factor that will encourage this is the difficulty of enforcing copyright where the copying is done by private individuals for their own use.

Another technical innovation which has worried the music, film and broadcasting industries is the development of copying devices such as home music centres with twin cassette decks and video recorders. The computer industry itself is extremely vulnerable to copying as many computer programs can be copied very easily. Attempts to restrict or stop the sale of twin cassette music centres failed as was noted in Chapter 6. It had been argued and, indeed it was suggested in a White Paper, that a levy should be imposed on the sale of blank audio cassette tape as a means of retrieving some of the profit lost as a result of copying.[134] However, this proposal did not survive in the Copyright, Designs and Patents Act 1988.

Copying of broadcasts, cable programmes, films and audio recordings is likely to increase as technology improves. For example, the introduction of digital audio tape (DAT), compact discs and mini-disks permit the making of copies of better quality than was previously possible.[135] In terms of the law, there is little that can be done as regards copying in the home, for private purposes apart from imposing a levy on blank media. The only workable alternative is for anti-copying technology to be developed and applied to recordings that are made available to the public. However, this may have a negative effect in that, for some, the very fact that the recordings can be copied is an important factor in the decision to purchase or hire. For example, a person who buys a compact disc of music to be played at home might also like to make a copy on audio tape to play in his car whilst driving to and from work although, strictly, this infringes copyright.[136]

Attempts at making computer programs difficult to copy have been made for some time. Some consist of a 'dongle', a piece of computer hardware that plugs into a computer. When the computer program is run, it checks to see if the dongle is in place before continuing. Other forms of copy-protection involve the scrambling of the program code on the magnetic disk or alterations to the disk

132 The British Copyright Council, *Reprographic Copying of Books and Journals*, 1985, p.5. The Society of Authors and the Publishers Association are members of the British Copyright Council.

133 An early example is the Performing Right Society. Under the Copyright Act 1956, there was a statutory recording licence. Any person could make records to be sold by retail as long as they paid the copyright owner 6¼ per cent of the ordinary retail selling price. This has been abolished by paragraph 21 of Schedule 1 to the Copyright, Designs and Patents Act 1988. A Public Lending Right Scheme was introduced by the Public Lending Right Act 1979 to distribute an annual sum of money amongst authors of literary works loaned out by public libraries.

134 *Intellectual Property and Innovation* Cmnd 9712 (London: HMSO, 1986). The proposed levy did not extend to short tapes used, predominantly, for computer programs, nor to video tape. Blank tape levy schemes appear to work effectively in some European countries, especially in Germany.

135 See Cornish, W.R. *Intellectual Property: Patents, Copyright, Trade Marks and Allied Rights* (London: Sweet & Maxwell, 2nd edn., 1989) at p.350.

136 Generally, the use of anti-copying techniques used with computer programs have had such a negative effect. Apart from the copying problem, such devices may make the program less convenient to use in practice.

directory. Inevitably, it was not long before devices and software designed to overcome these attempts at copy-protection appeared on the market. For example, relatively inexpensive computer software could be obtained to make copies of 'protected' programs costing many hundreds of pounds, often sold ostensibly as having some legitimate but unlikely use.

There can be little sympathy for those who make and sell devices deliberately designed to permit the copying of works that are copy-protected. They are now controlled by section 296 of the Copyright, Designs and Patents Act 1988 which provides that the making, importation, sale or hire, etc. of devices or means specifically designed or adapted to circumvent copy-protection of works issued to the public in electronic form are to be treated as an infringement of copyright. Furthermore, publishing information to enable or assist the circumvention of copy-protection is similarly treated. However, this is actionable only by the copyright owner and, presumably, an exclusive licensee of the copyright owner and the device or means or information must be directed to the form of copy-protection employed by the copyright owner.[137] In addition to devices and means intended to prevent or restrict copying, 'copy-protection' also includes those that are directed at impairing the quality of copies made from the original. Of course, these provisions are not just aimed at computer programs but also concern copy-protection of audio and visual works that are issued in an electronic form, which is widely defined in the Act by section 178. Some equipment can be used for making copies of sound and video recordings and computer programs legitimately, without infringing copyright, for example twin tape cassette machines, computer disk drives, 'double' video recorders. Even though such equipment can also be made to make unauthorized copies it will not fall within the scope of section 296 because it is not specifically designed to overcome copy-protection. Where equipment or software has lawful uses, it would obviously be unsatisfactory to ban its sale.[138]

FAX AND ELECTRONIC MAIL

Modern technology has seen the introduction of new methods of transmitting information. With facsimile transmission (fax), text and diagrams can be transmitted in a very short time using a telecommunications system to almost anywhere in the world. The material transmitted will usually already be written or printed on paper and there will be no difficulty in finding that copyright subsists in the material subject to the basic requirements of originality and qualification. If a person intercepts the transmission and makes a printed copy, normally this will be an infringement of copyright and the usual rules apply. However, if the person intercepting the transmission simply displays it on a computer screen without either making a printed copy or saving the information to magnetic disk, the issue will be whether the work in question has been copied. As the work concerned is most likely to fall within the 'original works' category, copying means reproducing the work in any material form, including storage in any medium by electronic means.[139] There is no definition of what a material form is but it is arguable that the presence of a work in the volatile memory of a computer (random access memory – RAM) does not constitute a material form as, in this form, the work will be lost once the computer is switched off or when

137 Section 101 provides that an exclusive licensee has the same rights as if the licence had been an assignment. Section 296 also contains provisions for delivery up and seizure of devices and means.

138 The music industry failed in its attempt to interfere with the sale of twin cassette music centres, see *CBS Songs Ltd.* v *Amstrad Consumer Electronics plc* [1988] 2 WLR 1191. In the United States, an attempt to ban the sale of the Betamax video recorder failed on similar grounds, *Sony* v *Universal City Studios* (1984) 104 US 774.

139 Section 17(2).

something else is loaded into the computer's RAM. In addition, the word 'storage' may connote a more permanent form of existence. However, other areas of law may be relevant to the interception of transmitted information. For example, under section 1 of the Interception of Communications Act 1985 it is an offence to intentionally intercept a communication during its transmission through a public telecommunications system. The law of breach of confidence may also assist if the information has the necessary quality of confidence about it, subject to it being possible to fix the eavesdropper with an obligation of confidence. The same principles apply, apart from the offence under the Interception of Communications Act 1985, to a person who uses surveillance equipment to detect and read or copy the display on a computer monitor.

Electronic mail is another method by which information can be transmitted. In this case it is less likely that there will be a written or printed copy of the information, especially if it is relatively short. For example, a person sending a message using electronic mail may simply type in the message at a computer keyboard and then transmit the message. The message may later be filed either by the sender or the receiver or by both, at which time it will be stored on magnetic disk. Once it is so stored there is no doubt that copyright is capable of subsisting in the work although it must be noted that, in the case of a simple and short message, there may be insufficient originality. The message may be accessed before it is sent, for example by a computer hacker, or it may be intercepted during sending. If the work does not, at that stage, exist in any other-form, it is unlikely that copyright will, as yet, subsist in it. Hence, there can be no infringement of copyright. By section 3(2) of the Copyright, Designs and Patents Act 1988, for copyright to subsist in a literary, dramatic or musical work, it must be recorded. Again, this suggests something more permanent, at least storage on magnetic disk or such like and the analogy with 'recording' for the purposes of the Forgery and Counterfeiting Act 1981 is not helpful.[140] Of course, if the work had been written on paper first then copyright will subsist in it but there still remains the question of infringement if the work is simply loaded directly from the telecommunications system into a computer's volatile memory. Of course, the offence under the Interception of Communications Act 1985 and the law of breach of confidence may still be relevant.

140 In *R v Gold* [1988] 2 WLR 984 it was held that a password and identification number held transiently in a computer's volatile memory were not recorded or stored for the purposes of the Forgery and Counterfeiting Act 1981.

If the work transmitted by electronic mail is simultaneously sent to more than one person, then it is possible that it falls within the meaning of a cable programme service. By section 7 of the Copyright, Designs and Patents Act 1988, a cable programme service is one consisting wholly or mainly in sending visual images, sounds or other information by means of a telecommunications system. This would appear to cover the sending of electronic mail to more than one recipient. However, section 7(2) excepts from the definition of a cable programme service one where there is some reciprocity between the sender and the recipients, that is where the persons receiving the information will respond and send information back to the original sender. But for the fact that this is required to be an essential feature, this exception would certainly cover electronic mail. The simple fact is that although the greatest use of electronic mail is to send and receive messages, this is not an essential feature because a person may make use of the facilities mainly for the purposes of receiving information without necessarily wishing to reply. Copyright in a cable programme is infringed by making a photograph of the whole or any substantial part of any image which is part of the cable programme. However, a photograph is a recording of light or radiation so that the copyright will not be infringed unless the image is stored on computer media. Incidentally, including a work in a cable programme service infringes the copyright subsisting in the work (except in the case of typographical arrangements of published editions).

FORMAT RIGHTS

Broadcasting is an extremely effective way of disseminating ideas and information to millions of people in a very short period of time. The success of broadcasting as a medium can have its disadvantages though, particularly as it firmly places ideas for such things as quiz shows and game shows within the public domain. Because copyright looks to the expression of the idea rather than the idea itself as the thing to be protected, ideas for programmes to be broadcast are relatively vulnerable. The law of confidence is of little use as, the moment the material has been broadcast, the quality of confidence will have been utterly destroyed.[141] A present concern for broadcasters and persons inventing and developing ideas for programmes is that the rights associated with them, the so-called 'format rights' seem to be weak in the extreme.[142]

It has been seen in Chapter 3, in the case of *Green* v *Broadcasting Corporation of New Zealand*,[143] that the dramatic format of a television show failed to attract copyright protection. There was, in effect, no expression to protect. There is no such thing as a format right recognized at law. It is up to devisers and commissioners of game shows and other television productions to make full use of existing intellectual property rights to protect their work and investment, for example by writing down details of the show including descriptions and diagrams and character profiles and writing out scripts in full. In this way, anyone copying the show's format may be liable for indirect infringement of these written materials. There is a possibility that names, insignia and the like can be registered as trade marks and any items designed for the show may be protected by design rights. In some circumstances, the law of passing off may also be useful to protect these 'format rights'.

141 However, the law of confidence may give remedies where an idea for a programme has been discussed with a television company and these remedies will continue after broadcasting to be available between the original parties to the discussions, see *Fraser* v *Thames TV Ltd.* [1984] 1 QB 44. Of course, third parties will be unaffected. The law of contract may also provide remedies in these situations.

142 The word 'right' is not used in its legal sense here.

143 [1989] RPC 700 (The Judicial Committee of the Privy Council).

9

European and international aspects of copyright

INTRODUCTION

The freedom to exploit intellectual property rights internationally is vital to the future growth of investment in the creative fields. But, even if the prospect of international trade in the work or article concerned is not contemplated, international protection cannot be ignored. For example, a copyright owner might intend only to sell a book or recording of music on the domestic market but pirate copies could be produced in a foreign country with weak intellectual property laws and imported into the domestic market, seriously damaging the copyright owner's commercial interests.

Of central importance is the state of law in the European Community. The United Kingdom became a member of the European Economic Community at the beginning of 1973 and with the coming of the single market, the interaction between United Kingdom intellectual property law and the Treaty of Rome is of utmost importance.[1] By Article 3 of the Treaty the aims of the Community include the elimination of quantitative restrictions on the import and export of goods and the abolition of obstacles to freedom of movement for persons, services and capital, ensuring that competition in the common market is not distorted. Exploitation of intellectual property may be in conflict with some of these aims and, although one might expect the main problems to result from patents or trade marks, there are several issues involving copyright. One thing to be borne in mind is that these aims are only applicable as regards trade between Member States. Another aim of the Community is the approximation of the laws of the Member States to the extent required for the proper functioning of the common market, that is the harmonization of laws. This is not a wholesale levelling of national differences or, at least, has not yet proven to be although domestic United Kingdom intellectual property law has been changed as a result and will be further changed in the near future.

1 This is the European Economic Treaty signed on 25 March 1957. Also signed in Rome on the same day was the Treaty establishing 'Euratom', the European Atomic Energy Community.

COPYRIGHT LAW AND THE TREATY OF ROME

By virtue of the European Communities Act 1972, Community law takes precedence over inconsistent domestic law. Section 2(1) of that Act states:

> All such rights, powers, liabilities, obligations and restrictions from time to time created or arising by or under the [Community] Treaties, and all such remedies and procedures from time to time provided for by or under the Treaties, as in accordance with the Treaties are without further enactment to be given legal effect or used in the United Kingdom shall be recognised and available in law, and be enforced, allowed and followed accordingly . . .

2 See for example, *Costa v ENEL* [1964] ECR 585 and *Internationale Handelsgesellschaft Case* [1970] ECR 1125.

Any doubts about the supremacy of European Community law over inconsistent domestic law were laid to rest well before the United Kingdom's entry on 1 January 1973.[2] The exercise of intellectual property rights might conflict with several provisions in the Treaty of Rome 1957 (the European Economic Treaty). Those provisions are:

- Articles 30-36 which promote the free movement of goods,
- Article 85 which prohibits restrictive trade practices,
- Article 86 which prevents the abuse of a dominant trading position.

Also, Article 7 of the Treaty provides that any discrimination on the grounds of nationality shall be prohibited. Therefore, one Member State may not exclude authors and performing artists from another Member State from the rights enjoyed by nationals. German law on copyright and related rights provided that non-German nationals could not rely on the provisions which prohibited the distribution of unauthorized recordings of performances given outside Germany. In *Collins v Imtrat Handelsgesellschaft mbH*[3], Phil Collins argued that this provision offended against Article 7 in an action relating to the distribution in Germany of a compact disc containing a recording made without his consent of one of his concerts given in the United States. On a reference to the Court of Justice for a preliminary ruling under Article 177, the Court confirmed that copyright and related rights fell within the scope of Article 7 and the principle of non-discrimination applied to those rights. This was so even though there was not yet full harmonization of copyright and related rights throughout the Community: they fell within the Treaty's provisions because of their effect on intra-Community trade in goods and services.

3 (unreported) *The Times*, 19 November 1993, Court of Justice of the European Communities.

The exercise of intellectual property rights may entail the control and dividing up of markets by the number and type of licence agreements entered into by the owner and the terms contained in them. For example, a United Kingdom company may own the copyright in a sound recording and decide to grant a licence to a Dutch company to make and sell copies in The Netherlands. A similar licence may be granted to a French company and both licence agreements may purport to prohibit either the Dutch or French company selling the recordings outside their respective countries. This would appear to interfere with the principle of the free movement of goods, especially if the recordings sell at different prices in different countries.

European Community law does recognize intellectual property rights. Article 222 of the Treaty of Rome states that nothing in the Treaty shall prejudice the rules in Member States governing the system of property ownership and intellectual property is undoubtedly a form of property. However, this refers to domestic law in Member States and, where the exercise of those rights interferes with the provisions of the Treaty, the rights will be compromised. Article 222 has to do with the *existence* of a right whereas Articles 30–36 are concerned with the *exercise* of that right. In principle, because copyright affords a weaker form of protection and does not lock away ideas as such, the possibility for conflict seems to be less than with patents or trade marks. However, there are a number of cases dealing with copyright licensing, disparity in protection between Member States, problems with collecting societies and issues similar to those occurring in the *British Leyland* spare parts case.[4] First, the reconciliation of copyright with the free movement of goods will be considered followed by the impact of Articles 85 and 86.

4 [1986] 2 WLR 400, discussed in Chapter 6.

The freedom of movement of goods and copyright

Article 30 of the Treaty states that, 'Quantitative restrictions on imports and all measures having equivalent effect [are] . . . prohibited between Member States' and Article 34 contains a similar provision as regards exports. Although Article 36 permits such restrictions and measures if they are for the protection of industrial and commercial property, the prohibitions have been held to apply to copyright and neighbouring rights.[5] The purpose of Articles 30 and 36 is to reconcile the requirements of the free movement of goods with the necessary respect for the legitimate exercise of exclusive rights in 'literary and artistic property'.[6] This has entailed the development of the doctrine of *exhaustion of rights* which is applied where the owner of the rights associated with copies of works that have been lawfully sold or distributed within a Member State attempts to use those rights to prevent the subsequent importation of the copies into another Member State. The doctrine is used to suppress the exercise of the rights in such circumstances. The European Court of Justice is prepared to recognize that certain activities fall within the normal exploitation of the work even though, at first sight, they may seem to be in conflict with Articles 30–36. For example, in *Bassett* v *Sociètè des Auteurs, Compositeurs et Editeurs de Musique (SACEM)*[7] a royalty of 8.25 per cent was charged by SACEM for playing records in a discotheque in Fréjus in France. The 8.25 per cent was calculated on the basis of a performing right and a mechanical reproduction right. In all other Member States, except Belgium, the mechanical reproduction rights were exhausted on an assignment to a manufacturer of phonograms and only a performance royalty had to be paid. The court held that Articles 30–36 did not prohibit the levying of the supplementary mechanical reproduction fee in addition to the usual performance fee even though the mechanical reproduction fee was not payable in the Member State where the recordings were first lawfully put on the market.[8] The extra royalty was seen as being part of the normal exploitation of the copyright and was not, therefore, an 'arbitrary discrimination or disguised restriction' on the trade between Member States.

Parallel imports

Parallel importing occurs when someone, often a third party, attempts to import copyright articles from one country, where they have been lawfully distributed,[9] to another country, usually against the copyright owner's wishes. However, any attempt to prevent or interfere with this will, at once, bring into question the applicability of Articles 30–36. In *Musik Vertrieb Membran GmbH* v *GEMA*,[10] Musik Vertrieb imported sound recordings into Germany from the United Kingdom and other Member States. The royalty fee paid, under the then statutory licence fee arrangements subsisting in the United Kingdom was 6.25 per cent.[11] There was no statutory licence system in place in Germany at the time but the normal royalty payable to the German collecting society, GEMA, was 8 per cent. GEMA therefore sued for the difference, 1.75 per cent. The European Court ruled that GEMA could not claim the difference on the basis of Articles 30–36 as the recordings had been put on the market with the consent of the copyright owner. However, the 'consent' in this case was not true consent as such but as a result of statutory licence. Nevertheless, the European Court appeared to accept that, on the facts, the owner had consented and it stated (at 166):

5 *Deutsche Grammophon GmbH* v *Metro-SB-Grössmarkte GmbH & Co.* [1971] ECR 487.

6 So it was stated in *EMI Electrola GmbH* v *Patricia Im- und Export Verwaltungsgesellschaft mbH* [1989] 2 CMLR 413. This reconciliation implies that protection should be refused to any abusive exercise of those rights which might tend to maintain or establish artificial boundaries within the Common Market.

7 [1987] ECR 1747. SACEM is a French collecting society which collects and distributes royalties in respect of the performing and mechanical reproduction rights for literary, dramatic and musical works.

8 The 8.25 per cent was made up of 6.6 per cent performance fee and 1.65 per cent mechanical reproduction fee.

9 Perhaps under a licence agreement.

10 [1981] ECR 147.

11 Copyright Act 1956, section 8. The statutory licence fee was abolished by the Copyright, Designs and Patents Act 1988.

> Articles 30 and 36 . . . [preclude] the application of national legislation . . . where those sound recordings are distributed on the national market after having been put into circulation in that other Member State by or with the consent of the owners of those copyrights . . .

This is to treat the notion of consent very widely and, in essence the *de jure* consent is looked for rather than *de facto* consent, although the right owner under a statutory licence is unlikely to refuse the royalties accrued in this way. However, it does appear that the Court may have changed its approach since the *Musik Vertrieb* case, as discussed below.

More recently, it has been held that Articles 30–36 did not prevent the working of national legislation to allow a copyright owner to rely on exclusive rights in order to prevent the sale in one Member State of copies of a work made in another Member State lawfully although without the consent of the copyright owner. So it was held in *EMI Electrola GmbH* v *Patricia Im- und Export Verwaltungsgesellschaft mbH*[12] in which copies of Cliff Richard recordings were made in Denmark, where exclusive rights under Danish copyright law had expired, and imported into Germany. However, such a restriction could not be justified on the ground of disparity of protection under national copyright laws where it constituted a means of arbitrary discrimination or a disguised restriction on trade between Member States. The question of whether an attempted restriction on parallel importing is controlled by Articles 30–36 appears to depend largely upon consent, that is whether the articles have been made available in the other country by the consent of the right owner, and it appears that the European Court is tending to move away from its decision in *Musik Vertrieb* and require actual rather than illusory consent.[13]

The above cases show the working of the doctrine of exhaustion. The sale or distribution of articles embodying a copyright work (or a patent or design right) in one Member State with the consent of the owner is said to exhaust the owner's rights to further control, exclusively, subsequent dealings in those articles.

A useful statement of important points regarding the application of Articles 30–36 to copyright was given in *Warner Bros. Inc.* v *Christiansen*,[14] which concerned video rental rights. At the time, there was no rental right in the United Kingdom once video films had been made and sold with the owner's consent, but there was such a right in Denmark. Warner Bros. made video films in the United Kingdom and granted a licence to a Danish company to make them there. A parallel importer bought videos in the United Kingdom and intended to hire them out in Denmark. The court ruled that an injunction against the parallel importer was justified and that the rental rights under Danish law were applicable and were not prohibited by Articles 30–36. The court further stated the principles that apply in terms of film copyright and Articles 30–36, including the following:

(a) The inclusion of an exclusive rental right among rights granted to copyright holders under national law constitutes a quantitative restriction under Article 30.

(b) The rights of the owner of a copyright work that are not touched by the rules of the Treaty are the exclusive rights of performance and reproduction.

12 [1989] 2 CMLR 413.

13 For example, in the patent case of *Pharmon BV* v *Hoechst AG* [1985] ECR 2281, a drug made under a compulsory licence was not made with the patentee's consent.

14 [1991] FSR 161.

(c) Where rental to the public constitutes a significant market and source of revenue for copyright owners and the only way for the latter to secure a share of that revenue is to grant an exclusive right to authorize such hiring out, national copyright laws conferring such an exclusive rental right are justified by Article 36(1).

(d) Where the copyright owner chooses to market copies of films in the form of videos in a Member State whose copyright law does not grant an exclusive rental right, that does not exhaust his rental right in another Member State whose law grants such a right. It is, therefore, permissible under Article 36 for him to enforce his rental right in the latter State and this also applies to copies imported from the former State.

These principles should also apply to sound recordings and computer programs. Surprisingly, there have not been any reported cases on the rental of computer programs. Of course, licence agreements for the acquisition of computer programs usually contain terms prohibiting the subsequent transfer or rental of the program. Such terms probably offend against Articles 30–36 of the Treaty if trade between Member States is adversely affected as a result.

Anti-competitive practices, Articles 85 and 86

Articles 85 and 86 are the main provisions to counter anti-competitive practices that may result from a cartel or from an abuse of a dominant position.[15] For example, all the manufacturers of vehicle tyres could get together and agree to raise their prices to a common level rather than try to compete in terms of the price each asks. The manufacturer of a motor vehicle might refuse to allow others to make spare parts for his vehicles. Article 85(1) makes agreements between undertakings and decisions by associations of undertakings and concerted practices that may affect trade between Member States illegal if they have, as their object or effect, the prevention, restriction or distortion of competition within the European Community. Particular agreements, decisions and concerted practices are stated to be those which:

(a) directly or indirectly fix purchase or selling prices or any other trading conditions;
(b) limit or control production, markets, technical development, or investment;
(c) share markets or sources of supply;
(d) apply dissimilar conditions to equivalent transactions with other trading parties, thereby placing them at a competitive disadvantage;
(e) make the conclusion of contracts subject to acceptance by the other parties of supplementary obligations which, by their nature or according to commercial usage, have no connection with the subject of such contracts.

Obviously, a licence agreement in relation to the exploitation of a work in which copyright subsists could be caught by Article 85(1). For example, a licence might state that the licensee must restrict his operation to a part of the European Community or that the licensee may only make a specified number of copies or that the licensee may not sell or distribute copies of similar works made by organizations that are rivals of the licensor. The European Court has made it clear that it will be prepared to act against exclusive copyright licences if they offend,[16] and, although intellectual property rights *per se* do not fall

15 A cartel is an association of independent organizations which have agreed to pursue a course of action which will benefit all of them such as fixing prices, unfair bidding practices and acceptance of contracts.

16 *Coditel v Ciné Vog Films* [1982] ECR 3381.

17 *Keurkoop v Nancy Kean Gifts BV* [1982] ECR 2853.

within the meaning of the term 'agreement' within Article 85(1), the exercise of an intellectual property right might well do so.[17] Terms within licence agreements, such as export bans, may be susceptible to control. To some extent it is a matter of whether the provision is part of the specific subject matter of the right and in *Re Ernest Benn Ltd.*[18] an export ban was objected to on the basis of Article 85(1). Exemption from the provisions of Article 85(1) are possible, either individually or through block exemption under Article 85(3) and a number of Commission Regulations have been passed giving block exemptions, for example in respect of patent licensing agreements and know-how licensing agreements.[19]

18 [1979] 3 CMLR 636.

19 Commission Regulations 2349/84 and 556/89 respectively. See Chapter 16 for a discussion of the exemptions in the context of patents.

20 [1991] 4 CMLR 248.

Reciprocal agreements between collecting societies protecting national interests do not fall foul of Article 85. In *Ministère Public* v *Tournier*[20] it was held that such collecting societies were pursuing legitimate aims where they sought to safeguard the rights and interests of their members, and contracts with users for that purpose could not be regarded as falling within the meaning of Article 85(1). However, this assumed that the practice was not excessive and did not go beyond what was necessary to achieve those legitimate aims.

Article 86 prohibits the abuse of a dominant position within the Common Market. It states:

> Any abuse by one or more undertakings of a dominant position within the common market or in a substantial part of it shall be prohibited as incompatible with the common market in so far as it may affect trade between Member States . . .

21 There may be a remedy under national law. For example, the UK Competition Act 1980, the Restrictive Trade Practices Act 1976 or the Fair Trading Act 1973.

Again, it must be noted that the abuse must affect trade between Member States and if it does not, there is no remedy under European Community law no matter how unfair the practice concerned is.[21] Four examples of abuse are given in Article 86:

(a) the imposition of unfair trading conditions or prices,
(b) the limitation of production, markets or technical developments,
(c) discrimination against some trading parties, and
(d) the imposition of unconnected supplementary obligations in contracts.

Examples would include the limitation of the supply of music recordings or video films in respect of some Member States, probably coupled with high prices. A supplementary obligation that would offend is where a publisher will only supply to retail outlets who agree not to buy from a rival publisher resident in another country.

22 [1979] ECR 461

What constitutes an abuse of a dominant position is not defined as such in Article 86 but in *Hoffmann-La Roche AG* v *E C Commission*[22] it was described as:

> an objective concept relating to the behaviour of an undertaking in a dominant position which is such as to influence the structure of the market where, as a result of the presence of the undertaking in question, the degree of competition is weakened and which, through recourse to methods different from those which condition normal competition . . . has the effect of hindering the maintenance of the degree of competition still existing in the market or the growth of that competition.

23 See *Leyland Daf Ltd.* v *Automotive Products plc* (unreported) *The Times* 9 April 1993, Court of Appeal.

Abuse is, therefore, directed at the use of methods different from normal commercial practices. Refusing to supply further goods until those already supplied have been paid for is outside Article 86.[23]

Merely occupying a dominant position does not automatically bring Article 86 into play. For example, a collecting society occupies a dominant position in its particular country of operation and in *Bassett* v *SACEM*[24] the French collecting society SACEM was occupying a dominant position but the exercise of its power was not an abuse as such. The European Court of Justice will not normally interfere unless some plain abuse is present. In *Volvo AB* v *Erik Veng (UK) Ltd.*,[25] Volvo refused to grant licences to spare part manufacturers and the court held that the proprietor of a protected design has a right to prevent third parties from manufacturing, selling or importing spare parts incorporating the design and that this was the very subject-matter of the right. Consequently, the court would not impose a compulsory licence because to do so would be to take away the essence of the right even though royalties would be payable. Volvo's decision to refuse to grant a licence was not, therefore, an abuse of its dominant position.[26]

This lack of interference with the exercise of rights is not absolute and in *Magill TV Guide/ITP, BBC and RTE*,[27] the European Commission effectively granted a compulsory licence in respect of listings for forthcoming television programmes even though the television companies concerned were refusing to make them available at all, except to their own publications. A distinction can be made between the Magill case and the Volvo case in that, although it refused to grant licences, Volvo did supply spare parts whereas in the Magill case, the listings were not made available in advance at all. The outcome of the Magill case has been enshrined in statutory form in the Broadcasting Act 1990, as section 176 imposes a duty to provide advance information about programmes broadcast by the BBC, the ITC and the Welsh Authority.[28]

A defendant sued for an infringement of copyright might, in desperation, advance a 'Euro-defence', for example under Article 86 of the Treaty. If nothing else, such a ploy might lengthen the proceedings especially if the case is referred to the European Court for a preliminary ruling under Article 177.[29] In *Ransburg-Gema AG* v *Electrostatic Plant Systems*[30] it was alleged that the defendant had infringed the copyright subsisting in certain drawings. The defendant entered a 'Euro-defence' claiming that the plaintiff was guilty of a breach of Article 86. In striking out the Euro-defences, Aldous J held that there must be a connection between the alleged actions of the plaintiff and the alleged breach under Article 86. The existence of an exclusive right and its exercise were not *per se* a breach of the Treaty of Rome. Further, to show this, the Euro-defence must be sufficiently detailed. In the earlier case of *Imperial Chemical Industries Ltd.* v *Berk Pharmaceuticals Ltd.*,[31] Megarry VC struck out Euro-defences because the defendant had failed to show a sufficient nexus between the alleged breach of Article 86 and the right claimed by the defendant, in that case, to imitate the plaintiff's get-up.

The occasions when the European Court will interfere with the normal exploitation of copyright are quite rare and the court seems to have achieved a fine balance between commercial exploitation and misuse of the right. The fact that copyright law is not harmonized throughout the Community has the effect of raising the status of, and hence the ability to rely on, national laws. Whether, in the course of time, if and when copyright laws are assimilated within the Common Market or a Community-wide copyright is achieved, the European Court will be more willing to intervene with the exploitation of copyright remains to be seen.

24 [1987] ECR 1747.

25 [1989] 4 CMLR 122.

26 Compare this with *British Leyland Motor Corp. Ltd.* v *Armstrong Patents Co. Ltd.* [1986] 2 WLR 400.

27 OJ [1988] L78/43.

28 It applies to the BBC's United Kingdom services, the ITC's regulated services, and, in addition, any national service regulated by the Radio Authority. In the absence of agreement as to the payment, the Copyright Tribunal has the power to fix payment. These provisions came into force on 1 March 1991.

29 This can take about 18 months.

30 [1990] FSR 287.

31 [1981] FSR 1.

HARMONIZATION

Unlike patent law and trade mark law, copyright varies considerably within the Member States of the Community. Harmonization in patent law has been largely achieved through the non-Community European Patent Convention and plans are well under way to grant Community-wide patents before too long. Trade mark harmonization was required by 1 January 1993[32] and a Euromark may become a reality in due course. However, copyright laws remain distinct and diverse amongst the Member States and this can be traced back to the development of copyright law with the strongly economic-biased English system standing in contrast to the French emphasis on the author's rights, for example with its *droite de suite,* the artist's resale right which requires that a percentage of the resale price of an artistic work is paid to the author.[33]

Although all the Member States are signatories to the Berne Convention there are still significant differences in copyright law and it will be some time before congruence can be achieved. This state of affairs does not mean that all thoughts of bringing together copyright laws have to be suppressed because there have been some moves towards this goal and a number of Council Directives have been issued and others are proposed. The first Directive in the copyright field was aimed at harmonizing the copyright protection of computer programs.[34] The need for this was, to some extent, a reflection of the diversity of copyright law between Member States and the undesirability of different treatments given the international spread of computer programs and the size and influence of the computer industry.

32 Council Directive to approximate the laws of the Member States relating to trade marks OJ [1987] L 40/1.

33 This right exists in Belgium, France, Germany, Italy and Luxemburg within the European Community. The right is exercisable even after the author's death, providing the work is still in copyright.

34 Council Directive of 14 May 1991 on the Legal Protection of Computer Programs, OJ [1991] L122/42.

Table 9.1 EC measures affecting copyright

Description	Compliance date	Reference	Comment
Directives Legal protection of computer programs	before 1 January 1993	OJ [1991] L122/42	Given effect by the Copyright (Computer Programs) Regulations 1992 (see Chapter 8).
Rental and lending rights and certain rights relating to copyright	not later than 1 July 1994	OJ [1992] L346/61	See Chapter 6.
Copyright and neighbouring rights relating to satellite broadcasting and cable retransmission	before 1 January 1995	OJ [1993] L248/15	See Chapter 8.
Proposals for Directives Term of protection of copyright and certain related rights	not later than 1 July 1997	OJ [1993] C 27/7	Without prejudice to acts of exploitation performed before 1 July 1994, see Chapter 3.
Legal protection of databases	before 1 January 1995	OJ [1993] C 194/144	See Chapter 8.

Further Directives have been adopted on rental and lending rights and satellite broadcasting and cable retransmission. There are proposals under consideration to deal with the term of copyright and the legal protection of databases. The Commission are also looking at home copying of sound and audiovisual recordings and moral rights. Table 9.1 on page 203 summarizes the legislative measures taken or proposed by the European Community that affect copyright and neighbouring rights.

Whilst it is unlikely that there will be an attempt at a wholesale bringing together of copyright law throughout the European Community in the near future, it is certainly possible that more moves will be made in respect of other copyright issues raised by the march of technology. The European Commission has published a Green Paper on copyright which might lay the foundations for future action in the area of copyright.[35]

INTERNATIONAL CONVENTIONS

The two international copyright conventions lay down minimum standards for copyright protection and provide for reciprocity of protection between those countries that have ratified the conventions. At the present time, each convention has a significant number of members (Berne has 102) and many countries, including the United Kingdom, having ratified both conventions. The United States of America, one of the original members of the Universal Copyright Convention has recently also joined the Berne Copyright Convention as has the Peoples' Republic of China. The Berne Copyright Convention is administered by the World Intellectual Property Organization and the Universal Copyright Convention by UNESCO, the United Nations Educational, Scientific and Cultural Organization. The Berne Copyright Convention dates from 1886 and has European origins. It has been and continues to be very successful but, as a means of encouraging other states to join an international copyright 'club', without requiring the Berne Copyright Convention to be watered down, the Universal Copyright Convention came into existence in 1952. One of the aims of this convention was to narrow the gap between the European concept of *droit d'auteur* and the common law countries' notion of copyright law based firmly on economic rights.[36] (This ignores the fact that the United Kingdom seems to have coped quite happily with the Berne Copyright Convention since its ratification in 1887.)

An examination of some of the provisions of the Berne Convention will give a feel for its influence on United Kingdom copyright law.[37] Article 1 of the Berne Convention states that:

> The countries to which this Convention applies constitute a Union for the protection of the rights of authors in their literary and artistic works.

However, 'literary and artistic works' are comprehensively defined by Article 2 as including 'every production in the literary, scientific and artistic domain, whatever may be the mode or form of its expression' and then goes on to give a comprehensive and wide list of examples. Protection is afforded also to translations, adaptations, arrangements of music and other alterations of a literary or artistic work: Article 2(3). Generally, the term of protection is the life of the author and 50 years after his death but countries in the Union may grant longer

35 *Copyright and the Challenge of Technology – Copyright Issues Requiring Immediate Action*, COM (88) 172.

36 For a history and detailed description of these conventions, see Stewart, S.M. *International Copyright and Neighbouring Rights* (London: Butterworths, 2nd edn., 1989), especially Chapters 5 and 6. Details of other international conventions, agreements and treaties are contained in this excellent text.

37 It is instructive to read the conventions, both of which are reproduced in Phillips, J. (ed.) *Butterworths Intellectual Property Law Handbook* (London: Butterworths, 1990).

38 Article 7.

39 Moral rights are provided for in article 6bis which came about as a result of the Rome Act (an Act modifying the Convention) in 1928. It took the United Kingdom just 60 years to comply.

40 Article 14ter.

41 Article 5(2).

42 Article III(1).

43 In any case, the use of a notice may help evidentially, for example as regards the date of origin of the work and whether the infringer knows or has reason to believe that copyright subsisted in the work.

44 The Satellite Convention 1974 and the Phonogram Convention 1971. The United Kingdom has ratified the latter. The Phonogram Convention is the source of the symbol (P) accompanied by the year of first publication. A 'phonogram' is an 'exclusively aural fixation' and excludes videograms, Article 1(a). Reciprocal rights are given to the producers of phonograms. Another convention is the Rome Convention for the Protection of Performers, Producers of Phonograms and Broadcasting Organizations, 1961 which has been ratified by the United Kingdom. See Chapter 10 on rights in performances.

45 *Tyburn Productions Ltd.* v *Conan Doyle* (unreported) *The Times*, 17 February 1990, Chancery Division, applying *Def Lepp Music* v *Stuart Brown* [1986] RPC 273.

46 Whilst accepting the territorial nature of copyright, doubts are raised in connection with transnational activities such as the international distribution of broadcasts and cable programmes, see Goltz, H. & Pritesche, K. U. 'Cable & Satellite Television – Copyright and Other Issues under German Law', [1988] 9 EIPR 261 at 263.

terms.[38] The text of the convention contains all the other main provisions such as the rights of the author in relation to the work, 'permitted' acts and for the author's moral rights.[39] The convention can be thought of as a basic statement of principle with the detailed implementation being left to the member countries. Both of the conventions allow ample scope for differences in implementation and many provisions are optional. For example, in the Berne Copyright Convention *droit de suite*, the artists resale right, is available 'only if legislation in the country to which the author belongs so permits'.[40] United Kingdom copyright law does not provide for this right and, therefore, United Kingdom artists do not have a right to a payment on the subsequent resale of their works.

The Universal Copyright Convention lacks the detail of the Berne Copyright Convention and takes a more 'broad brush' approach. Article 1 states:

> Each Contracting State undertakes to provide for the adequate and effective protection of the rights of authors and other copyright proprietors in literary, scientific and artistic works, including writings, musical, dramatic and cinematographic works, and paintings, engravings and sculpture.

The minimum term of protection shall not be less than the life of the author and 25 years after his death. One important difference between the conventions is that the Berne Copyright Convention requires no formalities – 'The enjoyment and the exercise of these rights shall not be subject to any formality'[41] – whereas the Universal Copyright Convention permits Contracting States to require compliance with formalities including deposit, registration, and the payment of fees. This has important implications for other countries, for to obtain reciprocal protection in a country having formalities, works must bear the copyright symbol © accompanied by the name of the copyright proprietor and the year of first publication 'placed in such a manner and location so as to give reasonable notice of claim to copyright'.[42] This explains the importance of using such a symbol in order to obtain the greatest possible international protection with respect to copyright works even though, in the United Kingdom, there is no requirement for such a notice.[43]

The international conventions have played and will continue to play an important role in the development of copyright law and in laying down minimum standards. In addition to the Berne and the Universal Copyright Conventions, there are other conventions dealing with copyright matters such as satellite broadcasts and phonograms.[44] The reciprocal protection initiated by the conventions has been instrumental in the protection of works of copyright on a much wider and more homogeneous scale than would otherwise have been the case.

Jurisdiction

If an infringement occurs in a foreign country, legal action must be taken in that particular country and the United Kingdom courts will not entertain disputes relating to foreign patents, copyright or trade mark laws.[45] Rights under intellectual property are territorial and only acts done within the United Kingdom infringe United Kingdom copyright.[46] In such a case, advantage should be made of the reciprocity arrangements, if applicable, to take action in the country where the infringement occurred. However, the transnational character of broadcasting can extend the geographical boundaries of copyright as in

BBC Enterprises Ltd. v *Hi-Tech Xtravision Ltd.*[47] where persons enabled or assisted to receive encrypted transmissions included persons outside the United Kingdom within the 'footprint' of the broadcasts for the purposes of section 298(2)(a) of the Copyright, Designs and Patents Act 1988.[48]

[47] [1991] 3 WLR 1.

[48] The offending decrypting apparatus was made in the United Kingdom and sold throughout Western Europe.

10

Rights in performances

INTRODUCTION

A well-known soprano gives a live performance of an operatic aria by W. A. Mozart. Unknown to the soprano, a member of the audience makes a recording of the performance on a magnetic tape and then, later, makes copies which he sells to the public without the singer's permission. Under copyright law, there is nothing that can be done to prevent the sale of the recordings of the performance. The music and lyrics are out of copyright so there is no infringement of the musical or literary work. Indeed, the only relevance of copyright law is that the person who made the recording without permission owns the copyright in it as a sound recording. Had the singer agreed a recording contract with a publisher, the publisher would be unable to use copyright law to prevent the sale of the unauthorized recordings, which have a separate and independent copyright to the publisher's recording. The authorized and unauthorized master recordings are coterminous and there is no link between them associated with the acts restricted by the copyright in the publisher's sound recording. There may still be problems if the music is protected by copyright because the owner of that copyright may be reluctant to pursue a claim for infringement with respect to one performance.

This state of affairs is clearly untenable and this 'loophole' in copyright law is closed by the law relating to performances. However, this area of law has only recently gained the status of a fully-fledged intellectual property right. The first law on the subject was the Dramatic and Musical Performers' Protection Act 1925 which provided criminal penalties in respect of the making of recordings of dramatic and musical performances without consent. This Act was basically re-enacted in 1958 and, by the Performers' Protection Act 1963, the provisions were extended to all the original works of copyright, that is literary, dramatic, musical and artistic works.[1] The Performers' Protection Act 1972 increased the maximum penalties available. However, these Acts only appeared to give rise to criminal liability and did not seem to give any civil remedies to performers or to those with whom the performers may have had recording contracts. The offences related to recording a live performance, broadcasting it, transmitting it via a cable distribution system or performing it in public without the consent of the original performers. The use of an unauthorized audio or audio-visual recording for the purpose of broadcasting, inclusion in a cable system, public performance and dealing with such unauthorized recordings were also offences.

The question as to whether the law gave a right to civil actions was considered both in respect of performers and recording companies. In *Rickless* v *United Artists Corp.*,[2] the defendant made a new film by using clips and outtakes (discarded excerpts) from previous Pink Panther films starring the late Peter Sellers. The plaintiff who owned the rights of Peter Seller's services as an

1 The purpose of the 1963 Act was to achieve compliance with the Convention for the Protection of Performers, Producers of Phonograms and Broadcasting Organizations (the Rome Convention), 26 October 1961.

2 [1988] 1 QB 40.

actor sued for, *inter alia,* breach of section 2 of the Dramatic and Musical Performers' Protection Act 1958 because the defendant failed to obtain the permission of the actor's executors. The trial judge awarded damages of US$ 1m and the defendant appealed to the Court of Appeal arguing that section 2 did not give rise to a private cause of action. The Court of Appeal dismissed the appeal confirming that section 2 of the Act conferred a right to civil remedies to the performer whose performance had been exploited without written consent in addition to imposing criminal penalties.[3] The basis for this decision was that, by imposing the criminal penalties, the Act imposed an obligation or prohibition for the benefit of a class of persons, in this case performers and, consequently, this gave a cause of action to any aggrieved performer. However, in *RCA Corp.* v *Pollard*[4] the Court of Appeal reluctantly found that the Acts did not give civil remedies to recording companies. This highlighted the problem that recording companies were having with 'bootleg' recordings and the regrettable lack of civil remedies under the 1958–1972 Acts.[5] The ease of making good quality bootleg recordings because of technological advances was of particular concern.

These problems were identified in the White Paper preceding the Copyright, Designs and Patents Act 1988.[6] That Act repealed the previous Acts in their entirety and replaced them with new provisions contained in Part II of the Act. In addition to giving a civil right of action to recording companies having an exclusive licence with the performer and confirming civil remedies for performers, the new provisions extend to live performances by a variety of artistes such as jugglers and acrobats and brings the criminal penalties and powers of search and seizure more in line with those available in copyright law.

Part II of the Copyright, Designs and Patents Act 1988 came into force on 1 August 1989. This area of law is largely new, rights in performances having been considerably expanded in comparison with previous law. The provisions are retrospective in that live performances that were made prior to the coming into force of the new law are protected but a right of action does not accrue in respect of acts carried out before that date.[7] In other words, new rights have been retrospectively granted but new liabilities have not been retrospectively imposed. For example, a live performance by a team of acrobats made in 1987 is protected. If a bootleg film was made of the performance, the making of the film did not infringe any intellectual property rights and there can be no legal action now in respect of it. However, if the person who made the film now decides to make and sell copies to the public, the acrobats can sue for infringement of their performers' right.[8]

Two separate and distinct rights are created by the 1988 Act: a performers' right and a recording right. The nature of the rights is somewhat peculiar as the rights are not transmissible except that a performer's right will pass on the death of the performer concerned.[9] However, by section 185(2)(b), the benefit of an exclusive recording licence may be assigned and by section 185(3)(b), a person may be assigned the benefit of a licence to make recordings for commercial exploitation.[10] Whether rights in performances are true property rights is, therefore, a moot point. The performers' right, in particular, has some features in common with the author's moral rights under copyright law. In other respects, the rights are very similar to copyright. Rights in performances subsist alongside and are independent of copyright, both the economic and moral

3 Applying the dictum of Lord Diplock in *Lonrho Ltd.* v *Shell Petroleum Co. Ltd.* [1982] AC 173.

4 [1983] Ch 135.

5 In this context, a 'bootleg' recording is one made without the permission of either the performer or the authorized recording company, if any.

6 *Intellectual Property and Innovation,* Cmnd. 9712 (London: HMSO, 1986). The problems had also been discussed earlier in the Whitford Committee Report, *Copyright and Designs Law,* Cmnd. 6732 (London: HMSO, 1977) and in the Green Paper, *Reform of the Law relating to Copyright, Designs and Performers' Protection,* Cmnd. 8302 (London: HMSO, 1981).

7 Section 180(3). Unless otherwise stated, in this chapter, statutory references are to the Copyright, Designs and Patents Act 1988.

8 Assuming the making of the copies was not in pursuance of arrangements made before the commencement of the new provisions. A person having an exclusive recording contract with the acrobats in relation to the performance may also sue because his recording rights have been infringed.

9 Section 192.

10 These provisions are concerned with qualification for the right.

rights. A fairly complex mosaic of rights might be involved. For example, a live performance might take place of a piece of music by a singer (Cynthia) and orchestra (Harvey and the Syncopators). The music was recently written by Filbert and the lyrics by Hamstein, who have assigned their copyrights to the Palm Beach Music Publishing Company. A television company (SKB TV) may have an exclusive recording contract with the singer and orchestra. If a person, John Silver, is in the audience and makes a bootleg recording with the intention of making copies for sale, then John has infringed the following rights:

(a) Palm Beach's copyright in the musical and literary work.
(b) The performers' right belonging to Cynthia and each and every member of the orchestra.
(c) SKB TV's recording right.

In addition, if John makes copies that are issued to the public but which do not mention the fact that the music was written by Filbert and Hamstein, they will have an action against John for infringement of their moral right of 'paternity'. If he sells or rents copies to the public, John will further infringe the copyrights.[11] The situation could be even more complex if the music is subject to an agreement with a collecting society or if SKB TV had assigned the benefit of the exclusive recording contract to another. John is therefore exposed to a veritable battery of civil actions but he is also liable to be prosecuted for offences under copyright law[12] and for dealing with illicit recordings.[13]

It is difficult to tell, as yet, how much use will be made of the rights in performances. These rights could be useful if, in the above example, the copyright owner is a foreign national and not particularly interested in suing in respect of the copyright infringement and the authors' moral rights have not been infringed. An added bonus is that it puts control into the hands of the performers themselves and persons having exclusive recording contracts. As yet there has been hardly any reported case law since the relevant provisions of the Copyright, Designs and Patents Act 1988 came into force.[14]

NATURE AND SUBSISTENCE OF THE RIGHTS

The rights are given to performers and persons having recording rights and their consent is required for the exploitation of the performance or the making of recordings.[15] Rights in performances should not be confused with 'performing rights'. This term is usually used to signify rights under copyright in relation to the acts of performing, showing or playing a work, in which copyright subsists in public. For example, where a retail store wishes to play background music, it will require the permission of the relevant copyright owners. The copyright performing rights are usually administered by collecting societies such as the Performing Right Society (in the United Kingdom).

A performance is a live performance given by one or more individuals which is a dramatic performance (including dance and mime), a musical performance, a reading or recitation of a literary work or a variety act or any similar presentation.[16] If a person sings live to a recorded backing track, for example in a 'karaoke bar', the live performance relates to the live singing only.[17] The meaning of 'recording' is important in terms of recording rights and infringement

11 He could have further liabilities arising from rental and lending rights provided for in pursuance of the rental and lending rights Directive.

12 Section 107(1).

13 Section 198(1).

14 One example is *Grower v British Broadcasting Corporation* [1990] FSR 595.

15 The performer's consent is required in relation to the performers' rights but the consent of either the performer or the person having the recording right is required in relation to the recording right.

16 Section 180(2).

17 However, there is also a public performance of the backing track and there will be an infringement of this unless permission to play the track has been obtained or a licence scheme is in operation and covers the playing of the particular backing track in question.

and is defined in section 180(2) as being a film or sound recording made directly from a live performance or made from a broadcast or cable programme including the performance or made directly or indirectly from another recording of the performance. Therefore, copies made from a master recording that was made during the performance count as being recordings.

For the rights to exist, certain qualification requirements must be satisfied. The performers' rights only subsist if the performance is a qualifying performance which, by section 181, means that it must be given by a qualifying individual or take place in a qualifying country. Section 206 defines a qualifying individual as being a citizen or subject of a qualifying country or a person who is resident in such a country. 'Qualifying country' means the United Kingdom and any other Member State of the European Economic Community and any other country designated by Order in Council under section 208, that is to countries enjoying reciprocal protection.[18]

For the recording right, by section 185, the person having recording rights who is a party to an exclusive recording contract with the performer or the assignee of the benefit of such a contract must be a qualifying person.[19] If not, then the right might still arise where a person who has been licensed to make recordings or to whom the benefit of such a licence has been assigned is a qualifying person. A qualifying person can be a qualifying individual or a body corporate formed under the law of the United Kingdom or of another qualifying country which carries on a substantial business activity in any qualifying country: section 206. It should be noted that the recording right can arise even though the performance is not a qualifying performance, so that an Italian film company having an exclusive recording contract to record the live performance of a juggler from North Korea which takes place in India will have recording rights which are enforceable in the United Kingdom even though the juggler himself has no rights in his own performance subject to United Kingdom law. The performance is not a qualifying performance because the juggler fails to meet the requirements for a qualifying individual and the performance does not take place in a qualifying country.[20]

The performer's right and the recording right endure for a period of 50 years from the end of the calendar year during which the performance was made.[21] Unlike most original works of copyright, the period of protection is fixed as soon as it is made and it not dependent upon a person's lifespan. This means that it is possible that a recording made without the performer's consent may be shown in public or broadcast when the performer is still alive, if the performance was more than 50 years ago. However, the decision in the *Rickless* case may still give rise to a separate civil right of action based on the offences which have no time limit.[22]

INFRINGEMENT

In considering infringement of the rights in performances, it will be easier to consider each right separately even though the infringements are similar. But before doing so, the meaning of 'illicit recording' must be explained (this is the equivalent of an infringing copy of a work in which copyright subsists, but there are some differences) as well as the meaning of 'consent'. By section 197, an illicit recording is:

18 This includes countries that are members of the Rome Convention for the Protection of Performers, Producers of Phonograms and Broadcasting Organizations, 1961.

19 An exclusive recording contract is a contract between the performer and another person under which that other person is entitled to the exclusion of all others, including the performer, to make recordings of one or more of his performances with a view to their commercial exploitation, section 185(1).

20 North Korea and India are not members of the Rome Convention.

21 Section 191. This will not be extended by the Directive on the term of protection.

22 See, De Frietas, D. 'The Copyright, Designs and Patents Act 1988 (4)' (1989) 133 *Solicitors Journal* 734 at 735. Section 180(4) states that the rights conferred are independent of 'any other right or obligation arising otherwise than under this Part'.

(a) for performer's rights, a recording of the whole or any substantial part of a performance made, otherwise than for private purposes, without the performer's consent;

(b) for the recording rights, a recording of the whole or any substantial part of a performance subject to an exclusive recording contract made, otherwise than for private purposes, without the consent of either the performer or the person entitled to the recording rights;

(c) a recording which is an illicit recording under the provisions of Schedule 2 to the Copyright, Designs and Patents Act 1988 (the permitted acts in relation to performances). This covers recordings, the making of which did not infringe the rights in performances because they were made for a permitted act, but which have been used subsequently outside the terms of the exception. For example, a recording made for educational purposes has been sold.[23]

23 See Schedule 2, para. 6(2).

The place where the recording was made is immaterial and there is no reason to believe that the question of substantiality will be construed otherwise than it is for copyright purposes.

The issue of consent is central to the infringement of the rights. There is no requirement for the consent to be in writing and, by section 193(1), consent may relate to a single specific performance, a number of performances or performances generally. Future and past performances are included, so that consent can be given retrospectively. Persons having any of the rights devolved to them are bound by consents given by previous right holders. This is strict and there are no exceptions for 'equity's darling'.

In the absence of express consent, it seems reasonable to suppose that it may be implied and it will be so implied if it is necessary and reasonable to do so. The same applies to the need to obtain consent if the intended use of a recording of a performance appears to exceed the terms of the original consent. However, consent given in respect of a particular use does not necessarily prohibit, by implication, other uses; something else must be shown, that is that the new intended use raises an implication that further consent is required. In *Grower* v *British Broadcasting Corporation*[24] the BBC had made a recording of a performance of 'Hoochie Coochie Man' by the Jimi Hendrix Experience for the immediate purpose of broadcasting on a radio programme hosted by Alexis Korner who had, at the invitation of Hendrix, joined in the performance, playing a guitar. It appeared that Korner had consented to the making of the recording and the broadcasting of that recording. In an agreement made in 1988, the BBC granted a licence to a Californian company in respect of the sound recording. The licence included a term that the Californian company obtain the consent of any artists who had contributed to the recording before exploiting the recording. The plaintiffs, the executors of Korner's estate, sued the BBC (as joint tortfeasor) on the basis that the Californian company had exploited the sound recording without their consent and that this was a breach of the performer's rights under Part II of the Copyright, Designs and Patents Act 1988. It was held, *inter alia*, that the plaintiff would have to establish that there was an implied term that the BBC either obtain the plaintiffs' consent to exploit the sound recording or that the BBC would guarantee that a licensee or assignee of the copyright in the sound recording would obtain the consent of all

24 [1990] FSR 595.

the performers and neither implication was necessary nor reasonable in the circumstances.[25]

Infringement of performer's rights

A performer's rights in a qualifying performance are infringed by any person who, without the performer's consent, does any of the following acts in relation to the whole or any substantial part of the performance:[26]

(a) makes a recording, otherwise than for his own private and domestic use;
(b) broadcasts live, or includes live in a cable programme service;
(c) by means of a recording which was, and which that person knows or has reason to believe was, made without the performer's consent, shows, plays in public, broadcasts or includes in a cable programme service;
(d) imports into the United Kingdom, otherwise than for his own private and domestic purposes, or, in the course of a business, possesses, sells, lets for hire, offers or exposes for sale or hire or distributes an illicit recording, which he knows is or has reason to believe is, an illicit recording.

Thus, as for copyright, there are secondary infringements associated with 'dealing' with illicit recordings. These approximate to, but do not exactly match, the criminal offences that also cover some of the 'primary' infringements. As can be seen in some of the infringements above, knowledge (actual or constructive) is required for the infringement to be made out. In some cases, knowledge is also important as regards the availability or quantification of damages.

Infringement of recording rights

Infringement of recording rights occurs in similar ways to infringement of performers' rights. However, there is no infringement of the recording right by a live broadcast or live inclusion in a cable programme service. For the 'making a recording' infringement, the consent required is that of either the performer or the person having the recording right and this also applies to public showing or playing and the broadcast or inclusion in a cable programme service of a recording of the performance. (Note that the broadcast or inclusion in a cable programme service in this case is not live – it relates to a recording of the performance.) The consent may have been given previously by the person then entitled to the recording rights.

Importing, possessing and dealing with illicit recordings, if done without consent, infringe the recording rights (as they do the performer's rights) but the consent needed here is that of the performer in the case of a qualifying performance or, otherwise, the consent of the person having the recording right.

EXCEPTIONS

The *Rickless* case has been criticized in that it gave civil rights in a way that was probably not intended by Parliament and this meant that such civil rights were without the comprehensive exceptions that apply to copyright and moderate its strength.[27] The fine balance usually maintained between the interests of the

25 Of course, the BBC owned the copyright in the sound recording. Neither was the BBC liable as joint tortfeasor as, although the BBC may have facilitated the infringement by the Californian company, it had not participated in it. It was, however, arguable that the making of a back-up copy of the recording was a breach of the Dramatic and Musical Performers' Protection Act 1958 and a breach of the agreement between Korner and the BBC.

26 See sections 182–184 for the infringements.

27 See Dworkin, G. & Taylor, R.D. *Blackstone's Guide to the Copyright, Designs and Patents Act 1988* (London: Blackstone, 1989) at p.127.

owners of intellectual property rights and the public was missing. The 1988 provisions remedy this in an extensive manner and a whole range of exceptions are made which, on the whole, are very similar to those available in copyright law. There are many cross references to the copyright provisions for definitions. The exceptions are contained in Schedule 2 to the Copyright, Designs and Patents Act 1988 and, although there is no room to discuss them here in detail, Table 10.1 should give some indication of their scope.[28]

28 For general principles, reference should be made to Chapter 7.

Table 10.1 Exceptions to infringement of rights in performances

Exception	Comment
Criticism, review and reporting current events (para. 2)	There is no exception for research and no requirement for a sufficient acknowledgement (but this may be required for copyright)
Incidental inclusion (para. 3)	As with copyright, deliberate inclusion is outside the exception
'Educational purposes' (paras 4-6)	Similar exceptions to those for copyright but less extensive
Copy required as a condition of export, e.g. article of cultural or historical importance (para. 7)	The long list of exceptions for libraries and archives for copyright are missing for performances
Public administration (paras 8-11)	Similar to copyright exceptions but not as many
Transfer of copies in electronic form (para. 12)	Allows the making of a back-up copy in some cases
Miscellaneous (paras 13-21) Recordings of spoken words Recordings of folk songs Club and society purposes	These are all very similar to the copyright exceptions

Broadcasts/cable programmes
Incidental recording for:
  Supervision and control
  Free public showing/playing
  Reception/retransmission
  Subtitled copies for hard of hearing, etc.
  Recording for archival purposes	

The Copyright Tribunal is, by section 190, given limited powers in respect of performances and a person who wishes to make a recording from an existing recording of a performance may ask the Tribunal to give consent where the identity or whereabouts of the performer cannot be ascertained by reasonable enquiry or where the performer unreasonably withholds his consent. In exercising this power, the Tribunal shall take into account:

(a) whether the recording from which the new recording is to be made was made with the performer's consent and is lawfully in the possession and control of the person proposing to make the new recording, and

(b) whether the making of the new recording would be consistent with the obligations and purposes of the parties to the arrangements under which the original recording was made.

Where the performer unreasonably withholds consent, the Tribunal may give consent only if satisfied that the performer's reasons do not include the protection of any of his legitimate interests, but it is for the performer to show what his reasons are and, in default, the Tribunal may make any such inference as it thinks fit. Where the Tribunal gives consent to the making of the further recording(s), it may make such order for payment as it thinks fit as being the appropriate consideration for the consent, unless the parties have agreed payment in the meantime.

REMEDIES

Infringement of any of the rights in a performance is actionable as a breach of statutory duty, by section 194. This would seem to include injunctions, damages and, as an alternative, accounts of profits. Damages are not available in respect of the making of a recording or a live broadcast or inclusion live in a cable programme service if, at the time, the defendant shows that he believed on reasonable grounds that the necessary consent had been given. For the secondary infringements, if the illicit recording was innocently acquired by the defendant or his predecessor in title, the only remedy for the infringement is damages not exceeding a reasonable payment in respect of the act complained of. By section 184(3), an illicit recording is innocently acquired if the person acquiring it did not know and had no reason to believe that it was an illicit recording.

In addition to the normal remedies, orders for delivery up of illicit recordings are available and there is a civil right of seizure of illicit recordings exposed for sale or hire at temporary premises after serving notice at a local police station.

OFFENCES

The criminal offences are similar to those under the previous Acts and are detailed in section 198. A person commits an offence if, without sufficient consent, he:

(a) makes for sale or hire, or
(b) imports into the United Kingdom, otherwise than for his private and domestic use, or
(c) possesses in the course of business with a view to committing an act infringing any of the rights in performances, or
(d) in the course of business
   (i)   sells or lets for hire, or
   (ii) offers or exposes for sale or hire, or
   (iii) distributes,

a recording which he knows, or has reason to believe, is an illicit recording.

The offences under (a), (b) and (d)(iii) are triable either way, carrying a maximum of 2 years' imprisonment and/or a fine. The other offences, including those described below are triable summarily only and carry a maximum penalty of a fine not exceeding level 5 on the standard scale or a term of imprisonment not exceeding six months or both.[29] It is also an offence, without sufficient consent, to cause a recording to be shown or played in public or to broadcast it or include it in a cable programme service; for the offence to be made out, it is required that the person concerned knows or has reason to believe that any of the rights in performances will be infringed as a result of his actions. None of the above offences are committed if the act comes within any of the exceptions in Schedule 2.

The meaning of 'sufficient consent' depends on whether the performance is a qualifying performance.[30] If it is, then it is the consent of the performer. Otherwise, and for the purposes of the offence of making for sale or hire, it is the consent of the performer or the person having the recording rights. For all the other offences involving a non-qualifying performance, it is the consent of the person having the recording rights. There are provisions for orders for delivery up in criminal proceedings (section 199), and for search warrants (section 200), and orders may be made for the disposal of illicit recordings (section 204). These provisions are similar to those available in respect of the copyright criminal offences.

Directors, managers, secretaries, and other similar officers of corporate bodies may also be liable where the offence is committed by a corporate body with their consent or connivance.[31] It is an offence for a person to falsely represent that he is authorized by any person to give the necessary consent in relation to a performance unless he believes, on reasonable grounds, that he is so authorized. This offence is triable summarily only and carries a maximum of imprisonment for a period not exceeding six months and/or a fine not exceeding level 5 on the standard scale.

SUMMARY

The statutory extension of performers' protection to give civil rights not only to performers but also to persons having exclusive recording contracts with those performers is welcome and is a direct response to the growing problem of bootleg recordings. The inclusion of variety acts, extending the scope beyond performances of the 'original works' category of copyright, is sensible as such performances are no less deserving of protection. The new law makes it more important than ever to ascertain the consent of *all* those taking part in a performance before making a recording and it could hinder future use of old recordings to make new recordings, for example by making a compilation of old recordings. The spectre of 'bit-part' actors withholding consent and preventing this future exploitation will be ever present in the minds of film and record companies.[32] This could have serious consequences for the British Broadcasting Corporation which have large numbers of recordings of television comedy and drama, much of which was broadcast live. However, the Copyright Tribunal is there as a last resort should the performer unreasonably withhold his consent. Of course, the old recordings must be of live performances, as opposed to a recording made in a studio.

---

29 Level 5 is currently £5,000.

30 Section 198(3).

31 Section 202. Both the officer and the corporate body are criminally liable.

32 Of course, employment and service contracts should provide for these rights in a way that facilitates future exploitation of the work.

Some measure of international protection is afforded through the Rome Convention of 1961 for the Protection of Performers, Producers of Phonograms and Broadcasting Organizations which has been ratified by a total of 44 states including the United Kingdom.

Part Three

THE LAW OF BREACH
OF CONFIDENCE

11

Introduction

This area of law is concerned with secrets of all kinds. They may be of a personal, commercial or industrial nature or concern the state and its administration. State secrets received a great deal of publicity a few years ago as a result of the publication of *Spycatcher* written by Peter Wright, a former assistant director of MI5, but it is in relation to trade secrets and business information that the law of confidence is of everyday importance. The vast majority of persons owe an obligation of confidence to others; all employees have a duty of confidence to their employers, consultants owe a duty to their clients, doctors have a duty of confidence in respect of their patients and solicitors are bound by a duty of confidence to their clients. The law of confidence also covers business transactions and negotiations and an obligation of confidence will be implied in a great many situations where there is no express agreement as to confidentiality.

Breach of confidence is a tort which lies in the domain of equity and is almost entirely based on case law. However, there is statutory recognition of the law of breach of confidence. For example, section 171(1) of the Copyright, Designs and Patents Act 1988 states that:

> Nothing in this Part [the part of the Act dealing with copyright law] affects . . . the operation of any rule of equity relating to breaches of trust or confidence

1 See *Lord Advocate v The Scotsman Publications Ltd.* [1990] AC 812 for a discussion of the Official Secrets Act 1989.

The notoriously widely drafted section 2 of the Official Secrets Act 1911, now replaced and narrowed by section 1 of the Official Secrets Act 1989[1], provided for a number of offences relating to the disclosure of confidential information to unauthorized persons.[2] Otherwise, disclosure of confidential information lies within the scope of the civil law and, being equitable, the law of confidence has proven to be reasonably flexible and a particularly useful adjunct to other intellectual property rights.

2 Section 2 became so infamous that juries had become inclined to acquit regardless of the evidence - for example, the trial and acquittal of the senior civil servant Clive Ponting for disclosure of cabinet minutes relating to the sinking of the *General Belgrano*, see *R v Ponting* [1985] Crim LR 318.

Whereas other rights such as copyright and patents are particularly useful when the subject matter is made public by exploitation by the right owner, the law of breach of confidence gives protection to things not released to the public or even part of the public. Indeed, this is the whole point of the law of confidence and its most useful feature is that an injunction can be obtained preventing an anticipated wrongful release or use of the information that is the subject matter of the confidence. In terms of patent law, confidence is vital to the grant of a patent as it is essential that details of the invention do not fall into the public domain before the filing of the patent application, otherwise the patent will be refused.[3] Confidence protects the invention and its detail. In some circumstances the inventor may decide to keep his invention secret in preference to obtaining a patent as the latter only gives a maximum of 20 years' protection. It depends on whether the information can be kept secret. As regards copyright, it has been seen that, as a matter of principle, copyright does not protect ideas, only the expression of ideas. However, confidence can and does protect ideas but only until such time as those ideas are published in some way.

3 An exception is made where the information has been released by a person acting in breach of confidence, Patents Act 1977, section 2(4). The requirement of novelty is, therefore, not compromised by a breach of confidence.

DEVELOPMENT OF THE LAW OF BREACH OF CONFIDENCE

The law of breach of confidence has had an erratic history. It largely developed in a spurt in the early to middle of the nineteenth century and then lay relatively dormant until the late 1940s when it was realized that this was an extremely useful area of law. Some of the early cases involved 'patent medicines'. There was obviously a lot of money to be made from these magic cures, bearing in mind that conventional medicine was still fairly primitive at this time and the public at large was relatively ignorant and uneducated. In *Morison* v *Moat*,[4] such a medicine was made known as 'Morison's Vegetable Universal Medicine'. There was a dispute between the son of the person who originally devised the recipe and the partner, Thomas Moat, who had improperly told his own son of the recipe. It was held that there was an equity against the defendant. It was a breach of faith and of contract by the partner, Thomas Moat, to tell his son of the secret who, therefore, derived his knowledge under a breach of faith and of contract and could not claim a title to the recipe. Although the term 'breach of confidence' was not used at this stage, it was clear that the breach of faith was actionable *per se* and was not dependant upon the existence of a contract. There was no contractual relationship between the son of the originator of the recipe and the son of the defendant.

Another important case which helped establish this area of law concerned etchings made by Queen Victoria and Prince Albert. The case is *Prince Albert* v *Strange*.[5] The Queen and Prince Albert made etchings for their own amusement, intended only for their own private entertainment, although they sometimes had prints made to give to friends. Some of the etchings were sent to a printer for impressions (prints) to be made from them. Whilst at the printers, it seemed that someone surreptitiously made some additional prints which came into the hands of the defendant who intended to display the prints in an exhibition to which the public could go on payment of an admission charge. The defendant advertised his intention to hold the exhibition and was sued by the Queen's Consort. It was held that relief would be given against the defendant even though he was a third party. The defendant had argued that the prints were not improperly taken but it was said that his possession must have originated in a breach of trust, a breach of confidence or a breach of contract and, therefore, an injunction was granted preventing the exhibition. Again, it was clear that relief was available without having to rely on a contractual relationship.

THE MODERN LAW OF BREACH OF CONFIDENCE

The law of breach of confidence began its renaissance about 40 or 50 years ago. It became apparent that this area of law was extremely well suited to protecting 'industrial property' during the development stages before other legal rights were able to afford protection.[6] Indeed, some industrialists had come to the conclusion that it was better to keep some details of their processes secret rather than obtain a patent which would mean that, eventually, the idea would fall into the public domain. However, it seems as if the significance of this area of law was not fully appreciated by law reporters. A number of important cases were reported in some series of law reports retrospectively, several years after the disposal of the cases.

4 (1851) 9 Hare 241.

5 (1849) 1 Mac & G 25.

6 'Industrial property' can be considered to include patent law, trade mark law and design law.

The first major case on the law of breach of confidence that laid the foundations for its modern form was *Saltman Engineering Co. Ltd. v Campbell Engineering Co. Ltd.*[7] The plaintiff owned the copyright in drawings of tools for use in the manufacture of leather punches. The defendant was given the drawings and instructed to make 5,000 of the tools at 3s 6d each. After completing the order, the defendant retained the drawings and made use of them for his own purposes. In finding for the plaintiff, holding that there was an implied condition that the defendant should treat the drawings as confidential and not make other use of them and should deliver the drawings with the tools made pursuant to the agreement,[8] Lord Greene MR described the nature of confidential information thus:

> The information, to be confidential, must, I apprehend, apart from contract, have the necessary quality of confidence about it, namely, it must not be something which is public property and public knowledge. On the other hand, it is perfectly possible to have a confidential document, be it a formula, a plan, a sketch, or something of that kind, which is the result of work done by the maker upon materials which may be available for the use of anybody; but what makes it confidential is the fact that the maker of the document has used his brain and thus produced a result which can only be produced by somebody who goes through the same process.[9]

Lord Greene also emphasized that an obligation of confidence is not limited to cases where the parties are in a contractual relationship, that the law will prevent an abuse of position by the recipient of confidential information. He also indicated that there need be nothing special about the information concerned and that others may be able to derive the information for themselves but will need to invest some effort to obtain that information. In other words, the recipient of confidential information will be prevented from making unfair use of the information outside that contemplated by the person giving it. It can be said that a person fixed with a duty of confidence is in an analogous position to that of a trustee; however, in the case of a person fixed with an obligation of confidence, the nature of that duty is always negative, that is he must not use or divulge the information outside the authority given to him by his confidant.

Megarry J further developed the action of breach of confidence and laid down a good working formula for the application of this area of law in the case of *Coco v A N Clark (Engineers) Ltd.*[10] The plaintiff, one Marco Paolo Coco, designed a moped engine and had entered into informal negotiations with the defendant with a view to the latter manufacturing the engine. In the end the negotiations broke down and no contract was executed between the plaintiff and the defendant. The plaintiff suggested that the defendant had deliberately caused the break down in negotiations with a view to making the engine without paying the plaintiff. When the defendant decided to manufacture its own engine to a design which closely resembled the plaintiff's design, the plaintiff sought an interlocutory injunction to prevent the defendant using confidential information given by the plaintiff for the purposes of a proposed joint venture.

Megarry J stated that the doctrine of confidence required three elements as follows:

(a) The information must have the necessary quality of confidence about it (using Lord Greene's definition in *Saltman*).

7 [1963] 3 All ER 413, also reported in (1948) 65 RPC 203.

8 There was no contract between the plaintiff and the defendant who had been sub-contracted to make the tools. The defendant was instructed to deliver up the drawings and an inquiry into damages was ordered.

9 [1963] 3 All ER 413 at 415.

10 [1969] RPC 41.

(b) The information must have been imparted in circumstances importing an obligation of confidence.

(c) There must be an unauthorized use of that information to the detriment of the party communicating it.

However, the plaintiff was not granted an injunction and had, at best, a weak case. Where information was communicated in the expectation that the plaintiff would be paid, it was doubtful whether an injunction was an appropriate remedy if there was subsequently a dispute. Megarry J ordered that the defendant should give an undertaking to pay a royalty of five shillings per engine made into a special joint bank account on trusts should the defendant manufacture the engines, pending the full trial. The formula used by Megarry J forms a useful basis for exploring the nature and scope of the law of breach of confidence and is used as a framework for the discussion in the following chapter.

The equitable nature of the law of breach of confidence was stressed by Ungoed-Thomas J in *Duchess of Argyll* v *Duke of Argyll*[11] where he said:

> These cases [*Prince Albert* v *Strange*, etc.] in my view indicate (1) that a contract or obligation of confidence need not be expressed but can be implied . . . (2) that a breach of confidence or trust or faith can arise independently of any right of property or contract other, of course, than any contract which the imparting of the confidence in the relevant circumstances may itself create; (3) that the court in the exercise of its equitable jurisdiction will restrain a breach of confidence independently of any right at law.

It is clear that an obligation will be implied in many situations but, as Ungoed-Thomas J acknowledges, the obligation may be created expressly by way of a contract (an express contractual obligation may run alongside or replace an obligation that would otherwise be imposed by equity). For example, a contract of employment or service may include terms imposing an obligation of confidence on one or both parties. Further, in some contracts, the subject-matter may be confidential information itself, for example where a designer gives details of his design to a manufacturer in return for royalties.

Being rooted in equity, the law of confidence retains a useful flexibility and it has been developed at an extraordinary rate by the courts over the last three or four decades. Nevertheless, the Law Commission recommended that this area of law be codified and a draft Bill was produced in 1981.[12] A major advantage of the law of breach of confidence has been its flexibility and the way in which it has been developed by the courts, freed from the straightjacket of statutory interpretation. It might be wondered, therefore, what would be gained by codifying this area of law, which works reasonably effectively, to replace it with sterile legislation. The Law Commission must have appreciated this as much of the draft Bill is couched in general terms and, indeed, the Law Commission stated:

> . . . we should emphasise that the legislative framework which we envisage would allow the Courts wide scope in applying its principles to differing situations and changing social circumstances.[13]

If this is the basis upon which the legislation would be founded it is difficult to see what advantage would be gained by its promulgation. Widely drafted legislation might have some unfortunate and unpredictable effects whilst the track

11 [1967] Ch 303 at 322.

12 The Law Commission, Law Comm. No. 110, *Breach of Confidence*, Cmnd 8388 (London: HMSO, 1981).

13 Para 6.1.

record of the courts in developing this area of common law has been good and there is no reason to believe that judicial common sense cannot provide for the future satisfactory development of the law of confidence. Such considerations may account for the fact that no moves have been made to codify the law of confidence and it would seem that codification is extremely unlikely in the foreseeable future.[14]

14 For a brief overview of the Law Commission's draft Bill, see Reid, B.C. *Confidentiality and the Law* (London: Waterlow, 1986) at p.190.

One area the draft Bill addressed was the position of persons improperly acquiring information, for example by industrial espionage. In many cases in the law of confidence, the information concerned has been divulged deliberately by the person who 'owns' the information. However, where a person acquires information by eavesdropping or other means such as computer hacking or other unauthorized taking or copying of information, it has not been clear whether an obligation of confidence exists. Perhaps the difficulty stems from one of the guidelines laid down by Megarry J in *Coco v A N Clark (Engineers) Ltd.*,[15] that is that the information must have been imparted in circumstances importing an obligation of confidence. This is an important point as, because of developments and improvements in areas of technology such as telecommunications, it is much easier for determined people to gain access to confidential information on a world-wide basis. In the case of *Prince Albert* v *Strange*,[16] the court did not know how the prints came into the defendant's possession, only that the prints must have been made surreptitiously. Nevertheless, the court was willing to give relief. It is possible that the principle as associated with this case can be applied to computer hackers and other persons gaining access to confidential material without permission, that is in respect to the improper acquisition of information, and that Megarry J's test is unduly restrictive.

15 [1969] RPC 41.

16 (1849) 1 Mac & G 25.

One final point that should be made before going on to examine the law of breach of confidence in more depth is that it has an Achilles' heel. An obligation of confidence cannot attach to a person who acquires the information innocently, without appreciating its confidential nature. Therefore, innocent third parties are generally free to use or divulge the information to others. The information has, in effect, fallen into the public domain and may be used freely. There would still be remedies against any person, owing an obligation of confidence who divulged the information to others or made use of the information without authority or permission. However, there is nothing the owner of the confidential information can do about others who have come into possession of the information in circumstances where they could not have appreciated that it was confidential apart from relying on the law of copyright or patent law, if appropriate. For example, if the confidential information is contained in a printed list of customers and a third party is given a copy of the list which he receives in good faith then the third party will be able to put the information to use by contacting the customers providing he does not make copies of the list. Of course, the circumstances in which the third party obtains the list should be such that he does not realize that the information is likely to be confidential; this is probably an objective test. That is, the circumstances and the nature of the information are such that it would be reasonable for the third party not to have realized that the information was confidential.

12

Nature of the law of confidence

INTRODUCTION

There is no fundamental right to privacy at English law. The law of confidence should not be confused with privacy. Invasions against privacy can be dealt with by an action for defamation or malicious falsehood but this course may not always be satisfactory, as in *Kaye v Robertson*[1] in which a journalist and a photographer gained access to Mr Gordon Kaye's private hospital room and took photographs and conducted an interview when Mr Kaye was in no fit state to be interviewed or to give consent. Mr Kaye, the actor from the television comedy series *'Allo 'Allo* had, whilst driving, been struck by a piece of wood and suffered severe head and brain injuries. In allowing in part the appeal against an injunction imposed by Potter J, the Court of Appeal judges were unanimous in their call for a legal right to privacy.[2] The Copyright, Designs and Patents Act 1988 gives a limited right to privacy in respect of certain photographs and films.[3] The law of breach of confidence may indirectly protect confidence if, for example, materials of a private nature have been shown or given to another to whom a duty of confidence attaches. The basic requirement for confidence is the existence of a duty which may be expressed or imputed from the circumstances.

The formula for a breach of confidence action given by Megarry J in *Coco v A N Clark (Engineers) Ltd.*[4] gives a good working structure to further examine the nature and extent of this area of law. To recap, for an action in breach of confidence, the following things are required:

(a) The information must have the necessary quality of confidence about it.
(b) The information must have been imparted in circumstances importing an obligation of confidence.
(c) There must be an unauthorized use of that information to the detriment of the party communicating it.

These points will now be analysed and discussed individually.

CONFIDENTIAL QUALITY

Nature of confidential quality

The sort of material protected may be technical, commercial or personal. Often the information will be related to commercial or industrial enterprise such as in the *Coco* case. The value of such information should not be taken for granted and it can be surprising how important some secrets are even though they may seem very mundane. For example, there was a dispute about a cockle bottling secret in which the cockle bottlers' greatest problem was discussed, being to achieve the right acidity level, that is strong enough to preserve the cockles

1 [1991] FSR 62.

2 For a discussion of this case and the need for a law of privacy see, Markesinis, B.S. 'Our Patchy Law of Privacy – Time to do Something about It', (1990) 53 MLR 802 and Prescott, P. 'Kaye v Robertson - a reply', (1991) 53 MLR 451. See also the Calcutt Committee Report *On Privacy and Related Matters* Cm 1102 (London: HMSO, 1990).

3 Section 85.

4 [1969] RPC 41.

The Times, 24 June 1986. In an earlier dispute which involved the same plaintiff who was a bottler of cockles and mussels, the founder of the plaintiff company had obtained £30,000 damages in respect of the copying of an onion peeling machine.

[1988] 1 Ch 457.

[1916] 1 Ch 261.

Because the analogy with copyright law in respect of works of a grossly immoral nature failed to find sympathy, the modern relevance of cases like *Glyn* v *Weston Feature Film Co. Ltd.* [1916] 1 Ch 261 must be doubted.

[1957] RPC 449.

Young's Patents (1943) 60 RPC 51.

In *Oxford* v *Moss* (1978) 68 Cr App R 183 it was held that information is not property for the purposes of theft.

[1976] FSR 345.

without being too strong so as to be unpleasant to taste.[5] Secrets of a personal nature are also protected, even if relating to sexual conduct of a lurid nature. It was held in *Stephens* v *Avery*[6] that there was no reason why such information, expressly communicated in confidence, could not be subject to an enforceable duty of confidence. The background to that case was the killing of Mrs Telling by her husband. Details of a sexual relationship between Mrs Stephens, the plaintiff, and Mrs Telling were disclosed in confidence to a friend, Mrs Avery, the defendant, who had published the information in a newspaper. Whilst a court would not protect information of a grossly immoral nature, on the basis of *Glyn* v *Weston Feature Film Co. Ltd.*[7], the difficulty in this instance was identifying what was grossly immoral. A general code of sexual morals accepted by the overwhelming majority of the public no longer existed and there was no common view that sexual conduct between consenting adults, two females in this case, was grossly immoral.[8] After all, the story was not so shocking so as to prevent the editor spreading the story across the pages of a major national newspaper for personal profit and it lay ill in the mouth of the defendant to claim that the law did not protect the confidentiality of information of this sort.

An objective test is applied to determine whether information is truly confidential. Simply marking a document with the words 'PRIVATE AND CONFIDENTIAL' will not suffice if the contents are commonplace and lie within the public domain such as a simple, straightforward recipe for bread which contains nothing unusual in terms of the ingredients or the methods to be employed in the mixing and baking of the dough. In *Dalrymple's Application*[9] a manufacturer distributed over 1,000 technical bulletins to members of a trade association, marking them 'CONFIDENTIAL' and including a statement on the front of the documents to the effect that the contents were not to be divulged to non-members. The material in the bulletins could not be regarded as confidential. Even distribution of a report marked 'PRIVATE AND CONFIDENTIAL' to only 10 out of 350 members of the British Cast Iron Research Association was fatal to confidentiality.[10]

The information does not have to be particularly special in any way and a compilation of already known information such as a list of customers can, when taken as a whole, be regarded as confidential. What makes such information worth protecting by confidence is the fact that time and effort has been expended in gathering, selecting and ordering the information. In other words, a competitor should not be permitted to take a short cut by 'stealing' information belonging to someone else – he should have to go through a similar process and discover the information for himself by his own labours.[11]

In *Thomas Marshall (Exports)* v *Guinle*,[12] the defendant was appointed as the managing director of the plaintiff company for ten years. The company's business largely concerned the purchase of clothing from Eastern Europe and the Far East and the sale of such clothing to retail outlets. The defendant's service agreement stated that he was not to engage in any other business without the company's consent and that he must not disclose confidential information. Further, after ceasing to be the managing director, he was not to use or disclose confidential information about the suppliers and customers of the plaintiff company. The defendant began to trade on his own account and on behalf of two companies in competition with the plaintiff company. When his service contract had another four-and-a-half years left to run, he purported to resign. It was held that the court would restrain the defendant from committing further breaches of his employment contract and that an interim injunction would be granted in respect of the defendant's breach of obligation of fidelity and good faith to his employer. Megarry VC suggested that four elements were important when testing for confidential quality:

(a) The information must be such that the owner believes that its release would be injurious to him or would be advantageous to his rivals or to others.
(b) The owner of the information must believe it to be confidential or secret and not already in the public domain.
(c) The owner's belief in (a) and (b) above must be reasonable.
(d) The information must be judged in the light of usages and practices of the particular trade or industry concerned.

According to this test, a certain amount of subjectivity is allowed on the part of the owner of the information but this is restricted by the requirement that the owner's beliefs must be reasonable. On this basis, it is possible that a duty of confidence could arise and attract legal remedies even if the information is actually in the public domain if the owner's contrary belief is reasonable. However, this is going too far and the author is not aware of any cases where information already in the public domain has been held to be confidential. Ultimately, the test must be objective.

Trade secret

The term 'trade secret' is often used in relation to confidential information associated with industrial and commercial activity. The classification of some forms of confidential information as trade secrets is important because the protection afforded by the law may depend upon it. Unfortunately, there is no satisfactory legal definition of the term.[13]

In *Herbert Morris Ltd* v *Saxelby*,[14] Lord Atkinson spoke of trade secrets thus (at 705):

> . . . trade secrets, such as prices, &c., or any secret process or things of a nature which the man [the defendant] was not entitled to reveal.

In that case, Lord Parker distinguished between detail: confidential information that was far too detailed to be carried away in the head was a trade secret whereas a general method or scheme that could be easily remembered cannot be regarded as a trade secret. At first instance, in *Faccenda Chicken Ltd.* v *Fowler*[15] Goulding J defined three classes of information being:

(a) information which, because of its trivial character or its easy accessibility from public sources, cannot be regarded as confidential,
(b) information which an employee must treat as confidential, but which, once learned, reasonably remains in the employee's head and becomes part of his skill and experience,
(c) specific trade secrets so confidential that a continuing duty of confidence applies even beyond the termination of employment or service contract.

This classification provides little guidance as to what precisely distinguishes a trade secret from information in the second category but it does show that such

13 See Coleman, A. *The Legal Protection of Trade Secrets* (London: Sweet & Maxwell, 1992), Chapter 2 for an exhaustive discussion of the meaning of 'trade secret'.

14 [1916] 1 AC 688.

15 [1985] 1 All ER 724.

information will be given less protection. In a restraint of trade case, *Lansing Linde Ltd.* v *Kerr*,[16] Staughton LJ spoke in terms of information that would be liable to cause real harm if it was disclosed to a competitor, provided it was used in a trade or business and the owner had either limited the dissemination of the information or at least not encouraged or permitted widespread publication. Butler-Sloss LJ stressed the need to take account of the changing nature of business and the need to take account of:

> . . . the wider context of highly confidential information of a non-technical or non-scientific nature . . . [17]

Whilst it is clear that a secret industrial process containing an inventive step is capable of being a trade secret, the position is less predictable in terms of confidential price lists, databases containing customer names and addresses and clients' accounts. The test of what can be remembered does not help as many new inventions may be easily remembered. Neither would it be realistic to limit trade secrets to inventions that are potentially patentable. Information relating to clients' credit ratings and the types of goods that they buy may be very valuable and, in the right circumstances, fall to be considered a trade secret. In *PSM International plc & McKechnie plc* v *Whitehouse & Willenhall Automation Ltd.*[18] drawings, quotations, price costing and business strategies were considered to rank as trade secrets.

Publication

If the information has been published or disclosed to third parties, it falls into the public domain and the law of confidence cannot prevent its subsequent use and further disclosure. A person who has received the information in circumstances such that he was not, or could not reasonably have been, aware of the confidential nature is free to make use of that information or to pass it on to others. However, even if the information has fallen into the hands of third parties because of a breach of confidence, there will be remedies available against the person in breach. When a patent is applied for, the specification of the invention is available for public inspection 18 months after the priority date. The protection afforded by the law of confidence is then lost, to be replaced by the patent, once granted.[19] The information is in the public domain even though it may be available only after a search at the Patent Office. In *Mustad & Son* v *Dosen*,[20] a case concerning information about a machine for the manufacture of fish hooks, it was held that publication through the master by obtaining a patent effectively destroys the servant's duty of confidence in respect of the subject-matter of the patent grant. However, this principle has been distinguished as regards a patent obtained by a third party.

In *Cranleigh Precision Engineering Ltd* v *Bryant*,[21] Bryant was the managing director of the plaintiff company which manufactured above ground swimming pools invented by Bryant. No patent had been granted in respect of the plaintiff's swimming pools. Patent agents, acting on behalf of the plaintiff informed Bryant of a rival invention known as the Bischoff patent which concerned a similar swimming pool but which lacked two special features which the plaintiff's design incorporated.[22] Bryant did not inform his co-directors of the Bischoff patent. Later, Bryant left and set up his own company and obtained an assignment of the Bischoff patent. He was sued, *inter alia*, for

16 [1991] 1 All ER 418.

17 at 270.

18 [1992] FSR 489.

19 Once the patent has been granted, the proprietor can sue for infringement in relation to acts done after the date of publication of the patent.

20 [1964] 1 WLR 109. This case was actually decided in 1928.

21 [1965] 1 WLR 1293.

22 The special features were a plastic strip clamping the inner and outer walls together and an overlapping interfit of the metal plates forming the outside wall of the swimming pool.

injunctions to restrain him and his company from making use of or disclosing information relating to the plaintiff's swimming pools.

It was argued on behalf of the defendant that, because knowledge of the Bischoff patent was in the public domain, there could be no breach of confidence. However, although details of the Bischoff patent could be inspected by anyone it was especially relevant to the plaintiff because of the possible effect of the Bischoff patent on the plaintiff's swimming pools and the possibility of a conflict over rights. Bryant had acted in breach of confidence in making use, as soon as he left the plaintiff's employ, of the information concerning the Bischoff patent and *its various effects on the plaintiff's position*. The case of *Mustad & Son* v *Dosen* was distinguished on the grounds that, in that case, the patent was granted to the master (employer), that is, publication was by the master of the person alleged to have committed the breach of confidence. In *Cranleigh Precision Engineering Ltd.* v *Bryant*, the publication was by another, Bryant's 'master' (the plaintiff) had never published anything, not even the specification for their swimming pool.

If the information has found its way into the public domain, the person who owed another an obligation of confidence in respect of that information may be prevented from making use of the information himself for a period of time. This is known as the 'springboard' doctrine. The person who was under an obligation of confidence is not allowed to use it as a springboard from which to launch his own project if to do so would be harmful to the person to whom the obligation was owed. In *Terrapin* v *Builders Supply Co. (Hayes) Ltd.*[23] it was said by Roxburgh J that:

> . . . a person who has obtained information in confidence is not allowed to use it as a springboard for activities detrimental to [the owner] and springboard it remains even when all the features have been published . . . [24]

However, the springboard effect does not last indefinitely. After all, if the information has been published, others are free to use it so why should the person who originally owed an obligation of confidence be restricted? Of course, one justification is that the information has been published because of a breach of that obligation. In *Roger Bullivant Ltd.* v *Ellis*,[25] the plaintiffs specialized in a type of construction work known as underpinning. This is a means of replacing defective foundations. The defendant who had been an employee of the plaintiff, with others, set up a rival business. It was discovered that the defendant had taken a copy of a card index of customers which had been compiled by the plaintiff. The defendant had deliberately made use of the card index and could not complain if the court restrained him from using it even though his obligation of confidence as an ex-employee was weaker and he would have been free to use information that he had simply remembered. It was said that the springboard doctrine would not normally extend beyond the period for which the unfair advantage gained would reasonably be expected to remain and the purpose of an injunction in such circumstances was not to punish the defendant but to protect the plaintiff. It was argued that the information was freely available elsewhere but, on the basis of *Robb* v *Green*[26] it was said that the defendant could not complain if the law was unable to distinguish between the information he was able to use and that which he could not.

23 [1967] RPC 375, actually decided in 1959.

24 Ibid. at 392.

25 [1987] FSR 172.

26 [1895] 2 QB 315.

Public interest

As with copyright, a defence of public interest is available in an action for breach of confidence. Of course, in many cases where this is relevant, there will be issues of both confidence and copyright such as where someone publishes a confidential document.[27] The courts will not respect an obligation of confidence if it is in the public interest that the confidential information is made known to the public at large or to a restricted class of the public, such as an official body. Public interest is relevant where it concerns the administration of justice – for example, the law of confidence cannot be used as a means of suppressing information concerning criminal conduct.[28] But it is wider than that and can cover matters about religion,[29] price-fixing[30] and about persons in the public eye. Three points about public interest are considered below; that is, where the proposed publication is potentially defamatory, where there is a conflict in public interests and, finally, as regards the scope and nature of the disclosure.

Potentially defamatory publication

It is recognized that the public has an interest in the truth. If a person intends to publish material which is clearly defamatory, there is little doubt that the courts would, if asked, grant an injunction preventing publication unless the defendant pleads justification. However, if a person has obtained information in confidence which might injure the reputation of another, he may be free to publish it if such publication can be said to lie within the public interest. This will apply particularly to information concerning the character of persons in the public limelight such as politicians and showbusiness personalities who actively seek publicity. Of course, public interest can only be realized if the information is true, and the courts will not usually restrain publication if the person intending to publish the information is likely to raise the defences of justification or fair comment if sued for defamation. In this respect, there is something to be said for the 'publish and be damned' attitude of the Duke of Wellington. After all, the aggrieved party has, if the information is untrue, remedies under the tort of defamation which can be quite effective bearing in mind the burden of proof in such an action.

In *Woodward* v *Hutchins*,[31] the defendant (Hutchins) was a public relations officer who worked for the plaintiffs, who were pop singers including Tom Jones, Englebert Humperdinck and Gilbert O'Sullivan. The singers wanted to be presented to the public in the best possible light in order to encourage large audiences to attend their concerts. The defendant went on tour with the singers and saw their 'goings on'. Later, when no longer engaged by the plaintiffs, he wrote articles about the plaintiffs' discreditable conduct including a case of adultery; it was a typical 'Sunday paper' story. The first article was published and the singers applied for an injunction to prevent further articles being published on the grounds that they were defamatory and had been written in breach of confidence. Lord Denning said that the public interest in the truth outweighed the public interest in protecting confidential information in this case. The remaining articles could be published, leaving the plaintiffs free to pursue a claim for damages in libel. The defendant had made it clear that he would plead justification if sued for defamation. An important factor in the decision is that the plaintiffs had sought publicity which was favourable to

27 For example, *Lion Laboratories Ltd.* v *Evans* 1984] 2 All ER 417, discussed n Chapter 7.

28 See *Gartside* v *Outram* 1857) 26 LJ Ch (NS) 113. However, in *Re Barlow Clowes Gilt Managers Ltd.* unreported) *The Times*, 13 une 1991, it was said that nformation received by iquidators in circumstances of onfidentiality and for the urposes of liquidation should ot be disclosed to defendants n collateral criminal roceedings unless there was a ompelling reason to divulge he information such as a court rder.

29 For example, in *Hubbard* v *osper* [1972] 2 QB 84, it was eld, *inter alia*, that it was in he public interest that details bout the Church of cientology be made known to he public.

0 *Initial Services Ltd.* v *utterill* [1968] 1 QB 396.

1 [1977] 2 All ER 751.

them and they could not, therefore, complain if the public were given true information showing them in a less favourable light.

This case can be seen as a considerable extension of the public interest defence to breach of confidence but it should be treated with care, considering its particular facts. For example, public interest would not apply if the person about whom the information applied had not previously sought publicity. One way of looking at *Woodward v Hutchins* is to say that it is really an instance of the public being disabused of a misrepresentation previously made to it by or on behalf on the plaintiffs.

Conflict of differing public interests

There may be more than one type of public interest involved where confidential information is concerned. Public interest can be served by the disclosure of certain types of information to a limited section of the public or to the public at large, depending on the nature of the information. However, the public interest can be best served by maintaining confidences generally, that is by discouraging potential breaches of confidences by a strong and certain law. For example, the public interest in maintaining confidences between doctors and their patients is extremely high. Sometimes there will be a conflict between these forms of public interest and the court must balance one against the other in coming to its decision.

In *W v Edgell*,[32] W had killed five people and had been diagnosed as suffering from paranoid schizophrenia. At his trial, his plea of diminished responsibility was accepted and he was detained without time limit under sections 60 and 65 of the Mental Health Act 1959.[33] Later, W's condition improved and his doctor recommended transfer to a regional secure unit. The doctor said that the illness was under control and W was no longer a danger provided he stayed on medication. The Home Secretary refused his consent to the transfer. W applied to a mental health review tribunal for discharge or transfer. Dr Edgell was instructed to examine W and make out a report. The report was unfavourable to W and Dr Edgell sent a copy to W's solicitor in the belief that it would be placed before the tribunal but W's solicitor withdrew the application. Dr Edgell heard of this and realized that there would not be a copy of his report on W's file for future reference. Being concerned at this, Dr Edgell sent a copy of his report to the Home Secretary. W complained that this was a breach of the confidential relationship between a patient and a doctor.

In the High Court, it was said that Dr Edgell owed a duty of confidence to W which was created and circumscribed by the particular circumstances of the case. Dr Edgell considered that W had a psychopathic personality and thought that W's solicitors intended to suppress the report. Because of this, Scott J considered that Dr Edgell also owed a duty to the public which required him to place before the proper authorities the results of his examination of W who was not an ordinary member of the public. W unsuccessfully appealed to the Court of Appeal. It was held that, although W had a personal interest to see that confidence he had reposed in Dr Edgell was not breached, the maintenance of a duty of confidence by a doctor to his patient was not a matter of private but of public interest. The public interest in maintaining confidence had to be balanced with the public interest in protecting others from possible violence. In

32 [1990] Ch 359.

33 Now sections 37 and 41 of the Mental Health Act 1983.

this case, the public interest in restrictive disclosure outweighed the public interest that W's confidences should be respected. Bingham LJ said:

> Only the most compelling circumstances could justify a doctor in acting in a way which would injure the immediate interests of his patient, as the patient perceived them, without obtaining his consent.[34]

34 [1990] Ch 359 at 423.

On the facts, Dr. Edgell acted very responsibly and, it would appear, under a sense of public duty. It is clear that breach of confidence in a relationship as sensitive as between doctor and patient would be legally permissible only under the most compelling and narrow circumstances.

Scope and nature of the disclosure

It is clear that, in some circumstances, whether the public interest defence applies depends on the scope and nature of the disclosure. Sometimes, a very restrictive disclosure will be appropriate such as in *W v Edgell*, and had that particular disclosure been made to a newspaper, the defendant would probably have lost his public interest defence. If there is a public interest in the disclosure, the judges will take into account the persons to whom the confidential information is communicated. For example, the public interest might be best served by disclosure to a responsible body rather than to the media.[35] Another, often related, factor might be whether the disclosure was done for gain or reward although this is not decisive.[36]

35 This was identified as a factor in *Lion Laboratories Ltd. v Evans* [1948] 2 All ER 417.

36 Profit was obviously a motive for publication in *Woodward v Hutchins*, above.

Simply because the confidentiality of information is breached for one particular purpose does not mean that it can be used for other purposes. Certain documents were seized legally by the police investigating a fraud case in *Marcel v Commissioner of Police of the Metropolis*.[37] It was held that the police were not entitled to disclose those documents to a third party to use in civil proceedings because the public interest in ensuring that the documents were used solely for public purposes appropriate to the powers of seizure conferred on the police outweighed the public interest in ensuring that all relevant information was available in civil proceedings. The police had a duty not to disclose such documents to third parties except by the order of the court. This case also provides another example of a conflict between two competing public interests.

37 [1991] 1 All ER 845. The documents were seized under the provisions in Part II of the Police and Criminal Evidence Act 1984.

OBLIGATION OF CONFIDENCE

The second requirement for an action in breach of confidence is that there must be an obligation of confidence which arises from the circumstances in which the information was imparted.[38] This obligation may arise by express agreement or prior notice or it may be implied by law, for example in a fiduciary relationship. Commonly, an obligation of confidence will be established and delineated by a contract which has express terms dealing with confidence or, in the absence of such terms, by implied terms depending on the nature of the contract. The obligation of confidence may extend beyond the termination of the contract. However, a contract is not essential and, frequently, the obligation will arise in preliminary negotiations for a contract even though the contract is never executed. It is axiomatic that an obligation of confidence will apply

38 per Megarry J in *Coco v A Clark (Engineers) Ltd.* [1969] RPC 41.

where there is a duty of good faith, for example between doctor and patient or between solicitor and client. However, the circumstances where the obligation will be appropriate are much wider than this and include business transactions, commercial negotiations, the relationship between husband and wife and, sometimes, disclosures to third parties. Four particular issues are considered below: express contractual terms imposing a duty of confidence, the employer/employee relationship, covenants in restraint of trade and the position of third party recipients.

Express contractual term

It is quite common for formal contracts to contain terms dealing with matters of confidence and imposing a duty on one or both parties not to use or disclose certain types of information. A computer software company engaged to write and install computer programs for a client will be expected not to divulge any details of the client's business to competitors. An advertising agency asked by a drinks manufacturer to mount an advertising campaign for a new brand of lager will be under a duty not to disclose information about the new product until after its launch. Of course, there will be an equitable duty but expressly providing for the duty in a contract means that it can be more stringent and focused in its scope. Breach of confidence will then constitute a breach of contract giving contractual remedies to the aggrieved party. Terms dealing with confidence, often imposing a reciprocal duty, are common in contracts between business organizations, between consultants and businesses engaging them and between employers and their employees, as discussed later.

As with any contractual term care must be taken in the drafting. The courts will not impose a duty of confidence to benefit a person other than that intended. In *Fraser* v *Evans*,[39] the plaintiff was a public relations consultant who had been engaged by the Greek government to prepare a report. The contract included an express term stating that the plaintiff must not divulge any of the information contained in the report during or after the currency of the contract. A copy of the report had been surreptitiously obtained and came into the hands of *The Sunday Times*. The plaintiff was granted an *ex parte* order restraining publication of the report or parts of it in the newspaper on the grounds that it would be defamatory and would be a breach of confidence. The plaintiff considered that an article based on the report would show him in a bad light. On the defendant's appeal, it was held that the plaintiff was not entitled to an injunction. Although the plaintiff owed a duty to the Greek government, no reciprocal duty was imposed by the contract, nor could such a duty be implied. The courts can only give effect to an obligation of confidence at the instance of the party to whom such obligation is owed. It was also held, *obiter,* that although the plaintiff owned the copyright in the report, this did not extend to preventing the use of the information contained within it, once again illustrating the distinction between idea and expression in copyright.

When items are distributed to the public or a limited section of the public, it can be assumed that confidential information embodied within those items will automatically lose its confidential quality and the person obtaining one of the items will not owe an obligation of confidence to its manufacturer. Other branches of intellectual property law are more appropriate such as patent law

39 [1969] 1 QB 349.

and copyright law. However, if the distribution occurs by way of a contract, the contract may include terms attempting to impose a continuing duty of confidence, for example by prohibiting dismantling or reverse engineering. In *K S Paul (Printing Machinery) Ltd.* v *Southern Instruments Ltd.*,[40] there were two defendants. The second defendant hired from the plaintiff a telephone answering machine which was enclosed in a box which concealed the workings of the machine. The contract of hire included a condition that the machine should not be removed from its installation position nor should it be interfered with. The machines were not available except under such conditions. The second defendant allowed the first defendant to remove the machine, dismantle and examine it. Access to the confidential information concerning the workings of the machine was thus obtained. An injunction was granted to the plaintiff restraining the use of confidential information obtained from the 'machines of the type hired by the plaintiffs . . . from any unlawful inspection of any such machines'. The contract of hire had effectively prolonged the effectiveness of confidence and applied to a third party who had been allowed by the hirer to dismantle the machine.

It is arguable that sales to the general public may not destroy the application of the law of breach of confidence if, by the very nature of the product, the secret information is not accessible or is only accessible after doing something which infringes some right or duty.[41] For example, if a computer program is licensed in object code form, the licensee, or any other person for that matter, will not be able to gain access to the ideas locked away in the program without carrying out reverse analysis of the program, an operation that will normally infringe the copyright subsisting in the program, unless falling within the scope of the permitted acts under copyright law.

Employer/employee relationship

An employee owes a duty of confidence to his employer and this duty may be expressly stated in the contract of employment and in any case will be implied by law. It can be said that an employee always has a duty to act in his employer's best interests together with a duty of good faith and this will obviously include a duty not to divulge confidential information about his employer's business to others without the consent of the employer. The sort of information concerned may be rather special, a 'trade secret' such as details of a technique to improve the strength or durability of a type of plastic, or it may be ordinary and mundane, such as details of the customers of the employer. There may be exceptions to this duty, for example if the information pertains to a criminal offence or it is in the public interest that the information is disclosed.

There is seldom any doubt about the duty owed by a present employee. Although the law will be quick to imply a duty of confidence, inclusion of terms dealing with this in a contract of employment at least have the effect of focusing the employee's attention on the question of confidence. If there are express terms in the contract of employment which attempt to strengthen this duty they must, of course, be clear and unambiguous.

Ex-employees

Many problems arise through the use or disclosure of confidential information by ex-employees and here the law is faced with a dilemma for, not only does

40 [1964] RPC 118.

41 For an American view of this possibility, see Davidson, D. M., 'Protecting Computer Software: A Comprehensive Analysis', (1983) 23(4) *Jurimetrics Journal*, 337 at 358.

the employer have an interest in maintaining confidence, but the employee has a competing interest in that he should be free to use his skill and knowledge to earn a living elsewhere. Much of attractiveness of a potential employee to other employers will be the fact that he has built up skill and experience in his previous employments and it may be difficult to separate this from a previous employer's confidential information. As a further complication, in some cases, the employment contract may contain terms trying to restrict an employee's use of confidential materials after the termination of employment. When there are no express terms, the employer will not be protected to any great extent. For example, if an ex-employee simply remembers some information about a few of his previous employer's customers there would be nothing to prevent the ex-employee using this information himself or putting it at the disposal of his new employer. Of course, it would be different if he deliberately memorized the customers' names or made a copy of them.[42] In the absence of an express term in the contract of employment dealing with confidentiality, it was said in *Printers and Finishers Ltd.* v *Holloway*[43] that there would be nothing improper in the employee putting his memory of particular features of his previous employer's plant at the disposal of his new employer. Even if there is an express term, the previous employer would have to show that the information was over and above the employee's normal skill in the job and amounted to a trade secret.

In *Northern Office Microcomputer (Pty.) Ltd.* v *Rosenstein*,[44] a case from the Supreme Court of South Africa involving the laws of copyright and trade secrets relating to computer programs, the problem of where to draw the line between the conflicting interests of an employee and his previous employer was considered. It was conceded by Marais J that:

> . . . the dividing line between the use by an employee of his own skill knowledge and experience and the use by him of his employer's trade secrets is notoriously difficult to draw.[45]

In recognizing that computer programs that were not commonplace should be eligible for protection as trade secrets, Marais J said that the protection given by the law of trade secrets in the context of ex-employees should be of a limited nature only and that all that should be protected was the employer's 'lead-time', the time to develop the program. That is, the advantage the employer has in getting his product to the market place first should be protected and nothing more. He went on to say that, in many cases, the employer's trade secrets were no more than the result of the application by an employee of his own skill and judgment, but if the employee was engaged specifically to produce that information then it can still amount to a trade secret. However, if the material was commonplace, there would be nothing to stop the ex-employee deriving the same or similar material again as long as he did not simply copy his employer's material. The employee would not have to 'wipe the slate of his mind clean' on the termination of his employment.

A test for employees and ex-employees' obligation of confidence

An important case which clarified the principles to apply in the employer/employee relationship is *Faccenda Chicken Ltd.* v *Fowler*.[46] This was about the alleged wrongful use by the defendant ex-employee, with a wonderfully

42 *Robb* v *Green* [1985] 2 QB 315. Making a copy of a list of customers would also be an infringement of copyright providing the list was original in copyright terms.

43 [1965] RPC 239.

44 [1982] FSR 124.

45 Ibid. at 138.

46 [1986] 1 All ER 617.

appropriate surname, of his employer's sales information, customers' names and addresses, the most convenient routes to customers, the most suitable times for delivery, prices charged and details of customers' usual orders, information which was, by its very nature fairly mundane and ordinary, but which was nevertheless, still within the scope of the law of breach of confidence. The employer's business was supplying fresh chickens from itinerant refrigerated vans to retailers and caterers. The defendant was engaged by the plaintiff as a sales manager and left the plaintiff company to set up in business on his own account, taking eight of the plaintiff's employees with him. He started selling fresh chickens from refrigerated vans in the same area that the plaintiff operated in. The employer's action for breach of confidence failed because the information was not of the type which an employee was bound, by an implied term in his contract of employment, not to use or disclose subsequent to the termination of employment. Neill LJ, delivering the judgment of the court, stated the Court of Appeal's views on the relevant principles to apply in cases involving confidentiality between master and servant:

(a) If there is a contract of employment the employee's obligations were to be determined from that contract.
(b) In the absence of any express terms, the employee's obligations would be implied.
(c) Whilst still in employment, there was an implied term imposing a duty of good faith or fidelity on the employee. This duty might vary according to the nature of the contract but would be broken if the employee copied or deliberately memorized a list of customers.
(d) The implied term imposing an obligation on the employee after the termination of his employment was more restricted than that imposed by the duty of fidelity. It might cover secret processes of manufacture or designs or special methods of construction or other information of a sufficiently high degree of confidentiality so as to be classed as a trade secret.
(e) To determine whether information fell within this implied term to prevent its use or disclosure by an ex-employee depended on the circumstances and attention should be given to the following:
    (i)   the nature of employment – a higher obligation might be imposed where the employee regularly handled confidential material;
    (ii) the nature of information – it should be an authentic trade secret or at least highly confidential;
    (iii) whether the employer stressed the confidential nature of the material; and
    (iv) whether the information could be easily isolated from other material the employee was free to use, this being useful evidentially rather than being a conclusive test.

On the last point, separability of information would tend to suggest that it was more likely that the information could be classed as confidential. The court left open the question of whether it would make any difference if the ex-employee used the information himself or whether he simply sold it to another. Although the decision in this case seems a trifle unfair in that the ex-employee calculatingly and deliberately took advantage of his employer's business and reputation it can be argued that the employer should have considered using a restrictive covenant which might have prevented the employee from competing in the area for at least a year or two. However, Mr Fowler was walking a thin line for in *Normalec v Britton*[47] the defendant decided to sell the same goods as his employer (electric bulbs and fittings) to the same customers he had been seeing on behalf of his employer. Worse still, the defendant did this while he was still in the employ of the plaintiff. The defendant was held to have a fiduciary duty to his employer who was entitled to the profits made by the defendant and the court also granted an injunction preventing the defendant from selling to the plaintiff's customers even after the termination of his employment.[48] The one major difference between this case and the *Faccenda Chicken* case is that here the activity was commenced whilst the defendant was still employed and while he still was under a duty of good faith or fidelity to his employer.[49]

Employer's obligation

The obligation of confidence arising from a contract of employment is not all one way. In many cases, the employer will owe a duty of confidence to his employees. An employer will hold information concerning the employee such as marital status, salary and career details. This information should not be divulged to others without the employee's permission except in circumstances where disclosure is permitted by express provision (for example, in pursuance of an attachment of earnings order)[50] or implied (for example, where salaries are calculated and paid by a third party). If the employee's details are stored on a computer, there will usually be restrictions on disclosure by virtue of section 5(2) of the Data Protection Act 1984.[51] Prospective employers also owe a duty of confidence in respect of *curricula vitae* submitted by job applicants.

Some employers operate employee suggestions schemes, usually with the possibility of rewards for suggestions having merit that will be used by the employer. By taking part in the scheme, an employee can be said to have waived his rights, if any, in the information he has disclosed in this way if his employer uses the information.[52]

However, if the employer does not make use of the information it seems that a duty of confidence will arise. In *Prout v British Gas plc*[53] the plaintiff, whilst employed by the defendant, submitted an idea for a new design of bracket for warning lamps placed around excavations. The bracket was supposed to be vandal-proof. The plaintiff was given an award by the defendant on the basis of its suggestions scheme but, later, the defendant said that it had no interest and agreed to allow the plaintiff to pursue a patent application on his own behalf. On the issue of confidence, it was held that there was a contractual or equitable duty of confidence imposed on the defendant, the employer. Although this duty would normally end once the idea was used in public for the first time without any objection from the employee, a fresh duty could arise if the employee gave notice of his intention to apply for a patent and would continue until the filing date of the application. In this particular case it was held that the employer was in breach of confidence by making use of the invention. This extension of duty beyond the first consensual public use could only apply where long-term trade or commercial secrecy was possible or where an application for legal protection

47 [1938] FSR 318.

48 In *Balston Ltd v Headline Filters Ltd.* [1990] FSR 385, an intention to set up in business in competition with the company of which he was a director was held not to conflict with the director's fiduciary duty to the company even though preliminary steps had been taken while he remained a director.

49 For an interesting description of this case and other dramatic intellectual property cases, see Pearson, H. and Miller, C. *Commercial Exploitation of Intellectual Property* (London: Blackstone, 1990) at pp. 3-5.

50 Attachment of Earnings Act 1971.

51 See *Rowley v Liverpool City Council* (unreported) 24 October 1989 (Court of Appeal). In this case disclosure was lawful under section 34(5) being required in the course of legal proceedings.

52 In some cases, the information will belong to the employer by virtue of the contract of employment.

53 [1992] FSR 478.

requiring novelty was envisaged. However, public use could easily destroy novelty and would do so in many cases.

Covenants in restraint of trade

An employer must be careful not to draft terms which are too wide in a contract of employment imposing a continuing duty of confidence after the employment has been terminated.[54] Terms that are too wide are in danger of being struck out by a court as being in restraint of trade. On appointment, an employee may agree to sign a contract restricting his use or disclosure of information concerning his employer's business or agreeing not to work for a competitor after the termination of the contract of employment.[55] Generally, such agreements will be enforced by the courts only if they are reasonable between the parties and not against the public interest. In particular, an employer cannot use the law of confidence to protect himself against future competition *per se*. If a term in the contract of employment is a clear attempt to prevent future competition rather than a legitimate means of protecting the employer's business interests, it will not be enforced by the courts.[56] Restrictive terms are usually referred to as covenants in restraint of trade and are frequently expressed in terms of preventing the employee working for a competitor or setting up a business in competition within a given area and for a given period of time.[57] These two factors, time and area, define the extent of the restraint. If the covenant is too wide in terms of either the courts are unlikely to enforce it and it is clear that the two factors must be considered together. In *Fitch v Dewes*,[58] a solicitor's clerk was prohibited from entering into the employment of another solicitor within a seven mile radius of Tamworth Town Hall. The restriction was indefinite in terms of time but nevertheless, because the geographic area was small, it was held to be valid. However, in *Herbert Morris Ltd. v Saxelby*,[59] a restriction that an engineer could not work for a competitor anywhere as an engineer for seven years was held to be void.[60] In any case, a restrictive covenant will not be enforced:

> unless the protection sought was reasonably necessary to protect a trade secret or to prevent some personal influence over customers being abused in order to entice them away.[61]

Geographical area will not be particularly relevant if the employer's business is carried out over the telephone or by facsimile transmission. A covenant prohibiting the former employee from carrying on a business as an employment agent within a 3,000 metre radius (about 1.9 miles) of the employer's place of business for a period of six months was held to be too wide in *Office Angels Ltd. v Rainer-Thomas*.[62] It was said that, as clients' orders were placed over the telephone, the location of the business was of no concern to them. Therefore, the area restriction was inappropriate.[63] However, even a small area restriction could be unduly restrictive if the area was one where most of the relevant business was undertaken.

If a covenant in restraint of trade is drafted too widely it will be void. The courts will not narrow it down to an acceptable level and apply that instead. In *J A Mont (UK) Ltd. v Mills*,[64] Simon Brown LJ said:

---

54 The same applies to independent consultants and the like engaged to perform some work.

55 Alternatively, such a promise might be extracted from the employee on payment of a settlement at the end of the contract of employment.

56 *Berkeley Administration Inc. v McClelland* [1990] FSR 505 and *Roberts v Northwest Fixings* [1993] FSR 281. The courts will not lend their aid to a determined attempt to stop competition.

57 It should be noted that such covenants are not always concerned with confidential information.

58 [1921] AC 158.

59 [1916] 1 AC 688.

60 For more on covenants in restraint of trade involving employees, see Rideout, R.W. *Rideout's Principles of Labour Law* (London: Sweet & Maxwell, 5th edn., 1989) and Selwyn, N. *Law of Employment* (London, Butterworths, 7th edn., 1992).

61 per Neill LJ in *Faccenda Chicken Ltd. v Fowler* [1986] 1 All ER 617 at 626.

62 [1991] IRLR 214.

63 The covenant was too wide because it went beyond that necessary to protect the employer's interests.

64 (unreported) *The Independent* 7 January 1993 (Court of Appeal).

. . . as a matter of policy, it seems to me similarly that the court should not too urgently strive to find within restrictive covenants *ex facie* too wide, implicit limitations such as alone could justify their imposition.

To construe covenants otherwise would encourage employers to draft their covenants deliberately in wide terms.[65] However, in *Littlewoods Organisation Ltd. v Harris*[66] Lord Denning MR adopted a much more relaxed approach to construction and a covenant that an employee

> . . . shall not at any time within twelve months . . . enter into a contract of service or other agreement of a like nature with GUS or any subsidiary thereto.

was interpreted as being limited to the mail order side of those parts of the GUS organization that operated in the United Kingdom. The distinction is that in this case, there had been an attempt to draw up a reasonable covenant.

Subject matter of covenants

There is some judicial confusion about the proper subject-matter of a covenant in restraint of trade in terms of confidential information. In *Faccenda Chicken*, Neill LJ suggested that only trade secrets or their equivalent could be protected by a restrictive covenant and that more mundane information could not. However, this was *obiter* (there was not a restrictive covenant imposed on the defendant) and it conflicts with Neill LJ's own description of the implied term imposed after termination of employment. The implied term protects trade secrets and, consequently, there is no need for a restrictive covenant in respect of them. In *Balston Ltd. v Headline Filters Ltd.*[67] Scott J declined to follow that part of Neill LJ's judgment to the effect that confidential information that could not be protected by an implied term *ipso facto* could not be protected by a suitably limited express covenant.[68] This accords with common sense as most business organizations possess information that would harm them or benefit others if divulged even though that information is not a trade secret or associated with one. By limiting the restriction the courts are seeking to arrive at an equitable balance between the interests of employer and employee alike.

Garden leave

Employers are often worried about the harm that can be caused to them by an employee working his notice. The employee might attempt to influence clients or remove confidential materials. It is not unknown for employees who have given or have been given notice of termination of their employment to be told to stay at home and 'enjoy the garden' during their period of notice. This 'garden leave' may last for some time if the employee is in a senior position subject to lengthy period of notice. If the employee attempts to work for another employer during his garden leave, the courts may act to restrain him.

Factors that may be relevant include the amount and nature of confidential information the employee had access to and the seniority of the employee. However, in *Provident Financial Group v Hayward*[69] the Court of Appeal refused to grant an injunction against an employee on garden leave because little of the period of notice remained, there was no evidence of a serious prospect that the employer's interests would be harmed and the employee worked in an administrative capacity, having access to very little confidential

---

65 See also *Mason v Provident Clothing and Supply Company Ltd.* [1913] AC 724.

66 [1978] 1 All ER 1026.

67 [1987] FSR 330, an interlocutory hearing.

68 At first instance, in *Faccenda Chicken Ltd. v Fowler* [1985] 1 All ER 724, Goulding J classified information available to employees in three categories. The second category, confidential information falling short of a trade secret was, he suggested, capable of being protected by a restrictive covenant. In the Court of Appeal, Neill LJ disagreed with this proposition.

69 [1989] 3 All ER 298.

information. It could also be argued that enforced garden leave is a breach of the contract of employment as an implied term is that the employer provides suitable work, if available.

Third party recipients

The general rule is that a third party who comes by the information without knowing it to be confidential or in circumstances where an obligation of confidence cannot be imposed is free to use the information or to disclose it as he sees fit especially if it entered the public domain. This is the one fundamental weakness of the law of breach of confidence – innocent third parties are largely unaffected by this area of law. They may, however, be subject to other rights, duties or liabilities. For example, the information may be in the form of a literary work and a question of infringement of copyright might be raised. Alternatively, use of the information may result in an action for passing off or its publication may be defamatory.

The position of the person who is not aware of the confidential nature of the information at the time it is disclosed to him but subsequently becomes so aware is less clear. In *Fraser* v Evans[70] Lord Denning MR said (at 361):

> No person is permitted to divulge to the world information he has received in confidence, unless he has just cause or excuse for doing so. Even if he comes by it innocently, nevertheless once he gets to know that it was originally given in confidence, he can be restrained from breaking that confidence.

It can be said that an equity fastens on the person's conscience once he discovers the confidential nature of the information. However, equitable remedies are discretionary and injunctive relief may not be given where it could cause hardship on their parties. The person to whom the information has been given might have performed work or made contracts with other persons in reliance of that information. This factor did not, however, prevent an Australian judge imposing injunctions on all the defendants (most of whom had unwittingly paid for the information).[71]

There will be circumstances where a third party will be bound by an obligation of confidence even though the owner of the information did not impart the information to the third party directly. The third party may receive confidential information knowing it to be confidential or in circumstances where a reasonable man would have suspected that it was confidential. In other cases, he may discover the confidential nature of the information subsequently. It appears that only when the recipient actually knows of the confidential nature will he be under an obligation not to use or divulge the information further. In *Fraser* v *Thames TV Ltd.*,[72] three actresses formed a rock group with the assistance of a manager and developed an idea for a TV series known as *The Rock Follies*. They discussed the idea orally with Thames TV in confidence and it was agreed that the actresses were to have first refusal should the series proceed. When Thames TV decided to proceed, one of the actresses could not get a release from another part and Thames TV replaced her with another actress.

It was held that the court would prevent a person disclosing an idea in written or oral form until it became general public knowledge, provided that:

70 [1984] 1 QB 44.

71 *Wheatley* v *Bell* [1984] FSR 16.

72 [1969] 2 All ER 101.

(a) the circumstances imputed an obligation of confidence, and

(b) the content was clearly identifiable, potentially attractive in a commercial sense and capable of being brought to fruition.

For a third party to be fixed with an obligation of confidence, he must know that the information was confidential and had been imparted in confidence. Even though it was disclosed to several people, it was disclosed to each and all of them in confidence. An argument by counsel for the defence that the idea lost its confidentiality when it was disclosed to others was rejected by Hirst J who said that the disclosure to others was plainly also in confidence and, therefore, confidence remained intact.[73] The actress who had been replaced was awarded very substantial damages.

A discussion of third party recipients is not complete without consideration of the position of a person who obtains the information surreptitiously, for example in circumstances involving industrial espionage. Can such a person be fixed with an obligation of confidence? At first sight it appears not, especially when the formula used in the *Coco* case is examined as it seems to suggest that the information is given voluntarily by its owner. There is very little case law on this point but in *Malone v Commissioner of Police*[74] Megarry VC was of the view that an eavesdropper would not owe a duty of confidence. *Malone* involved telephone-tapping, an activity which is now illegal under section 1 of the Interception of Communications Act 1985 which makes it an offence to intentionally intercept a communication during its transmission through a public telecommunications system.

In *Malone,* the telephone tap was lawful but Megarry VC spoke of unknown hearers and said that a person using a telephone to disclose confidential information must accept the risk of being overheard as that risk is inherent in the mode of communication. This case was distinguished in *Francome v Mirror Group Newspapers Ltd.*[75] where it was held that there was a serious issue to be tried on the basis of breach of confidence concerning information obtained by way of an illegal telephone tap. Although a person using a telephone takes the risk of being overheard because of imperfections or accidents, he does not willingly take the risk of an illegal tap. The same principle should apply to facsimile transmission. The sender takes the risk of the information being seen by persons, other than those to whom it is intended, who have access to the room where the receiving machine is installed. Even the risk of misdirection must be accepted. It must be questionable whether confidentiality can remain intact if a number of persons, other than those directly associated with the addressee such as secretarial staff, have an opportunity to read the contents of a facsimile transmission. Likewise, the status of a notice on the transmitted material to the effect that it is confidential and must not be read by anyone other than the addressee is doubtful. It should be noted that in the case of *Prince Albert v Strange,*[76] the court found for the plaintiff even though it was not known how the defendant had gained possession of the subject-matter, only that it must have been done surreptitiously. If the information in question contains personal data and is subsequently stored in a computer by the eavesdropper or spy, there may be an offence under the Data Protection Act 1984.[77]

---

73 See also *Franchi v Franchi* [1967] RPC 149.

74 [1979] 2 All ER 620.

75 [1984] 2 All ER 408

76 (1849) 1 Mac & G 25.

77 For example, by being an unregistered data user, section 5(1). In the unlikely event of the spy being registered under the Act, he may still be guilty of offences under section 5(2) relating to holding, obtaining, disclosing or transferring personal data. See Bainbridge, D.I. *Introduction to Computer Law* (London: Pitman, 2nd edn., 1993) at p.210.

UNAUTHORIZED USE

The final ingredient for an action for breach of confidence is an unauthorized use of the information to the detriment of the party communicating it. It will usually be fairly obvious when there has been an unauthorized use of confidential material. The use or disclosure complained of must be related to the nature of the obligation of confidence. For example, in an agreement between the owner of confidential information and a manufacturing company who are going to exploit it commercially on the basis of agreed royalty payments, the company will be permitted to use the information for the purposes detailed in the agreement. In addition, other use and subsequent disclosure may be implied. For example, the company may be able to divulge the information to subcontractors whilst stressing its confidentiality and to the company's own employees and to sister companies if part of a group. It is really a matter of construing the agreement.

If the information is a mixture of public and private materials then the recipient must be especially careful only to use that which is public, unless he has permission to use the private information. In *Seager* v *Copydex (No.1)*[78] the defendant designed a carpet grip using details from the public domain but also incorporating some ideas it had discussed with the plaintiff some years before. The defendant claimed it had forgotten about the latter so it was effectively a case of subconscious copying. Nevertheless and notwithstanding the 'innocence' of the defendant's actions, Lord Denning MR found for the plaintiff. It would appear, therefore, that the state of the mind of the person using the information in breach of confidence does not affect liability although it could be relevant when it comes to determining damages.

That there should be some detriment to the party communicating the information is doubtful.[79] In many cases, the justification for protecting confidences is that they are tied up with commercial activity, investment and marketing and industrial manufacture. In other words, confidence has an economic value to its owner who will have a vested interest to see that his competitors do not have access to the information, at least not without paying for it. But the law of breach of confidence has a tremendously wide scope and in some cases, economic considerations are largely irrelevant, for example where the disclosure of the information is likely to harm a person's public standing.

Where the information has economic value, it is easily understandable why the owner of the information would not want to see his competitors have some advantage from it. In *R* v *Licensing Authority ex parte Smith, Kline & French Laboratories Ltd.*,[80] SKF[81] originated a drug, known as Cimetidine to control gastric acid secretion and heal peptic ulcers. SKF marketed the drug under the name 'Tagamet' and obtained patents in respect of it in 1972 which were extended to 1992 on the basis that during the last four years the patents would be endorsed 'licences of right'.[82] SKF and others wishing to sell the drug had to obtain a product licence from the licensing authority. SKF objected to the licensing authority using confidential information submitted by SKF in support of its own application in order to consider other companies' applications for product licences. The High Court held that this was a breach of confidence but this was reversed in the Court of Appeal. The House of Lords upheld the Court

78 [1967] RPC 349.

79 For a discussion on this point, see Cornish, W. R. *Intellectual Property: Patents, Copyright, Trade Marks and Allied Rights* (London: Sweet & Maxwell, 2nd edn, 1989) at pp. 235–236.

80 [1989] 1 All ER 175.

81 Smith, Kline and French Laboratories Ltd.

82 The extension was by virtue of Schedule 1 to the Patents Act 1977. Under the Patents Act 1949, the maximum duration of a patent was 16 years.

of Appeal saying that the licensing authority, at its discretion and in the performance of its duties under the Medicines Act 1968 and Community law, had a right to make use of all the information provided by applicants for product licences in determining whether to grant other applications.[83] Two important factors were the protection of public health and the harmonization of the national laws through Member States.

Of course, this case has tremendous significance for originators of medicines and generic manufacturers. The originator has all the expense of research, development and, in particular, testing new drugs and medicines. If the drug or medicine was covered by patents then, theoretically, all the competitor has to do is to look up the patent specifications (being documents available for public inspection) and then, at the appropriate time, apply for a compulsory licence in respect of the patents or to have the patents endorsed 'licences of right'. However, the patent owner's monopoly will not be easily disturbed unless there is some evidence that the patent is not being worked or is being unfairly exploited in some way.[84] This reluctance to interfere with the monopoly provided by patents is justifiable in the context of something like a drug where a potential competitor could seriously undercut the originator because the former has not spent large sums of money on research and development.

REMEDIES

The whole rationale and justification for the law of breach of confidence is that it can and should be used to preserve secrets and confidences. Because of this the most appropriate remedy is the *quia timet* injunction which will be granted to prevent general publication or other disclosure of the subject-matter of the confidence. However, as previously noted, an injunction will not normally be granted if the aggrieved party complains that publication would be defamatory and the defendant is likely to raise a defence of justification or fair comment. In such a case, the courts will usually allow the defendant to publish and take the risk of paying damages, which could be considerable, should his defence in a defamation action fail. In some cases, an injunction may be granted to prevent the defendant making use of the information himself even though innocent third parties may be free to use it, the so-called 'springboard doctrine' discussed earlier in this chapter. However, normally, once the information has fallen into the public domain, an injunction will not be granted because it is ineffective, for example as in one of the *Spycatcher* cases, *Attorney-General v The Observer Ltd*.[85] In the House of Lords it was held that injunctions would not be granted against *The Observer* and *The Guardian* preventing them from reporting on the contents of *Spycatcher* because publication abroad had effectively destroyed the secrecy of its contents.[86]

Being equitable, injunctions are discretionary, and the decision to grant an injunction will be influenced by factors such as the 'innocence' of the defendant, for example in the case of non-deliberate use of information as in *Seager v Copydex (No. 1)*,[87] and whether an injunction is really necessary. In *Coco v A N Clark (Engineers) Ltd*,[88] the court decided that payment of damages in the form of royalties would be a sufficient remedy. Other considerations might be whether the plaintiff delayed in taking legal action, whether he was careless

83 Article 3 of EEC Directive 65/65 stated that no proprietary medical product could be marketed in a Member State unless authorized by a competent body of that State. A product licence was required under section 7(2) & (3) of the Medicines Act 1968 and the applicant had to supply a great deal of scientific material. Section 20(1)(b) of the Medicines Act 1968 was amended to take account of the streamlined procedure introduced by Directive 87/21/EEC which made it easier for generic applicants to obtain product licences. For example, results of tests were not required if the originator consented to the use of confidential information. The question basically was whether applicants for product licences could avoid supplying all the material required on the basis that the licensing authority could use the information supplied by SKF in their application.

84 See Chapter 14 for licences of right and compulsory licences. The latter are extremely rare and in 1992, no applications for compulsory licences under section 48(1) of the Patents Act 1977 were lodged. In the same year there were 4561 applications lodged by patentee for an entry to the effect that a licence is available as of right, section 46(1) Patents Act 1977.

85 [1989] AC 109.

86 *The Sunday Times* were in breach of confidence when it published an extract before copies of the book had become readily available in the United Kingdom and the newspaper was liable to account for the resulting profits. However, *The Sunday Times* could now continue with its further serialization of *Spycatcher*.

87 [1967] 2 All ER 415.

88 [1969] RPC 41.

with the information or whether he should have sought other legal means of protecting the information, for example by obtaining a patent.

If the information has been disclosed or used in some way in breach of confidence, then it will usually be too late for an injunction but damages may be available. Damages may be calculated on the basis of conversion, breach of confidence being in the nature of an equitable tort. The most thorough and comprehensive discussion of the relevant principles is to be found in *Seager* v *Copydex Ltd. (No. 2)*,[89] where it was said that the value of confidential information depends upon its nature, and one of the following two formulae would be appropriate:

89 [1969] RPC 250.

(a) If there is nothing very special about the information, and it could have been obtained by employing a competent consultant, then the value (for the purpose of damages) is the fee that consultant would charge.
(b) If the information is something special involving an inventive step, then the value is the price a willing buyer would pay for it.

If the information is commercial in nature and used in the manufacture of an object which is sold or hired, then it would seem that damages should be assessed on the basis of the fee the owner of the information reasonably might have expected had the information been used with his licence. Assessing damages for future infringement would be difficult using the second formula in *Seager* above. One might also question why a patent had not been applied for if there is an inventive step. A better approach would be that used in the *Coco* case where an order was granted to the effect that the defendant should pay into a trust account a royalty on engines made in the future.

If the information has been exploited commercially in breach of confidence, an account of profits may be more beneficial to the plaintiff. An account is an alternative to damages and, being an equitable remedy, is discretionary. In *Peter Pan Manufacturing Corp.* v *Corsets Silhouette Ltd.*[90] a manufacturer of brassières made use of confidential information under a licence agreement. After the expiry of a licence agreement, the manufacturer continued to use the information, clearly in breach of confidence. In an action for breach of confidence, the plaintiff asked for an account of profits based on the whole of the profits accruing from the brassières but the defendant claimed that the account of profits should be based only on the profit resulting from the wrongful use of the confidential information, that is the profit relating to the parts of the brassières incorporating the confidential information. The difference between the two sums was substantial and the plaintiff was awarded the higher sum because it was accepted by the court that the defendants would not have been able to make the brassières at all without the use of the confidential information.

90 [1963] RPC 45.

Finally, another equitable remedy which might be available, depending upon the circumstances, is an order for the destruction of articles that have been made by using the confidential information or which incorporate the tangible expression of such information. For example, an order for destruction of any of the brassières still held in stock by the defendant in the above case might have been appropriate. Such an order would not be granted as regards articles lawfully in the possession of third parties, unless somehow implicated in the breach of confidence.

Part Four

PATENT LAW

13

Patent law – background, basic principles and practical aspects

INTRODUCTION

Patent law concerns inventions that are new, involve an inventive step and are capable of industrial application. It is perhaps fitting that intellectual property law reserves a very special and powerful mode of protection for inventions that meet exacting standards. The grant of a patent effectively gives the inventor or, more commonly, his employer, a monopoly to work the invention to the exclusion of others for a period of time, not exceeding 20 years. The invention might concern a new or improved product, for example a new type of window lock or an improvement to the design of scaffolding clamps. Alternatively, the invention may concern some industrial process such as a new method of rustproofing motor car bodies or an improved method of making printed circuit boards for electronic equipment. Because of the strength of this form of property right, high standards are required, the invention must be new and it must involve an inventive step, that is it must be more than merely an obvious application of technology. Furthermore, the invention must be capable of industrial application and must not fall within certain stated exclusions. These requirements are explored in detail in the next chapter, suffice it to say for now that patents are not granted lightly and an application is subjected to a thorough examination process.

In common with other intellectual property rights, a patent is a form of personal property that may be assigned, licensed or charged by way of a mortgage. However, it is declared by section 30(1) of the Patents Act 1977 that a patent is not a thing in action, though why this should be so is incomprehensible.[1] Patent law grants a monopoly for a limited period of time in respect of an invention in return for disclosure of the details concerning the invention. These details are available for public inspection and are sufficiently detailed so that a person skilled in the particular art would be able to make practical use of the invention, in other words, he would be able to work the invention.[2] Disclosure is a central prerequisite for the grant of a patent and it must be total, with nothing of substance withheld, otherwise it might be difficult for others to make use of the invention once the patent has expired. In *Young v Rosenthal*,[3] Grove J said (at 31):

> Then he [the applicant] is bound so to describe it in his specification as that any workman acquainted with the subject . . . would know how to make it; and the reason of that is this, that if he did not do so, when the patent expired he might have some trade mystery which people would not be able actually to use in accordance with his invention (although they had a right to use it after his invention had expired), because they would not know how to make it.

1 On the other hand, copyright is a chose in action. The difference is of no consequence as assignment of patents is provided for by the Patents Act 1977.

2 Patent legislation uses the term 'a person skilled in the art'. This means a person (or team of persons) having knowledge and experience of the science or technology concerned.

3 (1884) 1 RPC 29.

The holding back of part of the invention runs counter to the whole rationale of patent law and such applications will be rejected or the applicant will be asked to modify and enlarge his disclosure accordingly.

After the expiry of the patent, the invention falls into the public domain and anyone is free to make use of it. One might wonder what the State or the general public get in return for this grant of privilege. The fact that the details of the invention are published means that competitors, researchers and the like have immediate access to this information which they may study and use subject to the scope of the infringing acts. The system benefits everyone by this because the wider availability of such information helps to spread and widen technical knowledge and, importantly, because investment is encouraged, wealth and employment are created and maintained. The whole patent transaction can be thought of as a bargain or contract between the inventor (or his employer) and the state, both parties bringing consideration to that contract[4] – see Table 13.1.

4 The person applying for the patent brings consideration in terms of fees and by adding his invention to the store of public information, ultimately giving his invention to the state or even the world at large.

Table 13.1 Patent consideration

Patent – concept of contract – consideration

Patentee's consideration	State's consideration
1. Details available for public inspection	1. Examination and search by Patent Office may assist in the drawing up or amendment of the application
2. Invention falls into the public domain on expiry	2. Wealth of information available at Patent Office will help in the framing of patent application
3. Some things can be done during the life of the patent (non-infringing acts) by others	3. The granting of a limited monopoly
4. The invention may be vulnerable to a compulsory licence	4. A priority date will be given assisting in applications in other countries
5. Competition law may impose restrictions on the exploitation of the patent	5. Useful evidential materials available, presumptions
6. Fees have to be paid	
7. The risk that the invention may be appropriated by the Crown (although payment may be made)	

Without a patent system, inventors and their employers would attempt to keep the details of the invention secret, relying on the law of confidence for protection. In some cases, it would be impossible to keep the details of the invention secret. For example, if it concerned a new type of gearing arrangement for a bicycle, anyone purchasing a bicycle with the new system fitted would be able to discover the inventive step by an examination of the gears, perhaps after dismantling them. However, if the invention concerned some new industrial process used for making bicycle gears, it might be possible to maintain secrecy because an inspection of the finished product would not necessarily disclose the manufacturing process. In the first case, obtaining a patent is the most effective way of protecting the invention and the investment incurred in developing it. Other ways do exist but are not usually as attractive. For example, the inventor will be first to the market place with his gear system and it could be several months or years before competitors can equip their factories and organize their production and marketing of a similar system. The duration of this lead-time is often proportional to the complexity of the technology required to put the invention into practice, although this lead-time might be dramatically reduced where the first product has to undergo rigorous safety testing and the competitor's product can largely avoid this by reliance on the testing of the first product. For example, in *R v Licensing Authority ex parte Smith, Kline & French Laboratories Ltd.*[5] information given by a drug manufacturer to a licensing authority, in order to obtain a product licence in respect of a drug, was used by the authority in determining whether to grant a product licence to a second manufacturer.

In the second case, where the invention relates to a process, the owner might still be well advised to seek patent protection because of the uncertainty of the law of confidence. This flawed form of legal protection is little better than useless if details of the invention fall into the hands of third parties who have acquired the information in good faith. Depending on how tight security measures can be made, a patent will usually be an attractive alternative to the law of breach of confidence. However, where secrecy can be assured, there is no need to obtain a patent and, indeed, the grant of a patent is a poor alternative as competitors will be able to find out about the process and gain a valuable insight into the way the patentee's business is likely to develop in the future. The invention will be available for anyone to use after expiry of the patent and compulsory licences might be available during its existence. If the secret can be maintained indefinitely, this will be preferable on all counts.

If the invention relates to a product rather than a process, it may be possible to register some aspects of the shape of the product as a design or it may fall within the unregistered design right. Additionally, there will be copyright in the drawings and written descriptions of the invention. However, copyright protection is a poor substitute for a patent as, in principle, copyright only protects the expression of an idea whereas a patent can protect from exploitation by others the idea that is encapsulated in the invention. The nature of patent protection was described by Buckley LJ in *Hickton's Patent Syndicate* v *Patents and Machine Improvements Co. Ltd.*[6] in the following terms:

> Every invention to support a patent must . . . either suggest a new way of making something . . . or it may mean the way of producing a new article altogether; but I think you are losing the grasp of the substance and seizing the shadow when you say that the invention is the manufacture as distinguished from the idea. It is much more true to say that the patent is for the idea as distinguished from the thing manufactured. No doubt you cannot patent an idea, which you have simply conceived, and have suggested no way of carrying out, but the invention consists in thinking of or conceiving something and suggesting a way of doing it.

5 [1989] 1 All ER 175. For a fuller discussion of this case on the law of confidence see Chapter 12

6 (1909) 26 RPC 339 at 348.

The strength of protection afforded to inventions through the patent system is one reason why patent protection is of a shorter duration than that available for works of copyright.

BRIEF HISTORICAL PERSPECTIVE

As with the origins and development of other intellectual property rights, England has a prime place in world history and has set the mould for patent rights internationally. It is no coincidence that England was the country were the first major steps towards an industrial society were taken. Whether this was a direct result of the patent system is arguable, but it is without doubt that patents had an important role to play in the Industrial Revolution. Before this, the origins of patent law can be seen emerging in medieval times. *Letters Patent* were open letters with the King's Great Seal on the bottom granting rights, often to foreign weavers and other craftsmen, allowing them to practise their trade. A Flemish weaver who wanted to practise his trade in England was granted a patent in 1331, one of the earliest recorded instances of a patent.[7] The regulation of trade was deemed to fall within the provenance of the Crown and letters patent proved to be a useful method of encouraging the establishment of new forms of industry and commerce, giving the Crown powerful control over trade. In this early form, there was no need for anything inventive, it had more to do with the practice of a trade and the granting of favours by the Crown. However, some letters patent were granted for inventions – for example, a patent was granted to John of Utyman in 1449 for his new method of making stained glass. Eventually, there was a strong need for an effective system that prevented unfair competition where, for example, one person had made some novel invention and wanted to stop others from simply copying it. A monopoly system developed in the reign of Elizabeth I and many letters patent were granted.

Monopolies are controversial. There are many dangers associated with monopolies, such as overcharging, manipulation of markets or a refusal to make the product available. *Darcy v Allen*[8] is an example of an early patent case which involved a monopoly for the making, importation and selling of playing cards. The patent was held to be invalid as being a common law monopoly although it appears to have been accepted that patents for new inventions could be legally valid. In the slightly later *Clothworkers of Ipswich Case*[9] patents of a limited duration were recognized. The Statute of Monopolies, 1623[10] gave recognition to patents as an exception to the general rule against monopolies by section 6 which stated:

> Provided . . . that any declaration before mentioned shall not extend to any letters patent and grants of privilege for the term of fourteen years or under . . . of the sole working or making of any manner of new manufactures within this realm, to the true and first inventor and inventors of such manufactures which others at the time of making such letters patent and grants shall not use, so as also they be not contrary to the law, or mischievous to the state, by raising prices of commodities at home, or hurt of trade, or generally inconvenient . . .

So, the true and first inventor was given 14 years in which he could exploit his invention to the exclusion of others. The section also makes it clear that the monopoly granted is not to be abused. Although there was a long way to go, the seeds of the modern patent system were sown.

7 For an early historical perspective, see Brett, H. *The United Kingdom Patents Act 1977* (Oxford: ESC Publishing, 1978) and Aldous, W., Young, D., Watson, A. and Thorley, S. *Terrell on the Law of Patents* (London: Sweet & Maxwell, 14th edn., 1990).

8 (1602) Co. Rep 84b.

9 (1614) Godbolt 252.

10 21 Jac 1 c.3. It seems that the world's first patents statute was passed in Venice in 1474, see Reid, B.C. *A Practical Guide to Patent Law* (London: Sweet & Maxwell, 2nd edn., 1993) at p.1.

Initially, there was no requirement for a written description of the invention to be provided by the applicant but this gradually became common practice. The descriptions, however, were not made publicly available. They became known, as they still are, as specifications. By 1718, the provision of a specification was often a requirement. The drafting of them could be quite important, as Arkwright discovered to his chagrin when his main patent for a water powered spinning machine was held to be invalid through want of detail in 1785.[11] Applications were still made to the Monarch, or later to the law officers of the Crown, and the system became difficult, long-winded and expensive. Charles Dickens wrote a critical exposé of it[12] and the system was overhauled by the Patent Law Amendment Act 1852. This saw the beginnings of the Patent Office and the opening of the Patent Office Library soon followed[13] as did a system for classifying patents.[14] The Patents, Designs and Trade Marks Act 1883 gave effect to the reciprocity provisions in the Paris Convention for the Protection of Industrial Property 1883. The 1883 Act also substituted the Seal of the Patent Office for the Monarch's Great Seal.

Until the early part of the twentieth century, patent applications were not searched for novelty. It was basically a deposit system, with applications simply being checked for satisfactory completion. However, as a result of the Patents Act 1902, novelty searches were commenced and the granting of patents became a much more exacting process. There were other Acts culminating in the Patents Act 1949 all of which can be seen as being developments based on the same traditions. However, the current Act, the Patents Act 1977 is different in that it was designed to take account of the European Patent Convention, which established the European Patent Office, and the yet to be introduced Community patent system. Since the coming into force of the 1977 Act, letters patent are no longer issued but, instead, a certificate from the Comptroller-General of Patents Designs and Trade Marks is provided. The maximum term of a patent has been extended from 16 years to 20 years.

JUSTIFICATION FOR PATENT RIGHTS

The conventional justification for a patent system has been briefly mentioned earlier in this chapter. In short, inventors and investors are rewarded for their time, work and risk of capital by the grant of a limited monopoly. This benefits society by stimulating investment and employment and because details of the invention are added to the store of available knowledge. Eventually, after a period of time, depending on how long the patent is renewed (subject to a maximum of 20 years),[15] anyone will be able to put the invention to use. This utilitarian approach found favour with great English philosophers such as Jeremy Bentham who argued that, because an invention involved a great deal of time, money and effort and also included a large element of risk, the exclusive use of the invention must be reserved for a period of time so that it could be exploited and thereafter used for the general increase of knowledge and wealth. He said that such exclusive use cannot:

> . . . otherwise be put upon any body but by the head of law: and hence the necessity and the use of the interposition of law to *secure* to an inventor the benefit of his invention.[16]

11 *R v Arkwright* (1785) 1 WPC 64. Arkwright was a barber from Bolton who left his business and nagging wife to pursue his interest in inventing.

12 Dickens, C. *A Poor Man's Tale of a Patent*, reprinted in Phillips, J. *Charles Dickens and the 'Poor Man's Tale of a Patent'* (Oxford: ESC Publishing, 1984). In a plea to end the considerable bureaucracy involved, the closing sentence ends with the sentiment '... England has been chaffed and waxed sufficient'. (One of the officials involved in the process was the Deputy Chaff-wax who appears to have been responsible for preparing the wax for the Sealer).

13 In 1855. Now known as the Science Reference and Information Service.

14 For a description of the period leading up to the 1852 Act, see Dutton, H.I. *The Patent System and Inventive Activity during the Industrial Revolution, 1750-1852* (Manchester: Manchester University Press, 1984).

15 Pharmaceutical patents can now be renewed up to a maximum of 25 years, Supplementary Protection Certificate for Pharmaceutical Products, EEC Regulation No. 1768/92, OJ [1992] L182/1 and Patents (Supplementary Protection Certificate for Medicinal Products) Rules 1992, SI 1992 No. 3162.

16 Bentham, J. *Manual of Political Economy*, reprinted in Stark, W. (ed.), *Jeremy Bentham's Economic Writings*, Vol. 1 (London: Allen & Unwin, 1952) at p.263.

Of course, the proprietor of a patent is likely to use this economic privilege to his advantage and the resulting product will be priced accordingly, subject to market forces. A high price may be asked which will reflect two factors, the cost of research and development required to bring the invention to fruition and the natural commercial desire to obtain a large profit. However, the owner of the patent (the proprietor) does not have *carte blanche* in this latter respect for the following reasons:

(a) Consumers have managed thus far without the invention and may continue to do so by refusing to pay high prices.

(b) The equation between volume of sales and profit margin must be considered. Sometimes a cheaper price will make more money for the owner of the patent by increasing sales disproportionately.

(c) The consuming public may not have a need for the invention and it may be difficult to attract sales at any price. The sad fact is that a great many inventions fail to be commercially viable.

(d) There are various safeguards and controls to prevent abuse of patents both in terms of domestic law (that is, United Kingdom law) and European Community law.

On the first point, John Stuart Mill, who strongly supported the patent system was considered by Smit to have:

> . . . adopted the rhetoric of the free market economy by suggesting that the reward depended on the invention proving to have economic value and that, in any event, only the users of the commodity created were paying for the increased price caused by the patent monopoly.[17]

A patent is, therefore, not necessarily a licence to print money and a great deal of market research and economic judgment is essential before embarking upon the development of inventions. Bearing in mind that most important patents are granted to corporate organizations, this is a highly significant factor. The days of eccentric inventors are by no means gone and simple and easily developed inventions are still a possibility, such as the Biro ball point pen or reflecting roadstuds ('cats' eyes'). But in most cases the advent of technology and its increasing complexity has necessitated substantial capital investment. The pharmaceutical industry is a good example of this; the cost of developing and testing new drugs requires large and long-term investment well before any rewards can be secured. Cursorily examined, the price charged for the finished product may seem exorbitant but could be the result of all sorts of preliminary and hidden costs associated with the invention. Speaking of the once popular exaggeration that drugs cost 'twopence a bucket to make and sell at £10 per pill', Walton points out that:

> What at first sight looks like profiteering, on examination turns out to be not so. What the drug houses sell is not a substance (whose manufacturing cost is commonly negligible) but a service. The cost of research – including the cost of all the abortive investigations – the clinical trials – the creation and maintenance of the market by initial and continuing promotion – the back-up servicing by the originating drug house which has at all times to deal with any slow to emerge problems caused by use of the drug – all this has to be paid for.[18]

17 Smit, D. van Zyl *The Social Creation of A Legal Reality: A Study of the Emergence and Acceptance of the British Patent System as a Legal Instrument for the Control of New Technology*, unpublished Ph.D. thesis, University of Edinburgh, 1980.

18 Walton, A. 'The Copyright, Designs and Patents Act 1988 (1)', (1989) 133 *Solicitors Journal* 646 at 650. Walton's comment was made in the context of compulsory licences, discussed in the following chapter.

These costs, which can be disproportionately large in comparison with the cost of manufacturing, will be incurred only by companies and organizations that can foresee a profitable return on them and the only way this can be guaranteed is to secure some form of legal protection that will ensure that this is a practical possibility. Without such protection another manufacturer would be able to come along, steal the idea and sell the product for far less than the originator could ever hope to. The other manufacturer would have the considerable advantage of not having to pay any of the costs identified by Walton except, perhaps, some minimal marketing costs.

The Industrial Revolution brought a great many pressures upon the patent system, eventually leading to major reforms starting with the Patent Law Amendment Act 1852. During the preceding period there was much debate about whether inventions should be afforded legal protection by the grant of patents and, indeed, in Switzerland and The Netherlands patent law was dismantled to be reintroduced later in the nineteenth century. The fact that this could happen and that the whole rationale for the granting of patents could be challenged in England now seems incredible. Nevertheless, the demise of the patent system was anticipated in the press, including *The Times* and *The Economist*.[19] Arguments for the abolition of the system centred around the detrimental effect of patents on competition and free trade.[20] Some commentators considered that patents had served their purpose and were no longer needed in a developed industrial society, whilst others saw patents as insidious and positively harmful, *The Economist* in 1851 noted that the granting of patents:

> . . . inflames cupidity, excites fraud . . . begets disputes and quarrels betwixt inventors, provokes endless lawsuits, makes men ruin themselves for the sake of getting the privilege of a patent, which merely fosters a delusion of greediness.[21]

Convincing arguments had to be developed by those keen to see the patent system retained and improved. Those arguments are still valid today and include:

(a) **The contract theory.** Temporary protection granted in reward for knowledge of new inventions.
(b) **The reward theory.** Inventors should be rewarded for making useful inventions and the law must be used to guarantee this reward so that inventors can receive sufficient recompense for their ingenuity.
(c) **The incentive theory.** By constructing a framework whereby invention is rewarded, this will act as an incentive to make new inventions and to invest the necessary time and capital. This is a forward-looking approach contrasted to the latter which is retrospective.
(d) **The natural law/moral rights theory.** Individuals have a right of property in their own ideas and this right should be protected from being usurped or stolen by others. (This is similar to moral rights in copyright law and accords with the rationale of French patent law, though until recently of little import in the United Kingdom where the emphasis has been on economic rights rather than moral rights.)

Of course, much of the dissatisfaction could be explained by the parlous state of patent law at the time. It was clear that something had to be done – either the patent system should be abandoned or it should be reformed and stream-

19 *The Times*, 29 May 1869; *The Economist*, 5 June 1869.

20 For a comprehensive description of the arguments for and against a patent system that were raging in the mid-nineteenth century, see Dutton, H.I. *The Patent System and Inventive Activity during the Industrial Revolution, 1750–1852* (Manchester: Manchester University Press, 1984), Chapter 1.

21 *The Economist*, 26 July 1851.

lined to meet the needs of a heavily industrialized society that depended on invention and innovation for future growth and prosperity. The arguments of the supporters of a strong patent system won the day and the latter course was taken. However, it should be appreciated that having a strong system of patent law is not a foregone conclusion and that there are some good reasons to the contrary. If patent law were to be abolished tomorrow, inventive activity would not cease altogether – other factors would come to the fore, such as the inventor's lead-time, that halcyon period before competitors can equip their factories and commence manufacture, when he has no competition. Depending upon the nature of the invention, that period may be sufficient to justify the initial expense associated with the putting of the invention to use. However, in many cases, the lead-time would be insufficient and the inventor would have to look to factors such as quality and value for money as a way of making the whole undertaking profitable and worthwhile. Trade marks and business goodwill are other ways in which the invention could be successfully exploited by the inventor or the owner of the patent. In spite of the arguments for and against patents, it is now unthinkable that the patent system would be abolished. Over the last 100 or so years, patents have become established on a world-wide basis with almost all the countries with developed industries having some form of patent protection for inventions.[22] Some industries, such as pharmaceuticals and electronics, would become stagnant without patent protection through lack of investment.

22 Even the USSR had patent laws. Mamiofa, I. E. 'The Draft of a New Soviet Patent Law', [1990] 1 EIPR 21.

PRACTICAL CONSIDERATIONS

Three possibilities present themselves to an inventor who is resolved on securing a patent for his invention. An application may be made for a United Kingdom patent, for a 'European' patent designating a number of member states of the European Patent Convention (EPC), or under the Patent Cooperation Treaty (PCT) designating some or all of the contracting states. In all cases, applications can be handled by the Patent Office in London. However, a European application can instead be filed direct with the European Patent Office in which case permission must first be obtained from the United Kingdom Patent Office which checks to see whether the application compromises national security.[23] The procedure for obtaining a United Kingdom patent will be described below, but first some definitions are given relating to the terms used and documents submitted.[24]

23 Section 23 of the Patents Act 1977. Unless otherwise stated, in this chapter statutory references are to this Act.

24 The procedure for a patent under the European Patent Convention is broadly similar. Patent Cooperation Treaty patents are somewhat different in that, after search and publication, applications must be made to the individual countries; this is known as entering the national phase and can be quite complex. The procedure for a United Kingdom patent is laid out in detail in the Patents Act 1977 and the Patents Rules 1990, SI 1990 No. 2384.

Filing date

This is the date when the application is received by the Patent Office. The application must contain a request for a patent, full identification of the applicant, a full description of the invention (the specification) and the filing fee.[25] All these things must be received before the application can be given a filing date. The filing date is important because it is the date used to determine the duration of the patent. That is, the 20 years maximum period available starts to run from the filing date.

25 Section 15(1).

Priority date

This will usually be the same as the filing date unless an earlier priority date is claimed as a result of a previous application made in the preceding 12 months if the present application is supported by matter disclosed in the earlier application. For example, an inventor may apply for a United Kingdom patent for his invention and then, within 12 months, apply for a patent at the European Patent Office, designating some other European states. The priority date will, in both cases, be the same, that is, the date of the filing of the United Kingdom application. The priority date is important because it is the state of the art at that date that is considered when judging the invention for novelty. It is also relevant in terms of infringement in that persons who in good faith have either done an act that would constitute infringement or have made effective and serious preparations for such an act before the priority date may continue to do so after the grant of the patent.[26]

26 Section 64.

Specification

This is a very important document, probably the most important item submitted by the applicant. The specification must contain a description of the invention, one or more claims together with any drawings required to illustrate the invention. The specification should fully describe the invention – anything omitted at this stage could have the effect of jeopardizing the application or cutting down the usefulness and scope of the patent should it be granted. The specification should also be sufficient so that a person skilled in the art can understand and work the invention. For example, if the invention concerns a new type of tow bar for a vehicle, the specification should be such that a skilled vehicle engineer would be able to make it. An example of a patent specification is given at the end of this chapter and should be referred to. It contains on the front page, the application number, date of filing,[27] the name and address of the applicant, inventors, agent and address for service, the classifications for the invention, a document cited by the examiner which may have a bearing on the novelty of the invention, field of search, title, abstract and, usually as here, a drawing. The little numbers in brackets alongside the entries are known as INID numbers and are used to standardize the layout of the page to help with the processing of the information contained on the page.[28] For example, on the front page of the sample application at the end of this chapter, (71) is the name of the applicant, (54) is the title of the invention, (57) is the abstract and (51) is the International Patent Classification. The remainder of the specification contains a detailed description of the invention and the claims. Sometimes there will be further drawings and there may be amendments to the claims.

27 This particular example does not have a priority date. Where the priority of an earlier application is claimed, a reference, the date and country of the earlier application will all be noted on the front page.

28 This system was devised by ICIREPAT, the International Committee for Information Retrieval by Examining Patent Offices.

Claims

The application will include a statement of the claims defining the invention for which protection is required. There will usually be several claims, some of which may be alternatives. The purpose of the claims is to define the limit of the monopoly and, therefore, they must be very carefully drawn up. The ideal situation from the applicant's point of view is a set of claims which give the widest scope to the invention without being rejected. The claims in the example should be carefully studied with this in mind. They provide a good example of the care and thoroughness that a patent agent employs on the drafting of claims.

By section 14(5) of the Patents Act 1977, the claims shall:

(a) define the matter for which the applicant seeks protection;
(b) be clear and concise;
(c) be supported by the description; and
(d) relate to one invention or to a group of inventions which are so linked as to form a single inventive concept.

The example at the end of the chapter is a good example of a group of inventions forming a single inventive concept. Claims 1, 20 and 39 relate to three different aspects – a beverage package, a method of packaging a beverage and a beverage when so packaged. Rule 22 of the Patent Rules 1990[29] states that where two or more inventions are claimed (whether in a single claim or in separate claims), and there exists between or among those inventions a technical relationship which involves one or more of the same or corresponding special technical features, then those inventions shall be treated as being so linked as to form a single inventive concept for the purposes of the Act. 'Special technical features' are defined as those technical features which define a contribution which each of the claimed inventions, considered as a whole, makes over the prior art.

Sometimes, an omnibus claim will be included, usually as the final claim, for example:

> the widget as substantially described hereinbefore with reference to the accompanying drawings.

The way claims are interpreted is important. By section 125(1) of the Act, the invention shall be taken to be that specified in a claim as interpreted by the description and any drawings contained in the specification. The extent of protection afforded by the grant of the patent is to be determined accordingly. But interpretation of claims can be wider than this and a purposive approach to interpretation is taken rather than a strict literal approach in accordance with the European Patent Convention. This feature is discussed in depth in Chapter 15.

Abstract

The abstract is simply a short summary of the patent description not exceeding 150 words.[30] The abstract must indicate the technical field to which the invention belongs and it should be clear about the technical problem and give some idea of the solution to that problem and the principal use or uses of the invention. It provides useful information to help in the searching process, for example when searching for anticipatory materials. Indeed it is a requirement that the abstract be drafted accordingly. By reading the abstract, it should be possible to determine whether it is necessary to consult the specification itself. Abstracts are included with other information in on-line and printed searching services.

Procedure for a United Kingdom patent[31]

The procedure described below applies where there has not been a declaration of priority from an earlier application. If there has been such a declaration, step

29 SI 1990 No. 2384, as amended by The Patents (Amendment) Rules 1992, SI 1992 No. 1142.

30 Rule 19, Patent Rules 1990, SI 1990 No. 2384.

31 The Patent Office produce some free literature on intellectual property. It is of excellent quality and of interest: *Patent Protection* and *How to Prepare a UK Patent Application*. These and others are available from The Patent Office, Marketing and Information Directorate, Cardiff Road, Newport, Gwent NP9 1RH.

(b) is different in that the claims and abstract must be filed within 12 months of the earliest priority date or within one month of the date of filing the application whichever is the later, but the form and search fee must be submitted within 12 months of the earliest declared priority date.

In simple terms, the application procedure is as follows.

(a) **File application:** submit application including a request for a patent, identification of the applicant (full name and address), description of the patent and the filing fee.

(b) **File claims, etc.:** within 12 months, file the claims, abstract, form requesting preliminary examination and search together with the search fee.

(c) **Preliminary examination and search:** the application will then be checked to ensure all necessary documents and forms have been filed and fees paid. The application will then go to a Patent Office examiner who will make a search, mainly amongst patent specifications to check for novelty and obviousness. After this a search report will be issued. This report helps the applicant to decide whether his invention is new and not obvious. In some cases, amendments may have to be made to the claims or description. Any amendment to the claims must not cover something not already disclosed in the specification as first filed.

(d) **Early publication:** the application will be published together with the search report and any amended claims received before date of publication. Normally, this takes place 18 months after the priority date.[32] The contents of the specification are no longer confidential and become part of the state of the art and may be used in judging the novelty of subsequent patent applications. The date of early publication is important because it is the date after which damages for infringement can be claimed. For example, if there is an infringement of the patent between the early publication and grant, assuming it is finally granted, an action in respect of that infringement can be commenced *after* the patent has been granted. Early publication is known as 'A' publication. The example at the end of the chapter is an 'A' publication.

(e) **Substantive examination:** this is the final stage before the grant of the patent. Within six months of the date of early publication, yet another form and fee has to be submitted to the Patent Office. The application will lapse if the form and fee are not received within those six months.[33] Once the patent application has been published and before grant any person may make written observations on the patentability of the invention. Reasons for the observations must be given and the Comptroller must consider the observations.[34] The specification is examined to see whether it complies with the requirements of the Patents Act 1977, especially whether the invention claimed is new and non-obvious, whether the description is adequate so that it can be carried out by a person skilled in the art concerned and whether the claims are clear and consistent with the description. It is common for the specification to require amendment in the light of objections raised by the examiner or for the claims to be narrowed. Once all the examiner's objections have been met, assuming they can be, the patent is granted. The patent as granted is published. This is known as 'B' publication.

[32] If there is no declared priority date, early publication takes place 18 months from the date of filing the application, rule 27, Patent Rules 1990, SI 1990 No. 2384.

[33] It is possible to obtain a one month extension.

[34] The person making the observations does not, as a result, become a party in any proceedings under the Act before the Comptroller, section 21. Under this provision, a person may claim that the invention is not new because he was working the invention before the priority date.

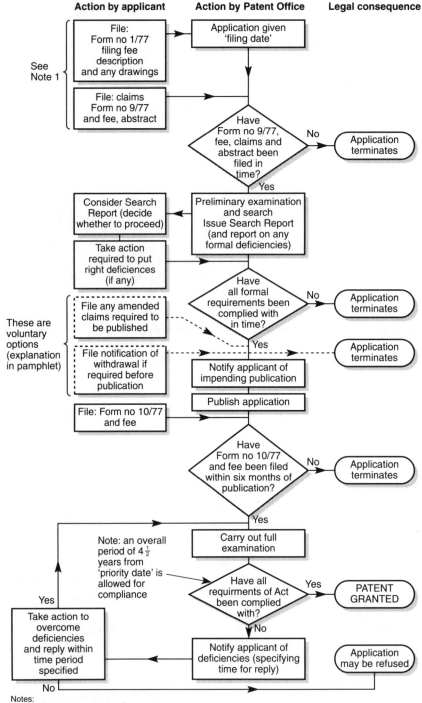

Figure 13.1 Flowchart of a UK patent application
(Reproduced by permission of the Controller of HMSO)

Figure 13.1 illustrates a flowchart for the UK patent application process. The pamphlet referred to in the chart is *Introducing Patents – A guide for inventors*, London: HMSO, 1988.

Altogether, four and a half years are allowed from the priority date to the satisfactory completion and submission of the specification. It can be seen that the shortest period is theoretically a little over 18 months but a period of between 2 and 3 years is more realistic. However, the Patent Office will consider shortening the publication period and the time between publication and full examination if the applicant can make out a good case. The initial grant is for four years. Thereafter the patent may be renewed annually up to a maximum of 20 years from the date of filing.

Cost of applying for a patent

The cost of applying for a patent can be quite high, apart from paying the appropriate fees to the Patent Office, the drawing up of the necessary documents and drafting of claims will usually take a considerable amount of time. Additionally, in most cases, the services of a patent agent will be required. Some of the main fees payable to the Patent Office in respect of a United Kingdom patent, as from 11 May 1992[35] are as follows:

35 Patents (Fees) Rules 1992, SI 1992 No. 616.

Filing fee	(Form 1/77)	£25
Request for preliminary examination and search	(Form 9/77)	£130
Request for substantive examination	(Form 10/77)	£130

Renewal fees – on a sliding scale varying from £110 for fifth year to £450 for twentieth and final year.

Of course, there are a whole range of other fees and forms for various purposes, for example, for amendments, assignments, restoration, etc. Applications for European Patent Convention patents and PCT patents are more expensive. For example, for an EPC patent or a PCT patent, the fees[36] are as follows:

36 These are the 1993 figures. Source: The Patent Office *Patent Protection*, July 1993.

	EPC	PCT
Filing	£258	£352 (plus £55 transmittal fee)
Search	£815	£1,030
Designation (per state)	£150	£85
Substantive examination	£1,202	National fee (varies) (plus EPO fee £1,288)
Grant	£601	National fee (varies)

It can be seen that obtaining a patent effective in several countries requires a considerable financial commitment, especially when the cost of preparing applications including translation into other languages and patent agent fees are taken into account. However, the increasing volume of patent activity clearly shows the attractiveness of this form of monopoly as a way of protecting inventions.

Classification system

Current and old patents have to be consulted for several reasons, the obvious one being to determine whether a 'new' invention has been anticipated and is, therefore, likely to be refused a patent on the grounds of lack of novelty. Other reasons relate to patent documents as a valuable source of information in terms of gaining information about competitors and a particular field of technology, seeing how certain problems have been tackled in the past, as a way of gaining inspiration and as a research tool. The Patent Office presently holds specifications and abstracts for every British patent dating from 1617, comprising around 2 million inventions, in addition to over 23 million patent publications from overseas. It will come as no surprise that some sort of classification scheme is needed to assist in searching for relevant documents. Patent abstracts and specifications are classified and indexed to make the task of searching easier. For example, for specifications, the system used is based on three elements, a section, a division and a heading. There are eight sections lettered from A to H as follows:

A   Human necessities
B   Performing operations
C   Chemistry and metallurgy
D   Textiles and paper
E   Civil engineering and building accessories
F   Mechanics, heating and lighting
G   Instrumentation
H   Electricity

In addition there is a 'division not specified'. Each section is divided into between two and eight divisions which are further divided into between two and 24 headings. As an example, the classification for toys is A6S (A6 being entertainments). Further subdivisions are used below the headings level and are known as terms which are developed and expanded pragmatically in response to volume of applications.

There is also a Universal Indexing Schedule and an International Patent Classification (IPC), the latter being used by the European Patent Office. The IPC is arranged in eight sections in a similar way to the United Kingdom classification. In practice, United Kingdom patent specifications will carry all three classifications. The Patent Office and the Science Reference and Information Service have access to several computer databases. Over 30 million patents have been published world-wide and that figure is being increased by around one million each year.

Patent agents

Persons wishing to apply for a patent normally use the services of a patent agent because of the complexity and technicality associated with patent applications and the importance of correctly defining the scope of the patent and extent of the claims. Although anyone can act for another in an agency capacity in respect of a patent application,[37] by section 276 of the Copyright, Designs and Patents Act 1988, only registered patent agents may describe themselves as patent agents or patent attorneys.[38] Communications between a client and his

37 Subject to restrictions under the European Patent Convention in relation to European patents, section 274 of the Copyright, Designs and Patents Act 1988.

38 Solicitors may also use the description patent attorney.

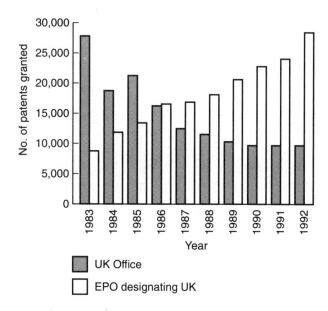

Figure 13.2 Patents granted 1983–1992

39 Section 280 of the Copyright, Designs and Patents Act 1988.

patent agent are privileged provided the agent is registered.[39] There is a professional body for patent agents, the Chartered Institute of Patent Agents. Chartered patent agents now have a right of audience in the Patents County Court.

Some statistics concerning UK and EPO patents

A patent is initially granted for four years after which a patent may be renewed annually. There are a large number of patent applications made each year for the United Kingdom alone, over 27,000 with nearly 230,000 renewals.[40]

40 The Patent Office, *Annual Report and Accounts 1992 to 1993*, (London: HMSO, 1993).

Around 46,000 applications were received by the European Patent Office of which around 93 per cent designated the United Kingdom. The number of patents renewed in 1992 ranged from 18,205 in the fifth year down to 3,633 which were renewed for their twentieth and final year. The total income from patent fees for the year ending 30 March 1993 received by the Patent Office was nearly £35 million. These figures indicate the importance of the patent system as perceived by inventors and their employers. Whilst United Kingdom based applicants account for approximately two-thirds of applications for United Kingdom patents, other countries such as the United States of America (7 per cent), Japan (6¼ per cent) and Germany (3½ per cent) are also significant sources of applications.

As time progresses, the role of the European Patent Office becomes increasingly important. This can be seen in Figure 13.2 which compares trends in the United Kingdom Patent Office and the European Patent Office in terms of numbers of patents granted.

Approaching one-third of applications are based on a claim to a priority in relation to an earlier application elsewhere. In 1992, a total of 557 patents were marked to the effect that licences are available as of right.[41] No compulsory

41 Under section 46(1) of the Act.

licences were granted under section 48(1) of the Act and there are no awards of compensation for employees making inventions of outstanding benefit to their employers under section 40 of the Act. A total of 52 patents were revoked, mainly by the Comptroller.

Success rates for patent applications cannot be directly obtained from the Patent Office's Annual Report. Because of the time lag in the grant of a patent, which may be as much as 3 to 4 years, it is not an easy task to determine what percentage of applications are successful, however, in 1992, 9,421 patents were granted in the United Kingdom. This should be compared with 27,178 applications made and 11,794 applications published in the same year bearing in mind that the grant will relate to applications made prior to 1992. The figures do, however, give a rough comparison.

Example patent application and specification

There follows a reproduction of a patent application made to the United Kingdom Patent Office (No. GB 2183592A). This is reproduced by permission of Guinness Brewing Worldwide Ltd. and their patent attorneys, Urquhart-Dykes & Lord. The application should be studied in the light of the description of the constituent parts of a patent specification given earlier in this chapter. The format of the specification and the high standard of draftsmanship should particularly be noted.

(12) **UK Patent Application** (19) **GB** (11) **2 183 592** (13) **A**

(43) Application published **10 Jun 1987**

(21) Application No **8529441**

(22) Date of filing **29 Nov 1985**

(71) Applicant
Arthur Guinness Son & Company (Dublin) Limited,

(Incorporated in Irish Republic),

St. James's Gate, Dublin 8, Republic of Ireland

(72) Inventors
Alan James Forage,
William John Byrne

(74) Agent and/or Address for Service
Urquhart-Dykes & Lord, 47 Marylebone Lane,
London W1M 6DL

(51) INT CL⁴
B65D 25/00 5/40

(52) Domestic classification (Edition I)
B8D 12 13 19 7C 7G 7M 7P1 7PY SC1
B8P AX
U1S 1106 1110 1111 B8D B8P

(56) Documents cited
GB 1266351

(58) Field of search
B8D
B8P
Selected US specifications from IPC sub-class B65D

(54) **Carbonated beverage container**

(57) A container for a beverage having gas (preferably at least one of carbon dioxide and inert (nitrogen) gases) in solution consists of a non-resealable container 1 within which is located a hollow secondary chamber 4, eg a polypropylene envelope, having a restricted aperture 7 in a side wall. The container is charged with the beverage 8 and sealed. Beverage from the main chamber of the container enters the chamber 4 (shown at 8a) by way of the aperture 7 to provide headspaces 1a in the container and 4a in the pod 4. Gas within the headspaces 1a and 4a is at greater than atmospheric pressure. Preferably the beverage is drawn into the chamber 4 by subjecting the package to a heating and cooling cycle. Upon opening the container 1, eg by draw ring/region 13, the headspace 1a is vented to atmosphere and the pressure differential resulting from the pressure in the chamber headspace 4a causes gas/beverage to be ejected from the chamber 4 (by way of the aperture 7) into the beverage 8. Said ejection causes gas to be evolved from solution in the beverage in the main container chamber to form a head of froth on the beverage. The chamber 4 is preferably formed by blow moulding and located below beverage level by weighting it or as a press fit within the container 1 by lugs 6 engaging the container walls, the container being preferably a can, carton or bottle. The chamber 4 may initially be filled with gas, eg nitrogen, at or slightly above atmospheric pressure, the orifice being formed by laser boring, drilling or punching immediately prior to locating the chamber 4 in the container 1.

The drawings originally filed were informal and the print here reproduced is taken from a later filed formal copy.

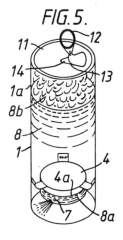

FIG.5.

Reference to UK Patent Application 2,183,592A is made with kind permission of Guinness Brewing Worldwide Limited and their Patent Attorneys, Urquhart-Dykes & Lord.

29 NOV 8529441

1/2

2183592

FIG.1.

FIG.2.

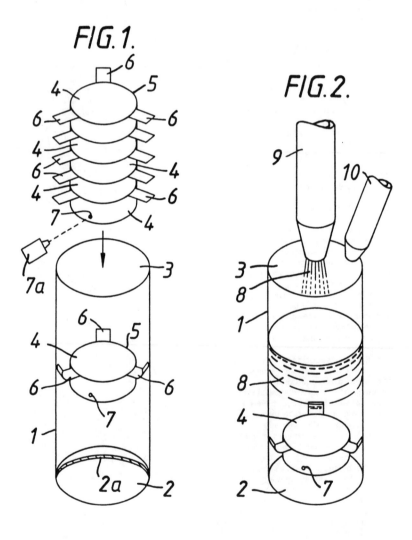

29 Nov 85 29441

2/2   2183592

FIG. 3.

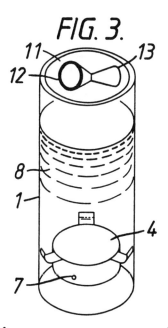

FIG. 4.

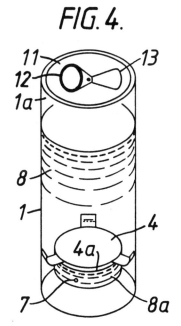

FIG. 5.

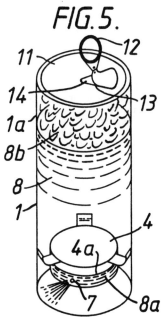

SPECIFICATION

A beverage package and a method of packaging a beverage containing gas in solution

5

Technical field and background art

This invention relates to a beverage package and a method of packaging a beverage containing gas in solution. The invention more particularly concerns
10 beverages containing gas in solution and packaged in a sealed, non-resealable, container which, when opened for dispensing or consumption, permits gas to be evolved or liberated from the beverage to form, or assist in the formation of, a head or froth on the
15 beverage. The beverages to which the invention relates may be alcoholic or non-alcoholic; primarily the invention was developed for fermented beverages such as beer, stout, ale, lager and cider but may be applied with advantage to so-called soft drinks
20 and beverages (for example fruit juices, squashes, colas, lemonades, milk and milk based drinks and similar type drinks) and to alcoholic drinks (for example spirits, liquers, wine or wine based drinks and similar).
25   It is recognised in the beverage dispensing and packaging art that the characteristics of the head of froth which is provided on the beverage by the liberation of gas from the beverage immediately prior to consumption are an important consideration to the
30 consumers enjoyment of the product and are therefore of commercial importance. Conventionally beverages of the type discussed above containing gas in solution and packaged in a non-resealable container (such as a can, bottle or carton) provide a
35 headspace in the container within which gas is maintained under pressure. Upon opening of the package, the headspace gas is vented to atmosphere and the beverage is usually poured into a drinking vessel. During such dispensing of the beverage it is
40 usual for gas in solution to be liberated to create the froth or head. It is generally recognised that when dispensing a beverage as aforementioned, the gas is liberated as a result of the movement of the beverage over a surface having so-called gas nucleation or ac-
45 tive sites which may be the wall of the drinking vessel into which the beverage is poured. There is therefore a distinct possibility with conventional beverage packages that upon opening of the container after storage and until the beverage is poured there-
50 from, the beverage will have little or no froth or head - such a headless beverage is usually regarded by the consumer as somewhat unattractive and unappealing especially where the beverage is to be drunk directly from the container. Admittedly it may be pos-
55 sible to develop a head or froth within the container by agitating or shaking the package (so that the movement of the beverage over the interior surface of the container causes the liberation of the gas in solution) but this is clearly inconvenient once the
60 container is opened and is inadvisable if the package is shaken immediately prior to opening as the contents tend to spray or spurt on opening.

There is therefore a need for a beverage package and a method of packaging a beverage containing
65 gas in solution by which the beverage is packaged in a non-resealable container so that when the container is opened gas is liberated from the beverage to form or assist in the formation of a head or froth without the necessity of an external influence being
70 applied to the package; it is an object of the present invention to satisfy this need in a simple, economic and commercially viable manner.

Statements of invention and advantages

75   According to the present invention there is provided a beverage package comprising a sealed, non-resealable, container having a primary chamber containing beverage having gas in solution therewith and forming a primary headspace comprising gas at
80 a pressure greater than atmospheric; a secondary chamber having a volume less than said primary chamber and which communicates with the beverage in said primary chamber through a restricted orifice, said secondary chamber containing beverage
85 derived from the primary chamber and having a secondary headspace therein comprising gas at a pressure greater than atmospheric so that the pressures within the primary and secondary chambers are substantially at equilibrium, and wherein said package is
90 openable, to open the primary headspace to atmospheric pressure and the secondary chamber is arranged so that on said opening the pressure differential caused by the decrease in pressure at the primary headspace causes at least one of the beverage and
95 gas in the secondary chamber to be ejected by way of the restricted orifice into the beverage of the primary chamber and said ejection causes gas in the solution to be evolved and form, or assist in the formation of, a head of froth on the beverage.
100   Further according to the present invention there is provided a method of packaging a beverage having gas in solution therewith which comprises providing a container with a primary chamber and a secondary chamber of which the volume of the secondary
105 chamber is less than that of the primary chamber and with a restricted orifice through which the secondary chamber communicates with the primary chamber, and charging and sealing the primary chamber with the beverage to contain the gas in solution and to
110 form a primary headspace in the primary chamber, and charging the secondary chamber with beverage derived from the primary chamber by way of said restricted orifice to form a secondary headspace in the secondary chamber whereby the pressures in both
115 the primary and secondary chambers are at equilibrium and gaseous pressures in both the primary and secondary headspaces are at a pressure greater than atmospheric so that, when the container is broached to open the primary headspace to atmos-
120 pheric pressure, the pressure differential caused by the decrease in pressure at the primary headspace causes at least one of the beverage and gas in the secondary chamber to be ejected into the beverage of the primary chamber by way of said restricted ori-
125 fice and the said ejection causes gas to be evolved from solution in the beverage in the primary chamber to form, or assist in the formation of, a head of froth on the beverage.

The present invention is applicable to a wide range
130 of beverages of the type as previously discussed and

where those beverages contain gas in solution which gas is intended to be liberated to form or assist in the formation of the head or froth on the beverage. Understandably the gas in solution must not detract
5 from, and should preferably enhance the characteristics required of the beverage and be acceptable for use with food products; preferably therefore the gas is at least one of carbon dioxide and inert gases (by which latter term is included nitrogen)
10 although it is to be realised that other gases may be appropriate.

The present invention was primarily developed for the packaging of fermented beverages such as beer, ale, stout, lager and cider where among the desirable
15 qualities sought in a head are a consistent and regular, relatively fine, bubble size; a bubble structure which is substantially homogeneous so that the head is not formed with large irregularly shaped and random gaps; the ability for the head or bubble
20 structure to endure during a reasonable period over which it is likely to be consumed, and a so-called "mouth-feel" and flavour whcih may improve the enjoyment of the beverage during consumption and not detract from the desirable flavour characteristics
25 required of the beverage. These desirable qualities are of course equally applicable to non-fermented beverages, for example with so-called soft drinks. Conventionally, beverages of the type to which the invention relates are packaged in a non-resealable
30 container which when opened totally vents the headspace to atmosphere, contain carbon dioxide in solution and it is the liberation of the carbon dioxide on opening of the package and dispensing of the beverage into a drinking vessel which creates the froth or
35 head; however, the head so formed has very few of the aforementioned desirable qualities - in particular it is usually irregular, lacks homogeneity and has very little endurance so that there is a tendency for it to collapse after a short period. It has been known for
40 approximately 25 years and as discussed in our G.B. Patent No. 876,628, that beverages having in solution a mixture of carbon dioxide gas and inert gas (such as nitrogen or argon) will, when dispensed in a manner whereby the mixed gases are caused to
45 evolve to develop the head or foam from small bubbles containing the mixture of carbon dioxide and, say, nitrogen gases, provide the desirable qualities for the head as previously discussed. Commericially the formation of the head by the use of mixed
50 gases as aforementioned has been widely employed in the dispensing of beverage in a draught system and on demand from a bulk container (such as a keg or barrel) where the gases are caused to evolve by subjecting the beverage to intense shear forces in
55 passing it under pressure through a set of small holes. Beverages, particularly stout, having a mixture of carbon dioxide and nitrogen gases in solution and dispensed in draught using the aforementioned technique have met with considerable commercial
60 success and it was soon realised that there was a need to make available for consumption a similar beverage derived from a small non-resealable container suitable for shelf storage and retail purposes. Research has indicated that to achieve the initia-
65 tion of a head on a beverage containing carbon

dioxide and inert gas such as nitrogen in solution it is necessary to provide so-called "active sites" which are regions where the beverage is subjected to a high local strain (such a strain being higher than the
70 cohesive force of the beverage). In these conditions the beverage prefers to generate a bubble of mixed gases instead of "bending around" the active site. It was found that an active site could be solid, liquid or gas such as granules, restrictor holes, rapid streams
75 of liquid or bubbles and the like. It was also found that ultrasonics could produce a "ghost" active site by the formation of extreme pressure gradients. There has however been a problem in providing an "active site" in a beverage packaged in a non-
80 resealable small container in a manner which is commercially and economically acceptable. During the past 25 years considerable expenditure has been devoted to research and development in an attempt to overcome the aforementioned problem. For ex-
85 ample, our G.B. Patent No. 1,588,624 proposes initiating the evolution of mixed carbon dioxide and nitrogen gases from a beverage by subjecting the beverage to ultrasonic excitement, by injecting a gas, liquid and/or foam into the beverage by use of a
90 syringe-type device, or by pouring the beverage over an excitation surface such as polystyrene granules. Although these latter proposals were successful in achieving the desired head formation, the necessity to use ancillary apparatus had commercial dis-
95 advantages (for example, it is unreasonable to expect a retail customer to have available an ultrasonic signal generator; also the steps required to effect initiation of the head following opening of the beverage package involved an inconvenient discipline and
100 time factor). In a further example our G.B. Patent No. 1,266,351 relates to a non-resealable package containing beverage having mixed carbon dioxide and inert gases in solution; in this disclosure a can or bottle has two chambers of which a larger chamber
105 contains the beverage while the smaller chamber is charged under pressure with the mixed gases. On opening of the can or bottle to expose the larger chamber to atmosphere, its internal pressure falls to atmospheric permitting the pressurised gas in the
110 small chamber to jet into the beverage by way of a small orifice between the two chambers. This jet of gas provides sufficient energy to initiate the formation of minute bubbles and thereby the head from the evolution of the mixed gases in the beverage
115 coming out of solution. By this proposal the small gas chamber is initially pressurised with the mixed gases to a pressure greater than atmospheric and from a source remote from the beverage; as a consequence it was found necessary, particularly in the
120 case of cans, to provide a special design of two chambered container and an appropriate means for sealing the smaller chamber following the charging of that chamber with the mixed gases (such charging usually being effected, in the case of cans, by injec-
125 ting the mixed gases into the small chamber through a wall of the can which then had to be sealed). Because of the inconvenience and high costs involved in the development of an appropriate two chambered container and the special facilities required for
130 charging the mixed gases and sealing the container,

the proposal proved commercially unacceptable.

The container employed in the present invention will usually be in the form of a can, bottle or carton capable of withstanding the internal pressures of the
5 primary and secondary chambers and of a size suitable for conventional shelf storage by the retail trade so that, the overall volume of the container may be, typically, 0.5 litres but is unlikely to be greater than 3 litres.
10 By the present invention a two chambered container is employed as broadly proposed in G.B. Patent No. 1,266,351; however, unlike the prior proposal the secondary chamber is partly filled with beverage containing gases in solution and the bever-
15 age in the secondary chamber is derived wholly from the beverage in the primary chamber so that when the contents of the primary and secondary chambers are in equilibrium (and the primary and secondary headspaces are at a pressure greater than atmosphe-
20 ric) immediately prior to broaching the container to open the primary headspace to atmosphere, the pressure differential between that in the secondary headspace and atmospheric pressure causes at least one of the beverage and the headspace gas in the
25 secondary chamber to be ejected by way of the restricted orifice into the beverage in the primary chamber to promote the formation of the head of froth without the necessity of any external influence being applied to the package. The pressurisation of
30 the headspace gas in the secondary chamber is intended to result from the evolution of gas in the sealed container as the contents of the container come into equilibrium at ambient or dispensing temperature (which should be greater than the tem-
35 perature at which the container is charged and sealed). Consequently the present invention alleviates the necessity for pressurising the secondary chamber from a source externally of the container so that the secondary chamber can be formed as a
40 simple envelope or hollow pod of any convenient shape (such as cylindrical or spherical) which is located as a discrete insert within a conventional form of can, bottle or carton (thereby alleviating the requirement for a special structure of can or bottle as
45 envisaged in G.B. Patent No. 1,266,351).

Although the head or froth formed by pouring wholly carbonated beverages tends to lack many of the desirable qualities required of a head as previously discussed; our tests have indicated that by
50 use of the present invention with wholly carbonated beverages (where the head is formed by injection of gas or beverage from the secondary chamber into the primary chamber) the resultant head is considerably tighter or denser than that achieved solely by
55 pouring and as such will normally have a greater life expectancy.

The beverage is preferably saturated or supersaturated with the gas (especially if mixed carbon dioxide and inert gases are employed) and the
60 primary chamber charged with the beverage under a counterpressure and at a low temperature (to alleviate gas losses and, say, at a slightly higher temperature than that at which the beverage freezes) so that when the container is sealed (which may be
65 achieved under atmospheric pressure using con-

ventional systems such as a canning or bottling line), the pressurisation of the primary and secondary headspaces is achieved by the evolution of gas from the beverage within the primary and secondary
70 chambers as the package is handled or stored at an ambient or dispensing temperature (greater than the charging temperature) and the contents of the container adopt a state of equilibrium. As an optional but preferred feature of the present invention, following
75 the sealing of the container, the package may be subjected to a heating and cooling cycle, conveniently during pasteurisation of the beverage. During such a cycle the gas within the secondary chamber is caused to expand and eject into the primary
80 chamber; during subsequent cooling of the package, the gas in the secondary chamber contracts and creates a low pressure or vacuum effect relative to the pressure in the primary chamber so that beverage from the primary chamber is drawn into the sec-
85 ondary chamber by way of the restricted orifice. By use of this preferred technique it is possible to ensure that the secondary chamber is efficiently and adequately charged with beverage and has the desired secondary headspace.
90 The restricted orifice through which the primary and secondary chambers communicate is conveniently formed by a single aperture in a side wall of the secondary chamber and such an aperture should have a size which is sufficiently great to alleviate
95 "clogging" or its obturation by particles which may normally be expected to occur within the beverage and yet be restricted in its dimensions to ensure that there is an adequate jetting effect in the ejection of the gas and/or beverage therethrough from the sec-
100 ondary chamber into the primary chamber to promote the head formation upon opening of the container. The restricted orifice may be of any profile (such as a slit or a star shape) but will usually be circular; experiments have indicated that a restricted
105 orifice having a diameter in the range of 0.02 to 0.25 centimeters is likely to be appropriate for fermented beverages (the preferred diameter being 0.061 centimetres). It is also preferred that when the package is positioned in an upstanding condition in which it is
110 likely to be transported, shelf stored or opened, the restricted orifice is located in an upwardly extending side wall or in a bottom wall of the secondary chamber and preferably at a position slightly spaced from the bottom of the primary chamber. It is also
115 preferred, particularly for fermented beverages, that when the contents of the sealed package are in equilibrium and the package is in an upstanding condition as aforementioned, the restricted orifice is located below the depth of the beverage in the
120 secondary chamber so that on opening of the container the pressure of gas in the secondary headspace initially ejects beverage from that chamber into the beverage in the primary chamber to promote the head formation. It is believed that such ejection
125 of beverage through the restricted orifice is likely to provide a greater efficiency in the development of the head in a liquid supersaturated with gas than will the ejection of gas alone through the restricted orifice; the reason for this is that the restricted orifice
130 provides a very active site which causes the bever-

age to "rip itself apart" generating extremely minute bubbles which themselves act as active sites for the beverage in the primary chamber, these extremely minute bubbles leave "vapour trails" of larger initia-
5 ted bubbles which in turn produce the head. Since the extremely minute bubbles are travelling at relatively high speed during their injection into the beverage in the primary chamber, they not only generate shear forces on the beverage in that chamber
10 but the effect of each such bubble is distributed over a volume of beverage much larger than the immediate surroundings of an otherwise stationary bubble.
   A particular advantage of the present invention is
15 that prior to the container being charged with beverage both the primary and secondary chambers can be at atmospheric pressure and indeed may contain air. However, it is recognised that for many beverages, particularly a fermented beverage, prolonged
20 storage of the beverage in contact with air, especially oxygen, is undesirable as adversely affecting the characteristics of the beverage. To alleviate this possibility the secondary chamber may initially be filled with a "non-contaminant" gas such as nitrogen (or
25 other inert gas or carbon dioxide) which does not adversely affect the characteristics of the beverage during prolonged contact therewith. The secondary chamber may be filled with the non-contaminant gas at atmospheric pressure or slightly greater (to allev-
30 iate the inadvertent intake of air) so that when the container is charged with the beverage, the non-contaminant gas will form part of the pressurised headspace in the secondary chamber. As previously mentioned, the secondary chamber may be formed
35 by an envelope or hollow pod which is located as a discrete insert within a conventional form of can, bottle or carton and such a discrete insert permits the secondary chamber to be filled with the non-contaminant gas prior to the envelope or pod being
40 located within the can, bottle or carton. A convenient means of achieving this latter effect is by blow moulding the envelope or pod in a food grade plastics material using the non-contaminant gas as the blowing medium and thereafter sealing the envelope
45 or pod to retain the non-contaminant gas therein; immediately prior to the pod or envelope being inserted into the can, bottle or carton, the restricted orifice can be formed in a side wall of the pod or envelope (for example, by laser boring). Immediately
50 prior to the container being sealed it is also preferable to remove air from the primary headspace and this may be achieved using conventional techniques such as filling the headspace with froth or fob developed from a source remote from the container and
55 having characteristics similar to those of the head which is to be formed from the beverage in the container; charging the primary chamber with the beverage in a nitrogen or other inert gas atmosphere so that the headspace is filled with that inert gas or nit-
60 rogen; dosing the headspace with liquid nitrogen so that the gas evolved therefrom expels the air from the headspace, or by use of undercover gassing or water jetting techniques to exclude air.
   Although the secondary chamber may be con-
65 structed as an integral part of the container, for the

reasons discussed above and also convenience of manufacture, it is preferred that the secondary chamber is formed as a discrete insert which is simply deposited or pushed into a conventional form
70 of can, bottle or carton. With cans or cartons such an insert will not be visible to the end user and many bottled beverages are traditionally marketed in dark coloured glass or plastics so that the insert is unlikely to adversely affect the aesthetics of the package. The
75 discrete insert may be suspended or float in the beverage in the primary chamber provided that the restricted orifice is maintained below the surface of the beverage in the primary chamber on opening of the container; for example the insert may be loaded or
80 weighted to appropriately orientate the position of the restricted orifice. Desirably however the insert is restrained from displacement within the outer container of the package and may be retained in position, for example at the bottom of the outer con-
85 tainer, by an appropriate adhesive or by mechanical means such as projections on the package which may flex to abut and grip a side wall of the outer container or which may engage beneath an internal abutment on the side wall of the outer container.
90
   Drawings
   One embodiment of the present invention as applied to the packaging of a fermented beverage such as stout in a can will now be described, by way of
95 example only, with reference to the accompanying illustrative drawings, in which:-
   Figures 1 to *4* diagrammatically illustrate the progressive stages in the formation of the beverage package in a canning line, and
100 *Figure 5* diagrammatically illustrates the effect on opening the beverage package prior to consumption of the beverage and the development of the head of froth on the beverage.

105 *Detailed description of drawings*
   The present embodiment will be considered in relation to the preparation of a sealed can containing stout having in solution a mixture of nitrogen and carbon dioxide gases, the former preferably being
110 present to the extent of at least 1.5% vols/vol and typically in the range 1.5% to 3.5% vols/vol and the carbon dioxide being present at a considerably lower level than the amount of carbon dioxide which would normally be present in conventional, wholly car-
115 bonated, bottled or canned stout and typically in the range 0.8 to 1.8 vols/vol (1.46 to 3.29 grams/litre). For the avoidance of doubt, a definition of the term "vols/vol" is to be found in our G.B. Patent No. 1,588,624.
   The stout is to be packaged in a conventional form
120 of cylindrical can (typically of aluminium alloy) which, in the present example, will be regarded as having a capacity of 500 millilitres and by use of a conventional form of filling and canning line appropriately modified as will hereinafter be described.
125 A cylindrical shell for the can 1 having a sealed base 2 and an open top 3 is passed in an upstanding condition along the line to a station shown in Figure 1 to present its open top beneath a stack of hollow pods 4. Each pod 4 is moulded in a food grade plastics
130 material such as polypropylene to have a short (say 5

270 *Patent law*

GB 2 183 592 A 5

millimetres) hollow cylindrical housing part 5 and a circumferentially spaced array of radially outwardly extending flexible tabs or lugs 6. The pods 4 are placed in the stack with the chamber formed by the
5 housing part 5 sealed and containing nitrogen gas at atmospheric pressure (or at pressure slightly above atmospheric); conveniently this is achieved by blow moulding the housing part 5 using nitrogen gas. The volume within the housing part 5 is approximately 15
10 millilitres. At the station shown in Figure 1 the bottom pod 4 of the stack is displaced by suitable means (not shown) into the open topped can 1 as shown. However, immediately prior to the pod 4 being moved into the can 1 a small (restricted) hole 7
15 is bored in the cylindrical side wall of the housing part 5. In the present example, the hole 7 has a diameter in the order of 0.61 millimetres and is conveniently bored by a laser beam generated by device 7a (although the hole could be formed by punching or
20 drilling). The hole 7 is located towards the bottom of the cylindrical chamber within the housing part 5. Since the hollow pod 4 contains nitrogen gas at atmospheric pressure (or slightly higher) it is unlikely that air will enter the hollow pod through the
25 hole 7 during the period between boring the hole 7 and charging of the can 1 with stout (thereby alleviating contamination of the stout by an oxygen content within the hollow pod 4).
The hollow pod 4 is pressed into the can 1 to be
30 seated on the base 2. Conventional cans 1 have a domed base 2 (shown by the section 2a) which presents a convex internal face so that when the pod 4 abuts this face a clearance is provided between the hole 7 and the underlying bottom of the chamber
35 within the can 1. It will be seen from Figure 1 that the diameter of the housing part 5 of the pod 4 is less than the internal diameter of the can 1 while the diameter of the outermost edges of the lugs 6 is greater than the diameter of the can 1 so that as the pod 4 is
40 pressed downwardly into the can, the lugs 6 abut the side wall of the can and flex upwardly as shown to grip the can side wall and thereby restrain the hollow pod from displacement away from the base 2.
The open topped can with its pod 4 is now displa-
45 ced along the canning line to the station shown in Figure 2 where the can is charged with approximately 440 millilitres of stout 8 from an appropriate source 9. The stout 8 is supersaturated with the mixed carbon dioxide and nitrogen gases, typic-
50 ally the carbon dioxide gas being present at 1.5 vols/vol (2.74 grams/litre) and the nitrogen gas being present at 2% vols/vol. The charging of the can 1 with the stout may be achieved in conventional manner, that is under a counterpressure and at a temperature of
55 approximately 0°C. When the can 1 is charged with the appropriate quantity of stout 8, the headspace above the stout is purged of air, for example by use of liquid nitrogen dosing or with nitrogen gas delivered by means indicated at 10 to alleviate contamina-
60 tion of the stout from oxygen in the headspace.
Following charging of the can 1 with stout and purging of the headspace, the can moves to the station shown in Figure 3 where it is closed and sealed under atmospheric pressure and in conventional manner
65 by a lid 11 seamed to the cylindrical side wall of the

can. The lid 11 has a pull-ring 12 attached to a weakened tear-out region 13 by which the can is intended to be broached in conventional manner for dispensing of the contents.
70 Following sealing, the packaged stout is subjected to a pasteurisation process whereby the package is heated to approximately 60°C for 15-20 minutes and is thereafter cooled to ambient temperature. During this process the nitrogen gas in the hollow pod 4a
75 initially expands and a proportion of that gas passes by way of the hole 7 into the stout 8 in the main chamber of the can. During cooling of the package in the pasteurisation cycle, the nitrogen gas in the hollow pod 4 contracts to create a vacuum effect
80 within the hollow pod causing stout 8 to be drawn, by way of the hole 7, from the chamber of the can into the chamber of the pod so that when the package is at ambient temperature the hole 7 is located below the depth of stout 8a within the hollow
85 pod 4.
Following the pasteurisation process the contents of the can 1 will stabilise in a condition of equilibrium with a headspace 1a over the stout 8 in the primary chamber of the can and a headspace 4a over the
90 stout 8a in the secondary chamber formed by the hollow pod 4 and in the equilibrium condition. With the sealed can at ambient temperature (or a typical storage or dispensing temperature which may be, say, 8°C) the pressure of mixed gases carbon dioxide
95 and nitrogen (which largely results from the evolution of such gases from the stout) is substantially the same in the headspaces 1a and 4a and this pressure will be greater than atmospheric pressure, typically in the order of 25lbs per square inch (1.72
100 bars).
The package in the condition shown in Figure 4 is typically that which would be made available for storage and retail purposes. During handling it is realised that the package may be tipped from its up-
105 right condition; in practice however this is unlikely to adversely affect the contents of the hollow pod 4 because of the condition of equilibrium within the can.
When the stout is to be made available for consumption, the can 1 is opened by ripping out the re-
110 gion 13 with the pull-ring 12. On broaching the lid 11 as indicated at 14 the headspace 1a rapidly depressurises to atmospheric pressure. As a consequence the pressure within the headspace 4a of the secondary chamber in the pod 4 exceeds that in the
115 headspace 1a and causes stout 8a in the hollow pod to be ejected by way of the hole 7 into the stout 8 in the primary chamber of the can. The restrictor hole 7 acts as a very "active site" to the supersaturated stout 8a which passes therethrough to be injected
120 into the stout 8 and that stout is effectively "ripped apart" to generate extremely minute bubbles which themselves act as active sites for the stout 8 into which are injected. These minute bubbles leave "vapour trails" of larger initiated bubbles which dev-
125 elop within the headspace 1a a head 8b having the previously discussed desirable characteristics.
It is appreciated that the headspace 1a occupies a larger proportion of the volume of the can 1 than that which would normally be expected in a 500 millilitre
130 capacity can; the reason for this is to ensure that

there is adequate volume in the headspace 1a for the
head of froth 8b to develop efficiently in the event, for
example, that the stout is to be consumed directly
from the can when the tear-out region 13 is removed.
5   Normally however the stout 8 will first be poured
from the can into an open topped drinking vessel
prior to consumption but this pouring should not
adversely affect the desirable characteristics of the
head of froth which will eventually be presented in
10   the drinking vessel.
    In the aforegoing embodiment the can 1 is charged
with stout 8 (from the source 9) having in solution the
required respective volumes of the carbon dioxide
and the nitrogen gases. In a modification the can 1 is
15   charged with stout (from source 9) having the carbon
dioxide gas only in solution to the required volume;
the 2% vols/vol nitrogen gas necessary to achieve
the required solution of mixed gas in the packaged
stout is derived from the liquid nitrogen dosing of
20   the headspace in the can.

CLAIMS

    1.   A beverage package comprising a sealed, non-
25   resealable, container having a primary chamber containing beverage having gas in solution therewith
and forming a primary headspace comprising gas at
a pressure greater than atmospheric; a secondary
chamber having a volume less than said primary
30   chamber and which communicates with the beverage in said primary chamber through a restricted orifice, said secondary chamber containing beverage
derived from the primary chamber and having a secondary headspace therein comprising gas at a pres-
35   sure greater than atmospheric so that the pressure
within the primary and secondary chambers are substantially at equilibrium, and wherein said package is
openable, to open the primary headspace to atmospheric pressure and the secondary chamber is arran-
40   ged so that on said opening the pressure differential
caused by the decrease in pressure at the primary
headspace causes at least one of the beverage and
gas in the secondary chamber to be ejected by way of
the restricted orifice into the beverage of the primary
45   chamber and said ejection causes gas in the solution
to be evolved and form, or assist in the formation of,
a head of froth on the beverage.
    2.   A package as claimed in claim 1 in which the
container has a normal upstanding condition with an
50   openable top and said secondary chamber has an
upwardly extending side wall or a bottom wall within
which said restricted orifice is located.
    3.   A packaged as claimed in either claim 1 or
claim 2 in which with the pressures within the
55   primary and secondary chambers substantially at
equilibrium the restricted orifice is located below the
depth of the beverage within the secondary
chamber.
    4.   A package as claimed in any one of the preced-
60   ing claims wherein the secondary chamber comprises a hollow and discrete insert within the container.
    5.   A package as claimed in claim 4 in which the
insert floats or is suspended in the beverage in the
65   primary chamber and means is provided for locating

the restricted orifice below the surface of the beverage in the primary chamber.
    6.   A package as claimed in claim 5 in which the
insert is weighted or loaded to locate the restricted
70   orifice below the surface of the beverage in the
primary chamber.
    7.   A package as claimed in claim 4 wherein
means is provided for retaining the insert at a predetermined position within the container.
75   8.   A package as claimed in claim 7 wherein the
container has a normal upstanding condition with an
openable top and said insert is located at or towards
the bottom of said container.
    9.   A package as claimed in either claim 7 or claim
80   8 wherein the insert comprises a hollow pod or envelope having means thereon for retaining it in position within the container.
    10.   A package as claimed in claim 9 wherein the
retaining means comprise flexible tab means which
85   engage a side wall of the container to retain the insert.
    11.   A package as claimed in any one of claims 4 to
10 wherein the insert comprises a hollow moulding.
    12.   A package as claimed in claim 11 when
90   appendant to claim 10 in which the container has a
side wall and the moulding is substantially cylindrical with radially extending tabs engaging the wall of
the container.
    13.   A package as claimed in any one of claims 4 to
95   12 in which the container has a base on which the
insert is located and said restricted orifice is located
in an upwardly extending side wall of the insert spaced from said base.
    14.   A package as claimed in any one of the pre-
100 ceding claims in which the beverage has in solution
therewith at least one of carbon dioxide gas and inert
gas (which latter term includes nitrogen).
    15.   A package as claimed in claim 14 in which the
beverage is saturated or supersaturated with said
105 gas or gases.
    16.   A package as claimed in any one of the pre-
ceding claims in which the container is in the form of
a can, bottle or carton.
    17.   A package as claimed in any one of the pre-
110 ceding claims in which the restricted orifice comprises a circular aperture having a diameter in the
range of 0.02 to 0.25 centimetres.
    18.   A package as claimed in any one of the pre-
ceding claims and comprising a fermented beverage
115 having in solution therewith carbon dioxide in the
range 0.8 to 1.8 vols/vol (1.46 to 3.29 grams/litre) and
nitrogen in the range 1.5% to 3.5% vols/vol.
    19.   A beverage package substantially as herein
described with reference to the accompanying illust-
120 rative drawings.
    20.   A method of packaging a beverage having
gas in solution therewith which comprises providing
a container with a primary chamber and a secondary
chamber of which the volume of the secondary
125 chamber is less than that of the primary chamber and
with a restricted orifice through which the secondary
chamber communicates with the primary chamber,
and charging and sealing the primary chamber with
the beverage to contain the gas in solution and to
130 form a primary headspace in the primary chamber,

and charging the secondary chamber with beverage derived from the primary chamber by way of said restricted orifice to form a secondary headspace in the secondary chamber whereby the pressures in both
5 the primary and secondary chambers are at equilibrium and gaseous pressures in both the primary and secondary headspaces are at a pressure greater than atmospheric so that, when the container is broached to open the primary headspace to atmos-
10 pheric pressure, the pressure differential caused by the decrease in pressure at the primary headspace causes at least one of the beverage and gas in the secondary chamber to be ejected into the beverage of the primary chamber by way of said restricted ori-
15 fice and the said ejection causes gas to be evolved from solution in the beverage in the primary chamber to form, or assist in the formation of, a head of froth on the beverage.

21. A method as claimed in claim 20 which com-
20 prises subjecting the sealed container to a heating and cooling cycle whereby gas within the secondary chamber is caused to expand and eject by way of the restricted orifice into the primary chamber and subsequently to contract and create a low pressure ef-
25 fect in the secondary chamber relative to the primary chamber to draw beverage from the primary chamber into the secondary chamber by way of said restricted orifice.

22. A method as claimed in claim 21 in which the
30 heating and cooling cycle comprises pasteurisation of the beverage.

23. A method as claimed in any one of claims 20 to 22 in which the container has an upstanding condition with an openable top and which comprises
35 locating the restricted orifice within an upwardly extending side wall or bottom wall of the secondary chamber.

24. A method as claimed in any one of claims 20 to 23 which comprises charging the secondary
40 chamber with beverage from the primary chamber to the extent that the restricted orifice is located below the depth of beverage in the secondary chamber.

25. A method as claimed in any one of claims 20
45 to 23 which comprises forming the secondary chamber by a discrete hollow insert located within the primary chamber of the container.

26. A method as claimed in claim 25 in which the hollow insert is to float or be suspended in the bever-
50 age in the primary chamber and which comprises loading or weighting the insert to locate the restricted orifice below the surface of the beverage in the primary chamber.

27. A method as claimed in claim 25 which com-
55 prises retaining the insert at a predetermined position within the container.

28. A method as claimed in any one of claims 25 to 27 which comprises forming the hollow insert having the restricted orifice in a wall thereof and loc-
60 ating the insert within the primary chamber prior to the charging and sealing of the primary chamber.

29. A method as claimed in any one of claims 25 to 28 which comprises forming the hollow insert by blow moulding.
65 30. A method as claimed in claim 29 which com-

prises blow moulding the hollow insert with gas for dissolution in the beverage so that said gas is sealed within the secondary chamber, and forming said restricted orifice in the wall of the insert immediately
70 prior to locating the insert in the primary chamber.

31. A method as claimed in claim 30 which comprises sealing said gas in the secondary chamber at atmospheric pressure or at a pressure slightly greater than atmospheric.
75 32. A method as claimed in any one of claims 25 to 31 which comprises forming the restricted orifice in the hollow insert by laser boring, drilling or punching.

33. A method as claimed in any one of claims 25
80 to 32 in which, prior to it being sealed, the container has an upstanding condition with an open top through which the primary chamber is charged with beverage and which comprises locating the insert through said open top to provide the secondary
85 chamber within the container.

34. A method as claimed in claim 33 when appendant to claim 27 which comprises press fitting the insert within the container so that during its location the insert engages with a side wall of the container to
90 be retained in position.

35. A method as claimed in any one of claims 20 to 34 which comprises, prior to sealing the primary chamber, purging the primary head space to exclude air.
95 36. A method as claimed in any one of claims 20 to 35 in which the gas comprises at least one of carbon dioxide gas and inert gas (which latter term includes nitrogen).

37. A method as claimed in claim 36 in which the
100 beverage is fermented and has in solution carbon dioxide in the range 0.8 to 1.8 vols/vol (1.46 to 3.29 grams/litre) and nitrogen in the range 1.5% to 3.5% vols/vol.

38. A method of packaging a beverage as
105 claimed in claim 20 and substantially as herein described.

39. A beverage when packaged by the method as claimed in any one of claims 20 to 38.

110 _____

Printed for Her Majesty's Stationery Office by
Croydon Printing Company (UK) Ltd, 4/87, D8991685.
Published by The Patent Office, 25 Southampton Buildings, London, WC2A 1AY,
from which copies may be obtained.

14

Requirements for patentability and ownership

INTRODUCTION

The long title to the Patents Act 1977 includes the aim of giving effect to certain international conventions on patents. The influence of the European Patent Convention, signed in Munich in 1973, is evident in the basic requirement for patentability. Article 52(1) of the European Patent Convention states that:

> European patents shall be granted for any new inventions which are susceptible of industrial application, which are new and which involve an inventive step.

Section 1(1) of the Patents Act 1977 requires the following conditions to be satisfied for a patent to be granted for an invention:

(a) the invention is new;
(b) it involves an inventive step;
(c) it is capable of industrial application;
(d) the grant of a patent for it is not excluded by subsections (2) and (3) below . . .

The similarities are even more pronounced when the exceptions in subsections (2) and (3) are compared to the equivalent provisions in the European Patent Convention. Because of the influence of the European Patent Convention on United Kingdom patent law, where appropriate, references will be made to the Convention and to judgments of the boards of appeal of the European Patent Office in Munich. The judgments are of persuasive authority and will normally be followed by United Kingdom judges. Congruity in the international development of patent law is seen as being of great importance. Indeed, section 130(7) of the Patents Act 1977 states a number of important provisions of the Act are declared to have, as nearly as practicable, the same effect in the United Kingdom as the corresponding provisions of the European Patent Convention, the Community Patent Convention and the Patent Co-operation Treaty.[1] In a case prior to the 1977 Act, Lord Parker LCJ said, in terms of Australian and New Zealand decisions:

1 Those provisions deal with, *inter alia*, patentability, infringement, burdens of proof and extent of invention.

> Finally one cannot shut from one's mind the desirability of having a homogeneous development of the law in all countries which have adopted our system of patent legislation. That desirability must result in a tendency of our Court to follow those decisions if it is possible to do so.[2]

2 *Swift's Application* [1962] RPC 37.

In the light of the United Kingdom's membership of the European Patent Convention, the same sentiments must now hold in respect of decisions of the European Patent Office. The same holds true as regards the Patent Co-operation Treaty.

The basic statement of the requirements for patentability, that is novelty, inventive step and industrial application followed by the exclusions from patentability, provide a good framework in which to explore the legal consequences and meaning of these words and phrases. The first point which must be made, however, is that the Patents Act 1977 contains no definition of what an invention is. Either this is because those responsible for drafting the Act felt that the task was too daunting or that a definition might later be seen as sterile and a fetter on the development of the law in tune with technological development. Another explanation is that they did not really know with any certainty. Many other common words from the world of technology cause similar problems, for example 'computer' or 'computer program'. A dictionary definition of 'invention' might talk in terms of an imaginative design or product or innovation or something produced for the first time. Schmookler gives a more rigorous definition and sub-divides inventions into process inventions and product inventions.[3] The former are new ways of producing something old and the latter are old ways of producing something new. Every invention can thus be considered to be a 'new combination of pre-existing knowledge which satisfies some want'.[4] On the other hand, innovation can be said to be the first use of an invention.[5] In practice, the lack of definition causes no problems because the basic requirements of novelty, inventive step and industrial application as defined in the statute and as interpreted by the courts produce an effective and practical explanation of 'invention' for the purposes of patent law.

BASIC REQUIREMENTS

Novelty

The invention must be new. It must not already be available to the public. The question of novelty (whether the invention is new) has a special meaning assigned to it by section 2(1) of the Patents Act 1977, which states that an invention is new if it 'does not form part of the state of the art'. Section 2(2) continues and describes the 'state of the art' as comprising all matter[6] made available to the public before the priority date of the invention whether by written or oral description, by use or in any other way.[7] This includes matter contained in other patent applications having an earlier priority date. Therefore, novelty is really a question of whether the invention has been 'anticipated', for example by a previous patent or by publication or use. The anticipating patent or publication could have occurred anywhere in the world as section 2(2) of the Act refers to public availability in 'the United Kingdom or elsewhere'. Whether publication in a limited circulation journal published in a remote part of South America would count is a moot point. Some sense of realism must be preserved and anticipatory matter does not include that which would not have been discovered during the course of a diligent search.[8]

By section 2(3), the state of the art includes matter in other patent applications published on or after the priority date of the invention being tested against the state of the art, provided the priority dates of those other applications are earlier. Patent applications are published 18 months after their priority date, unless withdrawn and this provision simply includes in the state of the art all those unpublished applications that have an earlier priority date. Thus, it is pos-

3 This is, indeed, the approach taken by the Patents Act 1977. The distinction is quite clearly seen in section 60, on infringement. Unless otherwise stated, in this chapter, statutory references are to the Patents Act 1977.

4 Schmookler, J. *Invention and Economic Growth* (Cambridge, Mass.: Harvard University Press, 1986) Chapter 1.

5 Dutton, H.I. *The Patent System and Inventive Activity During the Industrial Revolution 1750–1852* (Manchester: Manchester University Press, 1984) at p.9.

6 Whether a product, a process, information about either, or anything else (in other words, anything!).

7 The phrase 'made available to the public' was used in the definition of 'published' in section 101 of the Patents Act 1949 and should be given the same meaning, *PLG Research Ltd. v Ardon International Ltd.* [1993] FSR 197. At least one member of the public should be free in law and equity to use it.

8 *General Tire & Rubber Co. v Firestone Tyre & Rubber Co. Ltd.* [1972] RPC 457, per Sachs LJ. Section 130(1) defines 'published' as being made available to the public (in the United Kingdom or elsewhere) and a document shall be taken to be published if it can be inspected as of right at any place in the United Kingdom by members of the public, whether on payment of a fee or not. Given the enormous scale of publications held by the British Library, this is very wide.

sible for a patent application to be pre-empted by material that cannot, at the time of making the application, be discovered or inspected by the applicant.

Inventors may wish to demonstrate their invention to others, for example to secure investment or to show to potential licensees. If such demonstrations are held before the priority date the inventor runs a grave risk of jeopardizing his application by compromising the novelty of his invention. The inventor must be very careful not to disclose details of the invention but it may be safe to allow third parties to see a demonstration if this is held in private and the confidentiality of the event is stressed. In *Pall Corp.* v *Commercial Hydraulics (Bedford) Ltd.*,[9] the plaintiff sent samples of his claimed product (hydrophilic microporous membranes) to a potential customer for testing in comparison with other membranes. Other suppliers were present at the test which had been arranged. However, details of the nature and construction of the membrane were not disclosed and it was not possible to determine these details from a visual inspection of the membrane. After the patent had been granted, it was challenged on the basis that it had been made available to the public before the priority date. It was held, *inter alia,* that delivering samples in confidence to persons who knew that they were experimental and secret did not make the invention available to the public for the purposes of section 2(1) of the Act and did not, therefore, prejudice the novelty of the invention.[10]

It should be mentioned that, on the issue of novelty, cases under the Patents Act 1949 must be treated with caution as, under that Act, reasons for invalidity on the grounds of lack of novelty were somewhat different and prior secret use could invalidate a patent or be a reason for rejecting an application for a patent. In the 1949 Act a patent would be invalid if the invention was 'used in the United Kingdom before the priority date of the claim'[11] or if the invention 'is not new having regard to what was known or used before the priority date of the claim, in the United Kingdom'.[12] In *Quantel Ltd.* v *Spaceward Microsystems Ltd.*,[13] Falconer J made the point (at 108):

> [under the 1949 Act] there was no requirement that the prior dated use had to make the invention available to the public. Accordingly, cases of prior use decided under the 1949 Act *not* decided upon the criterion of whether the prior use made the patented invention available to the public, may no longer be good law. (original emphasis)

Now, under the 1977 Act, secret prior use, for example of a new industrial process by an employer-inventor whose employees are all sworn to secrecy, cannot anticipate the patent because it is not made available to the public.

Until recently, there was a general lack of authority on the meaning of prior experimental use in the context of anticipation. In *Prout* v *British Gas plc*[14] it was argued that a patent for an anti-vandal mounting bracket for a warning lamp was invalid because it had been used experimentally at a location on a public highway notorious for vandalism. However, Judge Ford held that the patent was valid nonetheless. There was some persuasive German authority that anticipatory use had to be more than mere trials in public and that the use of the finished invention was required. He also accepted that the repeal of the 1949 Act, particularly section 51(3) on trial use, revived the previous common law on the subject to the effect that experimental use to test the invention does not destroy the invention's novelty.[15]

9 [1990] FSR 329.

10 See also *Vax Appliances Ltd.* v *Hoover plc* [1991] FSR 307, decided along similar lines on the issue of prior use under the Patents Act 1949, section 32.

11 Section 14(1)(d) of the Patents Act 1949.

12 Section 32(1)(e) of the Patents Act 1949.

13 [1990] RPC 83.

14 [1992] FSR 478.

15 See also *Lux Traffic Controls Ltd.* v *Pike Signals Ltd.* [1993] RPC 107 in which it was held, *inter alia*, that field trials of a traffic lights controller did not destroy the novelty of the invention. However, making a prototype available to a person who was free in law and equity to examine it did disclose the invention.

To invalidate a patent on the grounds of lack of novelty the publication must amount to an enabling disclosure, it must be such that the public would be able to work the invention. If the published material does not adequately describe what is claimed there can be no loss of novelty. If someone else thought of the idea underlying the invention before the priority date, that alone would not be sufficient to invalidate the patent unless it was made available to the public. For example, in *Catnic Components Ltd.* v *C Evans & Co. (Builders Merchants) Ltd.*[16] a challenge on the grounds of lack of novelty by way of another person having a similar idea and making a model of a lintel failed even though the model had been shown to a number of people. The model was not the lintel (it was in fact too short to be used as a lintel) and, therefore, the plaintiff's patent for a new lintel was valid.

A prior publication which deals with a different problem to the one dealt with in the patent application could still amount to anticipation under old United Kingdom law. In *Molins* v *Industrial Machinery Co. Ltd.*,[17] an application was made in respect of a method of distributing tobacco evenly in the manufacture of cigarettes on a high-speed machine. The method involved pushing the tobacco in the same direction as the paper in which it would be wrapped. But this was held to have been anticipated by an earlier patent which used the same movement but in a slow-speed machine. This was so even though the movement in the older machine was not intended to cure the problem of uneven tobacco distribution. However, a carefully drafted application that is directed to a new purpose, not previously disclosed, might now succeed.[18] It has been accepted that the nature of novelty has been changed under Article 54 of the European Patent Convention and new purposes may be patentable and not anticipated by inherent prior disclosure.[19]

Anticipation is judged by considering how a prior publication, for example, would be construed by a person skilled in the art. This extension of the reasonable man test is essential as many technical publications are incomprehensible to the layperson. It is acknowledged that if the art is in a highly developed technology, it might be a matter of how it can be construed by a team of persons skilled in the particular art. This was accepted in *General Tire & Rubber Co.* v *Firestone Tyre & Rubber Co. Ltd.*,[20] in which the validity of Firestone's patent for making oil-extended rubber for tyres was challenged by an alleged infringer. Attacks on the validity of patents frequently come from defendants in infringement actions, where it is often the best form of defence and certainly puts the plaintiff to a great deal of additional trouble. As regards the rubber patent and the issue of anticipation, there had been a prior publication, but whether it related to Firestone's patent was ambiguous. It was said that if a prior publication contained a direction that was capable of being carried out in a manner which would infringe but would be at least as likely to be carried out in a way that would not do so, the patentee's claim would not be judged to be anticipated.[21] To anticipate the claim, the prior publication must contain a clear and unmistakable direction to do what the patentee claimed to have invented.

Finally, on the issue of novelty, matter that has been obtained unlawfully or in breach of confidence or has been divulged in breach of confidence is to be disregarded when considering the novelty of an invention.[22] In the case of a patent application, this covers the period of six months preceding the date of filing of the patent so that, effectively, if there has been a disclosure of the

16 [1983] FSR 401.

17 (1938) 55 RPC 31.

18 See the European Patent Office case of *Mobil Oil* [1990] OJ EPO 93, discussed later.

19 Falconer J recognized the changed nature of novelty in *Quantel Ltd.* v *Spaceward Microsystems Ltd.* [1990] RPC 83 at 108.

20 [1972] RPC 457.

21 It might, however, fail on the grounds of obviousness.

22 Section 2(4). Unlawfully obtained matter would include, for example a stolen model of something incorporating the invention or manufactured using the invention. Whether it applies to stolen information is less clear because of the difficulty with respect to theft of information, for example *Oxford* v *Moss* (1978) 68 Cr App R 183. However, details of the invention stored on a computer would be covered, as to gain access to them without authorization will usually be an offence under the Computer Misuse Act 1990, section 1. Of course, 'unlawfully' includes civil wrongs as well as criminal offences and could cover trespass and conversion.

invention because of a breach of confidence, for example by a potential manufacturer of products made in accordance with the invention who has been in negotiations with the inventor, there is a six-month time limit during which that disclosure will be ignored in the determination of novelty. There is provision for the inventor to display the invention at an international exhibition without this destroying the novelty of the invention subject to the inventor making a declaration and filing written evidence. The six-month time limit applies and the patent application must be filed within six months of the act of displaying the invention at the exhibition.[23]

One thing an inventor must be careful to avoid is anticipating his own invention, for example, by publishing details of it in an academic or trade journal before the priority date (normally the date of filing the application). However, to anticipate the invention, the publication must clearly describe the invention as claimed.[24] Tempting as it might be to publicize his ingenuity, the inventor would be advised to restrain his ego and keep the details of his invention secret and, in any dealings with advisors, potential manufacturers, assignees or licensees, to make it clear that discussion of the invention is in the strictest confidence.

New uses for old inventions

Old inventions may be patentable if the claims are directed to a new use. The new use will not be considered to be part of the state of the art. For inventions other than drugs for the treatment of humans and animals, new uses for old inventions may be patentable up to a point if there is some new technical effect, for example by combining two previous inventions in a new and non-obvious way.[25] However, in the case of drugs for the treatment of humans or animals, it appears that only the first use is patentable, although at first reading, section 2(6) gives the opposite impression. It states that the fact that the drug (substance or composition) already forms part of the state of the art does not prevent the new method of use from being patentable if 'the use of the substance or composition *in any such method* does not form part of the state of the art' (emphasis added). The key words are 'any such method' which seems to include the first use, at least on a strict literal interpretation. The omission of the word 'any' would clearly permit 'second use patents' and the only conclusion that can be reached is that the inclusion of the word 'any' was quite deliberate.[26] The literal approach, denying second use patents for drugs, was taken in the United Kingdom case of *John Wyeth's and Brothers Ltd.'s Application: Schering AG's Application*.[27] The background to the equivalent Convention provision does not seem to preclude a second patent where it involves a new use and in the European Patent Office case of *Eisai*[28] the Enlarged Board of Appeal held that:

(a) claims directed to the use of a product for the treatment of an illness in a human or animal body (when such use was the second or subsequent medical use) were equivalent to claims for a method of treatment of the human or animal body and therefore excluded from patentability,[29]

(b) claims directed to the use of a product for the manufacture of a medicament for a specified new therapeutic use were not lacking in novelty.[30]

23 Section 2(4). Rules 5 and 6 of the Patents Rules 1990, SI 1990 No. 2384 set out the detailed provisions.

24 *Lux Traffic Controls Ltd.* v *Pike Signals Ltd.* [1993] RPC 107. In that case a published paper did not describe the invention sufficiently clearly so as to make it known to the public.

25 See the discussion later on *Parks-Cramer Co.* v *G W Thornton & Sons Ltd.* [1966] RPC 407. Prior to the 1977 Act, there had to be novelty in the mode of using the old product as distinguished from novelty of purpose, *Lane-Fox* v *The Kensington and Knightsbridge Electric Lighting Co. Ltd.* (1892) 9 RPC 413.

26 In fact, article 54(5) of the European Patent Convention, the equivalent provision to section 2(6), also includes the word 'any'.

27 [1985] RPC 545. However, second use patents have been granted in Germany and have been recognized as a possibility in The Netherlands. See Paterson, G.D. 'The Patentability of Further Uses of a Known Product under the European Patent Convention' [1991] 1 EIPR 16.

28 [1985] OJ EPO 64.

29 Article 52(4) of the European Patent Convention – see also section 4(2) of the Patents Act 1977 which denies patentability to methods of treatment of the human or animal body by surgery or therapy or of diagnosis practised on the human or animal body.

30 Article 54 of the European Patent Convention, section 2 of the Patents Act 1977.

This is a fairly restrictive interpretation which does not apply to 'non-medical' inventions, that is those falling outside the scope of section 2(6) where the question of novelty depends on whether the new use for a new purpose had previously been made available to the public. Secret or hidden uses will not be considered to be grounds of objection.[31] In *Mobil Oil*, the example of a compound that had been previously known and used as a plant growth regulator was discussed. Imagine that it was later discovered that this same compound was effective also as a fungicide and the patent claim is for the use of the compound as a fungicide. The method of use is the same for both purposes, that is application to plants and, so, the only novelty that can be claimed is in the use of the compound as a fungicide rather than a growth regulator, that is in *the purpose of the use*. In such a case, the question of novelty has to be determined along basic principles, that is has that functional technical feature previously been made available to the public?

Inventive step

The invention must involve an inventive step. By section 3, this applies when the invention is not obvious to a person skilled in the art, having regard to all matter forming part of the state of the art but not including matter from patent applications with earlier priority dates which is published later than the priority date of the invention. This is different to the position concerning novelty as, normally, matter in earlier applications that has not yet been published is taken to be a part of the state of the art.[32] This information is used to test for novelty but not for inventive step.

The determination of whether matter forms part of the state of the art, that is the question of anticipation, is usually decided by application of a 'skilled worker test'. A similar test is used for deciding whether an invention involves an inventive step. However, this time, the test is provided for explicitly by the Act as being a question of obviousness judged from the objective standpoint of the notional skilled worker, a 'person skilled in the art'. The word 'obvious' does not have any special legal meaning and it has been said that it is not necessary to go beyond the dictionary definition and take it to mean 'very plain'.[33] It is manifestly evident that the notional skilled worker cannot be endowed with inventive faculties himself, however technical the art, otherwise all inventions could be considered to be obvious. The person skilled in the art is simply someone with a wide knowledge of the technology within which the invention lies (or a team of persons so skilled). The question becomes, would the invention be obvious to such a person or persons?[34] In some fields, a person skilled in the art who does not possess inventive faculties may be a contradiction, for example in the engineering professions where engineers are trained in problem-solving by the application of ingenuity, the very word 'engineer' sharing a common origin with the word 'ingenuity'. Perhaps the skilled worker should be limited to the technician level rather than that of the professional engineer.[35]

Obviousness is judged by looking at the invention as a whole and considering the entire state of the art at the relevant time. A process known as 'mosaicing' has occasionally been used to attack the validity of a patent by showing that it is obvious. This process consists of piecing together several unrelated bits of information in different documents which, when combined, are capable of

31 *Mobil Oil* [1990] OJ EPO 93.

32 See section 2(3).

33 *General Tire & Rubber* Co. v *Firestone Tyre & Rubber* Co. *Ltd.* [1972] RPC 457.

34 Conversely, if the invention is not obvious to skilled and inventive persons it must involve an inventive step, *Intalite International NV v Cellular Ceilings Ltd. (No.2)* [1987] RPC 537.

35 This is not to deny that technicians are devoid of inventive skills, quite the opposite. However, invention and ingenuity is less likely to be expected of them during the performance of their duties.

showing obviousness. But the use of such a technique is theoretically very unsound because, if this is the first time the mosaic has been constructed, that in itself is indicative of non-obviousness. If it were otherwise someone else would have pieced the bits together previously. In practice, mosaicing is unlikely to find favour in the courts, although there are exceptions, for example where it would be reasonable for the notional uninventive skilled worker to fit the pieces together, an unlikely phenomenon as the very act of mosaicing implies both detective and inventive skills.

Whether the invention is obvious is a question of fact. For example, in *Lux Traffic Controls Ltd.* v *Pike Signals Ltd.*,[36] the defendant claimed that the plaintiff's two patents in relation to traffic signal control systems were invalid on a number of grounds. The second patent was for a means of varying the 'inter-green' period, the safety period between the lights in one direction changing to red and before the lights in the other direction changed to green. It was argued that it was obvious. However, being unsupported by evidence, the court expressed surprise that the invention had not been proposed before, if that was the case. The invention may have been simple but it represented an advance and a technical contribution to the art.[37]

When obviousness has to be determined retrospectively, for example where the validity of a patent is in issue, commercial success is an important and telling factor that can be taken into account. If the invention fulfils a 'long-felt want', this is good evidence of non-obviousness. However, if commercial success is taken as a yardstick of non-obviousness, consideration must also be given to market forces. In *Technograph Printed Circuits Ltd.* v *Mills & Rockley (Electronics) Ltd.*,[38] the defendant alleged that the plaintiff's method of making printed circuit boards using a silk screen printing method was invalid because of obviousness and lack of novelty, relying on a prior United States patent relating to the manufacture of electrostatic shields and aerials. It was held that the plaintiff's patent was valid because the adaptation of the method described in the United States patent, where it was used in relation to three-dimensional objects, to printing a pattern on a flat circuit board was not an obvious step. Although the invention turned out to be an enormous commercial success this was some years later and the invention was not widely used for some years. Harman J said:

> It was objected that in fact it was not until ten years after the invention was published that it was commercially adopted . . . and it was argued from this that it was not a case of filling a long felt want. I do not accept this argument. In the years immediately following the war, manufacturers could sell all the machines they wanted using the old point-to-point wiring and had no need to trouble themselves with anything better.

Therefore, commercial success as an indicator of obviousness must be treated cautiously. Lack of immediate commercial success, as in the above case, might be explained by factors that have nothing to do with the obviousness of the invention. The correlation that the proprietor hopes will be confirmed by commercial success is that the invention cannot have been obvious because it clearly satisfies a demand and that demand would have been long since satisfied had the invention been obvious. Whilst this might be a reasonable assumption, the opposite is not tenable: lack of success does not necessarily directly equate to obviousness. Something might be highly inventive but it fails to sell because, put

36 [1993] RPC 107.

37 The first patent was held to be invalid through lack of novelty because prototypes had been made available to contractors who were able to examine them and such examination would have been sufficient to disclose the invention.

38 [1969] RPC 395.

simply, consumers have no desire for it. That commercial success as a measure of non-obviousness should be treated cautiously was confirmed by Mummery J in the Patents Court in *Molnlycke AB v Proctor & Gamble Ltd. (No. 3),*[39] a case involving a patent for disposable nappies, where he said that whether an invention was obvious was something which must be considered technically or practically rather than commercially. Commercial success might be relevant if it was due to the precise improvement which satisfied the long felt want but not if it was due to things such as appearance, get-up, price, marketing strategies or advertising campaigns.

The fact that it would be relatively inexpensive to experiment and to make prototypes is another point in favour of a finding of non-obviousness, especially when the problem that the invention sought to solve had existed for some time. So it was held in *Molnlycke A B v Proctor & Gamble Ltd.,*[40] in a subsequent case involving disposable nappies. It was argued that the plaintiff's dedicated fastening surface used for refastenable disposable nappies was obvious. The court disagreed because there had been an increasing need for multiple taping over a number of years and, had the idea been obvious, it would have occurred to someone much sooner especially as it would cost very little to make prototypes. The invention was not obvious even though some of the defendant's employees had the same idea before or at around the same time. The fact that a competitor has had the same idea does not affect the state of the art unless the competitor makes it available to the public or files a patent application in respect of it.

The invention may be the application of well-known technology to a particular problem, usually a new problem or an old one that has escaped attempts to solve it. Although novelty may be in issue, a second use of existing technology for a new purpose may still be acceptable on this point but, more importantly, the question of obviousness will be raised. Consideration of the magnitude of the problem and whether there have been many attempts to find a solution in the past all of which have proved to be unsuccessful will provide a useful rule of thumb. If such is the case, it can be presumed that the invention is not obvious and, again, the commercial success of the invention can prove to be a helpful factor in deciding obviousness. In *Parks-Cramer Co. v G W Thornton & Sons Ltd.,*[41] the invention was for a method of cleaning floors between rows of textile machines. There had been many attempts to find a satisfactory solution but none of them, unlike the present invention, actually worked. All the invention consisted of was an overhead vacuum cleaner which moved automatically up and down the rows between the machines. But, attached to the cleaners were long vertical tubes, reaching almost to the floor. In the High Court, the trial judge considered that the patent was invalid because it was obvious. He said that it was common knowledge to every competent housewife that dust could be removed from a floor by the passage of a vacuum cleaner.[42] However, the Court of Appeal held that the patent was valid. The many unsuccessful attempts by inventors to find a solution and the immediate commercial success of the invention denied the possibility of a finding of obviousness. Diplock LJ said:

> As in all other cases of obviousness, the question is one of degree. There may be an inventive step in recognizing that a problem exists at all; but given a problem which is

39 [1990] RPC 498.

40 [1992] FSR 549.

41 [1966] RPC 407.

42 Perhaps the judge should have used the term 'houseperson' instead.

known to exist which it is the object of the invention to solve, the question always is: 'Is the solution claimed by the patentee one which would have occurred to everyone of ordinary intelligence and acquaintance with the subject matter of the patent who gave his mind to the problem?[43]

The plaintiff was granted an injunction and an order was made for the delivery up or destruction of the infringing articles.

The courts have to draw a line somewhere when it comes to new uses of old technology and the question of obviousness. There must be a sufficient inventive step. Merely taking two older inventions and sticking them together will not necessarily be regarded as an inventive step. It is all a question of degree, and it is difficult to lay down hard and fast rules. For example, in *Williams* v *Nye*,[44] Williams took out a patent for an improved mincing machine made up from a combination of two old machines, a mincing machine and a filling machine. What he did was to take the cutter from one machine and simply replace it with the cutter from the other machine. When the plaintiff sued the defendant for infringement of the patent, the defendant claimed that the patent was invalid and this claim was successful because it was held that there was insufficient invention. However, the court accepted that a slight alteration might produce important results and be the result of great ingenuity. Cotton LJ said:

> . . . in order to maintain a patent there must be a substantial exercise of the inventive power or inventive faculty. Sometimes very slight alterations will produce very important results, and there may be in those very slight alterations very great ingenuity exercised or shown to be exercised by the Patentee.

Therefore, there seems to be a fine line drawn between what does and what does not constitute an inventive step. Even if the inventiveness appears at first sight trivial, the utility of the new invention and whether it is a significant improvement in the state of the art should be considered. Also one has to ask the obvious question, why did nobody else do it before? After all, many of the most successful inventions seem, in retrospect, to be very simple but simplicity should not be confused with obviousness.

Industrial application

Another requirement is that the invention is capable of industrial application. This requirement demonstrates the practical nature of patent law, which requires that the invention should be something which can be made industrially or that it relates to an industrial process.[45] An application for a patent that depends upon the use of hitherto undiscovered materials in its manufacture would be refused.[46] The invention has to be something that can be worked industrially and to some extent, this requirement distinguishes patents from other forms of intellectual property such as original works of copyright. It confirms the difference between 'industrial property' and copyright.

By section 4(1) an invention is capable of industrial application if it can be made or used in any kind of industry including agriculture. However, this does not cover methods of treatment of human or animal bodies by surgery, therapy or of diagnosis practised on human or animal bodies[47] but this exclusion does not extend to products consisting of substances or compositions used in any

43 [1966] RPC 407 at 418.

44 (1890) 7 RPC 62.

45 By section 4(1), 'industry' includes agriculture.

46 Under the 1949 Act, a patent could be invalidated on the grounds of inutility, section 32(1)(g).

47 Section 4(2). The reason is to ensure that medical practitioners (and veterinary surgeons) are not subjected to restraint by a patent when tending patients, *John Wyeth & Brother Ltd.'s Application: Schering AG's Application* [1985] RPC 545.

such methods.[48] Therefore, drugs are capable of industrial application and are patentable in principle. The words 'treatment' and 'diagnosis' imply an illness or disease of some kind which does not include conception or pregnancy, neither of which are considered to be illnesses.[49] Further, as treatment of the human or animal body is excluded, treatment to rid a person or animal of, for example, an infestation of lice, may be patentable if it is accepted that such treatment is directed towards the lice and not the human or animal body.[50]

The reason for the exclusion of surgery, therapy or diagnosis is probably a policy decision to prevent restrictions on the spread and adoption of new and improved methods of treatment – for example, if a surgeon develops a new and improved way to perform back surgery, it is in the public interest that such a method be available to all surgeons.[51] Nevertheless, this does not sit comfortably with the fact that drugs can be, and often are, patented. One difference between the surgeon and the drug company is that the former is in a profession were he is expected to pass on his knowledge to others (he will probably be very keen to publish his new technique) and will not expect financial recompense for his idea but will hope for kudos and the respect of colleagues whereas the drug company, operating in a competitive industry, needs a patent to justify investment in research and development.

Before the 1977 Act, the requirement equivalent to industrial application came from the phrase 'new manner of manufacture',[52] but it is no easy task to tell whether the change in phraseology makes any difference when it can be strongly argued that the requirement that the invention is capable of industrial application is totally unnecessary, especially when the exceptions contained in section 1(2) (discussed later) are considered, as these exceptions probably account for anything which might not have industrial application.[53] Otherwise, lack of industrial application may be relevant if the invention as claimed, simply does not work. This may be analogous to the provisions relating to inutility in the 1949 Act.[54]

There have been very few cases where the question of industrial application was at issue. One example under the 1949 Act, where the phrase used was 'manner of manufacture', was *Hiller's Application*.[55] An application for a patent for an improved plan for underground service distribution schemes for housing estates was turned down. The scheme involved the location of gas and water mains, electricity cables and storm and foul water drains. The alleged novelty lay in the idea of locating the main supply route alongside the road rather than underneath it with branches passing under the road at intervals serving adjacent houses. The appeal to the Patent Appeal Tribunal was turned down by Lloyd-Jacob J who said that the scheme could not constitute a 'manner of manufacture'. He did not need to trouble himself to go on to consider another possibly fatal objection to the application on the grounds of lack of novelty. There were other good grounds why the application should have been refused which were not really considered in the judgment, not the least being that it would give a disproportionate monopoly which would be certain to restrict the freedom of providers of public utilities. Finally, the scheme lacked an inventive step, being obvious and representing no more than good practice in the construction industry.

Another example of a refusal because the invention did not represent a new manner of manufacture was *C's Application*[56] in which an application in

48 Section 4(3).

49 See *Schering AG's Application* [1971] RPC 337 where a patent was granted to a method of contraception involving doses of gestagen. However, in 1936, an application in respect of 'improvements in pessaries' (contraceptive devices) was refused by exercise of the Royal Prerogative, *Riddlesbarger's Application* (1936) 53 RPC 57.

50 *Stafford-Miller's Application* [1984] FSR 258.

51 However, this does not prevent the surgeon from keeping his new technique secret which he may want to do if he works in the private sector and has built up a high reputation because of the effectiveness of his methods.

52 For example, section 101(1) of the Patents Act 1949.

53 However, the exception of surgery, therapy and diagnosis from industrial application is important.

54 Section 32(1)(g).

55 [1969] RPC 267.

56 (1920) 37 RPC 247.

57 [1969] RPC 646.

respect of an invention comprising a musical notation in which sharps and flats were printed in different colours and sizes compared to natural notes was refused. However, in *Pitman's Application*,[57] an application for a patent for an improved method of teaching pronunciation was allowed. The method involved visually conveying inflection and stress by using upper and lower case print and by the vertical displacement of the letters in relation to a median line. The arrangement was in the form of a printed sheet but the patent specification referred to the use of the sheet in conjunction with a reading machine. The invention possessed a definite mechanical purpose when considered together with the reading machine and was not simply a literary or intellectual arrangement of matter. In this way, the case is distinguishable from *C's Application*.

58 The phrase 'technical effect' derives from case law: it is not taken from the Patents Act 1977.

Industrial application can be equated with *technical effect*[58] and if there is some technical effect, that is if the use or working of the invention produces some tangible and physical consequences or if the invention is itself a physical entity (as opposed to information), then the requirement should be met. Technical effect is important when considering the scope of the exceptions to patent protection contained in section 1(2) of the Act, which is discussed below.

EXCLUSIONS FROM PATENTABILITY

One form of exclusion has already been described. The treatment or diagnosis in relation to human and animal bodies is excluded because this is not considered to be capable of an industrial application. Sections 1(2) and 1(3) of the Act contain a range of things that are excluded from patentability. Whilst, in many cases, these exclusions can be justified on the grounds of lack of technical effect, in some cases the exclusions are more controversial. For example, computer programs are excluded. The exclusions in section 1(2) can be classified as those necessary because of the nature of the subject-matter, either being information oriented and therefore more appropriately protected by copyright, or because they are too abstract and removed from immediate industrial application or manufacture. The exclusions in section 1(3) are based on policy considerations relating to social welfare, morality and ethics.

Exclusions in section 1(2)

Section 1(2) of the Patents Act 1977 states that anything which consists of the following (amongst other things – the list is not exhaustive) are not inventions for the purposes of the Act:

(a) a discovery, scientific theory or mathematical method;
(b) a literary, dramatic, musical or artistic work or any other aesthetic creation whatsoever;
(c) a scheme, rule or method for performing any mental act, playing a game or doing business, or a program for a computer;
(d) the presentation of information;[59]

59 These exclusions are derived from the European Patent Convention but the position is not far removed from earlier United Kingdom law because of the requirement that the invention was a 'manner of manufacture'. This would automatically exclude most of these things anyway.

However the section goes on to say that 'the foregoing provision shall prevent anything from being treated as an invention . . . only to the extent that a patent or application for a patent relates to that thing *as such*' (emphasis added). Herein lies the problem: the things in the list are not excluded totally and unequivocally but only if the patent application is directed towards the excluded thing itself.[60] This has caused some judicial differences in the way section 1(2) has been interpreted, especially in the context of computer programs. Before this is examined in detail, the nature of the other exclusions will be briefly discussed.[61]

A discovery, scientific theory or mathematical method

The things excepted in this category are the raw materials which are part of the stock-in-trade of scientists and if previously unknown ones are discovered, they should be available to all. But there is another reason why they cannot be patented and that is, by themselves, they have no technical effect. They have to be applied before there can be a technical effect and, therefore, an industrial application. But, in common with the other exclusions in section 1(2), these exclusions relate to patent applications for the stated things as such. If a mathematical formula is embodied into a measuring device, then that device itself may well be patentable.

The fact that mathematical theories cannot be patented is not new. In *Young v Rosenthal*,[62] there was an alleged infringement of a patent for improvements in the manufacture of corsets using seams arranged in diagonal patterns in accordance with a mathematical formula. In addressing the jury, Grove J said (at 31):

> An invention of an idea or mathematical principle alone, mathematical formula or anything of that sort could not be the subject of a patent. It must be a manufacture, and it must be a manufacture which is new in this realm.

The jury found that the plaintiff's invention had been copied by the defendant but that the patent was invalid because it was neither novel nor useful. The quote of Grove J confirms the view that there is a large overlap between section 1(2) and section 1(1)(c) (the industrial application requirement) and that one or other is unnecessary. This category is discussed further in the section devoted to computer programs, later in this chapter.

A literary, dramatic, musical or artistic work or any other aesthetic creation whatsoever

These works and creations are plainly the subject-matter of copyright law or design law, hence the exclusion. In most cases, these works will not be capable of industrial application and are thus excluded twice over. Copyright law is more suited to these types of works because a patent would give a protection that is too strong. Copyright does not provide a monopoly and the independent creation of similar works is permissible.[63] However, such works could be indirectly patented if they are part of some machine or process, for example in *Pitman's Application* discussed above.

A scheme, rule or method for performing any mental act, playing a game or doing business, or a program for a computer

Computer programs are discussed separately later in this chapter. It is not possible to stop people thinking or doing mental arithmetic, for example. If a patent were to be granted, say for a method of mental arithmetic, it would be

60 Thus, theoretically it should be possible to obtain a patent on an industrial application of a scientific theory though not for the theory itself.

61 The basic principles which have been developed in respect of the patentability of computer programs should also apply to the other excluded materials mentioned in section 1(2).

62 (1884) 1 RPC 29.

63 But a registered design enjoys a monopoly during its life.

unenforceable anyway. As far as playing games and doing business are concerned this means that it is not possible to patent, for example a new chess opening or a new method of assessing bids for large construction schemes.[64] However, copyright law may protect the expression of the scheme, rule or method and, depending upon the circumstances, the law of confidence could give some protection. Some of the things under this heading will not be capable of industrial application anyway (in a direct sense). Unlike most of the other items in this sub-category, computer programs are capable of being applied industrially and are often so used, for example by controlling an industrial process such as an electronically controlled furnace or in robotics.

64 On arithmetic, see *Re Gale's Patent Application* [1991] RPC 305 and, on methods of doing business, see *Re Merrill Lynch, Pierce Fenner and Smith Incorporated's Application* [1988] RPC 1 and [1989] RPC 561. Both of these cases are discussed in the section on computer programs below.

The presentation of information

This is another exception that can be best explained on the grounds that this is properly within the scope of copyright. If the information is presented in textual form, it will be a literary work; if it is represented as a flowchart then it will be an artistic work. Other ways of presenting information may give rise to other forms of copyright such as a film, sound recording or broadcast. If the information is presented orally without previously being recorded, then it will not be protected by copyright until it is so recorded. The law of confidence may also apply to the information presented. One example under this category that might otherwise have met the requirements for patentability was the old 'Swingometer' which was brought out on election days by the BBC. The original device was mechanical and used extensively by that likeable political broadcaster the late Bob MacKenzie to indicate predictions of the likely overall distribution of election successes between the two major parties.[65]

65 The latest computerized version as operated by Peter Snow somehow lacks the charm of its progenitor.

Computer programs

The exclusion from patentability of computer programs as such is in line with international trends as regards the legal protection of computer programs. Copyright is seen as the proper vehicle for the protection of computer programs although, when the Patents Act 1977 was being drafted, it was far from clear whether copyright did protect computer programs.[66] Even before the 1977 Act, computer programs were not generally patentable *per se* because they did not equate to a 'manner of manufacture', but there have been cases, both in the United Kingdom and in the United States where computer programs have been involved in applications for patents, usually as being part of a piece of machinery or an industrial process. Attempts to obtain a patent directly or indirectly for a computer program are a reflection of the perceived attractiveness of patents in terms of the relative strength of protection granted in comparison with copyright law, in spite of the shorter period of protection.

66 See Chapter 8.

Some commentators in the United States have argued for the direct protection of computer programs by the law of patent.[67] In the United States under the 'mental steps' doctrine, a patent cannot be granted for an invention consisting primarily of a mental activity or a mathematical algorithm.[68] In the leading case of *Diamond* v *Diehr*,[69] the United States Supreme Court eased the availability of patents for computer programs by developing a two stage test:

67 See, for example Bender, D. 'Computer Programs: Should They Be Patentable?' (1968) 68 *Columbia Law Review* 241.

68 For a comparative description of patent protection in the United States, Germany, France, Japan and Canada, see Hoffman, G., Grossman, J., Keane, P. and Westby, J. 'Protection for Computer Software: An International Overview: Part 2' [1989] 1 EIPR 7.

(a) Determine whether the mathematical algorithm is either directly or indirectly recited by the claim.

69 (1981) 450 US 175.

(b) Determine whether the claim, taken as a whole, merely recites a mathematical algorithm

This latter test requires the resolution of two further questions:

(a) Does the claim apply the mathematical formula in a structure or process, which considered as a whole, comprises a form of post-solution activity that fulfils a function of the patent laws?
(b) Is the post-solution activity significant? In other words, is the end-product merely a pure number as in *Benson* or *Flook,* or an applied solution that directly affects physical elements or controls process steps?[70]

In *Diamond* v *Diehr* the applicant was seeking to patent a process for curing synthetic rubber employing a mathematical formula used in a programmed digital computer. He was not seeking to patent a mathematical formula and the process was held to be patentable.[71] However, Webber argues that United States law and Australian patent practice have gone further and that, eventually, the patenting of computer programs as such will be allowed in those countries.[72]

Webber quotes the United States case of *Arrhythmia Research Technology Inc.* v *Corazonix Corp.*,[73] where, on appeal, it was held that a machine incorporating a process for analysing electro-cardiographic signals was patentable. A new test adopted by the Australian Patent Office is framed in terms of the production of some commercially useful effect. This seems wider than the current situation applying in the United Kingdom as neither the *Arrhythmia* case nor the Australian guideline reject an effect that is not external to a computer, that is a process that is entirely software based.

The rationale for the law as expressed in *Diamond* v *Diehr* is that a patent should not pre-empt or monopolize something, such as an algorithm or mathematical method that is, traditionally, not patentable. Nevertheless, allowing software based processes does not necessarily restrict algorithms and is not the same as granting patents for computer programs *as such*. It is just an alternative view of what constitutes a patentable technical effect. The position in the United States and Australia is not dissimilar to that subscribed to by the United Kingdom and the European Patent Office. It is really a question of the interpretation of what constitutes a technical effect. Two aspects concerning the patentability of computer programs which are of particular interest are the form of storage and the technical effect produced by running the program.

Mode of storage

In the United Kingdom, there were some patent applications involving computer programs prior to the 1977 Act where the important issue was whether the invention related to a manner of manufacture. For example, in *Gever's Application*,[74] data processing apparatus was arranged to work in a certain way by the use of punched cards. The purpose of the apparatus was to file world trade marks in such a way that they could be easily searched for similarity and prior registration. The patent application, concerning a piece of machinery which functioned in a certain way because of the punched cards, was allowed to proceed. The cards were described by Graham J as a 'manner of manufacture' because he considered that a punched card was analogous to a cam for

70 *Gottschalk* v *Benson* (1972) 409 US 63, *Parker* v *Flook* (1978) 437 US 584.

71 This case has been followed subsequently in the United States on a number of occasions.

72 Webber, D. 'Software Patents: A New Era in Australia and the United States?' [1993] 5 EIPR 181.

73 (1990) 22 USPQ 2d 1033.

74 [1970] RPC 91.

controlling the cutting path of a lathe. This was distinguished from a card that merely had written or printed material on it, intended to convey information to the human eye or mind and not meant to be ancillary to some machine by being specially shaped for that purpose. However, this approach is at odds with technical reality because, essentially, the form of storage of the computer program should not be relevant to the question of its patentability. Nevertheless, in another case, *Burrough's Corporation (Perkin's) Application*,[75] computer programs which controlled the transmission of data to terminals from a central computer (a communications system) were held to be the proper subject-matter of a patent because the programs were embodied in physical form. They were 'hard-wired', that is to say permanently embedded in the electronic circuits of the equipment. A more recent example of this artificial distinction between forms of storage of computer programs is the decision of Aldous J in *Re Gale's Patent Application*[76] where he suggested that a programmed ROM (read only memory) chip was patentable but the same program on a magnetic disk would not have been patentable. This inconsistent approach was remedied in the Court of Appeal where the operation of the program was seen to be all important and the mode of storage to be irrelevant. The applicant had developed a computer program to calculate square roots which was incorporated in read-only memory (ROM) circuitry and which did not produce any technical effect whatsoever. Nicholls LJ felt obliged to part company with Aldous J on the distinction between a claim relating to a magnetic disk containing a computer program and a ROM with particular circuitry. To hold otherwise would mean that any computer program would be patentable simply by installing it on a computer chip even if it produced no technical, physical or tangible effect. Such an approach would drive a coach and horses through section 1(2) as regards computer programs.

Technical effect

Two alternative approaches have been made to the question of the patent protection of inventions that include a computer program and the effect of the words 'as such' at the end of section 1(2). The first is that the patent application should be considered without the contribution of the excepted thing. For example, if a machine includes a computer program[77] it is then a question of whether the machine, without taking the computer program into account, adds anything to the state of the art. Does the machine, ignoring the computer program, meet the requirements for patentability? If the only novel and inventive step comes from or resides in the computer program itself, then the machine as a whole is not patentable. The judgment of Falconer J in the case of *Re Merrill Lynch, Pierce Fenner & Smith Incorporated's Application*[78] at first instance illustrates this approach.[79] The invention related to an improved data processing system for implementing an automatic trading market for securities. The system received and stored the best current bids, qualified customer buy and sell orders, executed orders, produced reports of trade particulars for customers and national stock reporting systems in addition to monitoring stock inventory and profit. The Principal Examiner of the Patent Office rejected the application for a patent and the appeal against his decision to the Patents Court was dismissed. It was held that where an invention involves any of the excluded mater-

75 [1974] RPC 147.

76 [1991] RPC 305.

77 Or if the invention incorporates a programmed computer.

78 [1988] RPC 1.

79 There was a further unsuccessful appeal to the Court of Appeal, *Re Merrill Lynch, Pierce Fenner and Smith Inc.* [1989] RPC 561.

ials in section 1(2), then the proper construction of the qualification in that sub-section requires that the Patent Office enquires into whether the inventive step resides in the contribution of the excluded matter alone. If the inventive step comes only from the excluded material, then the invention is not patentable because of section 1(2). However, in a somewhat contradictory statement, Falconer J said:

> If some practical (i.e. technical) effect is achieved by the computer or machine operating according to the instructions contained in the program, and such effect is novel and inventive (i.e. not obvious), a claim directed to that practical effect will be patentable, notwithstanding it is defined by that computer program.

The application failed because there was no practical or technical effect – the operation was entirely software based. However, the Technical Board of Appeal in the European Patent Office had previously taken a different approach although Falconer J considered that this was not inconsistent with his decision. He was later to be proved wrong.[80]

In *Vicom Systems Incorporated's Patent Application*,[81] a different approach was taken. This case concerned an application to the European Patent Office and the invention related to digital image processing, the process steps being expressed mathematically in the form of an algorithm. It was held by the Technical Board of Appeal that this claim was allowable. It was said that:

> . . . a claim directed to a technical process which process is carried out under the control of a program (be this implemented in hardware or in software), cannot be regarded as relating to a computer program as such within the meaning of Article 52(3) EPC, as it is the application of the program for determining the sequence of steps in the process and it is the process for which in effect protection is sought. Consequently, such a claim is allowable under Article 52(2)(c) and (3) EPC.[82]

Thus, in an application such as this, where the subject-matter of the invention is the technical effect produced by the operation of a computer program, the technical effect should be patentable, providing the other requirements are present, that is novelty, inventive step and industrial application. The patent is granted in relation to the technical effect and not the computer program as such and it should make no difference whether or not the inventive step resides in the computer program itself. This decision is entirely consistent with the Patents Act 1977 and the European Patent Convention and, on a purely logical basis, the method of implementing the invention should make not one iota of difference. Otherwise, a new and inventive technical effect would be patentable if it was implemented by mechanical means (for example, by using a diesel engine to power rods, cams and levers) but not if advantage was taken of modern technology by implementing the invention electronically using a programmed computer. Such a result would be absurd. It would provide a disincentive to apply robotics and computer control systems industrially. The *Vicom* case also confirms that there should be no distinction between different modes of storage (hardware or software) as regards patentability.

The apparent inconsistency between the United Kingdom approach and the European Patent Office approach was resolved and the European Patent Office's interpretation of the effect of the exclusions was approved of in *Genentech Inc.'s Patent*[83] which involved an application for a patent for the technical

80 The then current differences in interpretation of the scope of the exclusions from patent between the United Kingdom and the European Patent Office are described in Hart, R. J. 'Applications of Patents to Computer Technology - UK and the EPO Harmonisation?' [1989] 2 EIPR 42.

81 [1987] 2 EPOR 74, [1987] 1 OJ EPO 14.

82 Articles 52(2) and (3) of the European Patent Convention correspond to section 1(2) of the Patents Act 1977.

83 [1989] RPC 147.

application of a discovery relating to nucleotide sequences of DNA. A discovery, as such, is excluded by section 1(2), but an application which claimed the practical application of a discovery was not a claim for the discovery itself. It was held by the Court of Appeal that the practical application of a discovery could be patentable even though that practical application was obvious once the discovery was made. Dillon LJ said:

> In so far as a patent claims as an invention the practical application of a discovery, the patent does not, in my judgment, relate only to the discovery as such, even if the practical application may be obvious once the discovery has been made, even though unachievable in the absence of the discovery.

This apparent rejection of the need for an invention to involve an inventive step, that is that the invention is not obvious to the skilled worker, can be explained on the basis that, before the discovery was made, the invention could not have been obvious under any criteria. That the 'inventiveness' does not relate to the application of the discovery claimed but to the discovery itself makes this aspect of the decision questionable although it is justifiable in a practical sense because it rewards the work and investment associated with the making of the discovery.[84]

One issue that had not been fully resolved was the extent of the patentability of computer programs when installed or used in a conventional computer, for example if an item of computer hardware contains some computer software but the former is orthodox and the latter is new and contains an inventive step but the two together do not produce any external technical effect. In *Genentech Inc.'s Patent*,[85] Dillon LJ said at 240:

> It would be nonsense for the [Patents Act 1977] to forbid the patenting of a computer program, and yet permit the patenting of a floppy disc containing the computer program, or an ordinary computer when programmed with the program; it can well be said, as it seems to me, that a patent for a computer when programmed or for the disc containing the program is no more than a patent for the program as such.

This approach has been approved of in the Court of Appeal in *Re Merrill Lynch, Pierce Fenner & Smith Incorporated's Application*[86] where Fox LJ said that '. . . it cannot be permissible to patent an item excluded by section 1(2) under the guise of an article which contains that item' and, more recently, in *Re Gale's Patent Application*.[87] To hold otherwise would be to totally undermine the effect of section 1(2) and there must, therefore, be some technical effect that is novel and non-obvious which results from the use of the computer program and which is not limited to the mere device in which the program is contained or executed. If the only conceivable use of the computer program is running it in a computer there can be no patent. The European Patent Office has also adopted this stratagem in *IBM/Document Abstracting and Retrieving*[88] where an application for a patent for a method of automatically abstracting, storing and retrieving documents in an information storage and retrieval system was rejected by the Technical Board of Appeal. One crude but effective way of distinguishing between patentable and non-patentable computer programs (and other excluded materials) is to differentiate between intellectual and industrial uses of computer technology and to accept, as a rule of thumb, that intellectual effects are not patentable whereas industrial effects are.

84 In the *Genentech* case, there were at least five teams working independently on research directed towards the discovery. The research work was laborious, costly and success was by no means certain.

85 [1989] RPC 147.

86 [1989] RPC 561. See also *Re Wang Laboratories Inc.'s Application* [1991] RPC 463.

87 [1991] RPC 305.

88 [1990] EPOR 98.

Subsequent cases have confirmed the above approach. An application for a patent for an expert system shell[89] was refused in *Re Wang Laboratories Inc.'s Application*[90] because it was for nothing more than a computer program. When the system had been developed it did not form with the computer a new machine. Similarly, a claim in relation to a compiler program[91] was no more than a claim for the compiler program itself.[92] In Germany it has been confirmed that a similar approach applies and in *Re The Computer Generation of Chinese Characters*[93] a wordprocessing program using Chinese characters was not patentable because it did not solve a technical problem by a technical method nor did it make a technical contribution to the state of the art. It was mainly intellectual in nature and did not make use of methods beyond human intellectual activity.

Exclusions in section 1(3)

Further exclusions are contained in section 1(3) of the Patents Act 1977 and the things excluded can be considered to be so excluded mainly on policy grounds. For example, section 1(3)(a) excludes inventions, the publication or exploitation of which would be generally expected to encourage offensive, immoral or anti-social behaviour. Section 1(4) states that behaviour shall not be regarded as offensive, immoral or anti-social only because it is prohibited by law. Something more than mere illegality is required. It may be possible to obtain a patent for an invention which can be used in two ways, one of which is illegal. For example, an invention might relate to a radio transmitter/receiver that can be used lawfully by licensed radio amateur operators (radio 'hams') but other persons might use it to listen to or interfere with police transmissions or to broadcast without a licence. The fact that the radio set may have an unlawful use does not automatically debar it from patentability. To some extent, there is some discretion in the decision to accept the patent application, subject to appeal. It depends on whether the invention is expected to encourage the sort of behaviour described. Contraceptive devices no longer are considered to encourage immoral behaviour in the United Kingdom although they might be so considered in other countries that are parties to the European Patent Convention and which are predominantly Roman Catholic.[94] Examples of inventions which might be rejected as being expected to encourage offensive, immoral or anti-social behaviour might be a booby-trap bomb or a 'do-it-yourself' abortion kit. An invention that some might argue should have been excluded on the grounds of encouraging anti-social behaviour is the Sony 'Walkman'! However, bearing in mind the present social climate and degree of tolerance, it is unlikely that section 1(3)(a) will be used very often.

Section 1(3)(b) excludes from patentability varieties of animals or plants or any essentially biological process for the production of animals or plants. This does not extend to micro-biological processes or the products of such processes, for example brewer's yeast.[95] Plants may be protected under the Plant Varieties and Seeds Act 1964.[96] Under this Act, proprietary rights are granted to the breeders or discoverers of distinctive, uniform and stable plant varieties for a period not exceeding 30 years.[97] The rights are monopolistic in nature and are to produce and sell (or offer to sell) reproductive material of the plant variety.[98] The scheme is administered by the Plant Variety Rights Office under the control of the Controller of Plant Variety Rights.

89 An expert system shell is a program or suite of programs that allow a system developer to enter rules and facts to form an expert system directed towards providing solutions in particular knowledge domains. For example, a computer system that gives medical advice on stomach pains.

90 [1991] RPC 463.

91 A program used to create an object code version of a source code program.

92 *Re Hitachi Ltd.'s Application* [1991] RPC 415.

93 [1993] FSR 315.

94 For example, in *Schering AG's Application* [1971] RPC 337, a contraceptive method was not rejected but in *Riddlesbarger's Application* (1936) 53 RPC 57, the Royal Prerogative was exercised to refuse a patent for a contraceptive device. Prior to the 1977 Act, there was no direct equivalent to section 1(3).

95 Louis Pasteur obtained a patent for purified brewer's yeast in the United States of America in 1873. Eisenschitz, T.S. *Patents, Trade Marks and Designs in Information Work* (London: Croom Helm, 1987) at p.54. In *American Cyanamid Co. (Dann's) Patent* [1971] RPC 425, a method of producing antibiotics using micro-organisms was held to be patentable.

96 Amended by the Plant Varieties Act 1983.

97 Section 3 of the Plant Varieties and Seeds Act 1964. For trees and grapevines, the minimum period of protection is 25 years and for other plant varieties it is 20 years.

98 Section 4 of the Plant Varieties and Seeds Act 1964.

One problem with section 1(3)(b) is how to differentiate between biological and micro-biological processes. The distinction is of primary importance because the former are not patentable under any circumstances whilst the latter may qualify if the other requirements are satisfied. Micro-organisms can be considered to be very small independent units invisible to the naked eye and, to be patentable, some form of human intervention is required.[99] Genetic engineering processes and techniques are patentable and are likely to become of some importance. Patents have already been granted in the United Kingdom in relation to DNA.[100]

Genetic engineering

It is possible to obtain a patent in some countries for a new breed of animal, for example in the United States, but the scope of the exclusion in section 1(3)(b), and the corresponding provision of the European Patent Convention, Article 53(b), is unclear. The Board of Appeal of the European Patent Office granted a patent for a laboratory mouse that had been genetically altered (a transgenic animal) so as to be more likely to develop cancerous cells in a short period of time.[101] It was accepted that this mouse was not a new variety of animal and, as a result, not excepted from the grant of a patent. Obviously, this is a very sensitive, ethical issue and decisions in this area require careful consideration of animal rights and the potential benefits to man and animal alike. A proposal for a European Community Directive on the patentability of biotechnological inventions has been produced.[102]

The proposed Directive will remove the blanket exclusion that applies to biological material, defined as any self-replicating living matter and any matter capable of being replicated through a biological system or by any indirect means.[103] However, there will be a number of safeguards and certain things such as human bodies (whole or parts thereof), processes for modifying the genetic identity of the human body for non-therapeutic purposes contrary to the dignity of man and processes modifying the genetic identity of animals that are likely to inflict suffering or physical handicaps on them *without* any benefit to man or animal will not be patentable.[104] These exclusions could, for example, cover genetic processes to make humans more attractive or intelligent or to testing new drugs on animals containing human genes. The requirement for a benefit for man or animal is probably far too low a hurdle to jump. However, there remains a morality exception. Other provisions restate the existing law, for example section 4(2) on the unpatentability of methods of treatment of the human or animal body by surgery, therapy or diagnosis.[105]

There remains some opposition to these provisions in the European Parliament[106] but the importance of the technology and the scale of the potential benefits such as finding cures and treatments for many previously incurable and intractable diseases of man and animals, require that a solution is found that satisfies the promoters of scientific advancement and the many persons alarmed at the prospects of abuse. This will probably take some further discussion and consideration. Of course, refusing patents for biotechnological inventions does not prevent them and their use. That is a question of ethics best left to professional bodies and political decision makers rather than lawyers.

99 Eisenschitz, T.S., op cit at p.53.

100 For example, in *Genentech Inc.'s Patent* [1989] RPC 147. See Reid, B.C. *A Practical Guide to Patent Law* (London: Sweet & Maxwell, 2nd edn., 1993) at pp.23–24.

101 *Onco-Mouse/Harvard* [1990] EPOR 4 and [1990] EPOR 501. A number of oppositions to the patent remain to be heard.

102 Amended proposal for a Council Directive on the legal protection of biotechnological inventions OJ [1993] C44/36.

103 Article 2(2).

104 Article 2.

105 Article 8.

106 See Thurston, J. 'Recent EC Developments in Biotechnology' [1993] 6 EIPR 187.

OWNERSHIP AND DEALINGS IN PATENTS

The Patents Act 1977 contains a large number of provisions concerning the ownership (the owner of a patent is referred to as its proprietor) of patents, dealings with patents (assignment, licensing, mortgaging), Crown use, compulsory licences and licences as of right. The provisions are generally lengthy and complex. At the outset, a distinction has to be made between the inventor and the proprietor of a patent, although in some cases, the inventor will be the proprietor of the patent. The inventor of an invention is, by section 7(3), the actual devisor of the invention. Where the invention is the result of the combined efforts of two or more persons, they are the joint inventors of the invention. The proprietor is the person to whom the patent is granted and who, therefore, has the right to work the patent. If the inventor is not the proprietor of the patent, he has a right to be mentioned as being the inventor in any patent granted and in any published application.[107] Failure to identify the inventor may prevent an application from proceeding. A patent is a form of personal property,[108] but not a thing in action, and may be transferred, created or granted only in accordance with sections 30(2) to 30(7) inclusive. The availability of compulsory licences in certain circumstances prevents the abuse of the monopoly granted to the proprietor of the patent.

[107] Section 13(1).

[108] Section 30(1).

Proprietorship

Whilst any person can apply for a patent either on his own or jointly, it will only be granted to certain persons identified in section 7. Primarily, it will be granted to the inventor, or joint inventors, except where someone else has a better entitlement to it. This may arise through any enactment or rule of law, any foreign law or treaty or international convention or by any enforceable term in an agreement with the inventor that was entered into prior to the making of the invention. An example might be where an inventor is commissioned to produce an invention to overcome a particular problem. Equitable interests are not effective to make any other person entitled to the patent as far as the Act is concerned. The patent will be granted to the legal owner only, although any equitable owner may have a claim to the benefit accruing from the patent under a trust. Additionally, an invention made by an employee shall be taken to belong to his employer.[109] This situation might, in any case, be expressly covered by the contract of employment. Section 7(2)(c) also provides for the grant of a patent to a successor in title to the person who would otherwise have been entitled to the patent. To facilitate patent applications there is a rebuttable presumption that the person making the application is entitled to the grant of the patent. Where there are two or more proprietors of a patent, their ownership is equivalent to ownership as tenants in common, that is they are each entitled to an undivided share in the patent[110] and if one of the owners dies, his share passes under his will or by intestacy and does not automatically pass to the remaining owners. Each co-owner can do any act in respect of the invention without the consent of the other co-owners with some exceptions. For example, the consent of all is required for a licence, assignment or mortgage.

[109] Section 39.

[110] Section 36(1). In land law, a tenancy in common is an equitable tenancy in which each tenant is entitled to an undivided share (equal or unequal) in the land. Unlike a joint tenancy, there is no automatic right of survivorship.

An agreement between joint owners to the effect that one will forfeit his rights under certain circumstances, for example after failing to pay a share in the expenses related to renewing the patent, will not necessarily be considered to be void as a penalty clause. However, the court has an equitable jurisdiction to grant relief against forfeiture. It was held thus in *BICC plc* v *Burndy Corp.*[111] where the court granted an extension of time for payment of the agreed expenses associated with the upkeep of the patent.

111 [1985] RPC 273.

Employee inventors

The Act deals with employee inventors in far more detail than is the case, for example, in copyright law. The relevant provisions are of great import because a very large number of applications for the grant of a patent will concern inventions made by employees. 'Employee' is defined in section 130(1) as being a person who works or worked under a contract of employment or in employment under or for the purposes of a government department or a person who serves or who has served in the naval, military or air forces of the Crown. By section 39, an employee invention belongs to the employer in either of the following circumstances:

(a) The invention was made in the course of the employee's normal duties as an employee or, if not, in the course of duties specifically assigned to the employee providing that, in both cases, the circumstances are such that the invention might reasonably be expected to result from the carrying out of those duties (section 39(1)(a)).
(b) The invention was made in the course of the employee's duties which, at the time of making the invention, were such that the employee had a special obligation to further the interests of the employer's undertaking (section 39(1)(b)).

In all other circumstances, the invention belongs to the employee. These provisions apply as between the employee and the employer and would not, for example, affect any third party rights. They will apply where an employee's duties include making inventions in the normal course of his duties, for example where an employee is engaged in a research and development capacity. They would also apply where a workshop manager was given the task of trying to solve a particular problem with the employer's equipment or working practices and the manager makes the invention in the course of carrying out that task. They would not normally apply where, say, a clerical worker devises an invention which is of benefit to the employer's production line and which has nothing to do with the employee's normal duties and he has not been assigned any relevant specific duties.

The terms of the contract of employment, express or implied, will assist the court in determining whether the circumstances in which the invention was made fall into the above two categories. In *Electrolux Ltd.* v *Hudson*,[112] an employee of the plaintiff (a company making electrical appliances) invented, with his wife at home one evening, an adapter for a vacuum cleaner that would allow the use of any type of disposable bag in any make of vacuum cleaner taking disposable bags. At the time, the defendant was employed as a senior storekeeper. The plaintiff claimed entitlement to the patent for the invention on the basis of the defendant's contract of employment. However, it was held that the relevant term in the contract was too wide (it was probably too wide even for a person employed in a research capacity) and the court refused to imply an appropriate term because the employee was not employed to invent.

112 [1977] FSR 312.

Some further indication of the circumstances where an employee invention will or will not belong to the employer was given in the Patents Court in *Harris' Patent*.[113] The invention was for a slide valve for controlling the flow of material such as coal dust and was an improvement over the 'Wey' valve. Harris made the invention whilst he was a manager of the Wey valve department of R company, who were licensees of S, a Swiss company. Harris made the invention during the period after he was informed that he was to be made redundant and before he left the employ of R company. The patent was granted and the question of who was entitled to the patent was referred to the Comptroller under section 37. Harris' primary duty had been to sell Wey valves and R company had no research facilities and did not undertake any creative design. Major problems were referred to the Swiss company. It was held that the rights between an employee and employer were governed only by section 39. The employee's normal duties were the actual duties he was employed to perform. Any duty of fidelity owed to the employer did not assist in formulating those normal duties. Because R company never solved design problems it could not have been part of Harris' duties to provide solutions to problems and his duty in respect of problems was to report them for transmission to the Swiss company. Neither was the invention made in circumstances such that an invention might reasonably be expected to have resulted from the carrying out of the employee's normal duties. The invention did not fall within section 39(1)(b) – the employee's obligation was to sell Wey valves.

An employee might devise an invention that is of outstanding benefit to his employer in circumstances where the employer will be taken as being entitled to the patent. This might seem unfair because the benefit of the invention may far exceed the employee's salary for the period of time he has been involved with the invention. However, the employee has been given consideration for his work, that is his salary, and the employer will have been prepared to pay the employee his salary even if no useful invention resulted, simply as a speculative investment in the hope that a valuable invention would result. Even so, the employee may apply for compensation under section 40 which allows the Comptroller or a court to award compensation where the invention is of outstanding benefit to the employer and it is just to do so. Although there is little case law on the provisions, it is clear that the benefit must be out of the ordinary and not such as might be expected to result from the employee's normal duties.[114] In fact the use of the word 'outstanding' suggests that compensation will be awarded under these provisions only in exceptional circumstances.[115]

Section 41 lays down the basic principles for the calculation of the amount of the compensation, being an award that gives the employee a fair share in the benefit derived or expected to be derived. These provisions also apply where the invention initially belonged to the employee and he has subsequently assigned it to the employer or granted an exclusive licence to him. This might apply where, because of the employee/employer relationship, the employer is able to bring pressure to bear upon the employee. Of course, one way that the employer can avoid the compensation provisions where the employer is the person entitled to the patent is not to apply for a patent and to rely on the law of confidence. There are very few applications for compensation under section 40.[116]

It is conceivable that in some circumstances where the patent initially belongs to the employee, the equitable doctrine of undue influence might apply, for

113 [1985] RPC 19.

114 *G E C Avionics Patent* [1992] RPC 107.

115 *British Steel's Patent* [1992] RPC 117.

116 None were lodged in 1992. In 1991, two were lodged and heard but no compensation was awarded.

instance where an employee has been pressurized by his employer to assign the patent to his employer or grant an exclusive licence in favour of his employer and where the terms of the agreement are grossly unfavourable to the employee. However, the employee/employer relationship does not automatically give rise to a presumption of undue influence and the employee would have to prove the nature of the pressure. If the doctrine of undue influence does apply, the effect is to make the agreement voidable. Section 42 has a similar effect as it makes terms in contracts between an employee and his employer (or some other person at the request of the employer or through the employee's contract of employment) unenforceable if and to the extent that those terms attempt to diminish the employee's rights in inventions.

Dealing in patents

As with other forms of intellectual property, patents may be dealt with by way of assignment or licensing, either exclusive or otherwise. They may also be mortgaged or vest by operation of law as other personal property. For example, if the proprietor dies the patent will vest in the proprietor's personal representatives. Patent applications may also be dealt with, which is understandable considering the length of time that may pass before the patent is finally granted. Where there are two or more proprietors of a patent or application for a patent, the consent of all of them is required for a licence, assignment or mortgage.[117] By section 30(6), any purported assignment or mortgage of a patent or patent application is void unless it is in writing and signed by or on behalf of the parties to the transaction. An assent by a personal representative must be signed by or on behalf of the personal representative. Failure to adhere to these requirements could result in the patent having a legal owner and an equitable owner, which is unsatisfactory as only the proprietor or an exclusive licensee can sue for infringement of the patent. An equitable owner must join the legal owner in any proceedings.

A licence for the working of the invention may be granted under a patent or application for a patent by section 30(4). The licence may permit the making of sublicences and, unless the licence or sublicence provides otherwise, a licence or sublicence may be assigned or mortgaged. An exclusive licence is one conferring, to the exclusion of all others (including the proprietor or applicant), any right in respect of the invention to which the patent or the application relates.[118] An exclusive licensee has the same right as the proprietor to bring proceedings in respect of any infringement of the patent after the date of the licence agreement.[119] It is essential that assignments, mortgages and exclusive licences are registered at the Patent Office for two reasons. First, the result of section 33 is that registration of acquisition of property in a patent or application defeats earlier transactions, instruments or events that have not been registered (registration effectively gives proof of title) and, secondly, the subsequent proprietor of the patent or an exclusive licensee may be unable to obtain damages or an account of profits for any infringement of the patent.[120]

Licences as of right

The proprietor may, at any time after the grant of the patent, apply to the comptroller to indicate that licences as of right are available in respect of the

117 Section 36(3).

118 Section 130, the interpretation section.

119 Section 67. The proprietor shall be made a party to the proceedings.

120 Section 68.

patent.[121] This provision might be used by a proprietor who has been unable to exploit his patent to good effect. Whether making an entry in the register that licences are available as of right makes any difference is doubtful because, if the invention was commercially attractive in the first place, the proprietor should have had no difficulty in finding an organization willing to exploit the patent under an assignment or exclusive licence. However, apart from this form of free advertising, there is an added bonus for the proprietor because subsequent renewal fees are reduced by one half. If any person desires to take up the offer, the licence terms shall be as agreed between the parties or, failing agreement, upon such terms as may be settled by the Comptroller on the application of either party. The entry on the register to the effect that licences are available as of right may be later cancelled by application of the proprietor (section 47).

An entry on the register in respect of licences as of right may also come about from the operation of section 51, which concerns references to the Monopolies and Mergers Commission. This is an option open to the Comptroller where matters specified in the Commission's report operate, have operated or are likely to operate against the public interest.

In settling the terms of a licence of right (and a compulsory licence), the Comptroller must have regard to European Community Competition law. It had been the practice in the United Kingdom to allow a licensee of right to import the patented product from outside the European Community if the proprietor of the patent worked the patent by importing the product to the United Kingdom. However, if the proprietor manufactured the product within the United Kingdom, the licence of right would not allow the licensee to import the product from outside the European Community.[122] This was held by the European Court of Justice in *Generics (UK) Ltd.* v *Smith, Kline and French Laboratories Ltd.*,[123] to be discriminatory because it encouraged proprietors of patents to manufacture the patented product in their national territory rather than importing the product from other Member States.

Under the Patents Act 1949, the maximum term of a patent was 16 years but existing patents that were less than 11 years old when the 1977 Act came into force (on 1 June 1978) were extended to a maximum of 20 years subject to their being treated as endorsed 'licences of right' for the last four years of their life. However, because of the special problems with pharmaceutical products where the exploitation period is reduced because of the time taken to test and obtain a licence under the Medicines Act 1968, the proprietor of a patent for a product is allowed to file a declaration preventing licences as of right extending to pharmaceutical use.[124]

Compulsory licences

There has always been a danger that the proprietor of a patent will abuse the monopoly granted to him. For example, an inventor, Mary, develops an everlasting light bulb and obtains a patent for it. Brightlight Ltd., a manufacturer of conventional light bulbs, offers a large sum of money to Mary for an assignment of the patent to which she agrees. Brightlight then suppress the invention and do not put it to use, preferring to continue making conventional light bulbs. This state of affairs cannot exist as far as a patented invention is concerned because of the availability of compulsory licences under which others

---

121 Section 46.

122 This was the Comptroller's view of the provisions in sections 48(3) and 50(1) when the patent was not being worked in the United Kingdom. However, in *EC Commission* v *United Kingdom* [1993] FSR 1, it was held that section 48 offends against Article 30 of the Treaty of Rome, see later.

123 [1993] 1 CMLR 89.

124 Para. 4A, Schedule 1 to the Patents Act 1977, inserted by section 293 of the Copyright, Designs and Patents Act 1988. Patents for medicinal products may now be extended to a maximum of 25 years, Patents (Supplementary Protection Certificate for Medicinal Products) Rules 1992, SI 1992 No. 3162.

may work the invention against the wishes of the proprietor of the patent. Compulsory licences cover not only situations where a patent is not being worked, but also are available in other circumstances such as where demand for a product is not being met on reasonable terms.

Compulsory licences cannot be granted until after three years from the date of the grant of the patent, after which any person may apply for a licence under the patent and/or for an entry to be made on the register to the effect that licences are available as of right.[125] The grounds on which such application may be made are listed in section 48(3) and are:

125 Section 48(1).

(a) The invention is not being worked in the United Kingdom to the fullest extent that is reasonably practicable (assuming it is capable of being commercially worked in the United Kingdom).

(b) In the case of an invention which is a product, demand for it in the United Kingdom is not being met on reasonable terms or is being met substantially by importation.

(c) Where the invention is capable of being commercially worked in the United Kingdom and it is being prevented or hindered from being so worked by the importation of the product (in the case of a product invention) or by the importation of a product obtained directly by means of the process or to which the process has been applied (for a process invention).

(d) The proprietor refuses to grant a licence or licences on reasonable terms with the result that:

   (i) a market for the export of any patented product made in the United Kingdom is not being supplied, or

   (ii) the working or efficient working in the United Kingdom of any other patented invention which makes a substantial contribution to the art is prevented or hindered, or

   (iii) the establishment or development of commercial or industrial activities in the United Kingdom is being unfairly prejudiced.

(e) Because of conditions imposed by the proprietor on the grant of licences or on the disposal or use of the patented product or on the use of the patented process, the manufacture, use or disposal of materials not protected by the patent or the establishment or development of commercial or industrial activities in the United Kingdom is unfairly prejudiced.

It can be seen that the grounds are fairly wide and do not necessarily equate with the notion of abuse, for example where demand is being met by importation. Anyone can apply, even an existing licensee of the patent who shall not be estopped from applying for a compulsory licence because of any admission made by him, whether in such a licence or otherwise, or because he has accepted a licence in the first place.[126]

126 Section 48(8).

The grounds stated in section 48 are expressed in terms that focus upon the United Kingdom and, therefore, the proprietor of a patent can reduce the likelihood of a compulsory licence being granted if he manufacturers the product, if there is one, in the United Kingdom rather than manufacturing elsewhere and importing into the United Kingdom. The proprietor is encouraged to work his invention in the United Kingdom and this could easily fall foul of the free movement of goods principle enshrined in Article 30 of the Treaty of Rome. In particular, section 48(3)(b)(ii) which provides for compulsory licences where demand for a patented product being met to a substantial extent by importation can discriminate against imports from other Member States. This was held to offend against Article 30 in *EC Commission* v *United Kingdom*[127] and was not considered necessary to protect the specific subject-matter of the patent.[128] The other provisions in section 48(3) must be regarded as being subject to Article 30 of the Treaty of Rome. This also applies to the guidelines contained in section 50(1) on the Comptroller's exercise of his powers under section 48, discussed next. Appropriate amendments to the Patents Act 1977 can be expected soon.[129]

Guidelines for the exercise of the Comptroller's powers with respect to applications under section 48 are contained in section 50. The Comptroller shall take into account the following general purposes by section 50(1):

(a) The working of invention to the fullest extent that is reasonably practicable in the United Kingdom without undue delay if it is in the public interest for the invention to be worked on a commercial scale.

(b) Having regard to the nature of the invention, the inventor or other person entitled to the patent shall receive a reasonable remuneration.

(c) The interests of any person currently working or developing a patented invention in the United Kingdom shall not be unfairly prejudiced.

In determining whether to make an order or entry in the register, the Comptroller shall also take into account the nature of the invention, the time since publication of its grant, measures taken to make full use of the invention, the ability of a compulsory licensee (for example) to work the invention to the public advantage and the risks taken by that person. If the patent is being worked in the United Kingdom, it was held in *Research Corporation's (Carboplatin) Patent*[130] that it would normally run counter to policy to grant a licence of right (or compulsory licence) which permitted importation. Furthermore, if the price of the product was reasonable and demand at that price was being fully met, it was irrelevant to say that demand would be greater if the price was lower. The question is whether, in all the circumstances, the price being charged was reasonable.

The applicant for a compulsory licence must establish a *prima facie* case that the grounds relied upon apply. A mere suspicion will not be sufficient and an order for discovery will not be granted unless a *prima facie* case is raised by the applicant. In *Richco Plastic Co.'s Patent*[131] the only evidence that the applicant had was that the patentee had an associated company in the United Kingdom and an investigation at the United Kingdom Companies Registry which showed an entry for the company which did not refer to manufacturing costs but only to the costs of purchasing and importing. The application was dismissed as being an abuse of process.

Terms of licence as of right or compulsory licence

If the Comptroller has to settle the terms for a licence as of right or a compulsory licence he should do so with a view to securing, *inter alia*, that the proprietor of the patent received a reasonable remuneration having regard to the nature of the invention. This could only be done by considering what a willing licensor and a willing licensee would have agreed upon as a reasonable royalty

127 [1993] FSR 1.

128 Articles 36 and 222 discussed in Chapter 16.

129 The Patent Office, *Annual Report and Accounts* (London: HMSO, 1993) at p.30.

130 [1990] RPC 663. But this decision is now very questionable in the light of *EC Commission* v *United Kingdom* [1993] FSR 1, discussed above.

131 [1989] RPC 722.

132 [1987] RPC 327.

133 Section 41 allowed the Comptroller to grant compulsory licences, *inter alia*, for medical patents. He was obliged to secure that medicines would be available to the public at the lowest prices consistent with the patentee deriving a reasonable advantage for his patent rights. For a discussion of the effects of section 41 of the Patents Act 1949 and its demise in respect of pharmaceutical products, see, Walton, A. 'The Copyright, Designs and Patents Act 1988 (1)' (1989) 133 *Solicitors Journal* 646 at 650–651.

134 Although many of the provisions of the 1949 Act continue to apply to patents and applications existing on 1 June 1978 by virtue of the transitional provisions, section 41 did not. However, the courts still seek guidance from section 41, see *Shiley Inc.'s Patent* [1988] RPC 97.

135 [1964] RPC 391, approved by the Court of Appeal in *Allen & Hanburys Ltd.'s (Salbutamol) Patent* [1987] RPC 327.

136 [1990] RPC 203.

137 *Research Corporation's (Carboplatin) Patent* [1990] RPC 663.

138 [1988] RPC 97.

139 [1990] RPC 309.

to be paid for the rights granted under the licence as of right. So it was held in the Court of Appeal in *Allen & Hanburys Ltd.'s (Salbutamol) Patent*.[132] This would include taking account of the research and development costs and promotional costs incurred in creating and maintaining a market for the product. Regard should also be had for the reward deserved by the proprietor for his contribution to the art secured by an appropriate measure of profit upon the capital invested. It was suggested that this position is not unlike that pertaining under the compulsory licensing provisions in section 41 of the Patents Act 1949 which caused much concern in the drug industry.[133] The section 41 approach did not altogether die with the revocation of the 1949 Act.[134] It was held in *Geigy SA's Patent*[135] that three elements should be taken into account in calculating the licence fee: an allowance for research and development costs, an allowance for promotional costs and an appropriate uplift. The first two are the compensation element and the third is the reward element. However, the applicability of this test now seems in doubt, as discussed below.

The best way of determining what willing parties would agree upon is to look at comparable licences where these exist. In *Smith, Kline & French Laboratories Ltd.'s (Cimetidine) Patents*,[136] Lloyd LJ said (at 236):

> For my part I have no doubt that where close comparables exist, they provide by far the best and surest approach. There is no better guide to what a willing licensor and a willing licensee would agree than what other licensors and licensees have in fact agreed in comparable cases.

The presumption of willing parties to a licence could be extended to contemplate that they had a common understanding about future pricing policy and if price cutting was likely to ensue, the court should decide where the floor should be and what profits should be available calculated on that basis.[137]

Another possible method of calculating the terms is the 'profits available' approach in which the exercise is to determine what the available profits are and to divide these between the licensor and licensee. However, this is difficult to apply in practice and should be considered to be a last resort where there is nothing else to go on. It is accepted by the court that there are particular 'going rates' in specific industries. For example, in *Shiley Inc.'s Patent*,[138] which involved the settlement of terms for a licence of right in relation to a heart valve prosthesis, it was said the range of royalty in the mechanical engineering field was 5 to 7 per cent but the norm in the pharmaceutical industry was between 25 and 30 per cent. However, even though the patent was in the mechanical engineering field, being a mechanical surgical device, the royalty payable was set at 15 per cent because of factors such as the proprietor's pioneering work and the high profit margins in the particular technology.

The difference between the comparable licence and the section 41 approach can be quite large. In *American Cyanamid Co.'s (Fenbufen) Patent*,[139] Aldous J applied both of the methods (he considered the profits available method of no assistance because there was no clear evidence of how the profits should be split). He calculated that the royalty to produce a reasonable remuneration based on comparable licences was 27 per cent but that the application of the section 41 test gave between 45 and 54 per cent. He said that the section 41 royalty was not correct and the final figure awarded was 27 per cent uplifted to 32 per cent to take account of exceptional promotional costs.

The calculation of royalties in respect of compulsory licences and licences of right will continue to be a source of difficulty. It is not possible to lay down a strict percentage to be applied universally because of variations in development and promotional costs and there is a danger that the patentee will be robbed of his reward if the rate is set too low. Whilst it is essential that the incentive to invent is maintained it is important that certain inventions, especially related to drugs, are readily available at reasonable prices. The willing parties approach is by far the most satisfactory but sometimes there will be nothing to compare the licence with. In such circumstances, the old section 41 approach may still be of some assistance as the profits available approach is deeply flawed. For example, what happens if there are subsequent applications for licences of right? The patentee's remaining share of the available profit will be diluted still further.

CROWN USE

A patent is a right granted by the Crown and there are detailed provisions in the Act for Crown use. The forms of use covered are listed in section 55 and are declared not to be an infringement of the patent.[140] They are:

(a) **Product inventions**. To make, use, import, keep or sell or offer to sell it. Sale and offers to sell must be incidental or ancillary to the previously mentioned activities. To sell or offer to sell it for foreign defence purposes. For the production or supply of specified drugs and medicines, to dispose or offer to dispose of it otherwise than by selling it for any purposes.
(b) **Process inventions**. To use it or to do any of the above in relation to a product obtained directly by means of the process.
(c) **Specified drugs or medicines** (product inventions or the product of a process invention). To sell or offer to sell the drug or medicine.
(d) **Any type of invention**. To supply or offer to supply to any person the means, relating to an essential element of the invention, for putting the invention into effect. To dispose or offer to dispose of anything made, used, imported or kept which is no longer required for that purpose.

Crown use is subject to a royalty being paid to the proprietor of the patent but not in relation to things done before the priority date, unless done as a result of a confidential relevant communication.[141] The use must be for the services of the Crown and by any government department or any person authorized in writing by a government department. A health authority is, for the purposes of section 55, a government department. In *Dory* v *Sheffield Health Authority*,[142] the proprietor of a patent for machines for treating kidney stones sued the health authority for patent infringement. It was held that the use of the machines by the health authority was Crown use and that the authority exercised the functions of the Secretary of State which were devolved to the authority by the National Health Service Act 1977 and regulations made under that Act.

Section 57 deals with the rights of third parties that are affected by the Crown use and, fundamentally, prevents third-party rights interfering with the Crown use and apportions certain expenditure and royalty payments between the proprietor and an assignee of the patent or between the proprietor and an exclusive licensee. If the proprietor of the patent or an exclusive licensee suffers

140 See also section 56 which expands upon the meaning of some of the provisions and terms.

141 'Relevant communication' means, by section 55(9), a direct or indirect communication of the invention by the proprietor of the patent or any person from whom he derives title.

142 [1991] FSR 221.

loss from not being awarded a contract in relation to the invention where the invention is used for the services of the Crown, the government department concerned is under a duty to pay compensation.[143] Compensation is only payable to the extent that the contract could have been fulfilled from existing capacity and factors relevant to determining the loss are the profit that would have resulted from the contract and the extent to which manufacturing or other capacity was under-used.[144] The compensation is only calculable on the contract lost as a result of the Crown use and not for other contracts. The amount payable by way of royalties in respect of Crown use or the amount of compensation is to be agreed between the relevant government department and the proprietor with the approval of the Treasury but, in the absence of agreement, may be referred to the High Court[145] as may other disputes regarding Crown use, under section 58.

There are extended provisions for Crown use during a period of emergency which is a period declared to be so by Order in Council.[146] During a period of emergency, the powers exercisable by any government department or person authorized by a government department include the power to use the invention for any purpose that appears to the department to be necessary or expedient for one or more stated reasons, including the efficient prosecution of any war in which Her Majesty may be engaged, the maintenance of supplies and services essential to the life or well-being of the community and for assisting in the relief of suffering in any country outside the United Kingdom that is in grave distress as a result of war. However, to these are added some reasons which extend the meaning of 'emergency' somewhat, for example promoting the productivity of industry, commerce and agriculture and also for redressing the balance of trade, that is increasing exports and reducing imports.

Crown use may be involved where the invention concerns the country's defence and an order may have been given under section 22 prohibiting or restricting the publication or communication of information contained in the patent application. Failure to comply with such directions is an offence triable either way.[147] The wide powers under section 22 apply where the information is prejudicial to the defence of the realm or to the safety of the public. It could mean that an invention is kept secret and the exploitation of it by the proprietor is hindered or even prevented although the Secretary of State must keep the position under review from time to time (at least once a year). For example, in the early 1980s, an inventor devised a method of cryptography that was intended to be used for combating piracy of audio and video tapes and computer programs. However, and unfortunately for the inventor, it also had military uses and was subject to a section 22 direction.[148] As the apparent intention of the Ministry of Defence was not to use the invention but to keep it secret and prevent others from being able to use it, the unlucky inventor may not receive any income from his invention[149] unless some *ex gratia* payment is made. Had the inventor not tried to patent his invention he might have been able to exploit it relying on the law of confidence to protect his ideas.

143 Section 57A, added by the Copyright, Designs and Patents Act 1988, Schedule 5, para. 16(1).

144 Sections 57A(2) & (3).

145 In Scotland, the Court of Session and, in Northern Ireland, the High Court in Northern Ireland, section 130.

146 Section 59.

147 The maximum penalty on indictment is imprisonment for a period not exceeding 2 years and/or a fine. On summary conviction, the maximum penalty is a fine of £1,000, section 22(9).

148 *The Times*, 17 February 1984.

149 If it is used then, under section 55, royalties will be payable.

15

Patents: infringement, defences and remedies

INTRODUCTION

The strength of the rights granted by patent law is such that infringement of the patent and defences to infringement actions have to be carefully drawn out. Patent infringement is not measured in terms of whether a substantial part has been taken, as is infringement of a work of copyright, but there are difficulties where the invention has not been taken in its entirety by an alleged infringer, or some feature of the invention has been changed. In the latter case, the courts have to determine whether the variant infringes the patent. It is in the light of subsequent variants of an invention that the value of a precise and appropriate specification can be seen, not too wide to cause rejection of the application and not so narrow as to permit slight variations being lawfully made.

The scope of the infringing acts and the stated exceptions to infringement strive to achieve a balance between the interests of the proprietor and others, including his competitors. Reverse engineering[1] is permitted, *per se*, but is hardly necessary as a study of the patent specification, a public document, should be sufficient to determine how the invention works and what it does. Patent actions often involve challenges to the validity of the patent concerned and proprietors (or exclusive licensees) must be prepared to defend their patent. Commonly, challenges will be made on the grounds of anticipation or lack of inventive step. Partly because of this but mainly as a result of the technical nature of patents, litigation in this field tends to be expensive and time-consuming. Trials lasting several weeks and costs of up to £2 million are not unheard of.

As with other statute-based forms of intellectual property rights, with the single exception of trade marks, the culpability of the infringer is relevant in determining what remedies are available in a particular case. Like design law, there is a remedy for groundless threats of infringement proceedings, and, as is the case with registered designs, certificates of contested validity are available. There are also some criminal penalties associated with patents.

CHOICE OF COURT

Before looking in detail at infringement, defences and remedies, a brief word or two should be given on the choice of court for the hearing of a patent action.[2] In the past litigants were faced with little option but the inevitable expense associated with an action in the Patents Court, part of the Chancery Division of the High Court. Average costs in that court are estimated at £500,000.[3] The Patent Office itself has limited jurisdiction to hear certain matters, as governed by the 1977 Act, for example to grant compulsory licences and settle the terms

1 Sometimes referred to as reverse analysis. This occurs when the invention or the ideas underlying it are discovered by dismantling and inspecting articles made to the invention.

2 For a much fuller and detailed description, see Reid, B.C. *A Practical Guide to Patent Law* (London: Sweet & Maxwell, 2nd edn., 1993), chapters 7, 8 and 11.

3 Conn, D. 'Cut-price court in a spin', *The Times*, 23 November 1993.

of licences of right, to revoke patents, to award compensation to employees in respect of inventions of outstanding benefit to their employers, etc. Under section 61(3), with the agreement of the parties, the Comptroller may hear infringement actions. The Patent Rules 1990 lay down the procedural aspects.[4]

Following some speculation that the Patent Office should be given wider powers and a subsequent recommendation that a special county court to hear patents cases be set up'[5] the Patents County Court was established by virtue of Part VI of the Copyright Designs and Patents Act 1988.[6] The procedure is governed by normal county court procedures with some modification.[7]

The subject-matter of the jurisdiction of the Patents County Court is to hear proceedings relating to patents or designs and ancillary matters. The normal county court limits as to the damages that can be awarded do not apply and parties can be represented by a patent agent. Registered patent agents now have a right of audience in the Patents County Court.[8] The Patents County Court should result in speedier, less expensive hearings and, as might be expected, has been the target of brickbats and bouquets. In *Prout* v *British Gas plc*,[9] Sir Thomas Bingham MR said:

> [the Patents County Court] has not been in operation for very long and during the period that it has been in operation it has been conspicuously successful. Part of the source of that success has been that it has set out to be as economical of time and expense and as innovative in terms of procedure as possible, consistent always of course with the requirements of justice and the entitlement of the parties to a fair hearing.[10]

A number of criticisms are levelled at the court and its judge, Peter Ford and reported by Conn.[11] They include indecision and lack of firmness on the part of the judge. However, much of the trouble seems to stem from procedural difficulties which are being addressed by Judge Ford who states that the problems will be eased quickly, strengthening the court's *raison d'être* to provide easy access to litigation for persons and companies without large resources.

Inevitably, any new court must undergo its teething problems. It is reputed that the first seven decisions of the Patents County Court, tested in the Court of Appeal, were overturned.[12] The need for an inexpensive forum to hear patent disputes is, however, unquestionable and, in time, the Patents County Court should develop into a worthwhile and valued alternative to the Patents Court in the Chancery Division.

INFRINGEMENT

A patent may relate to a product or a process. If the invention is a process, it may be used to make a product. An example of a product invention is a new type of golf ball and an example of the latter is a new process for making ordinary golf balls. By section 130, a patented product is a product which is a patented invention or, in relation to a patented process, a product obtained directly by means of the process or to which the process has been applied.

Section 60[13] defines an infringement of a patent as the doing of any of the following things in relation to the invention without the proprietor's consent:

(a) **Product invention** – to make, dispose of, offer to dispose of, to use or import the product or to keep it, whether for disposal or otherwise.

4 SI 1990 No. 2384. The procedure for a section 61(3) reference is stated in rules 72 and 73.

5 *Intellectual Property and Innovation* Cmnd 9712 (London: HMSO, 1986) and the Oulton Committee Report (1987).

6 Also, see the Patents County Court (Designation and Jurisdiction) Order 1990, SI 1990 No. 1496.

7 For example, the Patents County Court may grant Anton Piller Orders and Mareva injunctions, sections 2 and 3 of the County Court Remedies Regulations 1991, SI 1991 No. 1222.

8 Section 292 of the Copyright, Designs and Patents Act 1988.

9 (unreported) 4 May 1993 (Court of Appeal).

10 This case was an appeal from the judgment of Judge Ford in the Patents County Court, [1992] FSR 478, on the question of costs.

11 Conn, D. op. cit.

12 Conn, D. op. cit.

13 Unless otherwise stated, in this chapter, statutory references are to the Patents Act 1977.

(b) **Process invention** – to use the process or offer it for use in the United Kingdom when the person concerned does so knowing, or where in the circumstances it would be obvious to a reasonable man, that such use would be
without the consent of the proprietor and would be an infringement of the
patent.

(c) **Process invention** – to dispose of or offer to dispose of, to use or import or
to keep (whether for disposal or otherwise) any product obtained directly
by means of the process.

(d) **All inventions** – to supply or offer to supply in the United Kingdom a
person (other than a licensee or other person entitled to work the invention)
with any of the means, relating to an essential element of the invention, for
putting the invention into effect. The alleged infringer must know, or it
must be obvious to a reasonable man in the circumstances, that those means
are suitable for putting, and are intended to put, the invention into effect in
the United Kingdom.[14]

The final type of infringement ('supplying the means') could occur where one
person supplies another with a kit of parts for the latter to assemble. This was
not an infringement before the 1977 Act came into force.[15] However, this
infringement does not apply to the supply, or offer to supply, of a staple commercial product unless made with the purpose of inducing an act that is an
infringement under any of the first three infringing acts above by the person
supplied (or the person to whom the offer was made).[16]

There are various exceptions to the above infringements and these will be
discussed in the section on defences. In the meantime, the scope of infringement
will be considered. The patent is granted on the basis of the specification and
the claims included in the application, perhaps after amendment. It is to these
documents that a court must turn to determine whether the patent has been
infringed. This is confirmed by section 125(1) which states that a patent shall,
unless the context otherwise requires, be taken to be that specified in a claim of
the specification as interpreted by the description and any drawings in the specification. The extent of the protection conferred by the patent is to be determined accordingly. Hence the importance of the claims.

If the alleged infringer has simply duplicated the product or process patented
then, subject to the defences or a challenge on the validity of the patent, there
should be no hesitation in finding that an infringement has occurred. But what
if the alleged infringer has not simply duplicated the invention but has introduced some changes, producing a variant? If this has happened, it is then a
matter of construing the patent specification and claims to find out whether the
grant extends to the variation. The alleged infringer is likely to suggest that his
variant lies outside the things claimed by the patent whilst the proprietor will
argue that the variant falls within the patent as granted. If the former is true,
then no matter how close to that dividing line the variant lies, there is no
infringement of the patent.

Interpretation of claims

A literal interpretation of the specification and claims is always a possibility,
given the predilection that many lawyers have for this approach. Nevertheless, a
literal approach to interpretation does not sit comfortably with the knowledge

14 This provision does not
apply to the proprietor of the
patent. So, for example, if the
proprietor grants an exclusive
licence to one person he does
not infringe by supplying the
means suitable for putting the
invention into effect to another
person. The proprietor will
probably be in breach of his
licence agreement with the first
person and the second person
will infringe the patent if he
works the invention.

15 The Act came into force
on 1 June 1978.

16 Section 60(3).

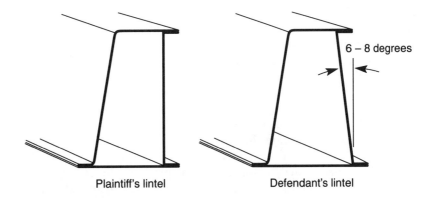

Figure 15.1 **Steel lintels in** *Catnic* v *Hill & Smith*

that patent specifications are written for scientists, engineers and technologists rather than for lawyers. Lord Reid disapproved a strict literal approach to the construction of a patent specification in *Rodi & Wienenberger AG v Henry Showell Ltd.*[17] where he said (at 378):

> . . . claims are not addressed to conveyancers: they are addressed to practical men skilled in the prior art, and I do not think that they ought to be construed with that meticulousness which was once thought appropriate for conveyancing documents.

Another way to resolve the question of infringement by a variant is to consider whether the differences between the variant and the patented invention are material, that is do they differ in essential or inessential respects? The invention claimed can be considered as comprising essential and non-essential integers (components), those that are fundamental to the invention and those that are not. If the alleged infringer has taken all of the essential integers then there is an infringement even if there are substantial differences in respect of the non-essential integers. This has been described by various judges as taking the 'pith and marrow' of the invention. However, when applying this principle, the scope of the patent claims is vital. Viscount Radcliffe said in *Van der Lely NV v Bamfords Ltd.*[18] (at 78):

> When, therefore, one speaks of theft or piracy of another's invention . . . and this 'pith and marrow' principle is invoked to support the accusation, I think that one must be very careful to see that the inventor has not by the actual form of his claim left open to the world the appropriation of just that property that he says has been filched from him . . .

In other words, the inventor must be very careful when drafting his claims to make sure that they are not framed too narrowly so that some slight and insignificant modification can be effected without infringing the patent. The essential integers claimed must be those very parts which the proprietor wishes to protect.

The 'pith and marrow' test still leaves the problem of interpretation and the question of construction of patent claims and variants came to a head in the case of *Catnic Components Ltd. v Hill & Smith Ltd.*[19] which involved several variants of steel lintels.[20] The plaintiff was a proprietor of a patent for steel lin-

17 [1969] RPC 367.

18 [1963] RPC 61.

19 [1982] RPC 183. This case concerned a patent granted under the 1949 Act but it has been accepted as being applicable to 1977 Act patents.

20 A lintel is a beam used to support some load, such as a wall, above an opening. For example, lintels are used above windows and doors to support the wall above and any transmitted loads.

tels that had a rear support member which was described as being vertical. Claim 1 of the specification described the rear support member as a 'second rigid support member extending *vertically* from or from near the rear edge of the first horizontal plate or part adjacent its rear edge' (emphasis added).[21] The defendant made a similar lintel but with the rear support member inclined between 6 and 8 degrees (depending on the particular model of lintel) from the vertical. Figure 15.1 gives an approximate representation in cross-section of one of the plaintiff's lintels and one of the defendant's lintels.

The strength of a steel lintel in this form of construction derives to some extent from the verticality of the rear member and the defendant's lintel had a reduced load bearing capacity compared to the plaintiff's lintel, but because of the small inclination from the vertical, this reduction was small.[22] The House of Lords found that the plaintiff's patent had been infringed – the defendant's argument that the verticality of the plaintiff's lintel was essential to its function and that, therefore, there was no pith and marrow infringement was rejected. It was confirmed that a purposive approach[23] should be adopted in the construction of patent specifications, Lord Diplock saying (at 243):

> A patent specification should be given a purposive construction rather than a purely literal one derived from applying to it the kind of meticulous verbal analysis in which lawyers are too often tempted by their training to indulge.

Lord Diplock identified the real crux of the matter as being whether practical persons, skilled in the art, would understand that strict compliance with a particular word or phrase was intended by the patentee to be an essential requirement of the invention. If so, any variant that did not comply would fall outside the claim regardless of whether it had any effect. If the variant does have a material effect, there is no infringement. Lord Diplock went on to suggest (and apply) a test that has become that favoured for deciding whether variants infringe.[24] The test comprises three questions:

(a) Does the variant have, in fact, a material effect on the way the invention worked? If the answer is 'yes', the variant falls outside the claim and does not infringe. If the answer is 'no', the second question is asked.

(b) Would it have been obvious, at the date of publication of the patent specification, to the informed reader (presumably a person skilled in the art) that the variant had no material effect? If the answer to this is 'no' then the variant falls outside the claim but if the answer is 'yes' the final question must be asked.

(c) Is it apparent to any reader skilled in the art that a particular descriptive word or phrase used in a claim cannot have been intended to exclude minor variants which would have no material effect upon the way in which the invention worked? If the answer to this is 'no' then the variant lies outside the claim but if 'yes' the variant infringes the patent.

Another way of expressing the third question is whether the skilled reader would understand from the language of the claim that strict compliance with the primary meaning of the claim was intended. Figure 15.2 shows a flowchart approach to the test.

21 Patent Specification No. 1298798 (GB).

22 For a 6 degree inclination from the vertical the reduction was only 0.6 per cent and for an 8 degree inclination the reduction was 1.2 per cent.

23 This is the modern equivalent of the 'mischief rule', that is the rule in *Heydon's Case* (1584) 3 Co Rep 7a. In other words, the word 'vertically' did not mean 'vertically' but 'vertically or nearly so'!

24 See for example, *A C Edwards Ltd. v Acme Signs & Displays Ltd.* [1990] RPC 621, concerning apparatus for displaying prices at petrol filling station forecourts, *Southco Inc. v Dzeus Fastener Europe Ltd.* [1990] RPC 587, which involved a lift and turn latch for a cabinet door and *Improver Corp. v Raymond Industries Ltd.* [1991] FSR 223, discussed later.

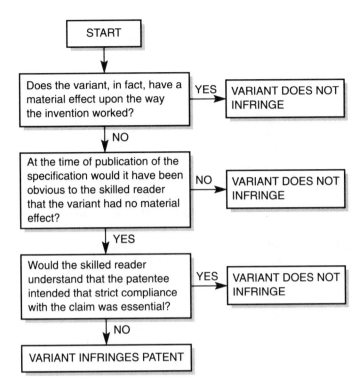

Figure 15.2 Flowchart – whether variant infringes patent

The *Catnic* test has become the basic test for infringements by variants. It can be criticized because it can lead to uncertainty. If a strict literal approach were to be adopted then a potential competitor wishing to make a non-infringing variant should be able to determine just how far he can go without infringing. It would also encourage persons drafting patent claims to use greater precision which would further reduce uncertainty. However, the purposive approach is broadly in line with the European Patent Convention and is here to stay.[25] Article 69 of the Convention accords with Section 125(1) in stating that the extent of protection shall be determined by the claims as interpreted by the description and drawings. The Protocol on the interpretation of Article 69[26] tries to strike a balance between certainty and second-guessing what the applicant had intended. It confirms that a strict literal approach is not to be used but that a position should be adopted 'between these extremes which combines a fair protection for the patentee with a reasonable degree of certainty for third parties'. In view of the immense sums involved in the exploitation of patents and the high cost of litigation it is submitted that an approach leaning towards certainty is preferable. However, it must be accepted that drafting legally precise claims for complex and highly technical inventions is no mean feat.

Equivalents

Sometimes the alleged infringement may contain mechanical equivalents, an alternative that works equivalently. A mechanical equivalent may be more than

25 In *Anchor Building Products Ltd.* v *Redland Roof Tiles Ltd.* [1990] RPC 283, it was held that the *Catnic* test was the same as that in the 1977 Act and the Protocol.

26 For a description of the impact of the Protocol, see Sherman, B. 'Patent Claim Interpretation: The Impact of the Protocol on Interpretation' (1991) 54 MLR 499.

a mere variant as in the *Catnic* case. It is then a question of deciding which are the essential integers of the claim in the pith and marrow approach to interpretation discussed above. For example, in *Rodi & Wienenberger AG v Henry Showell Ltd.*[27] it was held that replacing two 'U-shaped' bows in a flexible watch strap with a single large 'C-shaped' bow was not an infringement because the 'U-shaped' bow was an essential integer. Conversely, in *Marconi v British Radio Telegraph & Telephone*[28] the replacement of an auto-transformer with a two-coil transformer did not prevent a finding of infringement because the auto-transformer was not an essential integer.

The Court of Appeal in Hong Kong had to deal with a mechanical equivalent in *Improver Corp. v Raymond Industries Ltd.*[29] The plaintiff's patent was for a device, called the 'Epilady', for removing hair from arms and legs. The defendant imported and distributed a device that performed the same function and was called 'Smooth & Silky'.[30] It was held, applying the Diplock test in *Catnic*, that the first and second questions are questions of fact and the answers to them are not conclusive to the third question which was one of construction. Even a purposive construction might produce the conclusion that the patentee was confining his claim to the primary meaning and excluding the variant even though the variant might make no material difference and this would have been obvious at the time. On the evidence, there was no material difference, both devices trapped and plucked hair from the skin, and it was obvious that both worked in the same way. The answers to the first two questions in the flow-chart were therefore 'no' and 'yes' respectively and the third question fell to be determined. It was held that it was important to look at all the essential integers in the patent specification and claim and see if all those essential integers were present in the alleged infringement.[31] The alleged infringing device could perform the same task as long as it did so differently as regards at least on essential integer and this is so even if the difference had no material effect upon the way the invention worked.

The specification and claim must therefore be construed to determine what the essential integers are and these compared to the alleged infringing product or process. In the above case, the specification and claim referred to a helical spring that was rotated to pluck hairs. It was held that this was an essential integer and the fact the defendant used an elastomeric rod instead, even though this had no material effect on how the invention worked, indicated that the defendant's device did not infringe the patent. The skilled man, reading the patent specification and claim would have considered that the patentee had not intended to include such a variant. As the helical spring was rotated, its windings opened and closed up trapping and plucking out hairs. The defendant's device did the same thing but by using a rubber rod with slits in it. In a claim in the Patents Court involving the same devices, Hoffman J applied the *Catnic* test and his answers were 'no', 'yes' and 'yes' and therefore, in his opinion, the 'Smooth & Silky' hair remover did not infringe.[32]

The Epilady case is also interesting because it shows differences of approach to infringement and the effect of the protocol on the interpretation of Article 69. In Germany, in a parallel action involving the same parties and patent it was held that the defendant's rubber rod with slits in it infringed the Epilady patent.[33] Jacob suggests that there is an approach to infringement in Germany whereby a mechanical equivalent that is obvious will infringe even though the

27 [1969] RPC 367.

28 (1911) 28 RPC 181.

29 [1991] FSR 223.

30 The case was decided under the Patents Act 1977 which is in force in Hong Kong.

31 The word 'integer' is used to describe an element of an invention, assuming that it can be broken down into elements. The number of integers can be increased by adding to the claims by use of alternatives. For example, an offset eccentrically mounted widget which is attached to the mounting by magnetic means (claim 1) and a widget as in claim 1 which is attached to its mounting by plastic friction clips (claim 2).

32 *Improver Corp. v Remington Consumer Products Ltd.* [1990] FSR 181.

33 [1991] RPC 597.

4 Jacob, R. 'The Herchel Smith Lecture 1993', [1993] EIPR 312 at 313.

integer it replaces is an essential one.[34] Although the law on infringement by variants and mechanical equivalents is not settled it is suggested that the following tests should be used:

(a) Where the critical aspect of the alleged infringement is a minor variant, that is it does the same thing in the same way (as in the *Catnic* case), it should not escape an infringement action merely because of an inappropriately narrow choice of words.

(b) Where the aspect of the alleged infringement under consideration is a mechanical equivalent, that is it performs the same function but by different means (as in the *Improver* case) then, unless it is expressly covered by the claims as being an essential integer, there should be no infringement.

The application of the purposive approach may operate harshly on a defendant because, in an interlocutory hearing, it is likely to be used even more generously. The slightest hint of infringement might be sufficient to convince a judge that there is a serious issue to be tried. In *Beecham Group plc v J & W Sanderson Ltd*. Aldous J said:

> Patent claims are difficult to construe after a trial, and are even more difficult on motion without proper education as to the background and the technical effect of differences. This case is no exception, and I conclude that there is a serious issue to be tried as to whether the defendant's toothbrushes infringe claim 1.[35]

5 (unreported) 18 June 1993 Chancery Division).

Could it be that plaintiffs are given the benefit of doubt because of the purposive approach? This particular case concerned a patent for a toothbrush having a flexible handle by virtue of 'V-shaped' folds transverse to the handle. The defendant's toothbrush achieved flexibility by means of a helical spring or auger construction having coils connected to a central core. However, although Aldous J decided there was a serious issue to be tried, he refused an injunction after consideration of the balance of convenience, although he did order the defendant to pay 15 pence into a joint bank account for each toothbrush he sold.

Title to sue for infringement

The proprietor or exclusive licensee has title to sue for infringement of a patent. However if their interest has not been registered under section 32 they will not be entitled to damages or an account of profits in respect of infringements occurring before registration, unless registration takes place within six months, section 68. The court (or Comptroller) has a discretion to extend that period if satisfied that the interest was registered as soon as possible after providing it was not practicable to register sooner. If a party to proceedings is found not to have title to sue, he will be struck from the action as in *Bondax Carpets Ltd*. v

36 [1993] FSR 162.

Advance Carpet Tiles[36] where the third plaintiff was struck from the action. His contract with the second plaintiff had nothing to do with the rights under the patent.

One or more joint proprietors of a patent may bring an action for infringement without the concurrence of the others but they must be made parties to the proceedings.[37] The infringing acts are to be construed in the context of one or more joint proprietors of the patent subject to section 36. This means that the consent of the proprietor referred to in section 60 will usually require the con-

37 Section 66(2).

sent of each and every one of the proprietors of the patent. By section 67, the exclusive licensee of a patent has the same rights as the proprietor to bring an action for infringement committed after the date of the licence. In any action by an exclusive licensee, the proprietor shall be made a party to the proceedings.

DEFENCES

A person sued for an alleged infringement of a patent has several and varied escape routes. He might challenge the validity of the patent, claiming that it should be revoked because it has been anticipated or that it is obvious. Section 74 permits the defendant to put the validity of the patent in issue. This may also be done under certain other circumstances.[38] The defendant may claim that the patent has lapsed or expired or he may challenge the plaintiff's title to it or his right to sue. On the other hand, the defendant might be able to reduce his liability by showing that the patent is only partially valid. If the patent is only partially valid, the defendant will escape damages and costs in respect of the invalid part. By section 63, the plaintiff must show that the specification was framed in good faith and with reasonable skill and knowledge but even if he does, the court or Comptroller still have a discretion as to the date from which damages should be calculated and in respect of costs and expenses.

Apart from these points, other defences to an infringement action are:

(a) The act was done privately and not for commercial purposes: section 60(5)(a) – note the use of the conjunctive, the act must be both private and non-commercial.

(b) The act was done for experimental purposes relating to the subject matter of the invention: section 60(5)(b) – this might permit making the subject matter of the invention to see more clearly how it works.

(c) The act consists of the extemporaneous preparation in a pharmacy of a medicine for an individual in accordance with a registered medical or dental practitioner's prescription or consists of dealing with a medicine so prepared: section 60(5)(c) – pharmacists are excused, but the practitioner may be liable vicariously.

(d) Use in relation to certain ships, aircraft or vehicles temporarily or accidentally in the United Kingdom or crossing the United Kingdom: section 60(5)(d) to (f).[39]

(e) The act was done in good faith by the defendant before the priority date of the invention or he made in good faith effective and serious preparations to do such an act and the defendant claims under section 64 that he had the right to do the act or to continue to do the act. Alternatively the defendant may claim that he has obtained this right as being a partner of such a person or that he has acquired it with the relevant part of that person's business.

(f) The act complained of is not an infringing act, it does not fall within the meaning of infringement in section 60. For example, the alleged infringing article is a variant which differs in at least one essential integer from the claimed invention.

(g) The alleged infringing product or process lacks novelty or is obvious. Therefore, the patent claims are invalid if they cover the alleged infringe-

38 For example, on the application by any person that the invention is not a patentable invention or the person to whom the patent was granted was not entitled to it or that the specification does not disclose the invention clearly and completely enough, etc. (section 72), in proceedings in connection with alleged groundless threats of infringement proceedings (section 70), proceedings in respect of a declaration under section 71 and in disputes relating to Crown use, section 58. The 1949 Act contained some other specific grounds, for example false suggestion under section 32(1)(j), see *Intalite International NV v Cellular Ceilings Ltd. (No. 2)* [1987] RPC 537.

39 Including air space, internal and territorial waters. These exceptions apply to 'relevant' ships, aircraft, hovercraft and vehicles registered in or belonging to Paris Convention countries other than the United Kingdom. The provisions also apply to exempted aircraft under section 89 of the Civil Aviation Act 1982.

ment or, if valid, they cannot cover the alleged infringement. This is the 'Gillette' defence, from *Gillette Safety Razor Co.* v *Anglo-American Trading Co. Ltd.*[40]

(h) At the time of the infringement there was in force a contract or licence containing a condition or term void by virtue of section 44. This covers terms requiring the other party to purchase anything other than the patented product or prohibiting the acquisition of anything other than the patented product from a specified third party.

(i) The plaintiff's rights have been exhausted under European Community law. This might apply in terms of parallel importing, discussed in the next chapter.[41]

(j) A 'Euro-defence', based on Articles 30, 85 or 86 of the Treaty of Rome discussed in the following chapter.

(k) The defendant has an implied licence, for example to repair a product to which the patent relates. The principle of non-derogation from grant should also be available in some circumstances.

(l) The doctrines of estoppel and laches should apply. However, estoppel does not place a positive duty on a proprietor of a patent to publicize the patent or make enquiries, *Lux Traffic Controls Ltd.* v *Pike Signals Ltd.*[42] Inactivity on the part of the proprietor or exclusive licensee may bar him from the equitable remedies, in particular an interlocutory injunction. A warning may suffice to prevent the plaintiff's claim being barred by laches, *T J Smith & Nephew Ltd.* v *3M United Kingdom plc.*[43]

The claims may be central to the issue of infringement and validity. On the one hand, the defendant will want to show that the claims are narrow and do not extend to the alleged infringement. On the other hand, the defendant will argue that the claims are too wide and, hence, the patent is invalid or only partially valid because the claims embrace some material that lacks novelty or is obvious to the notional skilled worker. This may be particularly relevant in terms of the *Gillette* defence mentioned above where the defendant argues that his product lacks either novelty or an inventive step or, better still, both.

The section 44 defence may seem draconian from the proprietor's point of view (it is a complete defence) but its purpose is to discourage abuse of the patent monopoly. Section 44 makes void conditions or terms requiring the other party (for example, a licensee or purchaser of patented products) to acquire other products or to prohibit him from acquiring or using other products from third parties or using a patented process belonging to a third party. This severely limits the proprietor's ability to impose 'tying-in' clauses, for example where the proprietor grants a licence to work a patented process but insists that the licensee also acquires raw materials from the licensor and no-one else. Section 44(3) states that it is a defence to prove that a contract or licence containing a condition or term void under section 44 was in force at the time of the alleged infringement. The defendant to the action does not have to be a party to the contract or licence and may have no relationship whatsoever with the proprietor or his exclusive licensee.[44]

The fact that a contract is not subject to law in the United Kingdom does not prevent the operation of section 44 providing the contract in question concerns a United Kingdom patent. In *Chiron Corp.* v *Organon Teknika Ltd.*[45] one of

40 (1913) 30 RPC 465.

41 The Patents Act 1977 contains a specific provision in relation to the yet to be introduced Community Patent, section 60(4).

42 [1993] RPC 107.

43 [1983] RPC 92. Otherwise, the normal limitation period of six years applies, Limitation Act 1980.

44 There are some limitations, for example where the supplier or licensor was willing to supply the product or grant the licence on reasonable terms without the offending term or condition, section 44(4).

45 (Unreported) 25 February 1993 (Court of Appeal).

the plaintiffs had a patent valid in the United Kingdom relating to Hepatitis C Virus. It granted a licence to a co-plaintiff and a third party which contained a term requiring that the licensees purchase materials not covered by the patent claims. The licenses were subject to the law of New Jersey in the United States. It was held that, as far as the applicability of section 44 was concerned, it was irrelevant that the contract or agreement was governed by foreign law and it was also irrelevant that the foreign law in question did not include a provision having equivalent effect to section 44. United Kingdom patents were the concern of section 44 as were contracts affecting United Kingdom patents, whatever the law applicable to those contracts was. In the hearing in the Patents Court,[46] Aldous J described section 44 as being penal though the Court of Appeal disagreed with this description of the section. Strong measures are required to counter strong abuses.

46 [1993] FSR 324.

The section 64 defence (acts done in good faith before the priority date) is an important one as, in a particular industry, many organizations may be working towards the same goal at the same time. However, there is a period of limbo that can apply where the act, or preparations for the act, comes between the priority date and the date of publication of the specification. This may be relevant where a person suspects that a patent application has been filed that may cover the act by its claims. Although no damages can be awarded for acts done before publication they may be awarded if continued thereafter.[47] The person applying for the patent is unlikely to volunteer information concerning his patent at this stage and the person intending to do the act has either to take a chance or wait until publication. This may be unsatisfactory, particularly where some considerable initial expense is involved such as constructing a new factory or installing a new production line.

47 Section 69. Proceedings may not be brought until after the patent has been granted.

To take an example, say that Deuce Developments Ltd. commence making and selling extendible pruning shears for reaching high branches of fruit trees in November 1993. The shears incorporate a novel design of hinge but Deuce has not applied for a patent in respect of it. During April 1993, Metal Modes Ltd. filed an application for a patent in relation to a hinge. Deuce was not aware of this and Deuce did not start making serious and effective preparations to produce its shears until June 1993. When the patent specification was published, Deuce decided to change the design of its hinge so as not to infringe the patent, if granted. When the patent is granted to Metal Modes, it can do nothing about Deuce having made the shears prior to publication (it could have sued for damages as from the publication date had Deuce continued to make shears with the hinge as covered in the claims) but it can take action against persons who acquired the early shears with the infringing hinge if those persons are using them. This is an infringement under Section 60. However, they will be able to sue Deuce on the basis of a breach of Section 12(2) of the Sale of Goods Act 1979, the implied warranty of quiet possession to goods. The case of *Microbeads AC v Vinhurst Road Markings Ltd.*[48] gives an excellent example of the consequences of acts done between filing and publication of a patent that infringe and, as they were not a continuance of acts, or the result of serious and effective preparations, done before the priority date are not saved by section 64. In the *Microbeads* case road marking machines were made and sold after the priority date of the patent application made by a third party who later obtained a patent in respect of the machines.

48 [1975] 1 All ER 529.

Other points may be relevant, for example whether there is an express licence and, if so, whether it permits the acts complained of. Another way to escape liability is for the defendant to show that the plaintiff, if he claims to be an exclusive licensee, is indeed not an exclusive licensee or, even if he is, the acts complained of were performed before the licence took effect.[49] There is a presumption in favour of the proprietor under section 100 which states that if the patent in question has been granted for a process for obtaining a new product, the same product produced by anyone other than the proprietor or his licensee shall be taken to have been obtained by means of that patented process. This presumption is rebuttable on proof to the contrary and is relevant to infringement actions under section 60(1)(c), that is infringement of a process patent by disposing of, offering to dispose of, using, importing or keeping any product obtained directly by means of the process.

Groundless threats of infringement proceedings

There is a remedy for groundless threats of infringement proceedings and any person aggrieved can bring an action for a declaration that the threats are unjustifiable, an injunction against the continuation of those threats and damages for any losses sustained as a result of the threats.[50] The threats may be made by 'circulars, advertising or otherwise' and need not be directed against the person aggrieved. If the plaintiff satisfies the court that the threats were so made, the defendant then has the burden of proving that the acts in respect of which the proceedings were threatened were or would have been an infringement of the patent. Additionally, the patent must not be shown to be invalid in a relevant respect by the plaintiff. By section 70(4), these provisions do not apply where the threat relates to the making or importing of a product for disposal or of using a process. Notification of the existence of the patent does not constitute a threat of proceedings. Therefore, a timely letter pointing out that a certain invention is subject to a patent is not a threat. Examples of proceedings under section 70 are rare but one example is the case of *Bowden Controls Ltd. v Acco Cable Controls Ltd.*[51] in which the defendant had written to some of the plaintiff's customers threatening infringement proceedings. An injunction was granted to restrain the continuation of the threats because the plaintiff had a reasonable argument that the recipient of the defendant's letter would understand it to constitute a threat of infringement proceedings both against the recipient of the letter and the plaintiff. Although the defendant had an arguable case that section 70(4) applied, the plaintiff also had an arguable case that the threats were wider than the section 70(4) defence and the balance of convenience was in favour of an injunction.

By section 71, any person may apply to the court for a declaration that a certain act does not constitute an infringement of the patent, providing that a written application has been submitted to the proprietor accompanied by full details and the proprietor has refused or failed to give the acknowledgement requested. This enables a person to seek clarification as to whether his intended actions will infringe where the proprietor has been unhelpful on this question. It does not, however, apply to patent applications.

49 Section 130(1) defines 'exclusive licence' as a licence from the proprietor (or applicant for a patent) conferring on the licensee (including persons authorized by the licensee) and to the exclusion of all others (including the proprietor or applicant) any right in respect of the invention to which the patent or application relates.

50 Section 70.

51 [1990] RPC 427.

REMEDIES

The remedies available for infringement of a patent are an injunction, damages, an account of profits, an order for delivery up or destruction and a declaration that the patent is valid and has been infringed by the defendant.[52] However, damages and an account of profits are alternatives and may not, by section 61(2), both be awarded or ordered in respect of the same infringement. The question of infringement may be referred to the Comptroller if both parties (the proprietor and any other person who has allegedly infringed the patent) are willing, in which case remedies are limited to damages and/or a declaration.[53] Assessment of damages is discussed later.

'Innocent' infringers may escape some of the remedies. By section 62(1), neither damages nor an account of profits is available if the defendant can prove that, at the time of the infringement, he was not aware and had no reasonable grounds for supposing that the patent existed, the latter being a form of constructive notice. The application of the word 'patent' or 'patented' or words expressing or implying that a patent has been obtained for the product does not necessarily fix the defendant with constructive notice unless accompanied by the number of the patent or application. It would, however, be difficult for a defendant to prove to the court that he did not know of the existence of the patent if he copied a product to which the word 'Patented' was applied. The burden of proof, in this matter, lies with the defendant.

By section 25(4), there is, in effect, a period of six months' grace for payment of a renewal fee for a patent but, by section 62(2), in respect of any infringement done during this period, the court or the Comptroller has a discretion as to whether to award damages or make an order for an account of profits. Another provision relates to the situation where the infringement occurred before an amendment to the specification was allowed. In this case, damages are not available unless the court or the Comptroller is satisfied that the specification as published was framed in good faith and with reasonable skill and knowledge.[54]

By section 69, the applicant for a patent is able to sue for infringements which occurred between the publication of the application and the grant of the patent. It is also required that the act would, if the patent had been granted at the date of publication, have infringed the patent and the claims as published. The claims have to be interpreted by reference to the description and any drawings referred to in the description or claims.[55]

Damages may not be available or may be limited if the patent is found to be partially valid only by section 63. Damage and costs will not be available at all unless the court (or Comptroller as the case may be) is satisfied that the plaintiff has proved that the specification was framed in good faith and with reasonable skill and knowledge. Even then, the court or Comptroller has a discretion as to costs and as to the date from which damages should be calculated.

If the validity of a patent is challenged and it is found to be wholly or partially valid, the court (or Comptroller if the hearing is before him) may certify the finding and the fact that the validity was so contested, section 65(2). In any subsequent proceedings, including proceedings in the same action,[56] the proprietor can obtain his costs of the further proceedings on an indemnity basis if the judgment is made in his favour. A further certificate of contested validity may be granted.

52 Section 61.

53 Section 61(3).

54 Section 62(3).

55 Section 62(2) and (3) do not apply (discretion to refuse damages or an account of profits in relation to the further period for renewal or with respect to an amendment to the specification). There is, however, some discretion left to reduce damages if it would have been reasonable to expect that the patent would not have been granted or the act would not have infringed, section 69(3).

56 *Molnlycke AB v Proctor & Gamble Ltd.* [1992] FSR 549.

The award of damages or an order for an account of profits will not be possible if the plaintiff has not registered his interest in the patent.[57] A subsequent proprietor, for example one who has taken an assignment of the patent, must register his interest under section 33. The same applies for an exclusive licensee. Any infringement subsequent to the transfer or licence and before its registration gives no right to damages unless the registration takes place within six months of the relevant transaction, instrument or event or, if it was not practicable to register within that six month period, it was registered as soon as practicable after it.

Exceptionally, a court may refuse an injunction to restrain the defendant from further infringement. Aldous J refused an injunction in *Biogen Inc.* v *Medeva plc.*[58] The defendant, in its defence, claimed that the grant of an injunction would lead to loss of human life and/or avoidable damage to human health. The patent related to a vaccine for hepatitis B. However, the background facts were likely to change, the defendant's own vaccine might soon be approved or it may obtain a compulsory licence for the plaintiff's patent. In a previous case, Graham J said:

> A life-saving drug is in an exceptional position . . . it is at the least very doubtful if the court in its discretion even ought to grant an injunction . . . [59]

Of course, it must be recalled that, as an equitable remedy, the grant of an injunction is always discretionary. That is not to say that damages would not be appropriate in such cases.

Where there is an entry on the register to the effect that licences of right are available in respect of the patent and the defendant undertakes to take a licence, an injunction will not be granted against him. Also, the amount recoverable against him is limited to a maximum of double the amount that he would have paid had the infringing acts all been done under the licence.[60] It therefore makes sense for a person who is about to be sued for infringement to check whether licences of right are available for the patent concerned where there is any likelihood that damages will be assessed otherwise than on the basis of lost royalties and will be substantially more than the royalty payments under the licence of right.

Assessment of damages

The calculation of damages can give rise to complex considerations. The basic principle was stated by Lord Wilberforce in *General Tire & Rubber* Co. v *Firestone Tyre & Rubber Co. Ltd.*[61] in the following terms (at 185):

> As in the case of any other tort ... the object of damages is to compensate for loss or injury. The general rule at any rate in relation to 'economic' torts is that the measure of damages is to be, so far as possible, that sum of money which will put the injured party in the same position as he would have been in if he had not sustained the wrong.

If the proprietor has been exploiting the patent by granting licences to others in return for royalties, then his loss is the capitalized value of the royalties that the infringer would have paid had he taken a licence. For example, if the infringer had made 500 articles that were covered by the patent and the proprietor had granted others a licence to make such articles in return for a royalty of

57 Section 68.

58 (unreported) *The Times*, December 1992 (Chancery Division).

59 *Roussel-Uclaf* v *G D Searle & Co. Ltd.* [1977] FSR 125 at 131.

60 Section 46(3)(c). The defendant's undertaking can be made at any time before the final order in the proceedings without admission of liability, section 46(3A).

61 [1975] 2 All ER 173.

£30 per article, then the damages should be assessed at £15,000. This convenient method becomes less easy to use if the proprietor has granted licences in respect of the patent to different persons at different royalty rates. Alternatively, the royalty may be calculated as a percentage of the net sale price of the articles and the infringer has been selling them at a lower price than legitimate licensees.

The royalty method of calculation falls down altogether if the proprietor does not grant licences but works the patent himself. In this case it is a question of the profits lost as a result of the infringer's activities. Here, many factors may be relevant including the effect on the market place of the infringement. Particular issues include:

- Whether every sale of an infringing article represents a lost sale for the proprietor.
- Whether the proprietor would have sold other articles along with those lost sales (for example, the buyer may have also purchased non-patented articles in addition to the patented article) – these damages are often referred to as parasitic damages.
- Whether the infringer had generated additional interest in the patented article through his marketing efforts.
- What the effect on the market was by changing a monopoly into a duopoly (for example, did the proprietor have to reduce his prices to compete with the infringer).
- Typical profit margins for the category of article concerned.
- Whether the infringer had deliberately undercut the proprietor's sale price.

An instructive case on the issue of damages where the proprietor had no intention of licensing the patent is *Catnic Components Ltd.* v *Hill & Smith Ltd.*[62] which was a follow-up to the House of Lords' case on infringement of lintels by a variant.[63] The plaintiff's claim for damages was under the following heads:

62 [1983] FSR 512.

63 [1982] RPC 183.

(a) Loss of profits on each sale made by the defendant of infringing lintels – on the basis that every sale of the defendant's represented a lost sale by the plaintiff.
(b) Loss of profits on the sale of non-patented lintels that the plaintiff would have sold alongside the patented lintels – parasitic damages.
(c) A notional royalty of 20 per cent for any infringing lintels not subject to an award under (a) and (b) above.
(d) Compound interest at two per cent above clearing bank base rate.
(e) Exemplary damages on the sale at a large discount of infringing lintels by the defendant between the hearing in the House of Lords in the main action and the delivery of the judgment.

The defendant disputed these claims arguing that the plaintiff's lost sales, if any, were less than the defendant's sales of infringing lintels; that the plaintiff was not, in law, entitled to parasitic damages or exemplary damages and that interest payable should be simple interest at clearing bank rate *less* two per cent. The defendant conceded that the plaintiff was entitled to a royalty of two per cent on gross sales values.

It was held that it was proper to assume that each sale made by the defendant represented a lost sale unless the defendant could prove otherwise. A proper notional royalty rate was that which a potential licensee who had not yet entered the market would pay. No regard would be had to the fact that such a person could, instead, sell non-infringing lintels. On that basis, the appropriate royalty rate was seven per cent net of tax. Parasitic sales were not allowable as not being a direct and natural consequence of the infringement. Although the defendant's discounted sales made shortly before the House of Lords judgment fell within the second category of acts for which exemplary damages might be awarded (benefit to defendant far outweighed the potential loss) in *Rookes* v *Barnard*[64] it could not be awarded because there was no authority for it[65] Neither was there any authority for compound interest and the plaintiff was entitled only to simple interest calculated at clearing bank base rate plus two per cent.

UNITED KINGDOM COMPETITION LAW

A defendant may be able to set up a contravention of competition law as a form of defence. European Community Competition law has a major impact on the exploitation of intellectual property rights and is considered in the following chapter in some detail. United Kingdom competition law may still be relevant, however, particularly where the activity concerned does not affect trade between Member States of the European Community. It is, therefore, appropriate to consider the implications of United Kingdom law very briefly.[66] The Restrictive Trade Practices Act 1976 requires the registration of agreements between two or more parties containing, *inter alia*, restrictions on competition, prices or as to which customers to deal with. Schedule 3 to the Act contains a number of exemptions, for example licences or assignments in respect of patents if the restrictive terms concern the invention to which the patent relates or articles made by the use of the invention. If there are other restrictions beyond this, the agreement may be registrable. Vertical agreements, such as a normal licence agreement, are not affected by the Act. Generally, an intellectual property licence is not restrictive as it gives rights to a person who would not otherwise have those rights.[67]

The Competition Act 1980 is not unlike Article 85 of the Treaty of Rome and it allows the Director-General of Fair Trading to investigate (and possibly refer to the Monopolies and Mergers Commission) conduct that has the effect of restricting, distorting or preventing competition in connection with the production, supply or acquisition of goods in the United Kingdom. The Office of Fair Trading has identified three forms of anti-competitive practices being: the elimination of competition, restricting or preventing competition and, finally, distorting competition. It is possible for rights under patents to be used to achieve such results. However, the provisions apply only to organizations having a turnover in excess of £5 million per annum and at least a 25 per cent share of the relevant market.

Monopoly situations can be investigated by the Monopolies and Mergers Commission under the Fair Trading Act 1973. Mergers are also covered and clearance of mergers can be sought in advance. Indeed, section 51 of the Patents Act 1977 allows the Comptroller to take action (for example to declare that licences are available as of right) following a report of the Monopolies and Mergers Commission.

64 [1964] AC 1129.

65 *Broome v Cassell & Co.* [1972] AC 1027.

66 See Singleton, E.S. *Introduction to Competition Law* (London: Pitman, 1992).

67 *Re Ravenseft Properties Ltd.'s Application* [1978] QB 52.

CRIMINAL OFFENCES

Infringements of patents associated with selling, distributing and importing products that are subject to a patent are dealt with as civil wrongs and there are no criminal penalties for such dealings although, depending on the circumstances, trade description, forgery or trade mark offences may be committed. However, there are a number of offences provided for by the Patents Act 1977 but these do not directly relate to unauthorized dealing. Section 109 makes it an offence, triable either way, to make, or cause to be made, a false entry on the patents register. This also extends to writings purporting to be copies of such entries and to the use of such writings in evidence. The maximum penalty, on indictment is imprisonment for a term not exceeding two years and/or a fine. On summary conviction, the maximum penalty is a fine not exceeding £1,000.

Two offences deal with unauthorized claims with respect to patents. The first, by section 110, covers false representations that anything disposed of for value is a patented product, for example where the product has the words 'patented in the United Kingdom' or just simply the word 'patent' applied to it and there is no such patent. The second offence, in section 111, covers representations that a patent has been applied for in respect of any article disposed for value when this is not true or if the patent application has been withdrawn or refused. For both offences, a reasonable period of grace is allowed after the expiry or revocation of a patent or the refusal or withdrawal of an application to allow sufficient time to prevent the making or continuance of the representation. An example that would probably be deemed to fall within this period of grace is where an article to which a patent relates is being manufactured and has the word 'patented' embossed on it. Later, the patent is revoked. It would be expected that the person concerned would take immediate steps to prevent continuing application of the word 'patented' to the articles and that he would remove the word from his stock (if this is practicable) but he would not be expected to take action to remove the word from articles that he has sold to retailers. A further defence to these two offences is that the accused person had used due diligence to prevent the commission of the offence. The penalty for an offence under section 110 or 111 is a fine not exceeding level 4 on the standard scale, currently £2,500. These offences are triable summarily only.

Any person who uses on his place of business or on any document the words 'Patent Office' or any other words suggesting a connection between his place of business and the Patent Office, or indeed, that his place of business is the Patent Office, is guilty of an offence and will be liable on summary conviction to a fine not exceeding level 5 on the standard scale, currently £5,000.[68] An appropriate officer of a body corporate who consents or connives in the commission of any offence under the Act by that body corporate is also guilty of the relevant offence.[69] This also applies in the case of offences attributable to the neglect of the officer.[70] Appropriate officers are directors, managers, secretaries or other similar officers or any person purporting to act in such a capacity. Where the affairs of the corporation are managed by its members, then those members may be liable as if they were directors.

Finally, a person who is not a registered patent agent commits an offence by carrying on a business (otherwise than in partnership) under a name or description containing the words 'patent agent' or 'patent attorney' or, in the course of

68 Section 112.

69 Section 113(1).

70 Notice the difference between this provision and the equivalent provision for registered designs, where only consent and connivance bring criminal liability on the shoulders of the officer, mere negligence being insufficient (Registered Designs Act 1949, section 35A). Neither is neglect sufficient for criminal liability of officers of corporations in respect of the offence of fraudulent application of a trade mark under the Trade Marks Act 1938, see section 58A(5).

71 Section 276 of the
Copyright, Designs and
Patents Act 1988.

business, otherwise describes himself or permits himself to be described as a
'patent agent' or 'patent attorney'.[71] There are equivalent restrictions for part-
nerships and corporations. The maximum penalty is a fine not exceeding level 5
on the standard scale.

16

Patents in Europe

INTRODUCTION

More than with any other form of intellectual property right, it is difficult to reconcile patents with the provisions of the Treaty of Rome promoting the free movement of goods, controlling restrictive trade agreements and preventing the abuse of dominant trading positions. However, even here, the general principle is that patent rights are to be recognized and are not to be compromised lightly. For example, one of the block exemptions permitted under Article 85(3) concerns patent licensing agreements which contain certain types of terms.[1] For example, an exclusive licence in respect of all or part of the market does not offend against the provisions of Article 85(1) of the Treaty.[2] Nevertheless, there will be occasions when the European Court of Justice will interfere with the exercise of a patent right and the possibility of this must be borne in mind by proprietors of patents.[3]

Harmonization of patent law is not the issue it might once have been, thanks to the European Patent Convention. All the Member States of the European Community now belong to this Convention and some non-Community countries such as Austria, Switzerland and Sweden are full members of the Convention. It must be noted that the European Patent Office is not a Community organization although, when the Community Patent System comes into force, it will be administered by the European Patent Office.

This chapter is concerned primarily with the impact of the Treaty of Rome on the exercise of patent rights, followed by a discussion of the implications of the proposed Community Patent System. As regards the relevant Treaty provisions, reference should be made to Chapter 9 for a detailed description of them.

PATENTS AND THE TREATY OF ROME (EEC TREATY)

Points of conflict between patent law and the Treaty provisions as identified and set out in Chapter 9 are discussed here in the same overall structure. Reference should be made to that chapter for the basic principles which are, generally, also applicable to patent law. First we will consider the effects of Articles 30 to 36 promoting the free movement of goods, followed by Articles 85, prohibiting restrictive trade practices and, finally, Article 86, preventing the abuse of a dominant trading position.

It should be noted that there is a *de minimis* doctrine that applies in relation to Articles 85 and 86. Article 85 will not apply where the effect on the market is insignificant, see *Völk* v *Vervaecke*.[4] The Commission has also issued notices giving guidance, the latest dating from 1986 and provides quantitative guidance being that the goods or services covered by the agreement under consideration do not represent more than five per cent of the total market for such goods or

1 Commission Regulation (EEC) No. 2349/84 of 23 July 1984 (as amended, see [1993] 4 CMLR 177) on the application of Article 85(3) of the Treaty to certain categories of patent licensing agreements.

2 See Article 1 of the above regulations.

3 In particular, extreme care must be taken with the drafting of patent licences so as not to offend against the provisions of the Treaty of Rome. See Cawthra, B.I. *Patent Licensing in Europe*, (London: Butterworths, 2nd edn., 1986).

4 [1969] ECR 295.

services and the aggregate annual turnover of the participating undertakings is not more than 200 million ECU.[5] The criteria are for guidance only, however, and are not conclusive.

Role of national courts

National courts frequently are faced with cases in which issues under European Community law fall to be determined. For example, a defendant in a patent infringement action in the United Kingdom may plead a 'Euro-defence' based on Articles 30, 85 or 86[6]. Article 177 gives a discretion to national courts to refer questions on Community law to the European Court of Justice. However, by Article 177(3), the House of Lords must refer a matter concerning Community law to the Court of Justice.[7]

Article 177 references can take some time, currently around 18 months. Lord Denning spoke of the delay in *H P Bulmer Ltd.* v *Bollinger* SA[8] as being an important factor to be taken into account by a judge in deciding whether to refer a case to the Court of Justice. He went on to say that English judges should apply the Treaty of Rome themselves in most cases, using the European style of interpretation.

The Commission to the European Community is not opposed to a greater role being taken by national courts. Indeed, during 1993, it issued a notice on the cooperation between national courts and the Commission setting out their respective functions.[9] The main points are:

(a) The Commission has sole power to exempt certain types of agreement from Article 85(1).
(b) The simultaneous application of national competition law is compatible with the application of European Community law provided that it does not affect the effectiveness and uniformity of the latter.
(c) The Commission will concentrate on notifications, complaints and own-initiative proceedings of particular political, economic or legal significance. In the absence of any such criteria, notifications will normally be dealt with by comfort letters[10] and complaints should, as a rule, be dealt with by national courts.
(d) If the national courts can provide sufficient protection for the plaintiff, there will not normally be sufficient European Community interest to justify investigation. Of particular importance is the fact that national courts, in the enforcement of European Community competition law, can grant interim relief and award damages and costs.
(e) Nevertheless, national courts should avoid decisions that conflict with those taken or envisaged by the Commission. If the Commission has not ruled on a particular point, case law of the European Court of Justice and previous decisions of the Commission will provide guidance.

This reinforces John Major's principle of subsidiarity, leaving more decision-making to the Member States although this can result in an uneven application of legal rules which may, in turn, cause conflicts with the Treaty of Rome.

Patent law and the freedom of movement of goods

Article 30 prohibits quantitative restrictions on imports and all measures having equivalent effect between Member States. There is a derogation in Article 36

Notice on Agreements of Minor Importance OJ [1986] C231/2.

For example, Article 30 was pleaded in *The Wellcome Foundation Ltd.* v *Dispcharm Ltd.* [1993] FSR 433 and Article 86 was pleaded in *Chiron Corp.* v *Organon Teknika Ltd. (No. 2)* [1993] FSR 324 and in *Pitney Bowes Inc.* v *Francotyp-Postalia GmbH* [1991] FSR 72.

Note that Article 177 references still go to the European Court of Justice and not to the Court of First Instance.

[1974] 2 All ER 1226.

OJ [1993] C39/6.

See later in this chapter.

allowing prohibitions and restrictions on imports, exports or goods in transit that are justified on the grounds of protecting industrial and commercial property. However, such prohibitions and restrictions must not constitute a means of arbitrary discrimination or a disguised restriction on the free movement of goods. Although the doctrine of exhaustion of rights is clearly a result of Article 30, the prohibition therein applies to other situations also.

The manner in which compulsory licences are granted has conflicted with Article 30. In *EC Commission* v *United Kingdom*[11] it was held that a provision of national law (in this case section 48 of the Patents Act 1977) that equated a position where demand was being substantially met by importation from other Member States with insufficient exploitation of a patent giving rise to the grant of a compulsory licence offended against Article 30. It was not saved by Article 36 which protects the specific subject-matter of industrial property. The definition of what constitutes the specific subject-matter of a patent given in *Centrafarm BV* v *Sterling Drug Inc.*[12] was affirmed.

It is essential that trade between Member States is affected or likely to be affected by the restrictions or measure in question. The grant of a compulsory licence to work a patent subject to a prohibition on importation from outside the European Community did not affect trade between Member States in *Generics (UK) Ltd.* v *Smith, Kline and French Laboratories (UK) Ltd.*[13] The imposition of excessive prices in the United Kingdom did not, *per se*, affect trade between Member States.[14]

The doctrine of exhaustion of rights applies to patents as it does to trade marks, copyright and allied rights. The doctrine is that the owner or proprietor of an intellectual property right who consents to the marketing of a product or article in one Member State cannot use that right to prevent the importation of the product or article into another Member State or its subsequent sale. To this extent, the right is said to be exhausted by the first consensual marketing.[15] This leaves the proprietor of a patent with the dilemma of whether or not to exploit the patent in more than one Member State. Of course, this doctrine does not affect other patent rights, such as the right to prevent the making of the product or the use of the process that is the subject-matter of the patent. It is the right to prevent subsequent dealing and, particularly importation of the product which is touched by Article 30.

The effect of Article 30 on the exercise of a patent right is often brought into question in cases involving parallel importing. For example, in *Centrafarm BV* v *Sterling Drug Inc.*,[16] Sterling Drug were the proprietors of patents in the United Kingdom and The Netherlands in respect of a drug. It had United Kingdom and Dutch subsidiary companies and granted licences to both of them in respect of the drug. Due to government regulations in the United Kingdom, the drug cost approximately half there compared to the cost in The Netherlands. The United Kingdom company exported large quantities of the drug to The Netherlands, undercutting the Dutch company. It was held that this was permissible because the drug had been put on the market with the parent company's consent, thereby exhausting its rights under the patent. The Dutch subsidiary had wanted the parent company to exercise its patent rights to prevent the importation into The Netherlands of the drug made in the United Kingdom. It is difficult for a proprietor of patents in respect of the same invention in different Member States to maintain price differentials between those

11 [1993] FSR 1.

12 [1974] ECR 1147.

13 [1993] 1 CMLR 89. However, the criteria could be applied in such a way as to affect trade between Member States.

14 *Chiron Corp.* v *Organon Teknika Ltd. (No. 2)* [1993] FSR 324.

15 The doctrine was first formulated in *Consten and Grundig* v *Commission* [1966] ECR 299, a case concerning the scope of Article 85(1).

16 [1974] ECR 1147.

Member States. Purely economic considerations affecting the marketing of a product may be distorted and it could mean that a decision is taken not to market a product in a country where a low price would be appropriate or necessary.[17] However, for the exhaustion doctrine to apply, the marketing must have been with the consent of the patentee and in *Parke, Davis & Co.* v *Probel*[18] the exhaustion doctrine did not apply and the proprietor of a Dutch patent was able to prevent its importation into The Netherlands from Italy where the drug had been made without the consent of the patentee.[19]

The existence/exercise distinction is used by the European Court of Justice and it is only the exercise of the right that is controlled. It will be so controlled if it does not relate to the 'specific subject matter' of the right which was defined in the *Centrafarm* v *Sterling Drug* case as being:

> . . . the guarantee that the patentee, to reward the creative effort of the inventor, has the exclusive right to use an invention with a view to manufacturing industrial products and putting them into circulation for the first time, either directly or by the grant of licences to third parties, as well as the right to oppose infringements.

Of course, the proprietor or his licensee might attempt to use contractual methods to prevent the subsequent resale of the products and this, if it affects trade between Member States, will also be controlled. The fact of the matter is that, in the European context, the use of patents (or other intellectual property rights) to divide the market and maintain territorial boundaries is vulnerable to challenge and control. This may be a good thing; for example, where a manufacturer is deliberately operating price differentials for no other reason than to make unreasonable profit margins a parallel importer may soon put an end to this practice. However, there may be other good reasons for price differentials such as legal measures but such justifiable reasons may disappear or be less numerous as the single market is consolidated.

Anti-competitive practices and patents

Article 85 of the Treaty of Rome prohibits anti-competitive agreements and the like which have, as their object or effect, the distortion of competition within the Common Market. Two forms of agreement are relevant to the discussion: those which involve cross-licensing and agreements to pool intellectual property rights. For example, where two companies based in different Member States holding different patents in respect of a similar process (for example, the manufacture of engine castings) agree to share the exploitation of their patents, dividing up the Market between them. Another example might be where the patents pooled are complementary, for example where one relates to the casting of a part for an engine and the other relates to the finishing of the cast part and removal of the casting 'fins'. An example of a case where the Commission has taken action against a patent pooling agreement is *Re Video Cassette Recorders Agreement*.[20] Commission regulations allow block exemption in respect of the licensing of patents under certain circumstances, but this does not apply to pooled patents, joint venture patent agreements and cross-licensing, that is reciprocal patent licences.[21] It is also possible for an organization to apply to the Commission for individual exemption if the activity concerned does not fall within a block exemption. The block exemption is discussed later.

17 See Whish, R. *Competition Law* (London: Butterworths, 3rd edn., 1992), Chapter 19 for a discussion of this case and its implications in addition to a detailed discussion of the effect of United Kingdom and European Community law on anti-competitive practices.

18 [1968] ECR 55.

19 See also *Merck & Co. Inc.* v *Stephar BV* [1981] ECR 2063 where the facts were similar but Merck had consented to the manufacture of the drugs in Italy even though it had not a patent there. The availability of a licence in one Member State may also defeat the right to prevent imports made in another country without consent, *Allen and Hanbury* v *Generics (UK)* [1986] RPC 203.

20 [1978] CMLR 160. Upon leaving the 'pool', any member had to surrender its rights under the agreement but also had to allow the remaining members to continue to use its rights.

21 Commission Regulation (EEC) No. 2349/84 of 23 July 1984 on the application of Article 85(3) of the Treaty to certain categories of patent licensing agreements, article 5. This rule has been subject to some relaxation, Group Exemptions (Amendment) Regulation No.151/93.

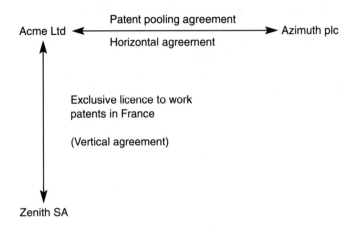

Figure 16.1 Horizontal and vertical agreements

In *Re Alcatel Espace and ANT Nachrichtentechnik*[22] there was an applica- 22 [1991] 4 CMLR 208. tion to the Commission for a negative clearance or individual exemption in respect of an agreement between a French and a German company, both involved in the manufacture of communication equipment, for the purposes of joint research and development, production and marketing activities. The agreement included a term to the effect that the relevant patents owned by each party (or to which each party was entitled) would be communicated to the other party who would be free to work each other's patents on a royalty-free, non-exclusive licence basis. First of all, the Commission held that the agreement offended against Article 85(1) because it would allocate research and development so that only one party would carry this out, that the agreement provided for the procurement by one party of equipment made by the other and that decision-making processes were to be allocated to common committees. The Commission considered all of these would restrict competition. The block exemption relating to research and development agreements was not applicable as the agreement went beyond its scope.[23] However, the Commission granted 23 Commission Regulation (EEC) No. 418/85 of 19 December 1984, as amended. an individual exemption under Article 85(3) for a period of ten years, subject to notification of changes in the agreement. The reasons given by the Commission are instructive:

(a) The planned cooperation would lead to improved technical solutions which would be discovered more rapidly and would contribute to technical progress which would benefit customers.
(b) The agreement only imposed restrictions necessary to the above objective. The fact that the agreement did not prohibit either party from engaging in other activities outside the scope of the agreement was an important factor.
(c) The nature of the market implied that separate marketing was not practicable.
(d) The parties' market share was not high.

Agreements of the type mentioned above are sometimes described as 'horizontal agreements' because they reflect mutuality of restrictions. On the other hand, a vertical agreement is simply one between licensor and licensee, for example where the proprietor of a patent grants an exclusive licence to a manufacturing company permitting that company to make, export and sell the product. Figure 16.1 shows an arrangement where two companies, Acme Ltd. and Azimuth plc have pooled their patents and Acme has subsequently granted an exclusive licence to Zenith SA to make and sell the product in France (the patent pooling agreement allows either party to grant such licences in respect of the pooled patents).

Both of these agreements could be invalid if challenged in as much as they affect trade between Member States. The types of terms that are likely to cause problems are those that attempt to extend the agreement or any part of it beyond the term of the patent, those which tie the licensee to the licensor, for example where the licensee agrees to purchase goods from the licensor that are unconnected with the patent in question, and terms which state that the licensor is not to work the patent in countries other than those included in the licence agreement.[24] It is certainly the case that any licence which includes some sort of exclusive right should be drawn up very carefully and specialist advice should be taken where there is any possibility of exploitation in more than one Member State or where the product is likely to be exported, with or without the consent of the parties to the agreement. However, some terms have been declared to be permissible, for example minimum royalty clauses and terms requiring minimum quantities of the product to be made by the licensee as they are properly within the normal exploitation of the patent and go to the specific subject matter of the patent. Terms that purport to prevent the licensee from challenging the validity of the patent or require him to refrain from competing with the licensor are likely to struck out by the Commission or European Court if they could affect inter-State trade.

A whole list of provisions in a licence agreement in respect of a patent and a trade mark were, according to the Commission in the case of *Velcro SA v Aplix SA*,[25] caught by Article 85(1), including:

(a) exclusivity preventing the licensor exploiting the patents and trade mark in the licensed territory or granting further licences there when the basic patents expired;
(b) an export ban preventing the licensee selling outside the licensed territory;
(c) the automatic extension of certain terms on the expiry of basic patents on the basis of improvement patents;
(d) an obligation to obtain manufacturing equipment exclusively from a named manufacturer;
(e) an obligation not to use specialized manufacturing machinery outside the licensed territory;
(f) an obligation on the parties not to compete with each other;
(g) an obligation to allow the licensor to acquire title to improvement patents in other Member States for improvements discovered by the licensee;
(h) a provision for the unilateral extension of the patent licence.

It cannot be disputed that the agreement in this case contained a great many provisions that were capable of affecting trade between Member States (the above list is not complete – there were other reasons why the agreement was caught by Article 85(1)). However, it is natural for commercial organizations to have their own interests at heart when drawing up licensing agreements and too much interference by the European Court can be criticized as being likely to

24 The case of *AIOP v Beyrard* [1976] 1 CMLR D14 concerned a provision which purported to allow the unilateral extension of the licence by the licensor. See also, *Kai Ottung v Klee & Weilbach* [1990] 4 CMLR 915, about an obligation to pay royalties after the expiry of a patent. The European Court considered that whether an agreement affected inter-State trade and thus offended against Article 85(1) was a matter for a national court to decide from the economic and legal context in which the agreement was concluded.

25 [1989] 4 CMLR 157.

restrict trade, the flow of information and collaboration by destroying the commercial viability of licences and other agreements. A comparison of the *Velcro* and *Alcatel Espace* cases indicates that the 'look and feel' of an agreement is very important: whether it prohibits certain activities or merely discourages them. For example, a collateral term insisting equipment is obtained only from the other party will be struck down but a term stating that equipment should or may be obtained from the other party may survive an attack based on Article 85(1). Another factor is that, in some cases, the complaint has not come from a third party whose trade has been affected adversely by the operation of the agreement but from one of the parties to the agreement itself, who is now trying to free himself of terms he had earlier expressly agreed to.

Exemption from Article 85(1)

The fact that exemption from Article 85(1) is available or can be obtained has already been mentioned. The effects of Article 85(3) which allows derogations from Article 85(1) will now be looked at in more detail. Article 85(3) permits the provisions of Article 85(1) to be declared inapplicable in the case of agreements that contribute to the improvement of the production or distribution of goods or to promoting technical or economic progress. Consumers must be allowed a fair share of the resulting benefit and such derogation from the force of Article 85(1) does not apply to agreements, decisions or concerted practices that:

(a) impose on the undertakings concerned restrictions which are not indispensable to the attainment of the above objectives;
(b) afford such undertakings the possibility of eliminating competition in respect of a substantial part of the products in question.

On the basis of Article 85(3), the Commission has issued regulations exempting certain patent licensing agreements from the application of Article 85(1), Commission Patent Licensing Regulation 1984.[26] There are other regulations affecting research and development, know-how licensing and franchise agreements. The patent licensing regulations contain three categories of obligations in licences to which only two undertakings are party. Some obligations are declared to be outside Article 85(1) – these are the *formal exemptions*. Others are not caught by Article 85(1) providing that they are generally not restrictive of competition – this list of obligations is known as the *white list*. Finally, there is the *black list* – obligations that are not exempted from the rigours of Article 85(1).

The block exemption applies to patent licences between two parties that contain one or more obligations that are mainly of a territorial nature. They are:

- an obligation of the licensor not to grant licences to others to exploit the inventions in the licensed territory as long as the licensed patent remains in force or to exploit it himself in such circumstances;
- an obligation on the licensee not to exploit in territories reserved for the licensor or other licensees as long as the patented product is protected by parallel patents in those territories;
- an obligation on the licensee not to pursue an active policy of putting the licensed product on the market in territories reserved for other licensees (for

26 Commission Regulation No. 2349/84 OJ [1984] L219/16, amended 1992, see [1993] 4 CMLR 177.

example, by specific advertising or opening a depot in those territories) providing the product is protected by parallel patents in those territories;

- an obligation not to export to territories reserved for other licensees for five years providing the product is protected by parallel patents in those territories (this is stronger than the previous obligation which requires an active policy – hence the limit of five years);
- an obligation on the licensee to use only the licensor's trade mark or get up, providing licensee can identify himself as manufacturer of licensed product.

The above exemption applies only in so far as the patent remains in force. If the patent expires in one or more Member States or a patent has not been acquired in the Member State in question, then the obligation will be subject to the full application of Article 85(1).

The block exemption will still apply if the agreement contains one or more of the following obligations providing that they are generally not restrictive of competition, the *white list*:

27 Such an obligation could be caught by section 44 of the Patents Act 1977 and provide a complete defence to an infringer, see the previous chapter.

- procurement of goods or services from licensor or as directed by licensor if necessary for the technically satisfactory exploitation of the invention[27];
- payment of a minimum royalty or manufacture of a minimum quantity;
- restriction of licensee's exploitation to one or more technical fields of application covered by the licensed patent;
- licensee not to exploit beyond termination of agreement (if patent still in force);
- licensee not to grant sublicences or to assign the licence;
- the marking of product with indication of patentee's name, licensed patent or licence agreement;
- licensee not to divulge know-how (can continue after expiry of agreement);
- to inform licensor of infringements, to take legal action and to assist in such legal action (but without prejudice to licensee's right to challenge the validity of the licensed patent);
- to observe specifications to achieve minimum quality;
- parties to communicate to each other experiences gained exploiting the invention and to grant to each other *non-exclusive licences* in respect of improvement patents;
- licensor to grant licensee more favourable terms than might be the case in subsequent licences.

In can be seen that, in most cases, these exemptions should cause no real difficulties and they can be seen as part of the normal exploitation of the patent. They acknowledge the fact that a patent licence cannot be restrictive, *per se*, because it gives rights that the licensee would not otherwise have. The black list terms, those where the block exemption cannot apply, include no-challenge terms (the licensee is not permitted to challenge the validity of the patent), arrangements for automatic extensions of the licence beyond the expiry of the

28 By section 45 of the Patents Act 1977, the licensee can give three months' notice to determine the licence after the patent has expired.

licensed patent,[28] restrictions on competition in respect of research and development, manufacture, use or sales except as provided for in the formal and white list exemptions, payment of royalties with respect to public domain know-how, quantitative restrictions, restrictions on the determination of prices, restrictions on classes of customers, obligations requiring the licensee to *assign rights* in improvements or new applications and where the licensee is induced, at the time of the agreement, to enter into collateral agreements that he does not want unless necessary for the exploitation of the licensed invention.

It is not unusual for a licensee (or the licensor himself) to make an invention that is ancillary to or supplements the invention that is the subject of the licence agreement. The licensor will be keen to obtain a right to make use of the improvement and the licence agreement may contain terms granting rights in any new patentable inventions or confidential know-how. However, it can be seen that whilst non-exclusive licences may be acceptable, an assignment of the new rights will not be. On the same basis, an exclusive licence will not generally be acceptable, unless there is some very good reason for it.

There is also provision for agreements that fall outside the block exemption to be individually exempted following notification to the Commission. The Commission may also give a negative clearance (or comfort letter). This means that the Commission can see no reason to intervene in the light of information available to the Commission at the time. An individual exemption under Article 85(3) is granted for a specific period of time which may be extended, an example being the *Re Alcatel Espace* case where an individual exemption was granted for 10 years.[29] The advantage of an Article 85(3) exemption over a negative clearance is that the former carries an immunity against fines imposed by the Commission whilst the latter does not.

29 [1991] 4 CMLR 208.

Abuse of a dominant trading position

The exploitation of a patent may offend Article 86 and the discussion in Chapter 9 on the refusal to grant licences in respect of copyright materials applies equally to patents. *In Chiron Corp. v Organon Teknika Ltd. (No. 2)*[30] Aldous J restated that a refusal to grant a licence to work an intellectual property right could not, *per se*, be an abuse of a dominant position. Therefore, refusal to grant a licence except on unfair or unreasonable terms was also not an abuse.[31]

The basic ingredients for an infringement of Article 86 were laid down in *Parke, Davis & Co. v Probel*[32] as:

(a) the existence of a dominant position;
(b) an improper exploitation of it; and
(c) the possibility that, as a result, trade between Member States may be affected.

Confirming that being in a dominant position is not sufficient by itself to bring Article 86 into play; something further is needed. An important factor indicating dominance is the ownership of intellectual property rights. In particular, ownership of a patent might constitute a considerable barrier to entry into the relevant market by third parties.

In *Tetra Pak Rausing SA v EC Commission*,[33] Tetra Pak, the world leaders in cartons and filling machines for liquid foods, especially aseptic packaging for UHT milk, through the acquisition of another company, obtained the exclusivity of a patent licence for an alternative process of sterilization.[34] Tetra Pak argued that Article 86 was inapplicable because a group exemption applied to the licence.[35] The European Court considered the implications of Article 86 and the relationship between Articles 85(1) and 86 and the effect of an exemption

30 [1993] FSR 324.

31 Following Hoffman J in *Pitney Bowes Inc. v Francotyp-Postalia GmbH* [1991] FSR 72 who, in turn, followed the European Court of Justice in *Volvo AB v Erik Veng (UK) Ltd.* [1989] 4 CMLR 122.

32 [1968] FSR 393.

33 [1991] 4 CMLR 334.

34 Tetra Pak had 92% of the European Community market in aseptic filling machines and 89% of the market for cartons.

35 Under Commission Regulations (EEC) No.2349/84 of 23 July 1984 (exemption from Article 85(1)).

under Article 85(3) on the operation of Article 86. It was held that Articles 85 and 86 were complementary in as much as they have a common objective in accordance with Article 3(f) – the institution of a system ensuring that competition in the common market is not distorted – but the Articles constitute two independent provisions addressing different situations. Therefore, an exemption under Article 85(3) cannot be such as to render Article 86 inapplicable. The fact that a company in a dominant position becomes more dominant through the acquisition of a patent licence does not, *per se,* constitute an abuse within Article 86. Account must be taken of the circumstances surrounding the acquisition, such as the effect on competition within the relevant market. The European Court upheld the Commission's finding that there had been an abuse of a dominant position. In a subsequent case, *Elopak Italia Srl* v *Tetra Pak (No. 2)*[36] it was held that Tetra Pak had been pursuing a policy of eliminating competition and the company was fined 75 million ECU.

A tying clause is one that requires a buyer of goods or licensee under a patent to obtain other goods or services or raw materials from the seller or licensor. For example, a company selling patented toothbrushes to retail outlets might insist that the company's toothpaste is also purchased by the outlets. The Patents Act 1977 can make such tying clauses void under certain circumstances and the existence of contracts or licenses containing them could provide a complete defence to an infringement action.[37] European Community law can also control such tying clauses if they conflict with Article 86. For example, in *Eurofix-Bauco* v *Hilti AG*[38], users of Hilti nail-guns used to fire nails into walls, were required to buy nails from Hilti when they bought cartridges for the guns. Other manufacturers made suitable nails. Hilti was fined 6 million ECU for this infraction of Article 86. The tying of the purchase of sailboards and rigs was also held to be an abuse of a dominant position in *Windsurfing International Inc.* v *EC Commission.*[39] Compulsory licences may not be liked by proprietors of patents but, if they are uncooperative in settling terms, that might be viewed as an abuse under Article 86 if the purpose is to delay the evil day when the licence is available. Hilti were held to have needlessly protracted proceedings for the grant of a licence of right in *Hilti AG* v *EC Commission.*[40] The Company had demanded a royalty of six times that finally adopted by the Comptroller of Patents. The patent had originally been granted under the Patents Act 1949 and an additional four years were allowed subject to licences being available as of right.[41]

THE COMMUNITY PATENT

The European Patent Convention has operated very successfully for a number of years and gives a patent that takes effect in those Member States specified by the proprietor. This Convention does not, however, provide a unitary European Community-wide patent system where a single grant automatically takes effect throughout the Community. The European Patent Convention can be seen as an important stepping stone towards the Community-wide patent and it is the intention of the European Community that this goal be achieved in the not too distant future. Plans have been around for some 18 years now and the Convention for a European Patent for the Common Market dates from 1975.[42] The

36 [1992] 4 CMLR 551.

37 Section 44.

38 OJ [1988] L 65/9.

39 [1986] ECR 611.

40 [1992] 4 CMLR 16.

41 Para. 4, Schedule 1 to the Patents Act 1977.

42 OJ [1976] L17/1. One problem that will have to be faced is that there are differences in membership of the European Community and the European Patent Convention. It is possible that the Community-wide patent might extend beyond the boundaries of the European Community. The reader must be careful to distinguish between the European Patent Convention, currently in operation, and the Community Patent Convention, to be implemented in the future.

latest version dates from 1989 and contains the procedures for bringing the patent system into operation.[43] It is obvious that the Community-wide patent will become popular once it is in place. The growth of business at the European Patent Office since its establishment gives a taste of what is to come.[44] The Community patent will grant a patent that has effect throughout the Community and, in the context of the breaking down of trade barriers and the single market, is of the utmost importance. The Community Patent Convention takes account of the developments in European Community law relating to the freedom of movement of goods and anti-competitive practices. For example, it expressly deals with the doctrine of exhaustion of rights. The Patents Act 1977 explicitly takes account of the Community Patent Convention giving direct legal effect to the Convention and decisions and cases under it.[45] By the 1989 Agreement (Article 10), before it can come into force, the Agreement must be ratified by all twelve signatory States. It will then become a reality three months after the last State ratifies.

The Community Patent will not replace national patents or the European Patent. All three systems will coexist. The pricing structures of the systems are likely to be such that it will not be economical to apply for anything other than a national patent if it is intended to exploit the invention in one country only. Alternatively, a European patent designating three or more Member States might be acceptable in some cases. However, for proprietors wishing to obtain full protection throughout the Community, the Community patent will be the most attractive.

Developments in Eastern Europe have important implications for the Community Patent and the European Patent. If more countries join the European Community, the geographical reach of the two Conventions may change. This could take some time, as patent law in countries wishing to join either Convention must be compatible with that laid down in the appropriate Convention. Other countries now appear to be keen to join the European Community and, in the case of Austria, there should be no problem as Austria has already ratified the European Patent Convention. The fact that European Patent Convention countries include some non-European Community countries, brings into question the availability of the Community Patent to such countries. The 1989 agreement allows non-European Community countries to join the Community Patent Convention by invitation on the basis of a special agreement. However, the administration of the Community Patent may become a problem, with different arrangements being established for different countries, perhaps with several grades of membership. Already, more countries wish to join the European Patent Convention, for example Monaco, Cyprus and Finland, and closer relations are being forged between the European Patent Office and patent authorities in the Czech Republic, Poland and other European countries.

43 Community Patent Agreement (89/695/EEC), 15 December 1989, OJ [1989] L401/1.

44 The Community-wide patent will also be administered by the European Patent Office.

45 Patents Act 1977, sections 86 and 87.

Part Five

DESIGN LAW

17

What is a design?

There are two forms of designs recognized by the law. One is the registered design provided for by the Registered Designs Act 1949, as amended, and the other is the design right provided for, along principles broadly analogous to copyright law, by Part III of the Copyright, Designs and Patents Act 1988.[1] A design is aspects of or features applied to an article, it is not the article itself and it should be noted that, in intellectual property law, the word 'design' has a restricted meaning. In normal usage the word 'design' can be taken to mean a plan or a scheme, which may be written or drawn, showing how something is to be constructed or how the elements of an item or article are arranged. Alternatively, a design may be a decorative pattern. In legal terms, a design is defined by reference to the provisions applicable to either the registered design or the design right, as appropriate.

Designs may be for functional articles, such as a can opener, a tool box, a container for frozen food or an exhaust pipe for a car. Articles which are functional in nature are generally, but not exclusively, in the province of the design right.[2] Alternatively, a design may relate to decorative articles or decorative features such as an attractive table lamp, an item of mass-produced furniture or a pattern applied to porcelain or pottery. Visually attractive designs which are intended to appeal to the eye, fall within the scope of registered designs. However, as will be seen, there is considerable overlap between the two rights. Whilst a purely functional object cannot be registered as a design (eye-appeal being a fundamental requirement), many registered designs also meet the requirements for the design right.

Design law is far from straightforward because of the overlap between the rights which apply and the extent of this overlap is not altogether clear. The complexity of design law is compounded by the transitional provisions that will apply for some years to come. In a few cases a design may be patentable if, for example, it relates to a function which has novelty, contains an inventive step, has industrial application and is not otherwise excluded from the grant of a patent. Usually, however, one of these requirements will be lacking and protection must be sought through registration of the design or by way of the design right, as appropriate. Occasionally, copyright may provide protection. This part of the book concentrates on registered designs and the design right. Copyright issues also will be discussed where they affect designs. If a design for an article meets the stringent requirements for patentability, it is obviously more fitting that a patent is obtained rather than relying solely on design law and, in some cases, an article may be protected by both patent and design law.

The law of designs has a reasonably long history dating back to the latter part of the eighteenth century and the Design Registry originated in the early part of the nineteenth century.[3] With the development of artistic copyright came problems of duplication of rights and the Copyright Act 1911, followed

1 Hereinafter referred to as the 'design right'.

2 Many functional articles also have eye-appeal. They have been so designed to make them more attractive to potential purchasers.

3 For a comprehensive description of the recent history of the law relating to designs, see Dworkin, G. & Taylor, R.D. *Blackstone's Guide to the Copyright, Designs and Patents Act 1988* (London: Blackstone, 1989) at pp.140–145.

by the Copyright Act 1956, attempted to remove the overlap between a regis-trable design and artistic copyright. This was modified by the Design Copyright Act 1968 which permitted dual protection to a design both as a registered design and under artistic copyright but reduced the term of copyright to 15 years.[4] If this was not bad enough, following the distinction between registrable and unregistrable designs highlighted in *Dorling v Honnor Marine Ltd.*,[5] a regrettable state of affairs arose.

The plaintiff in *Dorling v Honnor Marine* designed a sailing dinghy and granted a licence to the second defendant to build dinghies to the design and to make kits of parts on his behalf, all in accordance with the plaintiff's drawings. The relationship between the plaintiff and the second defendant broke down. Subsequently, the second defendant formed a limited company, the first defen-dant, to which he purported to assign his licence to build the dinghies. The design of the dinghy as a whole was registrable under the Registered Designs Act 1949 but it had not been registered. The individual parts, being purely functional, were not registrable.[6] By making a three-dimensional representation of the drawings in the form of parts for a boat, the defendants had infringed the copyright in the drawings. A defence based on section 10 of the Copyright Act 1956, which removed copyright protection from designs registrable under the Registered Designs Act 1949, failed because the parts, as opposed to the dinghy as an entirety, were not registrable. Thus, the outcome of the case was that if a design was aesthetic it was, subject to some other requirements, registrable under the Registered Designs Act 1949 and could be protected for 15 years.[7] If the design was purely functional it was not registrable but could attract artistic copyright through its drawings which would last for the remainder of the life of the author plus 50 years. Functional designs appeared to be far better protected than aes-thetic designs (not being works of copyright), an extremely anomalous situation.

The above unsatisfactory position can partly explain the House of Lords decision in *British Leyland Motor Corp. Ltd. v Armstrong Patents Co. Ltd.*,[8] concerning the reverse engineering of exhaust pipes which infringed indirectly the copyright in the drawings of the exhaust pipes. Their Lordships took the opportunity to partly redress the apparent imbalance between the protection for articles with eye-appeal and purely functional articles by using the principle of non-derogation from grant. Even if a design was registrable there was little incentive for registration as copyright in the drawings could still be enjoyed for 15 years, free of charge. In 1988, the last full year before the main provisions of the Copyright, Designs and Patents Act 1988 came into force, there were only 8,748 applications for registered designs received by the Design Registry.[9]

The law of designs has been radically affected by the Copyright, Designs and Patents Act 1988. It has not, however, been simplified although it is arguably more rational. The law prior to the coming into force of this Act will still be rel-evant for designs which where created or recorded before 1 August 1989. How-ever, it must be stressed that there was no design right before this date, it being an invention of the 1988 Act. Designs that were created or recorded before 1 August 1989 and which were not registrable under the Registered Designs Act 1949 continue to rely on copyright for protection. The law of registered designs remains but with some changes. Because of the complexity of this area of law, the remainder of this chapter is devoted to looking at and comparing the basic elements and definitions of registered designs and the design right, with

4 The Design Copyright Act 1968 and the Copyright Act 1956 were repealed in their entirety by the Copyright, Designs and Patents Act 1988.

5 [1965] Ch 1.

6 The Registered Designs Act 1949 requires that a registered design has eye-appeal.

7 This has now been extended to 25 years.

8 [1986] 2 WLR 400.

9 This compares with 30,471 patent applications received by the Patent Office in 1988 and 38,006 trade and service mark applications received by the Trade Marks Registry in the same year. *Patents, Designs and Trade Marks 1990*, 108th Annual Report of the Comptroller-General of Patents, Designs and Trade Marks (London: HMSO, 1990).

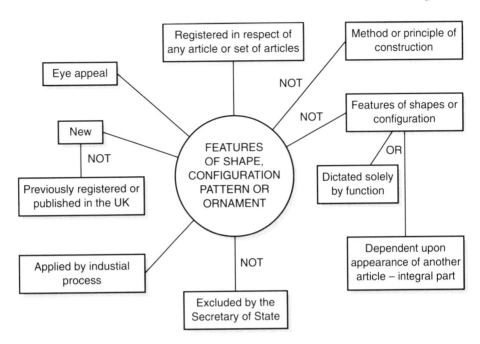

Figure 17.1 Registered designs

consideration of artistic copyright where appropriate. First, a brief description of the legal nature of the registered designs and design right is called for.

REGISTERED DESIGNS

The distinguishing feature for registered designs is that of eye-appeal. Although eye-appeal does not automatically bar a design from the design right, it is a definite requirement for a registered design. Whereas the design right applies mainly, but not exclusively, to functional designs, the law of registered designs applies to aesthetic articles. The word 'aesthetic' is chosen carefully to distinguish registered designs from artistic works of copyright. One problem that will be discussed later is ascertaining the boundaries of the description 'aesthetic' and, in particular, the relationship between 'artistic' and 'aesthetic'. One thing to notice at the outset is that although eye-appeal is a fundamental requirement for a design to be registered, it does not mean that the article to which the design applies cannot also be functional. An example is provided by telephone handsets or food containers which are designed to be attractive and yet are essentially functional articles. The Registered Designs Act 1949 does not require that aesthetic considerations are vital only that they are *material*.

For the purposes of the Registered Designs Act 1949, a 'design' means, by section 1(1):

> . . . features of shape, configuration, pattern or ornament applied to any article by an industrial process, being features which in the finished article appeal to and are judged by the eye . . .

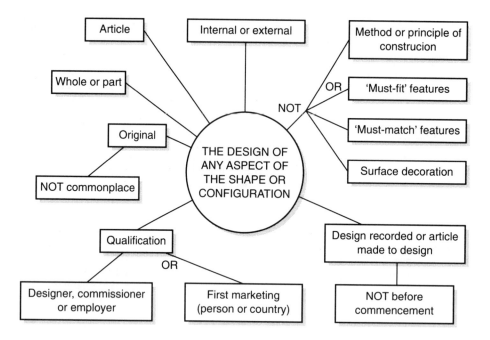

Figure 17.2 The design right

The design, to be registrable, must be 'new' and this means that it has not previously been registered or published in the United Kingdom prior to the date of application for registration. The creator of a registered design is, as with copyright, known as its author. Unlike copyright and the design right, there are no qualification requirements but there are some exceptions which are, in part, similar to those for the design right.[10] Figure 17.1 shows a representation of the right, the conditions and the exceptions (p.335).

10 Some of the exceptions are identically worded for both rights.

DESIGN RIGHT

A design right is declared by section 213(1) of the Copyright, Designs and Patents Act 1988 to be a property right which subsists in an original design. Section 213(2) defines a 'design' as 'the design of any aspect of the shape or configuration (whether internal or external) of the whole or part of an article'. The remainder of section 213 describes the requirements for a design. There are several similarities between the design right and copyright and, like copyright, the design right is automatic and does not depend on registration but requires some form of tangible expression. There are qualification requirements and the design must be 'original' for the right to subsist. Needless to say there are differences. A design is not original if it is commonplace in the design field in question at the time of its creation. This is probably a more stringent test than is the case with copyright. Figure 17.2 shows, in the form of a semantic net, the basic requirements for the design right.

Note that the design right applies to any aspect of the shape or configuration of the whole or part of an article, it does not apply to the article itself. Basically, for the design right to apply to a shape or configuration, it must be original (not commonplace) and it must be in some tangible form, that is recorded in a design document (alternatively, an article must have been made to the design) and the qualification requirements must be satisfied. The exceptions are similar to, but not identical with, those that apply to registered designs and can be justified on the basis that they prevent the right from becoming too strong or from working to the disadvantage of consumers requiring spare parts. A further exception is surface decoration which lies firmly within the scope of registered designs. The qualification requirements may be satisfied in one of three ways, first by reference to the designer[11] or, if the design is created under a commission or in the course of employment, by reference to the commissioner or employer and, finally, by reference to the person by whom and country in which articles made to the design are first marketed.

The design right is a new departure for intellectual property law in the United Kingdom and there was no equivalent right before the 1988 Act although certain features of shape and configuration may have had copyright protection. For example, a drawing of an article of a particular shape or configuration would have been an artistic work for copyright purposes. The design right provisions are not, however, retrospective and anything which would have qualified and which was recorded in a design document, or if an article had been to the design, before the commencement of the design right provisions[12] is excluded. That does not prevent the design right applying to a design that was conceived before 1 August 1989 but which was not recorded until after that date providing no articles were made to the design in the meantime.

REGISTERED DESIGNS AND THE DESIGN RIGHT

Design right is often described as applying to functional designs. However, that is not necessarily the sole domain of the design right. There is no reason why a new and attractive design cannot be subject to the design right if it relates to the shape or configuration of some article even though it would be expected that it should be registered as a design. An example might be a design for a drinking tankard which is a new shape or has a new shape of handle, made by an industrial process and which, its maker hopes, people will buy for the visual attractiveness of its shape. This should qualify for both rights. One advantage of seeking registration under the Registered Designs Act 1949 is that the period of protection is potentially longer.[13] However, the overlap between the design right and registered designs is not complete. The design right cannot apply to surface decoration but this is clearly within the scope of registered designs. Because registered designs have a requirement of eye-appeal, features of shape or configuration which are internal cannot be registered as designs but can be subject to the design right.[14] Nevertheless, in many cases a design will be registrable under the Registered Designs Act 1949 and yet still be subject to the design right. There are no provisions for abrogating one of these rights in favour of the other. Indeed, the Copyright, Designs and Patents Act 1988 explicitly recognizes the dual existence of the rights, section 224 raising a presumption that an assignment of the registered design automatically carries with it an assignment of the design right where the proprietor of the registered design and the owner of the design right are one and the same person.[15]

11 The term 'designer' is used here rather than 'author'; basically the two terms are equivalent.

12 1 August 1989.

13 A maximum of 25 years' protection is available for a registered design whereas the maximum duration of the design right is 15 years, or 10 years during which it is exploited commercially.

14 If the outer surface of the article is transparent and the feature can be seen, the design may be registrable after all.

15 There is a reciprocal presumption in section 19(3B) of the Registered Designs Act 1949 and section 19(3A) of that Act which requires that the registration of an interest under a registered design will not be made unless the registrar is satisfied that the person entitled to the interest is also entitled to the corresponding interest in the design right, if it subsists.

One final point is that the requirement for eye-appeal for registration of a design appears to have been strengthened. Now aesthetic considerations must be taken into account to a material extent by person acquiring or using articles to which the design has been applied. It remains to be seen what effect this has on applications for registration. Certainly, some prior registrations would be suspect if this requirement were to be applied to them.

DESIGN RIGHT AND COPYRIGHT

Design law may also overlap with copyright protection. Between 1969 and 1 August 1989, an extremely powerful and wide-ranging form of protection for functional designs was to have a drawing from which the article was made. If a person copied the article, he would infringe the copyright in the drawing even though he had never seen it, no matter how mundane the article was.[16] The only provisos were that the drawing should meet the originality requirements for copyright, not an onerous standard by any means, and a person who was not an expert in that field could recognize the drawing from the article. Even the mass-produced and, in the judges' opinions, vulgar furniture in *George Hensher Ltd.* v *Restawhile Upholstery (Lancs.) Ltd.*[17] would have been protected by copyright, indirectly, had some drawings been made which bore a two-dimensional resemblance to the furniture. Additionally, a design may overlap with other forms of copyright works such as sculptures and works of artistic craftsmanship. The design may be recorded in a document in which copyright subsists as a literary work, including computer data, or the design document may be a photograph.

To reduce this overlap, the Copyright, Designs and Patents Act 1988 contains two provisions, sections 236 and 51(1) respectively. The first is that where a work consisting of or including a design is itself protected by copyright, the design right is suppressed in favour of the copyright.[18] If what is done is an infringement of the copyright in the work, then an action lies under copyright law and not for infringement of the design right. That is, if the articles made to the design are themselves works of copyright, they will be protected by copyright rather than by the design right. This could be so if the articles are works of artistic craftsmanship, for example a hand-made wooden toy or an item of jewellery.[19] The second exception applies to cancel out the possibility of indirect copyright infringement by copying the article embodying the design. If an article is made to the design or a copy of an article made to the design is made, this does not infringe the copyright in a design document or model recording or embodying the design.[20] A design document is any record of the design and includes drawings, written descriptions, photographs and computer data.[21] Therefore, if the design is recorded in a drawing and a person makes an article using that drawing, he does not infringe the copyright in the drawing although he does, of course, infringe the design right. However, if the person makes a photocopy of the drawing instead, then the copyright in the drawing will be infringed in that instance but any subsequent making of articles from the copy of the drawing will infringe design right only.

As another example, consider a design recorded as computer data, for example as a series of numbers describing the three-dimensional co-ordinates of the

16 For example, see *L B (Plastics) Ltd.* v *Swish Products Ltd.* [1979] RPC 551 and, of course, *British Leyland Motor Corp. Ltd.* v *Armstrong Patents Co. Ltd.* [1986] 2 WLR 400.

17 [1976] AC 64.

18 Section 236.

19 Section 52 of the Copyright, Designs and Patents Act 1988 might apply, reducing the term of copyright to 25 years if the articles are not hand-made or more than 50 are made, see Copyright (Industrial Processes and Excluded Articles) (No. 2) Order 1989, SI 1989 No. 1070. Such a design could also be registrable.

20 Section 51 of the Copyright, Designs and Patents Act 1988.

21 Section 263.

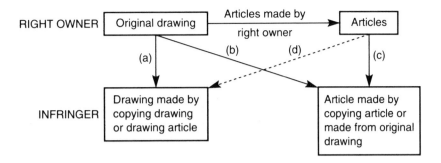

Figure 17.3 Design right and copyright

design. Without permission, a person copies the computer data onto a magnetic disk and takes the copy away. Later, he prints out the computer data and uses the information to make articles or he may, for example, enter the computer data into a computer-controlled lathe so that it can be used to make articles to the design. There are two infringements here. First, the copyright in the computer data (probably as a literary work, being a table or compilation) has been infringed by making a copy of it. This infringement is not suppressed by the design right. Secondly, by making articles, the design right is infringed. In this case, the copyright in the computer data is not infringed because it is not an infringement of a literary work to make three-dimensional work of it,[22] but even if the copyright had been infringed, say in the case of a drawing, section 51 of the Copyright, Designs and Patents Act 1988 would operate to suppress that copyright. The effect of section 51 can be seen diagrammatically in Figure 17.3.

In Figure 17.3, a design is recorded in a drawing. Articles have been made to the design. It is assumed that copyright does not subsist in the articles *per se*, for example as works of artistic craftsmanship. A person obtains a drawing and one original article and does one of the following things without the permission of the rights owner:

(a) copies the drawing (directly),
(b) makes articles from the drawings,
(c) makes articles from the original article,
(d) makes a drawing from the original article.

By doing act (a) the person will infringe the copyright in the drawing. Both acts (b) and (c) will infringe the design right and act (d) may infringe the copyright or the design right (this is discussed below).

An exercise in mental gymnastics can be had by considering the interaction between sections 51(1), 226(1)(b) and 236 of the Copyright, Designs and Patents Act 1988. Add to this the question: does making a copy of an article made to a design (as stated in section 51(1)) include making a copy in two dimensions? If the answer to this question is in the affirmative, there is only an action for infringement of design right based on section 226(1)(b) which gives the design right owner the exclusive right to make a design document for the purposes of enabling articles to be made to the design. However, if the answer

22 *Brigid Foley Ltd. v Ellot* [1982] RPC 433.

to the question is 'no', there is potentially an infringement of copyright and the design right because section 51(1) fails to operate and by section 236 an action will lie in copyright only under section 17 (copying). One speculative consideration is that if section 51(1) does apply to a two-dimensional representation of a design, for example a drawing, and the drawing is copied for purposes other than making articles to the design, for example to study the technology used in the manufacture of the articles, then copying the drawing may escape both copyright and design right liability. Section 51(1) removes copyright protection from the drawing and section 226(1) does not extend to making a design document for other purposes.[23]

23 Note that copying in terms of both copyright and the design right may be indirect.

ARTISTIC, AESTHETIC OR FUNCTIONAL

Contemplating the Copyright, Designs and Patents Act 1988 and the Registered Designs Act 1949 might lead one to think that a design (in a wide sense) can be classified as being artistic, aesthetic or functional. This classification, as sensible as it might at first sight appear, is not without difficulties. It is tempting to try to place an article into one of these categories because of the rational, but false, assumption that each category directly relates to a particular legal right. For example, an article that is artistic should be protected by copyright, an article that has aesthetic qualities should be registered as a design and a functional article should fall under the wing of the design right. If only things were that simple. We have already seen that there is an overlap between these various rights; this is recognized statutorily by sections 51(1), 224 and 236 of the Copyright, Designs and Patents Act 1988 and sections 19(3A) and 19(3B) of the Registered Designs Act 1949. We have also seen how the issue of dual concurrent protection is dealt with.

Table 17.1 Everyday and legal meaning of words

Word	Everyday meaning	Legal meaning
Artistic	Pertaining to art or artists. having some special quality, the result of imaginative skill	Depends on type of works, e.g. graphic work, photograph, sculpture or collage – no artistic quality required at all. Other works, e.g. works of artistic craftsmanship, some indefinable quality required CDPA 1988, s.4 [24]
Aesthetic	Attractive, artistic, some sense of beauty which appeals to the eye. Often taken to mean something less than artistic. Something made by a craftsman.	Features of shape, configuration, pattern or ornament which appeal to and are judged by the eye. RDA 1949, s.1.
Functional	Having a practical use irrespective of visual appearance	Not defined even indirectly. The design right applies to any aspect of the shape or configuration of an article CDPA 1988, s.213

CDPA 1988 – Copyright, Designs and Patents Act 1988
RDA 1949 – Registered Designs Act 1949

24 See *George Hensher Ltd. v Restawhile Upholstery (Lancs.) Ltd.* [1976] AC 64 and *Merlet v Mothercare plc* [1986] RPC 115.

There are two difficulties which make a one-for-one correlation between the classification of a work and the form of legal protection troublesome. The first has to do with the fact that the legal meaning of words such as artistic, aesthetic and functional does not necessarily equate with their everyday meaning as Table 17.1 indicates.

The word artistic can thus have an extensive legal meaning, much wider than its normal sense and can apply to something that could be described as utilitarian, for example an engineering drawing which represents an article that is purely functional. The second problem stems from the fact that there is an overlap even in the everyday meaning of these words and the way in which certain articles may be described. For example, a piece of art deco pottery, such as that designed by Clarice Cliff, can certainly be said to be aesthetic, some might argue that it is artistic. But, whether it be a teapot or a milk jug, it also has a functional purpose. The same applies to many items which can be described as both functional and aesthetic for, being functional, an item does not cease to be aesthetic – the two descriptions are not mutually exclusive. Many people see beauty in articles which have been designed purely and intrinsically for their functional character. A good example is the steam engine enthusiast. An train engine like the 'Mallard' was designed primarily for functionality, its streamlined appearance being the result of a desire to reduce wind resistance, yet few would deny that it has beauty.[25]

25 However, in *Dorling* v *Honnor Marine Ltd.* [1965] Ch 1, Danckwerts L J doubted whether the shape of a boat fell within the meaning of a registered design, it being necessarily functional in his opinion.

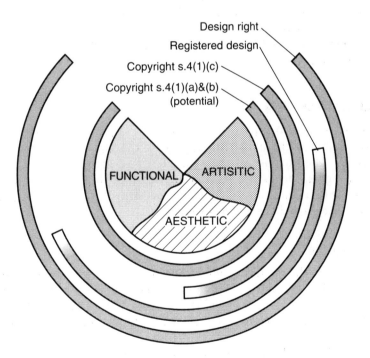

Figure 17.4 Potential scope of rights in designs

Figure 17.4 gives an indication of the scope of rights in relation to objects which are artistic, aesthetic or functional. The centre is the territory where an article can be placed according to its character. It can be seen that the boundaries between artistic and aesthetic and between aesthetic and functional are not straight lines, reflecting the impossibility of drawing a precise boundary. The outer arcs show the various rights and their extent in relation to the description of an article as being artistic, aesthetic or functional. It can be seen that some of these, potentially, cover the whole spectrum whilst others fade away as we move around the diagram. The difficulty in matching rights to specific articles where they lie in the 'grey' areas should be quite clear.

Of course, this is an oversimplification and many other requirements and exceptions apply. For instance, a design right can only apply to aspects of shape or configuration whereas some artistic works and some registrable designs are two-dimensional, some three-dimensional. Dual protection is partly but not completely curtailed.

One of the dilemmas facing the owner of a design that has some sort of eye-appeal is whether or not to attempt to seek registration of the design.[26] Registration, if the design is accepted, is preferable because of a potentially longer period of protection and stronger form of protection afforded. Registration is not particularly expensive. But, failure to register on the basis that the design is probably protected by the design right is dangerous as there is often no way of knowing whether the design right applies to a design short of litigation. Although registration of a design is not conclusive proof that the design meets all the requirements for registration, at least it indicates that the design does, in all probability, do so. The advice has to be: if in doubt, apply for registration. Another reason in favour of registration is that it demonstrates that the owner of the design takes his legal rights seriously, especially if the registration number is affixed to articles made to the design.

PARTICULAR EXAMPLES

The following articles are considered in the light of the different rights (registered design, design right and artistic copyright) that might apply to the design of the article. The purpose of the examples is to highlight the differences between the rights, their synthesis and inter-relationship. Where referred to, statutes are abbreviated thus: CDPA – Copyright, Designs and Patents Act 1988, RDA – Registered Designs Act 1949.

Porcelain figurine

Artistic copyright: The figurine could be considered to be a sculpture. The original model and the cast (mould) could also be sculptures (s.4(2) CDPA) as long as they are 'original' (s.1(1)(a) CDPA) irrespective of artistic quality (s.4(1) CDPA). Drawings and preliminary sketches could also be protected by copyright.[27]

Registered design: If the shape or configuration (or any surface decoration applied to the figurines) is 'new' (s.1(2) RDA) then the design of the figurines can be registered.[28] A figurine is unquestionably designed to appeal to the eye.

26 This was even more crucial under the Copyright Act 1956 which, by section 10(1), excluded copyright protection from a design which was fundamentally registrable under the Registered Designs Act 1949. The Design Copyright Act 1968 changed this.

27 By section 52 and pursuant regulations, if more than 50 figurines are made by an industrial process and marketed, the term of copyright is reduced to 25 years. It would appear from the wording of section 52 that this would apply to the original model, the cast(s) and any drawings, the figurines being three-dimensional copies of the drawings.

28 Works of sculpture are excluded from registration by the Registered Designs Rules 1989 (SI 1989 No. 1105), regulation 26, but only in as much as they are not 'casts or models used or intended to be used as models or patterns to be multiplied by any industrial process'. A model from which a cast will be made so that figurines can be mass-produced is, therefore, registrable.

Design right: If the shape or configuration is 'original' (s.213(1) CDPA), that is not commonplace, then the design right applies.

It appears that all three rights apply. Copyright is not suppressed because the articles are artistic works (s.51(1) CDPA). An advantage of registering the design is that no causal link is required for infringement to be proved (s.7 RDA).[29] However, copyright is wider in terms of the types of infringement, for example if a figurine is shown in television broadcast.[30] But copyright does not prevent similar works being created by independent effort. The existence of the design right is illusory because if the act complained of infringes copyright, the design right is suppressed (s.236 CDPA). Finally, it should be noted that the rights could be owned by different persons. For example, if a self-employed sculptor is commissioned to make the original model, he will own the copyright but the commissioner will, providing he has paid money or money's worth, be entitled to register the design on his own behalf.

Mass-produced furniture

Artistic copyright: It is unlikely that the furniture itself will be a work of artistic craftsmanship.[31] In principle, any drawings may be protected as will be other materials such as computer data describing the three-dimensional shape of the furniture. But this protection will be limited by s.51 CDPA to direct copying only, for example photocopying the original drawing. Copyright might subsist in any document, such as a drawing, recording the design of a pattern to be applied to the covers to be fitted to the furniture.

Registered design: If the shape or configuration is 'new' and has eye-appeal (s.1(2) RDA) then the design may be registered. If the furniture has patterned covers or an embossed surface, this too may be registrable separately. This might be useful if a particular line of furniture is produced with a choice from several different designs of covers, each of which are new and have eye-appeal. However, any aspects of the shape or configuration which relate to a method or principle of construction or are related to the function the furniture has to perform are excluded. Therefore, if the furniture has a distinctive shape that results only from the way it is made or the fact that it is designed for sitting upon, the design is not registrable. Obviously, in deciding whether to buy a particular suite of furniture, the appearance is a material factor.

Design right: This will apply if the shape or configuration applied to the furniture is 'original' (s.213(1) CDPA). Because the furniture is not itself an artistic work, the design right is not suppressed and runs alongside any registrations in respect of the design. Patterned covers and the like will not, however, be subject to the design right as these are features of surface decoration.

Some of the differences between registered designs and the design right may be important in this case. For example, duration is potentially longer for a registered design. Also, the exceptions are not quite the same. For the design right, features of shape and configuration which relate to the function of the article may be protected if not covered by the 'must-fit' and 'must-match' exceptions whereas for a registered design, functional features are totally excluded. Methods and principles of construction are excepted from both rights. There are also slight differences in the ownership provisions for the two rights.

29 For example, in copyright, for infringement by copying, the original thing (or a copy of it) must have been copied from directly or indirectly. However, damages are not available against innocent infringers, section 9 of the Registered Designs Act 1949.

30 But the number of restricted acts is less for artistic works than it is for the other original works. For example, by the Copyright, Designs and Patents Act 1988, the making of an adaptation is not an act restricted by the copyright in an artistic work, section 21. Nor is it an infringement to show an artistic work in public, section 19.

31 See *George Hensher Ltd. v Restawhile Upholstery (Lancs.) Ltd.* [1976] AC 64. In some cases, where the furniture has some particular artistic quality, it may be the subject of artistic copyright as a work of artistic craftsmanship. Past examples would include art deco or art nouveau furniture. It might also apply to hand crafted furniture.

Copyright in any drawing or painting showing the design of the surface deco-ration could run alongside a design registration. At first sight, the advantage of registering a design can be doubted. However, there are important differences in terms of infringement and ownership which can make registration as a design a more attractive proposition.

Can opener

Artistic copyright: It is unlikely that it could be considered to be a sculpture even if the handle and casing is injection moulded. Copyright, in principle, again will subsist in any drawings subject to s.51(1) CDPA.

Registered design: If the design has not previously been registered or published and has eye-appeal and is not governed by function then the design may be reg-istrable. Many such articles which are essentially functional may be designed also for eye-appeal. Some people are more willing to buy or to pay more for functional articles if they look attractive. Even a container with a neck in the shape of a duck's neck for toilet disinfectant has been registered as a design as has been a container for false teeth.

Design right: If the shape of the can opener is not commonplace, the design right may apply in so far as the design does not encompass a method or princi-ple of construction or it is not dictated by the shape of the cans it has to be placed against so that it may be used to open them.

Design right and the rights under design registration can subsist concurrently in the design but copyright is not relevant. However, design right could also apply to the shape or configuration of any internal mechanism of the can opener if original. If the casing has a pretty pattern printed or embossed on it, that pattern could be the subject of a separate design registration.

Moulded plastic tray for processed food

Artistic copyright: Although the moulded tray has shape, it is unlikely that it would be considered to be a sculpture.[32] However, sculptures are protected irre-spective of artistic quality and it could be possible to consider the original model from which the trays were made to be a sculpture. Any copyright in drawings for the tray is likely to be suppressed by s.51(1) CDPA.

Registered design: If new, the shape may be registrable. The eye-appeal require-ment can be satisfied in two ways, first from the point of view of the food processor who wants to make his chicken steaks (or whatever) to look as attractive as possible to potential customers. Secondly, the customers them-selves will be influenced in their purchasing decision by the appearance of the product. The amount of money expended on packaging is ample proof of the importance of attractive containers for food. Although largely irrelevant as to reasons associated with use from the customers' point of view, aesthetic consid-erations are important in the context of acquisition from the food processor's viewpoint.

Design right: If original, the shape of the tray will be protected by the design right.

Registration of the design of food containers is very common and rewards the effort expended in the creation of designs intended to show off the food to best commercial effect.

32 However, in the New Zealand case of *Wham-O Manufacturing Co. v Lincoln Industries Ltd.* [1985] RPC 127, it was held that a wooden model from which moulds for 'Frisbees' were made was a sculpture and the moulds and Frisbees were engravings. Copying a finished Frisbee infringed all these copyrights and the copyright in the working drawings.

OWNERSHIP - DIFFERENCES BETWEEN RIGHTS

The differences in the ownership provisions between artistic copyright, registered designs and the design right have already been alluded to. Before proceeding over the next two chapters to consider the registered design and the design right in more detail it will be useful to look briefly at these provisions comparatively. The fact that there are differences could be very inconvenient where a particular design attracts two forms of protection. The special provisions that apply, for example, in respect of Crown copyright are omitted for the sake of clarity. There are some differences in terminology. The person creating a work of copyright or a registered design is known as the 'author' whereas the creator of a design in which the design right subsists is called a 'designer'.[33] A copyright and a design right is owned by its 'owner' but for a registered design he is known as the 'proprietor'.

Artistic copyright: The author is the first owner of an artistic copyright unless he is an employee creating the work in the course of his employment in which case his employer is the first owner (s.11(1) and (2) CDPA).

Registered design: The author is the original proprietor of the design subject to two exceptions. The first is equivalent to the copyright provision for employees. The second exception is where the design is created under a commission in which case the commissioner is entitled to be the original proprietor provided the commission is for money or money's worth.

Design right: The designer is the first owner, subject to exceptions relating to employees and commissioned designs. As with registered designs, the commission must be for money or money's worth. A further provision applies to designs which qualify for the right by reference to the first marketing of articles made to the design. In this case, the person marketing the articles is the first owner of the right.

Table 17.2 shows the identity of potential first owners of the three rights. Which one it is will depend on the circumstances. For example, the first owner of a design right might be the designer, his employer or commissioner or the person responsible for the first marketing. For artistic copyright, the first owner can only be either the author or his employer.[34] Of course, the first owner may assign the right to another immediately upon its coming into existence or may agree to do so in respect of a future copyright or design.

[33] Statutory recognition is given to the fact that all these rights can be brought about by computer-generation and the provisions are equivalent for each of the rights.

[34] Ignoring section 11(3) of the Copyright, Designs and Patents Act 1988 which caters for Crown and parliamentary copyright and copyright belonging to certain international organizations.

Table 17.2 Potential first owners of rights in designs

Type of right	Creator of right known as	Owner of right known as	Potential identity of first owner from amongst			
			creator	employer	commissioner	marketer
Artistic Copyright	Author	Owner	**yes**	**yes**	no	no
Registered Design	Author	Proprietor	**yes**	**yes**	**yes***	no
Design Right	Designer	Owner	**yes**	**yes**	**yes**	**yes**

* only if the commission is undertaken for money or money's worth.

INTERNATIONAL ASPECTS

Unfortunately, the international protection of designs is far from satisfactory.[35] Although the World Intellectual Property Organization includes designs within its brief and there have been moves towards international protection, it has to be said that little has been achieved compared to the co-operation realized as regards copyright and patents. One reason for this is that design protection is effected in many different ways in different states. However, 22 states belong to the The Hague Agreement 1925 (not including the United Kingdom) which does go some way towards a unified system for registering designs by deposit without search.[36] Application for registration is made in Geneva but individual Member States can refuse within a certain period of time. However, registration in the United Kingdom is subject to a search to ensure that the design is new whereas some other countries operate a simple deposit system. The design right is, at the present time, unique to the United Kingdom, although designs that are subject to this right might fall within the sphere of other rights in different countries.

International protection of United Kingdom registered designs is automatically afforded in some countries (mainly Commonwealth countries) such as Bermuda, Botswana, Cyprus, Gibraltar, Hong Kong, Malaysia, Singapore and Uganda. Others extend protection by local re-registration of a United Kingdom design; these are Guernsey, Jersey, Malta, Montserrat, Tanzania, Trinidad and Tobago. Otherwise, if international protection is required for a design, it must be obtained by application to the appropriate states under their registered designs or petty patents systems.[37] There is, at least, the advantage of a six month priority arrangement for designs under the Paris Convention for the Protection of Industrial Property 1883. Some countries operate a law of unfair competition which could be useful in some cases. Of course, because of the much better international copyright position it may be possible to pursue actions for infringement of copyright in drawings in foreign states.

REFORM OF DESIGN LAW

Jehoram remarks that there is 'abundant evidence . . . that different national laws on intellectual property can restrict the free movement of goods within the Community'.[38] Indeed, the judgments in the case of *Volvo AB* v *Erik Veng (UK) Ltd.*[39] clearly indicate how lack of harmonization can emasculate European Community competition law. However, the disparate national treatment afforded to designs is unlikely to survive for much longer. The Commission to the European Community produced a Green Paper in June 1991 on the legal protection of industrial design.[40] This was influenced by a draft for European design law produced by the Max Planck Institute in Munich. There are two main thrusts in the Green Paper: first, a process of limited harmonization of design laws in Member States and, secondly, the implementation of a fully integrated Community system of design rights. Both the harmonization process and the Community Design system envisage a two tier model comprising a registered design and an unregistered design right. In some respects, that model is not unlike the system currently adopted in the United Kingdom. At the time of writing, a harmonization Directive is imminent (a draft was included in the Green Paper as was a comprehensive draft for the Community Design). The

35 For an excellent description of the international scene as regards designs, see Johnston, D. *Design Protection* (London: The Design Council, 3rd edn., 1989) especially Chapter 10 and Appendix A.

36 States which are signatories to The Hague Agreement include France, Germany, the Benelux countries, Italy and Spain.

37 A petty patent is like a weaker variety of patent which is used in some countries, for example Germany, Italy and Spain, as a half way house between full patents and registered designs. It is a means of affording protection for methods of construction and lesser inventive devices which would not qualify for a full patent. Petty patents are cheaper and of shorter duration than full patents.

38 Jehoram, H.C. 'The EC Green Paper on the Legal Protection of Industrial Design. Half Way down the Right Track - A View from the Benelux' [1992] 3 EIPR 75.

39 [1989] 4 CMLR 122.

40 Brussels, June 1991, 111/F/5131/91-EN. The Green Paper was not formally published but was circulated to interested parties. For a detailed description of the Green Paper's proposals, see Horton, A. A. 'Industrial Design Law: The Future for Europe' [1991] 12 EIPR 442.

Community Design proposal is outlined below, followed by a brief mention of the harmonization proposals.

Community design rights

The basic rationale of the two design right model is that there should be a formal right subject to registration that can last for up to 25 years and an informal right that can endure for a much shorter period of time (3 years is suggested in the Green Paper). The informal right will be particularly useful for those designs that have a relatively short period of time during which they are commercially viable, for example in the case of fashion clothing. It will be unnecessary to register such designs, the unregistered right giving all the protection required. For designs that may have a longer lifespan, registration can be delayed for up to one year allowing for test marketing without destroying the novelty of the design. Therefore, the owner of a design will be able to put articles made to the design on the market before deciding whether it is worthwhile going to the expense and trouble of registration. If the design is not particularly successful, the owner may decide not to bother registering the design (relying on the unregistered right for any copying that takes place). However, if the design is successful and it appears that this success will continue for some years to come, the owner can then apply for registration.

For both the formal and informal right, a design should have a distinctive character defined as being one that is 'not known to the circles specialized in the sector concerned operating within the Community' and 'through the overall impression it displays in the eyes of the relevant public, it distinguishes itself from any other design known to such circles'. Internal aspects will not be protected unless they can be perceived by the human senses. This would seem to exclude designs such as that in *Gardex Ltd.* v *Sorata Ltd.*[41] Designs that are dictated solely by technical function are excluded. However, in a denial of the United Kingdom requirement for eye-appeal for registered designs there will be no requirement that the appearance should be a material factor for either the registered or informal right.

The Green Paper contains an exception based on interconnections, that is, 'those features of the appearance of a product which must necessarily be reproduced in their exact form and dimensions in order to permit the product to which the design is applied to be assembled or connected with another product'. This is a 'must-fit' exception but there is not a 'must-match' exception equivalent to that for United Kingdom designs.

Harmonization

The Green Paper recognizes that national rights will have to subsist alongside the Community design rights for a period of time. Consequently, and in order to facilitate trade between Member States in the meantime, the Commission proposes that a process of harmonization should be begun in relation to registered designs. Therefore, a proposal for a Directive to harmonize national design rights is set out in the Green Paper. The main points covered by the harmonization Directive deal with the distinctive character test, the one year period of grace (allowing marketing without destroying novelty), the term of 25 years for registered designs and a 'must-fit' exception. The proprietor of the design

41 [1986] RPC 623. At least, as regards the underside of the shower tray. See the discussion of this case in the following chapter.

will have the exclusive right to prevent a third party, without permission, from making, offering, putting on the market or using a product to which the same design or one that creates an impression of substantial similarity is applied.[42] The right will extend to importing, exporting or stocking such a product for the above purposes. Some defences are proposed, for example in relation to acts done for private, non-commercial purposes, experimental purposes or for reproduction for the purpose of teaching design.

Latest proposals

A proposal for a European Parliament and Council Regulation on Community Design has been published proposing a two-tier system of registered and unregistered designs.[43] A proposed Directive to harmonize registered design systems has also been published.[44] The model of registered designs proposed in the harmonization Directive will be based on five-year periods of registration renewable in five-year blocks up to a maximum of 25 years. The definition of design is wide, being the appearance of the whole or part of a product resulting from the specific features of the lines, contours, colours, shape and/or its ornamentation. A design, to be registrable, must be new and have individual character. In a change from United Kingdom law, there is no requirement for the design to have 'eye-appeal'. However, there are a number of exclusions broadly equivalent to methods and principles of construction and the 'must-fit' exception.

Whilst the holder of a registered design will have exclusive rights to use the design, there are a number of exceptions to infringement, such as private or experimental purposes, in respect of teaching, and for foreign vessels temporarily in the territory of the Member State. There is a 'must-match' exception to infringement; however, this does not apply for the first three years. Thus, manufacturers of complex products such as motor vehicles will be able, through the registered design system, to prevent others making spare parts such as body panels for three years. The suggested date for implementation of the proposed Directive is 31 October 1996.

42 The draft Directive in the Green Paper refers to products rather than articles though it does not define 'product' except to state that it does not include a computer program or semiconductor product.

43 OJ [1994] C29/20.

44 OJ [1993] C345/14.

18

Registered designs

A system of registration for designs has been around since the early part of the nineteenth century. The initial demand for a system of registration came from the textile industry but now all manner of designs are registered, the most common kinds of designs being for toys, games and electrical goods. Design registration and patents were for a long time governed by common statutes, for example the Patents and Designs Act 1907, but they were separated in 1949 and the present statute dealing with registered designs is the Registered Designs Act 1949 which was amended by the Copyright, Designs and Patents Act 1988.[1] This latter Act includes a copy of the Registered Designs Act 1949, as amended, in Schedule 4, a very useful and helpful step. The amended version of the 1949 Act came into force on 1 August 1989.

1 Prior to this amendment, the right was referred to as the 'copyright in the registered design', the old section 7(1) of the Registered Designs Act 1949. Unless otherwise indicated, in this chapter, statutory references are to this Act.

REQUIREMENTS FOR REGISTRATION

A design may be registered in respect of any article or set of articles. A design means features of:

- shape
- configuration
- pattern or
- ornament

2 Section 1(1) of the Registered Designs Act 1949.

which are applied to an article by any industrial process, being features which in the finished article appeal to and are judged by the eye.[2] A design is thus not restricted to three-dimensions and surface decoration can come within the scope of registered designs as can designs applied to textiles or garments, for example a new and attractive motif applied to material for making dresses. The additional requirement for the appearance to be material in the acquisition or use of articles to which the design has been applied is discussed below though it remains to be seen how this will be interpreted by the Registrar and the courts. It was construed fairly liberally in the recent past.

A design may be registered for a set of articles. A set of articles is, by section 44, 'a number of articles of the same general character ordinarily on sale or intended to be used together, to each of which the same design, or the same design with modifications or variations not sufficient to alter the character or substantially to affect the identity thereof, is applied'. An example would be a design applied to cutlery with slight differences depending on the item concerned, whether the particular article is a knife or a fork. A suite of furniture where the same design is applied to a chair and a sofa would qualify as a set of articles. A chess set would not, as the intention of the designer is to produce pieces that can be distinguished from one another. The design of individual pieces such as the queen, rook and bishop will be different. The first part of the definition in section 44 applies but not the latter. The same principle applies to a typeface. However, if the pieces in a chess set are surmounted on plinths to which a new design has been applied, that design will be registrable for a set of articles, even though different chess pieces have different sized plinths. Similarly, a distinctive serif applied to all or most characters of a typeface may be registrable.[3] Whereas a single application for registration is acceptable for a set of articles, multiple applications must be made in the case of a design intended to be applied to more than one article not being part of a set of articles.[4] Thus, if the same design is to be applied to a kettle and to a plant pot, two separate applications must be made and two fees must be paid.

Applied to an article by any industrial process

The design must be applied to an article (or intended to be so applied). This might seem a simple and untroublesome prerequisite but 'article' is defined in section 44(1) of the Act as 'any article of manufacture and includes any part of an article if that part is made and sold separately'. It is in respect of parts of an article that difficulty can be met. In *Sifam Electrical Instrument Co. Ltd.* v *Sangamo Weston Ltd.*[5] it was held that the design on the front of an electric meter was not a part of an article under section 44(1) because it was not intended to be sold separately by the owner of the design. Graham J said (at 914):

> . . . on the whole I think the intention must be to grant registration only for such articles as are intended by the proprietor of the design to be put on the market and sold separately, such as for example a hammer handle, or the bit of a bradawl.

This judgment was cited with approval by the deputy High Court judge in *Ford Motor Co. Ltd. & Iveco Fiat SpA's Design Application*[6] where it was stated that door panels for vehicles, having no reality as articles of commerce apart from forming part of the complete vehicle, were not registrable. However, this is to deny the existence of a need for replacement parts and the very active market in manufacturing spare parts separately, in their own right. Perhaps a distinction could be made between selling parts of articles separately as accessories and selling them as replacement parts. However, the wording of the Act makes no such distinction.

The design must be applied by any industrial process. A definition of 'applied industrially' is given in rule 35 of the Registered Design Rules 1989[7] but this definition is made for the purposes of section 6 of the Act dealing with the industrial application in terms of corresponding designs relating to artistic works. It is not necessarily of universal application to the remainder of the Act and, in any case, only relates to quantity.

Modern technology may stretch the meaning of industrial application to its limits. For example, a typeface design would, in the past, be registrable. Individual characters would be registrable as would a common design aspect such as a new design of serif. A typeface used to be applied to articles, metal type ('hot metal'). However, most typefaces nowadays are stored as computer data in the form of software fonts. There are no articles to which the typeface design is applied industrially. Copyright protection remains for software typefaces which fall within the scope of artistic copyright.[8] Needless to say, all other forms of

3 Typefaces are less likely to be registrable nowadays because, usually they are contained in computer software and the design is not applied by an industrial process.

4 Rule 13 of the Registered Design Rules 1989, SI 1989 No. 1105.

5 [1973] RPC 899

6 [1993] RPC 399.

7 SI 1989 No. 1105.

8 Although not listed as a specific form of artistic work in section 4 of the Copyright, Designs and Patents Act 1988, sections 54 and 55 of that Act refer to the copyright in an artistic work consisting of the design of a typeface.

design that exist only in software (for example for an object to be displayed on a computer screen) and are not applied to an article fall outside the realms of registered designs. It is unlikely that, by any stretch of the imagination, the storage of data representing such a design on a magnetic disk could be perceived as being equivalent to the industrial application of a design to an article. Although such designs fail to be protected directly by copyright, this is of litle consequence as monopoly rights are granted by design registration.

Novelty

A further requirement is that the design must be new. It will neither be considered to be 'new' if it is the same as a design registered in a prior application, regardless of the nature of the article to which it was intended to be applied, nor if the design has been published in the United Kingdom prior to the date of application. This also applies to a design which differs only in immaterial details from such designs or in features that are variants commonly used in the trade. If a design is registered in respect of a particular article and the proprietor later wishes to register the same design in respect of other articles, the prior registration or publication of the design is ignored when considering whether the design is new.[9] Publication in breach of confidence or contrary to good faith is ignored in determining whether the design has been published.[10] If the design is applied to an article and that article is a copy of an artistic work, it is known as a 'corresponding design' and previous use of the artistic work does not prevent the design being new providing that the prior use does not include commercial exploitation of articles to which the design has been applied industrially.[11]

Prior to the amendments made by the Copyright, Designs and Patents Act 1988, the design had to be 'new or original' and, as this was qualified in the similar terms to the present requirement that a design should be 'new', it is unlikely that there has been any significant shift. That is, the design or a design substantially like it, as before, should not have been previously registered or published in the United Kingdom. In any case, the meaning of 'original' did not trouble the courts and the basic test was one of novelty. Although, in an extraordinary display of statutory interpretation, it was held by the Registered Designs Appeal Tribunal in *Aspro-Nicholas Ltd.'s Design Application*[12] that the 'or' in the phrase 'new or original' was not used in a disjunctive sense and, therefore, a design must be both new and original to qualify for registration. The courts have frequently had to deal with the question of novelty. In essence it is a matter of whether a design has been anticipated along patent lines. In *Rosedale Associated Manufacturers Ltd. v Airfix Products Ltd.*[13] it was held that the rules that apply to anticipation of patents also apply to registered designs. It has been observed that the contribution of the design to the store of human knowledge or experience might be another factor in determining novelty and where the contribution was slight, it would be unlikely that the court would find that the design was new.[14]

Eye-appeal

Before the changes made by the Copyright, Designs and Patents Act 1988, eye-appeal was the fundamental test for which features of a design could be

9 Section 4(1). This also applies to slight alterations.

10 See section 6. There are other provisions, for example with respect to the first and confidential order placed for an original textile design, exhibitions and disclosure to government departments.

11 Sections 6(4) and 6(5) of the Registered Designs Act 1949. This also applies to designs which differ only in immaterial details or in features which are variants commonly used in the trade. 'Applied industrially' is defined by rule 35 of the Registered Designs Rules 1989, SI 1989 No. 1105, as having the same meaning as for artistic works.

12 [1974] RPC 645. Another example where a judge interpreted an 'or' in a statute as 'and' is *Stock v Frank Jones (Tipton) Ltd.* [1978] 1 All ER 948.

13 [1957] RPC 239.

14 *Aspro-Nicholas Ltd.'s Design Application* [1974] RPC 645.

registered, that is, features 'which in the finished article appeal to and are judged solely by the eye'.[15] In *Amp Incorporated* v *Utilux Pty. Ltd.*,[16] it was said that there was no requirement for aesthetic or artistic appeal and that it was sufficient if the features in question were capable of being appreciated so as to make an impact on the eye.[17] However, in the House of Lords, Lord Reid said:[18]

> . . . 'judged solely by the eye' must be intended to exclude cases where a customer might choose an article of that shape, not because of its appearance but because he thought that the shape made it more useful to him.

In *Lamson Industries Ltd.'s Application*[19] Whitford J decided that a design for computer print-out paper having alternative coloured bands upon it was not registrable because the reason customers would buy the paper was that it would be easier to read and because information could be printed out on the paper more closely spaced. Customers would buy the paper because of its utility and not because of its appearance.

These cases demonstrated a fairly rigorous approach to eye-appeal. However, a more generous attitude was in evidence in the intervening years up to the changes to design law introduced by the Copyright Designs and Patents Act 1988. An extremely generous example is given in *Gardex Ltd.* v *Sorata Ltd.*[20] which concerned an alleged infringement of the design of a shower tray. The defendant challenged, *inter alia*, the registration of a shower tray including its underside as a design claiming that the shape of the underside was dictated solely by function. However, it was held that the under surface was intended to have aesthetic appeal and did not solely relate to a method or principle of construction and, therefore, the design was validly registered. This seems to be stretching eye-appeal to its limits as, once the shower tray had been installed, the underside would never be seen again. The plaintiff claimed that when he had created the design for the underside of the tray it had pleased him so much that he thought it worthy of design registration. This extraordinary claim seemed to find sympathy with the judge.

The test now seems to be more rigorous in that eye-appeal is still required but, in addition, the appearance of the article must be material. Whether the appearance is material involves a curious two-stage test.[21]

(a) With respect to articles of the same type as the particular article under scrutiny, are aesthetic considerations normally taken into account to a material extent by persons acquiring or using such articles? If the answer to this question is 'yes' then the appearance is material but if the answer is 'no' then the second stage of the test is invoked, that is;
(b) Would aesthetic considerations be taken into account to a material extent by persons acquiring or using articles to which the design in question has been applied? If the answer is 'yes' then the appearance is material despite the fact that it might not be material generally in respect of similar articles.

For example, a new shape of container may be designed for a liquid disinfectant. Theoretically, persons buying disinfectant should not and do not decide upon which brand to buy on the basis of aesthetic considerations. However, if a particular container has been designed to look attractive whilst standing on a bathroom shelf, the design may be registrable. Because of the change in emphasis in aesthetic characteristics, it is inevitable that some previously registered

15 Section 1(3) of the Registered Designs Act 1949 before amendment by the Copyright, Designs and Patents Act 1988.

16 [1970] RPC 397.

17 However, everything that can be seen has an impact upon the eye to a lesser or greater extent.

18 *Amp Incorporated* v *Utilux Pty Ltd.* [1972] RPC 103 at 108.

19 [1978] RPC 1.

20 [1986] RPC 623.

21 Section 1(3) of the Registered Designs Act 1949.

22 This situation may also arise because of changes to the exceptions to registrability.

23 Section 266(1) of the Copyright, Designs and Patents Act 1988. In addition, licences as of right are automatically available for such designs.

24 Another subtle change is that the phrase 'appeal to and are judged solely by the eye' has been changed to 'appeal to and are judged by the eye', section 1(1). This might make it easier for 'designer' functional articles to gain registration, such as a bottle opener in the shape of a hand.

25 The Registrar's full title is the Comptroller-General of Patents, Designs and Trade Marks.

designs would not meet the new standards for registration.[22] To deal with this problem, for designs which were registered in pursuance of an application made after 12 January 1988 and before 1 August 1989 but which would not be registrable under the new requirements, the design registration is limited to a maximum of ten years after 1 August 1989 providing it does not expire earlier in any event.[23]

The effects of this requirement of 'material appearance' are difficult to predict as it can be argued that even with the most functional of household objects appearance is a factor, especially in terms of their acquisition.[24] Goods have to vie with each other on supermarket shelves and an attractively shaped (and coloured) container or a functional article with an unusual design must have some impact upon buying decisions. The buying public have come to expect care and trouble to have been taken in the design of the outward appearance of articles and containers. The question is whether a particular make of article is preferred to another make because of appearance and one way of resolving this question might be to look at the relative price of 'designer' articles compared with plain unadorned articles that are purchased for the same function and which can perform that function just as efficiently. In other words, just how much money are people prepared to pay for the design?

Instead of considering the reasons for acquisition of articles, appearance may be a material factor in terms of usage. In most cases, if appearance is an important factor in the use of the article, it will also be a material factor in its acquisition. A great number of designs fall into this category, for example a set of dinner plates bearing an attractive pattern, cutlery, a table lamp, household ornaments and *objets d'art*, toys, curtain material, wallpaper and furniture. With respect to these types of articles, it is plain that, providing the other requirements are satisfied, they should qualify for registration. The difficulty lies in determining the position of articles which are normally acquired for their function but which have had, nevertheless, an attractive design applied to them perhaps in an effort to achieve a competitive edge or as a way of targeting a more discerning buyer who is prepared to pay a premium.

Exceptions

Even though a design is new it might not qualify for registration because section 1 of the Registered Designs Act 1949 contains some exceptions and others are provided for by statutory instrument. Additionally, the Registrar has a discretion to refuse an application generally or on the grounds that use of the design would be contrary to law or morality.[25] Designs which are expressly excluded by section 1(1) are:

(a) methods or principles of construction, or
(b) features of shape or configuration which are:
   (i) dictated solely by the article's function, or
   (ii) dependent upon the appearance of another article of which the article is intended by the design's author (creator) to form an integral part.

These exclusions serve two main purposes. They prevent the right from being too strong and hindering the development of new designs for similar articles or articles of a similar construction. Secondly, they allow, somewhat controversially, the manufacture of matching spare parts by others. This is the 'must match' exception and is identically worded to the equivalent exception for the design right.[26] In *Cow (PB) & Co. Ltd.* v *Cannon Rubber Manufacturers Ltd.*[27] the plaintiff had a registered design for rubber hot water bottles having a series of diagonally arranged ribs front and back. The claim to novelty lay in the shape or configuration of the bottle as shown in drawings. The defendant was sued for infringing the design and claimed that the registration was defective because it included a method or principle of construction and that it included features of shape and configuration dictated by function. Lloyd-Jacob J found for the plaintiff, confirming the validity of the design. The features claimed would not prevent the development of other designs for hot-water bottles, for example by using horizontal, vertical or criss-cross ribs.

Like patent law, registered design law gives rise to a monopoly and it is important that the protection offered does not extend too far. The equivalent to methods or principles of construction in patent law are discoveries, scientific theories and mathematical methods. One way of looking at methods or principles of construction and functions is to ask the question, is there any other way such articles could be made? Does the right prevent the making of similar articles to other designs? In *Amp Incorporated* v *Utilux Pty. Ltd.*[28] claims that the design was invalid on both of these grounds failed because it was conceivable that articles to perform the same function could be made in other shapes or sizes. In fact, because the Act states that features of shape or configuration which are dictated *solely* by function are excluded, this would seem not to operate if there is more than one shape or configuration that can be applied to an article so that a particular function can be performed. It is only when no alternative shapes or configurations are possible that the exclusion will apply. Of course, this exception only applies to those features so constrained and other features will still be registrable in principle. An example could be the pins on an electrical plug designed to fit a particular type of socket, the design of other parts of the plug being registrable. Another example might be the hull of a boat or the general shape of a sailing dinghy. In *Dorling* v *Honnor Marine Ltd.*[29] the question arose as to whether the shape of a completed sailing dinghy was registrable. Danckwerts LJ said (at 19):

> It was suggested that the one thing which was registrable was the shape of the completed dinghy . . . I feel the greatest doubt whether this was correct. I should have thought that the shape of the boat was necessarily functional.

Would this be true of a new shape of hull designed for performance and appearance or a new shape of sail which was both functional and attractive? Of course, the shape of a boat hull is dictated to some extent by its function – it has to comply with certain rules of hydrodynamics and physics so that it can perform its function efficiently. But a number of alternatives are feasible as evidenced by the large variety of shapes and profiles made, although many are the result of attempts to achieve the most efficient shape for the particular type of craft concerned. It is undeniable that, in the case of small vessels purchased for pleasure, eye-appeal is a factor in the design equation.

26 Apart from the use of the word 'designer' rather than 'author' (see section 213(3)(b)(ii) of the Copyright, Designs and Patents Act 1988), the design right also has a 'must-fit' exception which does not apply to the registered design which has a 'dictated solely by function' exception.

27 [1959] RPC 240.

28 [1970] RPC 397.

29 [1965] Ch 1. This case is notable in that it recognized indirect copyright infringement of drawings. An important aspect of the case was whether the shape of the boat was registrable because of the exception from copyright subsistence in anything which could have been registered as a design, section 10(1) Copyright Act 1956, now repealed.

'Must-match' exception

30 *British Leyland Motor Corp. Ltd.* v *Armstrong Patents Co. Ltd.* [1986] 2 WLR 400.

The importance of a right to a free market in spare parts was stressed in the *British Leyland* case.[30] The full application of design law to spare parts would work against such a free market. For example, if a vehicle manufacturer was allowed to register the shape of the body panels of his cars then he could charge exorbitant prices for replacement panels and refuse to grant licences to third party parts manufacturers or only grant licences in return for a hefty royalty. In the White Paper that preceded the Copyright, Designs and Patents Act 1988,[31] the Government spelt out its plans to exclude spare parts from the protection of the design right. Because some spare parts would be registrable as designs, the Government also stated its intention to extend the exclusion to the Registered Designs Act 1949.[32]

31 Intellectual Property and Innovation, Cmnd. 9712 (London: HMSO, 1986).

32 For example, 'protection would be available only for truly aesthetic, stand alone designs where competitors do not need to be able to copy such designs in order to compete effectively', per Lord Young of Graftham, H. L. Deb. 12 November 1987, Col. 1479.

The must-match exception is fairly narrow and applies only if the design features are dependent upon the appearance of another article and it is the author's intention that his articles form an integral part of the other article. An example is a door panel for a car. This obviously forms an integral part of the car. But the question is not so simple in relation to some spare parts. The question of registrability of spare parts for motor vehicles was considered in *Ford Motor Co. Ltd. & Iveco Fiat SpA's Design Applications*.[33] The judge classified spare parts in two groups. The first group which the judge decided were excluded by section 1(1)(b)(ii) from registration were main body panels, doors, bonnet lids, boot lids and windscreens.[34] He gave an example of a door panel as being an article which is intended by the author of the design to form an integral part of another article, being the vehicle. The second group of components, such as wing mirrors, wheels, seats and steering wheels can be made in a variety of designs to fit a particular vehicle as substitutions for the original parts whilst leaving the shape and general appearance of the vehicle unaffected. For example, the owner of a car might buy differently designed parts to give his car a sportier appearance. Such parts are registrable as designs provided the other requirements (for example, novelty) are satisfied.

33 [1993] RPC 399.

34 The judge also decided that these parts were not articles within the meaning in section 44 and unregistrable on this count also. The case is notable in that the judge considered the policy behind the changes to the Registered Designs Act 1949 and he considered some of the Parliamentary Debates, in accordance with the decision in *Pepper (Inspector of Taxes)* v *Hart* [1993] 1 All ER 42.

The fact that the main body panels of a vehicle are unlikely to be registrable as designs does not prevent the shape of the entire vehicle being registered. However, the degree of similarity in vehicle design must be taken into account and much of the overall shape of a vehicle will not be new. This is especially important when it comes to considering infringement and it may be that a comparison between the registered design and an alleged infringement will be concentrated on details rather than the overall shape.

Works primarily of a literary or artistic nature

35 SI 1989 No. 1105. These rules came into force at the same time as the amendments to the Registered Designs Act 1949 made by the Copyright, Designs and Patents Act 1988, that is, 1 August 1989.

Other exceptions have been provided for by statutory instrument, by rule 26 of the Registered Designs Rules 1989.[35] These excluded designs fall mainly within the scope of copyright and are:

(a) works of sculpture (but not casts or models for multiple articles made by any industrial process);
(b) wall plaques, medals and medallions;
(c) printed matter primarily of a literary or artistic character, including book jackets, calendars, certificates, coupons, dress-making patterns, greeting cards, labels, leaflets, maps, plans, playing cards, postcards, stamps, trade

advertisements, trade forms and cards, transfers and similar articles. Such items are left within the scope of full copyright protection only.

An identical list of items is excluded from the operation of section 52 of the Copyright, Designs and Patents Act 1988 which restricts copyright to 25 years for certain exploited artistic works.[36] In *Lamson Industries Ltd.'s Application*[37] it was held that computer print-out paper having alternating coloured bands on it was not an article consisting of printed matter primarily of a literary character.

Other exceptions

The Registered Designs Rules also allow the Registrar to insist on consent in respect of the use of portraits of Her Majesty or any member of the royal family, armorial bearings, flags of any country, insignia, etc.,[38] the consent being that of any official or other person as appears to the Registrar to be entitled to give such consent. If the design includes the portrait of a living or recently dead person then the Registrar may seek the consent of the person, if living, or the personal representative before proceeding with the registration.[39] The rules do not define 'recently dead' – presumably this lies within the Registrar's discretion.

Further exceptions lie within the Registrar's discretion. By section 3(3) of the Registered Designs Act 1949, the Registrar may refuse an application or accept it subject to modifications as he thinks fit. Additionally, by section 43(1), the Registrar will not register a design which, in his opinion, would be contrary to law or morality. In *Re Masterman's Application*[40] the Registrar had refused an application for registration of a design in respect of a Scots doll with a kilt which when lifted exposed male genitalia. The Registrar had objected on the basis of both sections 3(3) and 43(1) and because of the judgment of Evershed J in *La Marquise Footwear's Application*[41] disapproving of registration of designs showing representations of genitalia. It was held that the Registrar's decision should be exercised judicially, not administratively. A design which would offend the moral principles of right thinking members of society should not be registered but, in the present case, the worst that could be said about the design was that some people might find it distasteful and that would not be a good enough reason to deprive the applicant of protection against infringement of her design.

OWNERSHIP OF REGISTERED DESIGN

The person creating a design is known as the author of that design and the basic rule is that the author is entitled to be the original proprietor of the design.[42] There are exceptions to this basic rule and, if the design is commissioned for money or money's worth, the person commissioning the design is, by section 2(1A) of the Registered Designs Act 1949, the original proprietor. Otherwise, by section 2(1B), if the design is created by an employee in the course of employment, the employer is treated as the original proprietor. The person by whom the arrangements necessary for the creation of a computer-generated design are made is taken to be the author of the design. A computer-generated design (as with original works of copyright) is one which is generated by computer in circumstances such that there is no human author. What has already

36 Regulation 2, Copyright (Industrial Processes and Excluded Articles) (No. 2) Order 1989 SI 1989 No. 1070.

37 [1978] RPC 1.

38 Rule 24.

39 Rule 25.

40 [1991] RPC 89.

41 (1947) 64 RPC 27.

42 Section 2, Registered Designs Act 1949. Proprietorship is equivalent to ownership in copyright law.

been said in relation to computer-generated copyright works also applies here (see Chapter 5).

There is a difference as regards first ownership between registered designs and copyright in that commissioners of designs are automatically given the right of ownership of a registrable design. This little inconvenience is exaggerated when the ownership of the design right is considered because section 3(2) requires that a person making an application to register a design must also be the owner of the design right where it subsists concurrently in the design.[43] Usually, a person commissioning a design will be the proprietor of the registered design and will also be the owner of the design right. In some cases however, a design right will be owned by the person first marketing articles made to the design in the United Kingdom and this could be a different person to the intending proprietor of the registrable design. This is unlikely because the qualification requirements for the design right extend to Member States of the European Community and certain other designated countries. An example is, in relation to a design which is registrable and in which the design right is capable of subsisting, where a Chinese national resident in China is commissioned by a Saudi Arabian company to create the design. Articles made to the design are then marketed in the European Community by an Italian company. The Saudi-Arabian company would be entitled to register the design but for the fact that the Italian company is the owner of the design right. On the basis of section 3(2), an application for registration of the design in the United Kingdom must be refused. This ludicrous situation should not come about by assignment because, by section 19(3B), an assignment of the design right automatically includes an assignment of the registered design if their respective owners are one and the same and a contrary intention does not appear. Similarly, an assignment of a registered design automatically carries with it an assignment of the design right, unless the latter is owned by someone other than the proprietor of the registered design.[44] If the design right is later assigned without an assignment of the registered design, the court has the power to order rectification of the register on the application of any person aggrieved, section 20(1).[45]

Section 2(2) of the Registered Designs Act 1949 envisages the situation where the design or the right to apply the design to any article is assigned or is otherwise transmitted to another person. The transferee becomes the proprietor. Joint proprietorship is expressly provided for where one of the proprietors is the original proprietor and both are treated as being 'the proprietor'. No mention is made of other forms of joint proprietorship such as where a registered design is assigned to two third parties but this is implicit in the language of section 19. It is possible that transmission is limited to the application of the design in relation to specific articles only. There are provisions for registration of assignments of a registered design by section 19. This section confirms that a registered design can be dealt with in other ways, for example by a mortgage or licence. Equitable rights are not abrogated by the registration of a design. Proprietors, co-proprietors and persons with legal and equitable interests in a registered design may apply for registration of title or interest which will be done on proof of the same. A person having an interest must also show a corresponding interest in the design right where such right subsists in the design.[46] Although there is no express requirement for an assignment (or licence, for that matter) to be in writing, section 19(3) requires particulars to be entered on the register of

43 Indeed, Designs Form 2A, the application form for design registration, contains a declaration to the effect that the applicant claims to own any design right subsisting in the design.

44 Section 224 of the Copyright, Designs and Patents Act 1988.

45 The Registrar may also cancel the registration under section 11(2).

46 Section 19(3A).

an instrument or event by which the assignee derives title. It is obviously sensible for an assignment to be in writing and signed by the assignor especially as title has to be proved to the satisfaction of the Registrar.

RIGHTS GIVEN BY REGISTRATION AND INFRINGEMENT

Section 7 of the Registered Designs Act 1949 deals with the rights attendant upon registration of a design and also defines infringement of those rights. Registration of a design gives the registered proprietor certain exclusive rights in relation to articles embodying the design, that is an article in respect of which the design is registered and to which the design or one not substantially different has been applied. Those rights are:

(a) to make or import for sale or hire or for use for the purposes of a trade or business;
(b) to sell, hire or offer or expose for sale or hire.[47]

47 Section 7(1).

Any person who does any of the above acts without the licence of the registered proprietor infringes the right in the registered design. As with copyright law, the issue of substantiality is central to the question of infringement, however, for registered designs, the question appears to be one of comparing the differences between the two designs. For example, in *Matthew Swain Ltd.* v *Thomas Barker & Sons Ltd.*[48] a baking tray having right-angled goal-post shaped separating wires was held not to infringe a baking tray having semi-circular separating wires. The novel features of the design related to the separating wires. In *Benchairs Ltd.* v *Chair Centre Ltd.*,[49] concerning an alleged infringement of a design for a chair, it was said that the court should look at and compare the chairs made by the plaintiff and the defendant, separately and together and observe the similarities and differences. Whether the defendant's design was substantially different from the plaintiff's design was a matter of comparing the designs as a whole and that the supposed views on this matter of people buying or using articles made to the design was a relevant factor in making the comparison.

48 [1967] RPC 23.

49 [1974] RPC 429.

It is clear that what must be compared is not the articles as a whole but only those features which are the subject matter of the design registration. Where the design consists of more than one feature, the summation of the features should be used to determine whether infringement has occurred and it is insufficient if there is a resemblance in only one of the features if the summation of the designs being compared are substantially different.[50] In *Best Products Ltd.* v *F W Woolworth & Co. Ltd.*,[51] the plaintiff's design had been applied to a whistling kettle. The design comprised three features: the shape of the body, the shape of the handle and the shape of the spout. The defendant's kettle was held not to infringe because the spout on his kettle was substantially different from that on the plaintiff's kettle. The spout was an important and prominent feature of the design as a whole.

50 This is similar to the position pertaining to patent infringement.

51 [1964] RPC 226.

Novelty statements for registered designs are usually brief and not particularly specific. A common formula is 'the novelty of the design resides in the shape and/or configuration of the article shown in the representation'.[52] Sometimes, already-known features may be excluded (and coloured blue on the rep-

52 If the design relates to surface decoration, the words 'pattern and/or ornament' may be used instead.

resentation of the design) and there may be a disclaimer as to any words or numerals that appear in the design. The overall result is that the novelty statement is not usually particularly helpful in testing for infringement and it is the representation of the design that is more important.

Some designs are a totally new departure from what was already known, whereas others differ only by details from what was known before. In the former case comparison between the registered design and the alleged infringement should concentrate on the general form of the new design (where novelty is based on shape and configuration). However, where the novel features are restricted only to details, the comparison should concentrate on such details when testing for infringement. So it was held in *Gaskell & Chambers Ltd.* v *Measure Master Ltd.*[53] by Aldous J who decided that the plaintiff's registered design for a spirits dispenser as used in public houses was not infringed by the defendant's spirit measure. The plaintiff's dispenser was a substantial departure from the prior art and, although the defendant's design bore a family resemblance to the plaintiff's design, it was substantially different when judged as a whole. The similarities related to detail only.

Where a design is substantially different to what is already known, it might be advisable to make several applications to register the design – one for the overall shape and configuration and others for each novel detail. For example, if the design is for a new shape for a car that should be registered, of course. But other features such as the shape or configuration of the lamp clusters, wing mirrors, or bonnet fluting should, if new, be registered separately (subject to the exceptions relating to spare parts).

The decision as to whether another design infringed a registered design is based on a comparison of those features that appealed to and were judged by the eye. The relevant 'eye' is that of the interested customer who should be considered as looking at the two designs side by side. He should then go away and come back later to the alleged infringement. In this way, the court could conclude which design features would strike the eye and be remembered when deciding whether the designs were or were not substantially different.[54]

In some circumstances, the concept of 'imperfect recollection' may be used to test for substantial difference. For example, would an informed customer or potential customer, having an imperfect recollection, be likely to confuse the registered design with the alleged infringing design. The court will compare the design by looking through the eyes of this hypothetical customer on the basis that he would be interested in the particular design and not merely interested in obtaining an article of the particular type without caring about its design. In view of the 'aesthetic considerations' requirements,[55] this test should be relevant in all cases otherwise the design would have been refused registration. An example of the application of this test is given by the case of *Sommer Allibert (UK) Ltd.* v *Flair Plastics Ltd.*[56] The plaintiff registered a design to be applied to plastic garden chairs. The backrest had vertical grooves and the seat had grooves running from front to back. The defendant imported a plastic garden chair having horizontal grooves on the backrest and sideways grooves on the seats. After surviving an attack on the validity of the registration,[57] it was held in the Court of Appeal that the defendant's chairs did not infringe the design because no informed customer, even having imperfect recollection, would be likely to confuse the defendant's chair with the plaintiff's chair.

53 [1993] RPC 76.

54 *Gaskell & Chambers Ltd.* v *Measure Master Ltd.* [1993] RPC 76

55 Amendment to the Registered Designs Act 1949, made by the Copyright, Designs and Patents Act 1988.

56 [1987] RPC 599.

57 It had been claimed that the grooves were pattern or ornament and the registration was defective because it relied only upon features of shape and configuration. It was held that the grooves, being three-dimensional, were features of shape and configuration, regardless of the intention of applying them to the chairs. Other objections, raised on the basis that the design was similar to a prior registration and had been published prior to registration, also failed.

Infringement may also come about in other ways if done without the licence of the registered proprietor:

(a) making anything for enabling any such article to be made anywhere;[58]
(b) doing anything in relation to a kit which would infringe if done to the assembled article;
(c) making anything for enabling a kit to be made or assembled anywhere if the assembled article embodies the design.

58 Section 7(3) – the phrase used is 'in the United Kingdom or elsewhere'. 'Any such article' means any article in respect of which the design is registered and to which that design or one not substantially different has been applied.

A 'kit' means a complete or substantially complete set of components intended to be assembled into an article, section 7(4). However, there can be no infringement in respect of things done before the date that a certificate of registration was granted. Furthermore, there is no infringement of those features of shape or configuration of an article which are excluded by virtue of section 1(1)(b), if any. Reverse analysis of an article made to a design does not infringe, *per se,* but there might be an infringement depending upon how the knowledge thus gained is utilized.[59]

A would-be copier is defeated in attempting to overcome the right by making the article in a kit of parts. However, the protection does not extend to details which would not be registrable in their own right; for example, the right does not cover fastening devices used to assemble the parts. In *Dorling* v *Honnor Marine Ltd.*[60] Harman LJ said:

59 Reverse analysis, in this context, means taking an article apart and examining its component parts in order to determine the design attributes.

60 [1965] Ch 1.

> . . . I do not think that kits of parts are 'things made for enabling any such article to be made'. It is true that they may be parts of the article but they are not made in order to enable it to be made. If it were otherwise I do not see where one can stop: the words in their widest significance would include the screws and glue used to fasten the parts together.

DEFENCES TO INFRINGEMENT ACTIONS

Defences to an action for infringement of a registered design will, as is often the case with patent lawsuits, include an attack on the validity of the registration. For example, the defendant may choose to claim that:

(a) the design was not new when registered;[61]
(b) the registration has expired – this includes expiry by section 8(5) where a design was, at the time it was registered, a 'corresponding design' and the copyright has expired;[62]
(c) the design is primarily of a literary or artistic nature and excluded by the Registered Designs Rules 1989;[63]
(d) the design is contrary to law or morality and should not have been accepted for registration by the Registrar or he has otherwise exercised his discretion as to registration incorrectly (a judicial test).

61 Section 11 of the Registered Designs Act 1949 contains provisions concerning applications for cancellation of registration.

62 A 'corresponding design' is one which, in relation to an artistic work, if applied to an article would produce something which would be a copy of the artistic work, section 44 of the Registered Designs Act 1949.

63 SI 1989 No. 1105.

In any proceedings where the validity of a registered design is contested and the court holds that the registration is valid, it may certify that the validity of the registration was so contested, section 25 of the Registered Designs Act 1949. The effect of this is that, in future actions involving infringement of the design or its validity, the plaintiff is automatically entitled to his legal costs should the final award or order be made in his favour.

If there is no doubt about the validity of the registration, other defences that might be raised include:

(a) the plaintiff does not have *locus standi,* for example he is not the proprietor of the design;
(b) the alleged infringement does not relate to those details of the design claimed in the registration;
(c) the defendant's design is substantially different from that of the plaintiff;
(d) the alleged infringement occurred before registration (but the design right, if it also subsists in the design, could be infringed);[64]
(e) the alleged infringement only concerns those features left out of account when determining whether the plaintiff's design was registrable;[65]
(f) the act constituting the alleged infringement was done in good faith or seriously prepared for in good faith after expiry of the registration and before publication of an application for restoration of the right.[66]

A further possibility exists for an infringer when licences are available as of right in respect of the design. By section 11B, the defendant can undertake to take a licence on terms to be agreed or, failing agreement, on terms to be fixed by the Registrar. If the defendant makes such an undertaking, an injunction will not be granted against him and the amount recoverable in damages or by way of an account of profits shall not exceed double the amount that he would have paid had he obtained a licence on those terms before the earliest infringement. However, unlike the design right, registered designs will rarely be subject to licences as of right.

There is provision in the Registered Designs Act 1949 for a remedy against groundless threats of infringement proceedings whether by circulars, advertisement or otherwise.[67] The remedies for groundless threats of infringement proceedings are:

(a) a declaration to the effect that the threats are unjustifiable;
(b) an injunction against the continuation of the threats;
(c) damages, if any have been sustained – for example, the aggrieved party's business may have been detrimentally affected by the threats, his sales of the articles concerned may have been adversely affected.

It would seem that this provision extends to the situation where a person publicizes his views that another design infringes his registration and that he will take legal action for infringement. The burden of proof remains with the person making the threats, that is that the acts (or contemplated acts) complained of infringe the right in the registered design although the plaintiff would have to show that the registration is valid. Because of this, there is little, if anything, to be gained by making such threats and if they are without substance, the person making them could find himself liable for any harm caused to the other's business as a result of the threats. Another point is that suing for such groundless threats may precipitate an infringement action.[68]

REMEDIES

The Registered Designs Act 1949 does not specifically state what remedies are available although section 9 makes it clear that injunctions and damages are

64 Section 7(5).

65 Section 7(6).

66 Section 8B(4). In this situation, the person doing what would otherwise be an infringement may continue to do so even after restoration.

67 The scope of 'otherwise' could give rise to problems. For example, on the basis of the *ejusdem generis* rule of construction, would it extend to threats made over the telephone?

68 *Rosedale Associated Manufacturers Ltd.* v *Airfix Products Ltd.* [1957] RPC 239.

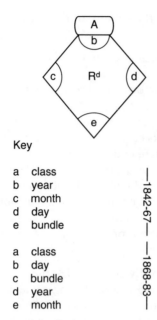

Key

a	class	┃
b	year	
c	month	1842-67
d	day	
e	bundle	┃

a	class	┃
b	day	
c	bundle	1868-83
d	year	
e	month	┃

Figure 18.1 Notice of design registration applied to articles
(Kindly supplied by the Design Registry)

possible remedies. Section 11B mentions an account of profits also. An award of damages is not available if the defendant can show that, at the time of infringement, he was not aware and had no reasonable grounds for supposing, that the design was registered.[69] It make good sense, therefore, for a notice to be placed upon articles incorporating the design. However, to be good, such a notice would have to include the registration number in addition to the word 'registered' or some abbreviation thereof. Merely affixing the words 'Registered Design' would, by section 9(1), appear to be insufficient but how, in such a case, a defendant could argue that he had no reasonable grounds for supposing that the design incorporated in the article was not a registered design is hard to imagine. An official form of notice was used in Victorian times to indicate registration, as shown in Figure 18.1.

Even if damages are not available because of lack of actual or constructive awareness of the right, section 9(2) makes it clear that an injunction still may be granted. An account of profits should also be available regardless of the defendant's lack of knowledge. Orders also may be granted for the destruction of or for the delivery-up of infringing articles.[70]

LICENCES – COMPULSORY AND AS OF RIGHT

Any person may apply to the Registrar for a compulsory licence in respect of a design which is not being applied to the articles for which it is registered to a reasonable extent.[71] This prevents an abuse of the registration by a proprietor who is happy to sit on the design and not exploit it for the time being. The Registrar may make any order he thinks fit. This will include the fixing of royalty

69 Section 9(1).

70 See, for example, *Cow (PB) & Co. Ltd. v Cannon Rubber Manufacturers Ltd.* [1959] RPC 240.

71 Section 10 of the Registered Designs Act 1949.

payments due under the compulsory licence. By section 10(2), an order for the grant of a compulsory licence shall take effect as if it were an executed deed. Licences available as of right in respect of a design may be provided for by the Registrar by making an entry on the register to that effect following application to the Registrar by the appropriate Minister or Ministers after a report by the Monopolies and Mergers Commission.[72] The report must contain conclusions that one of the following situations exists which operates or may operate against the public interest:

72 Section 11A.

(a) a monopoly situation;
(b) a merger situation which qualifies for investigation;
(c) a person engaged in an anti-competitive practice;
(d) a person pursuing a course of conduct covered by section 11 of the Competition Act 1980 (abuses of monopolies by nationalized industries).

Apart from declaring licences available as of right, the Registrar may cancel or modify any conditions in licences granted by the proprietor in respect of the registered design. Failing agreement as to the terms of a licence as of right, the Registrar has the power to fix those terms. There is an appeal procedure to an Appeal Tribunal constituted under section 28 of the Registered Designs Act 1949.

If a person has obtained the right to do an act which would have been an infringement by means of the time lag between expiry of the registration and notice of application for restoration of the right, that person may not grant a licence to another person to do that act although, if the act or the preparation for the act was done in the course of business, he may assign that right or it may transmit on his death to any person acquiring the relevant part of the business. He may also authorize any business partners for the time being to perform the act.

OFFENCES

There are three offences directly associated with registered designs and if such an offence is committed by a body corporate with the consent or connivance of an officer of the body such as a director, manager or secretary, that person in addition to the corporate body is guilty of the offence.[73] This also applies to persons purporting to act in such a capacity. By section 35, it is an offence for a person to falsely represent that a design applied to any article sold by him is registered in respect of that article. 'Represented' has a restricted meaning in that the offender has affixed the word 'registered', or any other word(s) to the effect that the design is registered, to the article, for example by stamping, engraving or impressing such word(s). Word of mouth is not sufficient. The liability appears to be strict albeit in a very narrow sense.

73 Section 35A.

For example, it is committed by a person selling the article who has impressed the word 'registered' believing that the design is subject to a valid registration and that he has the right to so mark the article.[74] This offence is triable summarily only and carries a fine not exceeding level 3 on the standard scale, currently £1,000. It is also an offence to mark articles in a like fashion after expiry of the right in a registered design. This offence could easily be com-

74 Section 35(2). Liability is strict in a narrow sense because it will not apply, for example, where the person is a dealer who sells such articles which were already marked when he obtained them. The person has to do the marking himself. However, other offences might be committed such as obtaining by deception; section 15 of the Theft Act 1968.

mitted by the proprietor of a recently expired design. However, selling articles to which a design relates after expiry of the design registration is not an offence providing the articles were marked before the expiry of the right.

Section 34 deals with the falsification of the register of designs. It is an offence, triable either way, to make or cause to be made either a false entry on the register or a counterfeit copy of a register entry. The falsification offence extends to producing, tendering or causing to be produced or tendered a counterfeit copy of an entry in the register in evidence. *Mens rea* is required for this offence, that is the person involved must know that the entry or written copy is false. Constructive knowledge is not sufficient. If tried on indictment, the maximum punishment is a term of imprisonment not exceeding 2 years or a fine or both. On summary conviction a person may be sentenced to imprisonment for a term not exceeding 6 months or a fine not exceeding the statutory maximum, currently £5,000, or both. Because the offence is worded 'makes or causes to be made', it could apply to the Registrar and his staff in addition to others.

Section 5 of the Registered Designs Act 1949 concerns requirements for secrecy in respect of designs which are relevant for defence purposes and allows the Registrar, subject to notification by the Secretary of State, to issue instructions prohibiting or restricting the publication or communication of information pertaining to the design. Written permission may also be required by a person resident in the United Kingdom before an application can be made outside the United Kingdom for the registration of a design of a prescribed class. Any person who fails to comply with such instructions or who makes or causes to be made such an application commits an offence under section 33 of the Act. The offence is triable either way and carries the same penalties as an offence under section 34.

REGISTRATION

The procedures for registration are comprehensively provided for by the Registered Designs Act 1949 and the Registered Designs Rules 1989 and reference to the relevant sections and rules should be made for the fine detail. Applications for registration are handled by the Designs Registry which is a branch of the Patent Office which publishes a document 'Design Registration' which outlines the procedures for registration.[75] There is no requirement that the proprietor is either a citizen of or resident in the United Kingdom, however by rule 8 of the Registered Designs Rules, he must have an address in the United Kingdom for service and this address will be entered on the register. The current fee for registering a design is £60.[76] There will be other expenses such as those incurred in the preparation of drawings or photographs and many proprietors use the services of an agent. Other fees are payable if, for example, a clerical error in the application has to be corrected. Following application, an examination and search is carried out at the Designs Registry and, if the Registrar does not object to the application, a Certificate of Registration will be issued. In straightforward cases, registration should be completed within about three to four months. Articles incorporating the design may be made or sold immediately following filing of the application although it should be noted that there can be no action for any infringement occurring before the date of grant of the certificate.

75 July 1993. This publication includes a specimen application.

76 Registered Designs (Fees) Rules 1990, SI 1992 No. 617. The fee for designs applied to lace or designs consisting mainly of stripes or checks applied to textiles is £35. The fee for a design applied to a set of articles is £90. The new scale of fees came into force on 11 May 1992.

Of course, if the design right also subsists in the design, an action may be based on this for such infringement.

It was anticipated that changes to design law, especially the removal of copyright protection of designs through their drawings would produce a rush of applications, especially after 1 August 1989 when the new provisions came into force. There was a slight increase in 1989 but the number of applications has fallen back and remains disappointing. The transitional arrangements may account for this as designs existing prior to 1 August 1989 can still enjoy copyright protection for their design documents until 1999.[77] For many designs created on or after 1 August 1989, the owner may hope to rely on the design right – although it does not give a monopoly right like the registered design.

Table 18.1 shows the numbers of applications and registrations for designs since 1985.[78] The proportion of foreign applicants is notable (a United Kingdom registration is accepted in a number of other countries with or without local re-registration). It should also be noted that the volume of registrations was much higher during Victorian times, often being in excess of 20,000 per annum.

77 Para. 19(1), Schedule 1, Copyright, Designs and Patents Act 1988. However, licences are available as of right.

78 The Patent Office, *Annual Report and Accounts 1992 to 1993* (London: HMSO, 1993).

Table 18.1 Registered design activity

Year	Applications	Proportion from foreign applicants %	Designs registered
1985	7,395	52.1	6,546
1986	7,844	55.3	7,167
1987	8,646	51.9	7,140
1988	8,748	55.5	8,049
1989	9,317	58.9	8,945
1990	8,566	55.1	9,171
1991	8,074	61.4	6,271
1992	8,267	66.8	8,175

Because of the time lag between application and grant, the annual totals for designs registered do not necessarily apply to applications made in the same calendar year. There is a priority system and the priority of an earlier application elsewhere may be claimed for up to six months.

Duration, renewal and restoration of lapsed registration

The initial registration period is five years from the date as of which the design is registered. Registration may be renewed for a second, third, fourth and fifth period of five years. Most designs have a limited commercial life and it is unlikely that many will be renewed for a fourth or fifth period. In 1992, a total of 3,465 designs were renewed for a second period and only 1,196 were renewed for a third period. It will be the year 2004 before any designs will be renewable for a fourth period as designs registered before 1 August 1989 can be registered for a maximum of 15 years only. There is, effectively, a period of six months' grace during which time the registration can be renewed without affecting its validity. If the design was first registered prior to 1 August 1989, the renewal must be made within that six month period otherwise the right is lost forever.[79] However, in relation to designs first registered on or after 1 August 1989, there is a further 6 months' period during which the right can be restored.[80] The Registrar publishes notices of applications for restoration but it is not an automatic right, the Registrar has a discretion and must be satisfied that the proprietor took reasonable care to see that the period of registration was extended in accordance with either section 8(2) or 8(4). If restoration is applied for and granted there are some effects as regards infringement of the right. Figure 18.2 applies to a design first registered on or after 1 August 1989.

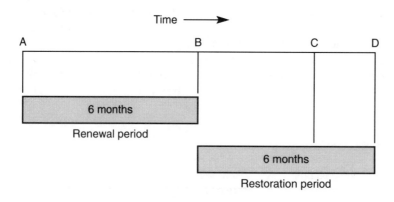

Figure 18.2 Renewal and restoration of registered design

In the diagram:
   A is the date of expiry of the registration
   B is the last date for renewal of the registration
   C is the actual date of an application for restoration
   D is the last date for application of renewal

Note that the restoration period only applies to designs registered on or after 1 August 1989.

Referring to Figure 18.2, during the period A to B the right may be renewed (providing it has not previously been renewed for a fifth period of five years) on payment of the appropriate renewal fee plus an additional fee of £18 per month. By section 8(4), the design is treated as if it had never expired. For the sake of argument, imagine that an application to restore the right is made at time C. Then, even if the restoration is permitted, a person may acquire rights in respect of the design if, during the period B to C, he began an act in good faith or made effective and serious preparations to do such an act.[81] If the registration is restored, acts which would normally have infringed the design which were done during the period A to B are treated as infringing acts as are continuations or repetitions of earlier infringing acts. However, an act which would have infringed which was carried out during the period B to C gives the proprietor no remedy unless it was a repeat of an earlier infringing act.[82] Fees for renewal are £130 for a second term and £210 for a third term. Restoration fees amount to £240 plus the renewal fee.[83]

79 Designs first registered prior to 1 August 1989 cannot be renewed beyond a third 5 year period.

80 Section 8A refers to a prescribed period during which the right can be restored. By Rule 41 of the Registered Designs Rule 1989, SI 1989 No. 1105, the prescribed period is 12 months from the date on which the right expired.

81 The right is to do the act or to continue to do the act, section 8A(4). Section 8A(5) allows business partners and acquirers of the person's business to do the acts.

82 Section 8A(3).

83 Registered Designs (Fees) Rules 1992, SI 1992 No. 617. The fees for renewal for the fourth and fifth terms have not yet been set. It will be some time before any designs will reach this stage.

INTERNATIONAL PROTECTION

Some countries, mainly belonging to the Commonwealth, recognize registration in the United Kingdom as being equivalent to registration in the country concerned. A large number of these countries (over 30) extend protection to United Kingdom registered designs without the need for local registration. These countries include Antigua, Bermuda, Botswana, Cyprus, Fiji, Ghana, Gibraltar, Hong Kong, Kenya, Malaysia, Sierre Leone, Singapore, Uganda and the Yeminite Arab Republic. Persons and organizations in these countries desiring protection for their designs normally register them at the United Kingdom Design Registry through an agent based in the United Kingdom.

Other countries and territories such as Guernsey, Jersey, Malta and Tanzania extend protection to United Kingdom registered designs, subject to local re-registration of the design.

If protection is required in another country, apart from those that recognize a United Kingdom registration, application must be made in each country for which protection is sought. The Paris Convention for Industrial Property 1883 has been ratified by most of the industrialized countries in the world and a person who has applied for registration of a design in any of the 102 convention countries is effectively given a priority with respect to applications to other convention countries made within 6 months following the first application.[84] However, a resident of the United Kingdom is forbidden to make such an application until after the expiry of six weeks from the United Kingdom application[85] or if directions prohibiting or restricting publication, etc. have been given by the Registrar. It has already been noted in the previous chapter that there is some variation in legal methods used by different countries for the protection of designs.

CROWN USE

In common with patents and the design right, the Crown can make use of the subject-matter of the right. As regards registered designs, Schedule 1 to the Registered Designs Act 1949 contains the necessary provisions. By paragraph 1(1), any government department may use, or authorize the use of, any registered design for the services of the Crown. Terms must be agreed, either before or after use, between the government department concerned and the registered proprietor with the approval of the Treasury. If agreement cannot be reached, the terms are to be determined by reference to the High Court. 'The services of the Crown' are defined in paragraph 1(6) and include:

(a) the supply to the government of a country outside the United Kingdom of articles required for the defence of that country or of any other country, subject to an agreement or arrangement involving Her Majesty's Government;

(b) the supply to the United Nations or any country belonging to the United Nations of articles required for any armed forces operating in pursuance of United Nations resolution, subject to an agreement or arrangement involving Her Majesty's Government.

84 Section 14(1). The applicant has to complete a declaration concerning the first application.

85 This is a result of section 5 of the Registered Designs Act 1949 which contains provisions for secrecy of certain designs. The Registrar has powers under this section to prohibit or restrict publication or the communication of information in respect of designs of a class notified by the Secretary of State as being relevant for defence purposes. The Secretary of State may then consider whether publication of the design would be prejudicial to the defence of the realm.

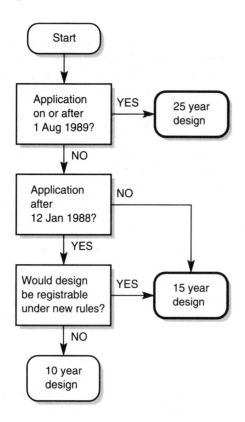

Notes: the periods relate to the maximum available subject to renewal. The '10 year' designs expire not later than 1 August 1989

Figure 18.3 Transitional provisions in relation to registrable designs

This is not an exhaustive definition, it merely indicates that the listed situations fall within the meaning of Crown use. It would also extend to use for the armed forces of the United Kingdom. Given the aesthetic nature of registered designs, it is unlikely that these provisions will be used to any great extent. An example could be where the design relates to an item of clothing or kit which could be used by soldiers. The only time payment will not be made is when the design has been recorded or applied by or on behalf of a government department prior to the date of registration.[86] This does not apply in respect of direct or indirect communications by the registered proprietor or any person through whom he derives title. The effect of this very limited provision is to allow free Crown use of a design independently and concurrently developed by a Government department.

86 Para. 1(2), Schedule 1.

TRANSITIONAL PROVISIONS

There are some transitional arrangements that will be effective for some years to come. These are necessary because of the changes in the law relating to registered designs. For designs registered in pursuance of an application filed on or after 1 August 1989, the maximum period for the registration is 25 years. For designs registered in pursuance of an application made before 1 August 1989, the normal maximum period is 15 years. However, if a design has been registered in pursuance of an application made after 12 January 1988 and before 1 August 1989 *and* that design would not now be registrable under section 1 of the Registered Designs Act 1949 as amended, the design registration must expire on 1 August 1999 unless it expires earlier in any event.[87] For such designs, licences have been available as of right since 1 August 1989 although, at the time of writing, no applications have been received by the Design Registry for licences as of right.

For designs that were created before 1 August 1989, the exclusion of copyright protection for design documents recording the design (or models embodying the design) does not operate for ten years after that date. Although directed at the design right this provision will also affect many of those registrable designs.[88] However, by paragraph 6(1) of Schedule 1 to the 1988 Act, copyright does not subsist in drawings of designs made before 1 June 1957.

The flowchart in Figure 18.3 shows these transitional provisions in relation to a design which existed prior to 1 August 1989.

EXAMPLE REGISTRATION

There follows an example of a registered design for the shape or configuration of a typists' chair including details from the certificate of registration.[89] Note the date of filing, date of grant and the priority date from an earlier application. There is a description of the article to which the design will be applied, the name and address of the proprietor and, in this case, an address for service in the United Kingdom (which is the agent's address). The novelty statement appears on the representation of the design. The design is reproduced with the permission of Fehlbaum & Co. and their agents Frank B Dehn & Co.

[87] Section 266(1) of the Copyright, Designs and Patents Act 1988.

[88] Para. 19, Schedule 1 to the Copyright, Designs and Patents Act 1988.

[89] Not all the representations are reproduced here.

DATE   13/ 9/1993.   PAGE   1

REGISTER ENTRY FOR DESIGN NUMBER   2029805

Date of Application. 16th March 1993

Date Application Treated as having been made under Section 14(2) of the Registered Designs Act 1949 as amended by the Copyright, Designs and Patents Act 1988 28th September 1992

Date as of which design registered 28th September 1992

Certificate of registration granted 19th July 1993

Article in respect of which design registered:
        'Chair

Name(s) and Address(es) of Proprietor(s):
        Fehlbaum & Co
        Kappeligasse 22
        CH-4125 Riehen
        SWITZERLAND

Address for Service
        Frank B Dehn & Co
        Imperial House
        15-19 Kingsway
        London
        WC2B 6UZ

FEHLBAUM & CO

2029805

The features of the design for
which novelty is claimed are the
shape and configuration of the
article shown in the representations.

Perspective view from
front and right side

Front elevation

19

Design right

INTRODUCTION

The introduction of the design right must be seen in the context of the history of design law prior to the enactment of the right.[1] Until the Design Copyright Act 1968, there was a gap in protection for designs which were primarily functional in nature. Copyright protected artistic works, patents were available for new inventions, and designs having eye-appeal could be protected by registration. However, a design having no eye-appeal, for example an overflow pipe for a washing machine, had no form of protection, *per se*.[2] The effect of the Design Copyright Act 1968 was to extend copyright protection to designs applied industrially for a period of 15 years from the end of the calendar year during which the relevant articles were first marketed. Eventually, by way of unanticipated judicial creativity, copyright was recognized as providing protection for functional designs through the medium of drawings for 50 years after the author's death.[3] Thus, unregistrable designs were given much longer protection than the 15 years maximum then available for registered designs.[4] Later, attempts were made to redress this inequality as in *British Leyland Motor Corp. Ltd. v Armstrong Patents Co. Ltd.*[5] It was seen to be important that persons buying articles that would need repairing during their life should be able to have access to a free market in spare parts and that, if a right in functional designs were to be established, some balance would have to be taken into account. Several options faced Parliament: it could introduce a petty patent system similar to that existing in some European countries, it could extend registered design law to include functional designs or it could leave protection to be gained via the medium of drawings. The White Paper that preceded the Copyright, Designs and Patents Act 1988[6] rejected all other solutions and suggested a new right that would apply, automatically, to original designs for three-dimensional articles broadly along copyright principles. A contrast can be made at once with registered designs for which protection is along lines analogous to patent law.

The Patent Office describe the design right as:

> a new intellectual property right which applies to original, non-commonplace designs of the shape or configuration of articles. . . . [It] is not a monopoly right but a right to prevent copying.[7]

Like copyright, the design right is a property right that is subject to qualification requirements. No formalities are required. However, the duration of the right is much less, being effectively no more than 10 years. The right only applies to designs for three-dimensional articles and there are some controversial exceptions which allow the making of spare parts by others. There is an overlap between this right and the right in a registered design and some designs

1 For a comprehensive and lively description of the background to the design right, see Walton, A. 'The Copyright, Designs and Patents Act 1988 (1)' (1989) 133 *Solicitors Journal* 646.

2 Other rights could subsist such as trade marks and passing off depending on the nature of the article.

3 Graham J in *Sifam* v *Sangamo* [1971] 2 All ER 1074, applying *Dorling* v *Honnor Marine Ltd.* [1965] Ch 1.

4 Section 10 of the Copyright Act 1956 effectively removed dual protection for registrable designs. The Design Copyright Act 1968 reinstated artistic copyright protection but limited it to 15 years for registrable designs.

5 [1986] 2 WLR 400.

6 *Intellectual Property and Innovation* Cmnd. 9712 (London: HMSO, 1986).

7 The Patent Office, *Designs: Basic Facts* (Newport: The Patent Office, 1992), at 6.

that are subject to the design right may also be registered. However, there are different requirements for the two rights and this overlap is not, therefore, absolute. Some functional designs cannot be registered and some registered designs fall outside the design right provisions. Examples of designs in which a design right is capable of subsisting are exhaust pipes and other parts for motor vehicles, tools, kitchen utensils, office equipment, packaging.

Design right is limited so that it will not usually extend to features that must be the shape they are so that they can fit or match another article. The design right is comparatively weak as it is not a monopoly right and it is of short duration. Furthermore, in the last five years of the right, licences are available as of right.

The design right came into existence on 1 August 1989 and is contained in Part III of the Copyright, Designs and Patents Act 1988. The provisions are not retrospective and designs that were expressed in a tangible form[8] prior to this date are not protected by the design right. Such designs may be protected through their preparatory drawings as section 51 of the 1988 Act does not apply for ten years to such designs, that is until 1 August 1999.[9] The design right provisions apply to England and Wales, Scotland and Northern Ireland. This may be extended to the Channel Islands, the Isle of Man or any colony by Her Majesty's Order in Council.[10]

As a result of compliance with a European Community Directive, the United Kingdom has afforded specific protection to the topographies of semiconductor products. This was done by means of the design right and the design right provisions of the Copyright, Designs and Patents Act 1988 were adapted to provide the required degree of protection. This special form of the design right is dealt with towards the end of this chapter.

SUBSISTENCE OF RIGHT

By section 213(1) of the Copyright, Designs and Patents Act 1988, for the design right to subsist in a design, it must be an original design. Furthermore, there is a requirement for qualification which must be satisfied and the design must be fixed in some tangible form by recording it in a design document or by making an article to the design. Computer-generated designs are defined in section 263(1) as designs generated by computer in circumstances such that there is no human designer. What has been said about computer-generated original works of copyright applies equally here and one can question whether there can ever be such a thing as a computer-generated design.[11] 'Design' means the 'design of any aspect of the shape or configuration (whether external or internal) of the whole or part of an article'.[12] The design right provisions also apply to articles made in a kit of parts being a complete or substantially complete set of components intended to be assembled into an article and it is possible that a design right subsists in a component as distinct from the design right in the assembled article.[13] However, as will be seen later, those features of components in the kit of parts which are shaped or configured specifically to match or fit other components are barred from design right protection.

In some respects the design right applies to a broader type of design than is the case with registrable designs. For example, the aspects of shape or configuration can be internal and may apply to part of an article. For a registered

8 Being recorded in a design document or having an article made to the design.

9 Para. 19, Schedule 1 to the Copyright, Designs and Patents Act 1988. Unless otherwise stated, in this chapter, statutory references are to this Act.

10 Section 255.

11 See Chapter 8.

12 Section 213(2).

13 Section 260.

design, the requirement for eye-appeal means that the features must be external unless the outside surface of the article is transparent. However, registered designs can also relate to parts of articles – for example, a new design of spout for a teapot will not be rejected simply because it relates only to a part of the teapot and not the whole pot. [14]

.4 In such a case, there may be disclaimer as to the rest of the rticle which may be coloured •lue on the representation and xcluded from the novelty tatement.

Exceptions

The design right is declared by section 213(3) not to subsist in:

(a) Methods or principles of construction.
(b) Features of shape or configuration which:
    (i) enable the article to be connected to, placed in, around or against another article so that either article may perform its function (the 'must-fit' exception), or
    (ii) are dependent upon the appearance of another article of which the article is intended by the designer (creator of the design) to form an integral part (the 'must-match' exception).
(c) Surface decoration.

15 [1987] RPC 599.

The first exception and the must-match exception are identical to those for registered designs but the surface decoration exception distinguishes the two rights. The must-fit exception is differently worded and probably narrower than the equivalent exception for registered designs. Registered designs can be applied to two-dimensional articles, such as a textile design whereas a design to which the design right applies must relate to shape or configuration. This could, as in the registered design case of *Sommer Allibert (UK) Ltd. v Flair Plastics Ltd.*,[15] apply to a raised surface pattern such as a relief or embossed pattern because that has three dimensions. In that case, it was confirmed that grooves in a garden chair were features of shape and configuration.

The must-fit and must-match exceptions have significant implications for the manufacturers of replacement parts. These exceptions are also relevant to manufacturers of accessory parts, for example a lamp to fit on a bicycle mounting or a dust cover for a typewriter. Because of the must-fit exception, the features that must accordingly be a certain shape or configuration can be made without infringing the design right. In the examples quoted this would extend to the connecting features of the lamp enabling it to be connected to the mounting bracket on the bicycle and the shape of the dust cover in as much as it had to be that shape to fit over the typewriter for which it was designed. Two points must be noted with respect to these exceptions:

(a) The exceptions do not extend to other features. For example, in the case of an exhaust system for a motor car, only those parts of the design that relate to the fixing of the exhaust system to the mounting brackets on the car and to the outlet at the engine manifold are excepted from the design right. These features of shape or configuration enable the exhaust to be fitted to the car body and to the engine so that the exhaust system can perform its function, that is the control of noise and engine emissions. Other features of the shape or configuration of the exhaust system may be subject to the right, for example if an unusual shape is selected for a silencer box (perhaps elliptical in cross-section rather than circular) that has nothing to do with the connection of the system to the car. A spare part manufacturer may copy the 'connecting' details but nothing else unless the other features are commonplace or any design right in them has expired. This seems to be less generous than the 'licence to copy' replacement parts granted by the House of Lords in *British Leyland Motor Corp. Ltd.* v *Armstrong Patents Co. Ltd.*[16]

16 [1986] 2 WLR 400.

(b) The other article referred to in section 213(3) could be made by the same person who makes the article we are interested in. For example, if a person manufacturers something comprising two articles (or an article that can be taken apart), then the connection between the articles will not be protected by the design right irrespective of the amount of research and development which may have been expended in the design of the connection.[17] The only time this exception cannot operate is if the connection is not relevant to the performance of function by either article. However, this would be highly unlikely.

17 'Connection' is taken in a wide sense here, covering all the situations described in section 213(3)(b).

Another example of the must-fit exception is where a manufacturer makes a television set and sells it together with a stand on which the set can be supported and swivelled around. The connection between the stand and the base of the television set (the mechanical interface) is not protected by the design right. All other features of the shape or configuration of both the television set and the stand are in principle – and subject to the other requirements such as originality – capable of design right protection. Another manufacturer can make replacement stands for the television sets copying details of the interface but no other details unless they are commonplace or if the design right in relation to them has expired.

The basic principles are the same as for the must-match exception. Again, the motor car can provide a good example. Consider replacement doors for a car. They obviously have to be a certain profile on the outside to match the sweep of the bodywork and would look extremely odd if they did not have this profile. The replacement doors also have to be a certain shape to fit the gap left for the door in the car body. All these features are excepted from the design right. However, most car doors have an inner skin which is hidden from view by upholstery (usually plastic). The inner skin often has holes for lightness and ribs for strength. The position and size of the holes and configuration of the ribs are irrelevant as regards appearance and, if their design is original, they may be protected by the design right and do not fall within the scope of the exception. Spare parts manufacturers must be aware of this and be careful not to copy those aspects of shape or configuration in which a design right might subsist and only copy those elements falling within the exceptions. It may be difficult, in many cases, to determine where the design right does and does not apply. Also, whether a particular right has expired could be extremely difficult to ascertain as there is not the benefit of a registration system and register that can be consulted to resolve such questions.

Originality

For a design right to subsist in a design it must be original. This is defined in the negative by section 213(4) which states that a design is not original if it is 'commonplace in the design field at the time of its creation'. What, then, does originality mean in the context of the design right? It is clear that it is not as high a standard as required for a registered design yet it appears to be more stringent than is usually the case in copyright which has been interpreted by judges to require simply that the work has originated from the author and has not merely been copied.[18] For a design to be registered it must be new, having not been previously registered or published in the United Kingdom in relation to the article to which the design is to be applied or any other article. This is a fairly high standard of originality. However, for the design right to apply to a design it must not be commonplace in the design field in question. As yet, there is little judicial guidance as to the meaning of this. In *C & H Engineering* v *F Klucznik & Sons Ltd*.[19] Aldous J said that the word original should be given the same meaning as it is in respect of copyright. That is, not copied but the independent work of the designer. He went on to say that this should be contrasted with the novelty requirement for registered designs. However, Aldous J continued (at 428):

> The word 'commonplace' is not defined, but [section 213(4)] appears to introduce a consideration akin to novelty. For the design to be original it must be the work of the creator and that work must result in a design which is not commonplace in the relevant field.

It is submitted that Aldous J goes too far in equating not being commonplace with novelty. The requirement of novelty must be more stringent because it permits no anticipation of the design whatsoever (although this is measured by registration or publication only).[20] However, a small number of articles may have been released onto the market or a representation of the design may have been published in a magazine with limited circulation and yet the design may still not be commonplace. It could be argued that a design will not be commonplace until a large number of persons working in, or knowledgeable about, the particular design field are familiar with the design.

The test of originality in the Act is very unsatisfactory and imprecise and it would have been better had a test of anticipation similar to that applying to patents been used. The *C & H Engineering* case has done nothing to bring predictability to the requirement of originality. Consider the following situations involving two designs which are similar and have been created by two designers Alice and Bernard. The designs, intended to be applied to a locking mechanism for sliding doors, have been created independently.

(a) Alice and Bernard create their designs and record them at around the same point in time.

(b) Alice and Bernard create their designs and record them at around the same point in time but there is a time difference in the marketing of articles made to the designs. Articles to which Alice's design has been applied reach the market place in advance of articles made to Bernard's design. In the meantime, articles to Alice's design do not sell in large numbers.

(c) Again, Alice and Bernard create and record their designs at the same time and articles made to Alice's design reach the market place first but this time large numbers of articles to Alice's design are sold before the appearance of articles made to Bernard's design.

18 For example, see the judgment of Lord Pearce in *Ladbroke (Football) Ltd.* v *William Hill (Football) Ltd.* 1964] 1 WLR 273.

19 [1992] FSR 421.

20 See section 1(4) of the Registered Designs Act 1949.

(d) Bernard does not create and record his design until after small numbers of articles made to Alice's design have been marketed or sold. (Bernard has not seen the articles.)

(e) Bernard creates and records his design after large numbers of articles made to Alice's design have been marketed and sold. (Again, Bernard does not see any of the articles to Alice's design.)

(f) Several other similar designs have been recorded and articles made to the designs have been marketed and sold before Bernard, in ignorance of these, creates his similar design.

In (a), (b) and (c) above, both Alice and Bernard have created designs in which the design right is capable of subsisting. The design was not commonplace at the time of its creation by Alice and by Bernard because the creation of the designs was coincident in time, or nearly so.[21] The fact that numbers of articles have been sold is irrelevant to the subsistence of the design rights and reference must be made to the time when the designs were created, at which time the design or variants of it was not commonplace. Situation (f) is easily dealt with – it is clear that at the time Bernard creates his design, the design has become commonplace in the design field. Situations (d) and (e) are less easy to distinguish but it is clear that the test will be applied objectively, probably through the eyes of an interested person, for example someone working in or knowledgeable about the design field in question. It is suggested that, if only small numbers of articles made to Alice's design have been sold, there is a possibility that Bernard's design can still attract the design right. This prompts another question as to whether it is sufficient that only one other example of a similar design has been created and applied to articles or whether the design, or variants of the design, are commonly used by a majority of designers in the particular design field. Incidentally, in none of the examples above does Bernard infringe Alice's design right.

Tangible form requirement

The design right springs into force when the design is recorded in a design document or, alternatively, when an article has been made to the design whichever happens first.[22] 'Design document' is defined by section 263, which contains minor definitions, as 'any record of a design, whether in the form of a drawing, a written description, a photograph, data stored in a computer or otherwise'. This would appear to cover virtually any form of recording and would be likely to include data stored on a compact disc, magnetic tape or a computer disk depending on the meaning of 'or otherwise'. Bearing in mind the wide variety of forms of storage mentioned specifically, it is certain that this will be construed very widely. The only difficulty could be with temporary storage and, on the basis of the House of Lords judgment in *R v Gold*,[23] temporary storage in a computer's volatile memory may not be sufficient although, as soon as the relevant data is copied onto a computer disk, this will be sufficient. One question which arises is whether storage on a removable computer disk is storage in a computer. However, this should be caught by the scope of the phrase 'or otherwise'.

Old designs cannot be resurrected by the design right because section 213(7) declares that the right does not subsist in designs that were recorded in a design

21 The time of the creation of a design may be of crucial importance in a case like this and the need for independent evidence as to the date of the creation of a design is a matter which should not be overlooked by designers, their employers and commissioners.

22 Section 213(6).

23 [1988] 2 WLR 984.

document or which have been applied to an article prior to the commencement of Part III of the Copyright, Designs and Patents Act 1988.[24]

Qualification

As with copyright law, some qualification requirements must be satisfied for the right to subsist in a design. These may be fulfilled by reference to the designer or, where relevant, the designer's employer or the commissioner of the design. A further route to satisfying the qualification requirements is through the first person who markets articles made to the design and the country in which that first marketing took place. There are, therefore, four possible routes to qualification. However, before the provisions can be understood, three terms used have to be defined: they are 'qualifying country', 'qualifying individual' and 'qualifying person'.[25]

'Qualifying country' means the United Kingdom and other Member States of the European Economic Community. Other countries may be added by Order in Council either under section 255 or section 256, the latter applying where the other country has reciprocal provisions for design rights. New Zealand, Hong Kong, the Channel Islands, the Isle of Man, Bermuda amongst others have been added to the list of qualifying countries by Order under section 256.[26]

'Qualifying individual' is a citizen, subject or person habitually resident in a qualifying country.[27]

'Qualifying person' means a qualifying individual or a body having legal personality including a body corporate which has been formed under the law of a qualifying country and which has, in any qualifying country, a place of business at which substantial business activity is carried out. In determining whether substantial business is carried out, no account is to be taken of dealings with goods which are, at all material times, outside the qualifying country. By section 263(1) 'business' includes a trade or profession.

The routes to qualification are by reference to:

(a) The designer, being the person who creates the design. If the design is computer-generated, the designer is taken to be the person by whom the arrangements necessary for the creation of the work are undertaken.[28] By section 218(2), a design qualifies for protection if the designer is a qualifying *individual* or, if the design is computer-generated, the designer is a qualifying person. A joint design is the result of collaboration between two or more designers such that their individual contributions are indistinct from one another.[29] A joint design qualifies if any of the designers is a qualifying individual (or a qualifying person for a computer-generated joint design). These provisions do not apply, however, if the design is created in the pursuance of a commission or in the course of employment.[30]

(b) The commissioner, if the design is commissioned and the commissioner is a qualifying *person* (section 219(1)). A commissioned design is one commissioned for money or money's worth.[31]

(c) The employer, if the design is created by the designer in the course of employment and the employer is a qualifying *person* (section 219(1)). Section 263(1) states that 'employee', 'employment' and 'employer' refer to employment under a contract of service or of apprenticeship. This definition is identical to that applying to copyright works.

---

24 The commencement date is August 1989.

25 Defined in section 217.

26 Design Right (Reciprocal Protection) (No. 2) Order 1989, SI 1989 No. 1294. Regulation 2 gives a full list of countries designated as enjoying reciprocal protection.

27 In respect of the United Kingdom, a citizen is a living person who is a British citizen or, in relation to a colony of the United Kingdom, a British Dependent Territories citizen in connection with that colony.

28 Section 214.

29 Section 259(1).

30 Section 218(1).

31 Section 263(1).

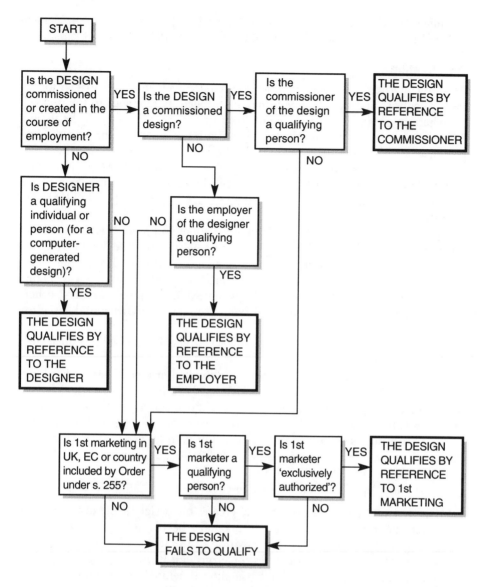

Figure 19.1 Qualification for the design right

(d) The first marketing of articles made to the design.[32] This can only apply if the other qualification requirements do not. In this case, the requirement is that the first marketing is done by a qualifying *person* exclusively authorized to put such articles on the market in the United Kingdom and it takes place in the United Kingdom, any other Member State of the European Economic Community or other country to which Part III of the Act has been extended by Order under section 255 but not to countries affording reciprocal protection included by Order under section 256. 'Exclusively authorized' refers (i) to authorization by the person who would have been the first owner of the right as designer, commissioner or employer had he (or it)

32 Section 220.

been a qualifying person including a person lawfully claiming under him and (ii) to exclusivity capable of legal enforcement in the United Kingdom.

In the case of a joint commission or a joint employment or joint marketing, the design qualifies if any of the commissioners, employers or marketers is a qualifying person. A design which would not otherwise qualify may so qualify for protection subject to specified requirements in an Order in Council so that an international obligation of the United Kingdom is fulfilled.[33] The flowchart shown in Figure 19.1 (opposite) sets out the various routes to qualification and their relationship.

33 Section 221.

Duration of design right

An important date in measuring the duration of a design right is the end of the calendar year during which the design was first either recorded in a design document or an article was made to the design. In other words this is the end of the calendar year during which the right came into existence. In the discussion below, this date is referred to as the 'end of the creation year'. The generosity of the law with regard to the duration of protection for functional designs through their drawings has been severely curtailed and now the maximum length of protection for a functional design by way of the design right is 15 years from the end of the creation year. In many cases, where the design has been commercially exploited, the period will be less than that. If articles made to the design have been made available for sale or hire, anywhere in the world by or with the licence of the owner of the right, within five years from the end of the creation year then, by section 216(1)(b), the design right expires ten years from the end of the calendar year during which that happened (the end of the first exploitation year).

The owner of the design right is given, effectively, ten years to exploit his design. However, during the last five years licences are available as of right.[34] The possible reduction in the term of protection from 15 years will not occur if articles made to the design have been offered for sale or hire by a person without the permission of the owner of the right, for example in the case of counterfeit articles, or if articles made to the design are placed in a public exhibition. However, if the owner of the design delays beyond the first five years, that will eat into the time he has in which to exploit the work. Figure 19.2 (p.382) shows how the duration rules work, assuming that, at some time, articles made to the design are made available for sale or hire.

34 Copyists must still beware of other areas of law which might apply to the articles such as registered design or passing off. In practice the owner will have little more than ten years depending on the time of year he commences offering articles for sale or hire.

35 Alternatively, because there are no formal registration requirements, it might be tempting to lie about the time the design was first put in a tangible form. That is, to keep quiet about a design that will not be exploited for several years. However, this might cause problems if, in the meantime, another person markets articles to a similar design. The best advice would be to have the design documents lodged with an independent person immediately it is created.

If period x is less than five years, then the total duration of the right, d, is $w + x + y + 10$ years, that is, $z = 10$ years (Date E + 10 years). However, if period x is more than five years, the total duration of the right, d, is $w + 15$ years (Date C + 15 years) and the period z is reduced accordingly. For example, if the design was created (and put in a tangible form) in April 1990 but articles made to the design were not made available for sale or hire until July 1997, the right expires at the end of year 2005. It is, therefore, important to commercially exploit the design within the first five years for maximum duration of commercial protection.[35]

Design rights will always expire at the end of a calendar year irrespective of the actual dates of creation or first exploitation. In the diagram, time interval A to B is of no relevance as regards the design right. Of course, during this period,

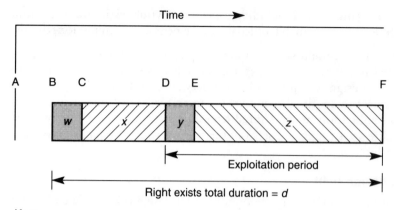

Key:
A – Designer has idea for a design
B – Design recorded in a design document or article made to
    design (creation)
C – End of calendar year during which creation happens
    (end of creation year)
D – Articles made to the design are made available for sale or hire
    (first exploitation)
E – End of calendar year during which articles to design are made
    available for sale or hire (end of first exploitation year)
F – Right expires.

Figure 19.2 Duration of design right

the design right has not yet been born and there is no remedy in design law if it
is reproduced, say from an oral description, although there may be a remedy
under the law of breach of confidence. If the oral description is recorded on
magnetic tape, with or without the permission of the designer, the right is born
because the design has been recorded in a design document and the definition of
design document in section 263(1) should be wide enough to include this form of
storage. The person recording the design will have no design right in it by reason
of having recorded it because rights are allocated by reference to the designer
who is the person who creates the design. The designer need not be the person
recording the design.[36] However, a person who records an oral description of a
design will have rights under copyright law in the sound recording thus created.

36 This point was made by
Aldous J in *C & H Engineering*
v *F Klucznik & Sons Ltd.*
[1992] FSR 421.

OWNERSHIP

The rules for first ownership of the design right are fairly straightforward and
the situation is more satisfactory than is the case with works of copyright where
the concept of an implied licence or of beneficial ownership may be called upon
to do justice. Of course, first ownership is conditioned by the route to qualification and four possibilities exist, there being a one to one correlation between
the qualifying individual or person and the first owner:

(a) Qualification by reference to designer, that is, in respect of a design not cre-
    ated either in the course of employment or in pursuance of a commission. In

37 The basic statements of
first ownership are contained in
section 215.

this case, the designer is the first owner of the design right.[37]

(b) Qualification by reference to the commissioner. The commissioner is the first owner of the design right.

(c) Qualification by reference to the employer (not being a design created in the pursuance of a commission). The employer is the first owner of the design right.

(d) Qualification by reference to the first marketing of articles made to the design. The person so marketing the articles is the first owner of the design right.

Joint first owners are possible where there is a joint design, being one created by two or more designers where the contribution of each is not distinct from the other(s), and a design will satisfy the qualification requirements if only one individual or person meets those requirements.[38] This leaves the problem of what rights the other joint designers, commissioners, etc. have in terms of ownership and the approach taken by the Act is that they have absolutely none. Only those individuals or persons who meet the qualification requirements are entitled to the design right.[39] For example, if a design is created by three self-employed designers, one being a British citizen, one being a citizen of France and the other being a Japanese citizen, as far as United Kingdom law is concerned, assuming the design was not created in pursuance of a commission, the joint first owners of the design will be the British citizen and the French citizen. The Japanese citizen will not be entitled to any ownership rights unless he qualifies by virtue of being habitually resident in a qualifying country. However, the ownership provisions are relatively generous in the scope of their reach and protection is afforded, for example, to citizens of Member States of the European Economic Community without there being any equivalent and reciprocal provisions for protection of functional designs created by British citizens. In all cases, the place the design was created is irrelevant.

38 If the designers'
contributions are distinct then
each will be regarded as the
sole designer in respect of his
own efforts, section 259(1).
The design is thus divisible and
can be regarded as a
combination of separate
designs which can owned by
different persons.

39 See sections 218(4), 219(3)
and 220(3).

Assignment and licensing

Design rights can be assigned but, by section 222(3), this must be done in writing and signed by or on behalf of the assignor. The right can also pass by testamentary disposition or by operation of law.[40] An assignment may be partial, limited to apply to not all the exclusive rights of the owner or limited in terms of duration. Licences may be granted by the owner and may be exclusive or otherwise. An exclusive licence, by section 225, must be in writing signed by or on behalf of the design right owner and an exclusive licensee has the same rights and remedies, except against the owner, as if the licence had been an assignment.[41] The Act contains provisions for the exercise of concurrent rights by the owner and an exclusive licensee.[42] Although there is little practical difference between an assignment or a licence, the latter is vulnerable if the design right is assigned to a purchaser in good faith for valuable consideration and without actual or constructive notice of the licence. This also applies to persons taking the right through a bona fide purchaser even if such other persons have knowledge of the licence or are made a gift of the design right. A future design right, one that will or may come into existence can be dealt with by assignment or licence just as an existing design right.[43]

40 An example of the latter
would be in the case of the
liquidation of a company that
owns a design right.

41 Section 234(1).

42 Section 235.

43 Section 223.

In the case of a design where there is an overlap between design right and a registered design – when both rights apply to a design – an assignment of the registered design right serves also to assign the design right if the proprietor of the registered design is also the person who owns the design right[44] and vice versa unless a contrary intention appears.[45] However, although it will be unusual, it is possible for the two rights to become separated, for example by an express term to the contrary in the document containing an assignment of either right. The automatic transfer of the other right is a presumption only. Of course, in such circumstances the person obtaining the one right will clearly know that the other right is not to be assigned to him and will be able to predict what he can and cannot do in relation to the design. If there is some doubt, for example if the words expressing the contrary intention are not clear, the *contra proferentum*[46] rule of construction might be applied by the court or a licence might be implied. At first sight, it might appear that the qualification requirements could frequently lead to separate ownership of the rights. However, by section 3 of the Registered Designs Act 1949, the Registrar will not entertain an application for registration of a design unless it is made by the person claiming to be the design right owner.[47]

Licences are available as of right in relation to the design right during the last five years of the subsistence of the right by section 237. If the parties are unable to agree terms they will be settled by the Comptroller-General of Patents, Designs and Trade Marks. This provision significantly weakens the design right. It could be argued that, because the design right is not a monopoly right and because it is further constrained by wide ranging exceptions, there is no need for this provision.

The would-be licensee under a licence as of right may be faced with one problem stemming from the lack formalities for the right. That problem is how to determine the date at which the design has five years left to run. It may be difficult to determine when the design was created or first commercially exploited. In the circumstances, the owner of the right is unlikely to be particularly helpful about dates. Another difficulty for the potential licensee is that other rights may apply such as the registered design and licences are unlikely to be available for such other rights.

RIGHTS OF OWNER AND INFRINGEMENT

By section 226(1), the owner of a design right subsisting in a design has the exclusive right to reproduce the design for commercial purposes by making articles to the design or by making a design document recording the design for the purpose of enabling such articles to be made. 'Commercial purposes' refers to things done with a view to the article in question being sold or hired in the course of business.[48] As the definition in section 226(2) of reproduction in relation to making articles to the design uses the word 'copying', the design right will not be infringed by a person who independently produces an article made to the same design. Copying a design by making articles exactly or substantially to the design is reproduction by making articles to the design but substantiality appears to be construed differently to its qualitative meaning in copyright law.

44 Section 224.

45 Section 19(3B) of the Registered Designs Act 1949.

46 This rule is used particularly in the context of exclusion clauses where a term that one person relies on to exclude or limit his liability (for example, under a contract where one party seeks to exclude his liability for breach of contract) is ambiguous. The court will usually take the meaning which is least favourable to the party seeking to rely on the term.

47 Section 19(3A) of the Registered Designs Act 1949 imposes similar requirements in respect of registration of an interest in a registered design. The applicant for registration has to sign a declaration to this effect.

48 Section 263(3).

Primary infringement

The design right is infringed by any person who does anything without the licence of the right owner which is by virtue of section 226 the exclusive right of the owner. In *C & H Engineering v F Klucznik & Sons Ltd.*[49] in an action brought by the plaintiff who claimed infringement of copyright in his drawings of lamb creep feeders, the defendant counterclaimed that the plaintiff had infringed his design right in pig fenders.[50] The pig fender in question had a round tube attached to the top edge. Apart from this tube, the design of the pig fender was commonplace. It was held that section 226 required the owner of the design right to show copying before infringement can be proved and, in this respect, the design right is similar to copyright. However, the test for infringement is different, requiring the alleged infringing article to be compared with the design document or model embodying the design to discover whether the alleged infringing article is made exactly to the design or substantially to that design. This requires an objective test, through the eyes of the person to whom the design is directed (in this case, a pig farmer), looking at the differences and similarities between the designs. In this particular case, Aldous J held that there was no infringement, the plaintiff's pig fender was not made to the defendant's design or made substantially to that design. The objective pig farmer would consider the two designs to be different but with a similar design feature, that is a round bar or tube around the top.

It has already been noted that the design right can apply to a part of an article but, in his interpretation of the test for infringement, Aldous J compared the design of the whole articles. This view is supported by the language of section 226(2) which speaks of reproduction in terms of producing articles (not parts of articles) exactly or substantially to the design. This weakens the right where it is applied or limited only to a part of an article and, as in the *C & H Engineering* case, a significant design improvement may accordingly go unprotected.

By using the test of the eye of the interested person Aldous J applied a test not dissimilar to that used for testing for infringement of registered designs. However, the design right can apply to an internal part of an article that may be concealed from view. Comparison of whole articles does not make sense in relation to internal designs and can only be undertaken when the alleged infringing article has been dismantled and the relevant part considered and compared with the equivalent part of the design document or article made to the design.

Indirect reproduction also infringes, and it is immaterial whether any intervening acts themselves infringe. Therefore, if reproduction is preceded by taking apart an article made to the design it will still be an infringement. However, if such 'reverse engineering' is done so that only non-protected elements can be copied, for example features that fall within the must-fit or must-match exceptions, then there will be no infringement of the design. Making a drawing of an article made to the design will only infringe if it is done for the purpose of enabling such articles to be made so that making a drawing to be displayed in an exhibition of drawings will not infringe. However, giving or selling the drawing to a manufacturer who intends to make the article would infringe if that was the purpose of making the drawing because it enables articles to be made to the design. It would appear from the language of section 226(1) that

50 A pig fender is a device placed around the entrance to a pig shelter to allow the sow to step out into the field whilst retaining the piglets.

the 'purpose of enabling' should be present at the time the drawing, or other design document, was made.

Secondary infringement

Another similarity with copyright law is the provisions for secondary infringement which approximate to commercial dealing with infringing articles, but there are no equivalent criminal penalties for infringement of the design right. An infringing article is one, the making of which to a particular design, was an infringement of the design right subsisting in that design.[51] The definition of 'infringing article' extends to articles which have been or are to be imported into the United Kingdom if their making in the United Kingdom would have been an infringement or a breach of an exclusive licence in respect to the design. A design document, however, is not an infringing article. Secondary infringement occurs when a person who, without the licence of the design right owner, does any of the following acts in relation to an article which is an infringing article and the person knows this or has reason to believe it to be so:

(a) imports into the United Kingdom for commercial purposes,
(b) has in his possession for commercial purposes,
(c) sells, hires or offers or exposes for sale or hire, in the course of a business.

It would seem that the knowledge requirement is the same as that for secondary infringement of copyright.[52] By section 228(4), there is a useful presumption in favour of the plaintiff that, when an article was made to the design in which the design right subsists or has subsisted, it was made at a time when the right subsisted unless the contrary can be proved. Bearing in mind that the plaintiff may be the only person with proof of the time the design right first arose, this is very favourable for the plaintiff.

EXCEPTIONS TO INFRINGEMENT

By section 236, if copyright subsists in a work which consists of or includes a design in which design right subsists, it is not an infringement of the design right to do anything which is an infringement of the copyright in the work. The overlap of actions between the design right and copyright is removed, leaving an action in copyright only. During the last five years of a design right, licences are available as of right[53] on terms to be fixed by the Comptroller-General of Patents, Designs and Trade Marks in the absence of agreement. The Secretary of State has the power to exclude by statutory instrument certain designs from the licence as of right provisions in order to comply with an international obligation or for purposes relating to reciprocal protection for British designs in other countries. Under section 245, the Secretary of State also has the power on the same basis to provide that certain acts do not infringe design right. In effect, this permits a reduction in the protection offered in respect of a foreign country if that country does not give full reciprocal protection to British designs.

If the owner of a design right imposes restrictive conditions in a licence or refuses to grant licences and, in the opinion of the Monopolies and Mergers Commission, this operates, has operated or is likely to operate against the public interest, the terms of such a licence may be varied or licences be declared

51 Section 228.

52 See the discussion of *L A Gear Inc.* v *Hi-Tec Sports plc* [1992] FSR 121 in Chapter 6.

53 This does not apply to the topography right, described later.

as being available as of right by means of powers under the Fair Trading Act 1973.[54]

There are similar provisions for Crown use of designs subject to the design right as there are for registered designs. These extend to 'health service purposes', that is the supply of articles for the purpose of providing pharmaceutical, general medical or general dental services. There are provisions for the settlement of terms and the award of compensation if the owner of the right or an exclusive licensee has suffered any loss as a result of not being awarded a contract because of Crown use.[55] It could be argued that the provisions for Crown use are inappropriate here since design right does not give rise to monopolies. In essence, design right is a form of copyright and there has never been Crown use in relation to works of copyright. However, the provisions may be important if the design is also registered. It would be a nonsense if Crown use applied to one right and not the other if both rights subsisted in the same design.

DEFENCES TO INFRINGEMENT ACTIONS

A person who has allegedly infringed a design right may plead several defences. Again, the best form of defence often is to attack the validity of the right. For example, a defendant might plead that:

(a) The right is not valid because the features copied fall within the exceptions, for example, they relate to a method or principle of construction.[56]
(b) The plaintiff's design is commonplace and, therefore, not original.[57]
(c) The qualification requirements are not satisfied in respect of the plaintiff's design.[58]
(d) The design right has expired.

Assuming that the design is valid, other defences which might be raised by the defendant include:

(a) The plaintiff does not have *locus standi*,[59] for example he is neither the owner nor the exclusive licensee.
(b) That the act does not fall within the scope of primary or secondary infringement.
(c) The defendant's articles are neither exactly nor substantially made to the plaintiff's design.
(d) The alleged infringement occurred before the right existed or after the right expired, but here the defendant has the burden of proof.
(e) In the case of an alleged secondary infringement, that the defendant did not know and had no reason to believe that the article was an infringing article.
(f) That the act complained of falls within one of the exceptions to infringement.

A further possibility exists for an infringer when licences are available as of right in respect of the design, as they are usually during the last five years of the right.[60] By section 239, the defendant can undertake to take a licence on terms to be agreed or, failing agreement, on terms to be fixed by the Comptroller. If the defendant makes such an undertaking, an injunction will not be granted against him, no order for delivery up will be made and the amount recoverable in damages or by way of an account of profits shall not exceed double the amount which he would have paid had he obtained a licence on the terms that would have been agreed or fixed by the Comptroller before the earliest infringement.

As with registered designs, there is provision for a remedy against groundless threats of infringement proceedings. The remedies for groundless threats of infringement proceedings are:

(a) a declaration to the effect that the threats are unjustifiable;
(b) an injunction against the continuation of the threats;
(c) damages, if any have been sustained as a result of the threats.

The burden of proof is on the person making the threats to show that the acts to which the threats relate to do, indeed, infringe or will infringe, his design right.

REMEDIES

An infringement is actionable by the design right owner but, by section 234, an exclusive licensee has, except against the design right owner, the same rights and remedies as if he were the owner of the right. Damages, injunctions, accounts or otherwise are available to the plaintiff as they are in respect to the infringement of any other property right.[61] However, an award of damages is not available in the case of a primary infringement, without prejudice to other remedies, if it is shown that, at the time of the infringement, the defendant did not know and had no reason to believe that the design right subsisted in the design.[62] In the case of a secondary infringement, a defendant who shows that the infringing article was acquired innocently by him or his predecessor in title will only be liable to pay damages not exceeding a reasonable royalty.[63]

The court has a discretion to award additional damages which are provided for by section 229(3) using an identical formula to that used for copyright under section 97(2). It is unlikely that additional damages will be awarded frequently as, usually, normal damages or an account of profits will be satisfactory.

Orders for delivery up, forfeiture or destruction of infringing articles are possible and proceedings can be brought for these forms of relief in county courts in England and Wales and Northern Ireland subject to the county court limit for actions in tort.[64]

61 Section 229.

62 Section 233(1).

63 Section 233(2). The meaning of 'innocently acquired' is given in section 233(3) being where the person did not know and had no reason to believe that the article was an infringing article.

64 Sections 230–232.

SEMICONDUCTOR TOPOGRAPHY DESIGN RIGHT

Integrated circuits are commonly known as 'silicon chips' or, quite simply, 'chips'. They are usually made from layers of materials by a process which includes etching using various 'masks' (templates) which are made photographically. The simplest integrated circuit consists of three layers, one of which is made from semiconductor material. A semiconducting material, in terms of its ability to conduct electricity, is one which lies between a conductor such as copper and an insulator such as rubber. Examples of semiconducting materials include silicon, germanium, selenium and gallium arsenide. A wafer of semicon-

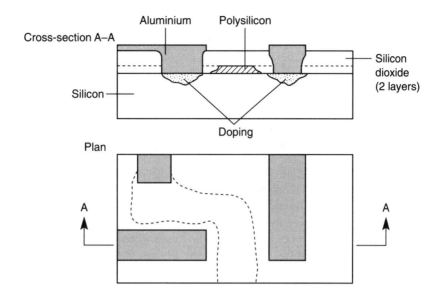

Figure 19.3 Representation of part of an integrated circuit

ductor material is coated with a layer of silicon oxide (an insulator) and the electronic components (for example, transistors) are formed by a process of diffusion (chemically doping the semiconductor material with impurities through holes etched through the oxide). Finally, an aluminium coating is applied which is partly evaporated using a mask, leaving behind the interconnections between components formed in the semiconductor layer. Figure 19.3 shows, diagrammatically, a plan view and cross-section of a tiny part of an integrated circuit.

The patterns formed by the processes of etching the layers and evaporation of the conductor make the electrical circuitry of the integrated circuit. These patterns represent the circuit design. The processes involved in the making of integrated circuits fall within the province of patent law and the first patents for integrated circuits were filed in the late 1950s. Licences were readily available and in 1961 the first chips were available commercially. Now that the early patents have expired and much of the know-how associated with making integrated circuits lies in the public domain, it is essential that the considerable effort that goes into the design and development of new integrated circuits is protected. The feature of an integrated circuit which is specifically protected in its own right is its topography.

History

The protection of semiconductor topographies has a fairly short history, as might be expected. Before legislation was introduced, it was possible that integrated circuits were protected by copyright through drawings or photographs. Most of the masks used in the manufacture were produced photographically and would be protected as photographs. The United States of America was the driving force behind the development of specific protection for semiconductor topographies and in 1984, the United States enacted the Semiconductor Chip

Protection Act which gave specific protection to the circuitry contained in the layers of semiconductors. The European Community felt duty bound to follow this lead on pain of loss of reciprocal protection for European designed topographies.[65] A Community Directive was issued and, under the authority of section 2(2) of the European Communities Act 1972, the Semiconductor Products (Protection of Topography) Regulations 1987 were made and came into force on 7 November 1987.[66] These regulations gave a right (called a 'topography right') in the layout of an integrated circuit. However, with the advent of the Copyright, Designs and Patents Act 1988, it was decided to replace these regulations with an amended version of the new design right by the Design Right (Semiconductor Regulations) 1989, which came into force on 1 August 1989.[67] The new right, referred to below as the 'semiconductor design right' draws heavily from Part III of the Copyright, Designs and Patents Act 1988 which deals with the unregistered design right but with some differences as far as semiconductor topographies are concerned. The problem with this is that we now have the situation where some sections of the 1988 Act are different depending on whether they are being applied to semiconductor designs or to design for other articles.[68]

Design Right (Semiconductor Regulations) 1989

The 1989 regulations are similar to the 1987 regulations in several respects; for example, it is the topography of a semiconductor which is protected being, by regulation 2(1), a design which is either:

(a) the pattern fixed, or intended to be fixed, in or upon –
   (i) a layer of a semiconductor product, or
   (ii) a layer of material in the course of and for the purpose of the manufacture of a semiconductor product, or
(b) the arrangement of the patterns fixed, or intended to be fixed, in or upon the layers of a semiconductor product in relation to one another.

'Semiconductor product' is also defined in regulation 2(1) and is:

> an article the purpose, or one of the purposes, of which is the performance of an electronic function and which consists of two or more layers, at least one of which is composed of semiconducting material and in or upon one or more of which is fixed a pattern appertaining to that or another function.

To be protected, the semiconductor topography must be original and it is not original if it is commonplace in the design field in question at the time of its creation, section 213(4) of the 1988 Act. As discussed earlier in this chapter, although 'original' is liberally interpreted in copyright law, the requirement that the topography is not commonplace is likely to lead to a much narrower interpretation. The qualification requirements are very similar to those for 'normal' designs with some minor differences.[69] In terms of the first marketing qualification rule, normally no account is to be taken of any sale or hire or any offer or exposure for sale or hire which is subject to an obligation of confidence.[70] On the international scene, there are reciprocity arrangements with several non-European Community countries such as the United States, Switzerland and Japan.[71]

65 For a discussion on the American approach and other possibilities for protection of integrated circuits, see Tapper, C. *Computer Law* (London: Longman, 4th edn., 1989) at pp.131–133.

66 SI 1987 No. 1497.

67 SI 1989 No. 1100 as amended by the Design Right (Semiconductor Topographies) (Amendment) Regulations 1991 and 1992, SI 1991 No. 2237 and SI 1992 No. 400. It is arguable that the 1987 regulations were a model for the new design right, see Cornish, W.C. *Intellectual Property: Patents, Copyright, Trade Marks and Allied Rights* (London: Sweet & Maxwell, 2nd edn., 1989) at p.391.

68 A similar situation to that pertaining to the Trade Marks Act 1938. Some provisions have alternative forms depending on whether they relate to a trade mark or a service mark.

69 For semiconductor products, the regulations substitutes different sections and parts of sections into the Copyright, Designs and Patents Act 1988. For example, a new section 217 is substituted.

70 Regulation 7. This does not apply if any of these things have previously been done or in terms of a Crown obligation.

71 Part II of the Schedule to the regulations.

72 Regulations 4 and 5.

The ownership provisions are very similar to those for the normal design right, however, the qualification provisions are slightly changed and commissioners or employers do not have to be qualifying persons.[72] The right given is as with normal designs and, on the whole, infringement (primary and secondary) is similarly defined but reproduction of the design privately for non-commercial aims is specifically excluded from the scope of the right as is an equivalent to some of the permitted acts, including fair dealing, in copyright. Section 226(1A)(b) allows reproduction for the purpose of analysing or evaluating the design or analysing, evaluating or teaching the concepts, processes, systems or techniques embodied in it. This can be seen as paving the way for reverse analysis of existing semiconductors in the development of new, non-competing, products. This is reinforced by regulation 8(4) which states that it is not an infringement of the semiconductor design right to create another original topography as a result of such analysis or evaluation or to reproduce that other topography.[73] As regards reverse analysis, a limiting factor will be the requirement for the new topography to be original and not commonplace. Regulation 8(5) retains the substantiality test for infringement. Secondary infringement does not apply if the article in question has previously been sold or hired within the United Kingdom by or with the licence of the owner of the right or within the European Economic Community or Gibraltar by or with the consent of the person who, at the time, was entitled to import it or sell it within the appropriate territory. Thus, the doctrine of exhaustion of rights applies to semiconductor topographies.

73 At first sight, this seems to defeat the whole object of the regulations but although reproducing the topography is permitted, reproducing by making articles is not. In some respects, this provision is similar to the decompilation right in relation to computer programs.

The duration of the semiconductor design right depends on if and when the topography is commercially exploited. A new section 216 is substituted for semiconductor products. Normally, the right endures for ten years from the end of the year in which it was first commercially exploited (anywhere in the world). However, if the right is not commercially exploited within fifteen years of the creation of the topography, the right expires fifteen years from the time the topography was first recorded in a design document or the time when an article was first made to the design, whichever is the earlier. Contrary to the position with other designs in which the design right subsists, licences as of right are not available during the last five years of the semiconductor design right. However, licences may be declared available as of right as a result of a report from the Monopolies and Mergers Commission as with other designs. Remedies for infringement are as for the design right generally.

The topography right is a result of international pressure, especially from the United States. However, because section 51 of the Copyright, Designs and Patents Act 1988 removes protection from design documents (in effect), the protection for topographies in the United Kingdom is now significantly weaker than it was before. Although copying a topography will infringe the copyright in the photographic masks and section 236 suppresses the design right in favour of copyright, it cannot apply as section 51 means that the copyright in the photographic masks are not infringed by making a semiconductor product to the same design.

Part Six

BUSINESS GOODWILL AND REPUTATION

20

Trade marks

INTRODUCTION

Trade marks are a diverse and familiar feature in both industrial and commercial markets. Trade marks have long been used by manufacturers and traders to identify their goods and distinguish them from goods made or sold by others. In Roman times it was common for pottery to be embossed or impressed with a mark, for example a representation of a dolphin or the maker's initials, as a visit to the British Museum will testify. Merchants' marks were used in commerce in Britain from the thirteenth century, William Caxton used the mark W74C and gold and silver articles were hallmarked as early as the fourteenth century.[1] By the end of the sixteenth century it was very common for shopkeepers to erect signs illustrating their trade. Traders took to using cards bearing their name and address often accompanied by a device of some sort, an early form of business card. The industrial revolution saw an enormous growth in the use of names and marks in advertising and the modern trade mark was born. Some of the nineteenth century marks were glorious in their pictorial detail.[2]

Marks are a very valuable form of intellectual property because marks become associated with quality and consumer expectations in a product or service. Some goods become almost synonymous with their trade name, for example Hovis bread, the soft drink Coca-Cola, Mars confectionery bars, Nescafé coffee, Hamlet cigars, Domestos bleach, Cadbury chocolate, Levi jeans, etc. Coupled with intensive advertising campaigns, the utility of marks to their owners as marketing weapons is plain to see and trade marks usually will be vigorously defended.

It is difficult to estimate the economic value of the power of symbolism in marketing. For example, the value of the CocaCola trade mark must be immense when one considers the size of world-wide sales in what could be described as a beverage based on a formula for an unexceptional syrup. Symbolism here is also reinforced by the shape of the Coca-Cola bottle (based on the shape of the coca bean) which was designed to prevent the dissipation of the company image resulting from the variety of bottles made.[3] Why else would such an expensive and impractical form of packaging be used? As a matter of interest, an attempt to register the Coca-Cola bottle itself as a trade mark in the United Kingdom failed.[4] However, the use of a similar shaped bottle by competitors could amount to passing off. Advertising permits the creation of an image associated with a product that might have nothing at all to do with the qualities of the product itself. An old example was the advertising describing a particular brand of menthol tipped cigarettes as being 'fresh as a mountain stream', creating an image completely contrary to medical evidence of the harm that can be done by smoking.[5]

1 Hallmarking is now covered by the Hallmarking Act 1973.

2 A practical and descriptive history of trade marks is to be found in Caplan, D. & Stewart, G. *British Trade Marks and Symbols* (London: Peter Owen, 1966).

3 A great deal of this beverage is now sold in cans, but the shape of the bottle is still in evidence in the form of a curved white stripe alongside the name.

4 *In re Coca-Cola Co.* [1986] 2 All ER 274, discussed later. Under the new Trade Marks Act, this bottle should be registrable.

5 Eisenschitz makes this point and emphasizes the power of such advertising, see Eisenschitz, T.S. *Patents, Trade Marks and Designs in Information Work* (London: Croom Helm, 1987) at pp.168–169.

A trade mark is described by the Patent Office as:

> . . . an identification symbol . . . which is used in the course of trade to enable the purchasing public to distinguish one trader's goods from the similar goods of other traders.[6]

The word 'used' is important. A trade mark must be used or intended to be used in relation to certain goods.[7] A fundamental principle is that there is a connection between a trader and the goods in question and there can be no such connection if the mark is not being used even though it might have been so used in the past. A mark that is dormant is susceptible to challenge on the grounds of validity and may be revoked for lack of use. Another important aspect is that the mark must be distinctive in some way, and this basic fact limits the scope of signs or symbols that can be used as marks. Ownership of a mark, referred to as proprietorship, gives what can be described as a restricted monopoly in that mark. A registered trade mark is a property right. It is limited by reference to the classes of goods or services against which the mark is registered and, also, by way of exceptions to the rights granted to proprietors. Trade marks are afforded legal protection through a system of examination, publication and registration. Marks can be registered in one or more of the 34 classes of goods and eight classes of services.[8]

A related area of law is called *passing off*. This can be likened to a common law version of trade mark law and, indeed, both of these areas of law share a common background. Passing off, in relation to goods, can be said to be the use by a person on his own goods of an unregistered mark or get-up belonging to another person with the intention of passing off the goods as being those of that other person.[9] Quite often, a particular set of circumstances will give rise to the possibility of a cause of action in both trade mark law and passing off. Indeed, it is usual to add a claim for passing off in a trade mark action because of the risk of the registration being held invalid. The somewhat wider scope of passing off could also be important. Passing off is dealt with in the following chapter. Another, less used area of law is trade libel. A remedy under this might be available, for example, where one trader falsely and maliciously claims that goods of another trader are not genuine.[10]

The law relating to trade marks is substantially civil law, but there are criminal penalties associated with the fraudulent application of marks. Other areas of criminal law may be relevant, depending on the circumstances, such as trade descriptions, theft, forgery and deception offences.

Rationale

Trade marks can be seen as serving two main purposes: to protect business reputation and goodwill and, secondly, to protect consumers from deception, that is to prevent the buying public from purchasing inferior goods or services in the mistaken belief that they originate from or are provided by another trader. As a form of consumer protection this area of law has been an effective weapon against counterfeit and inferior goods, considerably strengthened by the recent introduction of draconian criminal penalties for the fraudulent application of trade marks. However, as far as the control of the use of marks in the civil courts is concerned, the action lies with the proprietor of the mark and consumers are protected indirectly through the self-interest of those with property

6 The Patent Office, *Registering a Trade or Service Mark* (Newport: The Patent Office, 1992).

7 There is an exception – defensive registration of well-known marks, under the 1938 Act.

8 The classification system for trade and service marks can be seen in Appendix 2 to this book.

9 This is passing off in its traditional sense. 'Get-up' could include the appearance of goods, packaging or the general manner in which the goods are displayed, advertised or sold.

10 *Thomas* v *Williams* (1880) 14 Ch D 864.

rights in trade marks. Another way of justifying a system of trade marks is that it gives effect, to some extent, to the European notion of unfair competition.

Brief history

Although the application of distinguishing marks to goods has a long history, the law relating to trade marks is relatively young, going back to the early part of the nineteenth century.[11] However, an earlier example of an abuse of a mark is the case of *Southern* v *How*[12] where one clothier applied another's mark to his own inferior cloth which gave rise to an action in deceit. Because of the importance of obtaining injunctions against infringers of marks, the Court of Chancery became popular for pursuing actions concerning marks, although the common law courts also began to hear such actions, for example in *Sykes* v *Sykes*[13] where some basic principles were laid down. However, it soon became clear that this area of law needed clarifying and strengthening and pressure grew from traders for an effective statute which would provide for a system of registration like that adopted in France. One of the problems of litigation had been that the owner of the mark might have to prove his title to the mark every time an infringer came along and proving title depended on establishing a good-will associated with the mark, a problem that is still present in passing off actions. This increased the expense and the uncertainty of legal proceedings.

The first statute was the Trade Marks Registration Act 1875 which established a register for trade marks and which was extremely successful judging by the number of registrations applied for. The very first mark registered was one used for beer, a label for pale ale bearing the famous Bass red triangle (see Figure 20.1), the United Kingdom's No.1 trade mark which is still registered as a trade mark today and still very much in use.[14] These particular marks have been infringed on many occasions, especially in the nineteenth and the early part of the twentieth century. Bass plc reckon that they have had to deal with some 1,900 examples of infringement of their red triangle mark. Retrospectively, this can be seen as very flattering, as a measure of perceived quality and reputation of Bass ales and beers. In 1862 the Merchandise Marks Act was passed. This was a forerunner to the present Trade Descriptions Act 1968 and, *inter alia*, made it a criminal offence to forge a trade mark.

After some amending legislation, trade mark law was consolidated in the Patents, Designs and Trade Marks Act 1883. A later consolidating statute, the Trade Marks Act 1905, gave a statutory definition of 'trade mark' for the first time and a later amending statute, the Trade Marks Act 1919, divided the register into Part A and Part B marks. Registration in Part A was subject to more stringent requirements but gave better protection in terms of remedies than Part B. Then came the Trade Marks Act 1938 which consolidated the 1905 and the 1919 statutes together with the Trade Marks (Amendment) Act 1937 which was instantaneously enacted and repealed on the day the 1938 Act came into force, 27 July 1938. The 1938 Act is an outstanding example of intricate and difficult draftsmanship which has attracted judicial criticism, in particular section 4(1), dealing with rights and infringement in relation to Part A marks, being described by Mackinnon LJ as being of 'fuliginous obscurity'.[15]

Following recommendations made in a Green Paper,[16] the Trade Marks (Amendment) Act 1984 was passed and this made amendments to the 1938 Act

11 For a history of the legal development of trade marks and passing off, see Blanco White, T.A. & Jacob, R. *Kerly's Law of Trade Marks & Trade Names* (London: Sweet & Maxwell, 12th edn., 1986).

12 (1618) Popham 144.

13 (1824) 3 B & C 541.

14 Bass also registered two similar marks and the red triangle device on its own in the same year.

15 *Bismag v Amblins (Chemists) Ltd.* (1940) 57 RPC 209 at 237. 'Fuliginous' simply means obscure.

16 *Intellectual Property Rights and Innovation* Cmnd. 9117 (London: HMSO, 1983).

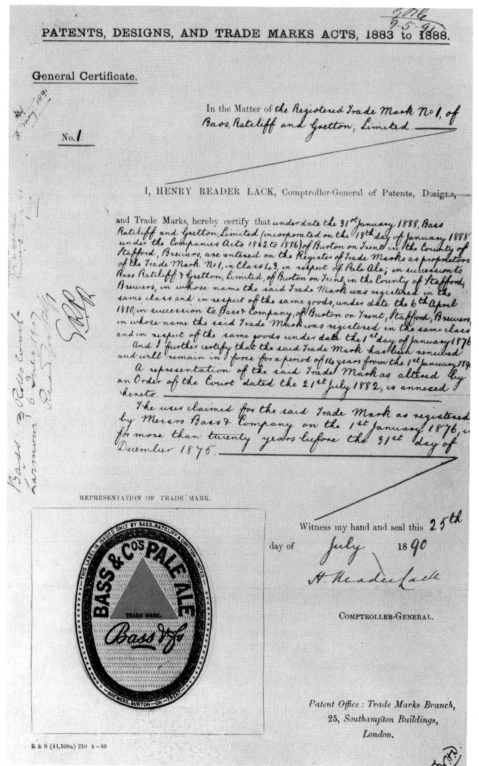

Figure 20.1 Britain's oldest registered trade mark (reproduced by permission of Bass plc)

and extended the scheme to service marks which can be registered in respect of services such as laundries and banking.[17] These provisions came into force on 1 October 1986 and made a bad Act worse. The way the amendments were made required two copies of the 1938 Act to be used and, indeed *Kerly's Law of Trade Marks and Trade Names*[18] has the two copies on facing pages. Prior to this, marks could only be registered in respect of goods. Finally, further amendments were made by the Patents, Designs and Trade Marks Act 1986 and the Copyright, Designs and Patents Act 1988. It can be seen that the complexity of the 1938 Act was not alleviated, only added to.

At the time of writing the second edition of this book a new Trade Marks Bill is before Parliament. Primarily to implement the European Community Directive to approximate the laws of Member States relating to trade marks,[19] the new Bill makes provisions for the proposed Community Trade Mark and to enable the United Kingdom to give effect to the Madrid Protocol relating to the international registration of trade marks, 1989. The opportunity has also been taken to make some much needed improvements to trade mark law and to bring it up to date. The Bill should receive the Royal Assent during 1994.

Layout of this chapter

Given the imminence of far-reaching changes to trade mark law, the latter part of this chapter contains a detailed examination of the new Bill. However, it was considered appropriate to retain and update the main content of this chapter from the first edition on the Trade Marks Act 1938. There are several reasons for this. First, the law under the 1938 Act (although still current at the time of writing, referred to as the old law) will remain effective to some extent under the transitional provisions. For example, infringements occurring before the commencement of the new Act will still be governed by the old law. Secondly, an understanding of the old law will help the reader to appreciate why some of the changes were necessary. Thirdly, knowledge of the old law will assist in the process of understanding the new law. Finally, much of the prior case law (though by no means all of it) will still be relevant and provide authority for the meaning and interpretation of the new law. For example, case law on distinctiveness, deception and non-use will remain valid.

The old law is described and discussed first followed by an examination of the law with comparison to the old law, where appropriate. Finally, at the end of the chapter, there is some discussion of trade marks in the context of European Community competition law.

The 'Old' Law

This section of the chapter contains an examination of trade mark law under the Trade Marks Act 1938, as amended. Under those provisions, distinction was made between trade marks and service marks, registrations for service marks commencing in 1986. That distinction is not made in the new law. Unless otherwise stated, in this part of the chapter statutory references are to the Trade Marks Act 1938. First, the nature of a trade mark is discussed.

17 Previously service industries relied on the law of passing off.

18 op. cit.

19 OJ [1989] L40/1.

WHAT IS A TRADE MARK?

Before the meaning of 'trade mark' can be appreciated, the scope of the word 'mark' must be established. Section 68(1) of the Trade Marks Act 1938, the interpretation section, defines a 'mark' as:

> a device, brand, heading, label, ticket, name, signature, word, letter, numeral or any combination thereof.[20]

A brand was added to the list of marks to cover marks made by a hot implement such as a branding iron, although there have been suggestions that brand names might also be included in this category. A title on the top of a page of printed material is an example of a heading. Labels and tickets typically contain words and/or devices printed on a material such as paper or card, intended to be affixed to goods. It must be noted that the definition of 'mark' given in section 68(1) is not exhaustive and even the colour combination of an article has been accepted for registration as a trade mark. In *Smith, Kline and French Laboratories Ltd.* v *Sterling Winthrop Group Ltd.*,[21] Smith, Kline and French applied to register coloured capsules for drugs as trade marks. The capsules were made in two halves, one coloured the other transparent, through which individual pellets could be seen. Registration was applied for in respect of the whole external appearance of the capsules. It was argued that a colour combination was not a trade mark within the meaning of section 68(1). It was accepted by the defendant, however, that these capsules had become sufficiently distinctive so that the use by other manufacturers would probably be actionable as passing off. It was held that there was nothing in the Trade Marks Act 1938 to exclude a mark that covers the whole surface of the goods, nor was there anything to prevent a three-dimensional object being a trade mark. The distinctiveness of the capsules was an important factor – the capsules were 'inherently adapted' to distinguish the goods of Smith, Kline and French from other traders.[22]

However, a line will be drawn and, as a comparison to the above case, in *In re Coca-Cola Co.*[23] an application was made to register the famous Coca-Cola bottle as a trade mark. Originally, the shape of the bottle had been protected as a design under the Patents and Designs Act 1907 but the registration had expired in 1940. The House of Lords was not sympathetic. Lord Templeman said that the concept of allowing a container to be registered as a trade mark raised the spectre of a total and perpetual monopoly in such containers. He thought that a rival manufacturer should be free to sell any container or article of a similar shape providing it was labelled or packaged differently in such a way as to avoid confusion as to the origin of the goods in the container. Lord Templeman was critical of the *Smith, Kline & French* case saying that it might lead to an undesirable monopoly in colours, but that the case did not create an undesirable monopoly in goods or containers. However, the argument for allowing colour combinations to be registered now seems uncontroversial and an attack on the validity of the registration of the copper and black colour combination used for Duracell batteries failed, the Patents Court treating this point as well settled in *Duracell International Inc.* v *Ever Ready Ltd.*[24] Also, in *Smith, Kline & French Laboratories Ltd.'s Cimetidine Trade Mark*[25] it was accepted that a colour mark was registrable in principle, although in that case,

20 The definition in respect to a service mark is more restrictive, omitting brands, headings, labels and tickets, section 1(7) of the Trade Marks (Amendment) Act 1984.

21 [1976] RPC 511

22 This is an important requirement for registration in Part A of the register, section 9(3)(a).

23 [1986] 2 All ER 274.

24 [1989] RPC 731.

25 [1991] RPC 17.

it was held that an application to register the colour pale green as a trade mark for pharmaceuticals (for the drug Tagamet) must fail because it was not sufficiently distinctive.

A distinction which can be made between the apparently conflicting cases is that, in the successful applications, it was the surface of the article at issue whereas, in *In re Coca-Cola,* it was the container. The drug capsule was meant to be swallowed whole whereas the bottle would be thrown away or returned after the contents had been consumed. In all the cases, copying of the features claimed as registrable as trade marks by other traders would probably amount to passing off. The container monopoly argument does not hold water and there is room for much diversity in the shape of containers.[26]

It has already been stated that it is important that a mark be used or intended to be used. This is borne out in the definition of 'trade mark' in section 68(1) which is:

> a mark . . . used or proposed to be used in relation to goods for the purpose of indicating, or so as to indicate, a connection in the course of trade between the goods and some person having the right either as proprietor or registered user to use the mark, whether with or without any indication of the identity of that person.[27]

The mark must be used or intended to be used. Token use will not suffice.[28] Such intention must be bona fide otherwise there are grounds for removal of the mark from the register under section 26(1). The registration of a 'ghost mark' is not bona fide and the objection under section 26(1) is not answered by token use. In *Imperial Group Ltd.* v *Philip Morris & Co. Ltd.*[29] the plaintiff wished to use the name 'Merit' for a new brand of cigarettes. However, that word would probably not be registrable as a trade mark, being a laudatory name. Nevertheless, and with the intention of protecting that name, the plaintiff registered the name 'Nerit' instead. When the defendant launched a new cigarette in the United States under the name 'Merit', the plaintiff made token use of 'Nerit' by marketing about one million cigarettes under this name so that the Nerit mark could not be expunged on the basis of non-use. This plan failed as it was held not to be bona fide and it was ordered to be expunged by the Court of Appeal.

There must be use in the relation to goods in the course of trade. In *Cheetah Trade Mark*[30] the defendant bought herbicide in Belgium made by the plaintiff and then imported it into the United Kingdom where he resold it. The herbicide was the same as that sold in the United Kingdom by the plaintiff but it had a different mark to the plaintiff's registered trade mark on the container. However, the defendant used the plaintiff's trade mark on delivery notes and invoices. The plaintiff sued for infringement of the trade mark but the defendant argued that the use of the trade mark complained of was not in the course of trade. However, it was held that use on delivery notes and invoices was still use in the course of trade. This was so even though the invoices were submitted long after sale and delivery of the containers of herbicide. The marks on invoices were also used in relation to the herbicide though not accompanying it on delivery.[31]

Use in relation to goods does not extend to services rendered on goods. Thus, indicating a connection in the course of trade does not extend to repairers of goods. In *Aristoc* v *Rysta Ltd.*[32] a repairer of silk stockings could not register a

---

26 In principle, containers will be registrable under the new law.

27 A service mark is defined in similar terms, subject to a more restricted list of possible 'marks', in relation to services and a business connection with the provider of those services, section 1(7) of the Trade Marks (Amendment) Act 1984.

28 See *Imperial Group Ltd.* v *Philip Morris & Co. Ltd.* [1982] FSR 72.

29 [1982] FSR 72.

30 [1993] FSR 263.

31 In *Esquire Electronics Ltd* v *Roopanand Bros.* [1985] RPC 83 it was held in the Supreme Court of South Africa that a trade mark recorded digitally on a video tape was not used in relation to the tape itself, the physical object. However, this was reversed on appeal, [1991] RPC 425.

32 [1945] AC 68.

mark applied to stockings indicating that they had been repaired by him, there was no connection in the course of trade between the repairer and the stockings.[33] Similarly, in respect of service marks, the provision of 'retail services', which are but an adjunct to the principal business of the applicant and not charged for as such, is not sufficient for showing a connection in the course of business between the applicant and the services provided. In *Dee Corp. plc*[34] applications were made by well-known retailers Dee, Homebase and Boots for the registration of a service mark in respect of the provision of retail services such as the provision of advice and information to customers, car parking, credit facilities, etc. Even the playing of background music was included. The Court of Appeal dismissed the appeal against refusal to register the marks as service marks because the applicants were not trading in the services, they were merely ancillary to their principal business. The services were not provided for money or money's worth as required by section 1(7) of the Trade Marks (Amendment) Act 1984 when read with section 68(1) of the 1938 Act as amended by the former Act.[35] However, it was conceded that the provision of crèche facilities could qualify as the service was charged for separately.

The person using the mark does not have to be the registered proprietor and the definition in section 68(1) shows that the connection can be between the registered user and the goods. For example, a large United States corporation might have an English subsidiary and the former is the proprietor whilst the latter is the registered user.[36] Another situation where a registered user may be found is in the field of franchising, that is the contractual licensing of trade names, get-up and know-how – in other words, a licence agreement where the subject matter is the intellectual property rights connected with the form of business.[37] Examples of franchise operations are 'Spud-U-Like', 'Tie Rack', 'Kentucky Fried Chicken'. The franchiser may grant a series of franchises to different persons over the country and he may register a series of agreements. One danger might occur where the franchiser, the proprietor of the trade or service mark, does not intend to use the mark himself as this could make registration susceptible to revocation under section 26 through non-use. However, by section 28(2), use by a registered user is deemed to be use by the proprietor for the purposes of section 26.

Certification trade marks may be registered in accordance with section 37 and Schedule 1. These are marks which associations of traders may use to be applied to goods certified by them, for example, as being of a particular nature or quality. An example is 'Stilton' cheese.

REQUIREMENTS FOR REGISTRATION[38]

Application for registration of a trade mark or service mark must, by section 17(1), be made by the person claiming to be the proprietor of the mark. The register is divided into Part A marks and Part B marks. The distinction between these is not an easy one to make and there are differences in terms of the protection afforded and the strength of the registration in terms of challenges on its validity. Registration in Part A is more desirable and most applications will be made for this. However, if the high standards for Part A are not satisfied, Part B registration may be offered.[39] Distinctiveness is an essential requirement for

33 Such a mark could be registered as a service mark nowadays.

34 [1990] RPC 159.

35 See also *Re The Solid Fuel Advisory Service Service Mark* [1990] RPC 535.

36 Registered users and their rights are dealt with in section 28.

37 See Abell, M. *The Franchise Option: A Legal Guide* (London: Waterlow, 1989) for a description of franchising and its legal consequences.

38 Other arrangements exist for the registration of Sheffield marks for metal goods, the register being held by the company of cutlers in Hallamshire, section 38 and schedule 2. A record called 'The Manchester record' is used for trade marks registered for textile goods, section 39.

39 Section 17(3). In 1992, 25 per cent of all registrations were in Part B; The Patent Office, *Annual Report and Accounts 1992 to 1993* (London: HMSO, 1993).

Part A registration of non-word marks whereas a Part B trade mark must be capable of distinguishing the connection between the proprietor and his goods from goods without such a connection. In essence the difference between Part A and Part B marks can be said to be in terms of distinctiveness. Part A marks are generally more distinctive than Part B marks. Although this is an oversimplification, it might assist in understanding the following description of the requirements for registrability.

Part A marks

Section 9 lays down the requirements for registration in Part A of the register. The mark must contain at least one of the following:

(a) a company, individual or firm name, represented in a special or particular manner;
(b) the signature of the applicant or his predecessor in business;
(c) an invented word or words;
(d) a word or words having no direct reference to the character or quality of the goods and not being a geographical name or surname (according to its ordinary significance);
(e) any other distinctive mark – but a name, signature, word or words not falling in any of the above categories will only be registrable on evidence of distinctiveness.

Distinctiveness is expressly mentioned only in relation to the last category. However, the other categories could be said to be distinctive 'by definition' and this is borne out by the use of the phrase 'any other distinctive mark' in section 9(1)(e). 'Distinctive', by section 9(2), means:

> . . . adapted, in relation to the goods in respect of which a trade mark is registered or proposed to be registered, to distinguish goods with which the proprietor of the trade mark is or may be connected in the course of trade from goods in the case of which no connection subsists, either generally or, where the trade mark is registered or proposed to be registered subject to limitations, in relation to use within the extent of the registration.

This is a good example of the verbosity of some of the provisions in the Act. In essence, this means that the mark has been adapted to distinguish the proprietor's goods from those of other traders. Section 9(3) goes on to suggest factors to be taken into account when determining what is distinctive and states that the tribunal shall have regard to the extent to which:

(a) the trade mark is inherently adapted to distinguish, and
(b) by reason of the use of the trade mark or any other circumstances the trade mark is in fact adapted to distinguish.

The first part is a question of law and refers to the nature of the mark itself whilst for the second part it appears that it is a question of fact but the equivalent phrase 'in fact capable of distinguishing' has been held to be capable of distinguishing in law.[40] Being inherently adapted to distinguish means that the mark is '. . . adapted of itself, standing on its own feet'.[41] An invented word that has never been used before is a good example of such a mark. The Registrar and the courts will generally treat with scepticism arguments that a mark is

40 *York Trailer Holdings Ltd. v Registrar of Trade Marks* [1982] FSR 111.

41 per Harman LJ in *Weldmesh Trade Mark* [1966] RPC 220 at 228.

factually adapted to distinguish and registration will not automatically be afforded simply because a mark has become a household name.[42] If the applicant relies on use for other goods as 'other circumstances' to show a mark is in fact adapted to distinguish, the claimed association must be fully demonstrated. The fact that a mark might be distinctive in a particular area may not be sufficient as in *Registrar of Trade Marks* v *W & G Du Cros Ltd.*[43] where two marks 'W & G', one stylized, the other simply in block letters, were refused registration even though it was recognized that the marks had become distinctive in London through their use on motor cabs. Another factor in that case, is that registration would make it difficult for other traders to use their own initials if they happened to be W & G. Each category in section 9(1) is considered below in more detail.

Names

The name may be that of an individual, a firm or a company. It may be an adopted trade name used by, say, a sole trader or a partnership. Of course, there are some types of marks which will be refused registration, for example if the mark is deceptive or likely to cause confusion.[44] The requirement that the name should be represented in a special or particular manner ensures that the mark should be distinctive and to allow the honest use of their own names by other traders. Normally, the representation of a name in normal type will be refused registration. In *Standard Cameras Ltd.'s Application*,[45] the name Robin Hood represented in a stylized way with the letters 'R' and 'd' showing an archer and a target respectively was accepted for registration.

Signatures

A signature is, *prima facie*, distinctive and a signature mark can be especially effective because of its personal connotations and it shows that the proprietor is very confident about the quality of his goods. Examples include the Cadbury mark used for chocolate.

Invented words

The word or words must be newly coined and must convey no obvious meaning to the ordinary Englishman.[46] An invented word will be refused if it sounds like an existing word or is suggestive of the quality of goods. However, in *Eastman Photographic Materials Co. Ltd.'s Application.*[47] the word 'Solio' was declared to be registrable by the House of Lords even though it had been refused registration as a trade mark for photographic papers because it sounded like the sun and could refer to the character of the particular goods. The Earl of Halsbury LC decided that 'Solio' was an invented word that did not indicate the character or quality of the goods but recognized that, in such cases, the line is difficult to draw. He offered the made up word 'Cheapandgood' as being an example that would clearly be unregistrable. Nevertheless, it seems that an invented word does not have to be totally devoid of meaning. One way of predicting whether an invented word is registrable is to consider whether its registration would make it difficult for other traders to describe their own goods or whether it would be an unnecessary fetter on the English language as used in business. An invented word will not be registered as a trade or service mark if, when

42 *Laura Ashley Trade Mark* [1990] RPC 539.

43 [1913] AC 624.

44 Sections 11 and 12.

45 (1952) 69 RPC 125.

46 per Parke J in *Phillipart* v *Whiteley Ltd.* (1908) 25 RPC 565.

47 [1898] AC 571.

spoken, it sounds the same as an ordinary word. In *re Edward Ripley and Son's Application*[48] an application was made in respect of the word 'PIRLE' which had been formed by rearranging the applicant's surname with the 'Y' missing. The reason for refusal was that 'PIRLE' when pronounced sounded exactly like a word which had an ordinary meaning and which could not, itself, be registered. Lindley MR, in his extremely brief judgment, stressed the importance of not imposing an unjustifiable monopoly on the public.[49] However, in the light of modern shopping practices where self-service is common, the sound of a mark may diminish in importance. Examples of invented words which have been refused registration in Part A are 'ORLWOOLA', 'TRAKGRIP', 'SCOTCHLITE', 'UNEEDA'. Examples of invented words successfully registered in Part A are 'KODAK', 'PORTAKABIN', 'DUSTIC', 'PRIMASPORT' and 'WHISQUEUR'.

Words not having a direct reference to the character or quality of goods

If a word has a direct reference to the character or quality of the goods in question it will not be registered. Otherwise, the fair and honest description of his goods by another trader might be hampered. Laudatory words (words praising the goods or services concerned) have a direct reference to the character or quality of goods or services, are not registrable in Part A and will only be registered in Part B if the word or words do not make it difficult for other traders to describe their own goods. The phrase 'I Can't Believe its Yogurt' was refused registration in Part A as being a laudatory phrase.[50] Words that are descriptive without necessarily being laudatory will also be refused Part A registration, as in *Re The Solid Fuel Advisory Service Service Mark*[51] and words such as NEXT and ALWAYS that might find a use in advertising a product will also be refused.[52]

Misspelling an otherwise descriptive word does not make it registrable and in *Electrix Ltd.* v *Electrolux Ltd.*,[53] a company making electrical apparatus sought to register the word 'ELECTRIX' as a trade mark. The company had used the name on their vacuum cleaners since 1933 and claimed distinctiveness on this basis but, nevertheless, it was held that the word 'ELECTRICS' (correctly spelt) was inherently incapable of registration because it is a word that other traders might reasonably want to use in the course of their business. That is, it is a word which has a direct reference to the character or quality of the goods concerned. Therefore, 'ELECTRIX' was also unsuitable for registration because trade marks appeal to the ear as well as the eye. An objection to registration of a word in its proper spelling applied equally to a word which was merely its phonetic equivalent.

Examples of marks thus refused are 'PUSSIKIN' for cat food, 'EARTHMASTER' for mechanical excavators 'TASTEE-FREEZ' for ice-cream and 'OVEN CHIPS' for chips. On the other hand, 'WELDMESH' for wire mesh, 'HOTPOINT' for electrical goods, 'NATIONAL' for cash registers and 'DUSTIC' for adhesives have all been accepted.[54]

Geographical names and surnames are not normally permitted under this category. This is to stop a trader monopolizing a particular name that would have unduly restrictive consequences but a sense of reality must be maintained. The 'bona fide use' defence may be relevant in this respect. An argument that a

48 (1898) 15 RPC 151.

49 See also *Electrix Ltd.* v *Electrolux Ltd.* [1960] AC 722 where the word 'Electrix' was refused registration. In *Compaq Computer Corp.* v *Dell Computer Corp. Ltd.* FSR 93, Aldous J questioned whether the mark 'Compaq' was correctly registered, being phonetically similar to 'Compact'.

50 *I CAN'T BELIEVE ITS YOGURT Trade Mark* [1992] RPC 533. It was, however, accepted for Part B of the register.

51 [1990] RPC 535. Part B registration was also refused.

52 NEXT Trade Mark [1992] RPC 455

53 [1960] AC 722.

54 Although, often, registration will only be allowed in Part B.

prefix mark 'PORTA' used with a collection of endings could prevent the use of the word 'Portadown', a town in Northern Ireland, was rejected in *Portakabin Ltd. v Powerblast Ltd.*[55] because it was said that any trader using the name of the town when describing his place of business or as a bona fide description of the character or quality of his goods could rely on the defence to infringement contained in section 8. Exceptionally, registration may be granted if the name is very distinctive with respect to the goods, examples being 'CHARTREUSE' for liqueurs and 'APOLLINARIS' for mineral waters from a spring of that name in Germany. The applicant has a heavy burden to discharge to show that the mark will be recognized as a trade mark rather than a place name[56] and it is fairly difficult to obtain registration for English and well-known foreign place names. Examples of refusals on this basis include 'LIVERPOOL' for cables, 'YORKSHIRE' for metal tubes, 'YORK' for trailers, 'KENT' for cigarettes and 'PHOENIX' for sportswear. However, 'ARCTIC' was accepted for bananas.

It is not unusual for an applicant wishing to register a name that sounds like or is the same as a geographical name to commission a survey to attempt to show that there is no danger of confusion.[57] For the evidence to be convincing, the survey must be statistically valid and sufficiently representative so that its results are capable of generalization. The sample size must be not too small and the questions asked are also important. For example, in *PHOENIX Trade Mark*[58] there was a survey carried out among 50 people in the Kingsway area of London by asking the question 'What does the word PHOENIX signify to you?'. Forty-two per cent said it was a bird rising from the ashes and only eight per cent identified it as a town. However, the survey was criticized because the sample size was far too small and the location too limited to give a valid representation of the general public reaction. The survey was directed at establishing the paramount signification of the word and in *CANNON Trade Mark*[59] this was held by the Court of Appeal to be irrelevant. To be of any assistance, apart from its other defects, the survey should have enquired about the ordinary signification of the word, followed by a second question 'And what else?' The Supreme Court of New South Wales said that survey evidence could be admissible either as direct evidence of public impressions and opinions or as original data which could provide the basis for expert evidence on the public opinion.[60] The Court further held that it did not need help in evaluating the survey evidence and deciding whether it could make generalizations on the basis of it.

A surname will not be registered if its ordinary signification is as a surname. Therefore, the name 'SMITH' is fundamentally unregistrable, although it might be as a signature or if represented in a special manner. Surnames, as such, will only be registered upon clear evidence that the name is distinctive and not normally taken to be a surname. As regards the use of a person's own name, section 8 provides a safeguard, permitting the bona fide use by a trader of his own surname.[61] Some surnames are also geographical names and are, in principle, doubly unregistrable under section 9(1)(d).

Any other distinctive mark

This includes device marks such as signs, symbols, pictures, labels and combinations of words and devices. They should be sufficiently distinctive, in accordance with sections 9(2) and 9(3), as discussed earlier. A symbol comprising a

---

55 [1990] RPC 471.

56 *KENT Trade Mark* [1985] RPC 117.

57 For example, *KENT Trade Mark* [1985] RPC 117 and *AVON Trade Mark* [1985] RPC 43. Surveys have also been used in passing off actions relating to character merchandising (see the following chapter).

58 [1985] RPC 122.

59 [1980] RPC 519.

60 *The Ritz Hotel Ltd. v Charles of the Ritz* [1989] RPC 333.

61 The law of passing off may also be important here – see *Harrods Ltd. v R Harrod Ltd.* (1924) 41 RPC 74.

simple pentagon on its own was not registrable. Laudatory epithets cannot be registered regardless of proof of use. In *Re Fantastic Sam's Service Mark*[62] it was held that the combination of 'Fantastic' with the possessive form of a familiar Christian name was not distinctive and could not be accepted under section 9(1)(e) for Part A registration. The application was made in respect of hairdressing services and the common practice of hairdressers using their Christian names reinforced the view that the phrase was not distinctive.

In determining whether a composite mark, for example one made up of letters, words and symbols, is distinctive it is wrong to dissect the mark into its individual components. The mark as a whole should be judged. In *Diamond T Motor Car Company*[63] it was held that a mark comprising a large letter 'T' dissected by the word 'DIAMOND', the whole being enclosed in a diamond shape made with a double line, was distinctive and was registrable subject to the applicant disclaiming any right to the exclusive use of a diamond-shaped border and the word 'DIAMOND'.[64]

Monograms and combinations of three or more letters will usually be registered on proof of distinctiveness, such as 'B.S.A.' and the John Player Special JPS monogram. Usually, at least three letters are needed and those comprising a single letter or only two letters are rarely accepted.[65] However, an attempt to have the British Petroleum 'BP' mark expunged failed because the mark, in a shield, had become very distinctive due to extensive use over the whole country for a long period of time.[66] Even numeral trade marks exist, an example being the '4711' mark used for eau-de-Cologne which was registered with and without a scroll and bell device.[67]

Conclusive validity of Part A marks

One advantage a Part A mark has over a Part B mark is that of validity. For Part A marks, after the expiry of the first seven years of registration (that is, upon first renewal) the original registration of the mark shall be taken as being valid in all respects.[68] There are two exceptions: first where the registration was obtained by fraud and, secondly, if the mark offends against section 11 being deceptive, immoral or scandalous. Thus, the question of validity of the original registration is not just a presumption and, unless the exceptions apply, it cannot be challenged in legal proceedings. Another presumption which applies to all marks facilitates the proof of title by a proprietor suing for infringement.[69]

Part B marks

Section 10 describes the standard required for registration in Part B of the register. The mark must be capable of distinguishing the trader's goods (or services) from those of other traders. Matters which can properly be taken into account are the extent to which:

(a) the trade mark is inherently capable of distinguishing, and
(b) by reason of the use of the trade mark or any other circumstances the trade mark is in fact capable of distinguishing.

Where there has been no use, it is necessary to consider the inherent nature of the mark. It was held that the phrase 'I CAN'T BELIEVE ITS YOGURT' was registrable in Part B because, although borderline, it passed the first test in

62 [1990] RPC 531.

63 [1921] 2 Ch 583.

64 Registration may be granted subject to a disclaimer as regards common or non-distinctive material, section 14.

65 *Registrar of Trade Marks v W & G Du Cros Ltd.* [1913] AC 624, 'W & G' mark refused.

66 *British Petroleum Co. v European Petroleum Distributors* [1968] RPC 54.

67 *R J Reuter & Co. Ltd. v Mulhens* [1954] Ch 50.

68 Section 13.

69 Section 46.

Section 10.[70] The mark had been accepted against Class 42 (other services) but refused against class 29 (coffee, tea, etc.) for yoghurt and yoghurt products. It was held that a useful test to apply was to consider how honest traders would be affected by allowing the registration and whether it would embarrass them. There was a range of phrases – at one end a phrase might be a mere exhortation to buy – at the other end it was a trader's name for his goods. In between those extremes it would be necessary to show that the phrase had a branding function as well as being an advertising slogan.

The fundamental distinction between a Part A non-word mark (that is, 'any other distinctive mark') and a Part B mark is that the former must be 'adapted to distinguish' whereas the latter is 'capable of distinguishing'. The difference between these phrases is subject to some doubt; however, a reasonable interpretation seems to be that the phrase 'adapted to distinguish' means that the mark is, in fact and in law, distinctive and the phrase 'capable of distinguishing' means that the nature of the mark is such that it is likely to become distinctive, perhaps after use of the mark. Sargant LJ described the meaning of 'capable of distinguishing' thus:

> [for Part B] . . . it is not necessary for the applicant to prove that the mark has actually become distinctive. It is sufficient for him to satisfy the Registrar that it is not incapable of becoming distinctive.[71]

The requirement has generally been taken to be much less stringent than for Part A. It appears that it is sufficient if the mark is likely to become distinctive, in the sense above, in the future when the mark is used in relation to the goods and services. However, if this is so, what is the meaning of 'inherently capable of distinguishing'? Although the Registrar has a discretion to accept marks in Part A and Part B (the language of section 9 and 10 is in terms of a mark being registrable rather than saying that a complying mark must be registered), whether a mark is capable of distinguishing may be more a matter for an opponent to disprove rather than the applicant to demonstrate.

Section 10(2) permits regard to be had to factual capability of distinguishing, for example, by use of the mark, in determining whether the mark is capable of distinguishing. However, in *York Trailer Holdings Ltd.* v *Registrar of Trade Marks*[72] it was held that, for Part B registration, capability of distinguishing was also a question of law. In that case, application was made to register 'YORK' for lorry trailers and containers. It was said in the House of Lords that, being a geographical name, the word was not in law capable of distinguishing the applicant's trailers from those of other traders even though it was accepted that the word had, through extensive use, become 100 per cent distinctive of the applicant's trailers and containers. It is clear that such a mark could not have been registered in Part A, being a well-known geographical name, but it is equally clear that anyone else trading in the same types of goods in relation to which the word 'YORK' was used would surely be guilty of passing off. However, the possibility of success in a passing off action is not an essential element in showing infringement of a trade mark, nor in opposition proceedings.[73]

A mark that has been registered in Part B does not necessarily qualify for Part A registration if, with the passage of time, it becomes 100 per cent distinctive. In *Weldmesh Trade Mark*[74] an application to register the word 'Weldmesh', used for steel mesh used in the construction industry, was refused.

70 *I CAN'T BELIEVE ITS YOGURT Trade Mark* [1992] RPC 533.

71 *Davies v Sussex Rubber Co.* (1927) 44 RPC 412 at 425.

72 [1982] FSR 111.

73 *Berlei (UK) Ltd.* v *Bali Brassiere Co. Inc.* [1969] 2 All ER 812.

74 [1965] RPC 590.

The mark had previously been registered in Part B and had become 100 per cent distinctive through use. Nevertheless the Court of Appeal confirmed the Registrar's decision that the mark was not registrable under Part A as the mark was too descriptive. In effect 'capable of distinguishing' did not mean 'capable of becoming distinctive within the sense required for section 9 registration'. On this basis, promotion of marks from Part B to Part A, for marks which through use have become very distinctive, is by no means to be taken for granted.

Even though the requirements for Part B are not as strict as for Part A, a mark will not be registered if to do so would interfere with the legitimate freedom of traders to describe their goods or services.[75]

MARKS WHICH MAY NOT BE REGISTERED

A trade or service mark will not be registered if it is deceptive, disentitled to protection, contrary to law or morality, scandalous or if it conflicts with earlier marks. Further, by the Trade Marks and Service Marks Rules 1986, some marks are prohibited and others are subject to the Registrar's discretion. A mark may be deceptive in one or more of several ways. For example, it may create a misleading impression about the nature or quality of the product or services concerned or it may be deceptive because it is likely to be confused with another similar trade mark registered by another person.

Mark identical with or resembling a registered mark

By section 12(1) a mark shall not be registered if it is identical with a mark already registered by another proprietor in respect of the same class of goods or services. Nor will the second mark be registered if it so nearly resembles the first mark as to be likely to deceive or cause confusion. In *Univer Trade Mark*[76] it was held that UNIVER for cardio-vascular preparations for humans nearly resembled UNIVET for veterinary preparations and registration was accordingly refused. The goods in relation to which the two marks were used were also in the same class.

Section 12(1) is only a bar to registration if the first mark is registered in respect of 'the same goods or description of goods'.[77] To decide whether goods are of the same description the classification used for purposes of registration is not appropriate. This may seem unfortunate but the ultimate test is whether confusion is likely to follow and the applicant will bear the onus of showing that there will be no confusion if the consequences of this would be serious.[78] The factors to be taken into account in deciding whether goods are of the same description were stated by Romer J, finding that shoes and shoe polish were not goods of the same description, in *Jellinek's Application*[79] as follows:

(a) The nature and composition of the goods.
(b) The respective uses of the goods.
(c) The trade channels through which the goods would be bought and sold.

The last factor was stressed in *Invicta Trade Marks*[80] in which an application for registration of INVICTA for fungicide was allowed even though a similar mark already existed for fungicide but which was used for different purposes.

75 *NEXT Trade Mark* [1992] RPC 455. This would be a reason for refusal in both Part A and Part B. See also *Re The Solid Fuel Advisory Service Service Mark* [1990] RPC 535.

76 [1993] RPC 239.

77 For service marks, section 12(1) extends not only to services but to goods associated with the particular services or class of services.

78 *Univer Trade Mark* [1993] RPC 239.

79 (1946) 63 RPC 59.

80 [1992] RPC 541.

Examples of marks refused on the grounds of section 12(1) are:

- UCOLITE – earlier mark COALITE (fuel)
- HUNTSMAN – earlier mark SPORTSMAN (both cherry brandy)
- An application showing a picture of three pigs was refused because of a prior word mark THREE PIGS BRAND (bacon)

However, in *Coca-Cola Co. of Canada Ltd.* v *Pepsi-Cola Co. of Canada Ltd.*,[81] it was held that 'PEPSI-COLA' was not too close to COCA-COLA even though the suffix 'COLA' was a word that had become common and descriptive of a type of beverage.[82]

Section 12(2) makes an exception in the case of honest concurrent use, or other special circumstances, so that occasionally an identical or resembling mark may be registered in the same class of goods or services subject to any conditions or limitations imposed on the second mark or its use. If there is any doubt about the rights of the two proprietors, the Registrar may delay registration until after this has been resolved.[83] This might apply where two persons have used identical or similar marks for at least five years or more in all honesty and have built up goodwill in ignorance of the use of the mark by the other company. Even though one has been registered, the second may be accepted for registration. There is no minimum period laid down as being acceptable.[84]

Lord Tomlin set out some criteria for deciding if the second mark should be registered in such circumstances in *Pirie's Application*[85] as follows:

(a) the likelihood of confusion that may arise from the use of both marks;
(b) whether the original choice and subsequent use of the second mark was honest – it could be honest even if the second company knew of the existence of the first mark if they believed there would be no confusion, this being a subjective test;
(c) the length of time that the second mark has been used – five years was deemed sufficient in the Pirie Case, but normally the Registrar might expect more;
(d) whether there was evidence of confusion in actual use;
(e) whether the second company's trade is larger than the first company's trade – if so, this fact may help the second company's application.

This list is not exclusive – all the surrounding circumstances must be considered in addition. An example of such a registration is 'ABERMILL BOND' for paper, the earlier mark being 'HAMERHILL', also for paper. The 'ABERMILL BOND' mark had been used for six years and the owner of the mark had built up a substantial trade.

Mark deceptive

Here we are concerned with other forms of deceptiveness under section 11, for example, where it concerns the quality or nature of the goods. In particular circumstances there may be an overlap between section 11 and section 12(1) as a mark that is very similar to a mark already registered in respect of the same goods falls foul of section 12(1) but can also be described as being likely to deceive or cause confusion under section 11. For example, in *Berlei (UK) Ltd.* v *Bali Brassiere Co. Inc.*[86] the plaintiff who had a registered trade mark 'Berlei' complained that the defendant's mark 'Bali' would be likely to deceive or cause

81 (1942) 59 RPC 127 (Judicial Committee of the Privy Council).

82 See also *Re Primasport Trade Mark* [1992] FSR 515.

83 Section 12(3).

84 A period of just over two years has been accepted in exceptional circumstances, *Peddie's Applications* (1944) 61 RPC 31.

85 (1933) 50 RPC 147.

86 [1969] 2 All ER 812.

confusion in the sense within section 11, both marks being for brassieres and corsets. The House of Lords agreed. The distinction between these two provisions is not usually important in this respect but it should be noted that section 11 is not restricted to similarity with existing trade marks. It might, for example, apply where the prior mark has never been registered as a trade mark.

The wording of section 11 is curious, stating that it shall not be lawful to register a mark 'the use of which would, by reason of its being likely to deceive or cause confusion or otherwise, be disentitled to protection in a court of justice . . .'. This clearly covers marks that are prohibited from registration under section 12(1) if such marks are not otherwise legally protectable, for example under the law of passing off. Because the origin of this provision is the Trade Marks Registration Act 1875 which spoke in terms of a court of equity, it is reasonable to think that the protection meant is that available in equity, for example under the law of passing off. The addition of the words 'or otherwise' may cover a situation where the owner of the mark is not entitled to the court's protection in respect of the mark because of the operation of estoppel.

The deceptiveness may relate to the origin of the goods, either by connection with the proprietor, or by false reference or implication as to the place of manufacture. For example, the use of a mark including the words 'Forrest' and 'London' by a watchmaker operating in Coventry who had no connection with London or a firm known as Forrest of London was held to be intended to deceive.[87] In *Boots Pure Drug Co.'s Trade Mark*[88] an application for registration of the mark 'Livron', a combination of the words 'liver' and 'iron', for a medicine was turned down because a rival company had an establishment at the town of Livron in France. The quality of the goods might be involved such as where the word 'Dairy' is used as part of the description of a synthetic material, for example, 'DAIRY GOLD' for a synthetic margarine.

A mark will not be registered if its use is likely to be a danger to the public, for example if a mark used for a medicine is confusingly similar to one used for a poison. An example of such a mark is 'JARDEX' for a poisonous disinfectant when there was already a meat extract called 'JARDOX'.[89]

Section 11 also prohibits the registration of marks which are contrary to law or morality and any scandalous design. This could cover something defamatory, obscene or particularly offensive, for example a mark having racist undertones. It is difficult to say where the line would be drawn in terms of sexual immorality, bearing in mind the more tolerant attitude in applying similar provisions to registered designs and patents. Section 11 is expressed in the imperative but, in reality, the Registrar still has an element of discretion (which can, of course, be challenged) in determining, for example, whether a mark is contrary to morality, this being a question of fact. However, whether a mark is contrary to law must be a question of law.

Trade Marks and Service Marks Rules 1986 and registration

Rules 15 to 19 of the Trade Marks and Service Marks Rules 1986 control the registration of certain other marks by prohibiting the registration of such marks or by giving the Registrar discretion as to whether or not they be accepted. Marks, the use of which would be an offence under certain statutory provisions, are absolutely prohibited by rule 15(1). These concern the Red Cross,

[87] *Hill's Trade Mark* (1893) 10 RPC 113.

[88] (1937) 54 RPC 129.

[89] See also *Univer Trade Mark* [1993] RPC 239 concerning an application to register a mark for a medicinal preparation to be used to treat humans where there already existed a registration for a similar mark used for a preparation to treat animals.

Royal Arms and the word Anzac.[90] If the proposed use would not be an offence under the appropriate statutes, the Registrar then has a discretion. The Registrar must give special consideration to other marks, such as representations of the Royal crests, armorial bearings, national flags, Her Majesty or any member of the Royal Family, matter leading to an inference of Royal patronage or authorization.[91] Also controlled by requiring the Registrar to give special consideration are marks that are capable of being an offence under section 35 of the Registered Designs Act 1949 (false representation of design as being registered), sections 110 or 111 of the Patents Act 1977 (unauthorized claim of patent rights or that a patent has been applied for) and a word or words suggestive of copyright or similar protection suggesting that infringement of a trade or service mark is a criminal offence.[92]

Marks including municipal, corporate and institutional arms, names, etc. may be refused registration unless the consent of the appropriate person has been obtained.[93] Consent is also required by rule 18 for representations or names of living persons or persons who are recently dead, in the latter case, the consent shall be obtained from the executors or other legal representatives. If the name or description of any goods or services appears on the mark, the Registrar may refuse to register the mark in other classes and he may even refuse to register the mark in the appropriate class unless given an assurance that the name or description will be varied if the mark is used for other goods or services.[94] For example, suppose a firm of brewers, Bloggs & Co. wish to register a mark comprising the words 'BEEZER' and 'Fine Ales' arranged around a representation of a barrel. If Bloggs & Co. apply to register this mark for class 32 (beer, ale and porter, etc.) the Registrar may require an assurance that the words 'Fine Ale' and, perhaps, the barrel, will be omitted in any further application. The Registrar may refuse an application for the mark as it stands for class 33 (wines, spirits and liqueurs) but might accept a variation for this class with the words 'Fine Table Wines' substituted.

REGISTRATION PROCEDURE[95]

Registration is open to any person, whether or not a British citizen or subject, who claims to be the proprietor of the trade mark or service mark which is used or is intended to be used in the United Kingdom. Thus, foreign companies can secure registration of trade marks in the United Kingdom. Applications are made to the Trade Marks Registry at the Patent Office in London or Newport, Gwent but applications for textile marks may be made at the Manchester branch of the Trade Marks Registry. Applications for marks for metal goods, in the case of an applicant carrying on business in or within six miles of Hallamshire may instead be made to the Cutlers' Company of Sheffield.

Applications with a number of representations of the trade or service mark must be made for each class of goods or services in which it is desired to register the mark as provided for by the Rules. The Registrar then examines the application to make sure that the mark is registrable, for example that it is distinctive and not deceptive, and makes a search amongst registered marks to ensure that the application does not conflict with existing registrations. The Registrar may impose limitations, for example in respect of the colours used for

90 The statutes are, the Geneva Conventions Act 1957, section 6; the Patents Act 1977, section 92(2) and the Anzac (Restriction on Trade Use of Word) Act 1916.

91 Rule 16.

92 Even though the fraudulent application or use of a trade mark is an offence, section 58A.

93 Rule 17. The appropriate person is the person appearing to the registrar as being entitled to give consent.

94 Rule 19.

95 Registration procedure is provided for by the Trade Marks and Service Marks Rules 1986, SI 1986 No. 1319.

97 The plaintiff was the proprietor of the famous Bass red triangle mark who had opposed the defendant's application which was held by the House of Lords to be registrable because it was an old mark, in use since before 1875 and registrable as such under section 9 of the Trade Marks Act 1905. The Registrar may also require a disclaimer in respect of certain parts of the mark.

98 Trade Marks and Service Marks (Fees) Rules 1992, SI 1992 No. 1069. This scale of fees came into effect on 11 May, 1992. There is no difference in the fees for Part A or Part B registration.

99 Rule 68 of the Trade Marks and Service Marks Rules 1986, SI 1986 No. 1319.

100 Rules 107–113 of the Trade Marks and Service Marks Rules 1986, SI 1986 No. 1319 contain the procedural details.

101 *Job Trade Mark* [1993] FSR 118.

102 [1984] FSR 199.

103 Character merchandising is also relevant in terms of passing off and the law appears to have recently taken a much more realistic view on this matter – see the following chapter.

the mark as in *Bass, Ratcliff & Gretton Ltd.* v *Nicholson & Sons Ltd.*[96] where an outline triangle containing the letter 'N' inside was allowed subject to the colours being white and black only.[97] If the mark is accepted by the Registrar, it is advertised in the *Trade Marks Journal* and within one month of publication any person may give notice of his intention to oppose the mark. If this is done, the Registrar will set a date for a hearing after completing the evidence. If the mark is unopposed within the period allowed or such opposition has been unsuccessful, the mark will be entered on the register on payment of the registration fee and a certificate of registration will be issued. Initial registration is for seven years after which time the registration can be renewed indefinitely in 14 year tranches. Usually, application is made for registration in Part A of the register. If there is any doubt as to whether the mark complies with the requirements for Part A, Part B registration may be offered instead. The fees at the time of writing are £185 for application with a renewal fee of £275.[98] There is provision for restoration of a mark in respect of which the registration has lapsed.[99] The restoration fee is £100 and the cost of a defensive registration is £185.

The popularity of trade and service marks can be seen in the volume of business in the Trade Marks Registry. In 1992 there were 29,850 applications for registration of trade marks, 6,118 applications for registration of service marks and 18,013 trade mark registrations were renewed (including 430 lapsed registrations which were restored and renewed). In 1992, the number of registrations granted was 26,211 in Part A and 8,926 in Part B.

By section 28, a person other than the proprietor of the mark may be registered as a registered user in respect of all or any of the goods (or services) for which the mark has been registered.[100] The use by the registered user is deemed by section 28(2) to be use by the proprietor. Certain requirements must be fulfilled. The arrangement must not be contrary to the public interest and must not amount to or facilitate trafficking in trade or service marks. The proprietor must exercise some control over the registered user's activities otherwise the arrangement could be deemed to be trafficking in trade marks.[101] In *Holly Hobbie Trade Mark*,[102] an application to register the Holly Hobbie mark (a drawing of a little girl in distinctive dress known as a Holly Hobbie) was turned down even though the mark had been previously used by the owner of the mark in the United States of America for greeting cards and the like. The mark was registered in the United States as a trade mark and the owner granted licences to allow others to apply the mark to suitable goods. The House of Lords held that mark could not be registered in the United Kingdom as a trade mark because the owner intended to grant licences in such a way that the mark was being dealt with primarily as a commodity in its own right and that there would be no real trade connection between the owner of the mark and the goods to which the mark was to be applied. The application would tend to facilitate trafficking in the mark. Thus, the activity known as 'character merchandising' cannot be facilitated by means of trade mark law.[103] This decision results from a correct application of the Trade Marks Act 1938 but does not accord with commercial reality proving that the Act is now showing its age. Lord Bridge of Harwich was reluctant to dismiss the appeal from the owner of the mark against the refusal to register it and he said (at 202):

. . . though I can find no escape from s.28(6) of the Act of 1938, I do not hesitate to express my opinion that it has become a complete anachronism and that the sooner it is repealed the better.

However, relief may now be available under the law of passing off[104] and the new Trade Marks Act will repeal this provision originally intended to protect consumers. Subject to any agreement between them, a registered user may call upon the proprietor to institute legal proceedings to prevent infringement, that is to apply for an injunction. If the proprietor neglects to do so within two months of the request, the registered user may institute proceedings against the proprietor for infringement.[105]

Defensive registration can be applied for by proprietors of very well-known trade and service marks.[106] This allows a proprietor who has a registration in respect of certain classes of goods or services to register the mark for other goods or services even though he does not intend to use the mark for such other goods and services. This gives a valid registration regardless of the fact that the proprietor does not use and does not intend to use the mark in relation to the classes of goods and services to which the defensive registration applies. However, defensive registration will only be granted if the mark is so well known that there is a serious likelihood of confusion. Defensive registration can be applied for only in relation to invented word marks. A good example is the word 'KODAK'.

By section 21 marks may be registered as a series. This would apply where the marks are similar, for example 'KEDS', 'PRO-KEDS' and 'KEDDETTE',[107] and are registered in respect of the same goods or description of goods. Such marks, being associated marks, are only assignable or transmissible as a whole and not separately.[108]

ASSIGNMENT

Proprietorship of a registered trade or service mark is a form of property and a very valuable form at that. Before the 1938 Act, a registered trade mark was not assignable without the business goodwill associated with it. For example, a trader might sell his business to a third party who would, naturally, wish to take an assignment of any trade mark used by the original trade. However, in recognition of the growing asset value of trade marks, section 22 of the Act, subject to any rule of law or equity to the contrary, permits the assignment or transmission of a registered mark with or without the goodwill of a business. However, this will not be allowed if the result would be to vest the right to use the mark in relation to the same goods or services or the same description of goods or services to more than one person.[109] If the proposed assignment is without the goodwill of a business there is a time condition to be satisfied by section 22(7). The proposed assignee must, within six months, apply to the Registrar for directions about advertising the assignment and must so advertise it as directed. Geographically divided assignments may be made as long as they do not conflict with the public interest: section 22(6). By section 22(3), unregistered marks are assignable if they are assigned at the same time and to the same person as registered marks used in relation to the same business and registered for all the goods for which the unregistered mark is assigned. Assignments must

104 *Reform of Trade Marks Law* Cm. 1203 (London: HMSO, 1990) at p.27.

105 Section 28(3).

106 Section 27 and rule 37.

107 *Re Keds Trade Mark* [1993] FSR 72.

108 Section 23(1).

109 Section 22(4).

be notified to the Registrar by way of application to register the assignee's title and the assignee will be registered as the proprietor once the Registrar is satisfied of the assignee's title. Certain marks registered as associated marks can only be assigned or transmitted as a whole.[110] Registration of an associated mark is not complete until the fact of association has been entered in the association volume of the register. Until this has been done any assignment of the other mark only will be effective, notwithstanding that it should have been registered as an associated work.[111]

RIGHTS GIVEN BY REGISTRATION AND INFRINGEMENT

The rights given to the registered proprietor of a trade or service mark and the scope of infringement differs depending on whether registration is made in Part A or Part B of the register. Unfortunately, the provisions dealing with rights and infringement are some of the most complex on the statute book. First rights given and infringement of Part A marks will be discussed.

Part A marks

Section 4 of the Trade Marks Act 1938 defines the rights given by registration in Part A of the register and infringement of Part A marks. The main provisions are contained in subsection (1) which has been severely criticized by the judiciary. Section 4(1) is expressed in a single sentence of some 253 words. The meaning of section 4(1) came up for examination in *Bismag Ltd.* v *Amblins (Chemists) Ltd.*,[112] an early case on comparative advertising described in more detail later in this chapter. MacKinnon LJ, giving a dissenting judgment, admitted that he was unable to discover the meaning of section 4(1), saying (at 687):

> In the course of three days hearing this case I have, I suppose, heard s.4 . . . read, or I have read it for myself, dozens if not hundreds of times. Despite this iteration I must confess that, reading it through once again, I have very little notion of what the section is intended to convey . . . I doubt if the entire statute book could be successfully searched for a sentence of equal length which is of more fuliginous obscurity.

Lord Greene MR, although describing the language of section 4 as turgid and diffuse, claimed to be able to discover its meaning. By breaking section 4(1) down into smaller parts, the following meaning seems reasonable.[113] (The reference letters and numbers do not refer to section 4.)

A. The proprietor has the exclusive right to the use of the trade mark in relation to 'GOODS'.

B. Without prejudice to the generality of **A.** above, infringement occurs if 1 and 2 below or 1 and 3 below are satisfied:

    1. (a) use in the course of trade
        (b) of a mark identical with or nearly resembling the trade mark
        (c) in relation to 'GOODS'

and **2.** in such manner as to render the use of the mark likely to be taken as being use as a trade mark,

or **3.** in a case in which use is
        (a) use upon 'GOODS', *or*
        (b) in physical relation to 'GOODS', *or*

[110] Section 23.

[111] *Re Keds Trade Mark* [1993] FSR 72.

[112] [1940] 1 Ch 667.

[113] Note: 'GOODS' means goods of class against which mark is registered. The provision as it applies to services has similar effect although several changes are made to section 4 for service marks by the Trade Marks (Amendment) Act 1984.

(c) in an advertising circular, *or*

(d) in any other advertisement issued to the public;

use in such a manner as to render the use of the mark as:

(a) importing a reference to persons having right to use trade mark, *or*

(b) importing a reference to 'GOODS' with which the person having right to use mark is connected in course of trade

The basic rule is given in **A.** above. The proprietor has the exclusive right to use the mark in relation to the class or classes of goods (or services) against which it is registered and any other person using the mark in relation to goods or services falling within this class or classes infringes the proprietor's right. The right is, however, subject to some exceptions given in section 4 and in sections 7 and 8; these will be discussed later. This basic rule seems fairly straightforward. The part of section 4(1) that leads to difficulties in interpretation is the part which starts 'without prejudice to the generality of the foregoing words'. What then follows is a description of certain acts which are deemed to infringe the right. These can be read as being examples of infringement of the basic right or as enlarging the right. Certainly, if the alleged infringement is clear use of the trade mark in relation to goods for which the mark is registered, there is no need to look further – the right is infringed. Textbooks usually state that the infringing use must be done in the course of trade, which of course it must be for the specific examples of infringement in section 4(1)(a) and (b). However, the basic statement of right does not mention the use being in the course of trade. It is submitted that the infringement need not be in the course of trade as regards the basic right and that infringement occurs if a person uses the trade mark in relation to goods belonging to the class against which registration has been granted. Needless to say, it is highly unlikely that such use would not be in the course of trade. An example might be where a sculptor makes a sculpture for an exhibition comprising several stacked tin cans and he places a mark very similar to the 'Heinz' trade mark on them. Of course, for section 4(1)(a) and (b), the use must be in the course of trade and this means trade in relation to goods of the classification covered by the registration.

A simplistic view of the principle of infringement which has much to recommend it is that taken by Lord Greene MR in *Saville Perfumery Ltd.* v *June Perfect Ltd.*[114] where he said:

> . . . infringement consists in using the mark as a trade mark, that is, as indicating origin.

However, this fails to take into account the 'importing a reference' infringement in section 4(1)(b). The statement may make more sense in terms of the registrability of a mark and in *Aristoc Ltd.* v *Rysta Ltd.*,[115] Lord Greene's statement was quoted with approval as one of the reasons why a trade mark, 'Rysta', could not be registered in respect of the repair of silk stockings.[116]

Normally, infringement will be clear, for example where a person fixes a mark on his goods that is identical to or nearly resembling a trade mark belonging to someone else and which is registered for the appropriate class of goods. 'Nearly resembling' means that the mark is likely to deceive or cause confusion. The 'importing a reference' example of infringement given in section 4(1)(b) was an addition to trade mark law introduced in the 1938 Act as a result of the

114 (1939) 58 RPC 147 at 161.

115 [1945] AC 68.

116 Another reason was that the word 'Rysta' so nearly resembled 'Aristoc' in sound so as to be likely to deceive or cause confusion.

117 (1934) 51 RPC 110.

decision in *Irving's Yeastvite Ltd.* v *Horsenail*[117] where it was held that the comparative advertising of the defendant's product as a substitute for the plaintiff's product 'YEASTVITE' by reference to that trade mark was not an infringement. On this basis alone, it can be claimed that the infringement described in section 4(1)(b) is in addition to the basic exclusive right of the proprietor. It was intended to prevent comparative advertising involving the use of another's trade mark. A cynical view is that the extreme verbosity of section 4(1) compared to its prior equivalent can only be explained by saying that the legislature intended to make some change to the law.

Section 4(1)(b) is particularly relevant in terms of advertising but it must be done in such a way that the goods referred to are clearly identifiable as being the goods of the proprietor of the trade mark and those actually being offered are not the genuine goods. Blanco White and Jacob make the point that it might not always be an easy matter to identify the goods being offered and that a trap order may be needed to prove infringement.[118] The advertising circular or other advertisement issued to the public mentioned in section 4(1)(b) included a manual issued to sales distributors in *Chanel Ltd.* v *L'Arome (UK) Ltd.*[119] Comparisons were made in the manual between the plaintiff's perfumes and the defendant's cheaper alternatives.

118 Blanco White T.A. and Jacob R., *Kerly's Law of Trade Marks and Trade Names* (London: Sweet & Maxwell, 12th edn., 1986) at p.267–268.

119 (unreported) *The Times*, 26 November 1992 (Court of Appeal).

120 The European Community has issued a draft Directive that would allow comparative advertising where it is fair, OJ [1991] C180/15.

Comparative advertising[120]

Comparative advertising has become fairly common lately. It occurs where one manufacturer compares the specification, performance and price of his product with a rival's product. For example, a particular make and model of car might be advertised by comparing its best features such as acceleration times and fuel consumption with the equivalent figures for a similar but different make of car which is mentioned by name. Such advertising might, though not always, involve the use of trade marks belonging to others. If it does, there is, in principle, a trade mark infringement.[121] In *Bismag Ltd.* v *Amblins (Chemists) Ltd.*[122] the plaintiff owned the trade mark in the word 'bisurated' as applied to a 'patent medicine', bisurated magnesia, which was sold under a published formula. The defendant was a pharmacist and sold the plaintiff's goods but also made up and sold a similar preparation called 'bismuthated magnesia'. The defendant published a pamphlet with a list of proprietary medicines sold by him but opposite was printed a list of medicines made by him that were similar in all respects but much less expensive than the proprietary medicines. It was held in the Court of Appeal, by a two to one majority, that the defendant had used the plaintiff's trade name as a convenient method of describing the merits of his own products and had infringed the plaintiff's exclusive rights under section 4(1) of the Trade Marks Act 1938. Lord Greene MR, applied section 4(1)(b) to the circumstances by the following steps:

121 There is relatively little litigation on comparative advertising. Reasons may include a wish to reciprocate or a concern that commencing an action in respect of such an activity might look as if the owner of the mark used was sensitive about the claims made about his products, that is that his product did not compare favourably with his competitor's product.

122 [1940] 1 Ch 667.

(a) The defendant had used the plaintiff's trade mark in two ways, one of which was legitimate as the trade mark of the plaintiff's goods, but the other use was as a mark forming by reference part of the description of his own goods in the course of trade and in relation to the goods with respect to which the mark was registered.

(b) The use was in an advertising circular or other advertisement.

(c) The mark was used in such a manner as to render the use of the mark likely to be taken to be importing a reference.
(d) The plaintiff had the right to use the mark – bisurated goods are goods with which the plaintiff had a connection in the course of trade.
(e) The defendant's use manifestly imported a reference to the plaintiff's goods.

In some cases, it can be argued that the use by the defendant of the plaintiff's trade mark in advertising does not infringe because such use does not relate to the plaintiff's product but, rather, to the plaintiff's business. This argument found favour in *Pompadour Laboratories Ltd.* v *Frazer*[123] where the phrase used by the defendant in advertising his hair lacquer, 'Frazer's Chemicals have manufactured hair lacquer for Pompadour Laboratories Limited for several years', was held to be a reference to the plaintiff's name and not to his trade mark.[124] If this line of argument is taken by the defendant, it is a question of fact for the court to decide. So it was held in *News Group Newspapers Ltd.* v *Mirror Group Newspapers (1986) Ltd.*[125] where the defendant had used the plaintiff's masthead *The Sun*, amongst others, in an advertisement placing it under the phrase 'Yes, Prime Minister' so as to indicate that the defendant's newspaper was the only one which opposed the Prime Minister. The advertisement was a 'knocking' advertisement indicating that the plaintiff's newspaper blindly followed the Prime Minister's views. Aldous J took the view that the advertisement must have referred to the newspaper rather than the plaintiff's business. An injunction was awarded restraining publication of further copies of the advertisement.[126] This seems eminently sensible and it is hard to see how such advertising could do other than refer to the product concerned.

It is possible to use a trade mark otherwise than in a trade mark sense and in *Mothercare UK Ltd.* v *Penguin Books Ltd.*[127] the publication of a book by the defendant with the title *Mother Care/Other Care* was held not to infringe the plaintiff's 'Mothercare' trade mark because the words were being used in a descriptive sense and not a trade mark sense. The fact that the plaintiff had conducted surveys of the public to show evidence of confusion was criticized by Dillon LJ as being unhelpful.[128] Another example is provided by the case of *Mars GB Ltd.* v *Cadbury Ltd.*[129] where it was held that the use by the defendant of the phrase 'Treat Size', used in relation to his packets of miniature chocolate bars, did not infringe the plaintiff's 'TREETS' trade mark, registered in Part A for confectionery. The plaintiff's use was not use as a trade mark, neither was it likely to deceive or cause confusion.

Part B marks

The rights given by registration and infringement thereof are for Part B marks much the same as for Part A marks with one important exception.[130] In an infringement action, if the defendant establishes to the satisfaction of the court that the use of which the plaintiff complains is not likely:

(a) to deceive or cause confusion, or
(b) to be taken as indicating a connection in the course of trade between the goods and the proprietor or registered user having the right to use the trade mark,

then, injunctive or other relief shall not be granted to the plaintiff.[131] In other

---

123 [1966] RPC 7.

124 See also *Harrods Ltd.* v *Schartz-Sackin & Co. Ltd.* [1986] FSR 490. The case involved alleged passing off, and breach of contract. In the Court of Appeal, allegations of trade mark infringement and passing off were dropped, leaving the question of breach of contract to be determined, [1991] FSR 209. It was held that a clause restricting the use of the plaintiff's name by the defendant in a concession agreement did not survive the termination of the agreement.

125 [1989] FSR 126.

126 However, in a later hearing, Hoffman J discharged the interlocutory injunction because of the plaintiff's inordinate and inexcusable delay in proceeding with the action, (unreported) *The Times*, 18 December 1990 (Chancery Division).

127 [1988] RPC 113. This case also involved a claim in passing off and this aspect is discussed in the following chapter.

128 See also *Smith Kline & French Laboratories Ltd.'s Cimetidine Trade Mark* [1991] RPC 17 where Gibson J said that survey evidence would seldom be convincing because of problems associated with sampling and the avoidance of leading questions. He suggested that it would probably be prohibitively costly to conduct a meaningful survey. In any case, whether a mark is 'in fact capable of distinguishing' is a question of law not fact.

129 [1987] RPC 387.

130 Section 5(1) states, in unnecessarily intricate language, that the rights given for a Part B registration are the same as for a Part A registration.

131 Section 5(2).

132 It might not be registrable in Part A, being a geographical name.

133 This infringement is provided for in section 6.

134 Para. 4, Schedule 1 to the Trade Marks (Amendment) Act 1984.

135 Of course, such persons will not be liable for breach of contract, not being a party to the original contract. Persons deriving title through a bona fide purchaser also take free of the obligation.

136 [1983] FSR 313.

words, if the defendant can show that his use of a mark does not cause both of the above, the trade mark right is ineffective. The provisions for service marks are similar. In view of this limitation it may be very hard to prove infringement of a part B mark by importing a reference to it. An example might be the phrase 'If you like Everest mint chocolates you'll love our Matterhorn choice mints' where the word Everest is registered in Part B for Class 30 goods (including confectionery).[132] Although a technical infringement, the proprietor of the Everest mark would not be able to prevent the use of the phrase in advertising by the manufacturer of the Matterhorn mints because of the section 5(2) defence. However, it is the defendant who bears the burden of proof.

Infringement by breach of restrictions

This applies to both Part A and Part B marks.[133] However, it does not apply to service marks.[134] A proprietor or registered user of a registered trade mark may make a written contract with another, being the purchaser or owner of goods, who agrees that he will not do any of five specified acts. If he then does one of those acts he is treated as infringing the trade mark in addition to being in breach of contract. This applies also to third parties to whom title to the goods has subsequently passed unless that person is a bona fide purchaser for money or money's worth in good faith before receiving notice of the obligation.[135] The specified acts are:

(a) applying the trade mark to goods after they have been altered or repackaged;

(b) the alteration, part removal or obliteration of the trade mark;

(c) where the trade mark is on the goods and other matter (such as packaging), the total or partial removal or obliteration of the mark from the goods whilst leaving the mark on the other matter;

(d) where the trade mark is on the goods, applying another trade mark to the goods;

(e) where the trade mark is on the goods, adding any other matter in writing which is likely to injure the reputation of the trade mark.

Trap orders

If the proprietor of a registered trade mark believes that his mark is being infringed, it should not be necessary to apply for an Anton Piller order for the purpose of obtaining and preserving evidence of the infringement. It will usually be possible to buy the examples of the product to which the alleged infringing mark has been applied. For example, in *Systematica Ltd.* v *London Computer Centre Ltd.*[136] it was pointed out that the plaintiff could have freely walked into the defendant's shop and purchased copies of the alleged infringing computer programs.

Several test purchases can be made to build up a pattern of infringement. It may serve a useful purpose to frame a request for the product in such a way as to demonstrate clearly that there is a significant chance of confusion, especially if the mark is registered in Part B. Such orders for goods are referred to as 'trap orders' and are commonly used as a means of obtaining evidence of infringement both in relation to trade marks and passing off actions. It is obvious that the way the order is placed is important and it should be done in a clear, unambiguous and fair way. Trap orders may, indeed, be essential if the trade mark infringement occurs in an advertisement to verify that the goods or services being offered in fact are not those of the proprietor or a registered user.

EXCEPTIONS

Certain exceptions to infringement are specifically provided for by the Act. Section 4, the Part A rights and infringement section, contains some exceptions that apply equally to Part B marks. Section 7 prevents interference by a trade mark proprietor or registered user with pre-existing rights and section 8 permits bona fide use of names and bona fide description of the character or quality of goods.

Section 4 exceptions

A trade or service mark may be entered upon the register subject to conditions or limitations. For example, a disclaimer may be required for part of the mark that is common to the trade or service. The rights given by registration are obviously subject to any such conditions or limitations by section 4(2).[137] Section 4(3)(a) applies to goods that may have been used in the manufacture of other goods, for example a mark applied to cloth which is made into a dress by a person to whom the cloth has been supplied. This covers two situations: first, where the proprietor (or registered user) has applied the mark and not subsequently removed or obliterated it. For example, the cloth might have the mark 'Novoweave' printed along the edge of rolls of cloth. The dressmaker buying the cloth makes it up into dresses and the mark may be visible on the inside of seams. The dressmaker does not infringe the trade mark by making, advertising and selling the dresses. The second situation is where the proprietor or registered user of the mark has expressly or impliedly consented to the use of the mark; for example, where the dressmaker advertises her dresses as being made from genuine 'Novoweave' cloth, the proprietor of the mark may be taken to have impliedly consented by selling the material to a dressmaker.

In *Accurist Watches Ltd.* v *King*,[138] third parties made watches for the registered user of the plaintiff's trade mark and applied the trade mark to the watches. The registered user became insolvent and the third parties retook possession of quantities of the watches by virtue of retention of title clauses in their contracts with the registered user who was not to obtain good title to the watches until he had paid for them. The third parties sought to sell the watches and the plaintiff sued for trade mark infringement and passing off. Remarking that retention of title clauses could be ineffective otherwise, the court held that the makers of the watches had a complete defence under section 4(3)(a).

Section 4(3)(b) applies to goods adapted to form part of, or to be an accessory to other goods and obviously covers both the dress examples above, spare parts and accessories. A retailer selling replacement parts for cars will obviously need to refer to the make and model of the car (either of which may be registered trade marks) in advertising and selling these parts, for example by placing a card in his shop window stating that he has for sale 'tyres for Ford Granadas at only £23.00 each'. In terms of accessories, the advertisement might read 'roof

137 In *Diamond T Motor Co.'s Application* [1921] 2 Ch 583 a disclaimer was required in respect of some of the features of the mark such as the double line diamond border. Therefore, if another trader used a mark which included a double line diamond border, that would not infringe unless other features of the mark were the same or similar (nearly resembling).

138 [1992] FSR 80

rack suitable for Vauxhall Cavalier, only £15.00'. The use of the mark in this way must be 'reasonably necessary to indicate that the goods are so adapted'. It is clear that a trader can use the mark in making a bona fide description of his goods as long as he does not imply that the goods to which the adapted goods form a part, or the accessory, are not connected with the trade mark proprietor or registered user.[139]

Section 7 – anterior marks

The continuing use of a pre-existing mark cannot be restrained by subsequent registration of a similar mark (identical or nearly resembling). This provision applies where the pre-existing mark has been continuously used from a date anterior to the use of the other mark or the date of registration of that other mark, whichever is first. Such use or registration has to be in relation to the same goods or services to which the pre-existing mark has been applied. The pre-existing mark may be accepted for registration on the basis of honest concurrent use under section 12(2). The justification for this is that, otherwise, what was once lawful might become unlawful upon registration of the other mark. If both marks are in use in relation to the same goods or services, there may be a possibility of a passing off action. The fact of registration does not remove this possibility because section 2 makes it clear that the law of passing off is unaffected by the Trade Marks Act 1938. It is not inconceivable that, where two similar marks are involved only one of which is registered, the proprietor of one can bring a trade mark action against the other whilst that other proprietor can bring a passing off action in return. For example, Acme Ltd. owns a word mark 'WHIZZO' applied to toys and has used the mark continuously since 1975. It has never been registered as a trade mark. Zenith Ltd. owns a word mark 'WHEEZE' also used for toys which it has used continuously since 1974. This mark was registered in 1985. Between 1982 and 1986, Acme built up a reputation for high quality toys and the volume of its sales became much greater than Zenith's. Acme cannot register its mark and is not immune from a trade mark action because its use of the mark was not prior to Zenith's use of the similar mark. Zenith can, therefore, bring an action for trade mark infringement. On the other hand, since Acme has developed substantial goodwill, it may be able to sue Zenith in passing off. In practice, Acme should have objected to Zenith's application when it was published in the *Trade Marks Journal* and will probably claim that the Zenith mark should be removed from the register (expunged) on the grounds that the mark is deceptive.

Section 8 – bona fide use

Here permitted is the bona fide use of a person of his own name or that of his predecessor or the name of his own or predecessor's place of business. Also the bona fide description of the character or quality of goods or services is permitted providing to do so does not import a reference as in section 4(1)(b).[140] Because of the general prohibition of the registration of geographical names in Part A, it is unlikely that the use of names of places of businesses would otherwise offend. 'Bona fide' use means essentially honest use without an intention to either deceive or to cash in on another's reputation or goodwill. Deliberately changing one's surname will not be bona fide if such intention is present, for example where the owner of a small confectionery shop changes his name to 'Cadbury'.

139 Advertising a film (not being one made by Kodak) for a Kodak camera is permissible as long as a connection between Kodak and the film is not imputed even though Kodak is registered for both films and cameras. *Kodak Ltd. v London Stereoscopic* (1903) 20 RPC 337.

140 Or, in respect to trade marks only, as mentioned in section 37(3) – certification marks.

DEFENCES

A defence to an infringement action may include a claim by the defendant that one of the exceptions, described above, applies to the alleged infringement. Other defences include claims that:

(a) the plaintiff does not have title to the mark allegedly infringed, that is he is not the registered proprietor (or registered user) of the mark;

(b) the mark which has allegedly been infringed is not registered or the registration is invalid and the mark ought to be expunged from the register;[141]

(c) the acts complained of do not fall within the meaning of infringement, for example the mark has not been used by the defendant as a trade mark;[142]

(d) the mark is registered in Part B of the register and the defendant is able to show that the use complained of is not likely to deceive or cause confusion, etc.[143]

Other matters may give rise to a defence such as acquiescence, estoppel or delay.[144] Another situation advantageous to the defence is where the mark is being used fraudulently on the basis of the principle of *ex turpi causa non oritur actio*.[145] Unlike design law and patent law, there is no remedy for groundless threats of infringement proceedings.

REMEDIES

The remedies available, depending upon the circumstances are injunctions, damages or an account of profits as an alternative and destruction of or erasure of the marks. If the marks cannot be erased, an order for the destruction of the articles, advertising materials, etc., may be granted. As has already been mentioned, in the case of an infringement of a Part B mark, injunctive and other relief is not available if the defendant can show that the act complained of is not likely to deceive or cause confusion or be taken as indicating a connection in the course of trade between the goods or services and proprietor or registered user of the mark.[146] In other cases, the successful plaintiff is entitled to nominal damages as a matter of course and substantial damages if proved based on the loss actually caused to the plaintiff, for example as a result in a downturn in sales as a consequence of the infringement. Remoteness along tortious lines may be a factor but it may be possible in principle for a plaintiff to claim damages in respect of damage done to his reputation as a result of the infringer's goods or services being of an inferior quality. An account of profits may be available as an alternative to damages, bearing in mind that this is an equitable remedy.

OFFENCES

Section 58A of the Trade Marks Act 1938[147] makes it a criminal offence for a person:

(a) to apply a mark identical to or nearly resembling a registered mark to goods or ancillary material, for example, labelling or packaging; or

(b) to sell, let for hire, or offer or expose for sale or hire, or distribute

141 Bearing in mind the relative safety of Part A marks after 7 years (section 13). A mark may be removed, for example for non-use (section 26). Other reasons include cancellation of defensive marks, section (27(5)), with respect to registered users (section 28(10)), rectification under section 32 (e.g. for fraud), breach of conditions imposed, section 33.

142 Section 4(1).

143 Section 5(2).

144 See the passing off case of *Vine Products Ltd.* v *Mackenzie & Co. Ltd.* [1969] RPC 1, discussed in the following chapter.

145 A right of action cannot arise from an evil deed.

146 Section 5(2).

147 Inserted by virtue of the Copyright, Designs and Patents Act 1988, section 300.

    (i) goods bearing such a mark, or

    (ii) material bearing such a mark which is used or intended to be used for labelling, packaging or advertising goods; or

(c) to use material bearing such a mark in the course of a business for labelling, packaging or advertising goods, or

(d) to possess in the course of a business goods or material bearing such a mark with a view to doing any of the above mentioned things

when the person is not entitled to use the mark in relation to the goods in question and the goods are not connected in the course of trade with a person who is so entitled.

Possession in the course of business of goods or material bearing such a mark is an offence if it is done for the purpose of enabling or assisting another to do any of the things mentioned in (a) to (c) above. For all these offences, by section 58A(3), it is required that the act is done with a view to gain or intention to cause loss to another and that the person concerned intended that the goods were accepted as being connected in the course of trade with a person entitled to use the mark. It is a defence to show a belief, on reasonable grounds, of entitlement to use the mark in question. The maximum penalty available for any of the above offences is extremely severe and reflects the growing awareness of the considerable damage to commerce and industry by counterfeiting, apart from public safety issues. The offences are triable either way and on indictment the maximum is ten years' imprisonment and/or a fine, or on summary conviction, imprisonment not exceeding six months and/or a fine not exceeding the statutory maximum, currently £5,000. By section 58A(5) a director, manager, secretary or other similar officer may also be criminally liable if he consented to or connived in the offence.

There are, in respect of the section 58A offences, provisions for the delivery up and disposal of offending goods and materials.[148] A local authority weights and measures department can enforce section 58A and provisions under the Trade Descriptions Act 1968 are made to apply to section 58A offences, for example powers of search and seizure, powers to make test purchases, etc.

By section 283 of the Copyright, Designs and Patents Act 1988, a person or body corporate carrying on a business as, or holding himself or itself out to be, a 'registered trade mark agent' when in fact that person or that body is not a registered trade mark agent is liable to a fine on summary conviction not exceeding £5,000.[149]

Previously, the only criminal offences were under sections 59 and 60 of the Trade Marks Act 1938. Section 59 concerned making or causing to be made a false entry or a forged copy of a register entry or tendering a forged copy knowing it to be false. A person who does any of these is guilty of a summary offence.[150] Section 60 makes it an offence to falsely represent that a mark is registered or is registered in respect of certain goods, etc., for example by impressing goods with the expression 'Registered Trade Mark'. The maximum penalty is a fine not exceeding level 3 on the standard scale, currently £1,000. Of course, with respect to the fraudulent use of trade marks there may also be a criminal offence under the Trade Descriptions Act 1968.[151] Section 1 makes it an offence to apply a false trade description to goods or to supply or offer to supply goods to which a false trade description has been applied. By Section

148 Section 58B & 58C.

149 This extends to allowing himself to be so described or held out.

150 However, in the Isle of Man, the offence is punishable by 2 years' imprisonment with or without hard labour and/or a fine not exceeding £100 (section 59(2)).

151 Trading Standards Officers usually take action in such cases. It is possible, though unlikely, that an order for compensation could be made in favour of the trade mark proprietor or registered user.

2(1), a trade description includes a direct or indirect indication of the manufacturer, producer or processor of the goods. However, where the act clearly falls within section 58A of the Trade Marks Act 1938, trading standards officers will normally prosecute under that section, and section 58D facilitates this, because of the harsher maximum penalties available.

The 'New' Law

BACKGROUND

At the end of 1988, the Council of the European Community adopted a Directive aimed at harmonizing trade mark law throughout the European Community.[152] Although the basic principles of trade mark law are largely unaffected by the Directive there were, nevertheless, some significant and far-reaching changes required to be made to United Kingdom law.[153]

The Directive required compliance by 1 January 1993 but the United Kingdom failed to meet this deadline. This raised a number of issues concerning the direct effect of Directives as in *Publico Ministero* v *Ratti*[154] and speculation as to the liability of the United Kingdom to individuals suffering damage as a result of noncompliance.[155] For example, a trader might claim that he has experienced loss because his application to register a trade mark has been refused because it was unregistrable. On the basis of the Directive, the mark would be registrable. However, the existence of the law of passing off substantially reduces the possibility of the trader suffering loss in practice. Although, a possible scenario is where a new trader (A) uses a distinctive bottle for his perfume. Under the old law, following *In re Coca-Cola Co.*,[156] the bottle would not be registrable. If another trader subsequently uses a similar bottle, also for perfume, an action in passing off may not succeed because, being new to the market, A has not yet built up the required goodwill associated with his product and get-up. Had the bottle been registered as a trade mark, the second trader could be stopped from using a similar bottle.

A new Trade Marks Bill was introduced in the House of Lords in December 1993. It should receive the Royal Assent during 1994 (at around the publication of the second edition of this book). In the convening period between 1 January 1993 and the coming into force of the Trade Marks Act 1994, the Registrar has continued to apply the law in conformity with the 1938 Act and Rules made in pursuance of it. But, in *Marleasing* v *La Comercial Internacional de Alimentacion*,[157] it was held that national courts should interpret national laws in accordance with Community law so that, in respect of registration of marks and infringement thereto in particular, there is a conflict between the position taken by the Registrar and the position likely to adopted taken by the courts. The government can be criticized for putting the Registrar in a difficult position because of its delay in implementing the Directive.

The need for reform of United Kingdom trade mark law goes back to long before the Directive and the Trade Marks Act 1938 has been subject to much judicial criticism over the years, section 4 of which attracted the description 'fuliginous obscurity' by Mackinnon LJ in *Bismag Ltd.* v *Amblins (Chemicals) Ltd.*[158] But difficult and obscure though the 1938 Act is, the need for change is

152 Council Directive of 21 December 1988 to approximate the laws of Member States relating to trade marks OJ [1989] L40/1. A White Paper was published subsequently setting out the government's plans to conform with the Directive, *Reform of Trade Mark Law* Cm. 1203 (London: HMSO, 1990).

153 An early description of the changes was given in Groves, P. & Martino, T. 'Euromark: or How the EEC Brought UK Trade Mark Law into the 20th Century' (1990) 1 *European Business Law Review* 109.

154 [1980] 1 CMLR 96.

155 *Francovich & Boneface* v *Italian State* [1992] IRLR 84.

156 [1986] 2 All ER 274.

157 [1990] ECR I-4135.

158 [1940] 1 Ch 667 at 687.

also a reflection of changing advertising and commercial operators. The 1938 Act sought to prevent comparative advertising and failed to take account of character merchandising (by its prohibition of trafficking in trade marks, described by Lord Bridge in *Holly Hobbie Trade Mark*[159] as a complete anachronism). It was also too restrictive in the nature of marks that could be registered and the way the legislation was altered to provide for service marks by the Trade Marks (Amendment) Act 1984 was clumsy in the extreme.

The new Bill brings a welcome breath of fresh air to thinking on trade mark law. Although it is fairly lengthy, comprising 106 sections and five schedules, it makes significant and substantial reforms to this important area of law. Gone is the obscure drafting of the 1938 Act. The Bill, though not without difficulty, is clearly drafted and it paves the way for improvements in both the substantive and procedural law relating to trade marks. Greater provision is made for the international aspects of trade mark law, for example with respect to the proposed Community Trade Mark (or 'Euromark') and it will enable the United Kingdom to ratify the Madrid Agreement on the International Registration of Marks. Priority may be claimed from filings in Paris Convention countries made within the previous six months of the date of filing in the United Kingdom. As to be expected, the existing law of passing off is retained.

REGISTRABLE TRADE MARKS

The basic definition of what constitutes a registrable mark will be significantly widened. Clause 1(1) of the Bill defines a trade mark as being any sign capable of being represented graphically and which is capable of distinguishing the goods or services of one undertaking from another. This is considerably wider than the definition of a mark in the 1938 Act.[160] However, the Registrar and the courts did not previously take a particularly restrictive view of what constitutes a trade mark with the notable exception of *In re Coca-Cola*.[161] Even a two colour combination for a capsule for a drug was permitted by the House of Lords in *Smith, Kline & French Laboratories Ltd.* v *Sterling Winthrop Group Ltd.*[162] Perhaps, in the past, applicants have felt constrained to be conservative in their choice of marks on the basis of the language of the 1938 Act and we can expect to see more imagination used in the choice of trade marks.

Musical jingles, moving computer-generated images and perfumes may all be potentially registrable. Sounds, computer images and smells are all capable of graphical representation, by means of musical notation, computer data and chemical formulae respectively. However, a limiting factor will be the advertising of marks in the *Trade Marks Journal*. The main purpose of advertising is to enable other traders to see if the new marks are too similar to theirs or are otherwise unregistrable, for example by being descriptive of goods in the particular industry. This purpose could be defeated if the character of the mark is not readily apparent from an inspection of the journal and whilst it may not be unreasonable to expect a reader to play a music mark to appreciate its character it would be unfair to expect readers of the *Trade Marks Journal* to conduct complex chemical experiments to arrive at the mark. Three dimensional marks which have hitherto been disallowed should cause no difficulty as it is a simple matter to represent the shape of an article by means of plan and elevation draw-

159 [1984] FSR 199 at 202.

160 Section 68(1) and, for Part A marks, section 9.

161 [1986] 2 All ER 274.

162 [1976] RPC 511.

ings or, even better, a perspective view. Computer-generated images can treated in a similar manner, perhaps using a number of views. In practice, the Rules to be made in pursuance of the new Act will have to deal with the practicalities of registering new forms of marks[163] but they are also likely to impose restrictions that will suppress the wilder excesses of marketing imagination.

Some specific examples of trade marks are given in clause 1 being words (including personal names), designs, letters, numerals or the shape of goods or their packaging. This would allow the registration of distinctive containers and, although there are exceptions, this could include new and aesthetic designs, normally the province of the Registered Designs Act 1949. The effect of this will be to give a monopoly right in a design applied to a specific type of good for a period of potentially unlimited duration compared with a maximum of 25 years' protection for registered designs. However, one important proviso is stated in clause 3(2) and a sign will not be registered if it consists exclusively of the shape which gives substantial value to the goods or is necessary to obtain a technical result or results from the nature of the goods themselves. It is clear that things that are acquired or used by reason of their design, such as a household ornament, will not be registrable as a trade mark but the Design Registry has applied the eye-appeal requirement very generously in the past[164] and a great many designs do not add substantial value. Quasi-functional articles possessing an element of eye-appeal such as food packaging, display or vending apparatus might fall into this category and, in some cases, be registrable both as trade marks and designs.

Single register

The two-tier system comprising Part A marks, being those adapted to distinguish, and Part B marks, being capable of distinguishing, will be abolished. In fact, the lower threshold, capable of distinguishing, will be used and it is likely that this will have the same meaning as before, that is capable in time of becoming distinctive with use, or not incapable of becoming distinctive, per Sargant LJ in *Davies* v *Sussex Rubber Co.*[165] Service marks will no longer be treated differently to trade marks for goods and all marks, whether for goods or services, will be described as trade marks.[166]

Unregistrable signs

Inevitably, there are some important exceptions to the types of signs that can be registered as trade marks. Stating the obvious, clause 3(1)(a) says that signs failing to meet with the basic requirement in clause 1(1) are not registrable. Other unregistrable signs are those devoid of any distinctive character or that are closely associated with kind, quality, quantity, purpose, value or geographical origin, those that are deceptive or immoral and signs that have become customary in the current language or in the bona fide and established practices of the trade (clause 3(1)(b)–(d)) However, of these other signs, they may be registrable if they have acquired a distinctive character through use by the date of application. The effect of these provisions is fairly close to that under the old law. For example, geographical names could be registered in Part B on evidence of distinctiveness.[167]

163 The White Paper, *Reform of Trade Marks Law*, Cm 1203 (London: HMSO, 1990) alludes to the fact that the open ended definition of trade marks in the United States has not appeared to cause any particular administrative or legal problems. It is unlikely that applicants will have to deposit three-dimensional objects, computer disks or sound recordings.

164 For example, a design for a shower tray including its underside in *Gardex Ltd.* v *Sorata Ltd.* [1986] RPC 623.

165 (1927) 44 RPC 412 at 425.

166 There will be some minor differences flowing from the differing nature of goods and services. For example, the meaning of using a sign. For goods, this includes affixing the sign to goods or their packaging and, for services, it includes offering or supplying services under the sign, clause 9(4).

167 *Andorra Trade Mark* [1976] RPC 397 for motor vehicles.

'Shape marks' are a new departure but there are some bars to registration in clause 3(2). They will not be registered if they consist exclusively of shape resulting from nature of goods themselves or if necessary to obtain a technical result or if the shape gives substantial value to goods.[168] Clause 3(3) prohibits the registration of marks that are contrary to public policy or accepted principles of morality or if the mark is deceptive, for example as regards the nature, quality or geographical origin of the goods or services. Marks that, by virtue of their use, are prohibited in the United Kingdom by any enactment or rule of law or by any provision of Community law are likewise unregistrable. Thus, a word mark 'Somerset Champagne' would fail on several grounds, being deceptive in two ways regarding geographical origin and by contravening European Community Regulation 823/87.[169] Certain emblems are also unregistrable, such as the Royal arms, national flags and emblems of countries belonging to the Paris Convention and of certain international organizations (for example, the United Nations). Again, these provisions are similar to the exceptions provided for by the old law.[170] A final ground for refusal in clause 3 is if the application was made in bad faith. This could apply in the case of a 'ghost mark' such as the 'Nerit' mark in *Imperial Group Ltd.* v *Philip Morris & Co. Ltd.*[171]

All the grounds for refusal in clause 3 are described as being absolute grounds for refusal. Clause 5 contains relative grounds for refusal. They are so described because registrability depends upon the nature of the relationship between the mark and an earlier mark or right. A mark will not be registered if identical to an earlier mark for the same goods or services, clause 5(1). Trade marks are not registrable if there exists a likelihood of confusion on the part of the public where the mark is identical to an earlier mark for similar goods or services or if it is similar to an earlier mark for the same or similar goods or services, clause 5(2). To take some examples:

- *Splurge* is to be used for chocolate. There exists an earlier mark, also *Splurge*, that is also used for chocolate. The registration will be refused point blank. There is no need to consider whether there is a likelihood of confusion
- As above but the earlier mark is used for gum drops. Registration will not be allowed if there is a likelihood of confusion as the goods are similar (confectionery)
- As above but the earlier mark is used for garden equipment. The new mark should be registrable because there is very little, if any, likelihood of confusion (the goods to which the two marks are applied are different and will be sold at different trade outlets)
- *Splurge* is to be used for chocolate. An earlier mark also used for chocolate is *Splodge*. Registration will probably be refused because there is a likelihood of confusion

And so on.

An identical or similar mark is not registrable if the earlier mark has gained a reputation even though in different goods and there would be unfair advantage of the earlier mark or a detriment to the distinctive character of earlier mark, clause 5(3). Nor will a mark be registered if its use could be prevented by passing off or the enforcement of some other earlier right (for example, a registered design or copyright) by clause 5(4) unless consent is obtained and there is not a likelihood of confusion, clause 5 (5).

168 The latter could be registrable as designs.

169 As amended. This would also amount to passing off, see *Taittinger SA v Allbev Ltd.* [1993] FSR 641, discussed in the following chapter.

170 See the Trade Marks Rules 1986, SI 1986 No. 1319.

171 [1982] FSR 72.

An earlier mark is defined in clause 6. It is a United Kingdom mark, an international mark (designating the United Kingdom) or Community Trade Mark (CTM, when in force) having an earlier date of registration taking priority into account; a CTM with a valid claim to seniority from an earlier registered trade mark or international trade mark (designating the United Kingdom); a trade mark entitled to protection under the Paris Convention as a well-known mark. Included are marks with earlier application dates pending registration (subject to their being registered). Expired marks shall be taken into account for one year after expiry unless the Registrar is satisfied there was no bona fide use during the two years immediately preceding the expiry.[172]

By clause 7, the Secretary of State is given power to provide by order that a trade mark shall not be refused registration on any of the grounds mentioned in clause 5 (relative grounds for refusal) unless objection on that ground is raised in opposition proceedings by the proprietor of the earlier mark or other earlier right. In other words, the new Trade Mark Rules may require that opposition to registration is a prerequisite for the relative grounds for refusal. Proprietors of existing registered marks will need to be ever vigilant and inspect the *Trade Marks Journal* regularly. This will have the effect of raising a limited presumption in favour of the mark being registrable, removing the Registrar's discretion in this respect.[173]

REGISTRATION

By clause 28, an application to register a trade mark will require the submission of the following items:

- a request for registration,
- information regarding the identity and address of applicant,
- a statement of goods or services in relation to which it is sought to register the mark,
- a representation of the mark,
- the prescribed fee (application plus class fees).

Also required will be a statement that the trade mark is being used by applicant or with his consent in relation to those goods or services or that he has a bona fide intention to do so. The date of filing will be the date when all the necessary documents have been furnished to the Registrar, clause 29. This is the date of application. Clause 31 provides for priority from earlier filings for up to 6 months.[174] By clause 32, the priority provision may be extended to the Channel Islands or colony or other countries or territories enjoying reciprocal rights by way of treaty, convention, arrangement or engagement. The applicant or proprietor may disclaim part of a mark or agree to a limitation (for example, a territorial limitation) by clause 12. This will usually be in response to advice from the Registrar. Under the old law, the Registrar could impose disclaimers himself directly.[175]

Registration procedure

The registration procedure is laid out in clauses 33 to 38 of the Bill. The main stages are as follows:

172 One year will probably be the period allowed for restoration of a lapsed trade mark. It was under the old law, section 20(3) of the 1938 Act. Clause 39 provides for restoration but leaves the period to be laid down in Rules.

173 By section 17(2) of the 1938 Act, the Registrar had a discretion to refuse or accept an application. Thus, the Registrar could refuse to register a trade mark on the grounds, *inter alia*, that it would be likely to cause confusion, section 12(1) of the 1938 Act.

174 By clause 31(6) the right of priority from a Convention application can be assigned or otherwise transmitted with or without the application.

175 Section 14. See *Diamond T Motor Car Company* [1921] 2 Ch 583.

- **Examination** – to make sure that the requirements in the Act and Rules are satisfied. This will entail a search of earlier marks as the Registrar considers necessary. The opportunity will be given to the applicant to make representations and/or amend the application if the Registrar thinks that the requirements are not met, clause 33.
- **Publication** – in the prescribed manner. Any person may give notice within the prescribed period (to be set by Rules) of opposition in writing and stating the grounds for opposition. Additionally, any person may make observations in writing before registration without becoming a party to the proceedings on the application, clause 34.
- **Registration** – Where there has been no opposition (or, if there has been, the proceedings have been decided in favour of the applicant) then, unless it appears to the Registrar that the application was accepted in error, the mark shall be registered. The registration will then be published and a certificate issued to the applicant, clause 36.

By clause 35, the applicant may withdraw his application at any time or restrict the goods or services covered by application. Amendment is also allowed but only in respect of name or address of applicant, errors of wording or copying or obvious mistakes providing correction does not substantially affect the identity of the trade mark or extend the goods or services covered by application. Presumably, a disclaimer or territorial limitation made or accepted by the applicant by virtue of clause 12 does not amount to an amendment. Otherwise it would be disallowed by clause 35. If the applicant has second thoughts and wishes to make changes to the mark, for example by adding a laurel wreath around the mark, he would have to withdraw and re-apply. Once the mark has been advertised, the fact of withdrawal or restriction must be advertised. Amendments affecting the representation of the mark also require publication.

Clause 37 allows for provision to be made to split an application into several applications, to merge applications or registrations or to register a series of trade marks. A series of marks means a number of trade marks resembling each other as to their material particulars and differing only in non-distinctive matters so as not to substantially affect the identity of the mark. This is equivalent to the registration of series of marks as associated marks under the old law. However, there does not seem to be any limitation on the separate assignment of such marks as there is under the old law.[176]

176 Section 23 of the 1938 Act.

There will be a change to the duration of registration, by clause 38(1) initial registration will be for a period of ten years from the date of registration (date of filing) or an earlier date if the priority of a registration or application elsewhere is claimed. Renewals will be for further periods of ten years, clause 38(2). Clause 39 contains provisions for renewal, leaving the fine detail to be provided for by rules which will include provisions for late renewal (within six months subject to an additional fee) and restoration of marks removed from the register for want of renewal.

Generally, once registered, a trade mark may not be altered, clause 40. However, an alteration may be permitted where the mark includes the proprietor's name and address, for example where there is a change to the name or address or address of the proprietor, providing that the alteration does not substantially affect the identity of the mark. The alteration will be published and persons claiming to be affected by it may object.

By clause 68, registration of a person as proprietor of the mark is *prima facie* evidence of the validity of the original registration of a trade mark and any subsequent assignment or other transmission of it. This is equivalent to the presumption contained in section 46 of the 1938 Act.

TRADE MARKS AS PROPERTY

The Trade Marks Bill firmly states that a registered trade mark is an item of personal property (or, in Scotland, incorporeal moveable property) and, under the provisions of the Bill, trade marks are easily alienable. By clause 22, trade marks can be assigned or pass by testamentary disposition or by operation of law with or without the goodwill of a business. Although similar in principle to the equivalent provisions in the 1938 Act, they are expressed in much simpler language. Assignments may be partial in terms of:

- some but not all goods or services for which it is registered,
- use in a particular manner or in a particular locality.

Assignments or vesting assents are not effective unless in writing and signed by or on behalf of the assignor (or personal representative), clause 22(3). This also applies to an assignment by way of security.

The Bill provides clear rules for joint proprietorship of trade marks. By clause 21(3) each co-proprietor may do any act for his own benefit that would otherwise infringe but may not, by clause 21(4), without the consent of the other co-proprietors, grant a licence to use the mark or assign or charge his share.

The Bill has detailed provisions for licensing (exclusive, non-exclusive and sub-licences) unlike the 1938 Act.[177] A licence must be signed by or on behalf of the grantor, clause 23(2). Unless otherwise provided for, a licence is binding on the grantor's successor in title. Sub-licences are recognized as possible and, by clause 23(4), references in the Bill to licences include sub-licences. An exclusive licence is one authorizing the licensee, to the exclusion of all others including the proprietor, to use a registered trade mark, clause 24(1).

The Bill contemplates exclusive licensees and non-exclusive licensees commencing legal proceedings against infringers, although the right of a licensee to do this can be affected by the terms of the licence agreement.[178] The difference between exclusive and non-exclusive licensees are that, in the case of the former, the proprietor can prevent the licensee from suing if he includes an appropriate term in the licence but, in the case of non-exclusive licences, the proprietor must include a term permitting the sub-licensee to sue. In one case, he must act to take the right away, in the other he must act to grant it. Nevertheless, these provisions will, in many cases, strengthen the hand of persons using trade marks under a franchise agreement. The following transactions affecting registered trade marks must be registered on application to the Registrar by a person claiming to be entitled to an interest in or under the mark concerned by virtue of any such transaction by clause 25(1):

- an assignment of the mark or any right in it (this could include, for example the assignment of a licence),

177 Clauses 23 and 24.

178 Clause 16 covers the rights and remedies of exclusive licensees and clause 18 states the rights of non-exclusive licensees in relation to infringement.

- the grant of a licence under the mark,
- the grant of a security interest (fixed or floating charge) over the mark or any right in or under it,
- the making by personal representatives of a vesting assent in relation to the mark or any right in or under it,
- a court order (or order of other competent authority – for example, the Trade Marks Registrar rectifying the register) transferring the mark or any right in or under it.

By clause 25(2), until the application for registration of the transaction has been made, it is ineffective against a person acquiring a conflicting interest in or under the mark in ignorance of the transaction and any person claiming to be a licensee because of the transaction does not have any rights and remedies for infringement.[179] A person becoming a proprietor or licensee has six months to register his interest (the court has discretion to extend if it was not practicable to register within six months). Failure to register within that time will mean that the new proprietor or licensee cannot obtain damages or an account of profits in respect of infringements occurring between the date of the transaction and the date of registration of the interest, clause 25(3). No trusts shall be entered on the register but equities in relation to registered trade marks may be enforced as with other personal property, clause 26. This permits action by beneficial owners of trade marks, for example where the assignment is oral or unsigned and has not complied with the formalities required by clause 22(3). Of course, the remedies available to a beneficial owner are severely limited unless he joins the legal owner in the action.

[179] Under clauses 16 and 18 (action by exclusive and non-exclusive licensees).

As it may take some months between application and registration, the provisions in the Bill relating to assigning, licensing and registration are also effective in relation to an application to register a trade mark, clause 27. Thus, it is possible to grant an assignment or licence in respect of a trade mark before it has been formally registered.

The registered user provisions will be dealt with in the future by licence arrangements and, thankfully, the provisions against trafficking in trade marks are missing from the Bill signalling a meeting of the law and commercial reality. Holly Hobbie and her ilk will become registrable as trade marks by their owners and licences granted to persons wishing to use such marks on their goods without requiring any other link between the owner and user of the mark or any actual use of the mark by or on behalf of the owner. This will greatly benefit character merchandisers.

RIGHTS CONFERRED BY REGISTRATION

The proprietor (and exclusive licensee, if there is one) has exclusive rights which are infringed by use of mark without consent in the United Kingdom, clause 8(1). That clause continues by stating that the acts amounting to infringement are specified in clause 9 but this is narrower than the basic statement in clause 8 – use in the United Kingdom without consent. This is contradictory and clause 8(1) could be construed by considering that *any* use without consent in United Kingdom infringes. However, it is unlikely that such an interpretation will be placed on the scope of infringement.

The rights have effect from the date of registration, clause 8(3). This is the date of filing of the application as clause 36(3) makes this the date of registration. However, the proprietor cannot begin infringement proceedings before the date on which the mark is in fact registered, therefore, infringement proceedings cannot be brought until the day that registration is granted. The language in the two provisions is somewhat tautologous. Clause 36(3) states that the date the mark is in fact registered is the date of filing. Because it is retrospective it is none the less a question of fact. But, obviously no proceedings can be entertained until it is known that the mark has been registered.

The proprietor's rights will be constrained if he has acquiesced in the use of a later registered trade mark for a continuous period of five years. This also applies to the owner of an earlier unregistered mark.[180] By clause 44, the proprietor of the earlier mark will not be entitled to claim that the registration of the later mark is invalid unless the later registration was applied for in bad faith. Neither will the proprietor of the earlier mark be able to oppose the use of the later mark in relation to the goods or services for which it has been used. Therefore, proprietors of trade marks must scan the pages of the *Trade Marks Journal* regularly and monitor the use of other marks that are similar and be prepared to take action. The existence of a validly registered later mark under these provisions does not affect the validity of the earlier mark in as much as the proprietor of the later mark is not allowed to oppose the use of the earlier mark or right.

180 Or, for that matter, any other earlier right such as a copyright or design right.

INFRINGEMENT OF A REGISTERED TRADE MARK

The notorious section 4(1) of the 1938 Act will soon disappear and its replacement by much less turgid language will cause sighs of relief from judges in trade mark actions.[181] For an infringement to be made out, the person responsible must use a sign in the course of trade and, by clause 99, this includes any business or profession. Use of a sign means, in particular, by clause 9(4):

181 However, it will linger on for some time as the transitional provisions state that the old law will continue to apply to infringements committed before the commencement of the new Act, para. 4(1), Schedule 3 to the Bill.

- affixing to goods or packaging thereof,
- offering or exposing goods for sale, putting them on the market or stocking them for those purposes under the sign, or offering or supplying services under the sign,
- importing or exporting goods under the sign,
- use of the sign on business papers or in advertising.

Infringement extends to the spoken use of words as well as a visual representation where the registered trade mark consists of or includes words which are distinctive elements of the mark.[182]

182 Clause 9(6).

One type of infringement does not require proof of a likelihood of confusion on the part of the public. This is use in the course of trade of a sign *identical* to the trade mark in relation to *identical* goods or services against which the mark is registered, clause 9(1). Other infringements require proof of likelihood of confusion (including the likelihood of association) and are: use in the course of trade of a sign which is:

(a) **identical** to the trade mark in relation to goods or services **similar** to those against which the mark is registered, clause 9(2)(a), or

(b) **similar** to the trade mark in relation to **identical** or **similar** goods or services against which the mark is registered, clause 9(2)(b),

where the similarity is the reason for the likelihood of confusion.

A registered trade mark is also infringed by the use of a sign in the course of trade that, without due course, takes unfair advantage of, or is detrimental to the distinctive character or repute of a registered mark enjoying a reputation in the United Kingdom, clause 9(3). For this to apply, the sign must be:

(a) **identical** or **similar** to the trade mark, and
(b) used in relation to goods or services **NOT similar to** those against which the mark is registered

This should compensate for the loss of defensive registration which is not provided for in the Bill. If a person uses an identical mark to a registered trade mark but in relation to goods or services that are quite different to those against which the mark is registered and there is no likelihood of confusion then that use could infringe. For example, if a trader calls his new range of shoes 'Rolls Royce Shoes', very few persons would consider that the motor car company or the jet engine manufacturer[183] had suddenly started making shoes. However, such use of the mark could weaken the registered marks by a process of erosion or devaluation and jeopardize the high standing of the marks. This will mirror passing off where using another trader's name to impute a quality or goodwill could damage the goodwill associated with the name because of an erosion of its reputation or distinctiveness and is recognized as an actionable form of damage.[184]

By clause 9(5) a person who applies a registered mark to material intended to be used for labelling or packaging goods, as a business paper (for example, a company letterhead or a sheet of instructions accompanying goods), or for advertising goods or services shall be treated as a party to any infringing use if, when he applied the mark he knew or had reason to believe that the application of the mark was not authorized by the proprietor or a licensee.

As use of a trade mark includes use in advertising it seems that the bar against comparative advertising that caused so much trouble under the 1938 Act will prevail. This was introduced into section 4(1) of that Act as a result of a failure to find infringement against a comparative advertiser in *Irving's Yeastvite Ltd.* v *Horsenail*.[185] However, there is a European Community proposal for a Directive on comparative advertising that would allow it if carried out fairly.[186] There are a number of defences to infringement in the Bill, most of which are similar to those under the 1938 Act.

As usual in any civil legal action, the burden of proof is on the plaintiff. The proprietor bears the burden of proof as regards the use to which the mark has been put if the question arises, clause 96. This will not normally be a problem, given the availability of Anton Piller orders.

As mentioned earlier, in some cases, non-exclusive licensees will be able to sue for infringement. This is something of a novelty and is not provided for by copyright, patent or design law (there are no provisions for the exclusive licensee of a registered design to sue for infringement). This is in the Bill presumably because of franchise arrangements where the 'man on the ground' is in the best position to take action.

183 This is an example of a split trade mark. Both companies use the same mark.

184 See for example, *Taittinger SA* v *Allhev Ltd.* [1993] FSR 641, discussed in the following chapter.

185 (1934) 51 RPC 110.

186 OJ [1991] C180/15.

If the validity of a registered mark is contested and found to be valid, the court may give a certificate to that effect by clause 69. This mirrors section 47 in the 1938 Act. Such a certificate could prove useful in any subsequent proceedings as regards the award of costs in favour of the proprietor.

Remedies

Clause 13(2) states that the remedies for infringement of a registered trade mark are damages, injunctions, accounts or otherwise as is available in respect of infringement of any other property right. This would seem to allow additional damages as for copyright although it is difficult to envisage a situation when exemplary or punitive damages would be appropriate. The 1938 Act did not specifically mention any particular remedy.

Orders for delivery up of infringing goods, materials or articles from a person having them in his possession, custody or control in the course of business are available by clause 14(1). But, by clause 92(1), an order for delivery up is not available after the end of the period of six years from:

● (with respect to infringing goods) – the date on which the registered trade mark was applied to goods or their packaging,
● (with respect to infringing material) – the date on which the registered trade mark was applied to the material,
● (with respect to infringing articles) – the date on which they were made,

unless the proprietor of the mark was suffering from a disability or was prevented by fraud or concealment from discovering the facts entitling him to apply for the order. In these cases, the six years runs from the time when he ceased to be under a disability or when he could, with reasonable diligence, have discovered the facts, clause 92(2).[187]

Infringing goods, materials or articles are defined in clause 15. Infringing goods are those bearing (or those on which their packaging bears) an identical or similar mark, the application of which was an infringement or the same in respect of goods to be imported or where the sign has otherwise been used in relation to the goods so as to infringe. This does not affect the importation of goods that can legally be imported by virtue of any enforceable Community right, clause 15(3). Exhaustion of rights is covered by clause 11: that is, it is not an infringement to use the mark in relation to goods which have been put on the market by or with the consent of the proprietor. This does not extend to a situation where the proprietor has a legitimate reason to oppose further dealings, for example where the condition of the goods has subsequently been changed or impaired.

Infringing material is material that bears an identical or similar mark and is used (or is intended to be used) for labelling or packaging the goods or as a business paper or for advertising goods or services so as to infringe, clause 15(4). Infringing articles are those specifically designed or adapted for making copies of a sign identical to or similar to a registered trade mark and the person who has the article in his possession, custody or control knows or has reason to believe that the article has been or will be used to produce infringing goods or material, clause 15(5).

187 By clause 92(3), a disability, in England and Wales, has same meaning as in the Limitation Act 1980. Clause 93 contains provisions for orders for disposal of infringing goods, materials or articles. Orders for delivery up or disposal may be brought in a county court in England or Wales, section 94. By clause 14(2) no order shall be made under clause 14 unless the court also makes or it appears to the court that there are grounds for making an order under clause 93.

Clauses 52 to 54 provide for injunctive relief in favour of the proprietors of well-known marks (within the meaning of the Paris Convention for the Protection of Industrial Property), national emblems and the like of convention countries and emblems, etc. of certain international organizations. There are some notification requirements to be fulfilled by clause 55. If the application for registration of a trade mark is made by an agent of the proprietor, the proprietor may apply for a declaration of the invalidity of the registration or apply for rectification of the register so as to substitute his name as proprietor.

There is, as with design rights and patents, a remedy for groundless threats of infringement proceedings and this is a new departure for trade mark law.[188] Relief is a declaration that threats are unjustifiable, injunction against continuance and damages. The plaintiff is entitled to such relief unless the defendant shows that the act in respect of which proceedings were threatened was or would be an infringement. Mere notification that a mark is registered or that application has been made does not constitute a groundless threat by clause 19(4). However, the proceedings must be other than in respect of the application of the mark to goods or their packaging, importation of such goods or packaging or the supply of services under the mark, clause 19(1). Thus this remedy could apply to threats in respect of the acts of advertising or offering for sale.

Exceptions and defences

Compared to the 1938 Act, defences and exceptions are greatly simplified. The provisions under the old law relating to contracts between the proprietor or registered user and purchaser or owner of goods are gone. These infringements would be actionable under contract law anyway and their inclusion was somewhat of a mystery.

By clause 10(1), any person may use a registered trade mark to identify goods or services as those of the proprietor providing the use is:

- in accordance with honest practices in industrial *or* commercial matters (for example, a retailer using a trade mark to advertise goods), and
- is not such as to take unfair advantage of, or be detrimental to, the distinctive character or repute of the mark (this could apply in the case of fair comparative advertising).

Honest practices in industrial *and* commercial matters is also the test for non-infringing use in clause 10(2) by:

- the use of a person of his own name or address,
- indications describing the goods or services, for example kind, quality, quantity, purpose, value, geographical origin, etc.,
- use necessary to indicate the intended purpose of the product or service (particularly with respect to accessories or spare parts).

Earlier rights associated with trade identifiers, for example earlier unregistered names or marks, continually in use in the course of trade in a particular locality from before the first use of a trade mark now registered or its date of registration, whichever is earlier, may continue to be used without infringing by clause 10(3). The earlier right is deemed to apply in a locality if it has sufficient goodwill to be protected by the law of passing off there.

Where the plaintiff's complaint relates to the use of a registered mark by the defendant, he may be able to set up acquiescence on the part of the plaintiff if the defendant's use has been continuous for at least five years by clause 44. The defendant's registration must not have been applied for in bad faith. In principle, this is not dissimilar to the conclusive validity of Part A marks that have been registered for at least seven years under section 13 of the 1938 Act.

Where a registration has been subject to a disclaimer or is limited in some other way, for example where it is restricted to a specified territory, use of the mark covered by the disclaimer or limitation does not infringe.[189]

189 Clause 12.

A defendant might want to argue that the plaintiff's mark should be revoked. An application for revocation may be made by any person by clause 42(4). However, the proprietor's rights may still extend up to the date of revocation. Alternatively, the defendant might want to claim that the registration is invalid under clause 43 and an application may be made by any person. The defendant can also challenge the registration on the basis of the absolute grounds for refusal or relative grounds for refusal or, by virtue of clause 43(4), that the proprietor acted in bad faith. The last ground requires that the Registrar himself applies for the declaration but the defendant might be in a position to convince the Registrar that this is the case.

SURRENDER, REVOCATION AND INVALIDITY

The proprietor may surrender the registration in respect of some or all goods or services for which it is registered by clause 41. Rules may be made to deal with the manner of surrender and its effects in addition to the effect on others having rights in mark, such as licensees. Clause 42(1) lists the grounds for revocation of a registered trade mark as being:

- **non-use:** within five years of the date of completion of the registration procedure, the mark has not been put to genuine use in the United Kingdom by the proprietor or with his consent in relation to the goods or services for which it was registered and there are no proper reasons for non-use;
- **non-use:** genuine use has been suspended for an uninterrupted period of five years and there are no proper reasons for non-use;
- **that it has become a generic name:** because of the acts or inactivity of the proprietor the mark has become a common name in trade for a product or service for which it is registered (note the use of the word 'product' rather than 'goods'; presumably, the word product is narrower, being a type or a particular species of goods);
- **it is misleading:** because of the use made by the proprietor or with his consent in relation to the goods or services for which it is registered, the mark is liable to mislead the public (particularly in respect of the nature, quality or geographical origin of the goods or services in question).

By clause 42(2) 'use' in terms of revocation includes use in a different form providing this does not alter its distinctive character, and use in the United Kingdom includes affixing the mark to goods or packaging in the United Kingdom solely for export purposes.

Revocation will not be carried out on grounds of non-use if the use is commenced or resumed after five years but before application for revocation is made. However, there is a three-month period prior to the application for revocation and use within this period will be ignored unless preparations for a commencement or resumption of use is made before the proprietor became aware that an application for revocation might be made, clause 42(3). This deals with the possibility of the proprietor taking immediate steps to use the mark once he hears that someone intends to apply for revocation so as to defeat revocation proceedings. An application for revocation may be made by anyone to the Registrar or the court.[190] If proceedings before the court are pending, the application must be made to the court and, in other cases, the Registrar may refer the application to the court. Revocation may be whole or partial by clause 42(5). If a mark has been revoked, the proprietor's rights are deemed to cease from the date of the application for revocation or at an earlier date if the Registrar or the court is satisfied that the grounds for revocation existed earlier.[191]

Clause 43 states that a registration may be declared invalid because:

- the registration was made in breach of clause 3 (the absolute grounds for refusal). However, the registration shall not be declared invalid if in breach of clause 3(1)(b), (c) or (d) if the mark has subsequently acquired a distinctive character in relation to the goods or services for which it was registered;[192]
- the registration was contrary to clause 5 (relative grounds for refusal);
- in the case of bad faith (the Registrar may apply to court for declaration of invalidity).

Application may be made by anyone to the Registrar or the court, clause 43(3). If proceedings in the court are pending, the application must be made to the court and, in other cases, the Registrar may refer the application to the court. By clause 43(5), the declaration of invalidity may be partial in terms of the goods or services for which it is registered. The effect of a declaration of invalidity is that the registration will be deemed never to have been made – it is void *ab initio*, clause 43(6). However, this will not affect any transactions past and closed.

OFFENCES

The offence of fraudulent use of a trade mark and the provisions for delivery up and disposal of offending goods as well as enforcement is restated in language appropriate to that used elsewhere in the new Bill (clauses 86 to 88). There is a statutory defence where the relevant act was done before the date of publication of registration.[193] The offences of falsification of the register, etc. and falsely representing a trade mark as registered are also restated in modified language. The opportunity has been taken to update the penalties for the latter two. The former now becomes an offence triable either way with a maximum penalty on conviction on indictment of imprisonment for a term not exceeding two years or a fine or both.

190 Clause 42(4).

191 Clause 42(6).

192 Clause 43(1).

193 Clause 8(3). Civil remedies are not affected by this.

OTHER PROVISIONS

The Bill contains some forward looking provisions and includes the necessary mechanism for the United Kingdom to implement the Community Trade Mark once the necessary regulation has been adopted by the European Community. The Secretary of State will also be empowered to make the necessary provisions to enable the United Kingdom to ratify the protocol to the Madrid Agreement concerning the international registration of trade marks.

The position as regards trade mark agents is not changed and clauses 77 to 82 of the Bill are very similar to sections 282 to 284 of the Copyright, Designs and Patents Act 1988 (which will be repealed) and section 65 of the Trade Marks Act 1938. The Secretary of State is given the power to make rules authorizing the Registrar to refuse applications from certain persons to act as agents.[194]

The new Bill contains detailed provisions for collective marks and certification marks in Schedules 1 and 2 respectively.

194 For example, a person who has been convicted of an offence of describing himself as a registered trade mark agent when not so registered, etc. under clause 79. Previously dealt with by rules under section 40 of the 1938 Act.

TRANSITIONAL ARRANGEMENTS

Because of the radical overhaul of trade mark law brought about by the new Bill there is a need to deal fully with transitional arrangements, particularly for existing registered marks. Schedule 3 to the Bill contains the transitional provisions. Marks registered under the 1938 Act immediately before commencement of the new law are known as 'existing registered marks' and they shall be transferred to the new register whether or not they were registered in Part A or Part B. Disclaimers and limitations will also be transferred to the new register but not conditions. Any proceedings to expunge a mark will be determined under the old law.

The new law on infringement applies to existing registered marks as regards infringements occurring after the commencement of the new law but, if the infringement took place earlier, it will remain to be determined under the old law. However, an act done in relation to an existing registered mark before commencement can continue to be performed without infringing. This applies in particular with respect to marks registered under the honest concurrent use provisions in section 12(2) of the 1938 Act.

Other transitional provisions concern co-ownership, assignment and other dealings with trade marks, licensing and registered users, revocation and rectification. Pending applications will be dealt with under the old law and considered to be, once registered, an existing registered mark. Some existing trade marks are still classified according to the pre-1938 classification scheme but these will be brought into line with the present system of classification. The new periods of duration take effect immediately upon commencement for new marks as well as for existing registered marks. Thus, where an existing registered mark falls due for renewal on or after the commencement of the new law, it will be renewed for a period of ten years, regardless of when the fee is, in fact, paid.

SUMMARY

The new law makes significant improvements to trade mark law and, in terms of clarity, is worlds apart from the 1938 Act. It does much to bring trade mark law up to date and to take it forward to the twenty-first century. The main criticism is that the new law has taken so long to come to fruition, trade mark law should have been reformed at least 10 to 15 years ago. Perhaps the delay is explicable (though not excusable) because of the European Community's plans to harmonize this important area of intellectual property law. At least the new law takes full account of the international dimensions of trade mark law.

The Bill is forward looking in that it contains the mechanisms to allow the United Kingdom to give effect to the Community Trade Mark (CTM, discussed below) and the Madrid Agreement concerning the International Registration of Trade Marks. At the present time, the United Kingdom is not a party to this Act which contains 37 Member States (eight of which are European Community Member States).[195]

Even though the Bill is unlikely to suffer much change of any significance before Royal Assent (it is not a politically contentious Bill), the final face of trade mark law will not be fully appreciated until the new rules to accompany and flesh out the new Act have been passed. In many cases, the Bill does little but to provide the framework for the rules which are likely to be just as voluminous as the new Act. Nevertheless, proprietors and authorized users of trade marks must be pleased to see the demise of the 1938 Act and its arid, verbose language.

TRADE MARKS AND THE EUROPEAN COMMUNITY

There are several matters of interest in respect of trade marks and the European Community. National trade mark law is presently being harmonized throughout the Community, there are plans for a 'Euromark', a Community-wide trade mark registration system; and, finally, of interest are the effects of the Treaty of Rome's prohibition on unjustifiable restrictions on imports and exports, especially in terms of 'parallel importing'. The harmonization of trade mark law is discussed above in the description of the new United Kingdom trade mark law.

'Euromark'

For some time there have been plans to implement a single Community-wide trade mark system; the Community Trade Mark (CTM). The most recent proposal contains some 127 Articles and is a comprehensive and well-thought out document.[196] Whether the harmonization of national laws will turn out to be an important and key step towards a unified system of trade marks remains to be seen. There are serious difficulties to be overcome, not the least being that similar marks already have been registered by different proprietors in different Member States and reconciling these marks could be a tremendous task made more difficult because of the potentially indefinite duration of trade mark rights. It is planned that the Community Trade Mark (CTM) will have effect throughout the Community and only marks that can be so registered will be accepted. Therefore, the *Kaffee Hag* trade mark, discussed in the next section, could never become a CTM unless there is merger of ownership.

195 Apart from the United Kingdom, of the EC Member States, Denmark, Eire and Greece are not a party to the Madrid Agreement.

196 *Amended proposal for a Council Regulation on the Community Trade Mark* OJ [1984] C230/27.

The draft Directive gives a definition of 'trade mark' which is similar to that in the harmonization Directive except that the former does not state that the mark should be represented graphically but it does specifically allow colour combinations by Article 3. One interesting requirement is that a publisher of a dictionary, encyclopaedia or similar work must ensure that any reproduction of a CTM is accompanied by an indication that the mark is registered where it is likely to be taken as a generic name.[197] The duration of registration (initial and on renewal) will, by Article 14, be 10 years as it will soon be in the United Kingdom. There are detailed provisions for assignment and licensing and recognition of the right to use a mark as a property right. In particular, the right subsisting in the CTM may be charged as security for a loan or mortgage. Article 98a allows the use of a symbol comprising the Greek capital letter epsilon within a circle. However, it may be some time before the CTM becomes established and, because of the nature of trade marks, the success achieved by the European Patent Office in respect of patent applications is unlikely to be replicated easily.

Parallel imports and exhaustion of rights

Exhaustion of rights can best be described by means of an example. Say that a parent company, Bear Holdings plc, of a group of companies making teddy bears and other fluffy animals is located in the United Kingdom. It has a subsidiary company located and trading in France, called La Peluche SA. The parent company uses a trade mark on its goods. The French company has the right to use the mark in France only and is not permitted to export its teddy bears to the United Kingdom. The sale price of the teddy bears is considerably less in France. A third party entrepreneur buys a large number of the French bears and exports them to the United Kingdom where it sells them, undercutting Bear Holdings plc which would like to prevent the entrepreneur selling the bears in the United Kingdom.

The problem is one of reconciling the right to use a trade mark with the desirability of allowing the free movement of goods and preventing the partitioning of the market within the European Community. The European Court of Justice has not, until recently, been particularly keen on enforcing trade mark rights if there is any danger of competition being distorted. In the above example, the European Court of Justice would be unlikely to enforce the trade mark rights in favour of Bear Holdings plc even though this approach seems a little unfair in that Bear Holdings is experiencing competition from items made by a subsidiary company in circumstances outside the contemplation of either. However, one advantage of the European approach for consumers is that it does make it difficult for undertakings to maintain unjustifiable price differentials between Member States.

Articles 30–36 of the Treaty of Rome promote the free movement of goods by prohibiting unjustifiable restrictions on the import and export of goods. Article 36 permits derogations by Member States on several grounds provided that they do not constitute 'a means of arbitrary discrimination or a disguised restriction on trade'. These grounds include public morality, public policy, public security, the protection of health and life of humans, animals and plants, the protection of national treasures possessing artistic, historic or archaeological value, or the protection of *industrial and commercial property*.[198] It is not

197 Article 9. Proprietors of trade marks are usually vigilant and try to prevent a mark becoming a generic name, for example by asking others using the mark to make sure that the mark is acknowledged as a registered trade mark. Some marks that have become generic names include 'ASPIRIN', CELLULOID', 'NYLON' and 'ESCALATOR'.

198 The phrase 'industrial property' is usually taken as including patents, trade marks and designs.

199 [1993] FSR 263.

200 But, see *Centrafarm BV v American Home Products Corp.* [1979] 1 CMLR 326, discussed below.

201 [1974] 2 CMLR 480.

202 *Hoffman-La Roche v Centrafarm* [1978] ECR 1139.

203 [1979] 1 CMLR 326.

204 [1989] RPC 497.

205 The licence agreement between the parent company and the Brazilian subsidiary contained a clause declaring that no restrictions were to be placed on exports. This was held not to be equivalent to express consent and was narrowly interpreted because it was inserted so as to comply with Brazilian law. Express or implied consent will excuse an infringement of a trade mark, section 4(3)(b) Trade Marks Act 1938.

206 Oliver, P. 'Of Split Trade Marks and Common Markets' (1991) 54 MLR 587 at 589.

unusual for commercial undertakings to use different trade marks in different countries. This, in itself, does not demonstrate a disguised restriction on trade and some further evidence is required. In *Cheetah Trade Mark*,[199] the plaintiff who was also the proprietor of a United Kingdom registered mark sold herbicide in the United Kingdom and Belgium but used a different trade mark in Belgium. The defendant bought a quantity of the herbicide from the plaintiff in Belgium, bearing the Belgian mark, and imported and resold it in the United Kingdom without altering the packaging. He did, however, use the United Kingdom trade mark on his delivery notes and invoices. When challenged, the defendant unsuccessfully argued that the use of different trade marks by the plaintiff was a disguised restriction on trade between Member States and that the rights in the United Kingdom trade mark had been exhausted by the sale of the herbicide under the Belgian mark. Of course, it would have been quite remarkable if putting goods onto the market under one trade mark exhausted the rights under another, different, trade mark even though both marks might be owned by the same company.[200]

In *Centrafarm BV v Winthrop BV*,[201] Winthrop, a Dutch company, was part of the Sterling group of companies and Centrafarm bought and imported into The Netherlands, drugs made by another company in the Sterling group in the United Kingdom. It was held that Winthrop could not exercise its trade mark rights under Dutch law to prevent this as the marketing of the drug in the United Kingdom had exhausted that right. This exhaustion principle has been applied subsequently where the importer has repackaged the goods[202] and even where different marks were used in different countries and the importer has changed the mark accordingly. This happened in *Centrafarm BV v American Home Products Corp.*[203] where a drug was marketed in the United Kingdom under the name 'Serenid' and under the name 'Seresta' in The Netherlands. Both marks were owned by AHP and it was held that AHP could not prevent the parallel importing of the drugs as its use of several trade marks was intended to split up the market artificially contrary to Article 30. The United Kingdom courts have had the opportunity to consider parallel importing from Brazil in *Colgate-Palmolive Ltd. v Markwell Finance Ltd.*[204] The United States parent company of the United Kingdom company and the Brazilian company owned trade marks registered in the United Kingdom and similar marks registered in Brazil. The defendant imported into the United Kingdom and sold the toothpaste made in Brazil which was of a poorer quality than that made in the United Kingdom. The Court of Appeal held that the United Kingdom trade marks were infringed and the defendant's argument that the parent company had expressly or implicitly consented to the importation was rejected because it would amount to a misrepresentation to consumers as to the quality of the goods.[205] It may be that this approach will find sympathy in the European Court of Justice because of the hint of a deception as to quality operating on members of the public and this view has been borne out recently, indicating that there may be a less extremist view of trade marks than was the case previously.[206]

Split trade marks

The cases discussed above involve a common origin in terms of the goods themselves, that is the companies making the goods are associated in some way, as members of a group of companies. A rarer case involves a common origin with respect to the trade mark but the link stops there. The right to use the mark in different countries has become separated in some way. In *Van Zuylen Freres* v *Hag AG*,[207] Hag AG, a German company owned the 'Kaffee Hag' trade mark in Germany, Belgium and Luxembourg. After the Second World War, the rights to the mark in Belgium and Luxembourg were sequestrated and assigned to Van Zuylen who then attempted to use its trade mark rights to prevent the importation into Belgium of the German 'Kaffee Hag'. It was held that, in a much criticized decision, on the doctrine of common origin the Belgian trade mark could not be relied on to prevent the marketing in one Member State of a product lawfully made in another Member State under an identical mark. This is not really the exhaustion principle, because the German coffee had not been marketed by or with the consent, implied or otherwise, of the owner of the Belgian trade mark. However, the European Court has expressly disapproved of this decision[208] in *SA CNL-SUCAL NV* v *Hag GF AG*[209] in which the facts were almost the reverse of the previous *Kaffee Hag* case. This time the current owner of the Belgian mark sought to sell its *Kaffee Hag* in Germany. It was held that Articles 30–36 of the Treaty of Rome did not prevent national legislation from permitting an undertaking which owned a trade mark in a Member State from restraining the importation of similar goods bearing a similar mark from another Member State. The justification was that otherwise consumers would not be able to identify with any certainty the origin of the product and the owner of the mark in one Member State might be blamed for the poor quality of goods for which he was not responsible. The effect of the two *Kaffee Hag* cases is that both the Belgian and German owners can exclude the importation of the other's product into their respective countries. This accords with common sense in the very special circumstances. In the decision the European Court laid down some principles for such mutual exclusivity being that:

(a) the two marks are identical or confusingly similar,
(b) the products are similar, and
(c) there are no legal or economic links between the parties.[210]

This conforms with the decision in *Terrapin (Overseas) Ltd.* v *Terranova Industrie CA Kapferer & Co.*[211] where the German owner of the 'Terranova' trade mark for building materials could prevent the United Kingdom company registering the mark 'Terrapin' for prefabricated buildings. Two themes from the above decisions can be seen in the harmonization Directive. First, in the second *Kaffee Hag* case the possibility of confusion is a reason for refusing to register a mark, Article 3(1)(g) – deception as to the nature, quality or geographical origin of the goods or services. Secondly, Article 7(2) limits the exhaustion principle where there are legitimate reasons for a trade mark owner to oppose further commercialization of the goods, especially where the condition of the goods is changed or impaired.

Trade marks may be split for other reasons. It is not uncommon for a group of companies to divest itself of one of its subsidiary companies. This may be a result of normal commercial factors or it may be a result of a de-merger notice from the Monopolies and Mergers Commission. Where such a separation takes place, there may be provision in the necessary agreements concerning the ownership and use of intellectual property rights for mutual use of a trade mark with geographical limitations. For example, a Spanish parent company making and selling shoes has a subsidiary company in Wales which, *inter alia*, also

207 [1974] 2 CMLR 127.

208 Express disapproval of one of its earlier decisions by the European Court of Justice is something of a rarity in itself.

209 [1990] 3 CMLR 571.

210 For a discussion of the effects of this decision, see Oliver, P. op cit.

211 [1976] 2 CMLR 482.

makes and sells shoes. The same trade mark is used by both companies and is registered in several countries. The Welsh company is listed as a registered user in the United Kingdom. The Spanish parent company decides to sell the Welsh company and it is agreed that the United Kingdom registration will be assigned to the Welsh company. Furthermore, it is agreed that the Spanish company will not use its mark on shoes it exports to the United Kingdom for five years and the new owner of the Welsh company agrees not to export shoes from the United Kingdom bearing the trade mark. In *Eleco* v *Mitek*,[212] the Commission took a favourable view of a similar arrangement in terms of Article 85(1). However, it leaves to be determined the question of what happens when the agreement expires. Will the territorial ban continue on the basis of mutual exclusivity as in the latest 'Kaffee Hag' case? The issue of split trade marks is likely to cause many problems in the future and it has already been raised in a number of cases. For example, in *Job Trade Mark*,[213] it was held that it was relevant to consider, in the context of the single market, whether it would be in the public interest for a trade mark to have different proprietors in respect of the same goods in the United Kingdom and France.[214]

212 [1992] 4 CMLR 70.

213 [1993] FSR 118.

214 See also *Fyffes plc* v *Chiquita Brands International Inc.* [1993] FSR 83.

215 [1993] 1 CMLR 421.

Registrability and free movement of goods

The importance of ensuring the free movement of goods within the European Community is of such importance that the basic provisions for registration of marks in individual Member States can be compromised. In *Re The 'Quattro' Trade Mark*[215] the plaintiff made a motor car in Germany called the Audi Quattro and the name 'Quattro', meaning the numeral four in Italian, was registered as a trade mark in Germany. The defendant, a French manufacturer, started importing into Germany a model of car called 'E Quadra'. When the plaintiff objected, the defendant challenged the validity of the German registered mark. Under German law, there is a presumption that a foreign numeral should not be registered as a trade mark. However, this presumption can be overcome by showing a strong identity between the word and the applicant's goods. That was so in this case. However, this could affect trade between Member States, allowing the proprietor to restrict the import of goods from other countries with a numeral in their description, something that could not be registered as a trade mark in those other countries. Because of this danger and because it did not feel competent to decide the matter, the German Federal Supreme Court submitted the case to the European Court for a preliminary ruling under Article 177. If the answer confirms the German court's doubts about the validity of the mark, this would mean that provisions in national trade mark law excluding registration of marks on certain specified grounds would have to take into account languages and methods of selling in other Member States. For example, a mark that has a reference to the nature of character of goods is not registrable and 'Six-Pack' should not, therefore, be registrable in the United Kingdom for use with beers and other drinks sold in sets of six cans. The phrase also should be unregistrable in all other Member States no matter how distinctive it has become in those countries. Otherwise, a United Kingdom brewer would not be able to export cans of beer in sixes and described as a six-pack. That being so, there may be a number of trade marks whose registration is vulnerable as the use of foreign words for trade marks is not uncommon.

21

Passing off

INTRODUCTION

The law of passing off and trade mark law have common roots and therefore are, in many respects, very similar. Passing off is a tort and can be described as the common law form of trade mark law. Section 2 of the Trade Marks Act 1938 makes it clear that the law of passing off is unaffected by the Act.[1] Business 'goodwill' is protected by passing off and, whilst this may be associated with a particular name or mark used in the course of trade, this area of law is significantly wider than trade mark law in terms of the scope of materials that can be protected. The owner of the goodwill has a property right that can be protected by an action in passing off. Buckley LJ described the nature of the proprietary right thus:

> A man who engages in commercial activities may acquire a valuable reputation in respect of the goods in which he deals, or of the services which he performs, or of his business as an entity. The law regards such a reputation as an incorporeal piece of property, the integrity of which the owner is entitled to protect.[2]

He goes on to confirm that the property right is not a right in the name, mark or get-up itself but that it is a right in the reputation or goodwill of which the name, mark or get-up is the badge or vehicle. The words 'reputation' and 'goodwill' are often used interchangeably but it is really in connection with goodwill that passing off is concerned. It is possible, after all, to have a reputation without goodwill, the Russian monk Rasputin providing a good example of this. The existence of reputation (in this case a favourable one) without any associated goodwill was fatal to a claim in passing off in *Anheuser Busch Inc.* v *Budejovicky Budvar*.[3] The *Budweiser* name for beer was well known in the United Kingdom but, in the absence of a trading presence here, the plaintiff could not establish the necessary goodwill to sustain an action in passing off.

Quite often, passing-off actions will be brought in respect of an unregistered trade mark, a mark that has not been registered through deliberate inertia on the part of the owner of the mark, as a result of ignorance or because the mark fails to satisfy the requirements for registration. The great majority of cases will involve a mark in the wide sense, including containers and packaging, but business goodwill can be achieved and maintained in other ways and it is possible that business methods and get-up, marketing strategy and advertising themes can be protected by this useful area of law. Passing off actions have never been limited to goods and actions in respect to services have always been a possibility. However, it is clear that the tort applies in a business context, directly or indirectly, although in other circumstances a passing off type of activity could amount to defamation.[4]

1 Section 2 also states that no action is available under the Act for the infringement of an unregistered trade mark. The Trade Marks Bill 1993 is to the same effect, clause 2(2).

2 *H P Bulmer Ltd.* v *J Bollinger SA* [1978] RPC 79 at 93.

3 [1984] FSR 84.

4 For example, *Tolley* v *J S Fry & Sons Ltd.* [1931] AC 333

The main point about passing off is that goodwill has been developed and another trader might try to take advantage of that goodwill, to cash in on it to the detriment of the first trader. There are two main reasons why a trader would wish to pass off his goods or services as being those of another, established trader. The first is that by doing so, a significant portion of the established trader's custom might be captured because of confusion amongst the buying public as to whom they are dealing with. The second reason is that sales might be boosted by unjustifiably imputing a quality to the second trader's goods that is widely recognized in connection with the goods of the established trader. In both cases, the established trader suffers damage by a shortfall in trade but in the second case, the damage may be even more far-reaching in that he stands to lose his goodwill and reputation for quality goods if, because of the misrepresentation, the buying public associate the poor quality goods with him. Alternatively, the harm may be more subtle and result in a gradual degradation of the first trader's name or get-up.[5]

The preservation of business goodwill is the prime concern of passing off but the protection of consumers from deception is an ancillary effect. The New Zealand case of *Plix Products Ltd. v Frank M Winstone (Merchants)*[6] involved pocket packs for kiwi fruit. The plaintiff had a monopoly in such packs as a result of the sole approval of the plaintiff's design for such packs by the New Zealand Kiwifruit Authority. The case turned on copyright issues in addition to passing off and in the former it was established that copyright infringement could occur through a verbal description. On the passing off claim it was held that a cause of action in passing off depended on damage to the plaintiff's reputation and not upon the premise that purchasers might confuse the plaintiff's and the defendant's packs and obtain an inferior or different product to the one they thought they were acquiring.

Passing off may overlap with other rights, especially trade marks and copyright, and a given set of circumstances may give rise to an action involving two or more different rights. For example, in *Mothercare UK Ltd. v Penguin Books Ltd.*[7] the defendant published a book, first published in the United States, about bringing up children, entitled *Mother Care/Other Care*. The plaintiff, who operated a chain of retail shops selling various items for babies, small children and expectant mothers, sued for trade mark infringement and for passing off. It was held the defendant had not infringed the 'Mothercare' trade mark because it had not been used in a trade mark sense. On the passing off action it was said that, considering the title of the book as a whole, there had not been a misrepresentation by use of that title.[8] In *The Visual Connection (TVC) Ltd. v Ashworth Associates Ltd.*,[9] the plaintiff sued for infringement of copyright in photographs and for passing off resulting from the use by the defendant of the photographs, representing his business as that of the plaintiff.[10]

BASIC REQUIREMENTS FOR A PASSING OFF ACTION

In *Perry v Truefitt*[11] it was said by Lord Langdale MR that, 'a man is not to sell his own goods under the pretence that they are the goods of another trader'. That is, the law would restrain one trader from passing off his goods as being those of another trader. The essence of the action is a misrepresentation, either

5 This is a continuing concern for traders dealing with high quality goods. See the discussion about the 'Champagne' cases later in this chapter.

6 [1986] FSR 63.

7 [1988] RPC 113.

8 Dillon LJ considered the recent fashion of conducting surveys to be unhelpful. He also deplored the proliferation of affidavits, assertions and counter-assertions common when wealthy companies are involved in passing off, copyright or trade mark cases.

9 (unreported) 14 January 1986, Chancery Division.

10 See also *Columbia Picture Industries v Robinson* [1987] 1 Ch 38 in which the plaintiff alleged infringement of copyright and trade marks and passing off. The defendant admitted to these and injunctive relief and an inquiry as to damages was ordered but the plaintiff had to pay £10,000 to the defendant because of an abuse of the Anton Piller order.

11 (1842) 49 ER 749.

express or implied. This was expanded to include a situation where the origin of the goods was not at issue, rather it was the quality of the goods. In *Spalding & Bros v A W Gamage Ltd.*,[12] the plaintiff was a dealer in footballs described for some years as 'Orb' footballs and this description and descriptions including the word 'Orb' became distinctive of the plaintiff's footballs. The plaintiff sold a quantity of defective balls to a waste rubber merchant and, eventually, they fell into the hands of the defendant who advertised them as being 'Orb' balls. An injunction was granted in favour of the plaintiff and Lord Parker considered the nature of passing off, saying:

12 (1915) 84 LJ Ch 449.

> The more general opinion appears to be that the right [that is, the right to take action to prevent passing off] is a right of property . . . property in the business or goodwill likely to be injured by the misrepresentation.[13]

13 Ibid. at 450.

An important case in which the basic requirements for success in a passing off action were described in the House of Lords was *Erven Warnink Besloten Vennootschap v J Townend & Sons (Hull) Ltd.*[14] The plaintiffs made a liqueur called advocaat which came to be well known.[15] It was a high quality liqueur made from brandewijn, egg yolks and sugar which acquired a substantial reputation and sold in large quantities. The defendant decided to enter this market and made a drink called 'Keeling's Old English Advocaat' which was made from Cyprus sherry and dried egg powder, an inferior but less expensive drink compared to the plaintiffs'. This captured a large part of the plaintiffs' market in the United Kingdom but it could not be shown that consumers would mistake it for the plaintiffs' drink. Nevertheless, it was held that the reputation associated with the plaintiffs' product should be protected from deceptive use of its name by competitors even though the goodwill was shared by several traders. There was a misrepresentation made by the defendant calculated to injure the plaintiffs' business or goodwill and an injunction was granted in favour of the plaintiffs, there being no exceptional grounds of public policy why an injunction should not be granted. Lord Diplock laid down the essentials for a passing off action, derived from the case of *Spalding & Bros. v A W Gamage Ltd.*[16] and subsequent cases, as being:

14 [1979] AC 731.

15 The plaintiffs were representative of the Dutch manufacturers of Advocaat.

16 (1915) 84 LJ Ch 449.

- a misrepresentation,
- made by a trader in the course of trade,
- to prospective customers of his or ultimate consumers of goods or services supplied by him,
- which is calculated to injure the business or goodwill of another trader (in the sense that this is a reasonably foreseeable consequence) and,
- which causes actual damage to a business or goodwill of the trader by whom the action is brought or (in a *quia timet* action) will probably do so.

Lord Oliver reduced this list to three elements in *Reckitt & Colman Products Ltd. v Borden Inc.*[17] namely; the existence of the plaintiff's goodwill, a misrepresentation as to the goods or services offered by the defendant and damage (or likely damage) to the plaintiff's goodwill as a result of the defendant's misrepresentation. Nevertheless, the courts still prefer Lord Diplock's authoritative test.[18] In the *Erven Warnink* case, Lord Fraser proposed a different formula to that used by Lord Diplock. Lord Fraser said:

17 [1990] 1 All ER 873.

18 See, for example the judgments in *Taittinger SA v Allbev Ltd.* FSR 641.

It is essential for the plaintiff in a passing off action to show at least the following facts:- (1) that his business consists of, or includes, selling in England a class of goods to which the particular trade name applies; (2) that the class of goods is clearly defined, and that in the minds of the public, or a section of the public, in England, the trade name distinguishes that class from other similar goods; (3) that because of the reputation of the goods, there is goodwill attached to the name; (4) that he, the plaintiff, as a member of the class of those who sell the goods, is the owner of goodwill in England which is of substantial value; (5) that he has suffered, or is really likely to suffer, substantial damage to his property in the goodwill by reason of the defendants selling goods which are falsely described by the trade name to which the goodwill is attached. Provided these conditions are satisfied . . . the plaintiff is entitled to protect himself by a passing off action.[19]

The definitions given by Lords Diplock and Fraser can be seen as attempts to produce a generalized, all-purpose rule, but it is probable that their Lordships were too strongly influenced by the facts of the case before them. In particular, Lord Fraser's definition is far too narrow – being restricted to goods sold in England (although recognizing that trade reputation has a specific locality) – but he does specifically mention the need for a goodwill associated with the goods although this is implicit in Lord Diplock's statement. Lord Diplock talks in terms of goods and services and it is clear that a passing off action is available in respect of services. Lord Diplock, by using the phrase 'calculated to injure' seems to suggest some fraud or malice on the part of the defendant whilst Lord Fraser makes no such inference.[20] As will be seen later, relief can be given when the misrepresentation is unintentional; the action is not limited to goods; the geographical scope can extend outside the United Kingdom as far as the trade is concerned, and passing off is not limited to trade names as indicated by Lord Fraser. On the whole, Lord Diplock's definition is probably closer to the present legal position and seems to be the one most referred to. In subsequent cases, there has been some conflict about whether the Diplock and the Fraser test should be applied together.[21] It appears, however, that Lord Diplock's test is of more general application than Lord Fraser's test.

In most cases, the defendant will have deliberately used some name, mark or get-up designed to capture part of the plaintiff's business but a fraudulent motive is not essential to the tort.[22] Even if the passing off is 'innocent' relief may be granted. It depends mainly on whether the goodwill associated with the plaintiff's business is harmed because the nature or origin of the defendant's goods or services is misrepresented and the buying public or ultimate consumers are taken in by that misrepresentation. A statement which is true may give rise to the action. If a sole trader with a retail clothing business changes his name to Levi Strauss by deed poll, having the name signwritten above his shop is not a false misrepresentation but it is, nevertheless, likely to be restrained if the clothing manufacturer by that name sues for passing off.[23] Although it is generally accepted that honest use of one's own name is permitted, regardless of the fact that customers may be misled, such honest use must be done in a way so as not to exaggerate the connection. For example, in *Wright, Layman & Umney Ltd. v Wright*[24] the plaintiff had a wide reputation under the name 'Wright's', as in 'Wright's Coal Tar Soap'. The defendant, trading as 'Wright's Chemical Company' had, without any dishonesty on his part, passed off his goods as those of the plaintiff by using the name 'Wright's' in relation to them. Lord Greene MR said:

19 [1979] AC 731 at 755.

20 Lord Diplock later states that 'calculated to injure' does not require actual intention to injure. It is more to do with whether injury is a reasonably foreseeable consequence.

21 See *British Broadcasting Corp. v Talbot Motor Co. Ltd.* [1981] FSR 228 and *Bristol Conservatories Ltd. v Conservatories Custom Built Ltd.* [1989] RPC 455. In the former case, Megarry VC suggested that the two tests may have been cumulative but, in the latter, it was held that they were not cumulative. Lord Fraser's five probanda should be restricted to cases like *Erven Warnink* and not applied universally.

22 *Baume & Co. Ltd. v A H Moore Ltd.* [1958] RPC 226.

23 See *Croft v Day* (1843) 7 Beav. 84. However, a true statement that the defendant had operated the fine art department in the plaintiff's store was not passing off, *Harrods Ltd. v Schwartz-Sackin & Co. Ltd.* [1991] FSR 209.

24 (1949) 66 RPC 149.

A man may sell goods under his own name as his own goods. If he does so, he is doing no more than telling the truth. If there happens to be already on the market another trader of that name ... that is just his misfortune . . . provided that a man keeps within the limit of using his own name and does so honestly and *does not go beyond that*, nobody can stop him even if the result of him doing so leads to confusion.[25] [Emphasis added]

25 Ibid. at 151.

It is apparent from the above case that a trader can easily go beyond the limit of using his own name honestly and the original injunction was extended to prevent the use by the defendant of the name 'Wright' or 'Wright's' in a descriptive phrase applied to his products. It is difficult to see what use of his own name the defendant was left with and the spirit of the sweeping and generous statement by Lord Greene does not appear to have been reflected in his judgment, bearing in mind the defendant's real surname was 'Wright'.[26]

26 For a discussion of the limits of honest use of a name, see Young, D. *Passing Off* (London: Longman, 2nd edn., 1989) at pp. 94–97.

PLAINTIFF'S GOODWILL

Merely copying the name or style of another trader is not, *per se,* sufficient for a passing off action although it could give rise to an action for infringement of copyright if what is copied is more than a simple name, for example a logo. There must have been a goodwill associated with reputation which had been acquired by the plaintiff in relation to that name or style. Reputation comes about through consistent use, for example the phrase 'Camel Hair Belting' used by the plaintiff from 1879 to 1891 was considered by the jury in *Reddaway* v *Banham*[27] to have become distinctive of the plaintiff's belting even though it was entirely descriptive. In *County Sound plc* v *Ocean Sound plc*,[28] the phrase 'Gold AM' used in connection with broadcasts of 'golden oldies' was held not to have acquired goodwill because it was often used in conjunction with the name 'County Sound', it was immediately descriptive of a certain type of radio programme and did not indicate the source of such programmes. Nourse LJ acknowledged that, had the name been truly distinctive, that a goodwill in that name could have been acquired within a period of six months.

27 [1896] AC 199.

28 [1991] FSR 367.

If a trader has just started in business or just started using an unregistered mark or 'get–up' he may be unable to succeed in a passing off action. Although a newly registered trade mark has immediate protection, with passing off the plaintiff must be able to prove that he has built up a reputation around the name, mark or 'get–up'. That is, he has acquired a property in the goodwill associated with the subject matter.[29] It is not possible to lay down hard and fast rules as to the period of time taken to acquire protectable goodwill. It depends on the circumstances. If there is a great deal of commercial activity and advertising throughout the United Kingdom, goodwill could be acquired in a relatively short period of time even prior to the availability of the goods or services to which the goodwill relates. In *Stannard* v *Reay*[30] it was held that three weeks was sufficient time to build up goodwill in the name 'Mr. Chippy' for a mobile fish and chip van operating on the Isle of Wight. The central question is whether a sufficient reputation has been acquired and it is possible for the goodwill to be shared amongst a number of traders or businesses as the *Erven Warnink* case emphatically indicates.

29 Just as, in the law of real property, a person may acquire property rights by continued user, for example by prescription.

30 [1967] RPC 589.

Goodwill can exist even if the product or service to which it relates has not yet been made available if a significant proportion of the public knew about the product or service because of a great deal of publicity. So it was held in *British Broadcasting Corp. v Talbot Motor Co. Ltd.*[31] where there was evidence that a significant part of the public recognized the name CARFAX as distinctive of the BBC's traffic information system capable of being received in vehicles by special radios.

1 [1981] FSR 228.

It is important to consider how the goodwill is associated with the product or service concerned. This may, of course, be influenced by the form of an advertising campaign. In *Whitworth Foods Ltd. v Hunni Foods (International) Ltd.*[32] the defendant deliberately copied the plaintiff's containers for glacé cherries. Viewed from the top, the cartons were easily distinguishable because the two companies' names were represented differently and set on different colour backgrounds. However, from the side the cartons looked very similar (both carrying the words 'Glacé Cherries') and the plaintiff argued that if the cartons were displayed on supermarket shelves, stacked on top of one another with the plaintiff's and the defendant's cartons adjacent to each other, there was a danger of confusion. In considering the association of the plaintiff's reputation with the features of their carton, Hoffman J said that the plaintiff's goodwill was chiefly associated with their name and not the design of their containers and that this was confirmed by evidence of the plaintiff's advertising which was done in a general way without specific reference to their individual products.

2 (unreported) 20 October 1986, Chancery Division and Court of Appeal.

THE SCOPE OF PASSING OFF

Compared to trade mark law, the scope of passing off is quite wide and it can protect unregistrable business names, unregistered trade marks, advertising and general 'get-up', in fact anything that is distinctive of the plaintiff's goods, services or business. Trade mark law requires some use of the mark whereas in passing off, no express use or mention of a trade name is required, mere implication is adequate. For example, in *Copydex Ltd. v Noso Products Ltd.*,[33] the plaintiff had given a demonstration of their glue on television although the name of the product was not mentioned (this was before the days of commercial television and great care was taken not to mention trade names, even to the extent of covering over manufacturers names on items used in dramatic sketches). The defendant company also made glue and one of its salesmen gave a demonstration of its glue in a large retail store. During the demonstration a large card was displayed which bore the words:

33 (1952) 69 RPC 38.

> 'NOSO' here again!
>
> As shown on television 'Women's Hour'

When the plaintiff complained the defendant gave the court an undertaking not to do it again, otherwise an injunction would have been granted in favour of the plaintiff.

The scope of passing off can be considered in terms of the meaning of 'in the course of trade', the extent of marks and 'get-up' protected and geographical range.

In the course of trade

Although some judges have talked about passing off in relation to trade in goods, it is clear that it applies equally to services as well. Before service marks could be registered, this was of exceptional importance as the use of another's name in relation to the provision of services could only be actionable as passing off. In *Harrods Ltd. v R Harrod Ltd.*,[34] the plaintiff was a well-known company with a banking department but which was precluded from operating as a moneylender by the articles of association. The defendant registered a money-lending company under the 'fancy name'[35] of R Harrod Ltd., that is a name having nothing to do with his own name. This fact together with his advertising style showed that he was acting fraudulently in an attempt to gain advantage from these similarities and the plaintiff was granted an injunction to restrain the defendant from using that name.

'Trade' does not have to be primarily associated with commercial enterprise and in *British Medical Association v Marsh*[36] the plaintiff, a professional body constituted as a non-profit-making unincorporated association, was able to obtain an injunction to prevent the defendant passing off his business as that of the plaintiff's.[37] The Association had published analyses of 'quack medicines' because of concern that they were of no medical value and were being sold at excessive prices. The defendant started making up proprietary medicines from the Association's analyses and sold them in a drug store which had the letters 'B.M.A.' displayed in the window together with other references to the Association. To describe the Association's operations as being in the course of trade shows a certain elasticity of thought but it was said that the plaintiff's 'business' would be harmed because the passing off might cause existing members to leave the Association or to discourage potential members from joining. That is, existing and potential members might think that the defendant's activities were approved of or connected with the Association.

Such a robust view of trade and potential harm has not readily been embraced in cases involving individuals whose names have been used without their permission. In *McCullogh v Lewis A May Ltd.*[38] the plaintiff was a well-known children's broadcaster who used the name 'Uncle Mac'. The plaintiff had some physical infirmities. The defendant sold cereal under the name 'Uncle Mac' with indirect reference to the plaintiff's infirmities without the plaintiff's permission. It could be argued that, in such a situation, inferences might be drawn by the public seeing the cereal which might be harmful to the plaintiff. For example, it could be inferred that the plaintiff had to resort to allowing his nickname to be used in this way to earn more money and that to soil his hands with advertising was contrary to the image he was trying to maintain. However, it was held that the facts could not give rise to passing off because the plaintiff was in no way involved in the making or marketing of cereals, instead he was a broadcaster. There was no common field of activity.[39] The decision totally fails to take any account of the fact that many of the public buying and eating the cereal would assume that the plaintiff had given permission for his nickname to

34 (1924) 41 RPC 74.

35 It may have been so described because the Patents, Designs and Trade Marks Act 1883 permitted the registration of 'fancy words' although the phrase 'invented word' was soon to replace it.

36 (1931) 48 RPC 565.

37 More recently, in *British Diabetic Association v British Diabetic Society Ltd.* [1992] 11 EIPR D-242, it was held that an element indistinguishable from commercial goodwill could be attributed to a charity which was equally entitled to legal protection through an action in passing off.

38 (1948) 65 RPC 58.

39 The need for a common field of activity is discussed later in this chapter.

be used in such a fashion and the possibility that he might lose popularity as a broadcaster because of the lower regard in which media personalities involved with advertising were once held.

Where a personal name has been used without permission in order to promote a product or a service, there is always a possibility of an action in defamation.[40] 'Uncle Mac' may have stood a better chance had he sued in libel as Wynn-Parry J said: 'If it were anything, it were libel, as to which I say nothing'. In *Sim v H J Heinz Co. Ltd.*[41] Ron Moody, the actor, was engaged to read the commentaries for advertisements for the defendant's products to be broadcast on television. In making the commentaries, he mimicked the voice of another popular actor, Alistair Sim, who took objection. However, it was held that an injunction would not be granted, whether on the basis of defamation or passing off because there was no evidence of damage to the reputation of the plaintiff. Again there is no common field of activity, the plaintiff was in the business of acting and not in the business of making and selling soups and baked beans. It is certainly far less likely that the plaintiff's business goodwill would be harmed in cases such as this compared to the *Uncle Mac* case.

Extent of marks and 'get-up' protected

Passing off goes beyond the type of mark that is registrable as a trade mark and can apply in respect of containers and packaging.[42] In a controversial case which went all the way to the House of Lords, *Reckitt & Colman Products Ltd. v Borden Inc.*,[43] it was held that the Jif lemon was protected by the law of passing off. The Jif lemon is a plastic, lemon coloured and shaped receptacle in which the plaintiff's lemon juice was sold. The defendant sold lemon juice in a similar but not identical container (it was bigger, having a green cap and a flat side) and was restrained from passing off its lemon juice as that of the plaintiffs by use of a deceptively similar 'get-up'. Lord Bridge said that the result was to give the plaintiff a *de facto* monopoly on the container which was just as effective as a *de jure* monopoly and he commented on the fact that a trader selling lemon juice would never be allowed to register a lemon as a trade mark but that the plaintiff had achieved that result indirectly. However, Lord Bridge had to reluctantly agree that that was the outcome on the basis of the application of the law of passing off.[44] Lord Oliver said that all the main ingredients of a passing off action, namely goodwill, misrepresentation and damage, were present. The Jif lemon had been on sale since 1956 and a considerable goodwill had built up associated with it and it was likely that a good number of housewives would purchase the defendant's lemon juice in the belief that they were purchasing Jif lemons even though careful inspection would show that the defendant's lemons were not Jif lemons because of the different shape and the attached labels.[45] The essence of a passing off action was said to be a deceit practised on the public. Customers were to be taken as they were found, it being no answer to the claim that customers would not have been mistaken had they been 'more careful, more literate and more perspicacious'.

The decision seems outrageous in that the plaintiff appears to have obtained a practical monopoly in lemon-shaped containers for the sale of lemon juice. It is not, however, an absolute monopoly because the defendant could have marked his lemons in such a way as to prevent confusion, for example, by

---

40 An example where the plaintiff successfully sued in defamation is *Tolley v J S Fry & Sons Ltd.* [1931] AC 333 where a picture of the plaintiff was printed on the wrappers of chocolate bars.

41 [1959] 1 All ER 547.

42 The imminent changes to trade mark law will permit the registration of the shape of containers subject to some limitations. Trade Marks Bill 1993, clauses 1(1) and 3(2).

43 [1990] 1 All ER 873.

44 All judges from the trial judge up to and including the House of Lords judges came to the same conclusion as regards passing off.

45 However, it was accepted that the labels could easily become detached.

embossing his name in bold letters, coloured in bright green or red, on the back and front of his lemons, although this could prove prohibitively expensive. The decision does raise the question as to whether a greengrocer could ever be accused of passing off his natural lemons as Jif lemons! The fact that the decision probably stops just short of this reinforces the suspicion that, although seemingly based on a flawless exposition of the law of passing off, the decision goes too far and protection should have been denied as a matter of policy. Perhaps the House of Lords should have taken the bull by the horns and refused an injunction as long as the defendant took reasonable steps (reasonable in terms of cost) to distinguish his lemons from those of the plaintiff. The same rationale as was applied by the House of Lords in the trade mark case of *In re Coca-Cola Co.*[46] should have been adopted here. That is, that it was undesirable to afford a monopoly in a container. However, the law of trade marks will soon be changed to permit more readily the registration of marks relating to the shape of goods or their packaging.[47]

A less controversial decision which again takes account of the ability of purchasers to make subtle distinctions is the Privy Council case of *White Hudson & Co. Ltd.* v *Asian Organisation Ltd.*[48] in which the plaintiff had sold cough sweets wrapped in red cellophane in Singapore since 1953. The wrapper bore the word 'Hacks' and a list of ingredients. From 1958, the defendant also sold cough sweets of a similar colour and shape which were also wrapped in red cellophane but with the name 'Pecto' printed on the wrappers. It was held that the plaintiff had established a get-up in the red coloured wrapper that was distinctive of his cough sweets and there was a danger of confusion especially as few purchasers could read the words 'Pecto' and it was shown that many customers asked for 'red paper cough sweets'. Although no deception was proved on the part of the defendant, the get-up of the defendant's sweets was calculated to deceive and the injunction granted to the plaintiff in the Court of Appeal in Singapore was confirmed. To avoid confusion the defendants could have simply used a different colour for their wrappers or used a prominent symbol on the wrapper. The use of a different colour will not always be a realistic option, for example as in the Jif lemon case.

The protection of wrappers and containers by passing off is one example of the width of this area of law compared to trade marks, although the latter will soon catch up as a result of planned amendments to trade mark law so as to implement the European Directive on the harmonization of trade and service marks.[49] But passing off can go even further in the subject matter protected and can protect, in principle, anything associated with goodwill such as a method of doing business or a theme used in advertising. Of course, the less tangible the subject matter is, the less likely it is that the plaintiff can show that there has been or will be damage to his goodwill as a result of the defendant's misrepresentation. In *Cadbury-Schweppes Pty. Ltd.* v *Pub Squash Co. Pty. Ltd.*,[50] the plaintiff marketed a soft drink in Australia called 'Solo' which was sold in cans resembling beer cans bearing a medallion device. An intensive advertising campaign portrayed it as a drink associated with 'rugged masculine endeavour' and, in total contradiction of the popular image of the Australian male, it sold well. The defendant later started selling a comparable drink called 'Pub Squash' in similar cans with advertising in a similar vein. It was held that the plaintiff had failed to acquire an intangible property right associated with their advertising

46 [1986] 2 All ER 274.

47 Trade Marks Bill (this should receive the Royal assent during 1994) in compliance with the Council Directive of 21 December 1988 to approximate the laws of the Member States relating to trade marks, [1989] OJ L40/1. This is discussed in the previous chapter.

48 [1964] 1 WLR 1466.

49 Even when trade mark is changed, the law of passing off may prove wider in this respect as there will be some exceptions that will affect the registrability of marks.

50 [1981] 1 All ER 213 (The Judicial Committee of the Privy Council).

campaign because it never became a distinguishing feature of the product or generally associated with it. Although it was conceded that the defendant had deliberately taken advantage of the plaintiff's advertising campaign, the consuming public were not misled or deceived by this into thinking that Pub Squash was the plaintiff's drink. In other words, the plaintiff could show no damage resulting from the defendant's use of similar advertising and get-up.

The *Pub Squash* case shows that distinctiveness is important to success in a passing off action. If a name is descriptive this will reduce or even eliminate the possibility of it being distinctive of a particular trader's business. For example, in *Advance Magazine Publishing Inc. v Redwood Publishing Ltd.*,[51] the plaintiff published a food magazine entitled *GOURMET*. The defendant planned to publish, as part of a series of magazines, a food magazine called *BBC Gourmet Goodfood*. Harman J refused to grant interlocutory relief to the plaintiff. As the word 'gourmet' was descriptive, small differences in get-up would be sufficient to avoid confusion. Furthermore, the plaintiff had failed to establish an arguable case. The magazines were different when looked at alongside each other and, even though the defendant's title might be shortened to 'Gourmet' by purchasers, magazines were not usually sold by name over the counter but from racks from which purchasers would select the magazine they wished to buy.

Geographical range

If passing off by one trader is to damage another trader's interests in the goodwill he has acquired it should be reasonable to assume that there should be some overlap in the geographical location and extent of the catchment area of their respective businesses. For example, it might be assumed that a baker in Leeds operating under the name 'Melwood Bakeries' would not be able to restrain another baker using the same name in Dover but he might be able to restrain the use of the name by a baker in Bradford which lies relatively close to Leeds. Bearing in mind the basic test for passing off stated in its barest form as being a misrepresentation that causes damage to business goodwill, there is a possibility that people in Bradford will think that the bakery there and the one in Leeds are owned by the same person and the latter may lose sales as a result. Overlapping or contiguous geographical areas would seem to be precursor for a passing off action.

The narrow view above does not take account of future growth of businesses and this may be a reason for allowing passing off an expansive geographical range. For example, the baker in the above example may be ambitious and his business may grow so that eventually he has a chain of bakeries spanning the whole of England, including Dover.[52] The goodwill may even be in relation to activities in a different country. In *Maxim's Ltd. v Dye*,[53] the plaintiff, an English company, owned a world-famous restaurant in Paris known as 'Maxim's'. The defendant opened a restaurant in Norwich and also named it 'Maxim's'. It was held that the plaintiff had goodwill in England derived from the business in France which might be regarded as being prospective. The plaintiff might want to commence trading in England in the future and should be able to rely on the goodwill he had in connection with the name.[54] Such international extent of goodwill will not be common but if an international reputation has been achieved, there is a danger that another person carrying out business using the

51 [1993] FSR 449.

52 See, for example, *Brestian v Try* [1958] RPC 161 where the plaintiff who had hairdressing shops in London, Wembley and Brighton succeeded in obtaining an injunction to prevent the defendant using the same name in Tunbridge Wells.

53 [1977] 1 WLR 1155.

54 Compare with *Anheuser Busch Inc., v Budejovicky Budvar* [1984] FSR 84, discussed earlier.

same name could cause confusion and customers might think that they were dealing with the plaintiff's business. This is particularly so in the case of large multi-national organizations such as 'McDonalds'. The above case is also an example of a remedy being available without proof of any actual or immediate damage; indeed, the damage is purely speculative as the plaintiff might never open a restaurant in Norwich, England or the United Kingdom. The decision can be justified on the basis that, by his choice of name, the defendant attempted to cash in on the plaintiff's goodwill. Additionally, there is always the danger that had the defendant's food not been of a high quality that the plaintiff's reputation, which it enjoyed in the United Kingdom, might have been harmed as a consequence. Dilution of goodwill is also a possible factor.

THE NATURE OF THE MISREPRESENTATION

The misrepresentation or deception is not necessarily limited to an exact copy of a name, mark or 'get-up'. Similarity sufficient to result in confusion will do, an important factor being whether purchasers or consumers of the product or services have been or are likely to be misled. For trade marks, the litmus test is whether the second mark is identical to or nearly resembles the first mark to the extent that it is likely to deceive or cause confusion.[55] So too with passing off but set in the wider context of 'get-up'. In deciding whether the buying public (or the ultimate consumer) is likely to be misled or confused, it is not necessary to consider whether members of the public who are knowledgeable about the particular product or service are deceived and it may be sufficient if members of the public who have relatively little knowledge of the product or service are deceived or are likely to be deceived.

The public are not expected to be particularly knowledgeable about the product concerned. The reasonable man is no connoisseur of fine wines and exotic foods. In *J Bollinger* v *Costa Bravo Wine Co. Ltd. (No. 2),*[56] the plaintiff made the famous sparkling wine known as 'champagne' in the Champagne region of France. This drink has a very high reputation and is often bought for special occasions by people who do not purchase it regularly. The defendant imported into the United Kingdom a sparkling wine called 'Spanish Champagne' which was supposed to be like the plaintiff's product but made in Spain. The defendant claimed that by adding the word 'Spanish' this clearly indicated that the wine was not made in France and, because Champagne was such a well known product, only a tiny portion of ignorant, ill-educated persons would be misled. The defendant further claimed that the word 'champagne' had become a generic description. An injunction was granted preventing the use of the word 'champagne' by the defendant. It was held in the High Court that a substantial number of persons, whose life and education had not taught them much about the nature and production of wine, might want to buy champagne from time to time and these people might be misled by the description of the defendant's sparkling wine as 'Spanish Champagne'. The description 'Spanish Champagne' was intended to attract to the defendant's product the goodwill connected with the reputation of champagne and amounted to dishonest trading. Danckwerts J said '. . . it seems to me that close resemblance makes the counterfeit not less but more calculated to deceive . . .'. 'Champagne' had not become a generic

55 Section 4(1) Trade Marks Act 1938; it is also required that the use is likely to be taken as use as a trade mark or importing a reference to the person having the right to use the mark. The Trade Marks Bill 1993 expresses infringement by use of a similar mark in terms of likelihood of confusion on the part of the public, clause 9(2).

56 [1961] 1 All ER 561.

name because corresponding wines made elsewhere were not described using that word.

A misrepresentation that is ineffective because the public see through it is not actionable in passing off because one important and fundamental requirement is missing. In the absence of confusion there can be no harm to goodwill and, therefore, no damage to the plaintiff. In *Tamworth Herald Co. Ltd.* v *Thomson Free Newspapers Ltd.*,[57] the plaintiff's newspaper had been published since 1868 as the *Tamworth Herald*, a weekly newspaper selling at 23 pence at the time of the action. The defendant bought the rights in a weekly free newspaper called the *Tamworth Trader* and intended to change its name to the *Tamworth Herald & Post*. Both newspapers were circulated in the same geographical area and the plaintiff commenced a *quia timet* action for passing off but was refused an injunction. It was held by Aldous J that it was improbable that the recipients of the defendant's paper would believe it was published by the plaintiff. An example of the defendant's new 'masthead' included a reference that the paper was formerly the *Tamworth Trader*. Potential advertisers would obtain the address or telephone number from the newspapers themselves or from the Yellow Pages and would in neither case be under a misapprehension as to whom they were dealing with.[58] The possibility of confusion and subsequent damage to the plaintiff's goodwill was, therefore, remote.[59]

Acquiescence

A case with similar facts to the *J Bollinger* (Spanish Champagne) case demonstrates that acquiescence in an activity that could be passing off will defeat the plaintiff's claim. In *Vine Products Ltd.* v *MacKenzie & Co. Ltd.*,[60] the Spanish producers of sherry tried to prevent the use of that word as in British Sherry, South African Sherry, Cyprus Sherry, etc. The genuine drink derives it name from the Jerez region in Spain and is a high-quality product. However, similar fortified wines have been produced in other countries, for example Australia, South Africa and Cyprus and sold under names including the word 'sherry', for example 'British Sherry' and 'Cyprus Sherry'. There was no evidence of confusion amongst the wine-drinking public and these other wines had been so described for a considerable period of time. It was held that the word 'Sherry', standing alone meant a wine from Jerez and others would be prevented from using the word on its own. However, the use of other descriptions such as 'British Sherry' would not be restrained because of acquiescence on the part of the plaintiffs. In practice, each type of sherry from different countries had achieved, over a long period of time, its own individual and distinct reputations. For example, it could be said that 'Cyprus Sherry' is a very pleasant and inexpensive form of the wine whilst the Spanish variant retains its high reputation as the wine of the highest quality. It is self-evident that the owner of an unregistered trade mark or other name or mark or get-up should not delay in taking action against any person copying that mark, name or get-up.

Inverse passing off

It has been said that passing off can be one of two types:

- classical passing off, where B represents his goods as being those of A.

57 [1991] FSR 337.

58 Whether two business concerns having similar names can be easily distinguished in the Yellow Pages is a nice objective test for passing off.

59 That the word 'Herald' is commonly used in the newspaper industry was a factor. The plaintiff was also concerned about the possibility of confusion resulting from telephone canvassing but this would not happen if the canvassers followed their instructions carefully and it was wrong to assume that they would not do so.

60 [1969] RPC 1.

- extended passing off, where A uses a false description for his goods to impute some quality to his goods, for example as in the *Spanish Champagne* case or the *Advocaat* case.[61]

However, passing off is not necessarily limited to these two forms and the common law should develop in such a way to reflect the higher standards of consumer protection recently legislated for. Indeed, in the *Advocaat* case, Lord Diplock said that passing off ought to proceed upon a parallel rather than diverging course to the trend in legislation.[62] Inverse passing off (if it exists as a separate species) occurs where the defendant falsely claims that the plaintiff's goods or services are actually made by, or provided by, the defendant. For example, in *Bristol Conservatories Ltd. v Conservatories Custom Built Ltd.*[63] the defendant's salesmen showed potential customers photographs of conservatories as a sample of the defendant's workmanship. The photographs were, in fact, of the plaintiff's conservatories. The Court of Appeal had no doubt that this constituted passing off although refusing to describe it as inverse (or reverse) passing off.[64] Nevertheless, the boundaries of passing off are not fixed and false claims as to patents or testimonials may fall within its ambit.[65]

Misrepresentation by imputing authorization

Misrepresentation is not limited to the use of a name or a similar get–up and it can even extend to an act that implies that it is authorized or consented to by another person. Placing advertising leaflets inside magazines and newspapers is a fairly common activity nowadays and this may be done after the magazines and papers have been delivered to the newsagents with neither the permission nor the authority of the proprietors of the magazines and newspapers. An independent advertising company may approach newsagents and ask them to insert advertising leaflets and one complication is that, at this time, the title to the magazines and newspapers will have passed to the newsagent. Although such an activity by itself will not amount to passing off, it will do so if sufficient persons are likely to believe that the leaflets were inserted with the authority of the publishers of the magazines and newspapers. So it was held in the Court of Appeal in *Associated Newspapers (Holdings) plc v Insert Media Ltd.*[66] The mere fact that the advertisements had been inserted in the plaintiff's newspapers without its permission did not establish the existence of a misrepresentation and it was necessary to consider whether a substantial number of people would think that the insertion had been authorized by the proprietor of the newspaper. It had been shown that the essence of the plan to insert the advertising was the defendant's hope that it would be associated with the newspaper concerned, the *Daily Mail,* to the effect that the advertising would appear to have the newspaper's seal of approval. The plaintiff might thus suffer damage to its reputation and goodwill. The Court of Appeal rejected a suggestion that a disclaimer should be printed on the inserts on the grounds that it would not be effective.

This case represents a new extension to the law of passing off because, in the High Court, it was doubted that such an activity could amount to passing off.[67] However, it does illustrate the potential width of passing off and the way that it is capable of being developed to meet new mischiefs. Nevertheless, the case is unusual on its facts and the normal way of imputing authority will involve the

61 See Young, D. *Passing-Off* (London: Longman, 2nd edn., 1989) at pp. 5–8.

62 *Erven Warnink Besloten Vennootschap v J Townend & Sons (Hull) Ltd.* [1979] AC 731 at 743.

63 [1989] RPC 455.

64 For a discussion of inverse passing off, see Carty, H. 'Inverse Passing-Off: A suitable Addition to Passing-Off?' [1993] 10 EIPR 370.

65 For example *Copydex Ltd. v Noso Products Ltd.* (1952) 69 RPC 38 ('as shown on television') and *Lawrie v Baker* (1885) 2 RPC 213 where the defendant sold, as patented, articles that were not patented but the plaintiff held a patent such that consumers would think that the defendant was selling articles made to that patent.

66 [1991] 3 All ER 535.

67 *Mail Newspapers plc v Insert Media Ltd.* [1987] RPC 521.

use of a name or mark. For example, a person might falsely claim to be a member of a professional body and the body will be able to take action to have the claim withdrawn and not repeated.

Intention

The great majority of passing off cases involve a deliberate and calculated attempt to take advantage of the goodwill owned by another trader and associated with goods manufactured or sold by him or services supplied by him. However, a fraudulent motive is not necessary to a passing off action and, indeed, innocence is no defence,[68] the main thrust of the law of passing off being the protection of goodwill. In *Taittinger SA* v *Allbev Ltd.*[69] Peter Gibson LJ said:

> Lord Diplock's phrase 'calculated to injure', as he himself made plain, does not import a test of actual intention to injure: it is sufficient that this should be the reasonably foreseeable consequence of the misrepresentation.

In contrast, in some cases, a person may make a deliberate misrepresentation that is intended to boost the reputation and sales of his product or services but against which there is no legal remedy under the law of passing off.[70] Some examples of this will be seen later in the section on character merchandising. A reading of the cases does, however, give the impression that intention may be an influential factor in the court's decision-making process,[71] although a deliberate and fraudulent act of copying someone else's get-up will not amount to passing off if there is little danger of the public being deceived, as in *Whitworth Foods Ltd.* v *Hunni Foods (International) Ltd.*, discussed above, where the defendant had placed an order with the company making containers for the plaintiff for containers that were similar in shape and appearance.

Common fields of activity

Rights associated with registered trade marks are restricted in terms of the classes of goods and services against which the marks are registered. Therefore, if Trader A has a trade mark consisting of a representation of a Harp registered for Class 2 goods (paints, varnishes, lacquers, etc.) and Trader B copies this mark but only uses in respect of wines (falling within Class 33), Trader B does not infringe Trader A's trade mark, unless it is subject to a defensive registration in Class 33. Passing off is limited in a similar way in that there must be a common field of activity between the plaintiff and the defendant. There must be some common ground otherwise there can be no trespass to this form of intellectual property. The justification for this is that, if there is no common field of activity, there can be no damage to the plaintiff's goodwill because the public will not make a connection between the traders and their alternate fields of activity. For example, if Trader A uses the name 'Spright' for its margarine and, later, Trader B uses the same name for its bicycles there will be little danger of damage to Trader A's goodwill (irrespective of the quality of the bicycles) because the public are not likely to think that the bicycles are made by or with the licence of Trader A. An electric shaver called a 'Rolls Razor' would not normally be confused with the makers of 'Rolls Royce' motor cars; at best it indicates that the razor is claimed, rightly or wrongly, to be of high quality.

68 See *Baume & Co. Ltd.* v *A H Moore Ltd.* [1958] RPC 226.

69 [1993] FSR 641 at 667.

70 See for example, *McCullogh* v *Lewis A. May Ltd.* (1948) 65 RPC 58.

71 For example, see *Harrods Ltd.* v *R Harrod Ltd.* (1924) 41 RPC 74.

A simple example of the common field of activity doctrine was the case of *Granada Group Ltd. v Ford Motor Company Ltd.*[72] the outcome of which was that the Granada television group, famous for making the television serial *Coronation Street,* could not prevent the Ford Motor Company naming one of its cars the 'Ford Granada'. There was no danger of confusion because of the different fields of activity (television and motor cars) and, consequently, there was little possibility of the plaintiff's goodwill being harmed.[73] This decision accords with common sense as it is highly unlikely that ordinary members of the public, even those knowing nothing about cars, would think that the car had anything whatsoever to do with the television company. The test of common field of activity is concerned with making an objective determination of the likelihood of damage to goodwill. This can only occur if there is, at least, a possibility of confusion. Yet, the test can be criticized because the diversification of business concerns and their fields of activity make the application of the test imperfect. Many members of the public realize that some large companies have interests that are wide and disparate in nature. Whereas, with a registered trade mark that is very well known, it is possible to obtain a defensive registration,[74] effectively pre-empting its use by others in classes of goods or services for which the mark is not used by the proprietor, the common field of activity rule seems coarse and arbitrary in terms of well-known names, marks and get-ups. To make the issue more difficult is the general desire amongst judges not to restrict competition unduly.

Showing a determined flexibility, the law of passing off has developed to embrace a situation were a name or mark is very well known and in such cases, the boundaries of the activities may be moved, dramatically enlarging the field of play. In *Lego Systems A/S v Lego M Lemelstrich Ltd.,*[75] the very well-known Lego company, that makes coloured plastic construction bricks for children, was granted an injunction preventing the use of the name Lego by the defendant who was planning to use it for its plastic irrigation and garden equipment. The defendant had used the name Lego for its equipment in various other countries such as Israel but the plaintiff's children's bricks had become so well known, as had the name Lego in association with these bricks, that the House of Lords was of the opinion that confusion was extremely likely. In this case, the common field of activity was, effectively, coloured plastic.[76] If the plaintiff's business had not been so successful and on such a grand scale in the United Kingdom, the plaintiff's field of activity might have been restricted to children's coloured plastic construction bricks, a much narrower field. Note that the quality of the defendant's products was not an issue: once the danger of confusion is present, it is assumed that there is a possibility that the plaintiff's reputation will be harmed. Such harm can go beyond the quality of the products concerned and in the Lego case, harm could be the result of the public thinking that the company was no longer concentrating on children's construction kits and might not continue to make the kits and additional parts for them so that it might not be feasible for a child to build up a large collection of Lego bricks and materials over a long period of time.

The boundaries of the plaintiff's field of activity appear to be directly proportional to the magnitude of his goodwill: the greater the goodwill, the greater net of passing off will be cast and the more likely it is that the defendant will found to have committed passing off.

72 [1973] RPC 49.

73 The name 'Granada' could not have been registered in Part A of the register of trade marks, being a relatively well known geographical name, section 9 of the Trade Marks Act 1938. It is unlikely that it would be accepted for Part B registration.

74 The new Trade Marks Act will abolish defensive registration.

75 [1983] FSR 155, yet another case involving a survey of the public used in support of the plaintiff's argument that the public would be deceived.

76 See also, *Annabel's (Berkeley Square) v Schock* [1972] RPC 838, where it was held that there was a possibility of confusion between a night club and an escort agency as both could be considered to be night-time activities.

Character merchandising

A fictitious or fantastic character might be devised for a television series, a book or a film, for example Kojak, the Wombles, Thunderbirds, Popeye, Super Mario, Teenage Mutant Hero Turtles, etc. The person who devised the character or the person commissioning the design will want to maximize the financial return on the investment involved. One way of doing this is to licence others to sell articles to which a representation of, or the name of, the character is applied. Examples are very common: Mickey Mouse watches, Captain Scarlett figures and T-shirts, Pink Panther mugs, Postman Pat toys, etc. Using fictitious characters in order to sell ordinary items is known as character merchandising and is very popular, particularly with respect to children's toys, games and stationery. It is big business. The normal way it is done is for the merchandising organization to obtain a licence from the creator of the character permitting the application of a representation of the character to the articles. In a few cases, the creator of the character or the owner of the rights in the character will retail the articles direct. Character merchandising is not limited to fictitious characters. Many famous sportsmen and women and television personalities allow their name to be used for promotional purposes. In this case, unauthorized appropriation of their name or nickname may not be remediable either under the law of passing off or under copyright law but it may be actionable as being defamatory.[77]

Character merchandising is not a new phenomenon. Walt Disney characters in particular have been used in this way for some time. However, when this operation is related to intellectual property rights subsisting in such characters, some major gaps appear. Copyright can give a fair degree of protection, for example where a representation of the character infringes the copyright in a drawing of that character. For example, if a company wishes to sell a mug to which a picture of Mickey Mouse has been applied by transfer printing, this will infringe the copyright in the original drawings of Mickey Mouse. If a photograph is made from a Mickey mouse cartoon or film, whether to be reproduced and sold as photographs or used as a medium from which to prepare a representation for transfer printing, the copyright in the film will be infringed. If a doll or three-dimensional figure is made, then the copyright in the drawings will be infringed, as it was in the case of Popeye dolls which were held to infringe the cartoon drawings of the Popeye character in *King Features Syndicate Inc.* v *O and M Kleeman Ltd.*[78] But, difficulties arise where only the name of the character is used. We have seen in Chapter 3 that copyright will not be afforded to a title for a film or a book and that it was also denied to the word 'Exxon'.[79] Neither does copyright protect the name of a fictitious character. This can be seen as the working of the *de minimis* principle and a throwback to the judgment of Davey J in *Hollinrake* v *Truswell*[80] to the effect that a literary work should offer information, instruction or pleasure in the form of literary enjoyment.

All that is left to protect a name is the law of passing off, or in some cases, trade mark law. With respect to the latter, the question hinges simply on whether the merchandiser has applied the name to the same or similar goods. However, trade mark law could not be used to promote character merchandising because section 28(6) of the Trade Marks Act 1938 requires the Registrar to

77 See *McCullogh* v *Lewis A May Ltd.* (1948) 65 RPC 58 and *Tolley* v *J S Fry & Sons Ltd.* [1931] AC 333.

78 [1941] AC 417.

79 *Exxon Corporation* v *Exxon Insurance Consultants International Ltd.* [1981] 3 All ER 241.

80 [1894] 3 Ch 420.

refuse an application for registration of a registered user if it appears to him that this would tend to facilitate trafficking in the mark. The House of Lords confirmed that trade marks law was not to be used to facilitate character merchandising in confirming the Registrar's refusal to register the 'Holly Hobbie' device including a drawing of a young girl as a trade mark.[81] This mark had been very successfully exploited in the United States but the registered user provisions in the United Kingdom Act are a considerable hurdle. One way over this hurdle is to show that the proprietor of the mark is able to maintain strict quality control over the articles to which the mark is applied, so demonstrating a sufficient connection in the course of trade. However, in the Holly Hobbie case, the applicant was unable to show this, partly because of the enormous scale of the planned commercial activities.

Passing off may not be any more effective than trade mark law in the context of character merchandising because of the requirement of a common field of activity and without this there can be no harm to the owner of the name of the character. For example, if someone buys a 'Garfield' telephone, that person would not be likely to complain to the makers of the Garfield cartoons and comic strips if the telephone turns out to be faulty.[82] The general public probably have a much better understanding of character merchandising than the judges have, in the past, given them credit for.

In the South African case of *Lorimar Productions Inc.* v *Sterling Clothing Manufacturers (Pty) Ltd.*[83] the Supreme Court considered that character merchandising was not particularly well known and, in the absence of evidence to the contrary, it could not be assumed that the man in the street would have any knowledge of it. The plaintiff owned the rights in the television series *Dallas* and failed to show an association in the minds of the public between the goodwill in the series and clothing or restaurants owned by the defendant which used names, locations and titles from the series.

The case of *Tavener Rutledge Ltd.* v *Trexapalm Ltd.*,[84] involving the television detective character 'Kojak', demonstrates some of the deficiencies of the law as regards character merchandising. Kojak, played by Telly Savalas, was often seen in the series sucking a spherical lolly. The plaintiff made similar shaped lollies and used the word 'KOJAKPOPS' as a brand name for these lollies and quickly built up a substantial trade in respect of them. The plaintiff had not obtained the permission of the makers of the *Kojak* television series to use this name or to make similar shaped lollies. Some time later, the defendant started making similar lollies called 'KOJAK LOLLIES' and claimed to have a licence agreement with the owners of the television series allowing him to do this. The plaintiff commenced an action for passing off[85] and applied for an interlocutory injunction. The defendant claimed that there was a sufficient connection in the course of trade between the lollies and the owners of the Kojak name because there were provisions for quality control contained in the licence agreement between the defendant and the owner of the name, and because of this quality control arrangement there was a common field of activity. Nevertheless, the injunction was granted to restrain the defendant passing off his lollies as being those of the plaintiff. The plaintiff had built up a considerable reputation in his lollies and the introduction of a similar lolly would cause confusion. Walton J considered that the defendant's lollies were not as good value as the plaintiff's and, as a consequence, the plaintiff's reputation would be seri-

81 *Holly Hobbie Trade Mark* [1984] RPC 329. This limitation will not apply under the new Trade Marks Act.

82 For a discussion on trafficking in marks where this point is made, see Pearson, H. E. & Miller, C. G. *Commercial Exploitation of Intellectual Property* (London: Blackstone, 1990) at pp.216–217.

83 [1982] RPC 395.

84 [1977] RPC 275.

85 There was also a trade mark issue because the plaintiff had applied for a trade mark but, because the passing off action succeeded, it did not require consideration.

ously harmed. The licence agreement argument failed on the basis that there was no actual or potential field of activity between the owners of the television series and the plaintiff's business. The point had not been reached where the fact of quality control was so well known that the public would rely on the existence of the licence as a guarantee of the defendant's product. Indeed, the public, in general, were not to be taken as having any particular knowledge of character merchandising. Finally, Walton J confirmed that there is no property in a name or a word, *per se.*

A common field of activity is the key to an action in passing off and no more so than where character merchandising is involved. It is important for the parties to a licence agreement to construct a connection in the course of trade between the owner of the name, the licensor, and the goods or services to which the name is to be applied. One way to do this has been hinted at above and that is to establish a system of quality control so that the owner of the name has a part to play in the practical aspects of the marketing exercise. In this way, the reputation of the name's owner will be extended into the other fields of activity defined by the merchandising project. This approach was successful in Australia where a licence agreement for the making of soft toys of the Muppet characters contained quality control provisions[86] but has yet to find favour in the United Kingdom. It is submitted that the exercise of quality control must be known about by the public and that appropriate advertising, marketing and labelling of the goods can do much to spread the word, thus extending the fields of activity.

Even if the field of activity can be widened by careful licensing and advertising, there will still be cases where this will not be sufficient to provide a remedy, bearing in mind that the prospect of harm to goodwill is a fundamental requirement. If there is no obvious link, regardless of any character licences, then there is no remedy under the law of passing off although there may be copyright issues, particularly if a drawing of the character is used. *Wombles Ltd.* v *Wombles Skips Ltd.*[87] shows that a wide disparity in fields of activity is fatal to a claim in passing off. The Wombles are fictitious animals from a television series and are noted for cleaning up litter and putting it to good use. The plaintiff company owned the copyright in the books and drawings of the Wombles. Its main business was granting licences in respect of the characters; for example, it granted one such licence for waste-paper baskets for children. The defendant formed a company to lease builders' skips, containers used typically for building rubble. After considerable thought and remembering the Wombles' reputation for clean habits he decided to call his company Wombles Skips Ltd. and registered the company name accordingly. The plaintiff argued that the use of the name would lead some persons to conclude that the defendant's business was connected with the plaintiff and that there was a common field of activity because one of the licences was for waste-paper baskets. It was held that there was no common field of activity and this was an essential ingredient in a passing off action. Without a common field of activity there is no danger of confusion and, in this case, the similarity between the making and selling of waste-paper baskets and hiring out builders' skips was not strong enough. The plain fact of the matter was that it was highly improbable that ordinary members of the public would think that the skips were associated with the Wombles in any way, just as a link between Granada Television and Ford Granada cars is quite absurd. Such an association might be made, however, in the case of waste-paper baskets for children and Wombles toys and dolls.

86 *Children's Television Workshop Inc. v Woolworths (New South Wales) Pty. Ltd.* [1981] RPC 187.

87 [1977] RPC 99. This case may be difficult to reconcile with the *Lego* case. However, neither the *Wombles* case nor the *Kojak* case was mentioned in Falconer J's judgment.

Full legal protection of character merchandising has yet to find favour in the United Kingdom courts, although there are now signs that the position is changing. There is a contradiction in the way the law has tended to dislike this form of exploitation and the way in which it has given full protection to other forms of intellectual property rights. The owner of the character has made an investment of time and money in creating and developing the character. In many cases, the character is the result of substantial flair and imagination which should be no less deserving of protection than, say, literary and artistic works. Whilst it is clear that the law gives some protection, for example copyright subsisting in drawings of characters or in written thumbnail sketches of characters[88] and other descriptive material, there are some gaps, and it is with respect to names that the law seems to be least effective.

Consider the following possibilities concerning *Coronation Street* characters. What if the name 'Rover's Return' is used for a public house in the Salford area? What if a tobacco company starts marketing 'Mike Baldwin cigars' or, for those with longer memories, a trader starts selling 'Ena Sharples hairnets'? There seems to be little that the makers of the television series can do because of a lack of a common field of activity. But, there is a possibility that some portion of the public will take the use of names to indicate that the products have some seal of approval from the television company and have achieved certain standards. This might allow the traders concerned to overcharge for substandard goods. In attempting to cut back the degree of protection offered to the owners of fictitious characters and the like (and indeed, their licensees and franchisees), the courts may indirectly be encouraging unfair and undesirable trading practices whereby unscrupulous traders still manage to cash-in on someone else's reputation in a way which transcends the artificiality of compartmentalized fields of activity.

There have been recent signs of a change in heart. The case of *Mirage Studios v Counter-Feat Clothing Co. Ltd.*[89] is a good example, Browne-Wilkinson VC seeming to prefer the way in which Australian passing off law has developed compared to United Kingdom law. The facts of the case were that the plaintiff created the Teenage Mutant Hero Ninja Turtle characters and made and marketed cartoons, films and videos containing these characters. Part of the plaintiff's business involved licensing the reproduction of the characters on goods sold by licensees, that is character merchandising. It was almost inevitable that, in view of the success of the characters, someone else would wish to take an unfair advantage of the immense goodwill built up by the plaintiff. The defendant, without the plaintiff's permission, made drawings of humanoid turtle characters that were similar in appearance to the plaintiff's characters. They were not exact reproductions. The defendant then began to licence these drawings to garment manufacturers for the purpose of applying them to T-shirts and the like. The defendant claimed that there was no intellectual property rights either in the name or the idea of the 'Turtles'. The Vice-Chancellor granted an interlocutory injunction to the plaintiff on the basis of an arguable case in copyright and for passing off. He found passing off to have occurred by applying Lord Diplock's test in the *Advocaat* case. The misrepresentation made by the defendant was that a substantial number of the buying public would believe that the reproduction of the figures was the result of a licence between the owner of the rights in the original drawings of the turtles. The result of the

88 This protection might be less effective. Obviously, an unauthorized photocopy will infringe, but will there be copyright infringement if the nature of the character is copied by a rival? Perhaps there might be a possibility that the restricted act of public performance will be relevant if the rival character faithfully follows the written description.

89 [1991] FSR 145.

defendant's action would be that, because the public associated goods bearing the defendant's drawings with the creator of the cartoons, the plaintiff's good-will would be harmed by fixing representations of turtles to inferior goods. The potential value of the plaintiff's licensing rights would be seriously harmed. Furthermore, there was a sufficient link between the plaintiff and the goods to found a case in passing off. At last, it seemed an English judge was prepared to accept that the public are aware of character merchandising.

Browne-Wilkinson VC considered that the law as developed in Australia was sound and applied *Children's Television Workshop Inc.* v *Woolworths (New South Wales) Ltd.*[90] in which it was held that the defendant, by his unlicensed use of the Muppet characters, had misrepresented that he had a connection with the owner of the copyright in drawings of the characters and was a bona fide licensee of rights in the Muppets. The Vice-Chancellor managed to distinguish three English cases involving the Wombles, Kojak and the pop group 'Abba',[91] although he seemed unduly cautious about doing so. The three English cases are distinguishable very easily because they only involved a name and not a drawing and are still good law. The question is whether the *Mirage Studios* (Turtle) case has modified the requirement of a common field of activity for an action in passing off to succeed. Certainly, there is now a greater awareness of character merchandising amongst the public but it may be insufficient to found an argument that goodwill will be harmed by unlicensed use of names and representations of characters. The public may be aware that the creator of a fictitious character will licence its use in this way, but equally may be prepared to accept that other companies can use the characters without such a licence. There may be a connection between quality products and the creator of the character but the public may simply assume that cheaper, inferior goods are made without the creator's specific permission and the link between inferior goods and the creator, essential for a passing off action to succeed, is thus absent. Put crudely, do the public really care? Many members of the public probably think that the creator of the character has made enough money through films, books and cartoons.

One major criticism of the judgment in the *Mirage Studios* (Turtles) case is that the copyright issue alone should have been sufficient to dispose of it, and this will usually be so where representations of characters are used, whether two-dimensional or three-dimensional. In the future, fictitious names may be registrable as trade marks.[92] Browne-Wilkinson's views on passing off could be considered to be *obiter*. Where names are used, there must be a common field of activity for there to be a prospect of harm to goodwill. The only way a character merchandiser can establish a sufficient link is to exercise a form of control over the goods to which the character or its name is applied and this link must be such that sufficient numbers of the public are aware of it. This view is consistent with Australian law and prior United Kingdom law. We have not heard the last of legal actions concerning character merchandising.

DAMAGE TO GOODWILL

Damage to goodwill, or at least a probability that damage will ensue, is one of the essential requirements for a passing off action.[93] Damage may result in a number of ways and the diminution in the plaintiff's goodwill may be caused by:

90 [1981] RPC 187. He also approved of a similar decision, *Fido-Dido Inc.* v *Venture Stores (Retailers) Pty. Ltd.* 16 IPR 365.

91 *Wombles Ltd.* v *Wombles Skips Ltd.* [1977] RPC 99, *Tavener Rutledge Ltd.* v *Trexapalm Ltd.* [1977] RPC 275 and *Lynstad* v *Annabast Products Ltd.* [1975] FSR 488.

92 *Reform of Trade Mark Law* Cm. 1203 (London: HMSO, 1990).

93 *Erven Warnink Besloten Vennootschap* v *J Townend & Sons (Hull) Ltd.* [1973] AC 731 per Lords Diplock and Fraser. Lord Fraser spoke in terms of a real likelihood of suffering substantial damage to goodwill.

Figure 21.1 Elderflower Champagne bottle label

(a) lost sales because buyers confuse the defendant's products (or services) with those of the plaintiff,[94]

(b) the fact that the defendant's product is inferior to the plaintiff's product and buyers think the defendant's product is the plaintiff's,[95]

(c) erosion or debasement of a name that is exclusive and unique and which is used by the plaintiff (or a number of persons entitled to use it).

The case of *Taittinger SA v Allbev Ltd.*[96] provides a recent example of the last form of damage to goodwill.[97] The defendant, an English company made a non-alcoholic drink called Elderflower Champagne. Not surprisingly, it attracted the attention of the French makers of champagne who have taken legal action no less than 46 times in England to protect the name 'champagne'. The High Court judge found for the defendant. He applied Lord Diplock's test and, although he found all the other elements present, he decided that there was no real likelihood of serious damage to the plaintiff's undoubted goodwill. Elderflower Champagne was only £2.45 for a 75 cl bottle and had wording on the label to the effect that it was non-alcoholic. Davies J considered that only a small number of persons would be confused even though Elderflower Champagne was sold in bottles resembling champagne bottles. A representation of the label is shown in Figure 21.1.

The Court of Appeal allowed the plaintiff's appeal because use of the word 'champagne' by those not entitled to use it would inevitably diminish the goodwill associated with it. Peter Gibson LJ said (at 670):

> . . . it seems to me no less obvious that erosion of the distinctiveness of the name champagne in this country is a form of damage to the goodwill of the business of the champagne houses.

94 For example, see *Reddaway v Banham* [1896] AC 199.

95 For example, as in *Spalding & Bros. v A W Gamage Ltd.* LJ Ch 449.

96 [1993] FSR 641. The case also hinged on EC Council Regulation 823/87 (as amended by Regulation 2043/89) which limits the use of names for wines which refer to specified regions.

97 Other examples are provided by the *Erven Warnink* case (advocaat) and the *Spanish Champagne* case discussed earlier.

This can be seen as an extension of the tort of passing off because in the *Erven Warnink* case there was also a substantial diminution in the sales of the plaintiff's drink.[98] However, it could be argued that the plaintiff acquiesced in the use of the name 'champagne' by others as it had been used in the United Kingdom and elsewhere for a number of years to describe a variety of locally made products. For example, 'rhubarb champagne' and 'greengage champagne', *inter alia,* have been used to describe home-made wines as the extracts below taken from *Peggy Hutchinson's Home Made Wine Secrets*, published around the time of the Second World War, demonstrate.[99]

98 Russell, F. 'The Elderflower Champagne Case: Is this a Further Expansion of the Tort of Passing–Off?' [1993] 10 EIPR 379.

99 Hutchinson, P. *Peggy Hutchinson's Home Made Wine Secrets* (London: Foulsham & Co., undated). The preface for the book starts 'The recipes for this book were originally compiled in the days of plenty before the Second World War. Times have changed; some of the ingredients are no longer easy to obtain . . .'. I am indebted to Lorraine Keenan for finding this book.

GREENGAGE CHAMPAGNE

Ingredients:
    4lbs. greengages
    20 vine leaves
    1 gallon water
    4 lbs. sugar
    1 slice toast; 1 oz. yeast

Method:
1. Put the greengages and vine leaves in a bowl, cover with cold water. Take the vine leaves out in 3 days but mash and stir the plums for 8 days, then strain.
2. Then add the sugar and yeast spread on both sides of the toast and leave to ferment 14 days.
3. Skim and bottle.

Proof of damage

A plaintiff must be able to satisfy the court that he has, or will, suffer substantial damage to his goodwill. Mere speculation will rarely suffice. In many cases proof of damage is not only important in quantifying damages to be awarded to the plaintiff but also it may be essential in demonstrating that there has been a misrepresentation calculated to injure the plaintiff's goodwill. In the case of *Tamworth Herald Co. Ltd.* v *Thomson Free Newspapers Ltd.*,[100] the plaintiff did not put any evidence of actual confusion on the part of persons seeking to place advertisements in its newspaper. However, in some cases, particularly in interlocutory hearings, there will be no actual damage to put before the court. The plaintiff must be able to convince the judge that there is a risk of confusion amongst the public. This will help to show that there is a serious issue to be tried and the judge can then move on to consider the balance of convenience and whether an interlocutory injunction should be granted.

100 [1991] FSR 337

In *Morgan-Grampian plc* v *Training Personnel Ltd.*[101] the plaintiff published a series of magazines with titles beginning with the phrase 'What's New in . . .' and the defendant later changed the title of one of its publications to 'What's New in Training'. An interlocutory injunction was granted. There was a risk of confusion and the fact that it would be difficult to quantify damage in monetary terms helped to tilt the balance of convenience in favour of the plaintiff.

101 [1992] FSR 267.

It may be tempting to obtain evidence of damage through surveys and trap orders. Surveys are carried out for a number of reasons but, unless they are properly carried out, they will fail to impress the court. For example, in

Imperial Group plc v *Philip Morris Ltd.*[102] it was held that there was no passing off by the defendant who used black and gold packets for 'Raffles' cigarettes. The plaintiff made John Player Specials (JPS) cigarettes in black with gold lettering and a gold monogram. The plaintiff had used surveys to show that there was a high degree of association between the colours black and gold and the JPS cigarette. Whitford J criticized the survey techniques used and he laid down some guidelines if a survey is to have validity, being:

- the persons interviewed must be selected to represent a relevant cross-section of the public,
- the sample size must be statistically significant,
- the survey must be conducted fairly,
- all the surveys carried out must be disclosed fully (a 'warts and all' approach),
- all the answers given must be disclosed and made available to the defendant,
- no leading questions should be put to interviewees,
- interviewees must not be led to embark upon a field of speculation they would not otherwise have considered,
- instructions to interviewers must be disclosed,
- if the answers are to be coded for computer input, the coding instructions must also be disclosed.

In other words, good statistical methods must be used coupled with complete openness and disclosure. In many cases, fulfilling these requirements will result in the survey being prohibitively expensive.

Trap orders are often used to provide evidence of passing off. For example, an order may be placed by the plaintiff (or his agent) for genuine goods in the hope that the defendant will supply other goods instead. Trap orders should be fair and, preferably, in writing where this is possible. In effect, in executing a trap order, the plaintiff is representing himself as a bona fide customer – in other words, he himself is making a misrepresentation. This he is allowed to do and his solicitor is allowed to advise him that he may do this and to make the necessary arrangements.[103] If the defendant had been 'caught' by a trap order, he should be put on notice immediately so that he can recall the facts clearly.[104]

DEFENCES

Defences to a passing off action are fairly straightforward. In the case of the first (no confusion and thus no harm to goodwill), the defendant may commission a survey to demonstrate that there is no confusion although it is more likely that the plaintiff will commission such a survey to show the opposite. The utility of such surveys has been doubted, as mentioned above, and the main difficulty is ensuring objectivity. The defences to a passing off action include:

(a) The defendant's activities have not harmed and are not likely to harm the plaintiff's goodwill associated with the name, mark or get-up. This may be because there is no common field of activity or because there is no danger of confusion as to the origin or quality of the goods or services.[105]
(b) The passing off is not in the course of trade, that is the defendant is not using the name or get-up, in the course of trade.

102 [1984] RPC 293.

103 The 'clean hands' doctrine does not appear to apply to trap orders, see *Marie Claire Album SA* v *Hartstone Hosiery Ltd.* [1993] FSR 692.

104 *Cellular Clothing Co. Ltd.* v *G White & Co. Ltd.* (1952) 70 RPC 9 where a trap order was held to be unsatisfactory for want of notice.

105 This line of defence succeeded in *Wombles Ltd.* v *Wombles Skips Ltd.* [1977] RPC 99.

106 *McCullogh* v *Lewis A May Ltd.* (1948) 65 RPC 58.

107 *County Sound plc* v *Ocean Sound plc* [1991] FSR 367.

108 For example, see *Wright, Layman & Umney Ltd.* v *Wright* (1949) 66 RPC 149.

109 *Vine Products Ltd.* v *MacKenzie & Co. Ltd.* [1969] RPC 1 is an example of acquiescence.

110 *Habib Bank Ltd.* v *Habib Bank AG Zurich* [1982] RPC 1. This can be seen as a more positive form of acquiescence.

111 [1979] AC 731.

112 *Baume & Co. Ltd.* v *A H Moore Ltd.* [1958] RPC 226.

(c) The plaintiff has no trade interest to be harmed, that is the plaintiff is not using the name or mark in the course of trade.[106]
(d) The plaintiff has not established the existence of goodwill associated with the name, mark or get-up concerned.[107]
(e) The defendant is simply making honest use of his own name or company name. Nevertheless, the actual use must be carefully done so as not to appear as passing off.[108]
(f) The plaintiff has acquiesced in the defendant's use of the name or mark or has expressly or impliedly granted the defendant permission to use the name or mark, for example in a contract for the sale of a business including the goodwill.[109]
(g) The plaintiff is estopped from enforcing his rights under passing off because he has encouraged the defendant's act.[110]

According to the judgment of Lord Diplock in *Erven Warnink Besloten Vennootschap* v *J Townend & Sons (Hull) Ltd.*[111] the misrepresentation made by the defendant must be calculated to injure the plaintiff's business or goodwill. But, as mentioned earlier, innocence does not provide a defence to a passing off action[112] and whether the misrepresentation is intended or accidental should make no difference as to whether an injunction is available. One point about this is that, if knowledge was a factor, there might be difficulty concerning proof and, generally, other intellectual property rights are enforceable regardless of the defendant's state of knowledge although this may be relevant as to the availability of some of the remedies, especially damages.

REMEDIES

Remedies available are injunctions (including interlocutory injunctions) and/or damages or, as an alternative, an account of profits. Additionally, an order may be granted for the delivery up or destruction of articles to which the name or mark has been applied or, if possible, an order for the obliteration of such names or marks. A declaration may be sufficient if the defendant has agreed not to continue the acts complained of.

113 [1990] RPC 449.

Damages will usually be based upon the actual loss attributable to the passing off, that is resulting from the loss of sales experienced by the plaintiff. How else can harm to goodwill be measured? However, in some cases, damages may be calculated on a royalty basis, that is based on the amount that would have been payable by the defendant if he had sought a licence to use the name or mark from the plaintiff. This possibility was discussed in *Dormeuil Freres SA* v *Feraglow Ltd.*[113] although it was accepted that there was no authority to that effect. However, a royalty basis could be applicable if it would yield a greater amount than that attributable to loss of sales. Of course, it will always be difficult to calculate damages resulting from a loss of sales and each sale by the defendant does not necessarily represent a sale lost by the plaintiff. A lost sale in a strict sense occurs where a purchaser buys the defendant's goods thinking that they are the plaintiff's goods. However, some of the defendant's customers will not have heard of the plaintiff or even if they have, will realize that they are not dealing with the plaintiff. In the above case, the plaintiff reckoned that 75 per cent of the defendant's sales of cloth represented sales of which the plaintiff was deprived as a result of the passing off. The plaintiff also claimed damages on a royalty basis for the remaining 25 per cent of the defendant's sales and damages for damage to goodwill because the defendant's cloth was of an inferior quality. The plaintiff was awarded a total of £20,000 damages which included interest and the unrecovered costs expended in pursuing foreign manufacturers of infringing cloth.

If the passing off is of the extended variety as in *Erven Warnink*, the assessment of damages may prove very difficult. The same applies to inverse passing off. However, in many cases of this sort, the main remedy sought by the plaintiff will be an injunction, often at the interlocutory stage before any actual damage to the plaintiff's goodwill has been caused. In an interlocutory hearing, the fact that damages will be difficult to quantify should an injunction not be granted may be a factor, though not a conclusive one, to be taken into account.[114] In interlocutory hearings, the judge is entitled to take account of the behaviour of the parties as well as considering the balance of convenience. In *Dalgety Spillers Foods Ltd. v Food Brokers Ltd.*,[115] the defendant wrote to the plaintiff indicating an intention to market a snack food called Cup Noodles (the plaintiff already marketed Pot Noodles) and enclosing sample containers. The plaintiff acknowledged receipt of the letter but did not reply further. Nearly one year later, the defendant launched its product and, one month later, the plaintiff served a writ on the defendant claiming that the defendant was guilty of passing off. The judge refused to grant an interlocutory injunction. The defendant had shown a desire to act with due regard to the plaintiff's rights by making its intention plain but the plaintiff chose to ignore the warning, only taking action after the defendant had spent considerable time and expense in launching its product.[116]

Nominal damages will be available against a trader who commits passing off innocently (an injunction almost certainly will be granted in addition). An account of profits may be a possibility in relation to the period following the time when the innocent trader is disabused of his innocence if he continues the passing off beyond this time. The position of the innocent passer off was well put by Lord Parker in *Spalding & Bros. v A W Gamage Ltd.*[117] where he said:

> Nor need the representation be made fraudulently. It is enough that it has in fact been made, whether fraudulently or otherwise, and that damages may probably ensue, though the complete innocence of the party making it may be a reason for limiting the account of profits to the period subsequent to the date at which he becomes aware of the true facts. The representation is in fact treated as the invasion of a right giving rise at any rate to nominal damages, the enquiry being granted at the plaintiff's risk if he might probably have suffered more than nominal damages.[118]

If the defendant's actions infringe a trade or service mark as well as constituting passing off, the damages that may be awarded are not cumulative. However, if passing off (or trade mark infringement) and copyright infringement both occur in relation to the same events, then the damages for passing off and copyright infringement may well be accumulated.[119]

MALICIOUS FALSEHOOD

A tort that is related to passing off is that known as malicious falsehood, sometimes referred to as trade libel.[120] This could occur where someone publishes

114 See *Morgan-Grampian plc v Training Personnel Ltd.* [1992] FSR 267, cf. *Blazer plc v Yardley & Co. Ltd.* [1992] FSR 501.

115 (unreported) *The Times*, 2 December 1993 (Chancery Division).

116 At a full trial, the defendant should be able to raise the plaintiff's acquiescence as a defence or, alternatively the doctrine of estoppel might apply.

117 (1915) 84 LJ Ch 449.

118 Ibid. at 449.

119 *Columbia Picture Industries v Robinson* [1987] 1 Ch 38.

120 For a fuller description of this tort, see Blanco White, T.A. & Jacob, R. *Kerly's Law of Trade Marks and Trade Names* (London: Sweet & Maxwell, 12th edn., 1986) Chapter 18.

information that is capable of seriously damaging a trader's position or reputation. For example, one trader might unjustifiably state that another trader's goods are of poor quality or are counterfeit.[121] Advertising 'puff' and mere claims that one trader's goods are superior to those of another trader does not, *per se*, amount to malicious falsehood. For example, in *Hubbuck & Sons Ltd.* v *Wilkinson, Heywood & Clerk Ltd.*,[122] a published statement that the defendant's zinc paint had a slight advantage over the plaintiff's paint was held not to be a malicious falsehood, even if the statement had been made maliciously.

The basis of the action is a false statement made maliciously, that is without just cause or excuse. These two ingredients, falsity and malice are essential if the plaintiff is to succeed. The plaintiff failed in *White* v *Mellin*[123] where the defendant sold the plaintiff's infants' food after fixing labels to the wrappers stating that the defendant's food for infants was far more nutritious and healthful than any other. There was no proof that the statement was untrue or that it had caused damage to the plaintiff. Proof of financial loss is another requirement but this was relaxed by section 3 of the Defamation Act 1952 which states that proof of special damage is not necessary if the statement was calculated to cause pecuniary damage to the plaintiff:

(a) and was published in writing or some other permanent form, or,
(b) was made in respect of any office, profession, calling, trade or business held or carried on by him at the time of publication.

Prior to the Defamation Act 1952, proof of special damage was not always required and general damage such as a significant fall in a trader's turnover could be sufficient. In *Ratcliffe* v *Evans*,[124] the plaintiff carried on business under the name 'Ratcliffe & Sons'. The defendant published a weekly newspaper circulated in the area where the plaintiff's business was situated. One week the newspaper carried a statement implying that the plaintiff had ceased trading and that the firm known as 'Ratcliffe & Sons' no longer existed. Not surprisingly, this untrue statement caused the plaintiff to experience a fall in business activity. It was held in the Court of Appeal that an untrue statement maliciously published about a plaintiff's business which is intended to produce and does indeed produce a loss is actionable as a malicious falsehood. Evidence of general loss, as was the case here, as opposed to evidence of particular loss (for example, where a named customer takes his trade elsewhere as a result of the untrue statement) was admissible in evidence and was sufficient to support the action.

Other examples of trade libel include circulars suggesting that the plaintiff's goods were not genuine[125] and claims that the plaintiff was intending to make use of a patented invention the use of which had been abandoned earlier by the defendant as being inadequate.[126] Selling one class of the plaintiff's goods as a different class can amount to malicious falsehood and passing off. The defendant in *Wilts United Dairies Ltd.* v *Thomas Robinson Sons & Co. Ltd.*[127] obtained large quantities of the plaintiff's condensed milk that had been sold off by the Ministry of Food at a very low price on condition that it should be used for animal food, manufacturing or export. The milk was old (it had been stocked during the Second World War) and it was known that it deteriorated with age. The plaintiff always had required that retailers sold the cans of milk within six months. The defendant offered the old milk for sale for human consumption. It was held that the defendant had passed off one class of the plain-

121 This might also be a personal libel, depending upon the circumstances.

122 [1899] 1 QB 86.

123 [1895] AC 154.

124 [1892] 2 QB 524.

125 *Thomas* v *Williams* (1880) 14 Ch D 864.

126 *London Ferro-Concrete Co. Ltd.* v *Justicz* (1951) 68 RPC. The statement had been made in the hope that this would induce a contractor to divert a sub-contract to the defendant.

127 [1958] RPC 94.

tiff's milk (that is, old stock not fit for human consumption) as another class (normal quality) and this amounted to a malicious falsehood calculated to injure the plaintiff's reputation. In many respects, the basic principles in this case are the same as those applying to the passing off case of *Spalding & Bros. v A W Gamage Ltd.*,[128] discussed earlier in this chapter, where the defendant sold defective footballs made by the plaintiff as if they were of normal quality.

128 (1915) 84 LJ Ch 449.

Malicious falsehood could be a possibility where a trader engages in comparative advertising in a way in which the stated facts concerning the other traders' goods are untrue or misleading. In *Compaq Computer Corp. v Dell Computer Corp. Ltd.*[129] the defendant advertised using a photograph showing its computer and the plaintiff's computer side by side. Underneath were details of the two computers including price and performance. This information was selected so as to show off the defendant's computer as being the best value. However, the information was misleading, particularly as regards price. The defendant had indicated a heavily discounted price for its machine compared to the list price (undiscounted) of the plaintiff's machine. An interlocutory injunction was granted because, although the defendant intended to justify his statement, the test was whether a jury would reasonably conclude that the statement was true.[130] However, this case should be compared with *McDonald's Hamburgers Ltd. v Burgerking (UK) Ltd.*,[131] where it was held that an advertising campaign for 'Whopper' burgers using the slogan 'It's Not Just Big Mac' in close proximity with the phrase 'Unlike Some burgers, it's 100 per cent pure beef . . .' did not amount to a malicious falsehood. It did, however, constitute passing off.

129 [1992] FSR 93.

130 However, there is no entitlement to a jury in a malicious falsehood action, unlike the case with defamation. The case also involved a trade mark infringement although the judge considered that there was an arguable case that the trade mark 'Compaq' was invalid.

131 [1987] FSR 112.

In some cases there may be an overlap between malicious falsehood and defamation and, if that is so, it may be advantageous to bring an action in malicious falsehood as legal aid is not available for defamation. To do this is not an abuse of process even if the sole aim is to facilitate an application for legal aid and in spite of the fact that the defendant will thus be deprived of a right to elect trial by jury. So it was held in *Joyce v Sengupta*[132] in which a former lady's maid of the Princess Royal took action in respect of an allegation by the defendant (a reporter for the *Today* newspaper) that the plaintiff had stolen intimate letters belonging to the Princess Royal and handed them to the newspaper. Nicholls VC also confirmed that the effect of section 3 of the Defamation Act 1952[133] was not to limit damages to nominal damages only.

132 [1993] 1 All ER 897.

133 Proof of special damage unnecessary in certain cases.

Local authorities may not sue in defamation because to allow defamation actions by local authorities and other bodies run on political lines would be an undesirable fetter on the freedom of speech. The House of Lords so held in *Derbyshire County Council v Times Newspapers Ltd.*,[134] applying authorities from the United States, in particular, *New York Times Co. v Sullivan*.[135] Although the United States cases were related to the American Constitution provisions securing freedom of speech, the United Kingdom principle of public interest was just as valid. Previous United Kingdom law as expressed in *Bognor Regis UDC v Campion*[136] was unsatisfactory and this case was overruled by the House of Lords. In that case, the council had been awarded £2,000 in damages after the defendant had circulated a leaflet savagely attacking the Council. Of course, a personal individual such as a councillor or an officer of the council will be able to bring a libel action if his individual reputation was wrongly harmed. Indeed, the leader of Derbyshire County Council had brought a personal action based on the same facts as in the local authority action.

134 (unreported) *The Times*, 19 February 1993. The Court of Appeal decision to the same effect is reported in [1992] QB 770.

135 (1964) 376 US 254.

136 [1972] 2 QB 169.

SUMMARY

The establishment and development of passing off is a typically common law method of protecting traders' rights but it does have equivalents in other forms of jurisdiction, broadly falling under the heading of unfair competition. For example, in Germany, there is trade mark law like protection for the *Ausstattung* (get-up) of goods, packaging, their advertising and the like.[137] For traders contemplating operations overseas, it is obviously important to take precautions such as seeking registrations of trade marks. In terms of the Treaty of Rome, the law of passing off does not appear to pose any particular problems and, because of differences between trade mark law and the law of passing off, the difficulties experienced in respect of parallel importing and trade marks do not seem to occur. It is apparent that passing off provides a very useful remedy where there is no trade mark and the wider scope of passing off can be important in restraining unfair practices. However, the scope can sometimes appear to be too wide, as in the Jif lemon case, and there are certainly some defects and gaps, particularly in the field of character merchandising. Nevertheless, the law of passing off is alive and kicking and prevents a great deal of unfair appropriation of business goodwill. It still proves to be a useful supplement to trade mark law. In turn, the law of malicious falsehood provides a useful supplement to passing off. It should be noted that, in a significant number of cases where passing off is an issue, that criminal offences may have been committed such as making a false instrument,[138] obtaining by deception,[139] going equipped to cheat[140] in addition to offences under the Trade Descriptions Act 1968 and Consumer Protection Act 1987. A local trading standards officer is as likely to take an interest in an activity where a name or mark has been used without permission in circumstances where the public are likely to be deceived as is the trader whose name or mark it is.

137 For an overview of German intellectual property law as it applies to the appearance of articles including get-up, see Rohnke, C. 'Protection of External Product Features in West Germany' [1990] 2 EIPR 41.

138 Section 1 of the Forgery and Counterfeiting Act 1981.

139 Section 15 of the Theft Act 1968.

140 Section 25 of the Theft Act 1968.

Appendices

Appendix 1
Member States of selected international conventions*

* Reproduced by permission of WIPO. Lists valid on 15 October 1993.

Paris Convention for the Protection of Industrial Property

Paris Convention (1883), revised at Brussels (1900), Washington (1911), The Hague (1925),
London (1934), Lisbon (1958) and Stockholm (1967), and amended in 1979

(Paris Union)

Status on October 15, 1993

State	Date on which State became party to the Convention	Latest Act[1] of the Convention to which State is party and date on which State became party to that Act
Algeria	March 1, 1966	Stockholm: April 20, 1975[2]
Argentina	February 10, 1967	Lisbon: February 10, 1967
		Stockholm, Articles 13 to 30: October 8, 1980
Australia	October 10, 1925	Stockholm, Articles 1 to 12: September 27, 1975
		Stockholm, Articles 13 to 30: August 25, 1972
Austria	January 1, 1909	Stockholm: August 18, 1973
Bahamas	July 10, 1973	Lisbon: July 10, 1973
		Stockholm, Articles 13 to 30: March 10, 1977
Bangladesh	March 3, 1991	Stockholm: March 3, 1991[2]
Barbados	March 12, 1985	Stockholm: March 12, 1985
Belarus	December 25, 1991	Stockholm: December 25, 1991[2]
Belgium	July 7, 1884	Stockholm: February 12, 1975
Benin	January 10, 1967	Stockholm: March 12, 1975
Bolivia	November 4, 1993	Stockholm: November 4, 1993
Brazil	July 7, 1884	Stockholm, Articles 1 to 12: November 24, 1992
		Stockholm, Articles 13 to 30: March 24, 1975[2]
Bulgaria	June 13, 1921	Stockholm, Articles 1 to 12: May 19 or 27, 1970[3]
		Stockholm, Articles 13 to 30: May 27, 1970[2]
Burkina Faso	November 19, 1963	Stockholm: September 2, 1975
Burundi	September 3, 1977	Stockholm: September 3, 1977
Cameroon	May 10, 1964	Stockholm: April 20, 1975
Canada	June 12, 1925	London: July 30, 1951
		Stockholm, Articles 13 to 30: July 7, 1970
Central African Republic	November 19, 1963	Stockholm: September 5, 1978
Chad	November 19, 1963	Stockholm: September 26, 1970
Chile	June 14, 1991	Stockholm: June 14, 1991
China	March 19, 1985	Stockholm: March 19, 1985[2]
Congo	September 2, 1963	Stockholm: December 5, 1975
Côte d'Ivoire	October 23, 1963	Stockholm: May 4, 1974
Croatia	October 8, 1991	Stockholm: October 8, 1991
Cuba	November 17, 1904	Stockholm: April 8, 1975[2]
Cyprus	January 17, 1966	Stockholm: April 3, 1984
Czech Republic	January 1, 1993	Stockholm: January 1, 1993
Democratic People's Republic of Korea	June 10, 1980	Stockholm: June 10, 1980
Denmark[4]	October 1, 1894	Stockholm, Articles 1 to 12: April 26 or May 19, 1970[3]
		Stockholm, Articles 13 to 30: April 26, 1970
Dominican Republic	July 11, 1890	The Hague: April 6, 1951[2]
Egypt	July 1, 1951	Stockholm: March 6, 1975[2]
Finland	September 20, 1921	Stockholm, Articles 1 to 12: October 21, 1975
		Stockholm, Articles 13 to 30: September 15, 1970
France[5]	July 7, 1884	Stockholm: August 12, 1975
Gabon	February 29, 1964	Stockholm: June 10, 1975
Gambia	January 21, 1992	Stockholm: January 21, 1992
Germany	May 1, 1903	Stockholm: September 19, 1970
Ghana	September 28, 1976	Stockholm: September 28, 1976
Greece	October 2, 1924	Stockholm: July 15, 1976
Guinea	February 5, 1982	Stockholm: February 5, 1982
Guinea-Bissau	June 28, 1988	Stockholm: June 28, 1988
Haiti	July 1, 1958	Stockholm: November 3, 1983
Holy See	September 29, 1960	Stockholm: April 24, 1975
Hungary	January 1, 1909	Stockholm, Articles 1 to 12: April 26 or May 19, 1970[3]
		Stockholm, Articles 13 to 30: April 26, 1970[2]
Iceland	May 5, 1962	London: May 5, 1962
		Stockholm, Articles 13 to 30: December 28, 1984
Indonesia	December 24, 1950	London: December 24, 1950
		Stockholm, Articles 13 to 30: December 20, 1979[2]
Iran (Islamic Republic of)	December 16, 1959	Lisbon: January 4, 1962
Iraq	January 24, 1976	Stockholm: January 24, 1976[2]
Ireland	December 4, 1925	Stockholm, Articles 1 to 12: April 26 or May 19, 1970[3]
		Stockholm, Articles 13 to 30: April 26, 1970
Israel	March 24, 1950	Stockholm, Articles 1 to 12: April 26 or May 19, 1970[3]
		Stockholm, Articles 13 to 30: April 26, 1970
Italy	July 7, 1884	Stockholm: April 24, 1977

State	Date on which State became party to the Convention	Latest Act[1] of the Convention to which State is party and date on which State became party to that Act
Japan......................	July 15, 1899	Stockholm, Articles 1 to 12: October 1, 1975 Stockholm, Articles 13 to 30: April 24, 1975
Jordan....................	July 17, 1972	Stockholm: July 17, 1972
Kazakhstan.................	December 25, 1991	Stockholm: December 25, 1991[2]
Kenya.....................	June 14, 1965	Stockholm: October 26, 1971
Latvia....................	September 7, 1993[6]	Stockholm: September 7, 1993
Lebanon...................	September 1, 1924	London: September 30, 1947 Stockholm, Articles 13 to 30: December 30, 1986[2]
Lesotho...................	September 28, 1989	Stockholm: September 28, 1989[2]
Libya.....................	September 28, 1976	Stockholm: September 28, 1976[2]
Liechtenstein.............	July 14, 1933	Stockholm: May 25, 1972
Luxembourg................	June 30, 1922	Stockholm: March 24, 1975
Madagascar................	December 21, 1963	Stockholm: April 10, 1972
Malawi....................	July 6, 1964	Stockholm: June 25, 1970
Malaysia..................	January 1, 1989	Stockholm: January 1, 1989
Mali......................	March 1, 1983	Stockholm: March 1, 1983
Malta.....................	October 20, 1967	Lisbon: October 20, 1967 Stockholm, Articles 13 to 30: December 12, 1977[2]
Mauritania................	April 11, 1965	Stockholm: September 21, 1976
Mauritius.................	September 24, 1976	Stockholm: September 24, 1976
Mexico....................	September 7, 1903	Stockholm: July 26, 1976
Monaco....................	April 29, 1956	Stockholm: October 4, 1975
Mongolia..................	April 21, 1985	Stockholm: April 21, 1985[2]
Morocco...................	July 30, 1917	Stockholm: August 6, 1971
Netherlands[7]............	July 7, 1884	Stockholm: January 10, 1975
New Zealand[8]............	July 29, 1931	London: July 14, 1946 Stockholm, Articles 13 to 30: June 20, 1984
Niger.....................	July 5, 1964	Stockholm: March 6, 1975
Nigeria...................	September 2, 1963	Lisbon: September 2, 1963
Norway....................	July 1, 1885	Stockholm: June 13, 1974
Philippines...............	September 27, 1965	Lisbon: September 27, 1965 Stockholm, Articles 13 to 30: July 16, 1980
Poland....................	November 10, 1919	Stockholm: March 24, 1975[2]
Portugal..................	July 7, 1884	Stockholm: April 30, 1975
Republic of Korea.........	May 4, 1980	Stockholm: May 4, 1980
Republic of Moldova.......	December 25, 1991	Stockholm: December 25, 1991[2]
Romania...................	October 6, 1920	Stockholm, Articles 1 to 12: April 26 or May 19, 1970[3] Stockholm, Articles 13 to 30: April 26, 1970[2]
Russian Federation........	December 25, 1991	Stockholm: December 25, 1991[2]
Rwanda....................	March 1, 1984	Stockholm: March 1, 1984
San Marino................	March 4, 1960	Stockholm: June 26, 1991
Senegal...................	December 21, 1963	Stockholm, Articles 1 to 12: April 26 or May 19, 1970[3] Stockholm, Articles 13 to 30: April 26, 1970
Slovakia..................	January 1, 1993	Stockholm: January 1, 1993
Slovenia..................	June 25, 1991	Stockholm: June 25, 1991
South Africa..............	December 1, 1947	Stockholm: March 24, 1975[2]
Spain.....................	July 7, 1884	Stockholm: April 14, 1972
Sri Lanka.................	December 29, 1952	London: December 29, 1952 Stockholm, Articles 13 to 30: September 23, 1978
Sudan.....................	April 16, 1984	Stockholm: April 16, 1984
Suriname..................	November 25, 1975	Stockholm: November 25, 1975
Swaziland.................	May 12, 1991	Stockholm: May 12, 1991
Sweden....................	July 1, 1885	Stockholm, Articles 1 to 12: October 9, 1970 Stockholm, Articles 13 to 30: April 26, 1970
Switzerland...............	July 7, 1884	Stockholm, Articles 1 to 12: April 26 or May 19, 1970[3] Stockholm, Articles 13 to 30: April 26, 1970
Syria.....................	September 1, 1924	London: September 30, 1947
The former Yugoslav Republic of Macedonia.......	September 8, 1991	Stockholm: September 8, 1991
Togo......................	September 10, 1967	Stockholm: April 30, 1975
Trinidad and Tobago.......	August 1, 1964	Stockholm: August 16, 1988
Tunisia...................	July 7, 1884	Stockholm: April 12, 1976[2]
Turkey....................	October 10, 1925	London: June 27, 1957 Stockholm, Articles 13 to 30: May 16, 1976
Uganda....................	June 14, 1965	Stockholm: October 20, 1973
Ukraine...................	December 25, 1991	Stockholm: December 25, 1991[2]
United Kingdom[9].........	July 7, 1884	Stockholm, Articles 1 to 12: April 26 or May 19, 1970[3] Stockholm, Articles 13 to 30: April 26, 1970
United Republic of Tanzania...	June 16, 1963	Lisbon: June 16, 1963 Stockholm, Articles 13 to 30: December 30, 1983

State	Date on which State became party to the Convention	Latest Act[1] of the Convention to which State is party and date on which State became party to that Act
United States of America[10]....	May 30, 1887	Stockholm, Articles 1 to 12: August 25, 1973 Stockholm, Articles 13 to 30: September 5, 1970
Uruguay........................	March 18, 1967	Stockholm: December 28, 1979
Uzbekistan.....................	December 25, 1991	Stockholm: December 25, 1991[2]
Viet Nam.......................	March 8, 1949	Stockholm: July 2, 1976[2]
Yugoslavia.....................	February 26, 1921	Stockholm: October 16, 1973
Zaire..........................	January 31, 1975	Stockholm: January 31, 1975
Zambia.........................	April 6, 1965	Lisbon: April 6, 1965 Stockholm, Articles 13 to 30: May 14, 1977
Zimbabwe.......................	April 18, 1980	Stockholm: December 30, 1981

(Total: 114 States)

---

[1] "Stockholm" means the Paris Convention for the Protection of Industrial Property as revised at Stockholm on July 14, 1967 (Stockholm Act); "Lisbon" means the Paris Convention as revised at Lisbon on October 31, 1958 (Lisbon Act); "London" means the Paris Convention as revised at London on June 2, 1934 (London Act); "The Hague" means the Paris Convention as revised at The Hague on November 6, 1925 (Hague Act).

[2] With the declaration provided for in Article 28(2) of the Stockholm Act relating to the International Court of Justice.

[3] These are the alternative dates of entry into force which the Director General of WIPO communicated to the States concerned.

[4] Denmark extended the application of the Stockholm Act to the Faröe Islands with effect from August 6, 1971.

[5] Including all Overseas Departments and Territories.

[6] Latvia acceded to the Paris Convention (Washington Act, 1911) with effect from August 20, 1925. It lost its independence on July 21, 1940, and regained it on August 21, 1991.

[7] Ratification for the Kingdom in Europe, the Netherlands Antilles and Aruba.

[8] The accession of New Zealand to the Stockholm Act, with the exception of Articles 1 to 12, extends to the Cook Islands, Niue and Tokelau.

[9] The United Kingdom extended the application of the Stockholm Act to the territory of Hong Kong with effect from November 16, 1977, and to the Isle of Man with effect from October 29, 1983.

[10] The United States of America extended the application of the Stockholm Act to all territories and possessions of the United States of America, including the Commonwealth of Puerto Rico, as from August 25, 1973.

3. Berne Convention for the Protection of Literary and Artistic Works

Berne Convention (1886), completed at Paris (1896), revised at Berlin (1908),
completed at Berne (1914), revised at Rome (1928), at Brussels (1948),
at Stockholm (1967) and at Paris (1971), and amended in 1979

(Berne Union)

Status on October 15, 1993

State	Date on which State became party to the Convention	Latest Act[1] of the Convention to which State is party and date on which State became party to that Act
Argentina	June 10, 1967	Brussels: June 10, 1967 Paris, Articles 22 to 38: October 8, 1980
Australia	April 14, 1928	Paris: March 1, 1978
Austria	October 1, 1920	Paris: August 21, 1982
Bahamas	July 10, 1973	Brussels: July 10, 1973 Paris, Articles 22 to 38: January 8, 1977[11]
Barbados	July 30, 1983	Paris: July 30, 1983
Belgium	December 5, 1887	Brussels: August 1, 1951 Stockholm, Articles 22 to 38: February 12, 1975
Benin	January 3, 1961[12]	Paris: March 12, 1975
Bolivia	November 4, 1993	Paris: November 4, 1993
Brazil	February 9, 1922	Paris: April 20, 1975
Bulgaria	December 5, 1921	Paris: December 4, 1974[11]
Burkina Faso	August 19, 1963[13]	Paris: January 24, 1976
Cameroon	September 21, 1964[12]	Paris, Articles 1 to 21: October 10, 1974 Paris, Articles 22 to 38: November 10, 1973
Canada	April 10, 1928	Rome: August 1, 1931 Stockholm, Articles 22 to 38: July 7, 1970
Central African Republic	September 3, 1977	Paris: September 3, 1977
Chad	November 25, 1971	Brussels: November 25, 1971[2,4] Stockholm, Articles 22 to 38: November 25, 1971
Chile	June 5, 1970	Paris: July 10, 1975
China	October 15, 1992	Paris: October 15, 1992[6]
Colombia	March 7, 1988	Paris: March 7, 1988
Congo	May 8, 1962[12]	Paris: December 5, 1975
Costa Rica	June 10, 1978	Paris: June 10, 1978
Côte d'Ivoire	January 1, 1962	Paris, Articles 1 to 21: October 10, 1974 Paris, Articles 22 to 38: May 4, 1974
Croatia	October 8, 1991	Paris: October 8, 1991
Cyprus	February 24, 1964[12]	Paris: July 27, 1983[7]
Czech Republic	January 1, 1993	Paris: January 1, 1993
Denmark	July 1, 1903	Paris: June 30, 1979
Ecuador	October 9, 1991	Paris: October 9, 1991
Egypt	June 7, 1977	Paris: June 7, 1977[6,11]
Fiji	December 1, 1971[12]	Brussels: December 1, 1971 Stockholm, Articles 22 to 38: March 15, 1972
Finland	April 1, 1928	Paris: November 1, 1986
France	December 5, 1887	Paris, Articles 1 to 21: October 10, 1974 Paris, Articles 22 to 38: December 15, 1972
Gabon	March 26, 1962	Paris: June 10, 1975
Gambia	March 7, 1993	Paris: March 7, 1993
Germany	December 5, 1887	Paris, Articles 1 to 21: October 10, 1974[5] Paris, Articles 22 to 38: January 22, 1974
Ghana	October 11, 1991	Paris: October 11, 1991
Greece	November 9, 1920	Paris: March 8, 1976
Guinea	November 20, 1980	Paris: November 20, 1980
Guinea-Bissau	July 22, 1991	Paris: July 22, 1991
Holy See	September 12, 1935	Paris: April 24, 1975
Honduras	January 25, 1990	Paris: January 25, 1990
Hungary	February 14, 1922	Paris, Articles 1 to 21: October 10, 1974 Paris, Articles 22 to 38: December 15, 1972
Iceland	September 7, 1947	Rome: September 7, 1947[7] Paris, Articles 22 to 38: December 28, 1984
India	April 1, 1928	Paris, Articles 1 to 21: May 6, 1984[6,9,10] Paris, Articles 22 to 38: January 10, 1975[11]
Ireland	October 5, 1927	Brussels: July 5, 1959 Stockholm, Articles 22 to 38: December 21, 1970

State	Date on which State became party to the Convention	Latest Act[1] of the Convention to which State is party and date on which State became party to that Act
Israel...................	March 24, 1950	Brussels: August 1, 1951 Stockholm, Articles 22 to 38: January 29 or February 26, 1970[3]
Italy....................	December 5, 1887	Paris: November 14, 1979
Jamaica..................	January 1, 1994	Paris: January 1, 1994[6]
Japan....................	July 15, 1899	Paris: April 24, 1975
Kenya....................	June 11, 1993	Paris: June 11, 1993
Lebanon..................	September 30, 1947	Rome: September 30, 1947
Lesotho..................	September 28, 1989	Paris: September 28, 1989[6,11]
Liberia..................	March 8, 1989	Paris: March 8, 1989[6,11]
Libya....................	September 28, 1976	Paris: September 28, 1976[11]
Liechtenstein............	July 30, 1931	Brussels: August 1, 1951 Stockholm, Articles 22 to 38: May 25, 1972
Luxembourg...............	June 20, 1888	Paris: April 20, 1975
Madagascar...............	January 1, 1966	Brussels: January 1, 1966
Malawi...................	October 12, 1991	Paris: October 12, 1991
Malaysia.................	October 1, 1990	Paris: October 1, 1990[6]
Mali.....................	March 19, 1962[12]	Paris: December 5, 1977
Malta....................	September 21, 1964	Rome: September 21, 1964 Paris, Articles 22 to 38: December 12, 1977[11]
Mauritania...............	February 6, 1973	Paris: September 21, 1976
Mauritius................	May 10, 1989	Paris: May 10, 1989[6,11]
Mexico...................	June 11, 1967	Paris: December 17, 1974[6]
Monaco...................	May 30, 1889	Paris: November 23, 1974
Morocco..................	June 16, 1917	Paris: May 17, 1987
Namibia..................	March 21, 1990	Paris: December 24, 1993
Netherlands..............	November 1, 1912	Paris, Articles 1 to 21: January 30, 1986[14] Paris, Articles 22 to 38: January 10, 1975[15]
New Zealand..............	April 24, 1928	Rome: December 4, 1947
Niger....................	May 2, 1962[12]	Paris: May 21, 1975
Nigeria..................	September 14, 1993	Paris: September 14, 1993
Norway...................	April 13, 1896	Brussels: January 28, 1963[5] Paris, Articles 22 to 38: June 13, 1974
Pakistan.................	July 5, 1948	Rome: July 5, 1948[2] Stockholm, Articles 22 to 38: January 29 or February 26, 1970[3]
Paraguay.................	January 2, 1992	Paris: January 2, 1992
Peru.....................	August 20, 1988	Paris: August 20, 1988
Philippines.............	August 1, 1951	Brussels: August 1, 1951 Paris, Articles 22 to 38: July 16, 1980
Poland...................	January 28, 1920	Rome: November 21, 1935 Paris, Articles 22 to 38: August 4, 1990
Portugal.................	March 29, 1911	Paris: January 12, 1979[16]
Romania..................	January 1, 1927	Rome: August 6, 1936[2] Stockholm, Articles 22 to 38: January 29 or February 26, 1970[3,11]
Rwanda...................	March 1, 1984	Paris: March 1, 1984
Saint Lucia.............	August 24, 1993	Paris: August 24, 1993[11]
Senegal..................	August 25, 1962	Paris: August 12, 1975
Slovakia.................	January 1, 1993	Paris: January 1, 1993
Slovenia.................	June 25, 1991	Paris: June 25, 1991[7]
South Africa............	October 3, 1928	Brussels: August 1, 1951 Paris, Articles 22 to 38: March 24, 1975[11]
Spain....................	December 5, 1887	Paris, Articles 1 to 21: October 10, 1974 Paris, Articles 22 to 38: February 19, 1974
Sri Lanka...............	July 20, 1959[12]	Rome: July 20, 1959 Paris, Articles 22 to 38: September 23, 1978
Suriname.................	February 23, 1977	Paris: February 23, 1977
Sweden...................	August 1, 1904	Paris, Articles 1 to 21: October 10, 1974 Paris, Articles 22 to 38: September 20, 1973
Switzerland.............	December 5, 1887	Paris: September 25, 1993[8]
Thailand.................	July 17, 1931	Berlin: July 17, 1931[8] Paris, Articles 22 to 38: December 29, 1980[11]
The former Yugoslav Republic of Macedonia...	September 8, 1991	Paris: September 8, 1991[7]
Togo.....................	April 30, 1975	Paris: April 30, 1975
Trinidad and Tobago........	August 16, 1988	Paris: August 16, 1988
Tunisia..................	December 5, 1887	Paris: August 16, 1975[11]
Turkey...................	January 1, 1952	Brussels: January 1, 1952[7]
United Kingdom...........	December 5, 1887	Paris: January 2, 1990

State	Date on which State became party to the Convention	Latest Act[1] of the Convention to which State is party and date on which State became party to that Act
United States of America...	March 1, 1989	Paris: March 1, 1989
Uruguay...................	July 10, 1967	Paris: December 28, 1979
Venezuela.................	December 30, 1982	Paris: December 30, 1982[11]
Yugoslavia................	June 17, 1930	Paris: September 2, 1975[7]
Zaire.....................	October 8, 1963[12]	Paris: January 31, 1975
Zambia....................	January 2, 1992	Paris: January 2, 1992
Zimbabwe..................	April 18, 1980	Rome: April 18, 1980
		Paris, Articles 22 to 38: December 30, 1981

(Total: 102 States)

---

[1] "Paris" means the Berne Convention for the Protection of Literary and Artistic Works as revised at Paris on July 24, 1971 (Paris Act); "Stockholm" means the said Convention as revised at Stockholm on July 14, 1967 (Stockholm Act); "Brussels" means the said Convention as revised at Brussels on June 26, 1948 (Brussels Act); "Rome" means the said Convention as revised at Rome on June 2, 1928 (Rome Act); "Berlin" means the said Convention as revised at Berlin on November 13, 1908 (Berlin Act).

[2] This State deposited its instrument of ratification of (or of accession to) the Stockholm Act in its entirety; however, Articles 1 to 21 (substantive clauses) of the said Act have not entered into force.

[3] These are the alternative dates of entry into force which the Director General of WIPO communicated to the States concerned.

[4] In accordance with the provision of Article 29 of the Stockholm Act applicable to the States outside the Union which accede to the said Act, this State is bound by Articles 1 to 20 of the Brussels Act.

[5] This State has declared that it admits the application of the Appendix of the Paris Act to works of which it is the State of origin by States which have made a declaration under Article VI(1)(i) of the Appendix or a notification under Article I of the Appendix. The declarations took effect on October 18, 1973, for Germany, and on March 8, 1974, for Norway.

[6] Pursuant to Article I of the Appendix of the Paris Act, this State availed itself of the faculties provided for in Articles II and III of the said Appendix. The relevant declaration is effective until October 10, 1994.

[7] Subject to the reservation concerning the right of translation.

[8] Accession subject to reservations concerning works of applied art, conditions and formalities required for protection, the right of translation, the right of reproduction of articles published in newspapers or periodicals, the right of performance, and the application of the Convention to works not yet in the public domain at the date of its coming into force.

[9] This State declared that its ratification shall not apply to the provisions of Article 14_bis_(2)(b) of the Paris Act (presumption of legitimation for some authors who have brought contributions to the making of the cinematographic work).

[10] This State notified the designation of the competent authority provided by Article 15(4) of the Paris Act.

[11] With the declaration provided for in Article 33(2) relating to the International Court of Justice.

[12] Date on which the declaration of continued adherence was sent, after the accession of the State to independence.

[13] Burkina Faso, which had acceded to the Berne Convention (Brussels Act) as from August 19, 1963, denounced the said Convention as from September 20, 1970. Later on, Burkina Faso acceded again to the Berne Convention (Paris Act); this accession took effect on January 24, 1976.

[14] Ratification for the Kingdom in Europe.

[15] Ratification for the Kingdom in Europe. Articles 22 to 38 of the Paris Act apply also to the Netherlands Antilles and Aruba.

[16] Pursuant to the provisions of Article 14_bis_(2)(c) of the Paris Act, this State has made a declaration to the effect that the undertaking by authors to bring contributions to the making of a cinematographic work must be in a written agreement. This declaration was received on November 5, 1986.

5. Madrid Agreement Concerning the International Registration of Marks

Madrid Agreement (Marks) (1891), revised at
Brussels (1900), Washington (1911),
The Hague (1925), London (1934), Nice (1957) and Stockholm (1967), and amended in 1979

(Madrid Union)

Status on October 15, 1993

State[1]	Date on which State became party to the Agreement	Latest Act of the Agreement to which State is party and date on which State·became party to that Act
Algeria....................	July 5, 1972	Stockholm: July 5, 1972
Austria...................	January 1, 1909	Stockholm: August 18, 1973
Belarus[2].................	December 25, 1991	Stockholm: December 25, 1991
Belgium[2].................	July 15, 1892	Stockholm: February 12, 1975
Bulgaria..................	August 1, 1985	Stockholm: August 1, 1985
China[3]...................	October 4, 1989	Stockholm: October 4, 1989
Croatia...................	October 8, 1991	Stockholm: October 8, 1991
Cuba[3]....................	December 6, 1989	Stockholm: December 6, 1989
Czech Republic............	January 1, 1993	Stockholm: January 1, 1993
Democratic People's Republic of Korea...............	June 10, 1980	Stockholm: June 10, 1980
Egypt.....................	July 1, 1952	Stockholm: March 6, 1975
France[5]...................	July 15, 1892	Stockholm: August 12, 1975
Germany...................	December 1, 1922	Stockholm: September 19, or December 22, 1970[4]
Hungary...................	January 1, 1909	Stockholm: September 19, or December 22, 1970[4]
Italy.....................	October 15, 1894	Stockholm: April 24, 1977
Kazakhstan................	December 25, 1991	Stockholm: December 25, 1991
Liechtenstein.............	July 14, 1933	Stockholm: May 25, 1972
Luxembourg[2]..............	September 1, 1924	Stockholm: March 24, 1975
Monaco....................	April 29, 1956	Stockholm: October 4, 1975
Mongolia[3]................	April 21, 1985	Stockholm: April 21, 1985
Morocco...................	July 30, 1917	Stockholm: January 24, 1976
Netherlands[2,6]..........	March 1, 1893	Stockholm: March 6, 1975
Poland[3]..................	March 18, 1991	Stockholm: March 18, 1991
Portugal..................	October 31, 1893	Stockholm: November 22, 1988
Romania...................	October 6, 1920	Stockholm: September 19, or December 22, 1970[4]
Russian Federation........	December 25, 1991	Stockholm: December 25, 1991
San Marino................	September 25, 1960	Stockholm: June 26, 1991
Slovakia..................	January 1, 1993	Stockholm: January 1, 1993
Slovenia..................	June 25, 1991	Stockholm: June 25, 1991
Spain[7]....................	July 15, 1892	Stockholm: June 8, 1979
Sudan.....................	May 16, 1984	Stockholm: May 16, 1984
Switzerland...............	July 15, 1892	Stockholm: September 19, or December 22, 1970[4]
The former Yugoslav Republic of Macedonia...	September 8, 1991	Stockholm: September 8, 1991
Ukraine...................	December 25, 1991	Stockholm: December 25, 1991
Uzbekistan................	December 25, 1991	Stockholm: December 25, 1991
Viet Nam..................	March 8, 1949	Stockholm: July 2, 1976
Yugoslavia................	February 26, 1921	Stockholm: October 16, 1973

(Total: 37 States)

---

[1] All the States have declared, under Article 3*bis* of the Nice or Stockholm Act, that the protection arising from international registration shall not extend to them unless the proprietor of the mark so requests (the dates in parentheses indicate the effective date of the declaration in respect of each State): Algeria (July 5, 1972), Austria (February 8, 1970), Belarus (December 25, 1991), Belgium (December 15, 1966), Bulgaria (August 1, 1985), China (October 4, 1989), Croatia (October 8, 1991), Cuba (December 6, 1989), Czech Republic (January 1, 1993), Democratic People's Republic of Korea (June 10, 1980), Egypt (March 1, 1967), France (July 1, 1973), Germany (July 1, 1973) (October 25, 1967, in respect of the German Democratic Republic), Hungary (October 30, 1970), Italy (June 14, 1967), Kazakhstan (December 25, 1991), Liechtenstein (January 1, 1973), Luxembourg (December 15, 1966), Monaco (December 15, 1966), Mongolia (April 21, 1985), Morocco (December 18, 1970), Netherlands (December 15, 1966), Poland (March 18, 1991), Portugal (December 15, 1966), Romania (June 10, 1967), Russian Federation (December 25, 1991), San Marino (August 14, 1991), Slovakia (January 1, 1993), Slovenia (June 25, 1991), Spain (December 15, 1966), Sudan (May 16, 1984), Switzerland (January 1, 1973), the former Yugoslav Republic of Macedonia (September 8, 1991), Ukraine (December 25, 1991), Uzbekistan (December 25, 1991), Viet Nam (July 2, 1976) (May 15, 1973, in respect of the Republic of South Viet-Nam), Yugoslavia (June 29, 1972).

[2] As from January 1, 1971, the territories in Europe of Belgium, Luxembourg and the Netherlands are, for the application of the Madrid Agreement (Marks), to be deemed a single country.

[3] In accordance with Article 14(2)(d) and (f), this State declared that the application of the Stockholm Act was limited to marks registered from the date on which accession entered into force: China: October 4, 1989; Cuba: December 6, 1989; Mongolia: April 21, 1985; Poland: March 18, 1991.

[4] These are the alternative dates of entry into force which the Director General of WIPO communicated to the States concerned.

[5] Including all Overseas Departments and Territories.

[6] The instrument of ratification of the Stockholm Act was deposited for the Kingdom in Europe. The Netherlands, which had extended the application of the Stockholm Act to Aruba with effect from November 8, 1986, suspended that application as from that date for an indefinite period.

[7] Spain declared that it no longer wished to be bound by instruments earlier than the Nice Act. This declaration became effective on December 15, 1966. The Madrid Agreement (Marks) was thus not applicable between Spain and the following States between December 15, 1966, and the date indicated for each State: Austria (February 8, 1970), Hungary (March 23, 1967), Liechtenstein (May 29, 1967), Morocco (December 18, 1970), Viet Nam (May 15, 1973).

International Convention for the Protection of Performers, Producers of Phonograms and Broadcasting Organisations*

Rome Convention (1961)

Status on October 15, 1993

State	Date on which State became party to the Convention	State	Date on which State became party to the Convention
Argentina[1]	March 2, 1992	Honduras	February 16, 1990
Australia[1]	September 30, 1992	Ireland[1]	September 19, 1979
Austria	June 9, 1973	Italy[1]	April 8, 1975
Barbados	September 18, 1983	Japan[1]	October 26, 1989
Bolivia	November 24, 1993	Lesotho[1]	January 26, 1990
Brazil	September 29, 1965	Luxembourg[1]	February 25, 1976
Burkina Faso	January 14, 1988	Mexico[1]	May 18, 1964
Chile	September 5, 1974	Monaco[1]	December 6, 1985
Colombia	September 17, 1976	Netherlands[1,2]	October 7, 1993
Congo[1]	May 18, 1964	Niger[1]	May 18, 1964
Costa Rica[1]	September 9, 1971	Nigeria[1]	October 29, 1993
Czech Republic[1]	January 1, 1993	Norway[1]	July 10, 1978
Denmark[1]	September 23, 1965	Panama	September 2, 1983
Dominican Republic	January 27, 1987	Paraguay	February 26, 1970
Ecuador	May 18, 1964	Peru	August 7, 1985
El Salvador	June 29, 1979	Philippines	September 25, 1984
Fiji[1]	April 11, 1972	Slovakia[1]	January 1, 1993
Finland[1]	October 21, 1983	Spain[1]	November 14, 1991
France[1]	July 3, 1987	Sweden[1]	May 18, 1964
Germany[1]	October 21, 1966	Switzerland[1]	September 24, 1993
Greece	January 6, 1993	United Kingdom[1]	May 18, 1964
Guatemala	January 14, 1977	Uruguay	July 4, 1977

(Total: 44 States)

---

* The secretarial tasks relating to this Convention are performed jointly with the International Labour Office and Unesco.

[1] The instruments of ratification or accession deposited with the Secretary-General of the United Nations by the following States contain declarations made under the articles mentioned hereafter (with reference to publication in Le Droit d'auteur (Copyright) for the years 1962 to 1964 and in Copyright since 1965):
Australia, Articles 5(3) (concerning Article 5(1)(c)), 6(2), 16(1)(a)(i) and 16(1)(b) [1992, p. 301];
Austria, Article 16(1)(a)(iii) and (iv) and 1(b) [1973, p. 67];
Czech Republic, Article 16(1)(a)(iii) and (iv) [1964, p. 110];
Congo, Articles 5(3) (concerning Article 5(1)(c)) and 16(1)(a)(i) [1964, p. 127];
Denmark, Articles 6(2), 16(1)(a)(ii) and (iv) and 17 [1965, p. 214];
Fiji, Articles 5(3) (concerning Article 5(1)(b)), 6(2) and 16(1)(a)(i) [1972, pp. 88 and 178];
Finland, Articles 6(2), 16(1)(a)(i), (ii) and (iv), 16(1)(b) and 17 [1983, p. 287];
France, Articles 5(3) and 16(1)(a)(iii) and (iv) [1987, p. 184];
Germany, Articles 5(3) (concerning Article 5(1)(b)) and 16(1)(a)(iv) [1966, p. 237];
Ireland, Articles 5(3) (concerning Article 5(1)(b)), 6(2) and 16(1)(a)(ii) [1979, p. 218];
Italy, Articles 6(2), 16(1)(a)(ii), (iii) and (iv), 16(1)(b) and 17 [1975, p. 44];
Japan, Articles 5(3) (concerning Article 5(1)(c)) and 16(1)(a)(ii) and (iv) [1989, p. 288];
Lesotho, Article 16(1)(a)(ii) and (1)(b) [1990, p. 95];
Luxembourg, Articles 5(3) (concerning Article 5(1)(c)), 16(1)(a)(i) and 16(1)(b) [1976, p. 24];
Monaco, Articles 5(3) (concerning Article 5(1)(c), 16(1)(a)(i) and 16(1)(b) [1985, p. 422];
Netherlands, Article 16(1)(a)(iii) and (iv) [1993, p. ...];
Niger, Articles 5(3) (concerning Article 5(1)(c)) and 16(1)(a)(i) [1963, p. 155];
Nigeria, Articles 5(3) (concerning Article 5(1)(c)), 6(2) and 16(1)(a)(ii), (iii) and (iv) [1993, p. ...];
Norway, Articles 6(2) and 16(1)(a)(ii), (iii) and (iv) [1978, p. 133; in respect of 16(1)(a)(ii) modified: 1989, p. 288];
Slovakia, Article 16(1)(a)(iii) and (iv) [1964, p. 110]
Spain, Articles 5(3) (concerning Article 5(1)(c)), 6(2) and 16(1)(a)(iii) and (iv) [1991, p. 221];
Sweden, Article 16(1)(b) [1962, p. 138; 1986, p. 382];
Switzerland, Articles 5(3) (concerning Article 5(1)(b)) and 16(1)(a)(iii) and (iv) [1993, p. ...];
United Kingdom, Articles 5(3) (concerning Article 5(1)(b)), 6(2) and 16(1)(a)(ii), (iii) and (iv) [1963, p. 244]; the same declarations were made for Gibraltar and Bermuda [1967, p. 36; 1970, p. 108].

[2] Accession for the Kingdom in Europe.

Patent Cooperation Treaty

PCT (Washington, 1970), amended in 1979 and modified in 1984

(PCT Union)

Status on October 15, 1993

State	Date on which State became party to the Treaty	State	Date on which State became party to the Treaty
Australia...................	March 31, 1980	Latvia......................	September 7, 1993
Austria....................	April 23, 1979	Liechtenstein[4]...........	March 19, 1980
Barbados...................	March 12, 1985	Luxembourg.................	April 30, 1978
Belarus[1].................	December 25, 1991	Madagascar[5]..............	January 24, 1978
Belgium....................	December 14, 1981	Malawi.....................	January 24, 1978
Benin......................	February 26, 1987	Mali.......................	October 19, 1984
Brazil.....................	April 9, 1978	Mauritania.................	April 13, 1983
Bulgaria[1]................	May 21, 1984	Monaco.....................	June 22, 1979
Burkina Faso...............	March 21, 1989	Mongolia[6]................	May 27, 1991
Cameroon...................	January 24, 1978	Netherlands[6].............	July 10, 1979
Canada.....................	January 2, 1990	New Zealand................	December 1, 1992
Central African Republic....	January 24, 1978	Niger......................	March 21, 1993
Chad.......................	January 24, 1978	Norway[2]..................	January 1, 1980
China......................	January 1, 1994	Poland[7]..................	December 25, 1990
Congo......................	January 24, 1978	Portugal...................	November 24, 1992
Côte d'Ivoire..............	April 30, 1991	Republic of Korea..........	August 10, 1984
Czech Republic.............	January 1, 1993	Romania[1].................	July 23, 1979
Democratic People's Republic		Russian Federation[1]......	December 25, 1991
of Korea.................	July 8, 1980	Senegal....................	January 24, 1978
Denmark....................	December 1, 1978	Slovakia...................	January 1, 1993
Finland[2].................	October 1, 1980	Spain[4]...................	November 16, 1989
France[1], [3].............	February 25, 1978	Sri Lanka..................	February 26, 1982
Gabon......................	January 24, 1978	Sudan......................	April 16, 1984
Germany....................	January 24, 1978	Sweden[2]..................	May 17, 1978
Greece[4]..................	October 9, 1990	Switzerland[4].............	January 24, 1978
Guinea.....................	May 27, 1991	Togo.......................	January 24, 1978
Hungary[1].................	June 27, 1980	Ukraine[1].................	December 25, 1991
Ireland....................	August 1, 1992	United Kingdom[8]..........	January 24, 1978
Italy......................	March 28, 1985	United States of America[9],[10]..	January 24, 1978
Japan......................	October 1, 1978	Uzbekistan[1]..............	December 25, 1991
Kazakhstan[1]..............	December 25, 1991	Viet Nam...................	March 10, 1993

(Total: 61 States)

---

[1] With the declaration provided for in Article 64(5).

[2] With the declaration provided for in Article 64(2)(a)(ii).

[3] Including all Overseas Departments and Territories.

[4] With the declaration provided for in Article 64(1)(a).

[5] According to information received from the Minister for Foreign Affairs of Madagascar concerning international applications designating Madagascar, the industrial property legislation, adopted by the competent authorities, provides, among other things, for the prolongation of the time limits under Articles 22 and 39 until such time as the new patent legislation will, after its entry into force, permit the processing of patent applications in Madagascar. The said prolonged time limits will be fixed in a decree which will be promulgated in due course. The Government of Madagascar has expressed the desire that this information be conveyed to applicants using the PCT system and designating or electing Madagascar, or intending to do so, so that they may take cognizance of the possibility thus offered them validly to designate or elect Madagascar and to wait with the action required to start the national phase under Articles 22 and 39 until after the new legislation has entered into force and the time limits to be observed under it have been determined.

[6] Ratification for the Kingdom in Europe, the Netherlands Antilles and Aruba.

[7] With the declaration provided for in Article 64(2)(a)(i) and (ii).

[8] The United Kingdom extended the application of the PCT to the territory of Hong Kong with effect from April 15, 1981, and to the Isle of Man with effect from October 29, 1983.

[9] With the declarations provided for in Articles 64(3)(a) and 64(4)(a).

[10] Extends to all areas for which the United States of America has international responsibility.

INTERNATIONAL SEARCHING AUTHORITIES UNDER ARTICLE 16 OF THE PATENT COOPERATION TREATY

The Patent Offices of Australia, Austria, China (with effect from January 1, 1994), Japan, the Russian Federation, Spain, Sweden, the United States of America, and the European Patent Office.

INTERNATIONAL PRELIMINARY EXAMINING AUTHORITIES UNDER ARTICLE 32 OF THE PATENT COOPERATION TREATY

The Patent Offices of Australia, Austria, China (with effect from January 1, 1994), Japan, the Russian Federation, Sweden, the United Kingdom (in respect of demands for international preliminary examination made on or before May 28, 1993), the United States of America, and the European Patent Office.

Appendix 2
Trade mark classification for goods and services

Classification for goods (34 classes)

1. Chemicals used in industry, science and photography, as well as in agriculture, horticulture and forestry; unprocessed artificial resins, unprocessed plastics; manures; fire extinguishing compositions; tempering and soldering preparations; chemical substances for preserving foodstuffs; tanning substances; adhesives used in industry.

2. Paints, varnishes, lacquers; preservatives against rust and against deterioration of wood; colourants; mordants; raw natural resins; metals in foil and powder form for painters, decorators, printers and artists.

3. Bleaching preparations and other substances for laundry use; cleaning, polishing, scouring and abrasive preparations; soaps; perfumery, essential oils, cosmetics, hair lotions; dentifrices.

4. Industrial oils and greases; lubricants; dust absorbing, wetting and binding compositions; fuels (including motor spirit) and illuminants; candles, wicks.

5. Pharmaceutical veterinary and sanitary preparations; dietetic substances adapted for medical use, food for babies; plasters, materials for dressings; material for stopping teeth, dental wax; disinfectants; preparations for destroying vermin; fungicides, herbicides.

6. Common metals and their alloys; metal building materials; transportable buildings of metal; materials of metal for railway tracks; non-electric cables and wires of common metal; ironmongery, small items of metal hardware; pipes and tubes of metal; safes; goods of common metal not included in other classes; ores.

7. Machines and machine tools; motors (except for land vehicles); machine coupling and belting (except for land vehicles); agricultural implements; incubators for eggs.

8. Hand tools and implements (hand operated); cutlery; side arms; razors.

9. Scientific, nautical, surveying, electric, photographic, cinematographic, optical, weighing, measuring, signalling, checking (supervision), life saving and teaching apparatus and instruments; apparatus for recording, transmission or reproduction of sound or images; magnetic data carriers, recording discs; automatic vending machines and mechanisms for coin-operated apparatus; cash registers, calculating machines, data processing equipment and computers; fire-extinguishing apparatus.

10. Surgical, medical, dental and veterinary apparatus and instruments, artificial limbs, eyes and teeth; orthopaedic articles; suture materials.

11. Apparatus for lighting, heating, steam generating, cooking, refrigerating, drying, ventilating, water supply and sanitary purposes.

12. Vehicles; apparatus for locomotion by land, air or water.

13. Firearms; ammunition and projectiles; explosives; fireworks.

14. Precious metals and their alloys and goods in precious metals or coated therewith, not included in other classes; jewellery, precious stones; horological and chronometric instruments.

15. Musical instruments.

16. Paper, cardboard and goods made from these materials, not included in other classes; printed matter; bookbinding material; photographs; stationery; adhesives for stationery or household purposes; artists' materials; paint brushes; typewriters and office requisites (except furniture); instructional and teaching material (except apparatus); plastic materials for packaging (not included in other classes); playing cards; printers' type; printing blocks.

17. Rubber, gutta-percha, gum, asbestos, mica and goods made from these materials and not included in other classes; plastics in extruded form for use in manufacture; packing, stopping and insulating materials; flexible pipes, not of metal.

18. Leather and imitations of leather, and goods made of these materials and not included in other classes; animal skins, hides; trunks and travelling bags; umbrellas, parasols and walking sticks; whips, harness and saddlery.

19. Building materials (non-metallic); non-metallic rigid pipes for building; asphalt, pitch and bitumen; non-metallic transportable buildings; monuments, not of metal.

20. Furniture, mirrors, picture frames; goods (not included in other classes) of wood, cork, reed, cane, wicker, horn, bone, ivory, whalebone, shell, amber, mother-of-pearl, meerschaum and substitutes for all these materials, or of plastics.

21. Household or kitchen utensils and containers (not of precious metal or coated therewith); combs and sponges; brushes (except paint brushes); brush-making materials; articles for cleaning purposes; steel wool; unworked or semi-worked glass (except glass used in building); glassware, porcelain and earthenware not included in other classes.

22. Ropes, string, nets, tents, awnings, tarpaulins, sails, sacks and bags (not included in other classes); padding and stuffing materials (except of rubber or plastics); raw fibrous textile materials.

23. Yarns and threads, for textile use.

24. Textiles and textile goods, not included in other classes; bed and table covers.

25. Clothing, footwear, headgear.

26. Lace and embroidery, ribbons and braid; buttons, hooks and eyes, pins and needles; artificial flowers.

27. Carpets, rugs, mats and matting, linoleum and other materials for covering existing floors; wall hangings (non-textile).

28. Games and playthings; gymnastic and sporting articles not included in other classes; decorations for Christmas trees.

29. Meat, fish, poultry and game; meat extracts; preserved, dried and cooked fruits and vegetables; jellies, jams, fruit sauces; eggs, milk and milk products; edible oils and fats.

30. Coffee, tea, cocoa, sugar, rice, tapioca, sago, artificial coffee; flour and preparations made from cereals, bread, pastry and confectionery, ices; honey, treacle; yeast, baking-powder; salt, mustard; vinegar, sauces (condiments); spices; ice.

31. Agricultural, horticultural and forestry products and grains not included in other classes; live animals; fresh fruits and vegetables; seeds, natural plants and flowers; foodstuffs for animals, malt.

32. Beers; mineral and aerated waters and other non-alcoholic drinks; fruit drinks and fruit juices; syrups and other preparations for making beverages.

33. Alcoholic beverages (except beers).

34. Tobacco; smokers' articles; matches.

Classification for services (8 classes)

35. Advertising, business management; business administration; office functions.

36. Insurance; financial affairs; monetary affairs; real estate affairs.

37. Building construction; repair; installation services.

38. Telecommunications.

39. Transportation; packaging and storage of goods; travel arrangement.

40. Treatment of materials.

41. Education; providing of training; entertainment; sporting and cultural activities.

42. Providing of food and drink; temporary accommodation; medical, hygienic and beauty care; veterinary and agricultural services; legal services; scientific and industrial research; computer programming; services that cannot be placed in other classes.

Appendix 3
*EC Directive on rental right and lending right and on certain rights related to copyright in the field of intellectual property**

* European Communities Council Directive of 19 November 1992 (92/100/EEC). Reproduced by permission of the European Communities.

II

(Acts whose publication is not obligatory)

COUNCIL

COUNCIL DIRECTIVE 92/100/EEC

of 19 November 1992

**on rental right and lending right and on certain rights related to copyright in
the field of intellectual property**

THE COUNCIL OF THE EUROPEAN COMMUNITIES,

Having regard to the Treaty establishing the European Economic Community, and in particular Articles 57 (2), 66 and 100a thereof,

Having regard to the proposal from the Commission ('),

In cooperation with the European Parliament (²),

Having regard to the opinion of the Economic and Social Committee ('),

Whereas differences exist in the legal protection provided by the laws and practices of the Member States for copyright works and subject matter of related rights protection as regards rental and lending; whereas such differences are sources of barriers to trade and distortions of competition which impede the achievement and proper functioning of the internal market;

Whereas such differences in legal protection could well become greater as Member States adopt new and different legislation or as national case-law interpreting such legislation develops differently;

Whereas such differences should therefore be eliminated in accordance with the objective of introducing an area without internal frontiers as set out in Article 8a of the

(') OJ No C 53, 28. 2. 1991, p. 35 and
OJ No C 128, 20. 5. 1992, p. 8.
(²) OJ No C 67, 16. 3. 1992, p. 92 and Decision of 28 October
1992 (not yet published in the Official Journal).
(³) OJ No C 269, 14. 10. 1991, p. 54.

Treaty so as to institute, pursuant to Article 3 (f) of the Treaty, a system ensuring that competition in the common market is not distorted;

Whereas rental and lending of copyright works and the subject matter of related rights protection is playing an increasingly important role in particular for authors, performers and producers of phonograms and films; whereas piracy is becoming an increasing threat;

Whereas the adequate protection of copyright works and subject matter of related rights protection by rental and lending rights as well as the protection of the subject matter of related rights protection by the fixation right, reproduction right, distribution right, right to broadcast and communication to the public can accordingly be considered as being of fundamental importance for the Community's economic and cultural development;

Whereas copyright and related rights protection must adapt to new economic developments such as new forms of exploitation;

Whereas the creative and artistic work of authors and performers necessitates an adequate income as a basis for further creative and artistic work, and the investments required particularly for the production of phonograms and films are especially high and risky; whereas the possibility for securing that income and recouping that investment can only effectively be guaranteed through adequate legal protection of the rightholders concerned;

Whereas these creative, artistic and entrepreneurial activities are, to a large extent, activities of self-employed persons; whereas the pursuit of such activities must be made easier by providing a harmonized legal protection within the Community;

Whereas, to the extent that these activities principally constitute services, their provision must equally be facilitated by the establishment in the Community of a harmonized legal framework;

Whereas the legislation of the Member States should be approximated in such a way so as not to conflict with the international conventions on which many Member States' copyright and related rights laws are based;

Whereas the Community's legal framework on the rental right and lending right and on certain rights related to copyright can be limited to establishing that Member States provide rights with respect to rental and lending for certain groups of rightholders and further to establishing the rights of fixation, reproduction, distribution, broadcasting and communication to the public for certain groups of rightholders in the field of related rights protection;

Whereas it is necessary to define the concepts of rental and lending for the purposes of this Directive;

Whereas it is desirable, with a view to clarity, to exclude from rental and lending within the meaning of this Directive certain forms of making available, as for instance making available phonograms or films (cinematographic or audiovisual works or moving images, whether or not accompanied by sound) for the purpose of public performance or broadcasting, making available for the purpose of exhibition, or making available for on-the-spot reference use; whereas lending within the meaning of this Directive does not include making available between establishments which are accessible to the public;

Whereas, where lending by an establishment accessible to the public gives rise to a payment the amount of which does not go beyond what is necessary to cover the operating costs of the establishment, there is no direct or indirect economic or commercial advantage within the meaning of this Directive;

Whereas it is necessary to introduce arrangements ensuring that an unwaivable equitable remuneration is obtained by authors and performers who must retain the possibility to entrust the administration of this right to collecting societies representing them;

Whereas the equitable remuneration may be paid on the basis of one or several payments an any time on or after the conclusion of the contract;

Whereas the equitable remuneration must take account of the importance of the contribution of the authors and performers concerned to the phonogram or film;

Whereas it is also necessary to protect the rights at least of authors as regards public lending by providing for specific arrangements; whereas, however, any measures based on Article 5 of this Directive have to comply with Community law, in particular with Article 7 of the Treaty;

Whereas the provisions of Chapter II do not prevent Member States from extending the presumption set out in Article 2 (5) to the exclusive rights included in that chapter; whereas furthermore the provisions of Chapter II do not prevent Member States from providing for a rebuttable presumption of the authorization of exploitation in respect of the exclusive rights of performers provided for in those articles, in so far as such presumption is compatible with the International Convention for the Protection of Performers, Producers of Phonograms and Broadcasting Organizations (hereinafter referred to as the Rome Convention);

Whereas Member States may provide for more far-reaching protection for owners of rights related to copyright than that required by Article 8 of this Directive;

Whereas the harmonized rental and lending rights and the harmonized protection in the field of rights related to copyright should not be exercised in a way which constitutes a disguised restriction on trade between Member States or in a way which is contrary to the rule of media exploitation chronology, as recognized in the Judgment handed down in Société Cinéthèque v. FNCF (¹),

HAS ADOPTED THIS DIRECTIVE:

CHAPTER I

RENTAL AND LENDING RIGHT

Article 1

Object of harmonization

1. In accordance with the provisions of this Chapter, Member States shall provide, subject to Article 5, a right to authorize or prohibit the rental and lending of originals and copies of copyright works, and other subject matter as set out in Article 2 (1).

(¹) Cases 60/84 and 61/84, ECR 1985, p. 2605.

2. For the purposes of this Directive, 'rental' means making available for use, for a limited period of time and for direct or indirect economic or commercial advantage.

3. For the purposes of this Directive, 'lending' means making available for use, for a limited period of time and not for direct or indirect economic or commercial advantage, when it is made through establishments which are accessible to the public.

4. The rights referred to in paragraph 1 shall not be exhausted by any sale or other act of distribution of originals and copies of copyright works and other subject matter as set out in Article 2 (1).

Article 2

Rightholders and subject matter of rental and lending right

1. The exclusive right to authorize or prohibit rental and lending shall belong :

— to the author in respect of the original and copies of his work,

— to the performer in respect of fixations of his performance,

— to the phonogram producer in respect of his phonograms, and

— to the producer of the first fixation of a film in respect of the original and copies of his film. For the purposes of this Directive, the term 'film' shall designate a cinematographic or audiovisual work or moving images, whether or not accompanied by sound.

2. For the purposes of this Directive the principal director of a cinematographic or audiovisual work shall be considered as its author or one of its authors. Member States may provide for others to be considered as its co-authors.

3. This Directive does not cover rental and lending rights in relation to buildings and to works of applied art.

4. The rights referred to in paragraph 1 may be transferred, assigned or subjet to the granting of contractual licences.

5. Without prejudice to paragraph 7, when a contract concerning film production is concluded, individually or collectively, by performers with a film producer, the performer covered by this contract shall be presumed, subject to contractual clauses to the contrary, to have transferred his rental right, subject to Article 4.

6. Member States may provide for a similar presumption as set out in paragraph 5 with respect to authors.

7. Member States may provide that the signing of a contract concluded between a performer and a film producer concerning the production of a film has the effect of authorizing rental, provided that such contract provides for an equitable remuneration within the meaning of Article 4. Member States may also provide that this paragraph shall apply *mutatis mutandis* to the rights included in Chapter II.

Article 3

Rental of computer programs

This Directive shall be without prejudice to Article 4 (c) of Council Directive 91/250/EEC of 14 May 1991 on the legal protection of computer programs (¹).

Article 4

Unwaivable right to equitable remuneration

1. Where an author or performer has transferred or assigned his rental right concerning a phonogram or an original or copy of a film to a phonogram or film producer, that author or performer shall retain the right to obtain an equitable remuneration for the rental.

2. The right to obtain an equitable remuneration for rental cannot be waived by authors or performers.

3. The administration of this right to obtain an equitable remuneration may be entrusted to collecting societies representing authors or performers.

4. Member States may regulate whether and to what extent administration by collecting societies of the right to obtain an equitable remuneration may be imposed, as well as the question from whom this remuneration may be claimed or collected.

Article 5

Derogation from the exclusive public lending right

1. Member States may derogate from the exclusive right provided for in Article 1 in respect of public lending, provided that at least authors obtain a remuneration for such lending. Member States shall be free to determine this remuneration taking account of their cultural promotion objectives.

2. When Member States do not apply the exclusive lending right provided for in Article 1 as regards phonograms, films and computer programs, they shall introduce, at least for authors, a remuneration.

(¹) OJ No L 122, 17. 5. 1991, p. 42.

3.   Member States may exempt certain categories of establishments from the payment of the remuneration referred to in paragraphs 1 and 2.

4.   The Commission, in cooperation with the Member States, shall draw up before 1 July 1997 a report on public lending in the Community. It shall forward this report to the European Parliament and to the Council.

CHAPTER II

RIGHTS RELATED TO COPYRIGHT

Article 6

Fixation right

1.   Member States shall provide for performers the exclusive right to authorize or prohibit the fixation of their performances.

2.   Member States shall provide for broadcasting organizations the exclusive right to authorize or prohibit the fixation of their broadcasts, whether these broadcasts are transmitted by wire or over the air, including by cable or satellite.

3.   A cable distributor shall not have the right provided for in paragraph 2 where it merely retransmits by cable the broadcasts of broadcasting organizations.

Article 7

Reproduction right

1.   Member States shall provide the exclusive right to authorize or prohibit the direct or indirect reproduction :

— for performers, of fixations of their performances,
— for phonogram producers, of their phonograms,
— for producers of the first fixations of films, in respect of the original and copies of their films, and
— for broadcasting organizations, of fixations of their broadcasts, as set out in Article 6 (2).

2.   The reproduction right referred to in paragraph 1 may be transferred, assigned or subject to the granting of contractual licences.

Article 8

Broadcasting and communication to the public

1.   Member States shall provide for performers the exclusive right to authorize or prohibit the broadcasting by wireless means and the communication to the public of their performances, except where the performance is itself already a broadcast performance or is made from a fixation.

2.   Member States shall provide a right in order to ensure that a single equitable remuneration is paid by the user, if a phonogram published for commercial purposes, or a reproduction of such phonogram, is used for broadcasting by wireless means or for any communication to the public, and to ensure that this remuneration is shared between the relevant performers and phonogram producers. Member States may, in the absence of agreement between the performers and phonogram producers, lay down the conditions as to the sharing of this remuneration between them.

3.   Member States shall provide for broadcasting organizations the exclusive right to authorize or prohibit the rebroadcasting of their broadcasts by wireless means, as well as the communication to the public of their broadcasts if such communication is made in places accessible to the public against payment of an entrance fee.

Article 9

Distribution right

1.   Member States shall provide

— for performers, in respect of fixations of their performances,
— for phonogram producers, in respect of their phonograms,
— for producers of the first fixations of films, in respect of the original and copies of their films,
— for broadcasting organizations, in respect of fixations of their broadcast as set out in Article 6 (2),

the exclusive right to make available these objects, including copies thereof, to the public by sale or otherwise, hereafter referred to as the 'distribution right'.

2.   The distribution right shall not be exhausted within the Community in respect of an object as referred to in paragraph 1, except where the first sale in the Community of that object is made by the rightholder or with his consent.

3.   The distribution right shall be without prejudice to the specific provisions of Chapter I, in particular Article 1 (4).

4.   The distribution right may be transferred, assigned or subject to the granting of contractual licences.

Article 10

Limitations to rights

1. Member States may provide for limitations to the rights referred to in Chapter II in respect of :

(a) private use ;

(b) use of short excerpts in connection with the reporting of current events ;

(c) ephemeral fixation by a broadcasting organization by means of its own facilities and for its own broadcasts ;

(d) use solely for the purposes of teaching or scientific research.

2. Irrespective of paragraph 1, any Member State may provide for the same kinds of limitations with regard to the protection of performers, producers of phonograms, broadcasting organizations and of producers of the first fixations of films, as it provides for in connection with the protection of copyright in literary and artistic works. However, compulsory licences may be provided for only to the extent to which they are compatible with the Rome Convention.

3. Paragraph 1 (a) shall be without prejudice to any existing or future legislation on remuneration for reproduction for private use.

CHAPTER III

DURATION

Article 11

Duration of authors' rights

Without prejudice to further harmonization, the authors' rights referred to in this Directive shall not expire before the end of the term provided by the Berne Convention for the Protection of Literary and Artistic Works.

Article 12

Duration of related rights

Without prejudice to further harmonization, the rights referred to in this Directive of performers, phonogram producers and broadcasting organizations shall not expire before the end of the respective terms provided by the Rome Convention. The rights referred to in this Directive for producers of the first fixations of films shall not expire before the end of a period of 20 years computed from the end of the year in which the fixation was made.

CHAPTER IV

COMMON PROVISIONS

Article 13

Application in time

1. This Directive shall apply in respect of all copyright works, performances, phonograms, broadcasts and first fixations of films referred to in this Directive which are, on 1 July 1994, still protected by the legislation of the Member States in the field of copyright and related rights or meet the criteria for protection under the provisions of this Directive on that date.

2. This Directive shall apply without prejudice to any acts of exploitation performed before 1 July 1994.

3. Member States may provide that the rightholders are deemed to have given their authorization to the rental or lending of an object referred to in Article 2 (1) which is proven to have been made available to third parties for this purpose or to have been acquired before 1 July 1994. However, in particular where such an object is a digital recording, Member States may provide that rightholders shall have a right to obtain an adequate remuneration for the rental or lending of that object.

4. Member States need not apply the provisions of Article 2 (2) to cinematographic or audiovisual works created before 1 July 1994.

5. Member States may determine the date as from which the Article 2 (2) shall apply, provided that that date is no later than 1 July 1997.

6. This Directive shall, without prejudice to paragraph 3 and subject to paragraphs 8 and 9, not affect any contracts concluded before the date of its adoption.

7. Member States may provide, subject to the provisions of paragraphs 8 and 9, that when rightholders who acquire new rights under the national provisions adopted in implementation of this Directive have, before 1 July 1994, given their consent for exploitation, they shall be presumed to have transferred the new exclusive rights.

8. Member States may determine the date as from which the unwaivable right to an equitable remuneration referred to in Article 4 exists, provided that that date is no later than 1 July 1997.

9. For contracts concluded before 1 July 1994, the unwaivable right to an equitable remuneration provided for in Article 4 shall apply only where authors or performers or those representing them have submitted a request to that effect before 1 January 1997. In the absence of agreement between rightholders concerning the level of remuneration, Member States may fix the level of equitable remuneration.

Article 14

Relation between copyright and related rights

Protection of copyright-related rights under this Directive shall leave intact and shall in no way affect the protection of copyright.

Article 15

Final provisions

1. Member States shall bring into force the laws, regulations and administrative provisions necessary to comply with this Directive not later than 1 July 1994. They shall forthwith inform the Commission thereof.

When Member States adopt these measures, they shall contain a reference to this Directive or shall be accompanied by such reference at the time of their official publication. The methods of making such a reference shall be laid down by the Member States.

2. Member States shall communicate to the Commission the main provisions of domestic law which they adopt in the field covered by this Directive.

Article 16

This Directive is addressed to the Member States.

Done at Brussels, 19 November 1992.

For the Council
The President
E. LEIGH

Appendix 4
EC Directive on the coordination of certain rules concerning copyright and rights related to copyright applicable to satellite broadcasting and cable retransmission*

* European Communities Council Directive of 27 September 1993 (93/83/EEC).
Reproduced by permission of the European Communities.

II

(Acts whose publication is not obligatory)

COUNCIL

COUNCIL DIRECTIVE 93/83/EEC
of 27 September 1993
on the coordination of certain rules concerning copyright and rights related to copyright applicable to satellite broadcasting and cable retransmission

THE COUNCIL OF THE EUROPEAN COMMUNITIES,

Having regard to the Treaty establishing the European Economic Community, and in particular Articles 57 (2) and 66 thereof,

Having regard to the proposal from the Commission ([1]),

In cooperation with the European Parliament ([2]),

Having regard to the opinion of the Economic and Social Committee ([3]),

(1) Whereas the objectives of the Community as laid down in the Treaty include establishing an ever closer union among the peoples of Europe, fostering closer relations between the States belonging to the Community and ensuring the economic and social progress of the Community countries by common action to eliminate the barriers which divide Europe;

(2) Whereas, to that end, the Treaty provides for the establishment of a common market and an area without internal frontiers; whereas measures to achieve this include the abolition of obstacles to the free movement of services and the institution of a system ensuring that competition in the common market is not distorted; whereas, to that end, the Council may adopt directives for the coordination of the provisions laid down by law, regulation or administrative action in Member States concerning the taking up and pursuit of activities as self-employed persons;

(3) Whereas broadcasts transmitted across frontiers within the Community, in particular by satellite and cable, are one of the most important ways of pursuing these Community objectives, which are at the same time political, economic, social, cultural and legal;

(4) Whereas the Council has already adopted Directive 89/552/EEC of 3 October 1989 on the coordination of certain provisions laid down by law, regulation or administrative action in Member States concerning the pursuit of television broadcasting activities ([4]), which makes provision for the promotion of the distribution and production of European television programmes and for advertising and sponsorship, the protection of minors and the right of reply;

(5) Whereas, however, the achievement of these objectives in respect of cross-border satellite broadcasting and the cable retransmission of programmes from other Member States is currently still obstructed by a series of differences between national rules of copyright and some degree of legal uncertainty; whereas this means that holders of rights are exposed to the threat of seeing their works exploited without payment of remuneration or that the individual holders of exclusive rights in various Member States block the exploitation of their rights; whereas the legal uncertainty in particular constitutes a direct obstacle in the free circulation of programmes within the Community;

([1]) OJ No C 255, 1. 10. 1991, p. 3 and
   OJ No C 25, 28. 1. 1993, p. 43.
([2]) OJ No C 305, 23. 11. 1992, p. 129 and
   OJ No C 255, 20. 9. 1993.
([3]) OJ No C 98, 21. 4. 1992, p. 44.

([4]) OJ No L 298, 17. 10. 1989, p. 23.

(6) Whereas a distinction is currently drawn for copyright purposes between communication to the public by direct satellite and communication to the public by communications satellite; whereas, since individual reception is possible and affordable nowadays with both types of satellite, there is no longer any justification for this differing legal treatment;

(7) Whereas the free broadcasting of programmes is further impeded by the current legal uncertainty over whether broadcastsing by a satellite whose signals can be received directly affects the rights in the country of transmission only or in all countries of reception together; whereas, since communications satellites and direct satellites are treated alike for copyright purposes, this legal uncertainty now affects almost all programmes broadcast in the Community by satellite;

(8) Whereas, furthermore, legal certainty, which is a prerequisite for the free movement of broadcasts within the Community, is missing where programmes transmitted across frontiers are fed into and retransmitted through cable networks;

(9) Whereas the development of the acquisition of rights on a contractual basis by authorization is already making a vigorous contribution to the creation of the desired European audiovisual area; whereas the continuation of such contractual agreements should be ensured and their smooth application in practice should be promoted wherever possible;

(10) Whereas at present cable operators in particular cannot be sure that they have actually acquired all the programme rights covered by such an agreement;

(11) Whereas, lastly, parties in different Member States are not all similarly bound by obligations which prevent them from refusing without valid reason to negotiate on the acquisition of the rights necessary for cable distribution or allowing such negotiations to fail;

(12) Whereas the legal framework for the creation of a single audiovisual area laid down in Directive 89/552/EEC must, therefore, be supplemented with reference to copyright;

(13) Whereas, therefore, an end should be put to the differences of treatment of the transmission of programmes by communications satellite which exist in the Member States, so that the vital distinc-tion throughout the Community becomes whether works and other protected subject matter are communicated to the public; whereas this will also ensure equal treatment of the suppliers of cross-border broadcasts, regardless of whether they use a direct broadcasting satellite or a communications satellite;

(14) Whereas the legal uncertainty regarding the rights to be acquired which impedes cross-border satellite broadcasting should be overcome by defining the notion of communication to the public by satellite at a Community level; whereas this definition should at the same time specify where the act of communication takes place; whereas such a definition is necessary to avoid the cumulative application of several national laws to one single act of broadcasting; whereas communication to the public by satellite occurs only when, and in the Member State where, the programme-carrying signals are introduced under the control and responsibility of the broadcasting organization into an uninterrupted chain of communication leading to the satellite and down towards the earth; whereas normal technical procedures relating to the programme-carrying signals should not be considered as interruptions to the chain of broadcasting;

(15) Whereas the acquisition on a contractual basis of exclusive broadcasting rights should comply with any legislation on copyright and rights related to copyright in the Member State in which communication to the public by satellite occurs;

(16) Whereas the principle of contractual freedom on which this Directive is based will make it possible to continue limiting the exploitation of these rights, especially as far as certain technical means of transmission or certain language versions are concerned;

(17) Whereas, in ariving at the amount of the payment to be made for the rights acquired, the parties should take account of all aspects of the broadcast, such as the actual audience, the potential audience and the language version;

(18) Whereas the application of the country-of-origin principle contained in this Directive could pose a problem with regard to existing contracts; whereas this Directive should provide for a period of five years for existing contracts to be adapted, where necessary, in the light of the Directive; whereas the said country-of-origin principle should not, therefore, apply to existing contracts which expire before

1 January 2000 ; whereas if by that date parties still have an interest in the contract, the same parties should be entitled to renegotiate the conditions of the contract ;

(19) Whereas existing international co-production agreements must be interpreted in the light of the economic purpose and scope envisaged by the parties upon signature ; whereas in the past international co-production agreements have often not expressly and specifically addressed communication to the public by satellite within the meaning of this Directive a particular form of exploitation ; whereas the underlying philosophy of many existing international co-production agreements is that the rights in the co-production are exercised separately and independently by each co-producer, by dividing the exploitation rights between them along territorial lines ; whereas, as a general rule, in the situation where a communication to the public by satellite authorized by one co-producer would prejudice the value of the exploitation rights of another co-producer, the interpretation of such an existing agreement would normally suggest that the latter co-producer would have to give his consent to the authorization, by the former co-producer, of the communication to the public by satellite ; whereas the language exclusivity of the latter co-producer will be prejudiced where the language version or versions of the communication to the public, including where the version is dubbed or subtitled, coincide(s) with the language or the languages widely understood in the territory allotted by the agreement to the latter co-producer ; whereas the notion of exclusivity should be understood in a wider sense where the communication to the public by satellite concerns a work which consists merely of images and contains no dialogue or subtitles ; whereas a clear rule is necessary in cases where the international co-production agreement does not expressly regulate the division of rights in the specific case of communication to the public by satellite within the meaning of this Directive ;

(20) Whereas communications to the public by satellite from non-member countries will under certain conditions be deemed to occur within a Member State of the Community ;

(21) Whereas it is necessary to ensure that protection for authors, performers, producers of phonograms and broadcasting organizations is accorded in all Member States and that this protection is not subject to a statutory licence system ; whereas only in this way is it possible to ensure that any difference in the level of protection within the common market will not create distortions of competition ;

(22) Whereas the advent of new technologies is likely to have an impact on both the quality and the quan-

tity of the exploitation of works and other subject matter ;

(23) Whereas in the light of these developments the level of protection granted pursuant to this Directive to all rightholders in the areas covered by this Directive should remain under consideration ;

(24) Whereas the harmonization of legislation envisaged in this Directive entails the harmonization of the provisions ensuring a high level of protection of authors, performers, phonogram producers and broadcasting organizations ; whereas this harmonization should not allow a broadcasting organization to take advantage of differences in levels of protection by relocating activities, to the detriment of audiovisual productions ;

(25) Wheres the protection provided for rights related to copyright should be aligned on that contained in Council Directive 92/100/EEC of 19 November 1992 on rental right and lending right and on certain rights related to copyright in the field of intellectual property (¹) for the purposes of communication to the public by satellite ; whereas, in particular, this will ensure that peformers and phonogram producers are guaranteed an appropriate remuneration for the communication to the public by satellite of their performances or phonograms ;

(26) Whereas the provisions of Article 4 do not prevent Member States from extending the presumption set out in Article 2 (5) of Directive 92/100/EEC to the exclusive rights referred to in Article 4 ; whereas, furthermore, the provisions of Article 4 do not prevent Member States from providing for a rebuttable presumption of the authoriztion of exploitation in respect of the exclusive rights of performers referred to in that Article, in so far as such presumption is compatible with the International Convention for ˙the Protection of Performers, Producers of Phonograms and Broadcasting Organizations ;

(27) Whereas the cable retransmission of programmes from other Member States is an act subject to copyright and, as the case may be, rights related to copyright ; whereas the cable operator must, therefore, obtain the authorization from every holder of rights in each part of the programme retransmitted ; whereas, pursuant to this Directive, the authorizations should be granted contractually unless a temporary exception is provided for in the case of existing legal licence schemes ;

(¹) OJ No L 346, 27. 11. 1992, p. 61.

(28) Whereas, in order to ensure that the smooth operation of contractual arrangements is not called into question by the intervention of outsiders holding rights in individual parts of the programme, provision should be made, through the obligation to have recourse to a collecting society, for the exclusive collective exercise of the authorization right to the extent that this is required by the special features of cable retransmission; whereas the authorization right as such remains intact and only the exercise of this right is regulated to some extent, so that the right to authorize a cable retransmission can still be assigned; whereas this Directive does not affect the exercise of moral rights;

(29) Whereas the exemption provided for in Article 10 should not limit the choice of holders of rights to transfer their rights to a collecting society and thereby have a direct share in the remuneration paid by the cable distributor for cable retransmission;

(30) Whereas contractual arrangements regarding the authorization of cable retransmission should be promoted by additional measures; whereas a party seeking the conclusion of a general contract should, for its part, be obliged to submit collective proposals for an agreement; whereas, furthermore, any party shall be entitled, at any moment, to call upon the assistance of impartial mediators whose task is to assist negotiations and who may submit proposals; whereas any such proposals and any opposition thereto should be served on the parties concerned in accordance with the applicable rules concerning the service of legal documents, in particular as set out in existing international conventions; whereas, finally, it is necessary to ensure that the negotiations are not blocked without valid justification or that individual holders are not prevented without valid justification from taking part in the negotiations; whereas none of these measures for the promotion of the acquisition of rights calls into question the contractual nature of the acquisition of cable retransmission rights;

(31) Whereas for a transitional period Member States should be allowed to retain existing bodies with jurisdiction in their territory over cases where the right to retransmit a programme by cable to the public has been unreasonably refused or offered on unreasonable terms by a broadcasting organization; whereas it is understood that the right of parties concerned to be heard by the body should be guaranteed and that the existence of the body should not prevent the parties concerned from having normal access to the courts;

(32) Whereas, however, Community rules are not needed to deal with all of those matters, the effects of which perhaps with some commercially insignificant exceptions, are felt only inside the borders of a single Member State;

(33) Whereas minimum rules should be laid down in order to establish and guarantee free and uninterrupted cross-border broadcasting by satellite and simultaneous, unaltered cable retransmission of programmes broadcast from other Member States, on an essentially contractual basis;

(34) Whereas this Directive should not prejudice further harmonization in the field of copyright and rights related to copyright and the collective administration of such rights; whereas the possibility for Member States to regulate the activities of collecting societies should not prejudice the freedom of contractual negotiation of the rights provided for in this Directive, on the understanding that such negotiation takes place within the framework of general or specific national rules with regard to competition law or the prevention of abuse of monopolies;

(35) Whereas it should, therefore, be for the Member States to supplement the general provisions needed to achieve the objectives of this Directive by taking legislative and administrative measures in their domestic law, provided that these do not run counter to the objectives of this Directive and are compatible with Community law;

(36) Whereas this Directive does not affect the applicability of the competition rules in Articles 85 and 86 of the Treaty,

HAS ADOPTED THIS DIRECTIVE:

CHAPTER I

DEFINITIONS

Article 1

Definitions

1. For the purpose of this Directive, 'satellite' means any satellite operating on frequency bands which, under telecommunications law, are reserved for the broadcast of signals for reception by the public or which are reserved

for closed, point-to-point communication. In the latter case, however, the circumstances in which individual reception of the signals takes place must be comparable to those which apply in the first case.

2. (a) For the purpose of this Directive, 'communication to the public by satellite' means the act of introducing, under the control and responsibility of the broadcasting organization, the programme-carrying signals intended for reception by the public into an uninterrupted chain of communication leading to the satellite and down towards the earth.

(b) The act of communication to the public by satellite occurs solely in the Member State where, under the control and responsibility of the broadcasting organization, the programme-carrying signals are introduced into an uninterrupted chain of communication leading to the satellite and down towards the earth.

(c) If the programme-carrying signals are encrypted, then there is communication to the public by satellite on condition that the means for decrypting the broadcast are provided to the public by the broadcasting organization or with its consent.

(d) Where an act of communication to the public by satellite occurs in a non-Community State which does not provide the level of protection provided for under Chapter II,

(i) if the programme-carrying signals are transmitted to the satellite from an uplink situation situated in a Member State, that act of communication to the public by satellite shall be deemed to have occurred in that Member State and the rights provided for under Chapter II shall be exercisable against the person operating the uplink station ; or

(ii) if there is no use of an uplink station situated in a Member State but a broadcasting organization established in a Member State has commissioned the act of communication to the public by satellite, that act shall be deemed to have occured in the Member State in which the broadcasting organization has its principal establishment in the Community and the rights provided for under Chapter II shall be exercisable against the broadcasting organization.

3. For the purposes of this Directive, 'cable retransmission' means the simultaneous, unaltered and unabridged retransmission by a cable or microwave system for reception by the public of an initial transmission from another Member State, by wire or over the air, including that by satellite, of television or radio programmes intended for reception by the public.

4. For the purposes of this Directive 'collecting society' means any organization which manages or administers copyright or rights related to copyright as its sole purpose or as one of its main purposes.

5. For the purposes of this Directive, the principal director of a cinematographic or audiovisual work shall be considered as its author or one of its authors. Member States may provide for others to be considered as its co-authors.

CHAPTER II

BROADCASTING OF PROGRAMMES BY SATELLITE

Article 2

Broadcasting right

Member States shall provide an exclusive right for the author to authorize the communication to the public by satellite of copyright works, subject to the provisions set out in this chapter.

Article 3

Acquisition of broadcasting rights

1. Member States shall ensure that the authorization referred to in Article 2 may be acquired only be agreement.

2. A Member State may provide that a collective agreement between a collecting society and a broadcasting organization concerning a given category of works may be extended to rightholders of the same category who are not represented by the collecting society, provided that :

— the communication to the public by satellite simulcasts a terrestrial broadcast by the same broadcaster, and

— the unrepresented rightholder shall, at any time, have the possibility of excluding the extension of the collective agreement to his works and of exercising his rights either individually or collectively.

3. Paragraph 2 shall not apply to cinematographic works, including works created by a process analogous to cinematography.

4. Where the law of a Member State provides for the extension of a collective agreement in accordance with the provisions of paragraph 2, that Member States shall inform the Commission which broadcasting organizations are entitled to avail themselves of that law. The Commission shall publish this information in the *Official Journal of the European Communities* (C series).

Article 4

Rights of performers, phonogram producers and broadcasting organizations

1. For the purposes of communication to the public by satellite, the rights of performers, phonogram producers and broadcasting organizations shall be protected in accordance with the provisions of Articles 6, 7, 8 and 10 of Directive 92/100/EEC.

2. For the purposes of paragraph 1, 'broadcasting by wireless means' in Directive 92/100/EEC shall be understood as including communication to the public by satellite.

3. With regard to the exercise of the rights referred to in paragraph 1, Articles 2 (7) and 12 of Directive 92/100/EEC shall apply.

Article 5

Relation between copyright and related rights

Protection of copyright-related rights under this Directive shall leave intact and shall in no way affect the protection of copyright.

Article 6

Minimum protection

1. Member States may provide for more far-reaching protection for holders of rights related to copyright than that required by Article 8 of Directive 92/100/EEC.

2. In applying paragraph 1 Member States shall observe the definitions contained in Article 1 (1) and (2).

Article 7

Transitional provisions

1. With regard to the application in time of the rights referred to in Article 4 (1) of this Directive, Article 13 (1), (2), (6) and (7) of Directive 92/100/EEC shall apply. Article 13 (4) and (5) of Directive 92/100/EEC shall apply *mutatis mutandis.*

2. Agreements concerning the exploitation of works and other protected subject matter which are in force on the date mentioned in Article 14 (1) shall be subject to the provisions of Articles 1 (2), 2 and 3 as from 1 January 2000 if they expire after that date.

3. When an international co-production agreement concluded before the date mentioned in Article 14 (1) between a co-producer from a Member State and one or more co-producers from other Member States or third countries expressly provides for a system of division of exploitation rights between the co-producers by geographical areas for all means of communication to the public, without distinguishing the arrangement applicable to communication to the public by satellite from the provisions applicable to the other means of communication, and where communication to the public by satellite of the co-production would prejudice the exclusivity, in particular the language exclusivity, of one of the co-producers or his assignees in a given territory, the authorization by one of the co-producers or his assignees for a communication to the public by satellite shall require the prior consent of the holder of that exclusivity, whether co-producer or assignee.

CHAPTER III

CABLE RETRANSMISSION

Article 8

Cable retransmission right

1. Member States shall ensure that when programmes from other Member States are retransmitted by cable in their territory the applicable copyright and related rights are observed and that such retransmission takes place on the basis of individual or collective contractual agreements between copyright owners, holders of related rights and cable operators.

2. Notwithstanding paragraph 1, Member States may retain until 31 December 1997 such statutory licence systems which are in operation or expressly provided for by national law on 31 July 1991.

Article 9

Exercise of the cable retransmission right

1. Member States shall ensure that the right of copyright owners and holders or related rights to grant or refuse authorization to a cable operator for a cable retransmission may be exercised only through a collecting society.

2. Where a rightholder has not transferred the management of his rights to a collecting society, the collecting society which manages rights of the same category shall be deemed to be mandated to manage his rights. Where more than one collecting society manages rights of that category, the rightholder shall be free to choose which of those collecting societies is deemed to be mandated to manage his rights. A rightholder referred to in this paragraph shall have the same rights and obligations resulting from the agreement between the cable operator and the collecting society which is deemed to be mandated to manage his rights as the rightholders who have mandated that collecting society and he shall be able to claim those

rights within a period, to be fixed by the Member State concerned, which shall not be shorter than three years from the date of the cable retransmission which includes his work or other protected subject matter.

3.   A Member State may provide that, when a rightholder authorizes the initial transmission within its territory of a work or other protected subject matter, he shall be deemed to have agreed not to exercise his cable retransmission rights on an individual basis but to exercise them in accordance with the provisions of this Directive.

Article 10

Exercise of the cable retransmission right by broadcasting organizations

Member States shall ensure that Article 9 does not apply to the rights exercised by a broadcasting organization in respect of its own transmission, irrespective of whether the rights concerned are its own or have been transferred to it by other copyright owners and/or holders of related rights.

Article 11

Mediators

1.   Where no agreement is concluded regarding authorization of the cable retransmission of a broadcast. Member States shall ensure that either party may call upon the assistance of one or more mediators.

2.   The task of the mediators shall be to provide assistance with negotiation. They may also submit proposals to the parties.

3.   It shall be assumed that all the parties accept a proposal as referred to in paragraph 2 if none of them expresses its opposition within a period of three months. Notice of the proposal and of any opposition thereto shall be served on the parties concerned in accordance with the applicable rules concerning the service of legal documents.

4.   The mediators shall be so selected that their independence and impartiality are beyond reasonable doubt.

Article 12

Prevention of the abuse of negotiating positions

1.   Member States shall ensure by means of civil or administrative law, as appropriate, that the parties enter and conduct negotiations regarding authorization for cable retransmission in good faith and do not prevent or hinder negotiation without valid justification.

2.   A Member State which, on the date mentioned in Article 14 (1), has a body with jurisdiction in its territory over cases where the right to retransmit a programme by cable to the public in that Member State has been unreasonably refused or offered on unreasonable terms by a broadcasting organization may retain that body.

3.   Paragraph 2 shall apply for a transitional period of eight years from the date mentioned in Article 14 (1).

CHAPTER IV

GENERAL PROVISIONS

Article 13

Collective administration of rights

This Directive shall be without prejudice to the regulation of the activities of collecting societies by the Member States.

Article 14

Final provisions

1.   Member States shall bring into force the laws, regulations and administrative provisions necessary to comply with this Directive before 1 January 1995. They shall immediately inform the Commission thereof.

When Member States adopt these measures, the latter shall contain a reference to this Directive or shall be accompanied by such reference at the time of their official publication. The methods of making such a reference shall be laid down by the Member States.

2.   Member States shall communicate to the Commission the provisions of national law which they adopt in the field covered by this Directive.

3.   Not later than 1 January 2000, the Commission shall submit to the European Parliament, the Council and the Economic and Social Committee a report on the application of this Directive and, if necessary, make further proposals to adapt it to developments in the audio and audiovisual sector.

Article 15

This Directive is addressed to the Member States.

Done at Brussels, 27 September 1993.

For the Council
The President
R. URBAIN

Bibliography

Books

Abell, M. *The Franchise Option: A Legal Guide* (London: Waterlow, 1989)

Aldous, W., Young, D., Watson, A. and Thorley, S. *Terrell on the Law of Patents* (London: Sweet & Maxwell, 14th edn., 1990)

Bainbridge, D.I. *Introduction to Computer Law* (London: Pitman, 2nd edn., 1993)

Bainbridge, D.I. *Software Copyright Law* (London: Pitman, 1992)

Bainbridge, D.I. *Intellectual Property: How to Identify, Protect and Exploit your Company's Assets* (London: Pitman, 1993)

Bentham, J. *Manual of Political Economy*, reprinted in Stark, W. (ed.) *Jeremy Bentham's Economic Writings* Vol. 1 (London: Allen & Unwin, 1952)

Blanco White, T.A. & Jacob, R. *Kerly's Law of Trade Marks & Trade Names* (London: Sweet & Maxwell, 12th edn., 1986)

Brett, H. *The United Kingdom Patents Act 1977* (Oxford: ESC Publishing, 1978)

The British Copyright Council, *Reprographic Copying of Books and Journals* (London: British Copyright Council, 1985)

Caplan, D. & Stewart, G. *British Trade Marks and Symbols* (London: Peter Owen, 1966)

Cawthra, B.I. *Patent Licensing in Europe* (London: Butterworths, 2nd edn., 1986)

Coleman, A. *The Legal Protection of Trade Secrets* (London: Sweet & Maxwell, 1992)

Cornish, W.R. *Intellectual Property: Patents, Copyright, Trade Marks and Allied Rights* (London: Sweet & Maxwell, 2nd edn., 1989)

Cornish, W.R. (ed.) *Materials on Intellectual Property* (Oxford: ESC Publishing, 1990)

Davenport, N. *The United Kingdom Patent System: A Brief History* (Havant: Mason, 1979)

Davies, G. & Hung, M.E. *Music and Video Private Copying* (London: Sweet & Maxwell, 1993)

Dickens, C. *A Poor Man's Tale of a Patent*, reprinted in Phillips, J. *Charles Dickens and the 'Poor Man's Tale of a Patent'* (Oxford: ESC Publishing, 1984)

Dutton, H.I. *The Patent System and Inventive Activity during the Industrial Revolution, 1750-1852* (Manchester: Manchester University Press, 1984)

Dworkin, G. & Taylor, R.D. *Blackstone's Guide to the Copyright, Designs and Patents Act 1988* (London: Blackstone, 1989)

Eisenschitz, T.S. *Patents, Trade Marks and Designs in Information Work* (London: Croom Helm, 1987)

Gallafent, R.J., Eastaway, N.A., Dauppe, V.A.F. *Intellectual Property: Law and Taxation* (London: Longman, 4th edn., 1992)

Hohfeld, W.N. *Fundamental Legal Conceptions as Applied in Judicial Reasoning*, reprinted in part in Lloyd, Lord (of Hampstead) *Introduction to Jurisprudence* (London: Stevens, 4th edn., 1979)

Irish, V. (ed.) *Intellectual Property: A Manager's Guide* (London: McGraw-Hill, 1991)

Jacob, R. & Alexander, D. *A Guidebook to Intellectual Property* (London: Sweet & Maxwell, 4th edn., 1993)

Johnston, D. *Design Protection* (London: The Design Council, 3rd edn., 1989)

Laddie, H., Prescott, P. & Vittoria, M. *The Modern Law of Copyright* (London: Butterworths, 1st edn., 1980)

Lehmann, M. & Tapper, C.F. (eds) *A Handbook of European Software Law* (Oxford: Clarendon Press, 1993)

Lloyd, I. *Information Technology Law* (London: Butterworths, 1993)

Marett, P. *Information Law and Practice* (London: Gower, 1991)

McFarlane, G. *Copyright through the Cases* (London: Waterlow, 1986)

Merkin, R. *Copyright, Designs and Patents: The New Law* (London: Longman, 1989)

The Patent Office – various publications of interest available from the Marketing and Information Directorate, Cardiff Road, Newport, Gwent. NP9 1RH

Pearson, H. & Miller, C. *Commercial Exploitation of Intellectual Property* (London: Blackstone, 1991)

Phillips, J. (ed) *Butterworths Intellectual Property Law Handbook* (London: Butterworths, 1990)

Phillips, J. & Firth, A. *Introduction to Intellectual Property Law* (London: Butterworths, 2nd edn., 1990)

Phillips, J., Durie, R. and Karet, I. *Whale on Copyright* (London: Sweet & Maxwell, 4th edn., 1993)

Prime, T. *The Law of Copyright* (London: Fourmat, 1992)

Reed, C. (ed) *Computer Law* (London: Blackstone, 2nd edn., 1993)

Reid, B.C. *Confidentiality and the Law* (London: Waterlow, 1986)

Reid, B.C. *A Practical Guide to Patent Law* (London: Sweet & Maxwell, 2nd edn., 1993)

Schmookler, J. *Invention and Economic Growth* (Cambridge, Mass: Harvard University Press, 1986)

Selwyn, N. *Law of Employment* (London: Butterworths, 7th edn., 1992)

Singleton, E.S. *Introduction to Competition Law* (London: Pitman, 1992)

Skone-James, E.P., Mummery, J., Rayner-James, J.E. & Garnett, K.M. *Copinger and Skone-James on Copyright* (London: Sweet & Maxwell, 13th edn., 1991)

Sterling, J.A.L. *Intellectual Property Rights in Sound Recordings, Film and Video* (London: Sweet & Maxwell, 1992)

Stewart, S.M. *International Copyright and Neighbouring Rights* (London: Butterworths, 2nd edn., 1989)

Tapper, C. *Computer Law* (London: Longman, 4th edn., 1989)

Tootal, C. *The Law of Industrial Design* (Bicester: CCH Editions, 1990)

Wadlow, C. *The Law of Passing Off* (London: Sweet & Maxwell, 1990)

Whish, R. *Competition Law* (London: Butterworths, 3rd edn., 1992)

Young, D. *Passing Off* (London: Longman, 2nd edn., 1989)

Reports

Annual Report of the European Patent Office 1992 (Munich: European Patent Office, 1993)

Anton Piller Orders: A Consultation Paper Lord Chancellor's Department, 1992.

The Banks Report *Committee to Examine the Patent System and Patent Law* Cmnd 4407 (London: HMSO, 1970)

The Calcutt Committee *Report on Privacy and Related Matters* Cm 1102 (London: HMSO, 1990)

Intellectual Property and Innovation Cmnd 9712 (London: HMSO, 1986)

Intellectual Property Rights and Innovation Cmnd 9117 (London: HMSO, 1983)

The Law Commission, Law Comm No. 110 *Breach of Confidence* Cmnd 8388 (London: HMSO, 1981)

The Patent Office *Annual Report and Accounts 1992 to 1993* (London: HMSO, 1993)

Reform of the Law Relating to Copyright, Designs and Performers' Protection Cmnd 8302 (London: HMSO, 1981)

Reform of Trade Marks Law Cm 1203 (London: HMSO, 1990)

The Whitford Committee *Copyright - Copyright and Design Law* Cmnd 6732 (London: HMSO, 1977)

Journal articles

Anon 'Appellate Court gives Green Light to Reverse Engineering' (1991) 2 *Intellectual Property in Business Briefing* 3

Bainbridge, D.I. 'Computer-aided Diagnosis and Negligence' (1991) 31 *Medicine, Science and the Law* 127

Bainbridge, D.I. 'The Copyright Act: A Legal Red Herring' (1989) 1(8) *Computer Bulletin* 21

Bender, D. 'Computer Programs: Should They Be Patentable?' (1968) 68 *Columbia Law Review* 241

Benson, J.R. 'Copyright Protection for Computer Screen Displays' (1988) 72 *Minnesota Law Review* 1123

Carty, H. 'Inverse Passing-Off: A Suitable Addition to Passing-Off?' [1993] 10 EIPR 370

Chalton, S. 'Implementation of the Software Directive in the United Kingdom: The Effects of the Copyright (Computer Programs) Regulations 1992' [1993] 9 CLSR 115

Cornish, W.R. 'Interoperable Systems and Copyright' [1989] 11 EIPR 391

Davidson, D.M. 'Protecting Computer Software: A Comprehensive Analysis' (1983) 23(4) *Jurimetrics Journal* 337

de Freitas, D. 'The Copyright, Designs and Patents Act 1988 (2)' (1989) 133 *Solicitors Journal* 670

de Freitas, D. 'The Copyright, Designs and Patents Act 1988 (4)' (1989) 133 *Solicitors Journal* 733

Dworkin, G. 'Authorship of Films and European Commission Proposals for Harmonising the Term of Copyright' [1993] 5 EIPR 151

Goldblatt, M. 'Copyright Protection for Computer Programs in Australia: The Law since Autodesk' [1990] 5 EIPR 170

Goltz, H. & Pritesche, K.U. 'Cable & Satellite Television - Copyright and Other Issues under German Law' [1988] 9 EIPR 261

Groves, P. & Martino, T. 'Euromark: Or How the EEC Brought UK Trade Mark Law into the 20th Century' (1990) 1 *European Business Law Review* 109

Hart, R.J. 'Applications of Patents to Computer Technology - UK and the EPO Harmonisation?' [1989] 2 EIPR 42

Hoffman, G., Grossman, J., Keane, P. & Westby, J. 'Protection for Computer Software: An International Overview: Part 2' [1989] 1 EIPR 7

Horton, A.A. 'Industrial Design Law: The Future for Europe' [1991] 12 EIPR 442

Jacob, R. 'The Herchel Smith Lecture 1993' [1993] 9 EIPR 312

Jehoram, H.C. 'The EC Green Paper on the Legal Protection of Industrial Design. Half Way down the Right Track - A View from the Benelux' [1992] 3 EIPR 75

Lea, G. 'Database Law - Solutions beyond Copyright' [1993] 9 CLSR 127

Lurie, P.M. & Weiss, H.D. 'Computer Assisted Mistakes: Changing Standards of Professional Liability' (1988) II *Software Law Journal* 283

Mamiofa, I.E. 'The Draft of a New Soviet Patent Law' [1990] 1 EIPR 21

Markesinis, B.S. 'Our Patchy Law of Privacy - Time to Do Something about it' (1990) 53 MLR 802

Monotti, A. 'The Extent of Copyright Protection for Compilations of Artistic Works' [1993] 5 EIPR 156

Oliver, P. 'Of Split Trade Marks and Common Markets' (1991) 54 MLR 587

Paterson, G.D. 'The Patentability of Further Uses of a Known Product under the European Patent Convention' [1991] 1 EIPR 16

Pessa, P. 'Evaluating the idea-expression dichotomy: rhetoric or legal principle?' (1991) *Computer Law & Practice* March/April, 166

Prescott, P. '*Kaye v Robertson* - a reply' (1991) 53 MLR 451

Rohnke, C. 'Protection of External Product Features in West Germany' [1990] 2 EIPR 41

Sherman, B. 'Patent Claim Interpretation: The Impact of the Protocol on Interpretation' (1991) 54 MLR 499

Snell, T. 'Pirates run Aground as UK fights IT Crime' *Computing* 21 January 1993 at 13

Taylor, W.D. 'Copyright Protection for Computer Software after *Whelan Associates v Jaslow Dental Laboratory*' (1989) 54 *Missouri Law Review* 121

Thurston, J. 'Recent EC Developments in Biotechnology' [1993] 6 EIPR 187

Walton, A. 'The Copyright, Designs and Patents Act 1988 (1)' (1989) 133 *Solicitors Journal* 646

Webber, D. 'Software Patents: A New Era in Australia and the United States' [1993] 5 EIPR 181

Winfield, M.J. 'Expert Systems: An Introduction for the Layman' (1982) *Computer Bulletin* 6

Miscellaneous

British Copyright Council *Reprographic Copying of Books and Journals* (London: British Copyright Council, 1985)

Conn, D. 'Cut-price court in a spin' *The Times* 23 November 1993

Smit, D. van Zyl *The Social Creation of a Legal Reality: A Study of the Emergence and Acceptance of the British Patent System as a Legal Instrument for the Control of New Technology*, unpublished Ph.D. Thesis, University of Edinburgh, 1980

Index

Database of summaries of intellectual property cases

A computer database of summaries of the most important intellectual property cases is available. The database is a useful supplement to this book and it contains summaries of many of the cases discussed within it. The database comprises summaries of over 120 cases. (A database of summaries of 45 computer law cases will also be provided at no extra cost)

The database is provided complete with an easy to use, attractive and powerful computer program having advanced retrieval and editing facilities. The user of the database system may edit or add to the existing summaries. When installed on a hard disk, the program may be used to create new databases for case summaries and/or legislation, as required.

Particular features are:
- ◆ Easy to install and use complete with manual containing clear instructions
- ◆ Refined searching of the database is possible using AND/OR connectors
- ◆ Searching may be carried out at a number of levels
- ◆ Users may add their own case summaries to the database
- ◆ Users may create their own new databases
- ◆ Case summaries may be printed out
- ◆ Databases of legislation may be created
- ◆ May be used as an effective way to teach databases and text retrieval

The database and accompanying program is available on a 3½ inch disk (1.44MB) suitable for an IBM personal computer or equivalent computer running DOS with a 1.44MB capacity disk drive. A hard disk is desirable (though not essential). The system can be run from DOS or it can be run from the Windows environment (as a DOS program)

The database and accompanying program is available for the price of £11.99 for students and academics or £17.99 for practitioners. Very reasonable prices for class packs and site licences will be quoted. Send payment (cheque or postal order made payable to David Bainbridge) to the address below, allowing 21 days for delivery. Prices include post and packing for UK only.

Dr. David Bainbridge
Corporate Management Division
Aston Business School
Aston University
Aston Triangle
BIRMINGHAM
B4 7ET

Note: if entering new materials to the database or creating new databases, please take care to avoid infringing copyright (see Chapters 6 and 7 of this book).